SUND.

UNIFORM WITH THIS VOLUME

The Weekday Missal

THE SUNDAY MISSAL

*Sunday Masses for the Entire Three-year Cycle
Complete in One Volume
together with extracts from
the Sacramental Rites
and from* The Divine Office

RENEWED BY DECREE OF
THE MOST HOLY SECOND ECUMENICAL COUNCIL OF THE VATICAN,
PROMULGATED BY AUTHORITY OF POPE PAUL VI
AND REVISED AT THE DIRECTION OF POPE JOHN PAUL II.

ENGLISH TRANSLATION ACCORDING
TO THE THIRD TYPICAL EDITION

Edited by
Revd Dr Robin Gibbons
Illustrated by
Matthew Alderman

Texts approved for use in
England and Wales, Ireland, Scotland

Collins

Collins, a division of HarperCollins*Publishers*
77–85 Fulham Palace Road, London W6 8JB

First published in 1984
This edition 2011

ISBNs
978-0-00-745629-1 (blue)
978-0-00-745628-4 (red)
978-0-00-745712-0 (black deluxe)
978-0-00-745630-7 (white deluxe)

© copyright compilation and editorial matter 1975, 1976, 1977, 1982, 1984 and 2011 HarperCollins*Publishers*

Latin text © Libreria Editrice Vaticana, Vatican City State, 2008.
New English Translation 2010, granted recognition by the Congregation for Divine Worship and the Discipline of the Sacraments, for the dioceses of the Bishops' Conferences of England and Wales (Prot. N. 915/06/L, 28 March 2010), and Scotland, (Prot. N. 1021/07/L, 23 June 2010), and Ireland (Prot. N. 516/05/L, 18 June 2010).

The English translation and chants of the *Roman Missal* © 2010, International Commission on English in the Liturgy Corporation. All rights reserved.

The English translation of the Gospel Readings for the Palm Sunday Procession from the *Revised Standard Version* © 1946 by the Division of Christian Educators of the National Council of Churches of Christ in the United States of America.

The English translation of Psalms 23[24] and 46[47] from *The Revised Grail Psalms* © 2010 Conception Abbey/The Grail, admin. by GIA Publications, Inc., www.giamusic.com. All rights reserved.

Other extracts from scripture (excepting Psalm texts) from the *Jerusalem Bible* version of scripture, © 1966, 1967 and 1968, Darton, Longman and Todd and Doubleday & Company Inc.

Other psalm texts from *The Grail Psalms* © 1963 The Grail (England), published by Collins.

Latin Typical Edition, 1970.
Amended Latin Typical Edition, 1971.
Second Latin Typical Edition, 1975.
Third Latin Typical Edition, 2002.
Amended Latin Third Typical Edition, 2008.

Concordat cum originali: Jane Porter, 19 December 2011.
Nihil obstat: Father Anton Cowan, Censor.
Imprimatur: The Most Reverend Vincent Nichols, Archbishop of Westminster.
Westminster, 8 January 2012, Feast of the Epiphany of the Lord.

The *Nihil obstat* and *Imprimatur* are a declaration that a book or pamphlet is considered to be free from doctrinal or moral error. It is not implied that those who have granted the *Nihil obstat* or *Imprimatur* agree with the contents, opinions or statements expressed.

Printed and Bound in China by RR Donnelley

CONTENTS

Preface	*page* ix
Introduction	xi
How to Use the Sunday Missal	xiii
Tables	
I Gospel Reading for Year A	xiv
II Gospel Reading for Year B	xvi
III Gospel Reading for Year C	xviii
IV Second Reading for Sundays	xx
V Principal Celebrations of the Liturgical Year	xxi
Prayers: Preparation for Mass	xxii

THE ORDER OF MASS

The Introductory Rites	3
The Liturgy of the Word	10
The Liturgy of the Eucharist	15
Prefaces	19
The Eucharistic Prayers	59
Eucharistic Prayer I (The Roman Canon)	60
Eucharistic Prayer II	69
Eucharistic Prayer III	74
Eucharistic Prayer IV	79
The Communion Rite	85
The Concluding Rites	90
Blessings at the End of Mass	94
Prayers over the People	105
Appendix to the Order of Mass	
Chants for the Eucharistic Prayer and other musical settings	110
Eucharistic Prayers for Reconciliation	156
Eucharistic Prayer for use in Masses for Various Needs	165
Latin Texts	183
Prayers: Thanksgiving after Mass	187

SUNDAY MASSES

Year A	191
Advent	193
Christmas Time	208
Lent	243
First Scrutiny	263

Contents

Second Scrutiny	274
Third Scrutiny	285
Holy Week	290
Palm Sunday of the Passion of the Lord	290
Holy Thursday: Chrism Mass	329
Easter Triduum	339
Thursday of the Lord's Supper: Evening Mass	342
Friday of the Passion of the Lord	355
Easter Time	381
Easter Vigil	383
Season of Easter	428
Solemnities of the Lord in Ordinary Time	474
The Most Holy Trinity	474
The Most Holy Body and Blood of Christ	477
The Most Sacred Heart of Jesus	482
Sundays in Ordinary Time	487
Appendix to Year A: Musical Settings	598

Year B

Advent	617
Christmas Time	631
Lent	641
Season of Easter	663
Solemnities of the Lord in Ordinary Time	696
The Most Holy Trinity	696
The Most Holy Body and Blood of Christ	699
The Most Sacred Heart of Jesus	703
Sundays in Ordinary Time	707

Year C

Advent	817
Christmas Time	819
Lent	832
Season of Easter	841
Solemnities of the Lord in Ordinary Time	864
The Most Holy Trinity	897
The Most Holy Body and Blood of Christ	897
The Most Sacred Heart of Jesus	900
Sundays in Ordinary Time	904
	908

Contents

FEASTS OF THE LORD AND SOLEMNITIES

2 February	Presentation of the Lord	1029
19 March	St Joseph, Spouse of the Blessed Virgin Mary	1036
25 March	The Annunciation of the Lord	1040
24 June	The Nativity of John the Baptist: Vigil	1043
	Mass during the Day	1047
29 June	Saints Peter and Paul, Apostles: Vigil	1050
	Mass during the Day	1053
6 August	The Transfiguration of the Lord	1057
15 August	The Assumption of the Blessed Virgin Mary: Vigil	1061
	Mass during the Day	1064
14 September	The Exaltation of the Holy Cross	1067
1 November	All Saints	1071
2 November	Commemoration of the Faithful Departed	1074
9 November	Dedication of the Lateran Basilica	1080
8 December	The Immaculate Conception of the Blessed Virgin Mary	1084

National Calendars for England, Scotland and Wales

1 March	St David	1089
17 March	St Patrick	1092
23 April	St George	1095
30 November	St Andrew	1099

National Calendars for Ireland

17 March	St Patrick	1103

COMMON MASSES

Common of the Dedication of a Church   1106

THE SACRAMENTS

Christian Initiation of Adults
    Rite of Baptism   1114
    Rite of Confirmation   1115

Rite of Pardon and Reconciliation
    Individual Penitents   1117

Contents

Several Penitents with Individual
   Confession and Absolution ... 1119
Rite of Communion of the Sick ... 1124

MASSES FOR VARIOUS NEEDS AND OCCASIONS
For the Evangelization of Peoples ... 1127

FROM THE DIVINE OFFICE
Evening Prayer II ... 1135
   Week 1 ... 1135
   Week 2 ... 1141
   Week 3 ... 1144
   Week 4 ... 1147

Night Prayer (Compline) ... 1151
   After Evening Prayer I of Sundays ... 1151
   After Evening Prayer II of Sundays ... 1154

PRAYERS
For Various Occasions ... 1157
For the Dying ... 1161
To our Lady ... 1163

PREFACE

When Saint Paul wrote to the Early Church about the Mass he told them that he was handing on to them what he had received from the Lord himself (1 Cor 11:23). The Church in every age has taken great care to be faithful to that same tradition. This new translation of the Roman Missal hands on to us this great gift from the Lord.

The newly translated texts of the Missal will help to nurture and deepen our faith. The vast majority of them are inspired by Sacred Scripture and the Teachings of the Church. They will enrich the celebration of the Mass and, indeed, our own personal prayer. They will deepen our knowledge of the faith. They will assist our participation and encourage us to take into the world what we have received at the Altar.

As Pope Benedict XVI reminded the bishops during his recent visit: 'As we know, the sacred liturgy and its forms are written deeply in the heart of every Catholic. Make every effort to . . . render the celebration of the Roman Rite in your Dioceses a moment of greater grace and beauty, worthy of the Lord and spiritually enriching for everyone'. These newly translated texts will assist us in that renewal, deepening our understanding and assisting us to worship God in spirit and in truth.

✠Arthur Roche
Bishop of Leeds

INTRODUCTION

From the time of the apostles the Christian community has kept Sunday as the Lord's Day. Every Sunday is a celebration of the Resurrection, not just at Easter, and it is our fundamental feastday. Saint Basil wrote: 'Holy Sunday, the first fruits of all other days honoured by the Lord's resurrection' and Saint Augustine called Sunday 'a sacrament of Easter' distinct from the Sabbath day. Not only is Sunday the first day of the week, it is also the eighth day, the promise of eternal life. At the heart of Sunday is the Eucharistic assembly, for the Eucharist is the summit and source of Christian life, feeding and forming the Church. As the 'epiphany' of the Church, the celebration of the Eucharist opens us up to communion with each other and the universal Church throughout the world.

When the people of God gather to celebrate the Eucharist, Christ's Spirit is then present and active in the community, and is the source of their prayer, praise and proclamation of God's wonderful works. Christ is present to us in four different ways: firstly, he is present in the assembled people of God. For Christ promised: 'Where two or three are gathered in my name, there am I in their midst' (Mt 18:20). Secondly, Christ is present in the person of the minister, called the presider, who leads our prayers and helps us understand the words and actions of the liturgy. When he does this, the priest acts in the person of Christ and on our behalf. Thirdly, Christ is present in the Word of God. Whenever we celebrate the liturgy of the hours, the sacraments or Mass we hear scripture proclaimed for us. In Saint John's Gospel the prologue tells us the Christ is the Word made flesh, so each time we hear the Word of God Christ is there with us and for us. That is why the liturgy gives such a principal place to the readings – they are an essential element in the act of worship that is the Mass. The fourth and special presence of Christ is the 'eucharistic species', the bread and wine taken, blessed, broken and shared, which become for us his Body and Blood. When we receive these sacred elements in communion we become even more the Body of Christ. This cycle of presence is the liturgical action of the Church, the active celebration of all who participate in the offering of the Eucharist.

The liturgy also uses signs and symbols to help us understand and perceive the great mystery that is being celebrated. The fourfold presence of Christ is shown by several places that have their own symbolic importance. The assembly is seen in the gathering space but also in the font, the symbol of our baptism. The role of the presider is symbolised by his chair, from which he presides over the gathered assembly and directs the prayers; this is not to be confused with the Bishop's Cathedra, which has a different meaning. The ambo or lectern is a focal point for the proclamation of scripture, the place of the Word, but above all, the altar is the centre of 'thanksgiving that the Eucharist accomplishes', the table of the Lord where the sacrifice of the cross is made present. Because it is consecrated, fixed and freestanding, it signifies Christ Jesus the living stone (1 Pet 2:4). There are other signs that help us in our liturgical celebration, such as the use of lights and incense, the dignified vesture of the priest and ministers and the traditional liturgical colours that show us the particular season or feast.

When the priest greets the people with the words 'The Lord be with you', he is stating a fact – the Lord is with his people as they gather to celebrate the Eucharist. The Mass is a sacrifice of praise and thanksgiving. We obey the command of Christ, given to his apostles at the Last Supper, to do this in his memory. In the Mass, Christ offers himself to the Father as the sacrificial lamb of God, who takes away the sins of the world. And with himself, Christ offers us in his sacrifice, who by the Holy Spirit are made into the one Body of Christ, a living sacrifice of praise.

The Mass is an act of worship, in which all present acknowledge and praise God. The worshipping community is the people of God, won by Christ with his blood, called together by the Lord, and nourished by his Word. This people is called to offer God the prayers of the entire human family; it is brought together and strengthened in unity by sharing in the Body and Blood of Christ. The more the people enter into the mystery of the Eucharist by conscious, active and fruitful participation, the more they grow in holiness. As we listen to the Word of God, join in the prayers and song, offer the sacrifice and share the Lord's table together, so we become one body, which is Christ the Lord.

HOW TO USE THE SUNDAY MISSAL

The Sunday Missal gives the prayers and readings for Mass on every Sunday through the year, as well as other special occasions, and has all you need to prepare for the Mass, to follow the celebration itself, and to reflect on the readings and prayers afterwards. This short introduction is designed to help you find your way about this book.

Some parts of the Mass (the Ordinary) are used in every Mass, while others (the Proper) change from week to week or season to season. The Ordinary is to be found on pp.1-93, with instructions in boxes to tell you when to refer to other parts of the book. In some cases, such as the Preface (p.19 onward) or Eucharistic Prayer (p.59 onwards), the priest chooses which of the various choices to use each Sunday, whereas the texts of the Proper (e.g. the Entrance Antiphon and other chants, Collect, Prayer over the Offerings and Communion) are all set according to the week of the Church Year.

The Church Year starts with the season of Advent, which prepares for Christmas, then Christmas itself. Lent prepares us for Easter, with the season of Easter following. The rest of the year is called 'Ordinary Time', which accounts for around two-thirds of the year. Table V on p.xxi gives the dates of the moveable festivals and also tells you which 'Year' of readings to use – A, B or C. The texts for Year A begin on p.191, for Year B on p.615, and for Year C on p.817. From week to week you will probably want to keep a ribbon marker in the current week of the relevant year. Some of the texts used each year in Lent and for Easter are included in the section for Year A. Otherwise you can simply work through each year week by week, taking account of when Easter falls according to the table on p.xxi.

This book also contains the Proper texts for the Feasts of the Lord and Solemnities (starting on p.1029), and for the major feasts in the National Calendars (from p.1089). There are also Masses for other occasions and, from p.1135, some extracts from the Divine Office which give the form of Evening Prayer for Sundays as well as Night Prayer. There are also some prayers to help in preparation and thanksgiving for Mass as well as for other occasions.

Table I
ORDER FOR GOSPEL READING FOR SUNDAYS IN ORDINARY TIME
YEAR A: YEAR OF MATTHEW

In order to do justice to the intention of the Lectionary, the five great 'sermons' in Matthew's Gospel will of necessity be the focal points of preaching and instruction. The narrative sections, which are placed in between the sermons, are composed in such a way that there is a unity and coherence in the whole work. Discourse and narrative stand side by side, so that the narrative chapters prepare the way for what follows in the discourses. Recognising the way in which the Lectionary has reflected the structure of Matthew's Gospel will enable preachers and readers to see the context of the readings from one week to the next.

Unit I	**The figure of Jesus the Messiah**	**Sundays 1-2**
SUNDAY 1	The Baptism of Jesus	Mt 3:13-17
SUNDAY 2	The witness of John the Baptist	Jn 1:29-34

Unit II	**Christ's design for life in God's Kingdom**	**Sundays 3-9**
	Narrative:	
SUNDAY 3	The call of the first disciples	Mt 4:12-23
	Discourse:	
SUNDAY 4	The Sermon on the Mount (1)	Mt 5:1-12
SUNDAY 5	The Sermon on the Mount (2)	Mt 5:13-16
SUNDAY 6	The Sermon on the Mount (3)	Mt 5:17-37
SUNDAY 7	The Sermon on the Mount (4)	Mt 5:38-48
SUNDAY 8	The Sermon on the Mount (5)	Mt 6:24-34
SUNDAY 9	The Sermon on the Mount (6)	Mt 7:21-27

Unit III	**The spread of God's Kingdom**	**Sundays 10-13**
	Narrative:	
SUNDAY 10	The call of Levi	Mt 9:9-13
	Discourse:	
SUNDAY 11	The mission sermon (1)	Mt 9:36-10:8
SUNDAY 12	The mission sermon (2)	Mt 10:26-33
SUNDAY 13	The mission sermon (3)	Mt 10:37-42

Table I

Unit IV	**The mystery of God's Kingdom**	**Sundays 14-17**
	Narrative:	
SUNDAY 14	The revelation to the simple	Mt 11:25-30
	Discourse:	
SUNDAY 15	The parable sermon (1)	Mt 13:1-23
SUNDAY 16	The parable sermon (2)	Mt 13:24-43
SUNDAY 17	The parable sermon (3)	Mt 13:44-52
Unit V	**God's kingdom on earth The Church of Christ**	**Sundays 18-24**
	Narrative:	
SUNDAY 18	The feeding of five thousand	Mt 14:31-21
SUNDAY 19	Jesus walks on the waters	Mt 14:22-33
SUNDAY 20	The Canaanite woman	Mt 15:21-28
SUNDAY 21	Peter's confession: the primacy conferred	Mt 16:13-20
SUNDAY 22	The passion prophesied: discipleship	Mt 16:21-27
	Discourse:	
SUNDAY 23	The community sermon (1)	Mt 18:15-20
SUNDAY 24	The community sermon (2)	Mt 18:21-35
Unit VI	**Authority and invitation the ministry ends**	**Sundays 25-33**
	Narrative:	
SUNDAY 25	The parable of the labourers	Mt 20:1-16
SUNDAY 26	The parable of the two sons	Mt 21:28-32
SUNDAY 27	The parable of the wicked vinedressers	Mt 21:33-43
SUNDAY 28	The parable of the marriage feast	Mt 22:1-14
SUNDAY 29	Paying tribute to Caesar	Mt 22:15-21
SUNDAY 30	The greatest commandment	Mt 22:34-40
SUNDAY 31	Hypocrisy and ambition	Mt 23:1-12
	Discourse:	
SUNDAY 32	The final sermon (1)	Mt 25:1-13
SUNDAY 33	The final sermon (2)	Mt 25:14-30
Unit VII	**God's Kingdom fulfilled**	**Sunday 34**
SUNDAY 34	Christ the King	Mt 25:31-46

Table II
ORDER FOR GOSPEL READING
FOR SUNDAYS IN ORDINARY TIME

YEAR B: YEAR OF MARK

Mark's main interest is the person of Jesus himself. He follows Jesus through his public ministry in Galilee, outside Galilee and finally in Jerusalem itself immediately before the passion. The crisis is reached when the fundamental question is posed to the disciples: 'Who do you say I am?' Peter's confession of faith is, therefore, at the heart of Mark's Gospel. In the year of Mark the Lectionary observes faithfully the structure and message of the Gospel itself. One important peculiarity is that the Lectionary includes a major insert from the Gospel of John (Sundays 17-21: John 6 – the sermon on the 'Bread of Life'). This fits well into this part of Mark's Gospel, which is concerned with Jesus' revelation of himself, and is known as 'the Bread section'.

Unit I	**The figure of Jesus the Messiah**	**Sundays 1-2**
SUNDAY 1	The baptism of Jesus	Mk 1:6b-11
SUNDAY 2	The call of Andrew and his friend	Jn 1:35-42

Unit II	**The Mystery progressively revealed**	**Sundays 3-23**

Stage I	*Jesus with the Jewish crowds*	*Sundays 3-9*
SUNDAY 3	The call of the first apostles	Mk 1:14-20
SUNDAY 4	A day in Capernaum (1)	Mk 1:21-28
SUNDAY 5	A day in Capernaum (2)	Mk 1:29-39
SUNDAY 6	The cure of a leper	Mk 1:40-45
SUNDAY 7	The cure of a paralytic	Mk 2:1-12
SUNDAY 8	The question of fasting	Mk 2:18-22
SUNDAY 9	Violation of the Sabbath	Mk 2:23-3:6

Stage II	*Jesus with his disciples*	*Sundays 10-14*
SUNDAY 10	Serious criticism of Jesus	Mk 3:20-35
SUNDAY 11	The parables of the Kingdom	Mk 4:26-34
SUNDAY 12	The calming of the storm	Mk 4:35-41
SUNDAY 13	Jairus' daughter; the woman in the crowd	Mk 5:21-43
SUNDAY 14	Jesus rejected at Nazareth	Mk 6:1-6

Stage III	*Jesus manifests himself*	*Sundays 15-23*
SUNDAY 15	The mission of the twelve	Mk 6:7-13
SUNDAY 16	Compassion for the crowds	Mk 6:30-34

Table II   xvii

SUNDAY 17	The feeding of five thousand	Jn 6:1-15
SUNDAY 18	The bread of life (1)	Jn 6:24-35
SUNDAY 19	The bread of life (2)	Jn 6:41-52
SUNDAY 20	The eucharist	Jn 6:51-58
SUNDAY 21	Incredulity and faith	Jn 6:61-70
SUNDAY 22	Jewish customs	Mk 7:1-8. 14-15. 21
SUNDAY 23	The cure of a deaf-mute	Mk 7:31-37

Unit III   **The Mystery of the Son of Man**   **Sundays 24-34**

Stage I   *The 'Way' of the Son of Man*   *Sundays 24-30*

SUNDAY 24	Peter's confession of faith	Mk 8:27-35
SUNDAY 25	Passion and resurrection prophesied	Mk 9:29-36
SUNDAY 26	Instructions for disciples	Mk 9:37-42. 44. 46-47
SUNDAY 27	Marriage and divorce	Mk 10:2-16
SUNDAY 28	The problem of wealth	Mk 10:17-30
SUNDAY 29	The sons of Zebedee	Mk 10:35-46
SUNDAY 30	The cure of Bartimaeus	Mk 10:46-52

Stage II   *Final revelation in Jerusalem*   *Sundays 32-33*

SUNDAY 31	The first commandment	Mk 12:28b-34
SUNDAY 32	The widow's mite	Mk 12:38-44
SUNDAY 33	The last things	Mk 13:24-32

Stage III   *The fulfilment of the mystery*   *Sunday 34*

| SUNDAY 34 | The solemnity of Christ the King | Jn 18:33b-37 |

Table III
ORDER FOR GOSPEL READING FOR SUNDAYS IN ORDINARY TIME

YEAR C: YEAR OF LUKE

Luke's Gospel represents Jesus' journey from Galilee to Jerusalem – a journey which is completed in the Acts of the Apostles by the journey of the Church from Jerusalem 'to the ends of the earth'. The Lectionary in the year of Luke represents faithfully his 'Travel Narrative' (chapters 9-19) – Jesus' journey to death, to resurrection and his return to the Father (see Sundays 13-31). Luke's vision of the journey is not geographical or chronological. Rather it is seen as a journey for the whole Church and for the individual Christian, a journey towards suffering and glory. Each Gospel passage should mean a great deal more to preacher and reader when it is seen in the context of the whole programme of readings for Year C.

Unit I	**The figure of Jesus the Messiah**	Sundays 1-2
SUNDAY 1	The baptism of Jesus	Lk 3:15-16. 21-22
SUNDAY 2	The marriage feast at Cana	Jn 2:1-12

Unit II	**Luke's programme for Jesus' ministry**	Sundays 3-4
SUNDAY 3	Prologue. The visit to Nazareth (1)	Lk 1:1-4; 4:14-21
SUNDAY 4	The visit to Nazareth (2)	Lk 4:21-30

Unit III	**The Galilean Ministry**	Sundays 5-12
SUNDAY 5	*The call of the first apostles	Lk 5:1-11
SUNDAY 6	The sermon on the plain (1)	Lk 6:17. 20-26
SUNDAY 7	The sermon on the plain (2)	Lk 6:27-38
SUNDAY 8	The sermon on the plain (3)	Lk 6:39-45
SUNDAY 9	The cure of the centurion's servant	Lk 7:1-10
SUNDAY 10	*The Widow of Naim	Lk 7:11-17
SUNDAY 11	*Jesus' feet anointed: the sinful woman	Lk 7:36-8:3
SUNDAY 12	Peter's confession of faith	Lk 9:18-24

Unit IV	**The first part of the 'Travel Narrative': The qualities Jesus demands of those who follow him**	Sundays 13-23
SUNDAY 13	*The journey to Jerusalem begins	Lk 9:51-62
SUNDAY 14	*The mission of the seventy-two	Lk 10:1-12. 17-20
SUNDAY 15	*The Good Samaritan	Lk 10:25-37

Table III

SUNDAY 16	*Martha and Mary	Lk 10:38-42
SUNDAY 17	*The importunate friend	Lk 11:1-13
SUNDAY 18	*The parable of the rich fool	Lk 12:13-21
SUNDAY 19	The need for vigilance	Lk 12:32-48
SUNDAY 20	'Not peace but division'	Lk 12:49-53
SUNDAY 21	Few will be saved	Lk 13:22-30
SUNDAY 22	True humility	Lk 14:1. 7-14
SUNDAY 23	The cost of discipleship	Lk 14:25-33

Unit V — **The 'Gospel within the Gospel': the message of pardon and reconciliation – the parables of God's mercy** — **Sunday 24**

SUNDAY 24	*The lost coin, the lost sheep, and the prodigal son	Lk 15:1-32

Unit VI — **The second part of the 'Travel Narrative': the obstacles facing those who follow Jesus** — **Sundays 25-31**

SUNDAY 25	*The unjust steward	Lk 16:1-13
SUNDAY 26	*The rich man and Lazarus	Lk 16:19-31
SUNDAY 27	*A lesson on faith and dedication	Lk 17:5-10
SUNDAY 28	*The ten lepers	Lk 17:11-19
SUNDAY 29	*The unjust judge	Lk 18:1-8
SUNDAY 30	*The Pharisee and the tax collector	Lk 18:9-14
SUNDAY 31	*Zacchaeus	Lk 19:1-10

Unit VII — **The ministry in Jerusalem** — **Sundays 32-33**

SUNDAY 32	The resurrection debated	Lk 20:27-38
SUNDAY 33	The signs announcing the end	Lk 21:5-19

Unit VIII — **Christ the King: reconciliation** — **Sunday 34**

SUNDAY 34	*The repentant thief	Lk 23:35-43

Note: Passages marked with an asterisk are found only in the Gospel of Luke.

Table IV
ARRANGEMENT OF THE SECOND READING FOR THE SUNDAYS IN ORDINARY TIME

Sunday	Year A	Year B	Year C
2	1 Corinthians 1-4	1 Corinthians 6-11	1 Corinthians 12-15
3	"	"	"
4	"	"	"
5	"	"	"
6	"	"	"
7	"	2 Corinthians	"
8	"	"	"
9	Romans	"	Galatians
10	"	"	"
11	"	"	"
12	"	"	"
13	"	"	"
14	"	"	"
15	"	Ephesians	Colossians
16	"	"	"
17	"	"	"
18	"	"	"
19	"	"	Hebrews 11-12
20	"	"	"
21	"	"	"
22	"	James	"
23	"	"	Philemon
24	"	"	1 Timothy
25	Philippians	"	"
26	"	"	"
27	"	Hebrews 2-10	2 Timothy
28	"	"	"
29	1 Thessalonians	"	"
30	"	"	"
31	"	"	2 Thessalonians
32	"	"	"
33	"	"	"

Table V
PRINCIPAL CELEBRATIONS OF THE LITURGICAL YEAR

A.D.	Dominical Letter	Sunday Cycle	Ash Wednesday	Easter	Ascension	Pentecost	Ordinary Time Before Lent Up Until	Ordinary Time Before Lent Week	Ordinary Time After Easter Time From	Ordinary Time After Easter Time From Week	First Sunday of Advent
2000*	b A	B - C	8 March	23 April	1 June	11 June	7 March	9	12 June	10	3 December
2001	g	C - A	28 February	15 April	24 May	3 June	27 February	8	4 June	9	2 December
2002	f	A - B	13 February	31 March	9 May	19 May	12 February	5	20 May	7	1 December
2003	e	B - C	5 March	20 April	29 May	8 June	4 March	8	9 June	10	30 November
2004*	d c	C - A	25 February	11 April	20 May	30 May	24 February	7	31 May	9	28 November
2005	b	A - B	9 February	27 March	5 May	15 May	8 February	5	16 May	7	27 November
2006	A	B - C	1 March	16 April	25 May	4 June	28 February	8	5 June	9	3 December
2007	g	C - A	21 February	8 April	17 May	27 May	20 February	7	28 May	8	2 December
2008*	f e	A - B	6 February	23 March	1 May	11 May	5 February	4	12 May	6	30 November
2009	d	B - C	25 February	12 April	21 May	31 May	24 February	7	1 June	8	29 November
2010	c	C - A	17 February	4 April	13 May	23 May	16 February	6	24 May	8	28 November
2011	b	A - B	9 March	24 April	2 June	12 June	8 March	9	13 June	10	27 November
2012*	A g	B - C	22 February	8 April	17 May	27 May	21 February	7	28 May	8	2 December
2013	f	C - A	13 February	31 March	9 May	19 May	12 February	5	20 May	7	1 December
2014	e	A - B	5 March	20 April	29 May	8 June	4 March	8	9 June	10	30 November
2015	d	B - C	18 February	5 April	14 May	24 May	17 February	6	25 May	8	29 November
2016*	c b	C - A	10 February	27 March	5 May	15 May	9 February	5	16 May	7	27 November
2017	A	A - B	1 March	16 April	25 May	4 June	28 February	8	5 June	9	3 December
2018	g	B - C	14 February	1 April	10 May	20 May	13 February	6	21 May	7	2 December
2019	f	C - A	6 March	21 April	30 May	9 June	5 March	8	10 June	10	1 December
2020*	e d	A - B	26 February	12 April	21 May	31 May	25 February	7	1 June	9	29 November
2021	c	B - C	17 February	4 April	13 May	23 May	16 February	6	24 June	8	28 November
2022	b	C - A	2 March	17 April	26 May	5 June	1 March	8	6 June	10	27 November
2023	A	A - B	22 February	9 April	18 May	28 May	21 February	7	29 May	8	3 December

*Leap Year

PRAYERS:
PREPARATION FOR MASS

I am the living bread which has come down from heaven.
Anyone who eats this bread will live forever;
and that bread that I shall give
is my flesh, for the life of the world. *John 6:51*

This is what I received from the Lord and passed on to you: that on the same night he was betrayed, the Lord Jesus took some bread, and thanked God for it and broke it, and he said, 'This is my body, which is for you; do this as a memorial of me.' In the same way he took the cup after supper, and said, 'This cup is the new covenant in my blood. Whenever you drink it, do this as a memorial of me.' Until the Lord comes, therefore, every time you eat this bread and drink this cup you are proclaiming his death. Everyone is to recollect himself before eating this bread and drinking this cup. *1 Corinthians 11:23–26. 28*

The cup that we bless is a communion with the blood of Christ, and the bread that we break is a communion with the body of Christ. *1 Corinthians 10:16*

Worship God in a way that is worthy of thinking beings, by offering your living bodies as a holy sacrifice, truly pleasing to God. *Romans 12:1*

Examination of Conscience
If anyone should sin, we have our Advocate with the Father, Jesus Christ, who is Just; he is the sacrifice that takes our sins away. *1 John 2:1*

You shall love the Lord your God with your whole heart.
Do I really love God, my heavenly Father, with my whole heart, and try to obey his commandments?
    Do I hold the teaching of the Church?
    Do I profess my faith in God and in the Church publicly when necessary, and act as a Christian in public and in private?
    Do I put my trust in money, wordly goods, wordly influence?
    Have I always said my morning and evening prayers?
    Do I keep Sundays and the feasts of the Church? Have I obeyed the precept of yearly confession and Easter communion?

Prayers: Preparation for Mass

You shall love your neighbour as yourself.
Do I truly love other people, or do I use them for selfish ends?
Have I given scandal in word or action?

Consider my family life. Remember that children owe their parents love, obedience and respect, and should help them in spiritual or material need.
Parents should help their children by giving good example, exercising proper parental authority and giving them a Christian education.
Married people should love each other in thought, word and deed.
Single people should respect the integrity of others and of themselves, and live chastely.

Have I been a source of peace and happiness to those with whom I live or work?
Have I shared enough of what I have with those who need it – my money, my time, my concern?
Have I despised, or given offence to, the poor, the sick, the aged, foreigners, people of different race or habits from myself?

Am I just, conscientious, honest, in my work?
Do I pay a just wage to those who work for me? Have I squandered my employer's time or defrauded him in any way?
Do I tell the truth?
Have I violated the rights of other people to life, physical integrity, reputation, honour or property?
Have I stolen what is not mine? If so, have I made restitution?
If anyone has offended me or done me harm, have I been ready to make peace and to forgive, for the love of Christ?

Be perfect as your heavenly Father is perfect.
Do I really believe in eternal life, and live as if I believed in it?
Do I try to grow in the spirit, by reading and meditating the word of God, by sharing the life of Christ through the sacraments, by denying myself?
Do I make an effort to overcome my faults and sinful habits?
Do I use my time and talents as a good servant of the Lord God?
Do I bear the sorrows and difficulties of life with patience and faith?
Do I always try to live according to the law of the Holy Spirit, in the true freedom of the children of God, or am I in fact the slave of any passion?

Prayer of St Ambrose

Lord Jesus Christ,
I approach your banquet table
in fear and trembling,
for I am a sinner,
and dare not rely on my own worth,
but only on your goodness and mercy.
I am defiled by many sins in body and soul,
and by my unguarded thoughts and words.

Gracious God of majesty and awe,
I seek your protection,
I look for your healing.
Poor troubled sinner that I am,
I appeal to you, the fountain of all mercy.
I cannot bear your judgement,
but I trust in your salvation.
Lord, I show my wounds to you
and uncover my shame before you.
I know my sins are many and great,
and they fill me with fear,
but I hope in your mercies,
for they cannot be numbered.

Lord Jesus Christ, eternal king, divine and human,
crucified for humanity,
look upon me with mercy and hear my prayer,
for I trust in you.
Have mercy on me,
full of sorrow and sin,
for the depth of your compassion never ends.
Praise to you, saving sacrifice,
offered on the wood of the cross for me and for all.
Praise to the noble and precious blood,
flowing from the wounds of my crucified Lord Jesus Christ
and washing away the sins of the whole world.

Remember, Lord, your creature,
whom you have redeemed with your blood.
I repent of my sins,
and I long to put right what I have done.

Merciful Father, take away all my offences and sins;
purify me in body and soul,
and make me worthy to taste the holy of holies.

May your body and blood,
which I intend to receive, although I am unworthy,
be for me the remission of my sins,
the washing away of my guilt,
the end of my evil thoughts,
and the rebirth of my better instincts.
May it spur me on to works pleasing to you
and profitable to my health in body and soul,
and a firm defence
against the wiles of my enemies.
Amen.

(Tr. ICEL)

Prayer of St Thomas Aquinas before Holy Communion
Almighty, everlasting God,
I draw near to the sacrament of your only-begotten Son,
our Lord Jesus Christ.
I who am sick approach the physician of life.
I who am unclean come to the fountain of mercy;
blind, to the light of eternal brightness;
poor and needy, to the Lord of heaven and earth.
Therefore, I implore you, in your boundless mercy,
to heal my sickness, cleanse my defilement,
enlighten my blindness, enrich my poverty,
and clothe my nakedness.
Then shall I dare to receive the bread of angels,
the King of kings and Lord of lords,
with reverence and humility,
contrition and love,
purity and faith,
with the purpose and intention necessary
for the good of my soul.
Grant, I beseech you, that I may receive
not only the Body and Blood of the Lord,
but also the grace and power of the sacrament.
Most merciful God,
enable me so to receive the Body of your only-begotten Son,
our Lord Jesus Christ, which he took from the Virgin Mary,
that I may be found worthy to be incorporated
into his mystical Body, and counted among his members.
Most loving Father,
grant that I may one day see face to face

your beloved Son, whom I now intend to receive
under the veil of the sacrament,
and who with you and the Holy Spirit,
lives and reigns for ever,
one God, world without end. **Amen.**

(Tr. Stanbrook)

Invocation to the Holy Spirit
Lord Almighty,
send down upon this sacrifice your Holy Spirit.
May he declare this bread that we shall eat
to be the body of Christ,
and this cup that we shall drink
to be the blood of Christ.
May he strengthen and sanctify us
who eat this bread and drink this cup,
grant forgiveness of our sins
and deliver us from the wiles of the devil.
May he fill us with his presence
to make us worthy of Christ, your Son,
and obtain for us eternal life.

Adapted from *The Apostolic Constitutions*
4th century

For prayers of thanksgiving after Mass, turn to pp.187ff.
For other prayers, turn to pp.1157ff.

THE ORDER OF MASS

THE ORDER OF MASS

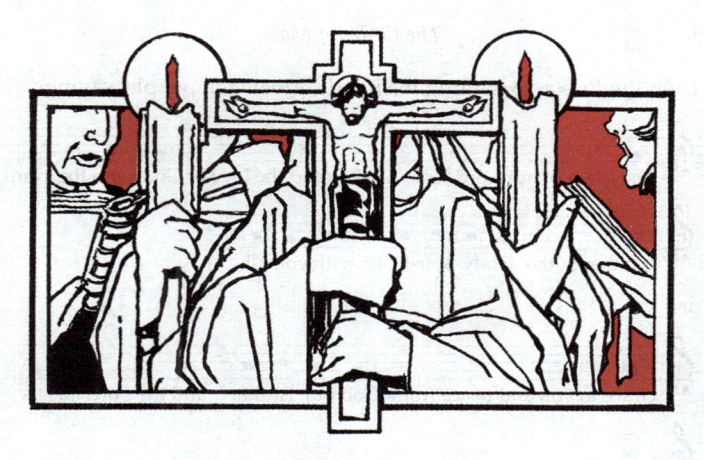

THE INTRODUCTORY RITES

When the people are gathered, the Priest approaches the altar with the ministers while the Entrance Chant is sung.

> **Entrance Chant:** turn to the Proper of the Mass of the Day, or a hymn is sung.

When he has arrived at the altar, after making a profound bow with the ministers, the Priest venerates the altar with a kiss and, if appropriate, incenses the cross and the altar. Then, with the ministers, he goes to the chair.

When the Entrance Chant is concluded, the Priest and the faithful, standing, sign themselves with the Sign of the Cross, while the Priest, facing the people, says:

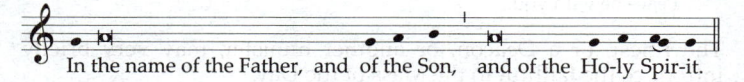

In the name of the Father, and of the Son, and of the Ho-ly Spir-it.

The people reply:

A-men.

The Order of Mass

Then the Priest, extending his hands, greets the people, saying:

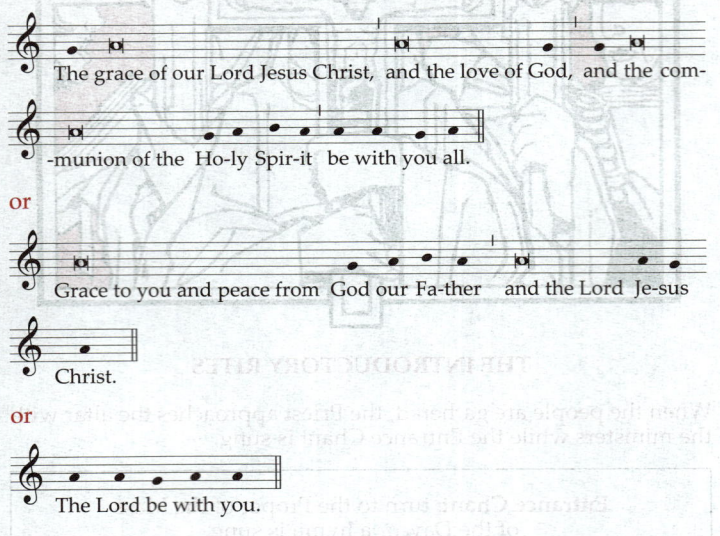

The grace of our Lord Jesus Christ, and the love of God, and the communion of the Holy Spirit be with you all.

or

Grace to you and peace from God our Father and the Lord Jesus Christ.

or

The Lord be with you.

The people reply:

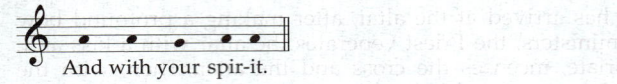

And with your spirit.

Instead of The Lord be with you, a Bishop says:

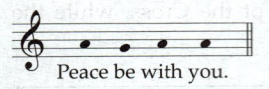

Peace be with you.

The Priest, or a Deacon, or another minister, may very briefly introduce the faithful to the Mass of the Day.

The Introductory Rites

Penitential Act*

(A musical setting for the Penitential Act may be found on p.147.)

Then follows the Penitential Act, to which the Priest invites the faithful, saying:

Brethren (brothers and sisters), let us acknowledge our sins,
and so prepare ourselves to celebrate the sacred mysteries.

A brief pause for silence follows. All say:

**I confess to almighty God
and to you, my brothers and sisters,
that I have greatly sinned,
in my thoughts and in my words,
in what I have done and in what I have failed to do,**

And, striking their breast, they say:

**through my fault, through my fault,
through my most grievous fault;**

Then they continue:

**therefore I ask blessed Mary ever-Virgin,
all the Angels and Saints,
and you, my brothers and sisters,
to pray for me to the Lord our God.**

The absolution by the Priest follows:

May almighty God have mercy on us,
forgive us our sins,
and bring us to everlasting life.

The people reply:

Amen.

---

or

The Priest invites the faithful to make the Penitential Act:

Brethren (brothers and sisters), let us acknowledge our sins,
and so prepare ourselves to celebrate the sacred mysteries.

A brief pause for silence follows.

---

*From time to time on Sundays, especially in Easter Time, instead of the customary Penitential Act, the blessing and sprinkling of water may take place (as in Year A, pp.418-21) as a reminder of Baptism.

The Priest then says:

Have mercy on us, O Lord.

The people reply:

For we have sinned against you.

The Priest:

Show us, O Lord, your mercy.

The people:

And grant us your salvation.

The absolution by the Priest follows:

May almighty God have mercy on us,
forgive us our sins,
and bring us to everlasting life.

The people reply:

Amen.

---

or

The Priest invites the faithful to make the Penitential Act:

Brethren (brothers and sisters), let us acknowledge our sins,
and so prepare ourselves to celebrate the sacred mysteries.

A brief pause for silence follows.

The Priest, or a Deacon or another minister, then says the following or other invocations with Kyrie, eleison (Lord, have mercy):

You were sent to heal the contrite of heart:

Lord, have mercy.   Or   Kyrie, eleison.

The people reply:

Lord, have mercy.   Or   Kyrie, eleison.

The Priest:

You came to call sinners:

Christ, have mercy.   Or   Christe, eleison.

The people:

Christ, have mercy.   Or   Christe, eleison.

The Introductory Rites

The Priest:

You are seated at the right hand of the Father to intercede for us:
Lord, have mercy.   Or   Kyrie, eleison.

The people:

Lord, have mercy.   Or   Kyrie, eleison.

The absolution by the Priest follows:

May almighty God have mercy on us,
forgive us our sins,
and bring us to everlasting life.

The people reply:

Amen.

The Kyrie, eleison (Lord, have mercy) invocations follow, unless they have just occurred in a formula of the Penitential Act.

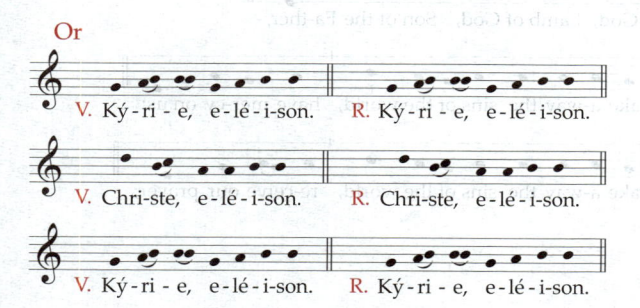

V. Lord, have mer-cy.   R. Lord, have mer-cy.

V. Christ, have mer-cy.   R. Christ, have mer-cy.

V. Lord, have mer-cy.   R. Lord, have mer-cy.

Or

V. Ký-ri-e, e-lé-i-son.   R. Ký-ri-e, e-lé-i-son.

V. Chri-ste, e-lé-i-son.   R. Chri-ste, e-lé-i-son.

V. Ký-ri-e, e-lé-i-son.   R. Ký-ri-e, e-lé-i-son.

The Order of Mass

Or

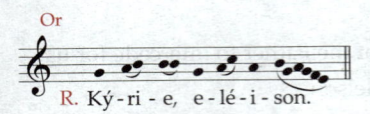

R. Ký-ri - e, e - lé - i - son.

Then, when it is prescribed, this hymn is either sung or said.

Glo-ry to God in the high-est,

and on earth peace to peo-ple of good will.

We praise you, we bless you, we a-dore you, we glo-ri-fy you,

we give you thanks for your great glo-ry,

Lord God, heav-en-ly King, O God, al - might-y Fa-ther.

Lord Je-sus Christ, On-ly Be-got-ten Son,

Lord God, Lamb of God, Son of the Fa-ther,

you take a-way the sins of the world, have mer-cy on us;

you take a-way the sins of the world, re-ceive our prayer;

The Introductory Rites

(musical notation)

you are seat-ed at the right hand of the Fa-ther, have mer-cy on us.

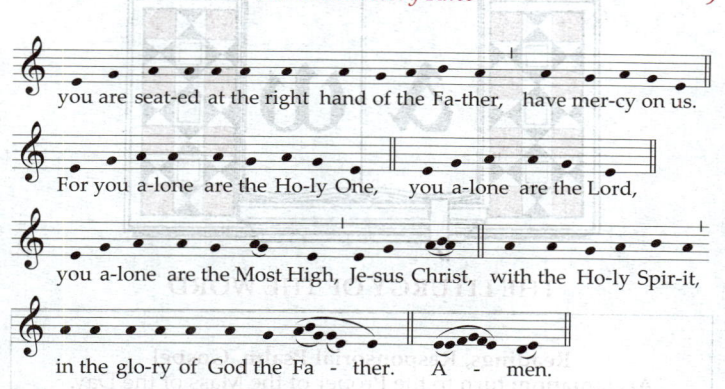

For you a-lone are the Ho-ly One, you a-lone are the Lord,

you a-lone are the Most High, Je-sus Christ, with the Ho-ly Spir-it,

in the glo-ry of God the Fa - ther. A - men.

When this hymn is concluded, the Priest, with hands joined, says:

Let us pray.

And all pray in silence with the Priest for a while.

> **Collect:** turn to the Proper of the Mass of the Day.

Then the Priest, with hands extended, says the Collect, at the end of which the people acclaim:

Amen.

THE LITURGY OF THE WORD

> **Readings, Responsorial Psalm, Gospel**
> **Acclamation:** turn to the Proper of the Mass of the Day.

The reader goes to the ambo and reads the First Reading, while all sit and listen.

(Musical settings for the following acclamations and responses may be found on p.150.)

To indicate the end of the reading, the reader acclaims:

The word of the Lord.

All reply:

Thanks be to God.

The psalmist or cantor sings or says the Psalm, with the people making the response.

After this, if there is to be a Second Reading, a reader reads it from the ambo, as above.

To indicate the end of the reading, the reader acclaims:

The word of the Lord.

All reply:

Thanks be to God.

There follows the Alleluia or another chant laid down by the rubrics, as the liturgical time requires.

Meanwhile, if incense is used, the Priest puts some into the thurible. After this, the Deacon who is to proclaim the Gospel, bowing profoundly before the Priest, asks for the blessing, saying in a low voice:

Your blessing, Father.

The Priest says in a low voice:

May the Lord be in your heart and on your lips,
that you may proclaim his Gospel worthily and well,
in the name of the Father, and of the Son, ✠ and of the Holy Spirit.

The Deacon signs himself with the Sign of the Cross and replies:

Amen.

If, however, a Deacon is not present, the Priest, bowing before the altar, says quietly:

Cleanse my heart and my lips, almighty God,
that I may worthily proclaim your holy Gospel.

The Deacon, or the Priest, then proceeds to the ambo, accompanied, if appropriate, by ministers with incense and candles. There he says:

The Lord be with you.

The people reply:

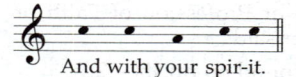

And with your spir-it.

The Deacon, or the Priest:

A reading from the holy Gospel according to ⎡ Mat-thew.
⎢ Mark.
⎢ Luke.
⎣ John.

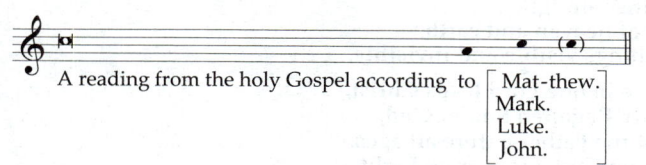

and, at the same time, he makes the Sign of the Cross on the book and on his forehead, lips, and breast.

The people acclaim:

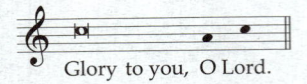

Glory to you, O Lord.

Then the Deacon, or the Priest, incenses the book, if incense is used, and proclaims the Gospel.

At the end of the Gospel, the Deacon, or the Priest, acclaims:

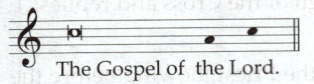

The Gospel of the Lord.

All reply:

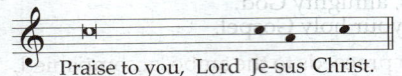

Praise to you, Lord Je-sus Christ.

Then he kisses the book, saying quietly:

Through the words of the Gospel
may our sins be wiped away.

Then follows the Homily, which is to be preached by a Priest or Deacon on all Sundays and Holydays of Obligation; on other days, it is recommended.

At the end of the Homily, the Symbol or Profession of Faith or Creed, when prescribed, is either sung or said:

(A musical setting of the Creed may be found on pp.150-52.)

I believe in one God,
the Father almighty,
maker of heaven and earth,
of all things visible and invisible.

I believe in one Lord Jesus Christ,
the Only Begotten Son of God,
born of the Father before all ages.
God from God, Light from Light,
true God from true God,
begotten, not made, consubstantial with the Father;
through him all things were made.
For us men and for our salvation
he came down from heaven,

The Liturgy of the Word

At the words that follow, up to and including and became man, all bow.

and by the Holy Spirit was incarnate of the Virgin Mary, and became man.

For our sake he was crucified under Pontius Pilate, he suffered death and was buried, and rose again on the third day in accordance with the Scriptures. He ascended into heaven and is seated at the right hand of the Father. He will come again in glory to judge the living and the dead and his kingdom will have no end.

I believe in the Holy Spirit, the Lord, the giver of life, who proceeds from the Father and the Son, who with the Father and the Son is adored and glorified, who has spoken through the prophets.

I believe in one, holy, catholic and apostolic Church. I confess one Baptism for the forgiveness of sins and I look forward to the resurrection of the dead and the life of the world to come. Amen.

Instead of the Niceno-Constantinopolitan Creed, especially during Lent and Easter Time, the baptismal Symbol of the Roman Church, known as the Apostles' Creed, may be used.

I believe in God, the Father almighty, Creator of heaven and earth, and in Jesus Christ, his only Son, our Lord,

At the words that follow, up to and including the Virgin Mary, all bow.

who was conceived by the Holy Spirit, born of the Virgin Mary, suffered under Pontius Pilate, was crucified, died and was buried; he descended into hell; on the third day he rose again from the dead; he ascended into heaven, and is seated at the right hand of God the Father almighty; from there he will come to judge the living and the dead.

**I believe in the Holy Spirit,
the holy catholic Church,
the communion of saints,
the forgiveness of sins,
the resurrection of the body,
and life everlasting. Amen.**

Then follows the Universal Prayer, that is, the Prayer of the Faithful or Bidding Prayers.

THE LITURGY OF THE EUCHARIST

When all this has been done, the Offertory Chant begins. Meanwhile, the ministers place the corporal, the purificator, the chalice, the pall, and the Missal on the altar.

It is desirable that the faithful express their participation by making an offering, bringing forward bread and wine for the celebration of the Eucharist and perhaps other gifts to relieve the needs of the Church and of the poor.

The Priest, standing at the altar, takes the paten with the bread and holds it slightly raised above the altar with both hands, saying in a low voice:

Blessed are you, Lord God of all creation,
for through your goodness we have received
the bread we offer you:
fruit of the earth and work of human hands,
it will become for us the bread of life.

Then he places the paten with the bread on the corporal.

If, however, the Offertory Chant is not sung, the Priest may speak these words aloud; at the end, the people may acclaim:

Blessed be God for ever.

The Deacon, or the Priest, pours wine and a little water into the chalice, saying quietly:

By the mystery of this water and wine
may we come to share in the divinity of Christ
who humbled himself to share in our humanity.

The Priest then takes the chalice and holds it slightly raised above the altar with both hands, saying in a low voice:

Blessed are you, Lord God of all creation,
for through your goodness we have received
the wine we offer you:
fruit of the vine and work of human hands,
it will become our spiritual drink.

Then he places the chalice on the corporal.
If, however, the Offertory Chant is not sung, the Priest may speak these words aloud; at the end, the people may acclaim:

Blessed be God for ever.

After this, the Priest, bowing profoundly, says quietly:

With humble spirit and contrite heart
may we be accepted by you, O Lord,
and may our sacrifice in your sight this day
be pleasing to you, Lord God.

If appropriate, he also incenses the offerings, the cross, and the altar. A Deacon or other minister then incenses the Priest and the people.

Then the Priest, standing at the side of the altar, washes his hands, saying quietly:

Wash me, O Lord, from my iniquity
and cleanse me from my sin.

(A musical setting for the Orate Frates *below may be found on p.152.)*

Standing at the middle of the altar, facing the people, extending and then joining his hands, the Priest says:

Pray, brethren (brothers and sisters),
that my sacrifice and yours
may be acceptable to God,
the almighty Father.

The people rise and reply:

May the Lord accept the sacrifice at your hands
for the praise and glory of his name,
for our good
and the good of all his holy Church.

The Liturgy of the Eucharist

> **Prayer over the Offerings:** turn to the Proper of the Mass of the Day.

Then the Priest, with hands extended, says the Prayer over the Offerings, at the end of which the people acclaim:

Amen.

THE EUCHARISTIC PRAYER

Then the Priest begins the Eucharistic Prayer.

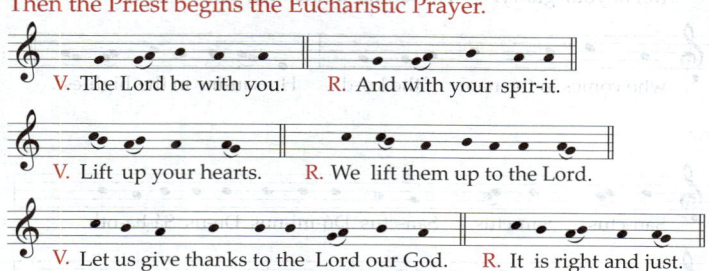

V. The Lord be with you. R. And with your spir-it.

V. Lift up your hearts. R. We lift them up to the Lord.

V. Let us give thanks to the Lord our God. R. It is right and just.

Extending his hands, he says:

The Lord be with you.

The people reply:

And with your spirit.

The Priest, raising his hands, continues:

Lift up your hearts.

The people:

We lift them up to the Lord.

The Priest, with hands extended, adds:

Let us give thanks to the Lord our God.

The people:

It is right and just.

The Priest, with hands extended, continues the Preface.

The Order of Mass

At the end of the Preface he joins his hands and concludes the Preface with the people, singing or saying aloud:

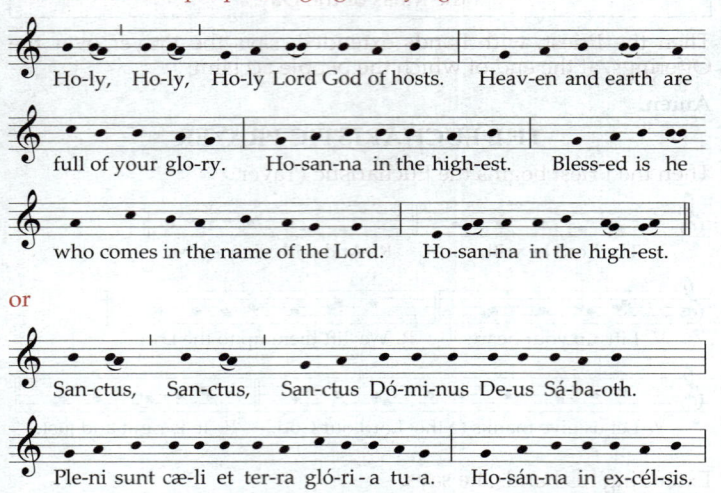

Holy, Holy, Holy Lord God of hosts. Heaven and earth are full of your glory. Hosanna in the highest. Blessed is he who comes in the name of the Lord. Hosanna in the highest.

or

Sanctus, Sanctus, Sanctus Dóminus Deus Sábaoth. Pleni sunt cæli et terra glória tua. Hosánna in excélsis. Benedíctus qui venit in nómine Dómini. Hosánna in excélsis.

PREFACES

PREFACE I OF ADVENT
The two comings of Christ

It is truly right and just, our duty and our salvation,
always and everywhere to give you thanks,
Lord, holy Father, almighty and eternal God,
through Christ our Lord.

For he assumed at his first coming
the lowliness of human flesh,
and so fulfilled the design you formed long ago,
and opened for us the way to eternal salvation,
that, when he comes again in glory and majesty
and all is at last made manifest,
we who watch for that day
may inherit the great promise
in which now we dare to hope.

And so, with Angels and Archangels,
with Thrones and Dominions,
and with all the hosts and Powers of heaven,
we sing the hymn of your glory,
as without end we acclaim:

Holy, Holy, Holy Lord God of hosts . . .

PREFACE II OF ADVENT
The twofold expectation of Christ

It is truly right and just, our duty and our salvation,
always and everywhere to give you thanks,
Lord, holy Father, almighty and eternal God,
through Christ our Lord.

For all the oracles of the prophets foretold him,
the Virgin Mother longed for him
with love beyond all telling,
John the Baptist sang of his coming
and proclaimed his presence when he came.

It is by his gift that already we rejoice
at the mystery of his Nativity,
so that he may find us watchful in prayer
and exultant in his praise.

And so, with Angels and Archangels,
with Thrones and Dominions,
and with all the hosts and Powers of heaven,
we sing the hymn of your glory,
as without end we acclaim:

Holy, Holy, Holy Lord God of hosts . . .

PREFACE I OF THE NATIVITY OF THE LORD
Christ the Light

It is truly right and just, our duty and our salvation,
always and everywhere to give you thanks,
Lord, holy Father, almighty and eternal God.

For in the mystery of the Word made flesh
a new light of your glory has shone upon the eyes of our mind,
so that, as we recognize in him God made visible,
we may be caught up through him in love of things invisible.

And so, with Angels and Archangels,
with Thrones and Dominions,
and with all the hosts and Powers of heaven,
we sing the hymn of your glory,
as without end we acclaim:

Holy, Holy, Holy Lord God of hosts . . .

PREFACE II OF THE NATIVITY OF THE LORD
The restoration of all things in the Incarnation

It is truly right and just, our duty and our salvation,
always and everywhere to give you thanks,
Lord, holy Father, almighty and eternal God,
through Christ our Lord.

For on the feast of this awe-filled mystery,
though invisible in his own divine nature,
he has appeared visibly in ours;
and begotten before all ages,
he has begun to exist in time;
so that, raising up in himself all that was cast down,
he might restore unity to all creation
and call straying humanity back to the heavenly Kingdom.

And so, with all the Angels, we praise you,
as in joyful celebration we acclaim:

Holy, Holy, Holy Lord God of hosts . . .

PREFACE III OF THE NATIVITY OF THE LORD
The exchange in the Incarnation of the Word

It is truly right and just, our duty and our salvation,
always and everywhere to give you thanks,
Lord, holy Father, almighty and eternal God,
through Christ our Lord.

For through him the holy exchange that restores our life
has shone forth today in splendour:
when our frailty is assumed by your Word
not only does human mortality receive unending honour
but by this wondrous union we, too, are made eternal.

And so, in company with the choirs of Angels,
we praise you, and with joy we proclaim:

Holy, Holy, Holy Lord God of hosts . . .

PREFACE OF THE EPIPHANY OF THE LORD
Christ the light of the nations

It is truly right and just, our duty and our salvation,
always and everywhere to give you thanks,
Lord, holy Father, almighty and eternal God.

For today you have revealed the mystery
of our salvation in Christ
as a light for the nations,
and, when he appeared in our mortal nature,
you made us new by the glory of his immortal nature.

And so, with Angels and Archangels,
with Thrones and Dominions,
and with all the hosts and Powers of heaven,
we sing the hymn of your glory,
as without end we acclaim:

Holy, Holy, Holy Lord God of hosts . . .

PREFACE OF THE BAPTISM OF THE LORD

It is truly right and just, our duty and our salvation,
always and everywhere to give you thanks,
Lord, holy Father, almighty and eternal God.

For in the waters of the Jordan
you revealed with signs and wonders a new Baptism,
so that through the voice that came down from heaven
we might come to believe in your Word dwelling among us,
and by the Spirit's descending in the likeness of a dove
we might know that Christ your Servant
has been anointed with the oil of gladness
and sent to bring the good news to the poor.

And so, with the Powers of heaven,
we worship you constantly on earth,
and before your majesty
without end we acclaim:

Holy, Holy, Holy Lord God of hosts . . .

PREFACE I OF LENT
The spiritual meaning of Lent

It is truly right and just, our duty and our salvation,
always and everywhere to give you thanks,
Lord, holy Father, almighty and eternal God,
through Christ our Lord.

For by your gracious gift each year
your faithful await the sacred paschal feasts
with the joy of minds made pure,
so that, more eagerly intent on prayer
and on the works of charity,
and participating in the mysteries
by which they have been reborn,
they may be led to the fullness of grace
that you bestow on your sons and daughters.

And so, with Angels and Archangels,
with Thrones and Dominions,
and with all the hosts and Powers of heaven,
we sing the hymn of your glory,
as without end we acclaim:

Holy, Holy, Holy Lord God of hosts . . .

PREFACE II OF LENT
Spiritual penance

It is truly right and just, our duty and our salvation,
always and everywhere to give you thanks,
Lord, holy Father, almighty and eternal God.

For you have given your children a sacred time
for the renewing and purifying of their hearts,
that, freed from disordered affections,
they may so deal with the things of this passing world
as to hold rather to the things that eternally endure.

And so, with all the Angels and Saints,
we praise you, as without end we acclaim:

Holy, Holy, Holy Lord God of hosts . . .

PREFACE III OF LENT
The fruits of abstinence

It is truly right and just, our duty and our salvation,
always and everywhere to give you thanks,
Lord, holy Father, almighty and eternal God.

For you will that our self-denial should give you thanks,
humble our sinful pride,
contribute to the feeding of the poor,
and so help us imitate you in your kindness.

And so we glorify you with countless Angels,
as with one voice of praise we acclaim:

Holy, Holy, Holy Lord God of hosts . . .

PREFACE IV OF LENT
The fruits of fasting

It is truly right and just, our duty and our salvation,
always and everywhere to give you thanks,
Lord, holy Father, almighty and eternal God.

For through bodily fasting you restrain our faults,
raise up our minds,
and bestow both virtue and its rewards,
through Christ our Lord.

Through him the Angels praise your majesty,
Dominions adore and Powers tremble before you.
Heaven and the Virtues of heaven and the blessed Seraphim
worship together with exultation.
May our voices, we pray, join with theirs
in humble praise, as we acclaim:

Holy, Holy, Holy Lord God of hosts . . .

PREFACE OF THE FIRST SUNDAY OF LENT
The Temptation of the Lord

It is truly right and just, our duty and our salvation,
always and everywhere to give you thanks,
Lord, holy Father, almighty and eternal God,
through Christ our Lord.

By abstaining forty long days from earthly food,
he consecrated through his fast
the pattern of our Lenten observance
and, by overturning all the snares of the ancient serpent,
taught us to cast out the leaven of malice,
so that, celebrating worthily the Paschal Mystery,
we might pass over at last to the eternal paschal feast.

And so, with the company of Angels and Saints,
we sing the hymn of your praise,
as without end we acclaim:

Holy, Holy, Holy Lord God of hosts . . .

PREFACE OF THE SECOND SUNDAY OF LENT
The Transfiguration of the Lord

It is truly right and just, our duty and our salvation,
always and everywhere to give you thanks,
Lord, holy Father, almighty and eternal God,
through Christ our Lord.

For after he had told the disciples of his coming Death,
on the holy mountain he manifested to them his glory,
to show, even by the testimony of the law and the prophets,
that the Passion leads to the glory of the Resurrection.

And so, with the Powers of heaven,
we worship you constantly on earth,

and before your majesty
without end we acclaim:

Holy, Holy, Holy Lord God of hosts . . .

PREFACE OF THE THIRD SUNDAY OF LENT
The Samaritan Woman

It is truly right and just, our duty and our salvation,
always and everywhere to give you thanks,
Lord, holy Father, almighty and eternal God,
through Christ our Lord.

For when he asked the Samaritan woman for water to drink,
he had already created the gift of faith within her
and so ardently did he thirst for her faith,
that he kindled in her the fire of divine love.

And so we, too, give you thanks
and with the Angels
praise your mighty deeds, as we acclaim:

Holy, Holy, Holy Lord God of hosts . . .

PREFACE OF THE FOURTH SUNDAY OF LENT
The Man Born Blind

It is truly right and just, our duty and our salvation,
always and everywhere to give you thanks,
Lord, holy Father, almighty and eternal God,
through Christ our Lord.

By the mystery of the Incarnation,
he has led the human race that walked in darkness
into the radiance of the faith
and has brought those born in slavery to ancient sin
through the waters of regeneration
to make them your adopted children.

Therefore, all creatures of heaven and earth
sing a new song in adoration,
and we, with all the host of Angels,
cry out, and without end acclaim:

Holy, Holy, Holy Lord God of hosts . . .

PREFACE OF THE FIFTH SUNDAY OF LENT
Lazarus

It is truly right and just, our duty and our salvation,
always and everywhere to give you thanks,
Lord, holy Father, almighty and eternal God,
through Christ our Lord.

For as true man he wept for Lazarus his friend
and as eternal God raised him from the tomb,
just as, taking pity on the human race,
he leads us by sacred mysteries to new life.

Through him the host of Angels adores your majesty
and rejoices in your presence for ever.
May our voices, we pray, join with theirs
in one chorus of exultant praise, as we acclaim:

Holy, Holy, Holy Lord God of hosts . . .

PREFACE I OF THE PASSION OF THE LORD
The power of the Cross

It is truly right and just, our duty and our salvation,
always and everywhere to give you thanks,
Lord, holy Father, almighty and eternal God.

For through the saving Passion of your Son
the whole world has received a heart
to confess the infinite power of your majesty,
since by the wondrous power of the Cross
your judgement on the world is now revealed
and the authority of Christ crucified.

And so, Lord, with all the Angels and Saints,
we, too, give you thanks, as in exultation we acclaim:

Holy, Holy, Holy Lord God of hosts . . .

PREFACE II OF THE PASSION OF THE LORD
The victory of the Passion

It is truly right and just, our duty and our salvation,
always and everywhere to give you thanks,

Lord, holy Father, almighty and eternal God,
through Christ our Lord.

For the days of his saving Passion
and glorious Resurrection are approaching,
by which the pride of the ancient foe is vanquished
and the mystery of our redemption in Christ is celebrated.

Through him the host of Angels adores your majesty
and rejoices in your presence for ever.
May our voices, we pray, join with theirs
in one chorus of exultant praise, as we acclaim:

Holy, Holy, Holy Lord God of hosts . . .

PREFACE OF PALM SUNDAY OF THE PASSION OF THE LORD
The Passion of the Lord

It is truly right and just, our duty and our salvation,
always and everywhere to give you thanks,
Lord, holy Father, almighty and eternal God,
through Christ our Lord.

For though innocent he suffered willingly for sinners
and accepted unjust condemnation to save the guilty.
His Death has washed away our sins,
and his Resurrection has purchased our justification.

And so, with all the Angels,
we praise you, as in joyful celebration we acclaim:

Holy, Holy, Holy Lord God of hosts . . .

PREFACE OF THE CHRISM MASS
The priesthood of Christ and the ministry of priests

It is truly right and just, our duty and our salvation,
always and everywhere to give you thanks,
Lord, holy Father, almighty and eternal God.

For by the anointing of the Holy Spirit
you made your Only Begotten Son
High Priest of the new and eternal covenant,
and by your wondrous design were pleased to decree
that his one Priesthood should continue in the Church.

For Christ not only adorns with a royal priesthood
the people he has made his own,
but with a brother's kindness he also chooses men
to become sharers in his sacred ministry
through the laying on of hands.

They are to renew in his name
the sacrifice of human redemption,
to set before your children the paschal banquet,
to lead your holy people in charity,
to nourish them with the word
and strengthen them with the Sacraments.

As they give up their lives for you
and for the salvation of their brothers and sisters,
they strive to be conformed to the image of Christ himself
and offer you a constant witness of faith and love.

And so, Lord, with all the Angels and Saints,
we, too, give you thanks as in exultation we acclaim:

Holy, Holy, Holy Lord God of hosts . . .

PREFACE I OF EASTER
The Paschal Mystery

It is truly right and just, our duty and our salvation,
at all times to acclaim you, O Lord,
but (on this night / on this day / in this time) above all
to laud you yet more gloriously,
when Christ our Passover has been sacrificed.

For he is the true Lamb
who has taken away the sins of the world;
by dying he has destroyed our death,
and by rising, restored our life.

Therefore, overcome with paschal joy,
every land, every people exults in your praise
and even the heavenly Powers, with the angelic hosts,
sing together the unending hymn of your glory,
as they acclaim:

Holy, Holy, Holy Lord God of hosts . . .

PREFACE II OF EASTER
New life in Christ

It is truly right and just, our duty and our salvation,
at all times to acclaim you, O Lord,
but in this time above all to laud you yet more gloriously,
when Christ our Passover has been sacrificed.

Through him the children of light rise to eternal life
and the halls of the heavenly Kingdom
are thrown open to the faithful;
for his Death is our ransom from death,
and in his rising the life of all has risen.

Therefore, overcome with paschal joy,
every land, every people exults in your praise
and even the heavenly Powers, with the angelic hosts,
sing together the unending hymn of your glory,
as they acclaim:

Holy, Holy, Holy Lord God of hosts . . .

PREFACE III OF EASTER
Christ living and always interceding for us

It is truly right and just, our duty and our salvation,
at all times to acclaim you, O Lord,
but in this time above all to laud you yet more gloriously,
when Christ our Passover has been sacrificed.

He never ceases to offer himself for us
but defends us and ever pleads our cause before you:
he is the sacrificial Victim who dies no more,
the Lamb, once slain, who lives for ever.

Therefore, overcome with paschal joy,
every land, every people exults in your praise
and even the heavenly Powers, with the angelic hosts,
sing together the unending hymn of your glory,
as they acclaim:

Holy, Holy, Holy Lord God of hosts . . .

PREFACE IV OF EASTER
The restoration of the universe through the Paschal Mystery

It is truly right and just, our duty and our salvation,
at all times to acclaim you, O Lord,
but in this time above all to laud you yet more gloriously,
when Christ our Passover has been sacrificed.

For, with the old order destroyed,
a universe cast down is renewed,
and integrity of life is restored to us in Christ.

Therefore, overcome with paschal joy,
every land, every people exults in your praise
and even the heavenly Powers, with the angelic hosts,
sing together the unending hymn of your glory,
as they acclaim:

Holy, Holy, Holy Lord God of hosts . . .

PREFACE V OF EASTER
Christ, Priest and Victim

It is truly right and just, our duty and our salvation,
at all times to acclaim you, O Lord,
but in this time above all to laud you yet more gloriously,
when Christ our Passover has been sacrificed.

By the oblation of his Body,
he brought the sacrifices of old to fulfilment
in the reality of the Cross
and, by commending himself to you for our salvation,
showed himself the Priest, the Altar, and the Lamb of sacrifice.

Therefore, overcome with paschal joy,
every land, every people exults in your praise
and even the heavenly Powers, with the angelic hosts,
sing together the unending hymn of your glory,
as they acclaim:

Holy, Holy, Holy Lord God of hosts . . .

The Eucharistic Prayer: Prefaces

PREFACE I OF THE ASCENSION OF THE LORD
The mystery of the Ascension

It is truly right and just, our duty and our salvation,
always and everywhere to give you thanks,
Lord, holy Father, almighty and eternal God.

For the Lord Jesus, the King of glory,
conqueror of sin and death,
ascended (today) to the highest heavens,
as the Angels gazed in wonder.

Mediator between God and man,
judge of the world and Lord of hosts,
he ascended, not to distance himself from our lowly state
but that we, his members, might be confident of following
where he, our Head and Founder, has gone before.

Therefore, overcome with paschal joy,
every land, every people exults in your praise
and even the heavenly Powers, with the angelic hosts,
sing together the unending hymn of your glory,
as they acclaim:

Holy, Holy, Holy Lord God of hosts . . .

PREFACE II OF THE ASCENSION OF THE LORD
The mystery of the Ascension

It is truly right and just, our duty and our salvation,
always and everywhere to give you thanks,
Lord, holy Father, almighty and eternal God,
through Christ our Lord.

For after his Resurrection
he plainly appeared to all his disciples
and was taken up to heaven in their sight,
that he might make us sharers in his divinity.

Therefore, overcome with paschal joy,
every land, every people exults in your praise
and even the heavenly Powers, with the angelic hosts,
sing together the unending hymn of your glory,
as they acclaim:

Holy, Holy, Holy Lord God of hosts . . .

PREFACE OF THE MYSTERY OF PENTECOST

It is truly right and just, our duty and our salvation,
always and everywhere to give you thanks,
Lord, holy Father, almighty and eternal God.

For, bringing your Paschal Mystery to completion,
you bestowed the Holy Spirit today
on those you made your adopted children
by uniting them to your Only Begotten Son.
This same Spirit, as the Church came to birth,
opened to all peoples the knowledge of God
and brought together the many languages of the earth
in profession of the one faith.

Therefore, overcome with paschal joy,
every land, every people exults in your praise
and even the heavenly Powers, with the angelic hosts,
sing together the unending hymn of your glory,
as they acclaim:

Holy, Holy, Holy Lord God of hosts . . .

PREFACE I OF THE SUNDAYS IN ORDINARY TIME
The Paschal Mystery and the People of God

It is truly right and just, our duty and our salvation,
always and everywhere to give you thanks,
Lord, holy Father, almighty and eternal God,
through Christ our Lord.

For through his Paschal Mystery,
he accomplished the marvellous deed,
by which he has freed us from the yoke of sin and death,
summoning us to the glory of being now called
a chosen race, a royal priesthood,
a holy nation, a people for your own possession,
to proclaim everywhere your mighty works,
for you have called us out of darkness
into your own wonderful light.

And so, with Angels and Archangels,
with Thrones and Dominions,
and with all the hosts and Powers of heaven,
we sing the hymn of your glory,
as without end we acclaim:

Holy, Holy, Holy Lord God of hosts . . .

PREFACE II OF THE SUNDAYS IN ORDINARY TIME
The mystery of salvation

It is truly right and just, our duty and our salvation,
always and everywhere to give you thanks,
Lord, holy Father, almighty and eternal God,
through Christ our Lord.

For out of compassion for the waywardness that is ours,
he humbled himself and was born of the Virgin;
by the passion of the Cross he freed us from unending death,
and by rising from the dead he gave us life eternal.

And so, with Angels and Archangels,
with Thrones and Dominions,
and with all the hosts and Powers of heaven,
we sing the hymn of your glory,
as without end we acclaim:

Holy, Holy, Holy Lord God of hosts . . .

PREFACE III OF THE SUNDAYS IN ORDINARY TIME
The salvation of man by a man

It is truly right and just, our duty and our salvation,
always and everywhere to give you thanks,
Lord, holy Father, almighty and eternal God.

For we know it belongs to your boundless glory,
that you came to the aid of mortal beings with your divinity
and even fashioned for us a remedy out of mortality itself,
that the cause of our downfall
might become the means of our salvation,
through Christ our Lord.

Through him the host of Angels adores your majesty
and rejoices in your presence for ever.
May our voices, we pray, join with theirs
in one chorus of exultant praise, as we acclaim:

Holy, Holy, Holy Lord God of hosts . . .

PREFACE IV OF THE SUNDAYS IN ORDINARY TIME
The history of salvation

It is truly right and just, our duty and our salvation,
always and everywhere to give you thanks,
Lord, holy Father, almighty and eternal God,
through Christ our Lord.

For by his birth he brought renewal
to humanity's fallen state,
and by his suffering, cancelled out our sins;
by his rising from the dead
he has opened the way to eternal life,
and by ascending to you, O Father,
he has unlocked the gates of heaven.

And so, with the company of Angels and Saints,
we sing the hymn of your praise,
as without end we acclaim:

Holy, Holy, Holy Lord God of hosts . . .

PREFACE V OF THE SUNDAYS IN ORDINARY TIME
Creation

It is truly right and just, our duty and our salvation,
always and everywhere to give you thanks,
Lord, holy Father, almighty and eternal God.

For you laid the foundations of the world
and have arranged the changing of times and seasons;
you formed man in your own image
and set humanity over the whole world in all its wonder,
to rule in your name over all you have made
and for ever praise you in your mighty works,
through Christ our Lord.

And so, with all the Angels, we praise you,
as in joyful celebration we acclaim:

Holy, Holy, Holy Lord God of hosts . . .

PREFACE VI OF THE SUNDAYS IN ORDINARY TIME
The pledge of the eternal Passover

It is truly right and just, our duty and our salvation,
always and everywhere to give you thanks,
Lord, holy Father, almighty and eternal God.

For in you we live and move and have our being,
and while in this body
we not only experience the daily effects of your care,
but even now possess the pledge of life eternal.

For, having received the first fruits of the Spirit,
through whom you raised up Jesus from the dead,
we hope for an everlasting share in the Paschal Mystery.

And so, with all the Angels, we praise you,
as in joyful celebration we acclaim:

Holy, Holy, Holy Lord God of hosts . . .

PREFACE VII OF THE SUNDAYS IN ORDINARY TIME
Salvation through the obedience of Christ

It is truly right and just, our duty and our salvation,
always and everywhere to give you thanks,
Lord, holy Father, almighty and eternal God.

For you so loved the world
that in your mercy you sent us the Redeemer,
to live like us in all things but sin,
so that you might love in us what you loved in your Son,
by whose obedience we have been restored to those gifts of yours
that, by sinning, we had lost in disobedience.

And so, Lord, with all the Angels and Saints,
we, too, give you thanks, as in exultation we acclaim:

Holy, Holy, Holy Lord God of hosts . . .

PREFACE VIII OF THE SUNDAYS IN ORDINARY TIME
The Church united by the unity of the Trinity

It is truly right and just, our duty and our salvation,
always and everywhere to give you thanks,
Lord, holy Father, almighty and eternal God.

For, when your children were scattered afar by sin,
through the Blood of your Son and the power of the Spirit,
you gathered them again to yourself,
that a people, formed as one by the unity of the Trinity,
made the body of Christ and the temple of the Holy Spirit,
might, to the praise of your manifold wisdom,
be manifest as the Church.

And so, in company with the choirs of Angels,
we praise you, and with joy we proclaim:

Holy, Holy, Holy Lord God of hosts . . .

PREFACE OF THE MYSTERY OF THE MOST HOLY TRINITY

It is truly right and just, our duty and our salvation,
always and everywhere to give you thanks,
Lord, holy Father, almighty and eternal God.

For with your Only Begotten Son and the Holy Spirit
you are one God, one Lord:
not in the unity of a single person,
but in a Trinity of one substance.

For what you have revealed to us of your glory
we believe equally of your Son
and of the Holy Spirit,
so that, in the confessing of the true and eternal Godhead,
you might be adored in what is proper to each Person,
their unity in substance,
and their equality in majesty.

For this is praised by Angels and Archangels,
Cherubim, too, and Seraphim,
who never cease to cry out each day,
as with one voice they acclaim:

Holy, Holy, Holy Lord God of hosts . . .

PREFACE OF THE MYSTERY OF THE INCARNATION
(25 March)

It is truly right and just, our duty and our salvation,
always and everywhere to give you thanks,
Lord, holy Father, almighty and eternal God,
through Christ our Lord.

For the Virgin Mary heard with faith
that the Christ was to be born among men and for men's sake
by the overshadowing power of the Holy Spirit.
Lovingly she bore him in her immaculate womb,
that the promises to the children of Israel might come about
and the hope of nations be accomplished beyond all telling.

Through him the host of Angels adores your majesty
and rejoices in your presence for ever.
May our voices, we pray, join with theirs
in one chorus of exultant praise, as we acclaim:

Holy, Holy, Holy Lord God of hosts . . .

PREFACE OF THE SACRED HEART
The Boundless Charity of Christ

It is truly right and just, our duty and our salvation,
always and everywhere to give you thanks,
Lord, holy Father, almighty and eternal God,
through Christ our Lord.

For raised up high on the Cross,
he gave himself up for us with a wonderful love
and poured out blood and water from his pierced side,
the wellspring of the Church's Sacraments,
so that, won over to the open heart of the Saviour,
all might draw water joyfully from the springs of salvation.

And so, with all the Angels and Saints,
we praise you, as without end we acclaim:

Holy, Holy, Holy Lord God of hosts . . .

PREFACE OF THE VICTORY OF THE GLORIOUS CROSS
(14 September)

It is truly right and just, our duty and our salvation,
always and everywhere to give you thanks,
Lord, holy Father, almighty and eternal God.

For you placed the salvation of the human race
on the wood of the Cross,
so that, where death arose,
life might again spring forth
and the evil one, who conquered on a tree,
might likewise on a tree be conquered,
through Christ our Lord.

Through him the Angels praise your majesty,
Dominions adore and Powers tremble before you.
Heaven and the Virtues of heaven and the blessed Seraphim
worship together with exultation.
May our voices, we pray, join with theirs
in humble praise, as we acclaim:

Holy, Holy, Holy Lord God of hosts . . .

PREFACE I OF THE MOST HOLY EUCHARIST
The Sacrifice and the Sacrament of Christ

It is truly right and just, our duty and our salvation,
always and everywhere to give you thanks,
Lord, holy Father, almighty and eternal God,
through Christ our Lord.

For he is the true and eternal Priest,
who instituted the pattern of an everlasting sacrifice
and was the first to offer himself as the saving Victim,
commanding us to make this offering as his memorial.
As we eat his flesh that was sacrificed for us,
we are made strong,
and, as we drink his Blood that was poured out for us,
we are washed clean.

And so, with Angels and Archangels,
with Thrones and Dominions,
and with all the hosts and Powers of heaven,
we sing the hymn of your glory,
as without end we acclaim:

Holy, Holy, Holy Lord God of hosts . . .

PREFACE II OF THE MOST HOLY EUCHARIST
The fruits of the Most Holy Eucharist

It is truly right and just, our duty and our salvation,
always and everywhere to give you thanks,
Lord, holy Father, almighty and eternal God,
through Christ our Lord.

For at the Last Supper with his Apostles,
establishing for the ages to come the saving memorial of the Cross,
he offered himself to you as the unblemished Lamb,
the acceptable gift of perfect praise.

Nourishing your faithful by this sacred mystery,
you make them holy, so that the human race,
bounded by one world,
may be enlightened by one faith
and united by one bond of charity.

And so, we approach the table of this wondrous Sacrament,
so that, bathed in the sweetness of your grace,
we may pass over to the heavenly realities here foreshadowed.

Therefore, all creatures of heaven and earth
sing a new song in adoration,
and we, with all the host of Angels,
cry out, and without end we acclaim:

Holy, Holy, Holy Lord God of hosts . . .

PREFACE OF THE MYSTERY OF THE PRESENTATION OF THE LORD
(2 February)

It is truly right and just, our duty and our salvation,
always and everywhere to give you thanks,
Lord, holy Father, almighty and eternal God.

For your co-eternal Son was presented on this day in the Temple
and revealed by the Spirit
as the glory of Israel and Light of the nations.

And so, we, too, go forth, rejoicing to encounter your Salvation,
and with the Angels and Saints
praise you, as without end we acclaim:

Holy, Holy, Holy Lord God of hosts . . .

THE MYSTERY OF THE TRANSFIGURATION
(6 August)

It is truly right and just, our duty and our salvation,
always and everywhere to give you thanks,
Lord, holy Father, almighty and eternal God,
through Christ our Lord.

For he revealed his glory in the presence of chosen witnesses
and filled with the greatest splendour that bodily form
which he shares with all humanity,
that the scandal of the Cross
might be removed from the hearts of his disciples
and that he might show
how in the Body of the whole Church is to be fulfilled
what so wonderfully shone forth first in its Head.

And so, with the Powers of heaven,
we worship you constantly on earth,
and before your majesty
without end we acclaim:

Holy, Holy, Holy Lord God of hosts . . .

PREFACE OF OUR LORD JESUS CHRIST, KING OF THE UNIVERSE

It is truly right and just, our duty and our salvation,
always and everywhere to give you thanks,
Lord, holy Father, almighty and eternal God.

For you anointed your Only Begotten Son,
our Lord Jesus Christ, with the oil of gladness
as eternal Priest and King of all creation,
so that, by offering himself on the altar of the Cross
as a spotless sacrifice to bring us peace,
he might accomplish the mysteries of human redemption
and, making all created things subject to his rule,
he might present to the immensity of your majesty
an eternal and universal kingdom,
a kingdom of truth and life,
a kingdom of holiness and grace,
a kingdom of justice, love and peace.

And so, with Angels and Archangels,
with Thrones and Dominions,
and with all the hosts and Powers of heaven,
we sing the hymn of your glory,
as without end we acclaim:

Holy, Holy, Holy Lord God of hosts . . .

PREFACE I OF THE DEDICATION OF A CHURCH
The mystery of the temple of God,
which is the Church

It is truly right and just, our duty and our salvation,
always and everywhere to give you thanks,
Lord, holy Father, almighty and eternal God,
through Christ our Lord.

For in this visible house that you have let us build
and where you never cease to show favour
to the family on pilgrimage to you in this place,
you wonderfully manifest and accomplish
the mystery of your communion with us.
Here you build up for yourself the temple that we are
and cause your Church, spread throughout the world,
to grow ever more and more as the Lord's own Body,
till she reaches her fullness in the vision of peace,
the heavenly city of Jerusalem.

And so, with the countless ranks of the blessed,
in the temple of your glory we praise you,
we bless you and proclaim your greatness, as we acclaim:

Holy, Holy, Holy Lord God of hosts . . .

PREFACE II OF THE DEDICATION OF A CHURCH
The mystery of the Church, the Bride of Christ
and the temple of the Spirit

It is truly right and just, our duty and our salvation,
always and everywhere to give you thanks,
Lord, holy Father, almighty and eternal God.

For in your benevolence you are pleased
to dwell in this house of prayer
in order to perfect us as the temple of the Holy Spirit,

supported by the perpetual help of your grace
and resplendent with the glory of a life acceptable to you.

Year by year you sanctify the Church, the Bride of Christ,
foreshadowed in visible buildings,
so that, rejoicing as the mother of countless children,
she may be given her place in your heavenly glory.

And so, with all the Angels and Saints,
we praise you, as without end we acclaim:

Holy, Holy, Holy Lord God of hosts . . .

PREFACE I OF THE BLESSED VIRGIN MARY
The Motherhood of the Blessed Virgin Mary

It is truly right and just, our duty and our salvation,
always and everywhere to give you thanks,
Lord, holy Father, almighty and eternal God,
and to praise, bless, and glorify your name
(on the Solemnity of the Motherhood / on the feast day / on the Nativity / in veneration)
of the Blessed ever-Virgin Mary.

For by the overshadowing of the Holy Spirit
she conceived your Only Begotten Son,
and without losing the glory of virginity,
brought forth into the world the eternal Light,
Jesus Christ our Lord.

Through him the Angels praise your majesty,
Dominions adore and Powers tremble before you.
Heaven and the Virtues of heaven and the blessed Seraphim
worship together with exultation.
May our voices, we pray, join with theirs
in humble praise, as we acclaim:

Holy, Holy, Holy Lord God of hosts . . .

PREFACE II OF THE BLESSED VIRGIN MARY
The Church praises God with the words of Mary

It is truly right and just, our duty and our salvation,
to praise your mighty deeds in the exaltation of all the Saints,
and especially, as we celebrate the memory of the Blessed Virgin Mary,
to proclaim your kindness as we echo her thankful hymn of praise.

The Eucharistic Prayer: Prefaces 43

For truly even to earth's ends you have done great things
and extended your abundant mercy from age to age:
when you looked on the lowliness of your handmaid,
you gave us through her the author of our salvation,
your Son, Jesus Christ, our Lord.

Through him the host of Angels adores your majesty
and rejoices in your presence for ever.
May our voices, we pray, join with theirs
in one chorus of exultant praise, as we acclaim:

Holy, Holy, Holy Lord God of hosts . . .

PREFACE OF THE IMMACULATE CONCEPTION OF THE BLESSED VIRGIN MARY
The mystery of Mary and the Church

It is truly right and just, our duty and our salvation,
always and everywhere to give you thanks,
Lord, holy Father, almighty and eternal God.

For you preserved the Most Blessed Virgin Mary
from all stain of original sin,
so that in her, endowed with the rich fullness of your grace,
you might prepare a worthy Mother for your Son
and signify the beginning of the Church,
his beautiful Bride without spot or wrinkle.

She, the most pure Virgin, was to bring forth a Son,
the innocent Lamb who would wipe away our offences;
you placed her above all others
to be for your people an advocate of grace
and a model of holiness.

And so, in company with the choirs of Angels,
we praise you, and with joy we proclaim:

Holy, Holy, Holy Lord God of hosts . . .

PREFACE OF THE ASSUMPTION OF THE BLESSED VIRGIN MARY
The Glory of Mary assumed into Heaven

It is truly right and just, our duty and our salvation,
always and everywhere to give you thanks,
Lord, holy Father, almighty and eternal God,
through Christ our Lord.

For today the Virgin Mother of God
was assumed into heaven
as the beginning and image
of your Church's coming to perfection
and a sign of sure hope and comfort to your pilgrim people;
rightly you would not allow her
to see the corruption of the tomb
since from her own body she marvellously brought forth
your incarnate Son, the Author of all life.

And so, in company with the choirs of Angels,
we praise you, and with joy we proclaim:

Holy, Holy, Holy Lord God of hosts . . .

PREFACE OF THE ANGELS
God glorified through the Angels (29 September, 2 October)

It is truly right and just, our duty and our salvation,
always and everywhere to give you thanks,
Lord, holy Father, almighty and eternal God,
and to praise you without end
in your Archangels and Angels.

For the honour we pay the angelic creatures
in whom you delight
redounds to your own surpassing glory,
and by their great dignity and splendour
you show how infinitely great you are,
to be exalted above all things,
through Christ our Lord.

Through him the multitude of Angels extols your majesty,
and we are united with them in exultant adoration,
as with one voice of praise we acclaim:

Holy, Holy, Holy Lord God of hosts . . .

PREFACE OF THE MISSION OF THE PRECURSOR
(24 June, 29 August)

It is truly right and just, our duty and our salvation,
always and everywhere to give you thanks,
Lord, holy Father, almighty and eternal God,
through Christ our Lord.

The Eucharistic Prayer: Prefaces

In his Precursor, Saint John the Baptist,
we praise your great glory,
for you consecrated him for a singular honour
among those born of women.

His birth brought great rejoicing;
even in the womb he leapt for joy
at the coming of human salvation.
He alone of all the prophets
pointed out the Lamb of redemption.

And to make holy the flowing waters,
he baptized the very author of Baptism
and was privileged to bear him supreme witness
by the shedding of his blood.

And so, with the Powers of heaven,
we worship you constantly on earth,
and before your majesty
without end we acclaim:

Holy, Holy, Holy Lord God of hosts . . .

PREFACE OF THE MISSION OF SAINT JOSEPH
(19 March, 1 May)

It is truly right and just, our duty and our salvation,
always and everywhere to give you thanks,
Lord, holy Father, almighty and eternal God,
and on the Solemnity of Saint Joseph
to give you fitting praise,
to glorify you and bless you.

For this just man was given by you
as spouse to the Virgin Mother of God
and set as a wise and faithful servant
in charge of your household,
to watch like a father over your Only Begotten Son,
who was conceived by the overshadowing of the Holy Spirit,
our Lord Jesus Christ.

Through him the Angels praise your majesty,
Dominions adore and Powers tremble before you.
Heaven and the Virtues of heaven and the blessed Seraphim
worship together with exultation.
May our voices, we pray, join with theirs
in humble praise, as we acclaim:

Holy, Holy, Holy Lord God of hosts . . .

PREFACE OF THE TWOFOLD MISSION OF PETER AND PAUL IN THE CHURCH
(29 June)

It is truly right and just, our duty and our salvation,
always and everywhere to give you thanks,
Lord, holy Father, almighty and eternal God.

For by your providence
the blessed Apostles Peter and Paul bring us joy:
Peter, foremost in confessing the faith,
Paul, its outstanding preacher,
Peter, who established the early Church from the remnant of Israel,
Paul, master and teacher of the Gentiles that you call.

And so, each in a different way
gathered together the one family of Christ;
and revered together throughout the world,
they share one Martyr's crown.

And therefore, with all the Angels and Saints,
we praise you, as without end we acclaim:

Holy, Holy, Holy Lord God of hosts . . .

PREFACE I OF APOSTLES
The Apostles, shepherds of God's people

It is truly right and just, our duty and our salvation,
always and everywhere to give you thanks,
Lord, holy Father, almighty and eternal God.

For you, eternal Shepherd, do not desert your flock,
but through the blessed Apostles
watch over it and protect it always,
so that it may be governed
by those you have appointed shepherds
to lead it in the name of your Son.

And so, with Angels and Archangels,
with Thrones and Dominions,
and with all the hosts and Powers of heaven,
we sing the hymn of your glory,
as without end we acclaim:

Holy, Holy, Holy Lord God of hosts . . .

PREFACE II OF APOSTLES
The apostolic foundation and witness

It is truly right and just, our duty and our salvation,
always and everywhere to give you thanks,
Lord, holy Father, almighty and eternal God,
through Christ our Lord.

For you have built your Church
to stand firm on apostolic foundations,
to be a lasting sign of your holiness on earth
and offer all humanity your heavenly teaching.

Therefore, now and for ages unending,
with all the host of Angels,
we sing to you with all our hearts,
crying out as we acclaim:

Holy, Holy, Holy Lord God of hosts . . .

PREFACE I OF SAINTS
The glory of the Saints

It is truly right and just, our duty and our salvation,
always and everywhere to give you thanks,
Lord, holy Father, almighty and eternal God.

For you are praised in the company of your Saints
and, in crowning their merits, you crown your own gifts.
By their way of life you offer us an example,
by communion with them you give us companionship,
by their intercession, sure support,
so that, encouraged by so great a cloud of witnesses,
we may run as victors in the race before us
and win with them the imperishable crown of glory,
through Christ our Lord.

And so, with the Angels and Archangels,
and with the great multitude of the Saints,
we sing the hymn of your praise,
as without end we acclaim:

Holy, Holy, Holy Lord God of hosts . . .

PREFACE II OF SAINTS
The action of the Saints

It is truly right and just, our duty and our salvation,
always and everywhere to give you thanks,
Lord, holy Father, almighty and eternal God,
through Christ our Lord.

For in the marvellous confession of your Saints,
you make your Church fruitful with strength ever new
and offer us sure signs of your love.
And that your saving mysteries may be fulfilled,
their great example lends us courage,
their fervent prayers sustain us in all we do.

And so, Lord, with all the Angels and Saints,
we, too, give you thanks, as in exultation we acclaim:

Holy, Holy, Holy Lord God of hosts . . .

PREFACE III OF SAINTS
The glory of Jerusalem, our mother (November 1)

It is truly right and just, our duty and our salvation,
always and everywhere to give you thanks,
Lord, holy Father, almighty and eternal God.

For today by your gift we celebrate the festival of your city,
the heavenly Jerusalem, our mother,
where the great array of our brothers and sisters
already gives you eternal praise.

Towards her, we eagerly hasten, as pilgrims advancing by faith,
rejoicing in the glory bestowed upon those exalted members of the Church
through whom you give us, in our frailty, both strength and good example.

And so, we glorify you with the multitude of Saints and Angels,
as with one voice of praise we acclaim:

Holy, Holy, Holy Lord God of hosts . . .

PREFACE I OF HOLY MARTYRS
The sign and example of martyrdom

It is truly right and just, our duty and our salvation,
always and everywhere to give you thanks,

Lord, holy Father, almighty and eternal God.

For the blood of your blessed Martyr N.,
poured out like Christ's to glorify your name,
shows forth your marvellous works,
by which in our weakness you perfect your power
and on the feeble bestow strength to bear you witness,
through Christ our Lord.

And so, with the Powers of heaven,
we worship you constantly on earth,
and before your majesty
without end we acclaim:

Holy, Holy, Holy Lord God of hosts . . .

PREFACE II OF HOLY MARTYRS
The wonders of God in the victory of the Martyrs

It is truly right and just, our duty and our salvation,
always and everywhere to give you thanks,
Lord, holy Father, almighty and eternal God.

For you are glorified when your Saints are praised;
their very sufferings are but wonders of your might:
in your mercy you give ardour to their faith,
to their endurance you grant firm resolve,
and in their struggle the victory is yours,
through Christ our Lord.

Therefore, all creatures of heaven and earth
sing a new song in adoration,
and we, with all the host of Angels,
cry out, and without end we acclaim:

Holy, Holy, Holy Lord God of hosts . . .

PREFACE OF HOLY PASTORS
The presence of holy Pastors in the Church

It is truly right and just, our duty and our salvation,
always and everywhere to give you thanks,
Lord, holy Father, almighty and eternal God,
through Christ our Lord.

For, as on the festival of Saint N. you bid your Church rejoice,
so, too, you strengthen her by the example of his holy life,

teach her by his words of preaching,
and keep her safe in answer to his prayers.

And so, with the company of Angels and Saints,
we sing the hymn of your praise,
as without end we acclaim:

Holy, Holy, Holy Lord God of hosts . . .

PREFACE OF HOLY VIRGINS AND RELIGIOUS
The sign of a life consecrated to God

It is truly right and just, our duty and our salvation,
always and everywhere to give you thanks,
Lord, holy Father, almighty and eternal God.

For in the Saints who consecrated themselves to Christ
for the sake of the Kingdom of Heaven,
it is right to celebrate the wonders of your providence,
by which you call human nature back to its original holiness
and bring it to experience on this earth
the gifts you promise in the new world to come.

And so, with all the Angels and Saints,
we praise you, as without end we acclaim:

Holy, Holy, Holy Lord God of hosts . . .

COMMON PREFACE I
The renewal of all things in Christ

It is truly right and just, our duty and our salvation,
always and everywhere to give you thanks,
Lord, holy Father, almighty and eternal God,
through Christ our Lord.

In him you have been pleased to renew all things,
giving us all a share in his fullness.
For though he was in the form of God, he emptied himself
and by the blood of his Cross brought peace to all creation.
Therefore he has been exalted above all things,
and to all who obey him,
has become the source of eternal salvation.

And so, with Angels and Archangels,
with Thrones and Dominions,
and with all the hosts and Powers of heaven,

we sing the hymn of your glory,
as without end we acclaim:

Holy, Holy, Holy Lord God of hosts . . .

COMMON PREFACE II
Salvation through Christ

It is truly right and just, our duty and our salvation,
always and everywhere to give you thanks,
Lord, holy Father, almighty and eternal God.

For in goodness you created man
and, when he was justly condemned,
in mercy you redeemed him,
through Christ our Lord.

Through him the Angels praise your majesty,
Dominions adore and Powers tremble before you.
Heaven and the Virtues of heaven and the blessed Seraphim
worship together with exultation.
May our voices, we pray, join with theirs
in humble praise, as we acclaim:

Holy, Holy, Holy Lord God of hosts . . .

COMMON PREFACE III
Praise to God for the creation and restoration of the human race

It is truly right and just, our duty and our salvation,
always and everywhere to give you thanks,
Lord, holy Father, almighty and eternal God.

For just as through your beloved Son
you created the human race,
so also through him
with great goodness you formed it anew.

And so, it is right that all your creatures serve you,
all the redeemed praise you,
and all your Saints with one heart bless you.
Therefore, we, too, extol you with all the Angels,
as in joyful celebration we acclaim:

Holy, Holy, Holy Lord God of hosts . . .

COMMON PREFACE IV
Praise, the gift of God

It is truly right and just, our duty and our salvation,
always and everywhere to give you thanks,
Lord, holy Father, almighty and eternal God.

For, although you have no need of our praise,
yet our thanksgiving is itself your gift,
since our praises add nothing to your greatness
but profit us for salvation,
through Christ our Lord.

And so, in company with the choirs of Angels,
we praise you, and with joy we proclaim:

Holy, Holy, Holy Lord God of hosts . . .

COMMON PREFACE V
The proclamation of the Mystery of Christ

It is truly right and just, our duty and our salvation,
always and everywhere to give you thanks,
Lord, holy Father, almighty and eternal God,
through Christ our Lord.

His Death we celebrate in love,
his Resurrection we confess with living faith,
and his Coming in glory we await with unwavering hope.

And so, with all the Angels and Saints,
we praise you, as without end we acclaim:

Holy, Holy, Holy Lord God of hosts . . .

COMMON PREFACE VI
The mystery of salvation in Christ

It is truly right and just, our duty and our salvation,
always and everywhere to give you thanks, Father most holy,
through your beloved Son, Jesus Christ,
your Word through whom you made all things,
whom you sent as our Saviour and Redeemer,
incarnate by the Holy Spirit and born of the Virgin.

The Eucharistic Prayer: Prefaces

Fulfilling your will and gaining for you a holy people,
he stretched out his hands as he endured his Passion,
so as to break the bonds of death and manifest the resurrection.

And so, with the Angels and all the Saints,
we declare your glory,
as with one voice we acclaim:

Holy, Holy, Holy Lord God of hosts . . .

PREFACE FOR THE UNITY OF CHRISTIANS
The unity of the Body of Christ, which is the Church

It is truly right and just, our duty and our salvation,
always and everywhere to give you thanks,
Lord, holy Father, almighty and eternal God,
through Christ our Lord.

For through him you brought us
to the knowledge of your truth,
so that by the bond of one faith and one Baptism
we might become his Body.

Through him you poured out
your Holy Spirit among all the nations,
so that in a wondrous manner
he might prompt and engender unity
in the diversity of your gifts,
dwelling within your adopted children
and filling and ruling the whole Church.

And so, in company with the choirs of Angels,
we praise you, and with joy we proclaim:

Holy, Holy, Holy Lord God of hosts . . .

PREFACE I FOR THE CELEBRATION OF MARRIAGE
The dignity of the marriage covenant

It is truly right and just, our duty and our salvation,
always and everywhere to give you thanks,
Lord, holy Father, almighty and eternal God.

For you have forged the covenant of marriage as a sweet yoke of harmony

and an unbreakable bond of peace,
so that the chaste and fruitful love of holy Matrimony
may serve to increase the children you adopt as your own.

By your providence and grace, O Lord,
you accomplish the wonder of this twofold design:
that, while the birth of children brings beauty to the world,
their rebirth in Baptism gives increase to the Church,
through Christ our Lord.

Through him, with the Angels and all the Saints,
we sing the hymn of your praise,
as without end we acclaim:

Holy, Holy, Holy Lord God of hosts . . .

PREFACE II FOR THE CELEBRATION OF MARRIAGE
The great sacrament of matrimony

It is truly right and just, our duty and our salvation,
always and everywhere to give you thanks,
Lord, holy Father, almighty and eternal God,
through Christ our Lord.

For in him you have made a new covenant with your people,
so that, as you have redeemed man and woman
by the mystery of Christ's Death and Resurrection,
so in Christ you might make them partakers of divine nature
and joint heirs with him of heavenly glory.

In the union of husband and wife
you give a sign of Christ's loving gift of grace,
so that the Sacrament we celebrate
might draw us back more deeply
into the wondrous design of your love.

And so, with the Angels and all the Saints,
we praise you, and without end we acclaim:

Holy, Holy, Holy Lord God of hosts . . .

PREFACE III FOR THE CELEBRATION OF MARRIAGE
Matrimony as a sign of divine love

It is truly right and just, our duty and our salvation,
always and everywhere to give you thanks,
Lord, holy Father, almighty and eternal God.

The Eucharistic Prayer: Prefaces

For you willed that the human race,
created by the gift of your goodness,
should be raised to such high dignity
that in the union of husband and wife
you might bestow a true image of your love.

For those you created out of charity
you call to the law of charity without ceasing
and grant them a share in your eternal charity.

And so, the Sacrament of holy Matrimony,
as the abiding sign of your own love,
consecrates the love of man and woman,
through Christ our Lord.

Through him, with the Angels and all the Saints,
we sing the hymn of your praise,
as without end we acclaim:

Holy, Holy, Holy Lord God of hosts . . .

PREFACE I FOR THE DEAD
The hope of resurrection in Christ

It is truly right and just, our duty and our salvation,
always and everywhere to give you thanks,
Lord, holy Father, almighty and eternal God,
through Christ our Lord.

In him the hope of blessed resurrection has dawned,
that those saddened by the certainty of dying
might be consoled by the promise of immortality to come.
Indeed for your faithful, Lord,
life is changed not ended,
and, when this earthly dwelling turns to dust,
an eternal dwelling is made ready for them in heaven.

And so, with Angels and Archangels,
with Thrones and Dominions,
and with all the hosts and Powers of heaven,
we sing the hymn of your glory,
as without end we acclaim:

Holy, Holy, Holy Lord God of hosts . . .

PREFACE II FOR THE DEAD
Christ died so that we might live

It is truly right and just, our duty and our salvation,
always and everywhere to give you thanks,
Lord, holy Father, almighty and eternal God,
through Christ our Lord.

For as one alone he accepted death,
so that we might all escape from dying;
as one man he chose to die,
so that in your sight we all might live for ever.

And so, in company with the choirs of Angels,
we praise you, and with joy we proclaim:

Holy, Holy, Holy Lord God of hosts . . .

PREFACE III FOR THE DEAD
Christ, the salvation and the life

It is truly right and just, our duty and our salvation,
always and everywhere to give you thanks,
Lord, holy Father, almighty and eternal God,
through Christ our Lord.

For he is the salvation of the world,
the life of the human race,
the resurrection of the dead.

Through him the host of Angels adores your majesty
and rejoices in your presence for ever.
May our voices, we pray, join with theirs
in one chorus of exultant praise, as we acclaim:

Holy, Holy, Holy Lord God of hosts . . .

PREFACE IV FOR THE DEAD
From earthly life to heavenly glory

It is truly right and just, our duty and our salvation,
always and everywhere to give you thanks,
Lord, holy Father, almighty and eternal God.

The Eucharistic Prayer: Prefaces

For it is at your summons that we come to birth,
by your will that we are governed,
and at your command that we return,
on account of sin,
to that earth from which we came.

And when you give the sign,
we who have been redeemed by the Death of your Son,
shall be raised up to the glory of his Resurrection.

And so, with the company of Angels and Saints,
we sing the hymn of your praise,
as without end we acclaim:

Holy, Holy, Holy Lord God of hosts . . .

PREFACE V FOR THE DEAD
Our resurrection through the victory of Christ

It is truly right and just, our duty and our salvation,
always and everywhere to give you thanks,
Lord, holy Father, almighty and eternal God.

For even though by our own fault we perish,
yet by your compassion and your grace,
when seized by death according to our sins,
we are redeemed through Christ's great victory,
and with him called back into life.

And so, with the Powers of heaven,
we worship you constantly on earth,
and before your majesty
without end we acclaim:

Holy, Holy, Holy Lord God of hosts . . .

THE EUCHARISTIC PRAYERS

EUCHARISTIC PRAYER I

(THE ROMAN CANON)

In all Masses, the Priest celebrant is permitted to sing parts of the Eucharistic Prayer, especially the principal parts. (See pp.110-46 for musical settings of these texts.)

In Eucharistic Prayer I, the Roman Canon, the words included in brackets may be omitted.

℣ The Lord be with you.
℟ **And with your spirit.**

℣ Lift up your hearts.
℟ **We lift them up to the Lord.**

℣ Let us give thanks to the Lord our God.
℟ **It is right and just.**

Then follows the Preface to be used in accord with the rubrics, which concludes:

Holy, Holy, Holy Lord God of hosts.
Heaven and earth are full of your glory.
Hosanna in the highest.
Blessed is he who comes in the name of the Lord.
Hosanna in the highest.

The Priest, with hands extended, says:

To you, therefore, most merciful Father,
we make humble prayer and petition
through Jesus Christ, your Son, our Lord:

He joins his hands and says:

that you accept

He makes the Sign of the Cross once over the bread and chalice together, saying:

and bless ✠ these gifts, these offerings,
these holy and unblemished sacrifices,

With hands extended, he continues:

which we offer you firstly
for your holy catholic Church.
Be pleased to grant her peace,
to guard, unite and govern her

Eucharistic Prayer I

throughout the whole world,
together with your servant N. our Pope
and N. our Bishop,*
and all those who, holding to the truth,
hand on the catholic and apostolic faith.

Commemoration of the Living.
Remember, Lord, your servants N. and N.

The Priest joins his hands and prays briefly for those for whom he intends to pray.

Then, with hands extended, he continues:

and all gathered here,
whose faith and devotion are known to you.
For them, we offer you this sacrifice of praise
or they offer it for themselves
and all who are dear to them:
for the redemption of their souls,
in hope of health and well-being,
and paying their homage to you,
the eternal God, living and true.

Within the Action.

In communion with those whose memory we venerate,
especially the glorious ever-Virgin Mary,
Mother of our God and Lord, Jesus Christ,
† and blessed Joseph, her Spouse,
your blessed Apostles and Martyrs,
Peter and Paul, Andrew,
(James, John,
Thomas, James, Philip,
Bartholomew, Matthew,
Simon and Jude;
Linus, Cletus, Clement, Sixtus,
Cornelius, Cyprian,
Lawrence, Chrysogonus,
John and Paul,
Cosmas and Damian)
and all your Saints;

---

*Mention may be made here of the Coadjutor Bishop, or Auxiliary Bishops, as noted in the *General Instruction of the Roman Missal*, no. 149.

we ask that through their merits and prayers,
in all things we may be defended
by your protecting help.
(Through Christ our Lord. Amen.)

PROPER FORMS OF THE *COMMUNICANTES*

On the Nativity of the Lord and throughout the Octave

Celebrating the most sacred night (day)
on which blessed Mary the immaculate Virgin
brought forth the Saviour for this world,
and in communion with those whose memory we venerate,
especially the glorious ever-Virgin Mary,
Mother of our God and Lord, Jesus Christ, †

On the Epiphany of the Lord

Celebrating the most sacred day
on which your Only Begotten Son,
eternal with you in your glory,
appeared in a human body, truly sharing our flesh,
and in communion with those whose memory we venerate,
especially the glorious ever-Virgin Mary,
Mother of our God and Lord, Jesus Christ, †

Thursday of the Lord's Supper

Celebrating the most sacred day
on which our Lord Jesus Christ was handed over for our sake,
and in communion with those whose memory we venerate,
especially the glorious ever-Virgin Mary,
Mother of our God and Lord, Jesus Christ, †

From the Mass of the Easter Vigil until the Second Sunday of Easter

Celebrating the most sacred night (day)
of the Resurrection of our Lord Jesus Christ in the flesh,
and in communion with those whose memory we venerate,
especially the glorious ever-Virgin Mary,
Mother of our God and Lord, Jesus Christ, †

On the Ascension of the Lord

Celebrating the most sacred day
on which your Only Begotten Son, our Lord,
placed at the right hand of your glory

our weak human nature,
which he had united to himself,
and in communion with those whose memory we venerate,
especially the glorious ever-Virgin Mary,
Mother of our God and Lord, Jesus Christ, †

On Pentecost Sunday

Celebrating the most sacred day of Pentecost,
on which the Holy Spirit
appeared to the Apostles in tongues of fire,
and in communion with those whose memory we venerate,
especially the glorious ever-Virgin Mary,
Mother of our God and Lord, Jesus Christ, †

With hands extended, the Priest continues:

Therefore, Lord, we pray:
graciously accept this oblation of our service,
that of your whole family;
order our days in your peace,
and command that we be delivered from eternal damnation
and counted among the flock of those you have chosen.

He joins his hands.

(Through Christ our Lord. Amen.)

From the Mass of the Easter Vigil until the Second Sunday of Easter

Therefore, Lord, we pray:
graciously accept this oblation of our service,
that of your whole family,
which we make to you
also for those to whom you have been pleased to give
the new birth of water and the Holy Spirit,
granting them forgiveness of all their sins;
order our days in your peace,
and command that we be delivered from eternal damnation
and counted among the flock of those you have chosen.

He joins his hands.

(Through Christ our Lord. Amen.)

Holding his hands extended over the offerings, he says:

Be pleased, O God, we pray,
to bless, acknowledge,
and approve this offering in every respect;
make it spiritual and acceptable,
so that it may become for us
the Body and Blood of your most beloved Son,
our Lord Jesus Christ.

He joins his hands.

In the formulas that follow, the words of the Lord should be pronounced clearly and distinctly, as the nature of these words requires.

On the day before he was to suffer,

*He takes the bread
and, holding it slightly raised above the altar, continues:*

he took bread in his holy and venerable hands,

He raises his eyes.

and with eyes raised to heaven
to you, O God, his almighty Father,
giving you thanks, he said the blessing,
broke the bread
and gave it to his disciples, saying:

He bows slightly.

Take this, all of you, and eat of it,
for this is my Body,
which will be given up for you.

He shows the consecrated host to the people, places it again on the paten, and genuflects in adoration.

After this, the Priest continues:

In a similar way, when supper was ended,

*He takes the chalice
and, holding it slightly raised above the altar, continues:*

he took this precious chalice
in his holy and venerable hands,

Eucharistic Prayer I

and once more giving you thanks, he said the blessing
and gave the chalice to his disciples, saying:

He bows slightly.

TAKE THIS, ALL OF YOU, AND DRINK FROM IT,
FOR THIS IS THE CHALICE OF MY BLOOD,
THE BLOOD OF THE NEW AND ETERNAL COVENANT,
WHICH WILL BE POURED OUT FOR YOU AND FOR MANY
FOR THE FORGIVENESS OF SINS.
DO THIS IN MEMORY OF ME.

He shows the chalice to the people, places it on the corporal, and genuflects in adoration.

Then he says:

The mys-ter-y of faith.

or

The mys-ter-y of faith.

And the people continue, acclaiming:

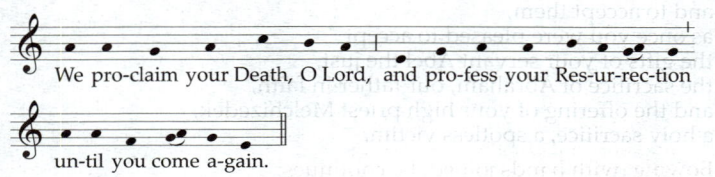

We pro-claim your Death, O Lord, and pro-fess your Res-ur-rec-tion un-til you come a-gain.

or

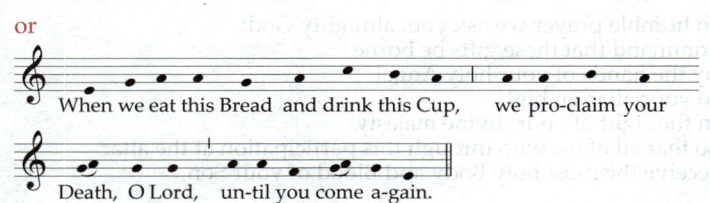

When we eat this Bread and drink this Cup, we pro-claim your Death, O Lord, un-til you come a-gain.

or

Save us, Saviour of the world, for by your Cross and Resurrection you have set us free.

Then the Priest, with hands extended, says:

Therefore, O Lord,
as we celebrate the memorial of the blessed Passion,
the Resurrection from the dead,
and the glorious Ascension into heaven
of Christ, your Son, our Lord,
we, your servants and your holy people,
offer to your glorious majesty
from the gifts that you have given us,
this pure victim,
this holy victim,
this spotless victim,
the holy Bread of eternal life
and the Chalice of everlasting salvation.

Be pleased to look upon these offerings
with a serene and kindly countenance,
and to accept them,
as once you were pleased to accept
the gifts of your servant Abel the just,
the sacrifice of Abraham, our father in faith,
and the offering of your high priest Melchizedek,
a holy sacrifice, a spotless victim.

Bowing, with hands joined, he continues:

In humble prayer we ask you, almighty God:
command that these gifts be borne
by the hands of your holy Angel
to your altar on high
in the sight of your divine majesty,
so that all of us, who through this participation at the altar
receive the most holy Body and Blood of your Son,

Eucharistic Prayer I

He stands upright again and signs himself with the Sign of the Cross, saying:

may be filled with every grace and heavenly blessing.

He joins his hands.

(Through Christ our Lord. Amen.)

Commemoration of the Dead

With hands extended, the Priest says:

Remember also, Lord, your servants N. and N.,
who have gone before us with the sign of faith
and rest in the sleep of peace.

He joins his hands and prays briefly for those who have died and for whom he intends to pray.

Then, with hands extended, he continues:

Grant them, O Lord, we pray,
and all who sleep in Christ,
a place of refreshment, light and peace.

He joins his hands.

(Through Christ our Lord. Amen.)

He strikes his breast with his right hand, saying:

To us, also, your servants, who, though sinners,

And, with hands extended, he continues:

hope in your abundant mercies,
graciously grant some share
and fellowship with your holy Apostles and Martyrs:
with John the Baptist, Stephen,
Matthias, Barnabas,
(Ignatius, Alexander,
Marcellinus, Peter,
Felicity, Perpetua,
Agatha, Lucy,
Agnes, Cecilia, Anastasia)
and all your Saints;
admit us, we beseech you,
into their company,
not weighing our merits,
but granting us your pardon,

He joins his hands.

through Christ our Lord.

And he continues:

Through whom
you continue to make all these good things, O Lord;
you sanctify them, fill them with life,
bless them, and bestow them upon us.

He takes the chalice and the paten with the host and, raising both, he says:

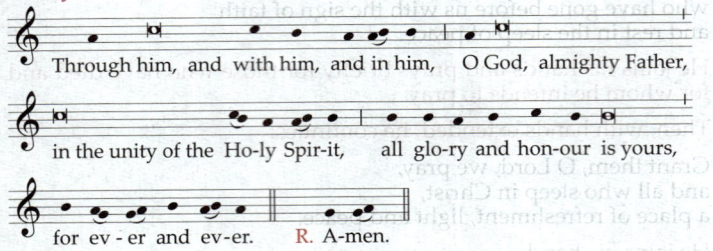

Through him, and with him, and in him, O God, almighty Father, in the unity of the Holy Spirit, all glory and honour is yours, for ev-er and ev-er. R. A-men.

The people acclaim:

Amen.

Then follows the Communion Rite, p.85.

EUCHARISTIC PRAYER II

Although it is provided with its own Preface (a musical setting for this can be found on pp.123-9), this Eucharistic Prayer may also be used with other Prefaces, especially those that present an overall view of the mystery of salvation, such as the Common Prefaces.

℣ The Lord be with you.
℟ **And with your spirit.**

℣ Lift up your hearts.
℟ **We lift them up to the Lord.**

℣ Let us give thanks to the Lord our God.
℟ **It is right and just.**

It is truly right and just, our duty and our salvation,
always and everywhere to give you thanks, Father most holy,
through your beloved Son, Jesus Christ,
your Word through whom you made all things,
whom you sent as our Saviour and Redeemer,
incarnate by the Holy Spirit and born of the Virgin.

Fulfilling your will and gaining for you a holy people,
he stretched out his hands as he endured his Passion,
so as to break the bonds of death and manifest the resurrection.

And so, with the Angels and all the Saints
we declare your glory,
as with one voice we acclaim:

Holy, Holy, Holy Lord God of hosts.
Heaven and earth are full of your glory.
Hosanna in the highest.
Blessed is he who comes in the name of the Lord.
Hosanna in the highest.

The Priest, with hands extended, says:

You are indeed Holy, O Lord,
the fount of all holiness.

He joins his hands and, holding them extended over the offerings, says:

Make holy, therefore, these gifts, we pray,
by sending down your Spirit upon them like the dewfall,

He joins his hands and makes the Sign of the Cross once over the bread and the chalice together, saying:

so that they may become for us
the Body and ✠ Blood of our Lord Jesus Christ.

He joins his hands.

In the formulas that follow, the words of the Lord should be pronounced clearly and distinctly, as the nature of these words requires.

At the time he was betrayed
and entered willingly into his Passion,

*He takes the bread
and, holding it slightly raised above the altar, continues:*

he took bread and, giving thanks, broke it,
and gave it to his disciples, saying:

He bows slightly.

Take this, all of you, and eat of it,
for this is my Body,
which will be given up for you.

He shows the consecrated host to the people, places it again on the paten, and genuflects in adoration.

After this, he continues:

In a similar way, when supper was ended,

*He takes the chalice
and, holding it slightly raised above the altar, continues:*

he took the chalice
and, once more giving thanks,
he gave it to his disciples, saying:

He bows slightly.

Take this, all of you, and drink from it,
for this is the chalice of my Blood,
the Blood of the new and eternal covenant,
which will be poured out for you and for many
for the forgiveness of sins.
Do this in memory of me.

Eucharistic Prayer II

He shows the chalice to the people, places it on the corporal, and genuflects in adoration.

Then he says:

The mys-ter-y of faith.

And the people continue, acclaiming:

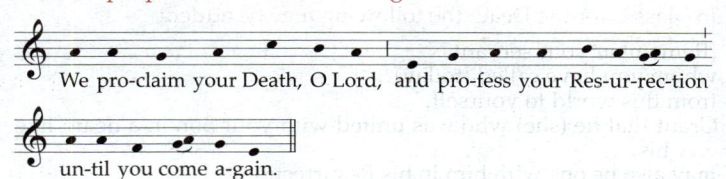

We pro-claim your Death, O Lord, and pro-fess your Res-ur-rec-tion un-til you come a-gain.

or

When we eat this Bread and drink this Cup, we pro-claim your Death, O Lord, un-til you come a-gain.

or

Save us, Sav-iour of the world, for by your Cross and Res-ur-rec-tion you have set us free.

Then the Priest, with hands extended, says:

Therefore, as we celebrate
the memorial of his Death and Resurrection,
we offer you, Lord,
the Bread of life and the Chalice of salvation,
giving thanks that you have held us worthy
to be in your presence and minister to you.

Humbly we pray
that, partaking of the Body and Blood of Christ,
we may be gathered into one by the Holy Spirit.

Remember, Lord, your Church,
spread throughout the world,
and bring her to the fullness of charity,
together with N. our Pope and N. our Bishop*
and all the clergy.

In Masses for the Dead, the following may be added:

[Remember your servant N.,
whom you have called (today)
from this world to yourself.
Grant that he (she) who was united with your Son in a death like his,
may also be one with him in his Resurrection.]

Remember also our brothers and sisters
who have fallen asleep in the hope of the resurrection,
and all who have died in your mercy:
welcome them into the light of your face.
Have mercy on us all, we pray,
that with the Blessed Virgin Mary, Mother of God,
with the blessed Apostles,
and all the Saints who have pleased you throughout the ages,
we may merit to be coheirs to eternal life,
and may praise and glorify you

He joins his hands.

through your Son, Jesus Christ.

He takes the chalice and the paten with the host and, raising both, he says:

---

*Mention may be made here of the Coadjutor Bishop, or Auxiliary Bishops, as noted in the *General Instruction of the Roman Missal*, no. 149.

Eucharistic Prayer II

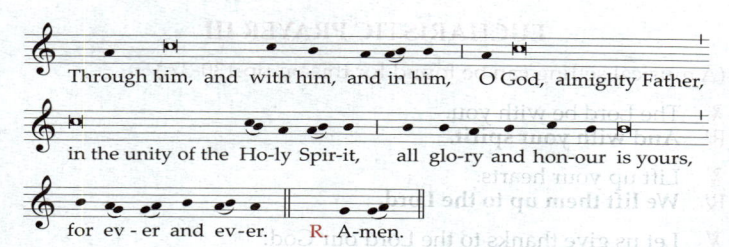

♪ Through him, and with him, and in him, O God, almighty Father, in the unity of the Holy Spirit, all glory and honour is yours, for ever and ever. ℟. Amen.

The people acclaim:

Amen.

Then follows the Communion Rite, p.85.

EUCHARISTIC PRAYER III

(A musical setting can be found for this on pp.130-37.)

℣ The Lord be with you.
℟ **And with your spirit.**

℣ Lift up your hearts.
℟ **We lift them up to the Lord.**

℣ Let us give thanks to the Lord our God.
℟ **It is right and just.**

Then follows the Preface to be used in accordance with the rubrics, which concludes:

Holy, Holy, Holy Lord God of hosts.
Heaven and earth are full of your glory.
Hosanna in the highest.
Blessed is he who comes in the name of the Lord.
Hosanna in the highest.

The Priest, with hands extended, says:

You are indeed Holy, O Lord,
and all you have created
rightly gives you praise,
for through your Son our Lord Jesus Christ,
by the power and working of the Holy Spirit,
you give life to all things and make them holy,
and you never cease to gather a people to yourself,
so that from the rising of the sun to its setting
a pure sacrifice may be offered to your name.

He joins his hands and, holding them extended over the offerings, says:

Therefore, O Lord, we humbly implore you:
by the same Spirit graciously make holy
these gifts we have brought to you for consecration,

He joins his handsand makes the Sign of the Cross once over the bread and chalice together, saying:

that they may become the Body and ✚ Blood
of your Son our Lord Jesus Christ,

He joins his hands.

at whose command we celebrate these mysteries.

Eucharistic Prayer III

In the formulas that follow, the words of the Lord should be pronounced clearly and distinctly, as the nature of these words requires.

For on the night he was betrayed

*He takes the bread
and, holding it slightly raised above the altar, continues:*

**he himself took bread,
and, giving you thanks, he said the blessing,
broke the bread and gave it to his disciples, saying:**

He bows slightly.

TAKE THIS, ALL OF YOU, AND EAT OF IT,
FOR THIS IS MY BODY,
WHICH WILL BE GIVEN UP FOR YOU.

He shows the consecrated host to the people, places it again on the paten, and genuflects in adoration.

After this, he continues:

In a similar way, when supper was ended,

*He takes the chalice
and, holding it slightly raised above the altar, continues:*

**he took the chalice,
and, giving you thanks, he said the blessing,
and gave the chalice to his disciples, saying:**

He bows slightly.

TAKE THIS, ALL OF YOU, AND DRINK FROM IT,
FOR THIS IS THE CHALICE OF MY BLOOD,
THE BLOOD OF THE NEW AND ETERNAL COVENANT,
WHICH WILL BE POURED OUT FOR YOU AND FOR MANY
FOR THE FORGIVENESS OF SINS.
DO THIS IN MEMORY OF ME.

He shows the chalice to the people, places it on the corporal, and genuflects in adoration.

Then he says:

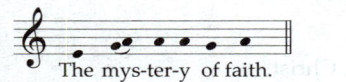

The mys-ter-y of faith.

And the people continue, acclaiming:

We proclaim your Death, O Lord, and profess your Resurrection until you come again.

or

When we eat this Bread and drink this Cup, we proclaim your Death, O Lord, until you come again.

or

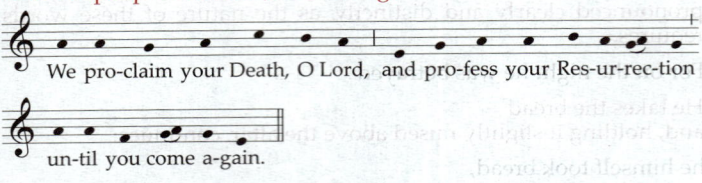

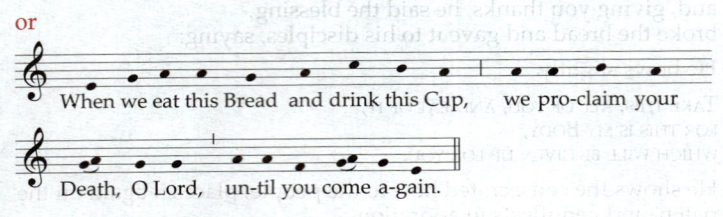

Save us, Saviour of the world, for by your Cross and Resurrection you have set us free.

Then the Priest, with hands extended, says:

Therefore, O Lord, as we celebrate the memorial
of the saving Passion of your Son,
his wondrous Resurrection
and Ascension into heaven,
and as we look forward to his second coming,
we offer you in thanksgiving
this holy and living sacrifice.

Look, we pray, upon the oblation of your Church
and, recognizing the sacrificial Victim by whose death
you willed to reconcile us to yourself,
grant that we, who are nourished
by the Body and Blood of your Son
and filled with his Holy Spirit,
may become one body, one spirit in Christ.

Eucharistic Prayer III

May he make of us
an eternal offering to you,
so that we may obtain an inheritance with your elect,
especially with the most Blessed Virgin Mary, Mother of God,
with your blessed Apostles and glorious Martyrs
(with Saint N.: the Saint of the day or Patron Saint)
and with all the Saints,
on whose constant intercession in your presence
we rely for unfailing help.

May this Sacrifice of our reconciliation,
we pray, O Lord,
advance the peace and salvation of all the world.
Be pleased to confirm in faith and charity
your pilgrim Church on earth,
with your servant N. our Pope and N. our Bishop,*
the Order of Bishops, all the clergy,
and the entire people you have gained for your own.

Listen graciously to the prayers of this family,
whom you have summoned before you:
in your compassion, O merciful Father,
gather to yourself all your children
scattered throughout the world.

† To our departed brothers and sisters
and to all who were pleasing to you
at their passing from this life,
give kind admittance to your kingdom.
There we hope to enjoy for ever the fullness of your glory

He joins his hands.

through Christ our Lord,
through whom you bestow on the world all that is good. †

He takes the chalice and the paten with the host and, raising both, he says:

---

*Mention may be made here of the Coadjutor Bishop, or Auxiliary Bishops, as noted in the *General Instruction of the Roman Missal*, no. 149.

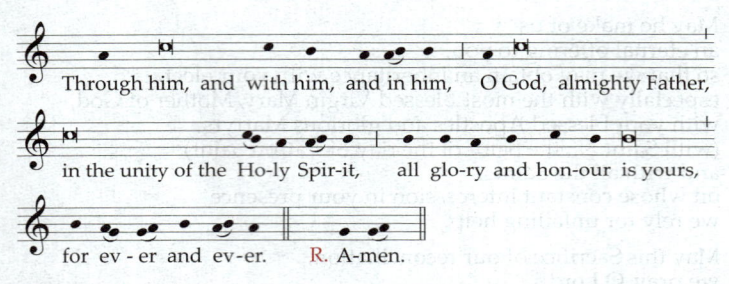

Through him, and with him, and in him, O God, almighty Father, in the unity of the Ho-ly Spir-it, all glo-ry and hon-our is yours, for ev-er and ev-er. R. A-men.

The people acclaim:

Amen.

Then follows the Communion Rite, p.85.

When this Eucharistic Prayer is used in Masses for the Dead, the following may be said:

† Remember your servant N.
whom you have called (today)
from this world to yourself.
Grant that he (she) who was united with your Son in a death like his,
may also be one with him in his Resurrection,
when from the earth
he will raise up in the flesh those who have died,
and transform our lowly body
after the pattern of his own glorious body.
To our departed brothers and sisters, too,
and to all who were pleasing to you
at their passing from this life,
give kind admittance to your kingdom.
There we hope to enjoy for ever the fullness of your glory,
when you will wipe away every tear from our eyes.
For seeing you, our God, as you are,
we shall be like you for all the ages
and praise you without end,

He joins his hands.

through Christ our Lord,
through whom you bestow on the world all that is good. †

EUCHARISTIC PRAYER IV

It is not permitted to change the Preface of this Eucharistic Prayer because of the structure of the Prayer itself, which presents a summary of the history of salvation (a musical setting can be found for this on pp.138-46).

℣ The Lord be with you.
℟ **And with your spirit.**

℣ Lift up your hearts.
℟ **We lift them up to the Lord.**

℣ Let us give thanks to the Lord our God.
℟ **It is right and just.**

It is truly right to give you thanks,
truly just to give you glory, Father most holy,
for you are the one God living and true,
existing before all ages and abiding for all eternity,
dwelling in unapproachable light;
yet you, who alone are good, the source of life,
have made all that is,
so that you might fill your creatures with blessings
and bring joy to many of them by the glory of your light.

And so, in your presence are countless hosts of Angels,
who serve you day and night
and, gazing upon the glory of your face,
glorify you without ceasing.

With them we, too, confess your name in exultation,
giving voice to every creature under heaven,
as we acclaim:

Holy, Holy, Holy Lord God of hosts.
Heaven and earth are full of your glory.
Hosanna in the highest.
Blessed is he who comes in the name of the Lord.
Hosanna in the highest.

The Priest, with hands extended, says:

We give you praise, Father most holy,
for you are great
and you have fashioned all your works
in wisdom and in love.

You formed man in your own image
and entrusted the whole world to his care,
so that in serving you alone, the Creator,
he might have dominion over all creatures.
And when through disobedience he had lost your friendship,
you did not abandon him to the domain of death.
For you came in mercy to the aid of all,
so that those who seek might find you.
Time and again you offered them covenants
and through the prophets
taught them to look forward to salvation.

And you so loved the world, Father most holy,
that in the fullness of time
you sent your Only Begotten Son to be our Saviour.
Made incarnate by the Holy Spirit
and born of the Virgin Mary,
he shared our human nature
in all things but sin.
To the poor he proclaimed the good news of salvation,
to prisoners, freedom,
and to the sorrowful of heart, joy.
To accomplish your plan,
he gave himself up to death,
and, rising from the dead,
he destroyed death and restored life.

And that we might live no longer for ourselves
but for him who died and rose again for us,
he sent the Holy Spirit from you, Father,
as the first fruits for those who believe,
so that, bringing to perfection his work in the world,
he might sanctify creation to the full.

He joins his hands and, holding them extended over the offerings, says:

Therefore, O Lord, we pray:
may this same Holy Spirit
graciously sanctify these offerings,

*He joins his hands
and makes the Sign of the Cross once over the bread and chalice together, saying:*

Eucharistic Prayer IV

that they may become
the Body and ✥ Blood of our Lord Jesus Christ

He joins his hands.

for the celebration of this great mystery,
which he himself left us
as an eternal covenant.

In the formulas that follow, the words of the Lord should be pronounced clearly and distinctly, as the nature of these words requires.

For when the hour had come
for him to be glorified by you, Father most holy,
having loved his own who were in the world,
he loved them to the end:
and while they were at supper,

He takes the bread
and, holding it slightly raised above the altar, continues:

he took bread, blessed and broke it,
and gave it to his disciples, saying:

He bows slightly.

Take this, all of you, and eat of it,
for this is my Body,
which will be given up for you.

He shows the consecrated host to the people, places it again on the paten, and genuflects in adoration.

After this, he continues:

In a similar way,

He takes the chalice
and, holding it slightly raised above the altar, continues:

taking the chalice filled with the fruit of the vine,
he gave thanks,
and gave the chalice to his disciples, saying:

He bows slightly.

Take this, all of you, and drink from it,
for this is the chalice of my Blood,
the Blood of the new and eternal covenant,

WHICH WILL BE POURED OUT FOR YOU AND FOR MANY
FOR THE FORGIVENESS OF SINS.

DO THIS IN MEMORY OF ME.

He shows the chalice to the people, places it on the corporal, and genuflects in adoration.

Then he says:

The mys-ter-y of faith.

And the people continue, acclaiming:

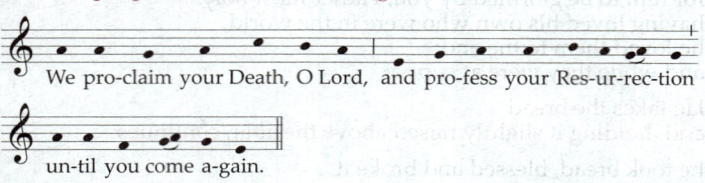

We pro-claim your Death, O Lord, and pro-fess your Res-ur-rec-tion un-til you come a-gain.

or

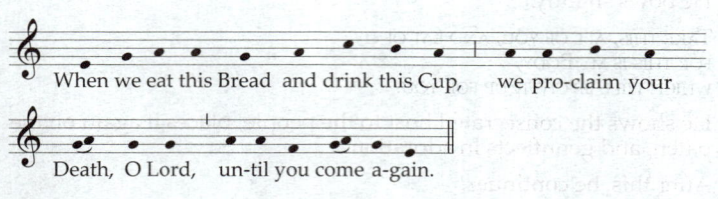

When we eat this Bread and drink this Cup, we pro-claim your Death, O Lord, un-til you come a-gain.

or

Save us, Sav-iour of the world, for by your Cross and Res-ur-rec-tion you have set us free.

Then, with hands extended, the Priest says:

Therefore, O Lord,
as we now celebrate the memorial of our redemption,

Eucharistic Prayer IV

we remember Christ's Death
and his descent to the realm of the dead,
we proclaim his Resurrection
and his Ascension to your right hand,
and, as we await his coming in glory,
we offer you his Body and Blood,
the sacrifice acceptable to you
which brings salvation to the whole world.

Look, O Lord, upon the Sacrifice
which you yourself have provided for your Church,
and grant in your loving kindness
to all who partake of this one Bread and one Chalice
that, gathered into one body by the Holy Spirit,
they may truly become a living sacrifice in Christ
to the praise of your glory.

Therefore, Lord, remember now
all for whom we offer this sacrifice:
especially your servant N. our Pope,
N. our Bishop,* and the whole Order of Bishops,
all the clergy,
those who take part in this offering,
those gathered here before you,
your entire people,
and all who seek you with a sincere heart.

Remember also
those who have died in the peace of your Christ
and all the dead,
whose faith you alone have known.

To all of us, your children,
grant, O merciful Father,
that we may enter into a heavenly inheritance
with the Blessed Virgin Mary, Mother of God,
and with your Apostles and Saints in your kingdom.
There, with the whole of creation,
freed from the corruption of sin and death,
may we glorify you through Christ our Lord,

He joins his hands.

---

*Mention may be made here of the Coadjutor Bishop, or Auxiliary Bishops, as noted in the *General Instruction of the Roman Missal*, no. 149.

through whom you bestow on the world all that is good.

He takes the chalice and the paten with the host and, raising both, he says:

Through him, and with him, and in him, O God, almighty Father, in the unity of the Ho-ly Spir-it, all glo-ry and hon-our is yours, for ev-er and ev-er. **R.** A-men.

The people acclaim:

Amen.

Then follows the Communion Rite, p.85.

THE COMMUNION RITE

After the chalice and paten have been set down, the Priest, with hands joined, says:

At the Saviour's command
and formed by divine teaching,
we dare to say:

He extends his hands and, together with the people, continues:

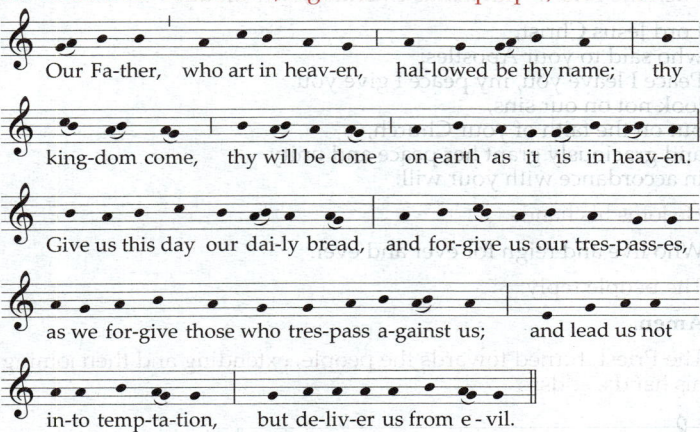

Our Father, who art in heaven, hallowed be thy name; thy kingdom come, thy will be done on earth as it is in heaven. Give us this day our daily bread, and forgive us our trespasses, as we forgive those who trespass against us; and lead us not into temptation, but deliver us from evil.

(Alternative musical settings of the Lord's Prayer, including the Latin text, may be found on p.153.)

With hands extended, the Priest alone continues, saying:

Deliver us, Lord, we pray, from every evil,
graciously grant peace in our days,

that, by the help of your mercy,
we may be always free from sin
and safe from all distress,
as we await the blessed hope
and the coming of our Saviour, Jesus Christ.

He joins his hands.

The people conclude the prayer, acclaiming:

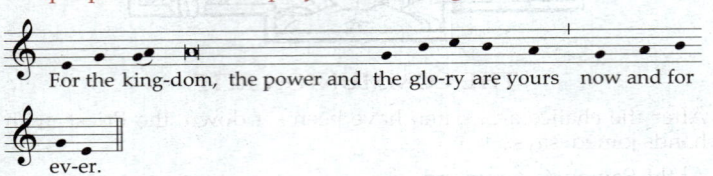

For the king-dom, the power and the glo-ry are yours now and for ev-er.

(A musical setting of the following prayer and response may be found on p.154.)

Then the Priest, with hands extended, says aloud:

Lord Jesus Christ,
who said to your Apostles:
Peace I leave you, my peace I give you,
look not on our sins,
but on the faith of your Church,
and graciously grant her peace and unity
in accordance with your will.

He joins his hands.

Who live and reign for ever and ever.

The people reply:

Amen.

The Priest, turned towards the people, extending and then joining his hands, adds:

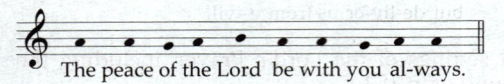

The peace of the Lord be with you al-ways.

The Communion Rite

The people reply:

And with your spir-it.

Then, if appropriate, the Deacon, or the Priest, adds:

Let us offer each other the sign of peace.

And all offer one another a sign, in keeping with local customs, that expresses peace, communion, and charity. The Priest gives the sign of peace to a Deacon or minister.

Then he takes the host, breaks it over the paten, and places a small piece in the chalice, saying quietly:

May this mingling of the Body and Blood
of our Lord Jesus Christ
bring eternal life to us who receive it.

Meanwhile the following is sung or said:

Lamb of God, * you take a-way the sins of the world,

have mer-cy on us.

Lamb of God, * you take a-way the sins of the world,

have mer-cy on us.

Lamb of God, * you take a-way the sins of the world,

grant us peace.

(An alternative musical setting of the Agnus Dei, including the Latin text, may be found on p.155.)

The invocation may even be repeated several times if the fraction is prolonged. Only the final time, however, is grant us peace said.

Then the Priest, with hands joined, says quietly:

Lord Jesus Christ, Son of the living God,
who, by the will of the Father
and the work of the Holy Spirit,
through your Death gave life to the world,
free me by this, your most holy Body and Blood,
from all my sins and from every evil;
keep me always faithful to your commandments,
and never let me be parted from you.

or

May the receiving of your Body and Blood,
Lord Jesus Christ,
not bring me to judgement and condemnation,
but through your loving mercy
be for me protection in mind and body
and a healing remedy.

(A musical setting of the following may be found on p.155.)

The Priest genuflects, takes the host and, holding it slightly raised above the paten or above the chalice, while facing the people, says aloud:

Behold the Lamb of God,
behold him who takes away the sins of the world.
Blessed are those called to the supper of the Lamb.

And together with the people he adds once:

**Lord, I am not worthy
that you should enter under my roof,
but only say the word
and my soul shall be healed.**

The Priest, facing the altar, says quietly:

May the Body of Christ
keep me safe for eternal life.

The Communion Rite

And he reverently consumes the Body of Christ.

Then he takes the chalice and says quietly:

May the Blood of Christ
keep me safe for eternal life.

And he reverently consumes the Blood of Christ.

After this, he takes the paten or ciborium and approaches the communicants. The Priest raises a host slightly and shows it to each of the communicants, saying:

The Body of Christ.

The communicant replies:

Amen.

And receives Holy Communion.

If a Deacon also distributes Holy Communion, he does so in the same manner.

If any are present who are to receive Holy Communion under both kinds, the rite described in the proper place is to be followed.

> **Communion Antiphon:** turn to the Proper
> of the Mass of the Day.

While the Priest is receiving the Body of Christ, the Communion Antiphon begins.

When the distribution of Communion is over, the Priest or a Deacon or an acolyte purifies the paten over the chalice and also the chalice itself.

While he carries out the purification, the Priest says quietly:

What has passed our lips as food, O Lord,
may we possess in purity of heart,
that what has been given to us in time
may be our healing for eternity.

Then the Priest may return to the chair. If appropriate, a sacred silence may be observed for a while, or a psalm or other canticle of praise or a hymn may be sung.

Then, standing at the altar or at the chair and facing the people, with hands joined, the Priest says:

Let us pray.

> **Prayer after Communion:** turn to the Proper of the Mass of the Day.

All pray in silence with the Priest for a while, unless silence has just been observed. Then the Priest, with hands extended, says the Prayer after Communion, at the end of which the people acclaim:

Amen.

THE CONCLUDING RITES

If they are necessary, any brief announcements to the people follow here.

Then the dismissal takes place. The Priest, facing the people and extending his hands, says:

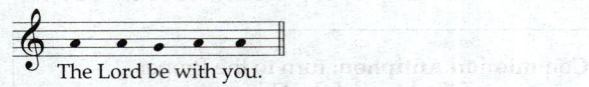

The Lord be with you.

The people reply:

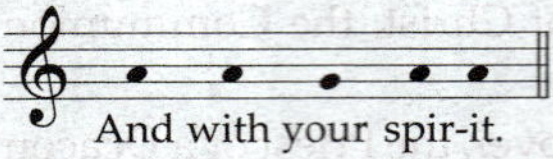

And with your spir-it.

The Priest blesses the people, saying:

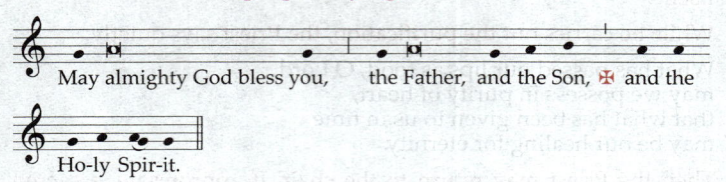

May almighty God bless you, the Father, and the Son, ✠ and the Ho-ly Spir-it.

The Concluding Rites

The people reply:

A-men.

> On certain days or occasions, this formula of blessing is preceded, in accordance with the rubrics, by another more solemn formula of blessing or by a prayer over the people (cf. pp.94-109.).

In a Pontifical Mass, the celebrant receives the mitre and, extending his hands, says:

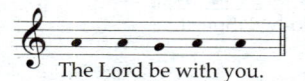

The Lord be with you.

All reply:

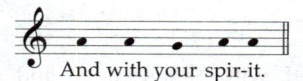

And with your spir-it.

The celebrant says:

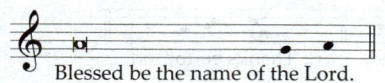

Blessed be the name of the Lord.

All reply:

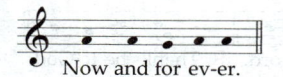

Now and for ev-er.

The celebrant says:

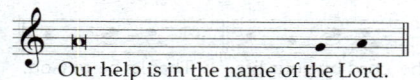

Our help is in the name of the Lord.

All reply:

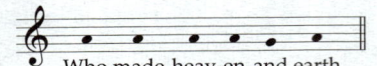

Who made heav-en and earth.

Then the celebrant receives the pastoral staff, if he uses it, and says:

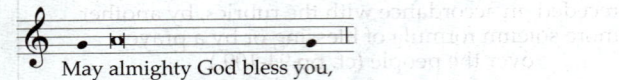

May almighty God bless you,

making the Sign of the Cross over the people three times, he adds:

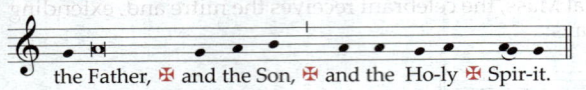

the Father, ✠ and the Son, ✠ and the Ho-ly ✠ Spir-it.

All:

A-men.

Then the Deacon, or the Priest himself, with hands joined and facing the people, says:

V. Go forth, the Mass is end-ed. R. Thanks be to God.

or

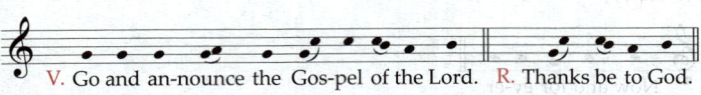

V. Go and an-nounce the Gos-pel of the Lord. R. Thanks be to God.

or

V. Go in peace, glorifying the Lord by your life. R. Thanks be to God.

The Concluding Rites

or

℣. Go in peace. ℟. Thanks be to God.

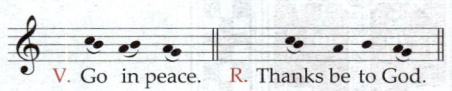

The people reply:

Thanks be to God.

At the Easter Vigil, on Easter Sunday, throughout the Easter Octave, and at Pentecost the following dismissal is used:

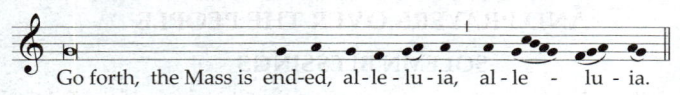

Go forth, the Mass is end-ed, al-le-lu-ia, al-le-lu-ia.

or

Go in peace, al-le-lu-ia, al-le-lu-ia.

The people reply:

Thanks be to God, al-le-lu-ia, al-le-lu-ia.

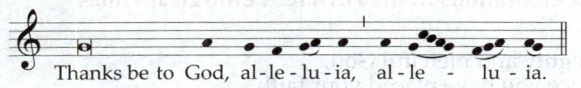

Then the Priest venerates the altar as usual with a kiss, as at the beginning. After making a profound bow with the ministers, he withdraws.

If any liturgical action follows immediately, the rites of dismissal are omitted.

BLESSINGS AT THE END OF MASS AND PRAYERS OVER THE PEOPLE

SOLEMN BLESSINGS

The following blessings may be used, at the discretion of the Priest, at the end of the celebration of Mass, or of a Liturgy of the Word, or of the Office, or of the Sacraments.

The Deacon or, in his absence, the Priest himself, says the invitation: Bow down for the blessing. The Priest, with hands extended over the people, says the blessing, with all responding: **Amen.**

I. For Celebrations in the Different Liturgical Times

Advent
May the almighty and merciful God,
by whose grace you have placed your faith
in the First Coming of his Only Begotten Son
and yearn for his coming again
sanctify you by the radiance of Christ's Advent
and enrich you with his blessing.
Amen.

As you run the race of this present life,
may he make you firm in faith,
joyful in hope and active in charity.
Amen.

So that, rejoicing now with devotion
at the Redeemer's coming in the flesh,

Blessings at the End of Mass

you may be endowed with the rich reward of eternal life
when he comes again in majesty.
Amen.

And may the blessing of almighty God,
the Father, and the Son, ✠ and the Holy Spirit,
come down on you and remain with you for ever.
Amen.

The Nativity of the Lord
May the God of infinite goodness,
who by the Incarnation of his Son has driven darkness from the world
and by that glorious Birth has illumined this most holy night (day),
drive far from you the darkness of vice
and illumine your hearts with the light of virtue.
Amen.

May God, who willed that the great joy
of his Son's saving Birth
be announced to shepherds by the Angel,
fill your minds with the gladness he gives
and make you heralds of his Gospel.
Amen.

And may God, who by the Incarnation
brought together the earthly and heavenly realm,
fill you with the gift of his peace and favour
and make you sharers with the Church in heaven.
Amen.

And may the blessing of almighty God,
the Father, and the Son, ✠ and the Holy Spirit,
come down on you and remain with you for ever.
Amen.

The Beginning of the Year
May God, the source and origin of all blessing,
grant you grace,
pour out his blessing in abundance,
and keep you safe from harm throughout the year.
Amen.

May he give you integrity in the faith,
endurance in hope,

and perseverance in charity
with holy patience to the end.
Amen.

May he order your days and your deeds in his peace,
grant your prayers in this and in every place,
and lead you happily to eternal life.
Amen.

And may the blessing of almighty God,
the Father, and the Son, ✢ and the Holy Spirit,
come down on you and remain with you for ever.
Amen.

The Epiphany of the Lord
May God, who has called you
out of darkness into his wonderful light,
pour out in kindness his blessing upon you
and make your hearts firm
in faith, hope and charity.
Amen.

And since in all confidence you follow Christ,
who today appeared in the world
as a light shining in darkness,
may God make you, too,
a light for your brothers and sisters.
Amen.

And so when your pilgrimage is ended,
may you come to him
whom the Magi sought as they followed the star
and whom they found with great joy, the Light from Light,
who is Christ the Lord.
Amen.

And may the blessing of almighty God,
the Father, and the Son, ✢ and the Holy Spirit,
come down on you and remain with you for ever.
Amen.

The Passion of the Lord
May God, the Father of mercies,
who has given you an example of love
in the Passion of his Only Begotten Son,

Blessings at the End of Mass

grant that, by serving God and your neighbour,
you may lay hold of the wondrous gift of his blessing.
Amen.

So that you may receive the reward of everlasting life from him,
through whose earthly Death
you believe that you escape eternal death.
Amen.

And by following the example of his self-abasement,
may you possess a share in his Resurrection.
Amen.

And may the blessing of almighty God,
the Father, and the Son, ✝ and the Holy Spirit,
come down on you and remain with you for ever.
Amen.

Easter Time
May God, who by the Resurrection of his Only Begotten Son
was pleased to confer on you
the gift of redemption and of adoption,
give you gladness by his blessing.
Amen.

May he, by whose redeeming work
you have received the gift of everlasting freedom,
make you heirs to an eternal inheritance.
Amen.

And may you, who have already risen with Christ
in Baptism through faith,
by living in a right manner on this earth,
be united with him in the homeland of heaven.
Amen.

And may the blessing of almighty God,
the Father, and the Son, ✝ and the Holy Spirit,
come down on you and remain with you for ever.
Amen.

The Ascension of the Lord
May almighty God bless you,
for on this very day his Only Begotten Son
pierced the heights of heaven

and unlocked for you the way
to ascend to where he is.
Amen.

May he grant that,
as Christ after his Resurrection
was seen plainly by his disciples,
so when he comes as Judge
he may show himself merciful to you for all eternity.
Amen.

And may you, who believe he is seated
with the Father in his majesty,
know with joy the fulfilment of his promise
to stay with you until the end of time.
Amen.

And may the blessing of almighty God,
the Father, and the Son, ✚ and the Holy Spirit,
come down on you and remain with you for ever.
Amen.

The Holy Spirit
May God, the Father of lights,
who was pleased to enlighten the disciples' minds
by the outpouring of the Spirit, the Paraclete,
grant you gladness by his blessing
and make you always abound with the gifts of the same Spirit.
Amen.

May the wondrous flame that appeared above the disciples,
powerfully cleanse your hearts from every evil
and pervade them with its purifying light.
Amen.

And may God, who has been pleased to unite many tongues
in the profession of one faith,
give you perseverance in that same faith
and, by believing, may you journey from hope to clear vision.
Amen.

And may the blessing of almighty God,
the Father, and the Son, ✚ and the Holy Spirit,
come down on you and remain with you for ever.
Amen.

Blessings at the End of Mass

Ordinary Time I
May the Lord bless you and keep you.
Amen.

May he let his face shine upon you
and show you his mercy.
Amen.

May he turn his countenance towards you
and give you his peace.
Amen.

And may the blessing of almighty God,
the Father, and the Son, ✚ and the Holy Spirit,
come down on you and remain with you for ever.
Amen.

Ordinary Time II
May the peace of God,
which surpasses all understanding,
keep your hearts and minds
in the knowledge and love of God,
and of his Son, our Lord Jesus Christ.
Amen.

And may the blessing of almighty God,
the Father, and the Son, ✚ and the Holy Spirit,
come down on you and remain with you for ever.
Amen.

Ordinary Time III
May almighty God bless you in his kindness
and pour out saving wisdom upon you.
Amen.

May he nourish you always with the teachings of the faith
and make you persevere in holy deeds.
Amen.

May he turn your steps towards himself
and show you the path of charity and peace.
Amen.

And may the blessing of almighty God,
the Father, and the Son, ✚ and the Holy Spirit,
come down on you and remain with you for ever.
Amen.

Ordinary Time IV
May the God of all consolation order your days in his peace
and grant you the gifts of his blessing.
Amen.

May he free you always from every distress
and confirm your hearts in his love.
Amen.

So that on this life's journey
you may be effective in good works,
rich in the gifts of hope, faith and charity,
and may come happily to eternal life.
Amen.

And may the blessing of almighty God,
the Father, and the Son, ✠ and the Holy Spirit,
come down on you and remain with you for ever.
Amen.

Ordinary Time V
May almighty God always keep every adversity far from you
and in his kindness pour out upon you the gifts of his blessing.
Amen.

May God keep your hearts attentive to his words,
that they may be filled with everlasting gladness.
Amen.

And so, may you always understand what is good and right,
and be found ever hastening along
in the path of God's commands,
made coheirs with the citizens of heaven.
Amen.

And may the blessing of almighty God,
the Father, and the Son, ✠ and the Holy Spirit,
come down on you and remain with you for ever.
Amen.

Ordinary Time VI
May God bless you with every heavenly blessing,
make you always holy and pure in his sight,

Blessings at the End of Mass

pour out in abundance upon you the riches of his glory,
and teach you with the words of truth;
may he instruct you in the Gospel of salvation,
and ever endow you with fraternal charity.
Through Christ our Lord.
Amen.

And may the blessing of almighty God,
the Father, and the Son, ✟ and the Holy Spirit,
come down on you and remain with you for ever.
Amen.

II. For Celebrations of the Saints

The Blessed Virgin Mary
May God, who through the childbearing of the Blessed Virgin Mary
willed in his great kindness to redeem the human race,
be pleased to enrich you with his blessing.
Amen.

May you know always and everywhere
the protection of her,
through whom you have been found worthy to receive
the author of life.
Amen.

May you, who have devoutly gathered on this day,
carry away with you the gifts of spiritual joys and heavenly rewards.
Amen.

And may the blessing of almighty God,
the Father, and the Son, ✟ and the Holy Spirit,
come down on you and remain with you for ever.
Amen.

Saints Peter and Paul, Apostles
May almighty God bless you,
for he has made you steadfast in Saint Peter's saving confession
and through it has set you on the solid rock of the Church's faith.
Amen.

And having instructed you
by the tireless preaching of Saint Paul,
may God teach you constantly by his example

to win brothers and sisters for Christ.
Amen.

So that by the keys of St Peter and the words of St Paul,
and by the support of their intercession,
God may bring us happily to that homeland
that Peter attained on a cross
and Paul by the blade of a sword.
Amen.

And may the blessing of almighty God,
the Father, and the Son, ✜ and the Holy Spirit,
come down on you and remain with you for ever.
Amen.

The Apostles
May God, who has granted you
to stand firm on apostolic foundations,
graciously bless you through the glorious merits
of the holy Apostles N. and N. (the holy Apostle N.).
Amen.

And may he who endowed you
with the teaching and example of the Apostles,
make you, under their protection,
witnesses to the truth before all.
Amen.

So that through the intercession of the Apostles,
you may inherit the eternal homeland,
for by their teaching you possess firmness of faith.
Amen.

And may the blessing of almighty God,
the Father, and the Son, ✜ and the Holy Spirit,
come down on you and remain with you for ever.
Amen.

All Saints
May God, the glory and joy of the Saints,
who has caused you to be strengthened
by means of their outstanding prayers,
bless you with unending blessings
Amen.

Blessings at the End of Mass

Freed through their intercession from present ills
and formed by the example of their holy way of life,
may you be ever devoted
to serving God and your neighbour.
Amen.

So that, together with all,
you may possess the joys of the homeland,
where Holy Church rejoices
that her children are admitted in perpetual peace
to the company of the citizens of heaven.
Amen.

And may the blessing of almighty God,
the Father, and the Son, ✠ and the Holy Spirit,
come down on you and remain with you for ever.
Amen.

III. Other Blessings

For the Dedication of a Church
May God, the Lord of heaven and earth,
who has gathered you today for the dedication of this church,
make you abound in heavenly blessings.
Amen.

And may he who has willed that all his scattered children
should be gathered together in his Son,
grant that you may become his temple
and the dwelling place of the Holy Spirit.
Amen.

And so, when you are thoroughly cleansed,
may God dwell within you
and grant you to possess with all the Saints
the inheritance of eternal happiness.
Amen.

And may the blessing of almighty God,
the Father, and the Son, ✠ and the Holy Spirit,
come down on you and remain with you for ever.
Amen.

In Celebrations for the Dead
May the God of all consolation bless you,
for in his unfathomable goodness he created the human race,
and in the Resurrection of his Only Begotten Son
he has given believers the hope of rising again.
Amen.

To us who are alive, may God grant pardon for our sins,
and to all the dead, a place of light and peace.
Amen.

So may we all live happily for ever with Christ,
whom we believe truly rose from the dead.
Amen.

And may the blessing of almighty God,
the Father, and the Son, ✛ and the Holy Spirit,
come down on you and remain with you for ever.
Amen.

PRAYERS OVER THE PEOPLE

The following prayers may be used, at the discretion of the Priest, at the end of the celebration of Mass, or of a Liturgy of the Word, or of the Office, or of the Sacraments.

The Deacon or, in his absence, the Priest himself, says the invitation: Bow down for the blessing. Then the Priest, with hands outstretched over the people, says the prayer, with all responding: **Amen**.

After the prayer, the Priest always adds: And may the blessing of almighty God, the Father, and the Son, ✠ and the Holy Spirit, come down on you and remain with you for ever. ℟ **Amen.**

1. Be gracious to your people, O Lord,
    and do not withhold consolation on earth
    from those you call to strive for heaven.
    Through Christ our Lord.

2. Grant, O Lord, we pray,
    that the Christian people
    may understand the truths they profess
    and love the heavenly liturgy
    in which they participate.
    Through Christ our Lord.

3. May your people receive your holy blessing,
    O Lord, we pray,
    and, by that gift,
    spurn all that would harm them
    and obtain what they desire.
    Through Christ our Lord.

4. Turn your people to you with all their heart,
    O Lord, we pray,
    for you protect even those who go astray,
    but when they serve you with undivided heart,
    you sustain them with still greater care.
    Through Christ our Lord.

5. Graciously enlighten your family, O Lord, we pray,
    that by holding fast to what is pleasing to you,
    they may be worthy to accomplish all that is good.
    Through Christ our Lord.

6. Bestow pardon and peace, O Lord, we pray,
   upon your faithful,
   that they may be cleansed from every offence
   and serve you with untroubled hearts.
   Through Christ our Lord.

7. May your heavenly favour, O Lord, we pray,
   increase in number the people subject to you
   and make them always obedient to your commands.
   Through Christ our Lord.

8. Be propitious to your people, O God,
   that, freed from every evil,
   they may serve you with all their heart
   and ever stand firm under your protection.
   Through Christ our Lord.

9. May your family always rejoice together, O God,
   over the mysteries of redemption they have celebrated,
   and grant its members the perseverance
   to attain the effects that flow from them.
   Through Christ our Lord.

10. Lord God, from the abundance of your mercies
    provide for your servants and ensure their safety,
    so that, strengthened by your blessings,
    they may at all times abound in thanksgiving
    and bless you with unending exultation.
    Through Christ our Lord.

11. Keep your family, we pray, O Lord,
    in your constant care,
    so that, under your protection,
    they may be free from all troubles
    and by good works show dedication to your name.
    Through Christ our Lord.

12. Purify your faithful, both in body and in mind,
    O Lord, we pray,
    so that, feeling the compunction you inspire,
    they may be able to avoid harmful pleasures
    and ever feed upon your delights.
    Through Christ our Lord.

13. May the effects of your sacred blessing, O Lord,
    make themselves felt among your faithful,

Prayers over the People

to prepare with spiritual sustenance the minds of all,
that they may be strengthened by the power of your love
to carry out works of charity.
Through Christ our Lord.

14. The hearts of your faithful submitted to your name,
entreat your help, O Lord,
and since without you they can do nothing that is just,
grant by your abundant mercy
that they may both know what is right
and receive all that they need for their good.
Through Christ our Lord.

15. Hasten to the aid of your faithful people
who call upon you, O Lord, we pray,
and graciously give strength in their human weakness,
so that, being dedicated to you in complete sincerity,
they may find gladness in your remedies
both now and in the life to come.
Through Christ our Lord.

16. Look with favour on your family, O Lord,
and bestow your endless mercy on those who seek it:
and just as without your mercy,
they can do nothing truly worthy of you,
so through it,
may they merit to obey your saving commands.
Through Christ our Lord.

17. Bestow increase of heavenly grace
on your faithful, O Lord;
may they praise you with their lips,
with their souls, with their lives;
and since it is by your gift that we exist,
may our whole lives be yours.
Through Christ our Lord.

18. Direct your people, O Lord, we pray,
with heavenly instruction,
that by avoiding every evil
and pursuing all that is good,
they may earn not your anger
but your unending mercy.
Through Christ our Lord.

19. Be near to those who call on you, O Lord,
    and graciously grant your protection
    to all who place their hope in your mercy,
    that they may remain faithful in holiness of life
    and, having enough for their needs in this world,
    they may be made full heirs of your promise for eternity.
    Through Christ our Lord.

20. Bestow the grace of your kindness
    upon your supplicant people, O Lord,
    that, formed by you, their creator,
    and restored by you, their sustainer,
    through your constant action they may be saved.
    Through Christ our Lord.

21. May your faithful people, O Lord, we pray,
    always respond to the promptings of your love
    and, moved by wholesome compunction,
    may they do gladly what you command,
    so as to receive the things you promise.
    Through Christ our Lord.

22. May the weakness of your devoted people
    stir your compassion, O Lord, we pray,
    and let their faithful pleading win your mercy,
    that what they do not presume upon by their merits
    they may receive by your generous pardon.
    Through Christ our Lord.

23. In defence of your children, O Lord, we pray,
    stretch forth the right hand of your majesty,
    so that, obeying your fatherly will,
    they may have the unfailing protection
    of your fatherly care.
    Through Christ our Lord.

24. Look, O Lord, on the prayers of your family,
    and grant them the assistance they humbly implore,
    so that, strengthened by the help they need,
    they may persevere in confessing your name.
    Through Christ our Lord.

25. Keep your family safe, O Lord, we pray,
    and grant them the abundance of your mercies,
    that they may find growth

through the teachings and the gifts of heaven.
Through Christ our Lord.

26. May your faithful people rejoice, we pray, O Lord,
to be upheld up by your right hand,
and, progressing in the Christian life,
may they delight in good things
both now and in the time to come.
Through Christ our Lord.

On Feasts of Saints

27. May the Christian people exult, O Lord,
at the glorification of the illustrious members of your Son's Body,
and may they gain a share in the eternal lot
of the Saints on whose feast day
they reaffirm their devotion to you,
rejoicing with them for ever in your glory.
Through Christ our Lord.

28. Turn the hearts of your people
always to you, O Lord, we pray,
and, as you give them the help of such great patrons as these,
grant also the unfailing help of your protection.
Through Christ our Lord.

APPENDIX

TO THE ORDER OF MASS

CHANTS FOR THE EUCHARISTIC PRAYER AND OTHER MUSICAL SETTINGS

EUCHARISTIC PRAYER I

or THE ROMAN CANON

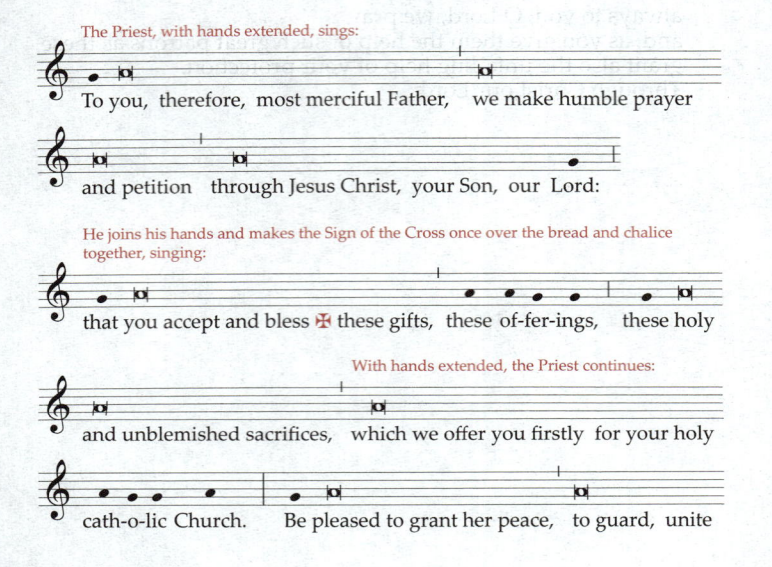

The Priest, with hands extended, sings:

To you, therefore, most merciful Father, we make humble prayer and petition through Jesus Christ, your Son, our Lord:

He joins his hands and makes the Sign of the Cross once over the bread and chalice together, singing:

that you accept and bless ✠ these gifts, these of-fer-ings, these holy

With hands extended, the Priest continues:

and unblemished sacrifices, which we offer you firstly for your holy cath-o-lic Church. Be pleased to grant her peace, to guard, unite

Appendix: Chants and other Musical Settings 111

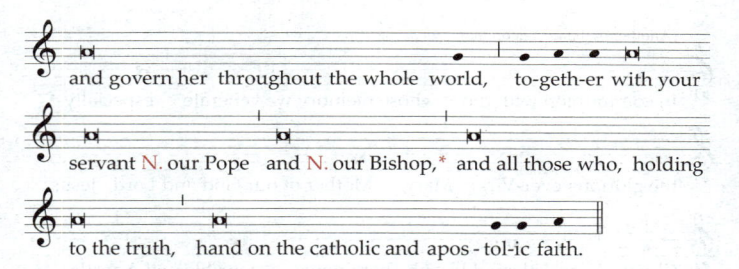

and govern her throughout the whole world, to-geth-er with your servant N. our Pope and N. our Bishop,* and all those who, holding to the truth, hand on the catholic and apos-tol-ic faith.

* Mention may be made here of the Coadjutor Bishop, or Auxiliary Bishops, as noted in the *General Instruction of the Roman Missal*, no. 149.

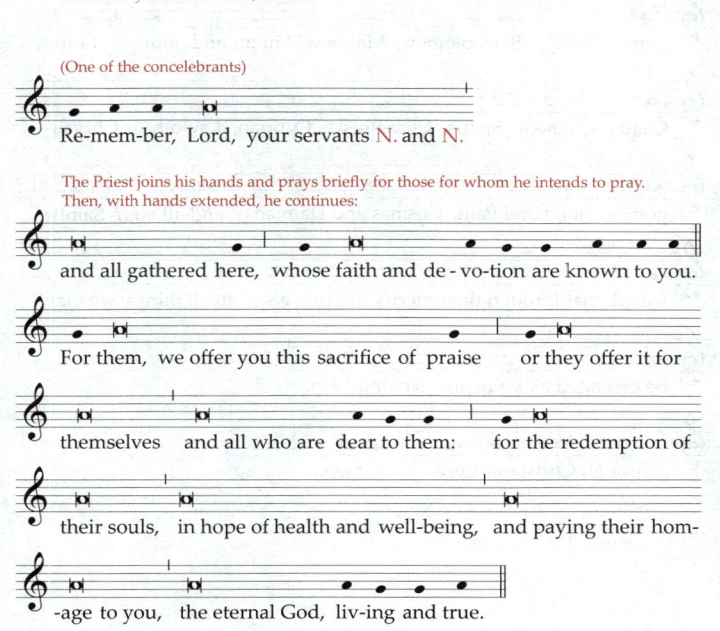

(One of the concelebrants)

Re-mem-ber, Lord, your servants N. and N.

The Priest joins his hands and prays briefly for those for whom he intends to pray. Then, with hands extended, he continues:

and all gathered here, whose faith and de-vo-tion are known to you. For them, we offer you this sacrifice of praise or they offer it for themselves and all who are dear to them: for the redemption of their souls, in hope of health and well-being, and paying their hom--age to you, the eternal God, liv-ing and true.

(Another of the concelebrants)

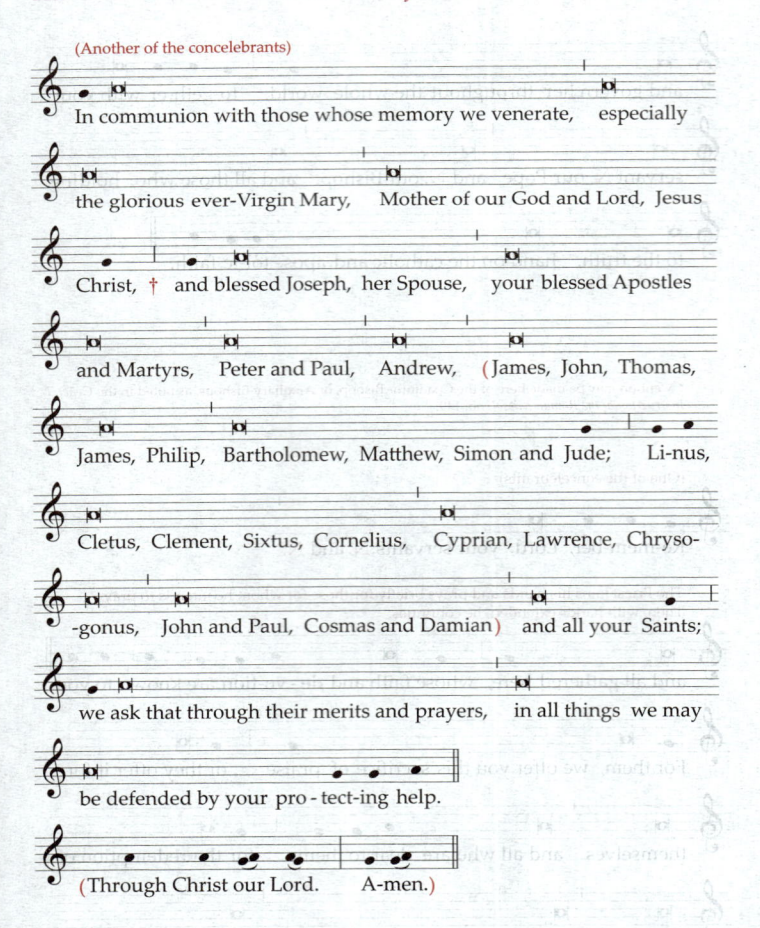

In communion with those whose memory we venerate, especially the glorious ever-Virgin Mary, Mother of our God and Lord, Jesus Christ, † and blessed Joseph, her Spouse, your blessed Apostles and Martyrs, Peter and Paul, Andrew, (James, John, Thomas, James, Philip, Bartholomew, Matthew, Simon and Jude; Linus, Cletus, Clement, Sixtus, Cornelius, Cyprian, Lawrence, Chrysogonus, John and Paul, Cosmas and Damian) and all your Saints; we ask that through their merits and prayers, in all things we may be defended by your pro‑tect‑ing help.

(Through Christ our Lord. A‑men.)

Appendix: Chants and other Musical Settings

PROPER FORMS OF THE *COMMUNICANTES* AND *HANC IGITUR*

On the Nativity of the Lord and throughout the Octave

Cel-ebrating the most sacred night/day on which blessed Mary the immaculate Virgin brought forth the Saviour for this world, and in communion with those whose memory we ven-er-ate, es-pe-cial-ly the glorious ever-Virgin Mary, Mother of our God and Lord, Jesus Christ, †

On the Epiphany of the Lord

Cel-ebrating the most sacred day on which your Only Begotten Son, eternal with you in your glory, appeared in a human body, truly sharing our flesh, and in communion with those whose memory we ven-er-ate, es-pe-cial-ly the glorious ever-Virgin Mary, Mother of our God and Lord, Jesus Christ, †

Thursday of the Lord's Supper

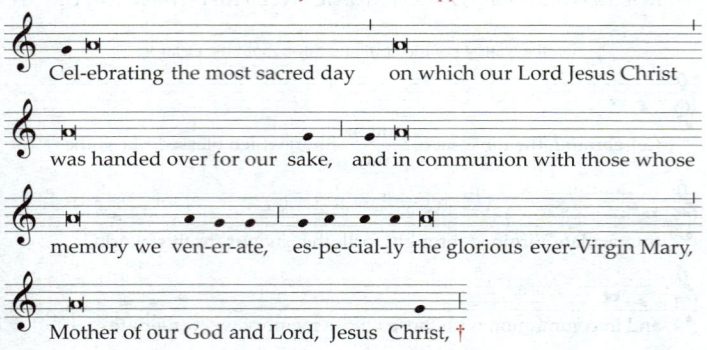

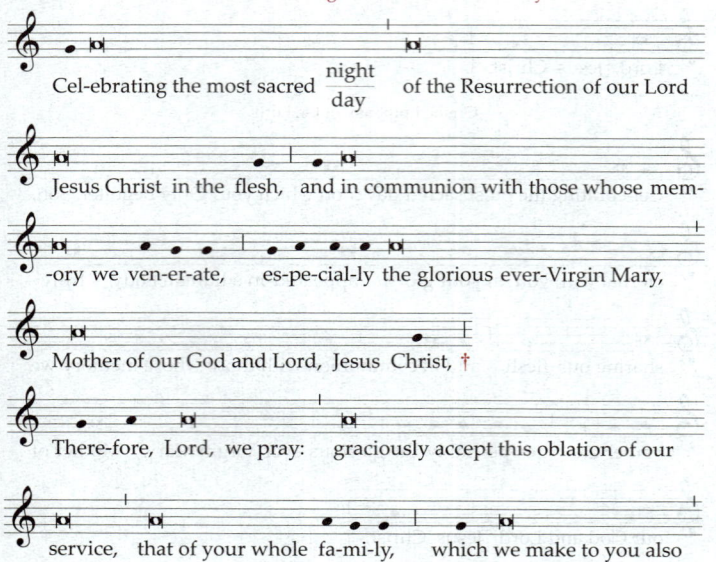

Cel-ebrating the most sacred day on which our Lord Jesus Christ was handed over for our sake, and in communion with those whose memory we ven-er-ate, es-pe-cial-ly the glorious ever-Virgin Mary, Mother of our God and Lord, Jesus Christ, †

From the Mass of the Easter Vigil until the Second Sunday of Easter

Cel-ebrating the most sacred night/day of the Resurrection of our Lord Jesus Christ in the flesh, and in communion with those whose mem-ory we ven-er-ate, es-pe-cial-ly the glorious ever-Virgin Mary, Mother of our God and Lord, Jesus Christ, †

There-fore, Lord, we pray: graciously accept this oblation of our service, that of your whole fa-mi-ly, which we make to you also

Appendix: Chants and other Musical Settings

for those to whom you have been pleased to give the new birth of water and the Holy Spirit, granting them forgiveness of all their sins; or-der our days in your peace, and command that we be delivered from eternal damnation and counted among the flock of those you have cho-sen.

(He joins his hands.)

(Through Christ our Lord. A-men.)

On the Ascension of the Lord

Cel-ebrating the most sacred day on which your Only Begotten Son, our Lord, placed at the right hand of your glory our weak human na-ture, which he had united to him-self, and in communion with those whose memory we ven-er-ate, es-pe-cial-ly the glorious ever- -Virgin Mary, Mother of our God and Lord, Jesus Christ, †

On Pentecost Sunday

Celebrating the most sacred day of Pentecost, on which the Holy Spirit appeared to the Apostles in tongues of fire, and in communion with those whose memory we venerate, especially the glorious ever-Virgin Mary, Mother of our God and Lord, Jesus Christ, †

With hands extended, the Principal Celebrant continues:

Therefore, Lord, we pray: graciously accept this oblation of our service, that of your whole family; order our days in your peace, and command that we be delivered from eternal damnation and counted among the flock of those you have chosen.

(He joins his hands.)

(Through Christ our Lord. Amen.)

Holding his hands extended over the offerings, he sings (together with the concelebrants):

Be pleased, O God, we pray, to bless, acknowledge, and approve

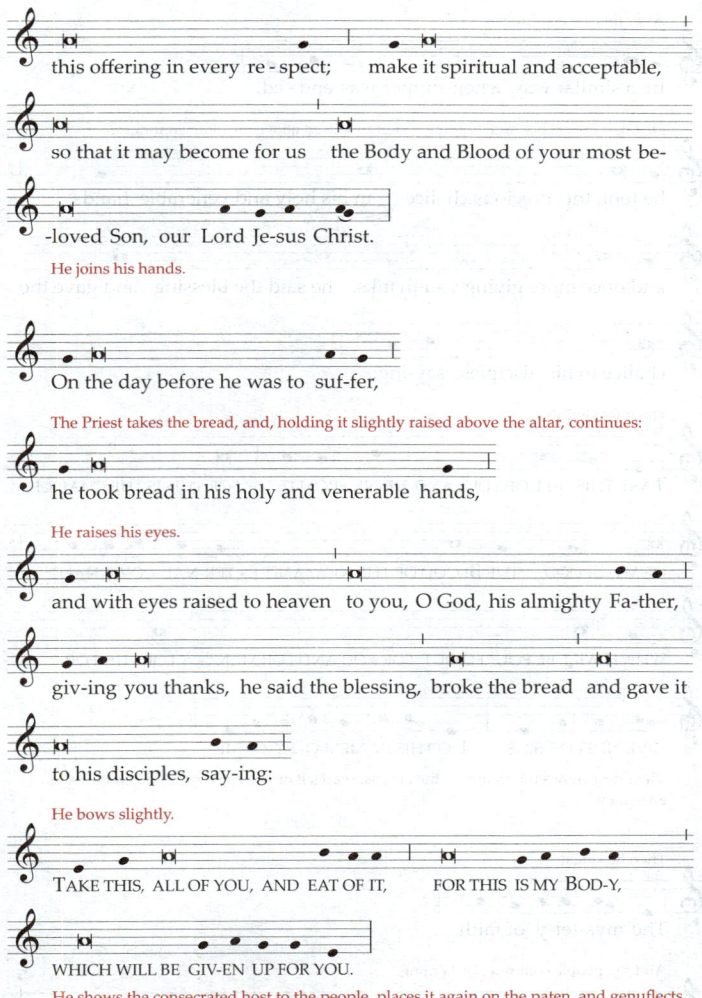

Appendix: Chants and other Musical Settings 117

this offering in every re-spect; make it spiritual and acceptable, so that it may become for us the Body and Blood of your most be-loved Son, our Lord Je-sus Christ.

He joins his hands.

On the day before he was to suf-fer,

The Priest takes the bread, and, holding it slightly raised above the altar, continues:

he took bread in his holy and venerable hands,

He raises his eyes.

and with eyes raised to heaven to you, O God, his almighty Fa-ther, giv-ing you thanks, he said the blessing, broke the bread and gave it to his disciples, say-ing:

He bows slightly.

TAKE THIS, ALL OF YOU, AND EAT OF IT, FOR THIS IS MY BOD-Y, WHICH WILL BE GIV-EN UP FOR YOU.

He shows the consecrated host to the people, places it again on the paten, and genuflects in adoration.

After this, he continues:

In a similar way, when supper was end-ed,

He takes the chalice and, holding it slightly raised above the altar, continues:

he took this precious chalice in his holy and venerable hands,

and once more giving you thanks, he said the blessing and gave the

chalice to his disciples, say-ing:

He bows slightly.

TAKE THIS, ALL OF YOU, AND DRINK FROM IT, FOR THIS IS THE CHALICE

OF MY BLOOD, THE BLOOD OF THE NEW AND E-TER-NAL COV-E-NANT,

WHICH WILL BE POURED OUT FOR YOU AND FOR MANY FOR THE FOR-

-GIVE-NESS OF SINS. DO THIS IN MEM-O-RY OF ME.

The Priest shows the chalice to the people, places it on the corporal, and genuflects in adoration.

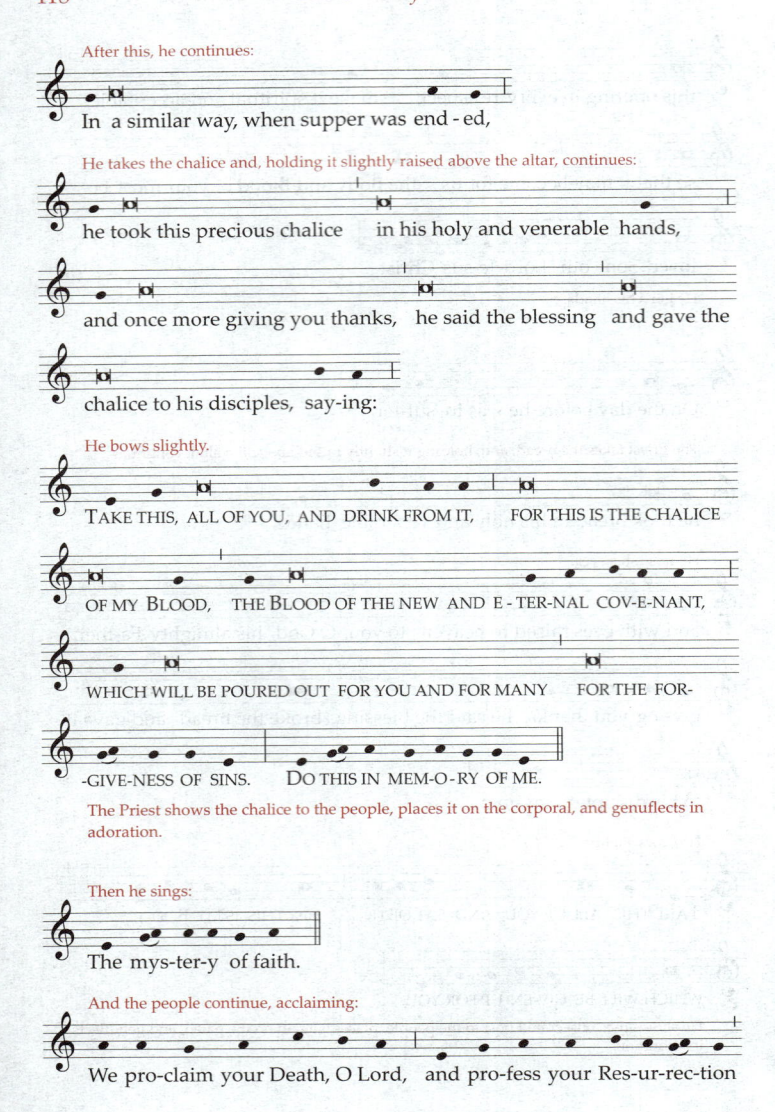

Then he sings:

The mys-ter-y of faith.

And the people continue, acclaiming:

We pro-claim your Death, O Lord, and pro-fess your Res-ur-rec-tion

Appendix: Chants and other Musical Settings 119

un-til you come a-gain.

Or:

When we eat this Bread and drink this Cup, we pro-claim your Death, O Lord, un-til you come a-gain.

Or:

Save us, Sav-iour of the world, for by your Cross and Res-ur-rec-tion you have set us free.

Then he, with hands extended, sings (one of the concelebrants):

There-fore, O Lord, as we celebrate the memorial of the blessed Passion, the Resurrection from the dead, and the glorious Ascension into heaven of Christ, your Son, our Lord, we, your servants and your holy people, offer to your glorious majesty from the gifts that you have giv-en us, this pure victim, this holy victim, this spotless vic-tim, the holy Bread of eternal life and the Chalice of ever-

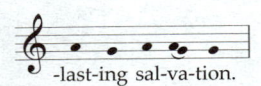

-last-ing sal-va-tion.

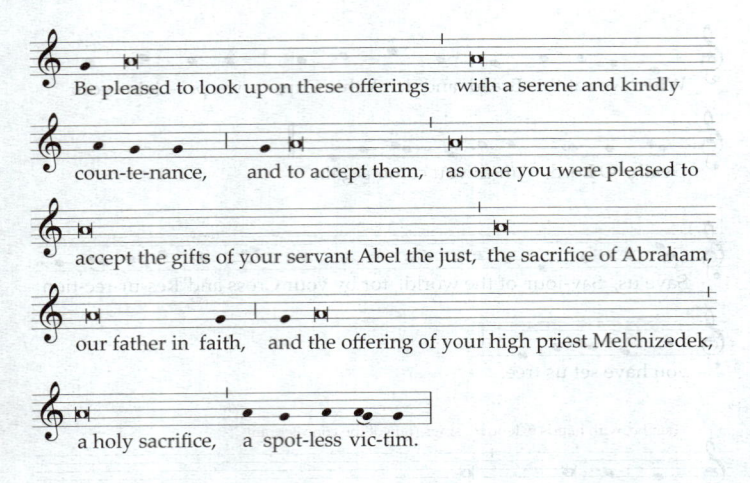

Be pleased to look upon these offerings with a serene and kindly coun-te-nance, and to accept them, as once you were pleased to accept the gifts of your servant Abel the just, the sacrifice of Abraham, our father in faith, and the offering of your high priest Melchizedek, a holy sacrifice, a spot-less vic-tim.

Bowing, with hands joined, he continues:

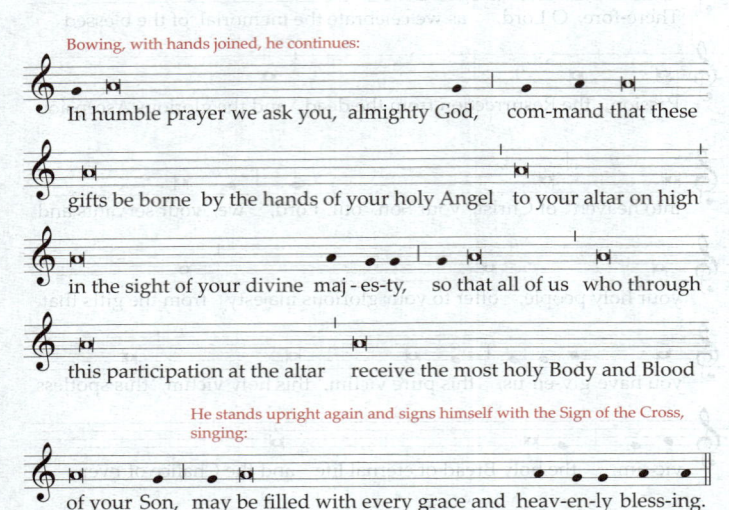

In humble prayer we ask you, almighty God, com-mand that these gifts be borne by the hands of your holy Angel to your altar on high in the sight of your divine maj-es-ty, so that all of us who through this participation at the altar receive the most holy Body and Blood

He stands upright again and signs himself with the Sign of the Cross, singing:

of your Son, may be filled with every grace and heav-en-ly bless-ing.

Appendix: Chants and other Musical Settings

(He joins his hands.)

(Through Christ our Lord. A-men.)

With hands extended, the Priest sings (one of the concelebrants):

Re-mem-ber also, Lord, your servants N. and N., who have gone before us with the sign of faith and rest in the sleep of peace.

He joins his hands and prays briefly for those who have died and for whom he intends to pray.
Then, with hands extended, he continues:

Grant them, O Lord, we pray, and all who sleep in Christ, a place of refreshment, light and peace. (He joins his hands.) (Through Christ our Lord. A-men.)

(Another of the concelebrants)
He strikes his breast with his right hand, singing: And, with hands extended, he continues:

To us, also, your servants, who, though sinners, hope in your abun--dant mercies, graciously grant some share and fellowship with your holy Apostles and Mar-tyrs: with John the Baptist, Stephen, Mat--thias, Barnabas, (Ignatius, Alexander, Marcellinus, Peter, Felicity,

Perpetua, Agatha, Lucy, Agnes, Cecilia, Anastasia) and all your Saints; ad-mit us, we beseech you, into their company, not weigh-ing our merits, but granting us your par-don,

He joins his hands.

through Christ our Lord.

And the Principal Celebrant continues, with hands joined:

Through whom you continue to make all these good things, O Lord; you sanctify them, fill them with life, bless them, and be-stow them up-on us.

He takes the chalice and the paten with the host and raising both, he sings (together with the concelebrants):

Through him, and with him, and in him, O God, almighty Father, in the unity of the Ho-ly Spir-it, all glo-ry and hon-or is yours, for ev-er and ev-er. R. A-men.

Then follows the Communion Rite.

Appendix: Chants and other Musical Settings

EUCHARISTIC PRAYER II

Although it is provided with its own Preface, this Eucharistic Prayer may also be used with other Prefaces, especially those that present an overall view of the mystery of salvation, such as the Common Prefaces.

V. The Lord be with you. R. And with your spirit.

V. Lift up your hearts. R. We lift them up to the Lord.

V. Let us give thanks to the Lord our God. R. It is right and just.

It is truly right and just, our duty and our salvation, always and everywhere to give you thanks, Father most holy, through your beloved Son, Jesus Christ, your Word through whom you made all things, whom you sent as our Saviour and Redeemer, incarnate by the Holy Spirit and born of the Virgin. Fulfilling your will and gaining for you a holy people, he stretched out his hands as he endured his Passion, so as to break the bonds of death and manifest the res-ur-rec-tion. And so, with the Angels and all the Saints we declare your glo-ry, as with one voice we ac-claim:

At the end of the Preface he joins his hands and concludes the Preface with the people, singing aloud:

Ho-ly, Ho-ly, Ho-ly Lord God of hosts. Heav-en and earth are full of your glo-ry. Ho-san-na in the high-est. Bless-ed is he who comes in the name of the Lord. Ho-san-na in the high-est.

The Principal Celebrant, with hands extended, sings:

You are indeed Holy, O Lord, the fount of all ho-li-ness.

He joins his hands and, holding them extended over the offerings, sings (together with the concelebrants):

Make holy, therefore, these gifts, we pray, by sending down your Spirit upon them like the dew-fall,

He joins his hands and makes the Sign of the Cross once over the bread and the chalice together, singing:

so that they may become for us the Body and ✠ Blood of our Lord

Appendix: Chants and other Musical Settings

Je-sus Christ.

He joins his hands.

At the time he was betrayed and entered willingly into his Pas-sion,

He takes the bread and, holding it slightly raised above the altar, continues:

he took bread and, giving thanks, broke it, and gave it to his dis-ciples, say-ing:

He bows slightly.

Take this, all of you, and eat of it, for this is my Bod-y,

which will be giv-en up for you.

He shows the consecrated host to the people, places it again on the paten, and genuflects in adoration.

After this, he continues:

In a similar way, when supper was end-ed,

He takes the chalice and, holding it slightly raised above the altar, continues:

he took the chalice and, once more giving thanks, he gave it to his disciples, say-ing:

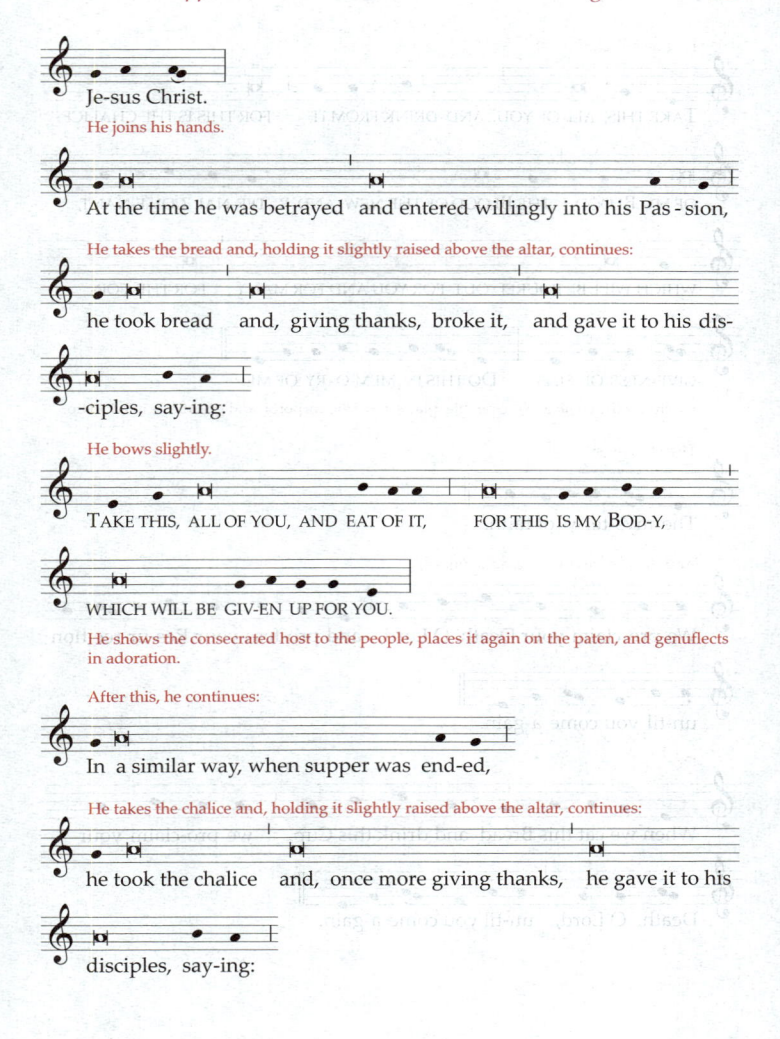

He bows slightly.

Take this, all of you, and drink from it, for this is the chalice of my Blood, the Blood of the new and eternal covenant, which will be poured out for you and for many for the forgiveness of sins. Do this in memory of me.

He shows the chalice to the people, places it on the corporal, and genuflects in adoration.

Then he sings:

The mystery of faith.

And the people continue, acclaiming:

We proclaim your Death, O Lord, and profess your Resurrection until you come again.

Or:

When we eat this Bread and drink this Cup, we proclaim your Death, O Lord, until you come again.

Appendix: Chants and other Musical Settings   127

Or:

Save us, Sav-iour of the world, for by your Cross and Res-ur-rec-tion you have set us free.

Then he, with hands extended, sings (one of the concelebrants):

There-fore, as we celebrate the memorial of his Death and Resur-rection, we offer you, Lord, the Bread of life and the Chalice of sal-vation, giv-ing thanks that you have held us worthy to be in your presence and minis-ter to you.

Hum-bly we pray that, partaking of the Body and Blood of Christ, we may be gathered into one by the Ho-ly Spir-it.

(One of the concelebrants)

Re-mem-ber, Lord, your Church, spread throughout the world, and bring her to the fullness of charity, together with N. our Pope and N. our Bishop * and all the cler-gy.

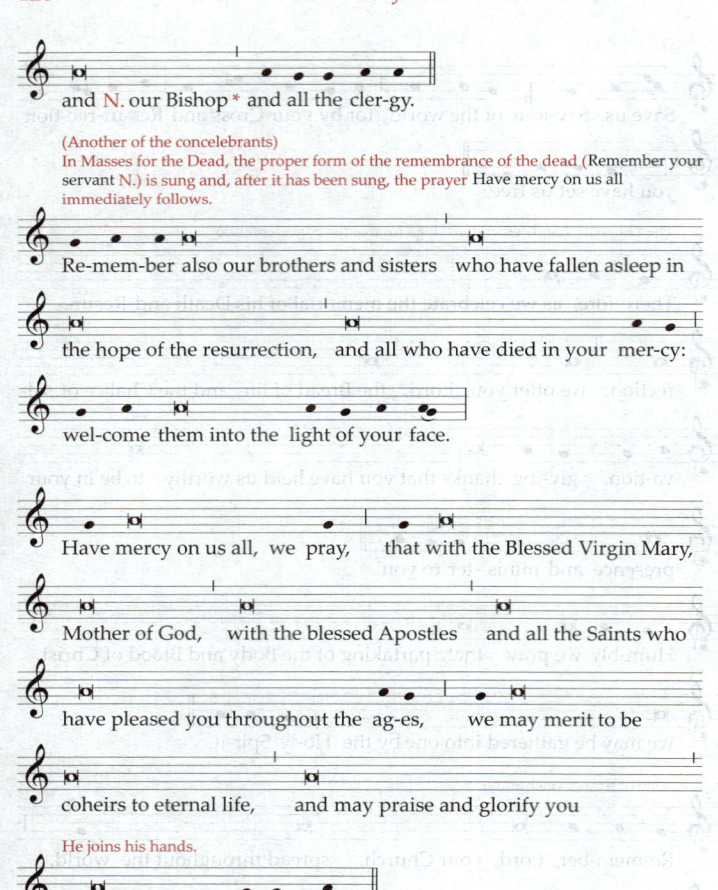

(Another of the concelebrants)
In Masses for the Dead, the proper form of the remembrance of the dead (Remember your servant N.) is sung and, after it has been sung, the prayer Have mercy on us all immediately follows.

Re-mem-ber also our brothers and sisters who have fallen asleep in

the hope of the resurrection, and all who have died in your mer-cy:

wel-come them into the light of your face.

Have mercy on us all, we pray, that with the Blessed Virgin Mary,

Mother of God, with the blessed Apostles and all the Saints who

have pleased you throughout the ag-es, we may merit to be

coheirs to eternal life, and may praise and glorify you

He joins his hands.

through your Son, Je-sus Christ.

* Mention may be made here of the Coadjutor Bishop, or Auxiliary Bishops, as noted in the *General Instruction of the Roman Missal*, no. 149.

Appendix: Chants and other Musical Settings

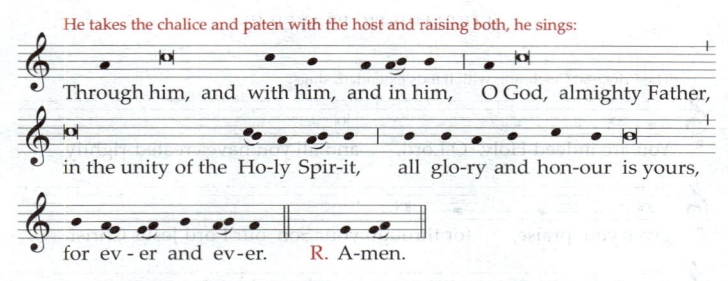

He takes the chalice and paten with the host and raising both, he sings:

Through him, and with him, and in him, O God, almighty Father, in the unity of the Ho-ly Spir-it, all glo-ry and hon-our is yours, for ev-er and ev-er. ℟. A-men.

Then follows the Communion Rite.

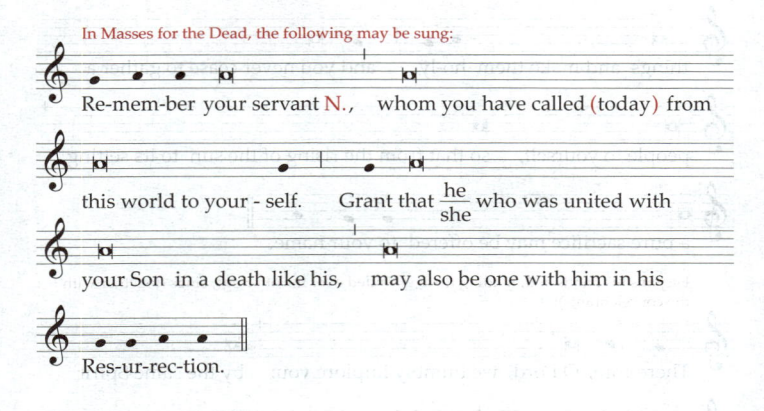

In Masses for the Dead, the following may be sung:

Re-mem-ber your servant N., whom you have called (today) from this world to your-self. Grant that $\frac{he}{she}$ who was united with your Son in a death like his, may also be one with him in his Res-ur-rec-tion.

EUCHARISTIC PRAYER III

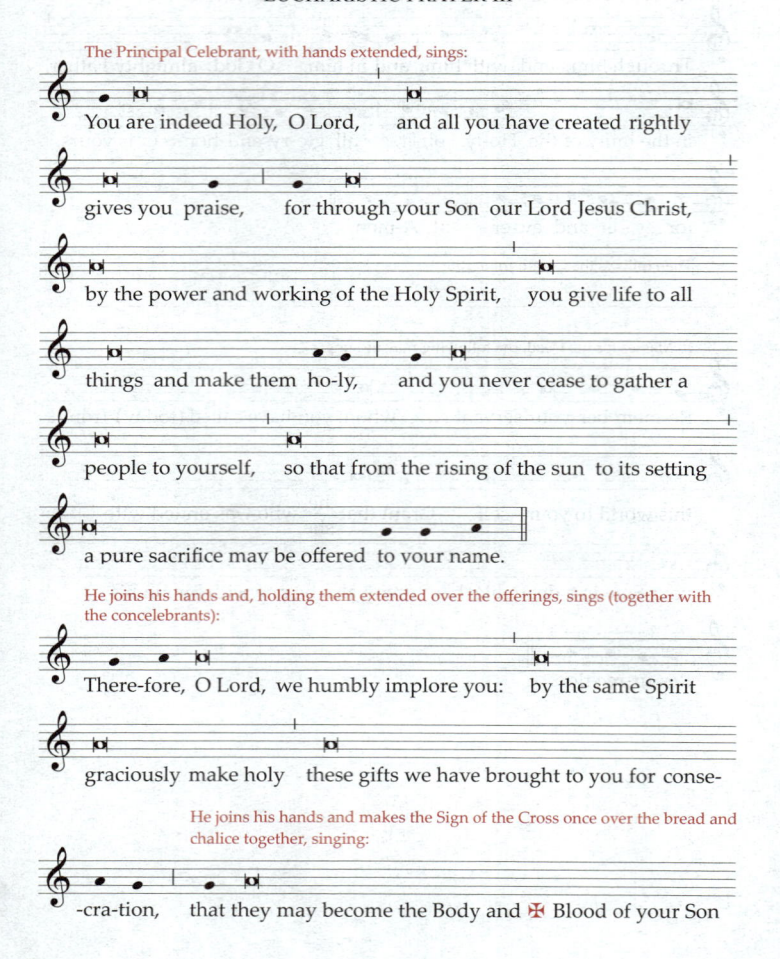

The Principal Celebrant, with hands extended, sings:

You are indeed Holy, O Lord, and all you have created rightly gives you praise, for through your Son our Lord Jesus Christ, by the power and working of the Holy Spirit, you give life to all things and make them ho-ly, and you never cease to gather a people to yourself, so that from the rising of the sun to its setting a pure sacrifice may be offered to your name.

He joins his hands and, holding them extended over the offerings, sings (together with the concelebrants):

There-fore, O Lord, we humbly implore you: by the same Spirit graciously make holy these gifts we have brought to you for conse-

He joins his hands and makes the Sign of the Cross once over the bread and chalice together, singing:

-cra-tion, that they may become the Body and ✠ Blood of your Son

Appendix: Chants and other Musical Settings

He joins his hands.

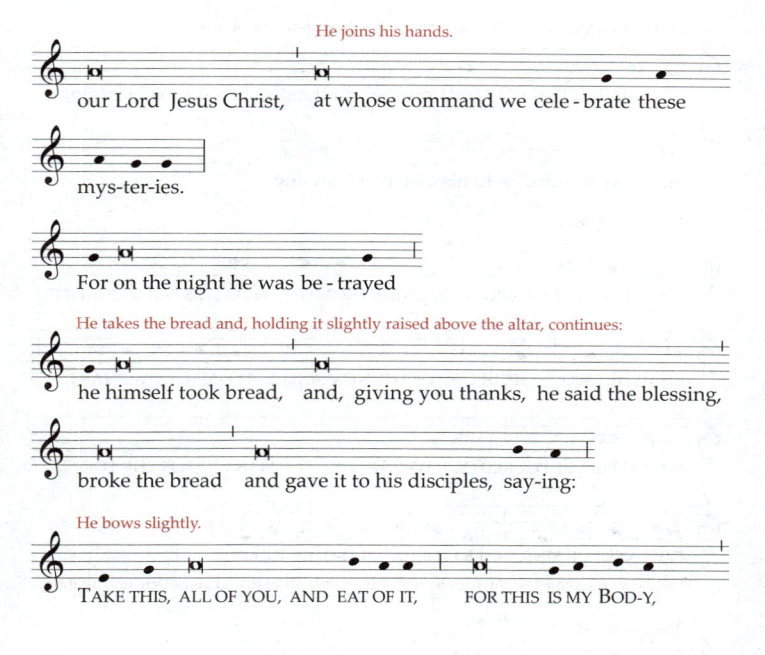

our Lord Jesus Christ, at whose command we cele-brate these mys-ter-ies.

For on the night he was be-trayed

He takes the bread and, holding it slightly raised above the altar, continues:

he himself took bread, and, giving you thanks, he said the blessing, broke the bread and gave it to his disciples, say-ing:

He bows slightly.

TAKE THIS, ALL OF YOU, AND EAT OF IT, FOR THIS IS MY BOD-Y, WHICH WILL BE GIV-EN UP FOR YOU.

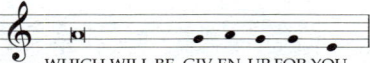

He shows the consecrated host to the people, places it again on the paten, and genuflects in adoration.

After this, he continues:

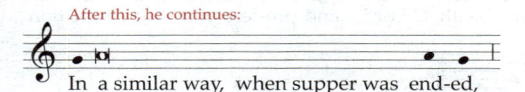

In a similar way, when supper was end-ed,

He takes the chalice and, holding it slightly raised above the altar, continues:

he took the chalice, and, giving you thanks, he said the blessing, and gave the chalice to his disciples, say-ing:

He bows slightly.

TAKE THIS, ALL OF YOU, AND DRINK FROM IT, FOR THIS IS THE CHALICE OF MY BLOOD, THE BLOOD OF THE NEW AND E-TER-NAL COV-E-NANT, WHICH WILL BE POURED OUT FOR YOU AND FOR MANY FOR THE FOR--GIVE-NESS OF SINS. DO THIS IN MEM-O-RY OF ME.

He shows the chalice to the people, places it on the corporal, and genuflects in adoration.

Then he sings:

The mys-ter-y of faith.

And the people continue, acclaiming:

We pro-claim your Death, O Lord, and pro-fess your Res-ur-rec-tion un-til you come a-gain.

Or:

When we eat this Bread and drink this Cup, we pro-claim your

Appendix: Chants and other Musical Settings

Death, O Lord, un-til you come a-gain.

Or:

Save us, Sav-iour of the world, for by your Cross and Res-ur-rec-tion you have set us free.

Then he, with hands extended, sings (one of the concelebrants):

There-fore, O Lord, as we celebrate the memorial of the saving Pas-sion of your Son, his wondrous Resurrection and Ascension into heaven, and as we look forward to his second com-ing, we offer you in thanksgiving this holy and liv-ing sac-ri-fice.

Look, we pray, upon the oblation of your Church and, recognizing the sacrificial Victim by whose death you willed to reconcile us to your-self, grant that we, who are nourished by the Body and

Blood of your Son and filled with his Holy Spirit, may become one body, one spir-it in Christ.

(One of the concelebrants)

May he make of us an eternal offering to you, so that we may obtain an inheritance with your e-lect, es-pecially with the most Blessed Virgin Mary, Mother of God, with your blessed Apostles and glori--ous Martyrs (with Saint N.)* and with all the Saints, on whose con--stant intercession in your presence we rely for un-fail-ing help.

(Another of the concelebrants)

May this Sacrifice of our reconciliation, we pray, O Lord, advance the peace and salvation of all the world. Be pleased to confirm in faith and charity your pilgrim Church on earth, with your servant N.

* the Saint of the day or Patron Saint

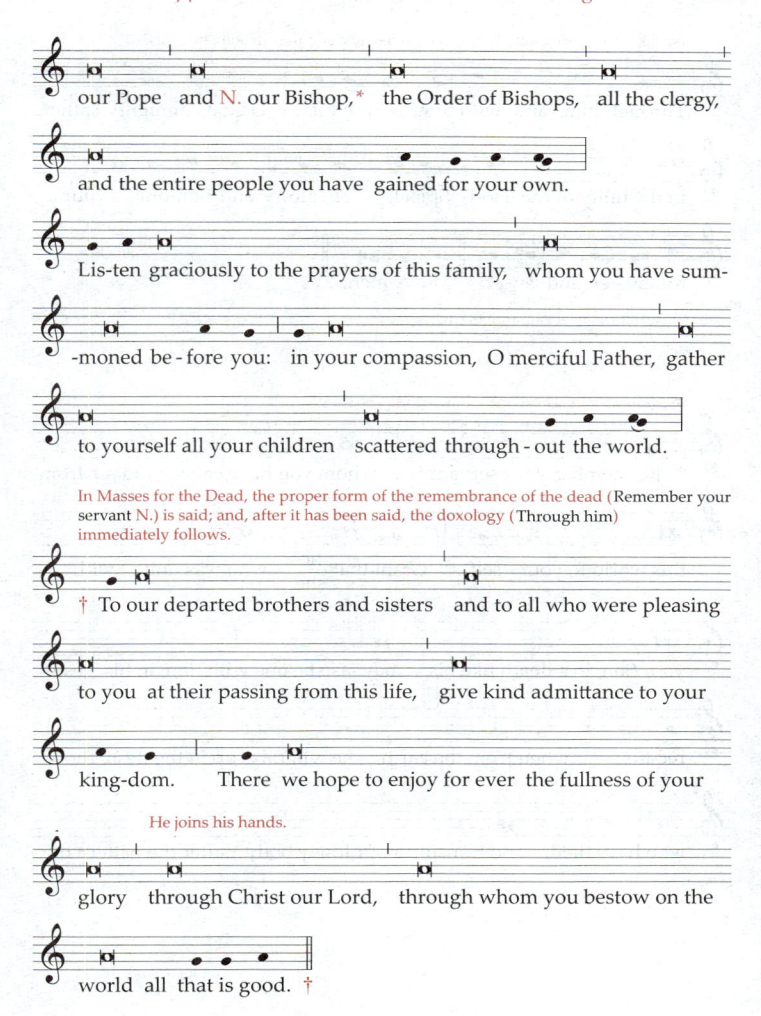

Appendix: Chants and other Musical Settings 135

our Pope and N. our Bishop,* the Order of Bishops, all the clergy, and the entire people you have gained for your own.

Lis-ten graciously to the prayers of this family, whom you have summoned be-fore you: in your compassion, O merciful Father, gather to yourself all your children scattered through-out the world.

In Masses for the Dead, the proper form of the remembrance of the dead (Remember your servant N.) is said; and, after it has been said, the doxology (Through him) immediately follows.

† To our departed brothers and sisters and to all who were pleasing to you at their passing from this life, give kind admittance to your king-dom. There we hope to enjoy for ever the fullness of your

He joins his hands.

glory through Christ our Lord, through whom you bestow on the world all that is good. †

* Mention may be made here of the Coadjutor Bishop, or Auxiliary Bishops, as noted in the *General Instruction of the Roman Missal*, no. 149.

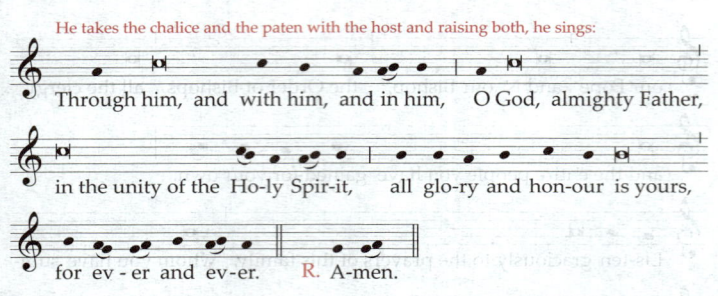

He takes the chalice and the paten with the host and raising both, he sings:

Through him, and with him, and in him, O God, almighty Father, in the unity of the Holy Spirit, all glory and honour is yours, for ev-er and ev-er. R. A-men.

Then follows the Communion Rite.

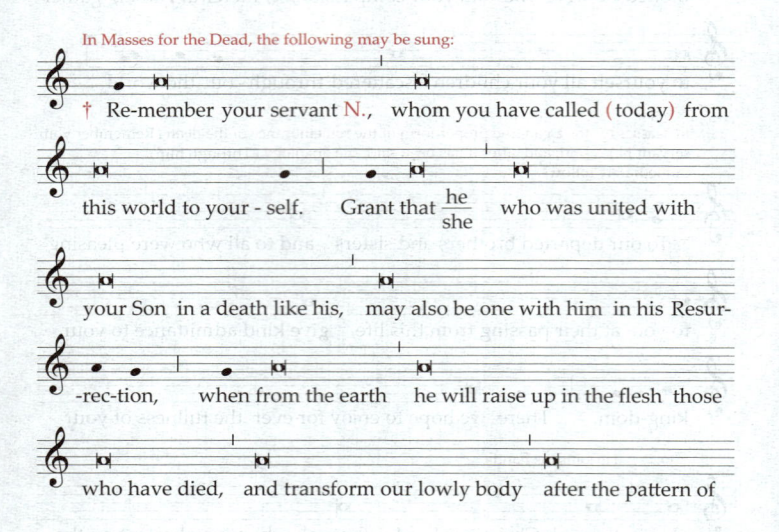

In Masses for the Dead, the following may be sung:

† Remember your servant N., whom you have called (today) from this world to yourself. Grant that he/she who was united with your Son in a death like his, may also be one with him in his Resurrection, when from the earth he will raise up in the flesh those who have died, and transform our lowly body after the pattern of

Appendix: Chants and other Musical Settings 137

his own glo-ri-ous bod-y.   To our departed brothers and sisters, too,

and to all who were pleasing to you   at their passing from this life,

give kind admittance to your king-dom.   There we hope to enjoy for

ever the fullness of your glory,   when you will wipe away every tear

from our eyes.   For seeing you, our God, as you are,   we shall be

He joins his hands.

like you for all the ages   and praise you without end,   through Christ

our Lord,   through whom you bestow on the world all that is good. †

EUCHARISTIC PRAYER IV

It is not permitted to change the Preface of this Eucharistic Prayer because of the structure of the Prayer itself, which presents a summary of the history of salvation.

V. The Lord be with you.   R. And with your spirit.

V. Lift up your hearts.   R. We lift them up to the Lord.

V. Let us give thanks to the Lord our God.   R. It is right and just.

It is truly right to give you thanks, truly just to give you glory, Father most holy, for you are the one God living and true, existing before all ages and abiding for all eternity, dwelling in unapproachable light; yet you, who alone are good, the source of life, have made all that is, so that you might fill your creatures with blessings and bring joy to many of them by the glory of your light. And so, in your presence are countless hosts of Angels,

Appendix: Chants and other Musical Settings

who serve you day and night   and, gazing upon the glory of your face, glorify you with-out ceas-ing. With them we, too, confess your name in ex-ul-ta-tion,   giving voice to every creature under heaven, as we ac-claim:

At the end of the Preface he joins his hands and concludes the Preface with the people, singing aloud:

Ho-ly, Ho-ly, Ho-ly Lord God of hosts. Heav-en and earth are full of your glo-ry. Ho-san-na in the high-est. Bless-ed is he who comes in the name of the Lord. Ho-san-na in the high-est.

The Principal Celebrant, with hands extended, sings:

We give you praise, Father most holy, for you are great and you have fashioned all your works in wisdom and in love. You formed man in your own image, and entrusted the whole world to his care, so that in serving you alone, the Creator, he might have dominion over all crea-tures. And when through disobedience he had lost your friendship, you did not abandon him to the domain of death. For you came in mercy to the aid of all, so that those who seek might find you. Time and again you offered them covenants and through the prophets taught them to look forward to sal-va-tion. And you so loved the world, Father most holy, that in the fullness of time you sent your Only Begotten Son to be our Sav-iour. Made incarnate by the Holy Spirit and born of the Virgin Mary, he shared our hu--man nature in all things but sin. To the poor he proclaimed the good news of salvation, to prisoners, freedom, and to the sorrow-

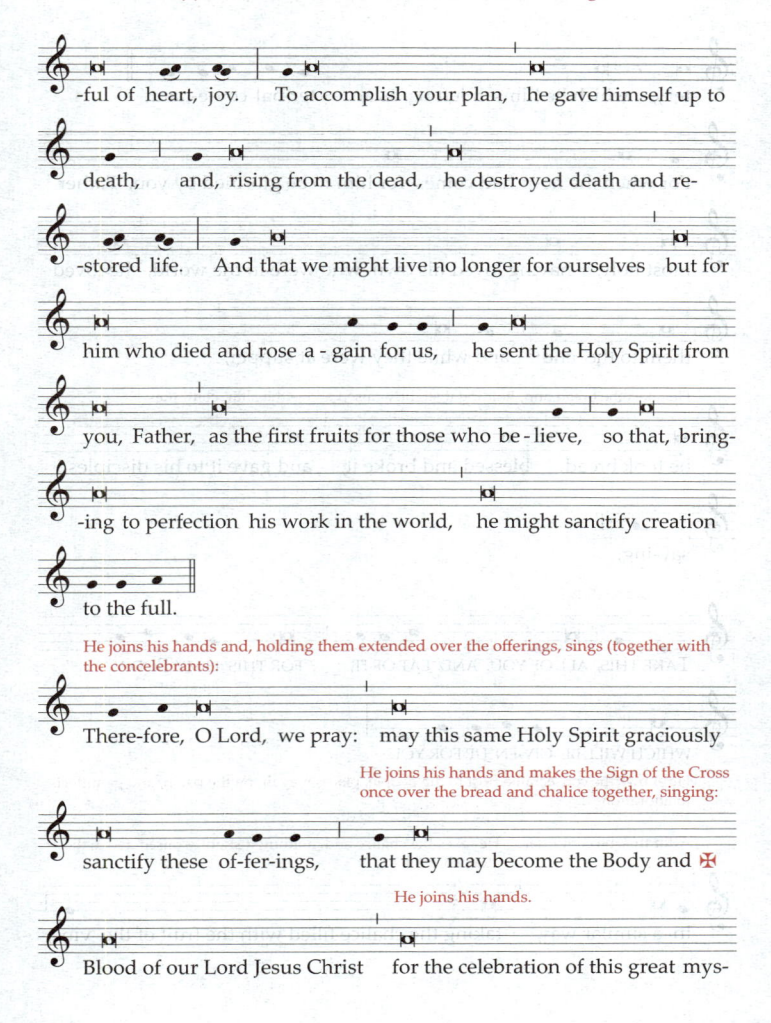

Appendix: Chants and other Musical Settings 141

-ful of heart, joy. To accomplish your plan, he gave himself up to death, and, rising from the dead, he destroyed death and re-stored life. And that we might live no longer for ourselves but for him who died and rose a-gain for us, he sent the Holy Spirit from you, Father, as the first fruits for those who be-lieve, so that, bring-ing to perfection his work in the world, he might sanctify creation to the full.

He joins his hands and, holding them extended over the offerings, sings (together with the concelebrants):

There-fore, O Lord, we pray: may this same Holy Spirit graciously

He joins his hands and makes the Sign of the Cross once over the bread and chalice together, singing:

sanctify these of-fer-ings, that they may become the Body and ✠

He joins his hands.

Blood of our Lord Jesus Christ for the celebration of this great mys-

-tery, which he himself left us as an e-ter-nal cov-e-nant.

For when the hour had come for him to be glorified by you, Father

most holy, having loved his own who were in the world, he loved

them to the end: and while they were at supper,

He takes the bread and, holding it slightly raised above the altar, continues:

he took bread, blessed and broke it, and gave it to his disciples,

say-ing,

He bows slightly.

TAKE THIS, ALL OF YOU, AND EAT OF IT, FOR THIS IS MY BOD-Y,

WHICH WILL BE GIV-EN UP FOR YOU.

He shows the consecrated host to the people, places it again on the paten, and genuflects in adoration.

After this, he continues: *He takes the chalice and, holding it slightly raised above the altar, continues:*

In a similar way, taking the chalice filled with the fruit of the vine,

Appendix: Chants and other Musical Settings

he gave thanks, and gave the chalice to his disciples, say-ing:

He bows slightly.

Take this, all of you, and drink from it, for this is the chalice of my Blood, the Blood of the new and e-ter-nal cov-e-nant, which will be poured out for you and for many for the for-give-ness of sins. Do this in mem-o-ry of me.

He shows the chalice to the people, places it on the corporal, and genuflects in adoration.

Then he sings:

The mys-ter-y of faith.

And the people continue, acclaiming:

We pro-claim your Death, O Lord, and pro-fess your Res-ur-rec-tion un-til you come a-gain.

Or:

When we eat this Bread and drink this Cup, we pro-claim your

Death, O Lord, un-til you come a-gain.

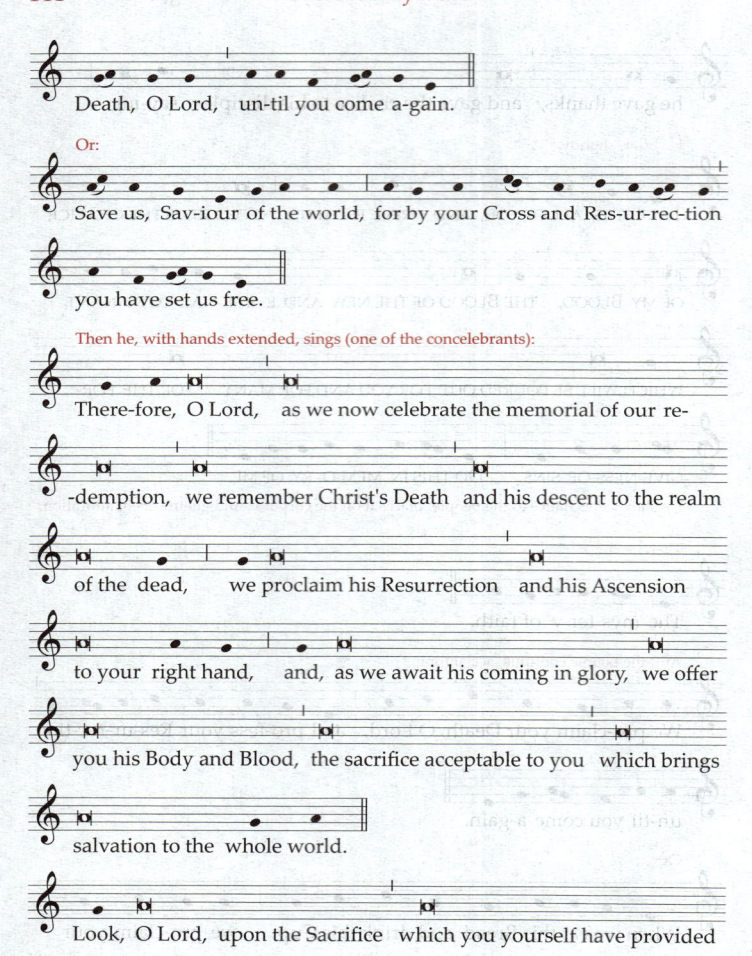

Or:

Save us, Sav-iour of the world, for by your Cross and Res-ur-rec-tion you have set us free.

Then he, with hands extended, sings (one of the concelebrants):

Therefore, O Lord, as we now celebrate the memorial of our redemption, we remember Christ's Death and his descent to the realm of the dead, we proclaim his Resurrection and his Ascension to your right hand, and, as we await his coming in glory, we offer you his Body and Blood, the sacrifice acceptable to you which brings salvation to the whole world.

Look, O Lord, upon the Sacrifice which you yourself have provided

Appendix: Chants and other Musical Settings 145

for your Church, and grant in your loving kindness to all who partake of this one Bread and one Chal-ice that, gathered into one body by the Holy Spirit, they may truly become a living sacrifice in Christ to the praise of your glo-ry.

(One of the concelebrants)

There-fore, Lord, remember now all for whom we offer this sac-ri-fice: es-pe-cial-ly your servant N. our Pope, N. our Bishop,* and the whole Order of Bish-ops, all the clergy, those who take part in this offering, those gathered here before you, your entire people, and all who seek you with a sin-cere heart. Re-mem-ber also those who have died in the peace of your Christ and all the dead,

* Mention may be made here of the Coadjutor Bishop, or Auxiliary Bishops, as noted in the *General Instruction of the Roman Missal*, no. 149.

whose faith you alone have known. To all of us, your children, grant, O merciful Father, that we may enter into a heavenly inheritance with the Blessed Virgin Mary, Mother of God, and with your Apostles and Saints in your kingdom. There, with the whole of creation, freed from the corruption of sin and death, may we glorify

He joins his hands.

you through Christ our Lord, through whom you bestow on the world all that is good.

He takes the chalice and the paten with the host and raising both, he sings:

Through him, and with him, and in him, O God, almighty Father, in the unity of the Holy Spirit, all glory and honour is yours, for ever and ever. R. Amen.

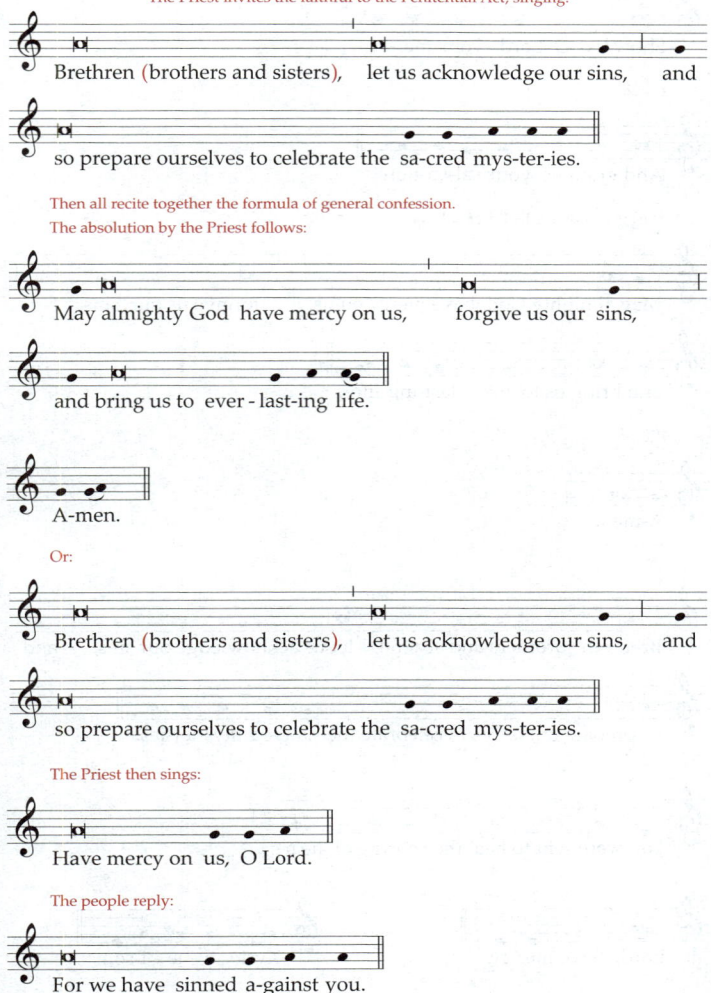

Appendix: Chants and other Musical Settings 147

PENITENTIAL ACT

The Priest invites the faithful to the Penitential Act, singing:

Brethren (brothers and sisters), let us acknowledge our sins, and so prepare ourselves to celebrate the sa-cred mys-ter-ies.

Then all recite together the formula of general confession.
The absolution by the Priest follows:

May almighty God have mercy on us, forgive us our sins, and bring us to ever-last-ing life.

A-men.

Or:

Brethren (brothers and sisters), let us acknowledge our sins, and so prepare ourselves to celebrate the sa-cred mys-ter-ies.

The Priest then sings:

Have mercy on us, O Lord.

The people reply:

For we have sinned a-gainst you.

The Order of Mass

Priest:

Show us, O Lord, your mer-cy.

People:

And grant us your sal-va-tion.

The absolution by the Priest follows:

May almighty God have mercy on us, forgive us our sins,

and bring us to ever-last-ing life.

People:

A-men.

Or:

Brethren (brothers and sisters), let us acknowledge our sins, and

so prepare ourselves to celebrate the sa-cred mys-ter-ies.

You were sent to heal the contrite of heart:

Lord, have mer-cy.   **Or:**   Kýrie, e - lé - i - son.

Appendix: Chants and other Musical Settings

People:

Lord, have mer-cy.   Or: Kýrie, e - lé - i - son.

Priest:

You came to call sin-ners:

Christ, have mer-cy.   Or: Christe, e - lé - i - son.

People:

Christ, have mer-cy.   Or: Christe, e - lé - i - son.

Priest:

You are seated at the right hand of the Father to inter-cede for us:

Lord, have mer-cy.   Or: Kýrie, e - lé - i - son.

People:

Lord, have mer-cy.   Or: Kýrie, e - lé - i - son.

The absolution by the Priest follows:

May almighty God have mercy on us,   forgive us our sins,

and bring us to ever-last-ing life.

A-men.

LITURGY OF THE WORD

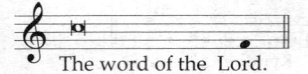

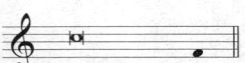

The word of the Lord.

Thanks be to God.

The word of the Lord.

Thanks be to God.

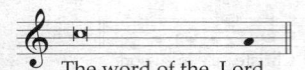

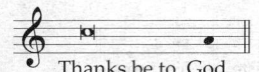

CREED

I be-lieve in one God, the Fa-ther al-might-y, mak-er of heav-en and earth, of all things vis-i-ble and in-vis-i-ble.

I be-lieve in one Lord Je-sus Christ, the Only Be-got-ten Son of God, born of the Father be-fore all a-ges. God from God, Light from Light, true God from true God, be-got-ten, not made,

Appendix: Chants and other Musical Settings

con-sub-stan-tial with the Fa-ther; through him all things were made. For us men and for our sal-va-tion he came down from

*At the words that follow, up to and including **and became man**, all bow.*

heav-en, and by the Ho-ly Spir-it was in-car-nate of the Vir-gin Mar-y, and be-came man.

For our sake he was cru-ci-fied un-der Pon-tius Pi-late, he suffered death and was bur-ied, and rose a-gain on the third day in accordance with the Scrip-tures. He as-cend-ed in-to heav-en and is seated at the right hand of the Fa-ther. He will come a-gain in glo-ry to judge the living and the dead and his kingdom will have no end.

I be-lieve in the Ho-ly Spir-it, the Lord, the giv-er of life, who proceeds from the Father and the Son, who with the Father and the Son is adored and glorified, who has spoken through the prophets. I believe in one, holy, catholic and apostolic Church. I confess one Baptism for the forgiveness of sins and I look forward to the resurrection of the dead and the life of the world to come. A - men.

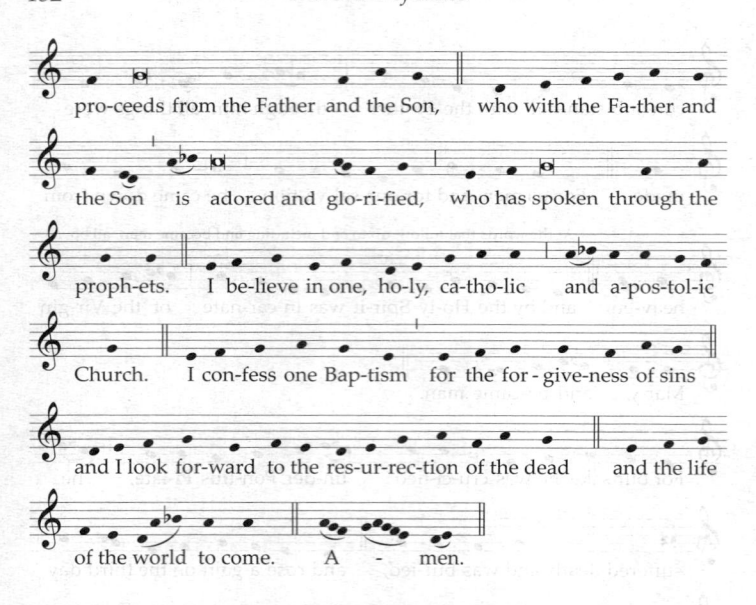

ORATE FRATRES

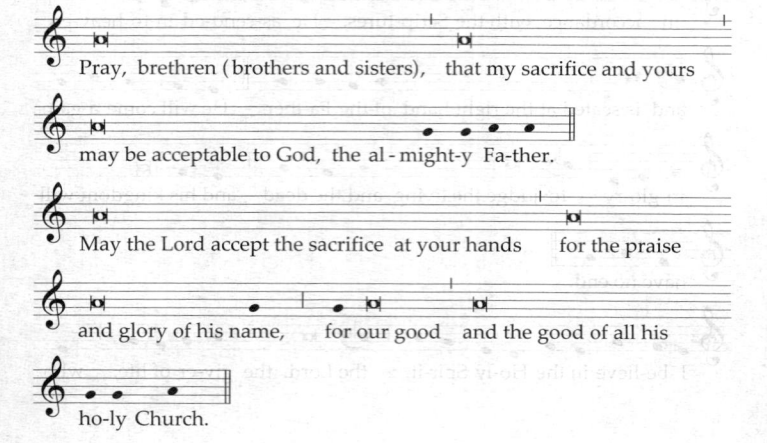

Pray, brethren (brothers and sisters), that my sacrifice and yours may be acceptable to God, the almighty Father.

May the Lord accept the sacrifice at your hands for the praise and glory of his name, for our good and the good of all his holy Church.

Appendix: Chants and other Musical Settings

THE LORD'S PRAYER

At the Saviour's command and formed by divine teaching,

we dare to say:

Pater noster, qui es in caelis: sanctificétur nomen tuum;

advéniat regnum tuum; fiat volúntas tua, sicut in caelo,

et in terra. Panem nostrum cotidiánum da nobis hódie;

et dimítte nobis débita nostra, sicut et nos dimíttimus

debitóribus nostris; et ne nos indúcas in tentatiónem;

sed líbera nos a malo.

Deliver us, Lord, we pray, from every evil, graciously grant peace

in our days, that, by the help of your mercy, we may be always free

from sin and safe from all distress, as we await the blessed hope

and the coming of our Saviour, Jesus Christ.

THE SIGN OF PEACE

Lord Jesus Christ, who said to your Apostles: Peace I leave you, my peace I give you, look not on our sins, but on the faith of your Church, and graciously grant her peace and unity in ac-

He joins his hands.

-cordance with your will. Who live and reign for ev-er and ev-er.

A-men.

The peace of the Lord be with you al-ways.

And with your spir-it.

Let us offer each other the sign of peace.

Appendix: Chants and other Musical Settings

AGNUS DEI

A-gnus De-i, * qui tol-lis pec-cá-ta mun-di: mi-se-ré-re no-bis.

A-gnus De-i, * qui tol-lis pec-cá-ta mun-di: mi-se-ré-re no-bis.

A-gnus De-i, * qui tol-lis pec-cá-ta mun-di: do-na no-bis pa-cem.

COMMUNION

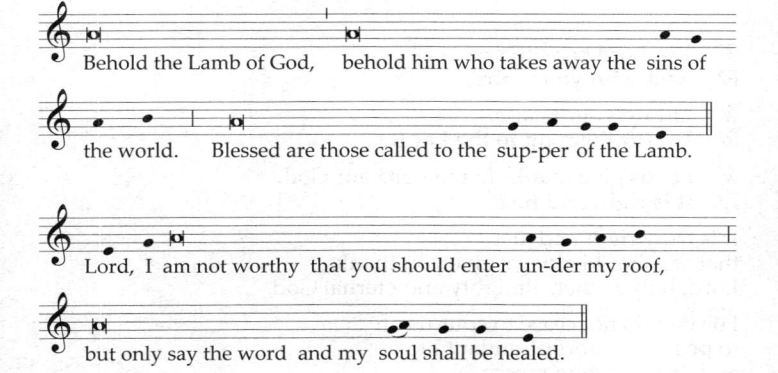

Behold the Lamb of God, behold him who takes away the sins of the world. Blessed are those called to the sup-per of the Lamb.

Lord, I am not worthy that you should enter un-der my roof, but only say the word and my soul shall be healed.

EUCHARISTIC PRAYERS
FOR RECONCILIATION

The Eucharistic Prayers for Reconciliation may be used in Masses in which the mystery of reconciliation is conveyed to the faithful in a special way, as, for example, in the Masses for Promoting Harmony, For Reconciliation, For the Preservation of Peace and Justice, In Time of War or Civil Disturbance, For the Forgiveness of Sins, For Charity, of the Mystery of the Holy Cross, of the Most Holy Eucharist, of the Most Precious Blood of our Lord Jesus Christ, as well as in Masses during Lent. Although these Eucharistic Prayers have been provided with a proper Preface, they may also be used with other Prefaces that refer to penance and conversion, as, for example, the Prefaces of Lent.

I

℣ The Lord be with you.
℟ **And with your spirit.**

℣ Lift up your hearts.
℟ **We lift them up to the Lord.**

℣ Let us give thanks to the Lord our God.
℟ **It is right and just.**

It is truly right and just
that we should always give you thanks,
Lord, holy Father, almighty and eternal God.

For you do not cease to spur us on
to possess a more abundant life
and, being rich in mercy,
you constantly offer pardon
and call on sinners
to trust in your forgiveness alone.

Never did you turn away from us,
and, though time and again we have broken your covenant,
you have bound the human family to yourself
through Jesus your Son, our Redeemer,
with a new bond of love so tight
that it can never be undone.

Even now you set before your people
a time of grace and reconciliation,
and, as they turn back to you in spirit,

Appendix: Eucharistic Prayers for Reconciliation

you grant them hope in Christ Jesus
and a desire to be of service to all,
while they entrust themselves
more fully to the Holy Spirit.

And so, filled with wonder,
we extol the power of your love,
and, proclaiming our joy
at the salvation that comes from you,
we join in the heavenly hymn of countless hosts,
as without end we acclaim:

Holy, Holy, Holy Lord God of hosts.
Heaven and earth are full of your glory.
Hosanna in the highest.
Blessed is he who comes in the name of the Lord.
Hosanna in the highest.

The Priest, with hands extended, says:

You are indeed Holy, O Lord,
and from the world's beginning
are ceaselessly at work,
so that the human race may become holy,
just as you yourself are holy.

He joins his hands and, holding them extended over the offerings, says:

Look, we pray, upon your people's offerings
and pour out on them the power of your Spirit,

He joins his hands and makes the Sign of the Cross once over the bread and chalice together, saying:

that they may become the Body and ✠ Blood

He joins his hands.

of your beloved Son, Jesus Christ,
in whom we, too, are your sons and daughters.

Indeed, though we once were lost
and could not approach you,
you loved us with the greatest love:
for your Son, who alone is just,
handed himself over to death,
and did not disdain to be nailed for our sake
to the wood of the Cross.

But before his arms were outstretched between heaven and earth,
to become the lasting sign of your covenant,
he desired to celebrate the Passover with his disciples.

In the formulas that follow, the words of the Lord should be pronounced clearly and distinctly, as the nature of these words requires.

As he ate with them,

*He takes the bread
and, holding it slightly raised above the altar, continues:*

he took bread
and, giving you thanks, he said the blessing,
broke the bread and gave it to them, saying:

He bows slightly.

Take this, all of you, and eat of it,
for this is my Body,
which will be given up for you.

*He shows the consecrated host to the people, places it again on the paten, and genuflects in adoration.
After this, he continues:*

In a similar way, when supper was ended,
knowing that he was about to reconcile all things in himself
through his Blood to be shed on the Cross,

*He takes the chalice
and, holding it slightly raised above the altar, continues:*

he took the chalice, filled with the fruit of the vine,
and once more giving you thanks,
handed the chalice to his disciples, saying:

He bows slightly.

Take this, all of you, and drink from it,
for this is the chalice of my Blood,
the Blood of the new and eternal covenant,
which will be poured out for you and for many
for the forgiveness of sins.
Do this in memory of me.

He shows the chalice to the people, places it on the corporal, and genuflects in adoration.

Appendix: Eucharistic Prayers for Reconciliation

Then he says:

The mystery of faith.

And the people continue, acclaiming:

**We proclaim your Death, O Lord,
and profess your Resurrection
until you come again.**

or

**When we eat this Bread and drink this Cup,
we proclaim your Death, O Lord,
until you come again.**

or

**Save us, Saviour of the world,
for by your Cross and Resurrection
you have set us free.**

Then the Priest, with hands extended, says:

Therefore, as we celebrate
the memorial of your Son Jesus Christ,
who is our Passover and our surest peace,
we celebrate his Death and Resurrection from the dead,
and looking forward to his blessed Coming,
we offer you, who are our faithful and merciful God,
this sacrificial Victim
who reconciles to you the human race.

Look kindly, most compassionate Father,
on those you unite to yourself
by the Sacrifice of your Son,
and grant that, by the power of the Holy Spirit,
as they partake of this one Bread and one Chalice,
they may be gathered into one Body in Christ,
who heals every division.

Be pleased to keep us always
in communion of mind and heart,
together with N. our Pope and N. our Bishop.*

Help us to work together
for the coming of your Kingdom,

---

*Mention may be made here of the Coadjutor Bishop, or Auxiliary Bishops, as noted in the *General Instruction of the Roman Missal*, no. 149.

until the hour when we stand before you,
Saints among the Saints in the halls of heaven,
with the Blessed Virgin Mary, Mother of God,
the blessed Apostles and all the Saints,
and with our deceased brothers and sisters,
whom we humbly commend to your mercy.

Then, freed at last from the wound of corruption
and made fully into a new creation,
we shall sing to you with gladness

He joins his hands.

the thanksgiving of Christ,
who lives for all eternity.

He takes the chalice and the paten with the host and, raising both, he says:

Through him, and with him, and in him,
O God, almighty Father,
in the unity of the Holy Spirit,
all glory and honour is yours,
for ever and ever.

The people acclaim:

Amen.

Then follows the Communion Rite, p.85.

II

℣ The Lord be with you.
℟ **And with your spirit.**

℣ Lift up your hearts.
℟ **We lift them up to the Lord.**

℣ Let us give thanks to the Lord our God.
℟ **It is right and just.**

It is truly right and just
that we should give you thanks and praise,
O God, almighty Father,
for all you do in this world,
through our Lord Jesus Christ.

Appendix: Eucharistic Prayers for Reconciliation

For though the human race
is divided by dissension and discord,
yet we know that by testing us
you change our hearts
to prepare them for reconciliation.

Even more, by your Spirit you move human hearts
that enemies may speak to each other again,
adversaries may join hands,
and peoples seek to meet together.

By the working of your power
it comes about, O Lord,
that hatred is overcome by love,
revenge gives way to forgiveness,
and discord is changed to mutual respect.

Therefore, as we give you ceaseless thanks
with the choirs of heaven,
we cry out to your majesty on earth,
and without end we acclaim:

Holy, Holy, Holy Lord God of hosts.
Heaven and earth are full of your glory.
Hosanna in the highest.
Blessed is he who comes in the name of the Lord.
Hosanna in the highest.

The Priest, with hands extended, says:

You, therefore, almighty Father,
we bless through Jesus Christ your Son,
who comes in your name.
He himself is the Word that brings salvation,
the hand you extend to sinners,
the way by which your peace is offered to us.
When we ourselves had turned away from you
on account of our sins,
you brought us back to be reconciled, O Lord,
so that, converted at last to you,
we might love one another
through your Son,
whom for our sake you handed over to death.

He joins his hands and, holding them extended over the offerings, says:

And now, celebrating the reconciliation
Christ has brought us,
we entreat you:
sanctify these gifts by the outpouring of your Spirit,

He joins his hands and makes the Sign of the Cross once over the bread and chalice together, saying:

that they may become the Body and ✢ Blood of your Son,
whose command we fulfil
when we celebrate these mysteries.

He joins his hands.

In the formulas that follow, the words of the Lord should be pronounced clearly and distinctly, as the nature of these words requires.

For when about to give his life to set us free,
as he reclined at supper,

He takes the bread and, holding it slightly raised above the altar, continues:

he himself took bread into his hands,
and, giving you thanks, he said the blessing,
broke the bread and gave it to his disciples, saying:

He bows slightly.

Take this, all of you, and eat of it,
for this is my Body,
which will be given up for you.

He shows the consecrated host to the people, places it again on the paten, and genuflects in adoration.

After this, he continues:

In a similar way, on that same evening,

He takes the chalice and, holding it slightly raised above the altar, continues:

he took the chalice of blessing in his hands,
confessing your mercy,
and gave the chalice to his disciples, saying:

Appendix: Eucharistic Prayers for Reconciliation

He bows slightly.

Take this, all of you, and drink from it,
for this is the chalice of my Blood,
the Blood of the new and eternal covenant,
which will be poured out for you and for many
for the forgiveness of sins.
Do this in memory of me.

He shows the chalice to the people, places it on the corporal, and genuflects in adoration.

Then he says:

The mystery of faith.

And the people continue, acclaiming:

**We proclaim your Death, O Lord,
and profess your Resurrection
until you come again.**

or

**When we eat this Bread and drink this Cup,
we proclaim your Death, O Lord,
until you come again.**

or

**Save us, Saviour of the world,
for by your Cross and Resurrection
you have set us free.**

Then the Priest, with hands extended, says:

Celebrating, therefore, the memorial
of the Death and Resurrection of your Son,
who left us this pledge of his love,
we offer you what you have bestowed on us,
the Sacrifice of perfect reconciliation.

Holy Father, we humbly beseech you
to accept us also, together with your Son,
and in this saving banquet
graciously to endow us with his very Spirit,
who takes away everything
that estranges us from one another.

May he make your Church a sign of unity
and an instrument of your peace among all people
and may he keep us in communion
with N. our Pope and N. our Bishop*
and all the Bishops
and your entire people.

Just as you have gathered us now at the table of your Son,
so also bring us together,
with the glorious Virgin Mary, Mother of God,
with your blessed Apostles and all the Saints,
with our brothers and sisters
and those of every race and tongue
who have died in your friendship.
Bring us to share with them the unending banquet of unity
in a new heaven and a new earth,
where the fullness of your peace will shine forth

He joins his hands.

in Christ Jesus our Lord.

He takes the chalice and the paten with the host and, raising both, he says:

Through him, and with him, and in him,
O God, almighty Father,
in the unity of the Holy Spirit,
all glory and honour is yours,
for ever and ever.

The people continue:

Amen.

Then follows the Communion Rite, p.85.

---

*Mention may be made here of the Coadjutor Bishop, or Auxiliary Bishops, as noted in the *General Instruction of the Roman Missal*, no. 149.

EUCHARISTIC PRAYERS FOR USE IN MASSES FOR VARIOUS NEEDS

I

The Church on the Path of Unity

The following form of this Eucharistic Prayer is appropriately used with Mass formularies such as, For the Church, For the Pope, For the Bishop, For the Election of a Pope or a Bishop, For a Council or Synod, For Priests, For the Priest Himself, For Ministers of the Church, and For a Spiritual or Pastoral Gathering.

℣ The Lord be with you.
℟ **And with your spirit.**

℣ Lift up your hearts.
℟ **We lift them up to the Lord.**

℣ Let us give thanks to the Lord our God.
℟ **It is right and just.**

It is truly right and just to give you thanks
and raise to you a hymn of glory and praise,
O Lord, Father of infinite goodness.

For by the word of your Son's Gospel
you have brought together one Church
from every people, tongue, and nation,
and, having filled her with life by the power of your Spirit,
you never cease through her
to gather the whole human race into one.

Manifesting the covenant of your love,
she dispenses without ceasing
the blessed hope of your Kingdom
and shines bright as the sign of your faithfulness,
which in Christ Jesus our Lord
you promised would last for eternity.

And so, with all the Powers of heaven,
we worship you constantly on earth,
while, with all the Church,
as one voice we acclaim:

Holy, Holy, Holy Lord God of hosts.
Heaven and earth are full of your glory.
Hosanna in the highest.

**Blessed is he who comes in the name of the Lord.
Hosanna in the highest.**

The Priest, with hands extended, says:

You are indeed Holy and to be glorified, O God,
who love the human race
and who always walk with us on the journey of life.
Blessed indeed is your Son,
present in our midst
when we are gathered by his love,
and when, as once for the disciples, so now for us,
he opens the Scriptures and breaks the bread.

He joins his hands and, holding them extended over the offerings, says:

Therefore, Father most merciful,
we ask that you send forth your Holy Spirit
to sanctify these gifts of bread and wine,

He joins his hands and makes the Sign of the Cross once over the bread and chalice together, saying:

that they may become for us
the Body and ✢ Blood

He joins his hands.

of our Lord Jesus Christ.

In the formulas that follow, the words of the Lord should be pronounced clearly and distinctly, as the nature of these words requires.

On the day before he was to suffer,
on the night of the Last Supper,

He takes the bread and, holding it slightly raised above the altar, continues:

he took bread and said the blessing,
broke the bread and gave it to his disciples, saying:

He bows slightly.

TAKE THIS, ALL OF YOU, AND EAT OF IT,
FOR THIS IS MY BODY,
WHICH WILL BE GIVEN UP FOR YOU.

Appendix: Eucharistic Prayers for Various Needs 167

He shows the consecrated host to the people, places it again on the paten, and genuflects in adoration.

After this, he continues:

In a similar way, when supper was ended,

He takes the chalice and, holding it slightly raised above the altar, continues:

he took the chalice, gave you thanks
and gave the chalice to his disciples, saying:

He bows slightly.

TAKE THIS, ALL OF YOU, AND DRINK FROM IT,
FOR THIS IS THE CHALICE OF MY BLOOD,
THE BLOOD OF THE NEW AND ETERNAL COVENANT,
WHICH WILL BE POURED OUT FOR YOU AND FOR MANY
FOR THE FORGIVENESS OF SINS.

DO THIS IN MEMORY OF ME.

He shows the chalice to the people, places it on the corporal, and genuflects in adoration.

Then he says:

The mystery of faith.

And the people continue, acclaiming:

**We proclaim your Death, O Lord,
and profess your Resurrection
until you come again.**

or

**When we eat this Bread and drink this Cup,
we proclaim your Death, O Lord,
until you come again.**

or

**Save us, Saviour of the world,
for by your Cross and Resurrection
you have set us free.**

Then the Priest, with hands extended, says:

Therefore, holy Father,
as we celebrate the memorial of Christ your Son, our Saviour,

whom you led through his Passion and Death on the Cross
to the glory of the Resurrection,
and whom you have seated at your right hand,
we proclaim the work of your love until he comes again
and we offer you the Bread of life
and the Chalice of blessing.

Look with favour on the oblation of your Church,
in which we show forth
the paschal Sacrifice of Christ that has been handed on to us,
and grant that, by the power of the Spirit of your love,
we may be counted now and until the day of eternity
among the members of your Son,
in whose Body and Blood we have communion.

Lord, renew your Church (which is in N.)
by the light of the Gospel.
Strengthen the bond of unity
between the faithful and the pastors of your people,
together with N. our Pope, N. our Bishop,*
and the whole Order of Bishops,
that in a world torn by strife
your people may shine forth
as a prophetic sign of unity and concord.

Remember our brothers and sisters (N. and N.),
who have fallen asleep in the peace of your Christ,
and all the dead, whose faith you alone have known.
Admit them to rejoice in the light of your face,
and in the resurrection give them the fullness of life.

Grant also to us,
when our earthly pilgrimage is done,
that we may come to an eternal dwelling place
and live with you for ever;
there, in communion with the Blessed Virgin Mary, Mother of
    God,
with the Apostles and Martyrs,
(with Saint N.: the Saint of the day or Patron)
and with all the Saints,
we shall praise and exalt you

---

*Mention may be made here of the Coadjutor Bishop, or Auxiliary Bishops, as noted in the *General Instruction of the Roman Missal*, no. 149.

Appendix: Eucharistic Prayers for Various Needs 169

He joins his hands.

through Jesus Christ, your Son.

He takes the chalice and the paten with the host and, raising both, he says:

Through him, and with him, and in him,
O God, almighty Father,
in the unity of the Holy Spirit,
all glory and honour is yours,
for ever and ever.

The people acclaim:

Amen.

Then follows the Communion Rite, p.85.

II

God Guides His Church along the Way of Salvation

The following form of this Eucharistic Prayer is appropriately used with Mass formularies such as, For the Church, For Vocations to Holy Orders, For the Laity, For the Family, For Religious, For Vocations to Religious Life, For Charity, For Relatives and Friends, and For Giving Thanks to God.

℣ The Lord be with you.
℟ **And with your spirit.**

℣ Lift up your hearts.
℟ **We lift them up to the Lord.**

℣ Let us give thanks to the Lord our God.
℟ **It is right and just.**

It is truly right and just, our duty and our salvation,
always and everywhere to give you thanks,
Lord, holy Father,
creator of the world and source of all life.

For you never forsake the works of your wisdom,
but by your providence are even now at work in our midst.
With mighty hand and outstretched arm
you led your people Israel through the desert.
Now, as your Church makes her pilgrim journey in the world,
you always accompany her
by the power of the Holy Spirit

and lead her along the paths of time
to the eternal joy of your Kingdom,
through Christ our Lord.

And so, with the Angels and Saints,
we, too, sing the hymn of your glory,
as without end we acclaim:

Holy, Holy, Holy Lord God of hosts.
Heaven and earth are full of your glory.
Hosanna in the highest.
Blessed is he who comes in the name of the Lord.
Hosanna in the highest.

The Priest, with hands extended, says:

You are indeed Holy and to be glorified, O God,
who love the human race
and who always walk with us on the journey of life.
Blessed indeed is your Son,
present in our midst
when we are gathered by his love
and when, as once for the disciples, so now for us,
he opens the Scriptures and breaks the bread.

He joins his hands and, holding them extended over the offerings, says:

Therefore, Father most merciful,
we ask that you send forth your Holy Spirit
to sanctify these gifts of bread and wine,

He joins his hands and makes the Sign of the Cross once over the bread and chalice together, saying:

that they may become for us
the Body and ✣ Blood

He joins his hands.

of our Lord Jesus Christ.

In the formulas that follow, the words of the Lord should be pronounced clearly and distinctly, as the nature of these words requires.

On the day before he was to suffer,
on the night of the Last Supper,

Appendix: Eucharistic Prayers for Various Needs

He takes the bread and, holding it slightly raised above the altar, continues:

he took bread and said the blessing,
broke the bread and gave it to his disciples, saying:

He bows slightly.

TAKE THIS, ALL OF YOU, AND EAT OF IT,
FOR THIS IS MY BODY,
WHICH WILL BE GIVEN UP FOR YOU.

He shows the consecrated host to the people, places it again on the paten, and genuflects in adoration.

After this, he continues:
In a similar way, when supper was ended,

He takes the chalice and, holding it slightly raised above the altar, continues:

he took the chalice, gave you thanks
and gave the chalice to his disciples, saying:

He bows slightly.

TAKE THIS, ALL OF YOU, AND DRINK FROM IT,
FOR THIS IS THE CHALICE OF MY BLOOD,
THE BLOOD OF THE NEW AND ETERNAL COVENANT,
WHICH WILL BE POURED OUT FOR YOU AND FOR MANY
FOR THE FORGIVENESS OF SINS.

DO THIS IN MEMORY OF ME.

He shows the chalice to the people, places it on the corporal, and genuflects in adoration.

Then he says:

The mystery of faith.

And the people continue, acclaiming:

**We proclaim your Death, O Lord,
and profess your Resurrection
until you come again.**

or

**When we eat this Bread and drink this Cup,
we proclaim your Death, O Lord,
until you come again.**

or

**Save us, Saviour of the world,
for by your Cross and Resurrection
you have set us free.**

Then the Priest, with hands extended, says:

Therefore, holy Father,
as we celebrate the memorial of Christ your Son, our Saviour,
whom you led through his Passion and Death on the Cross
to the glory of the Resurrection,
and whom you have seated at your right hand,
we proclaim the work of your love until he comes again
and we offer you the Bread of life
and the Chalice of blessing.

Look with favour on the oblation of your Church,
in which we show forth
the paschal Sacrifice of Christ that has been handed on to us,
and grant that, by the power of the Spirit of your love,
we may be counted now and until the day of eternity
among the members of your Son,
in whose Body and Blood we have communion.

And so, having called us to your table, Lord,
confirm us in unity,
so that, together with N. our Pope and N. our Bishop,*
with all Bishops, Priests and Deacons,
and your entire people,
as we walk your ways with faith and hope,
we may strive to bring joy and trust into the world.

Remember our brothers and sisters (N. and N.),
who have fallen asleep in the peace of your Christ,
and all the dead, whose faith you alone have known.
Admit them to rejoice in the light of your face,
and in the resurrection give them the fullness of life.

Grant also to us,
when our earthly pilgrimage is done,
that we may come to an eternal dwelling place
and live with you for ever;

---

*Mention may be made here of the Coadjutor Bishop, or Auxiliary Bishops, as noted in the *General Instruction of the Roman Missal*, no. 149.

Appendix: Eucharistic Prayers for Various Needs 173

there, in communion with the Blessed Virgin Mary, Mother of God,
with the Apostles and Martyrs,
(with Saint N.: the Saint of the day or Patron)
and with all the Saints,
we shall praise and exalt you

He joins his hands.

through Jesus Christ, your Son.

He takes the chalice and the paten with the host and, raising both, he says:

Through him, and with him, and in him,
O God, almighty Father,
in the unity of the Holy Spirit,
all glory and honour is yours,
for ever and ever.

The people acclaim:

Amen.

Then follows the Communion Rite, p.85.

III

Jesus, the Way to the Father

The following form of this Eucharistic Prayer is appropriately used with Mass formularies such as, For the Evangelization of Peoples, For Persecuted Christians, For the Nation or State, For Those in Public Office, For a Governing Assembly, At the Beginning of the Civil Year, and For the Progress of Peoples.

℣ The Lord be with you.
℟ **And with your spirit.**

℣ Lift up your hearts.
℟ **We lift them up to the Lord.**

℣ Let us give thanks to the Lord our God.
℟ **It is right and just.**

It is truly right and just, our duty and our salvation,
always and everywhere to give you thanks,
holy Father, Lord of heaven and earth,
through Christ our Lord.

For by your Word you created the world
and you govern all things in harmony.
You gave us the same Word made flesh as Mediator,
and he has spoken your words to us
and called us to follow him.
He is the way that leads us to you,
the truth that sets us free,
the life that fills us with gladness.

Through your Son
you gather men and women,
whom you made for the glory of your name,
into one family,
redeemed by the Blood of his Cross
and signed with the seal of the Spirit.

Therefore now and for ages unending,
with all the Angels,
we proclaim your glory,
as in joyful celebration we acclaim:

Holy, Holy, Holy Lord God of hosts.
Heaven and earth are full of your glory.
Hosanna in the highest.
Blessed is he who comes in the name of the Lord.
Hosanna in the highest.

The Priest, with hands extended, says:

You are indeed Holy and to be glorified, O God,
who love the human race
and who always walk with us on the journey of life.
Blessed indeed is your Son,
present in our midst
when we are gathered by his love
and when, as once for the disciples, so now for us,
he opens the Scriptures and breaks the bread.

He joins his hands and, holding them extended over the offerings, says:

Therefore, Father most merciful,
we ask that you send forth your Holy Spirit
to sanctify these gifts of bread and wine,

Appendix: Eucharistic Prayers for Various Needs

He joins his hands and makes the Sign of the Cross once over the bread and chalice together, saying:

that they may become for us
the Body and ✚ Blood

He joins his hands.

of our Lord Jesus Christ.

In the formulas that follow, the words of the Lord should be pronounced clearly and distinctly, as the nature of these words requires.

On the day before he was to suffer,
on the night of the Last Supper,

He takes the bread and, holding it slightly raised above the altar, continues:

he took bread and said the blessing,
broke the bread and gave it to his disciples, saying:

He bows slightly.

TAKE THIS, ALL OF YOU, AND EAT OF IT,
FOR THIS IS MY BODY,
WHICH WILL BE GIVEN UP FOR YOU.

He shows the consecrated host to the people, places it again on the paten, and genuflects in adoration.

After this, he continues:

In a similar way, when supper was ended,

He takes the chalice and, holding it slightly raised above the altar, continues:

he took the chalice, gave you thanks
and gave the chalice to his disciples, saying:

He bows slightly.

TAKE THIS, ALL OF YOU, AND DRINK FROM IT,
FOR THIS IS THE CHALICE OF MY BLOOD,
THE BLOOD OF THE NEW AND ETERNAL COVENANT,
WHICH WILL BE POURED OUT FOR YOU AND FOR MANY
FOR THE FORGIVENESS OF SINS.
DO THIS IN MEMORY OF ME.

The Order of Mass

He shows the chalice to the people, places it on the corporal, and genuflects in adoration.

Then he says:

The mystery of faith.

And the people continue, acclaiming:

**We proclaim your Death, O Lord,
and profess your Resurrection
until you come again.**

or

**When we eat this Bread and drink this Cup,
we proclaim your Death, O Lord,
until you come again.**

or

**Save us, Saviour of the world,
for by your Cross and Resurrection
you have set us free.**

Then the Priest, with hands extended, says:

Therefore, holy Father,
as we celebrate the memorial of Christ your Son, our Saviour,
whom you led through his Passion and Death on the Cross
to the glory of the Resurrection,
and whom you have seated at your right hand,
we proclaim the work of your love until he comes again
and we offer you the Bread of life
and the Chalice of blessing.

Look with favour on the oblation of your Church,
in which we show forth
the paschal Sacrifice of Christ that has been handed on to us,
and grant that, by the power of the Spirit of your love,
we may be counted now and until the day of eternity
among the members of your Son,
in whose Body and Blood we have communion.

By our partaking of this mystery, almighty Father,
give us life through your Spirit,
grant that we may be conformed to the image of your Son,
and confirm us in the bond of communion,

Appendix: Eucharistic Prayers for Various Needs 177

together with N. our Pope and N. our Bishop,*
with all other Bishops,
with Priests and Deacons,
and with your entire people.

Grant that all the faithful of the Church,
looking into the signs of the times by the light of faith,
may constantly devote themselves
to the service of the Gospel.
Keep us attentive to the needs of all
that, sharing their grief and pain,
their joy and hope,
we may faithfully bring them the good news of salvation
and go forward with them
along the way of your Kingdom.

Remember our brothers and sisters (N. and N.),
who have fallen asleep in the peace of your Christ,
and all the dead, whose faith you alone have known.
Admit them to rejoice in the light of your face,
and in the resurrection give them the fullness of life.

Grant also to us,
when our earthly pilgrimage is done,
that we may come to an eternal dwelling place
and live with you for ever;
there, in communion with the Blessed Virgin Mary, Mother of God,
with the Apostles and Martyrs,
(with Saint N.: the Saint of the day or Patron)
and with all the Saints,
we shall praise and exalt you

He joins his hands.

through Jesus Christ, your Son.

He takes the chalice and the paten with the host and, raising both, he says:

Through him, and with him, and in him,
O God, almighty Father,
in the unity of the Holy Spirit,
all glory and honour is yours,

---

*Mention may be made here of the Coadjutor Bishop, or Auxiliary Bishops, as noted in the *General Instruction of the Roman Missal*, no. 149.

for ever and ever.

The people acclaim:

Amen.

Then follows the Communion Rite, p.85.

IV
Jesus, Who Went About Doing Good

The following form of this Eucharistic Prayer is appropriately used with Mass formularies such as, For Refugees and Exiles, In Time of Famine or For Those Suffering Hunger, For Our Oppressors, For Those Held in Captivity, For Those in Prison, For the Sick, For the Dying, For the Grace of a Happy Death, and In Any Need.

℣ The Lord be with you.
℟ **And with your spirit.**

℣ Lift up your hearts.
℟ **We lift them up to the Lord.**

℣ Let us give thanks to the Lord our God.
℟ **It is right and just.**

It is truly right and just, our duty and our salvation,
always and everywhere to give you thanks,
Father of mercies and faithful God.

For you have given us Jesus Christ, your Son,
as our Lord and Redeemer.

He always showed compassion
for children and for the poor,
for the sick and for sinners,
and he became a neighbour
to the oppressed and the afflicted.

By word and deed he announced to the world
that you are our Father
and that you care for all your sons and daughters.

And so, with all the Angels and Saints,
we exalt and bless your name
and sing the hymn of your glory,
as without end we acclaim:

Appendix: Eucharistic Prayers for Various Needs 179

Holy, Holy, Holy Lord God of hosts.
Heaven and earth are full of your glory.
Hosanna in the highest.
Blessed is he who comes in the name of the Lord.
Hosanna in the highest.

The Priest, with hands extended, says:

You are indeed Holy and to be glorified, O God,
who love the human race
and who always walk with us on the journey of life.
Blessed indeed is your Son,
present in our midst
when we are gathered by his love
and when, as once for the disciples, so now for us,
he opens the Scriptures and breaks the bread.

He joins his hands and, holding them extended over the offerings, says:

Therefore, Father most merciful,
we ask that you send forth your Holy Spirit
to sanctify these gifts of bread and wine,

He joins his hands and makes the Sign of the Cross once over the bread and chalice together, saying:

that they may become for us
the Body and ✠ Blood

He joins his hands.

of our Lord Jesus Christ.

In the formulas that follow, the words of the Lord should be pronounced clearly and distinctly, as the nature of these words requires.

On the day before he was to suffer,
on the night of the Last Supper,

He takes the bread and, holding it slightly raised above the altar, continues:

he took bread and said the blessing,
broke the bread and gave it to his disciples, saying:

He bows slightly.

The Order of Mass

Take this, all of you, and eat of it,
for this is my Body,
which will be given up for you.

He shows the consecrated host to the people, places it again on the paten, and genuflects in adoration.
After this, he continues:

In a similar way, when supper was ended,

He takes the chalice and, holding it slightly raised above the altar, continues:

he took the chalice, gave you thanks
and gave the chalice to his disciples, saying:

He bows slightly.

Take this, all of you, and drink from it,
for this is the chalice of my Blood,
the Blood of the new and eternal covenant,
which will be poured out for you and for many
for the forgiveness of sins.

Do this in memory of me.

He shows the chalice to the people, places it on the corporal, and genuflects in adoration.

Then he says:

The mystery of faith.

And the people continue, acclaiming:

**We proclaim your Death, O Lord,
and profess your Resurrection
until you come again.**

or

**When we eat this Bread and drink this Cup,
we proclaim your Death, O Lord,
until you come again.**

or

**Save us, Saviour of the world,
for by your Cross and Resurrection
you have set us free.**

Appendix: Eucharistic Prayers for Various Needs

Then the Priest, with hands extended, says:

Therefore, holy Father,
as we celebrate the memorial of Christ your Son, our Saviour,
whom you led through his Passion and Death on the Cross
to the glory of the Resurrection,
and whom you have seated at your right hand,
we proclaim the work of your love until he comes again
and we offer you the Bread of life
and the Chalice of blessing.

Look with favour on the oblation of your Church,
in which we show forth
the paschal Sacrifice of Christ that has been handed on to us,
and grant that, by the power of the Spirit of your love,
we may be counted now and until the day of eternity
among the members of your Son,
in whose Body and Blood we have communion.

Bring your Church, O Lord,
to perfect faith and charity,
together with N. our Pope and N. our Bishop,*
with all Bishops, Priests and Deacons,
and the entire people you have made your own.

Open our eyes
to the needs of our brothers and sisters;
inspire in us words and actions
to comfort those who labour and are burdened.
Make us serve them truly,
after the example of Christ and at his command.
And may your Church stand as a living witness
to truth and freedom,
to peace and justice,
that all people may be raised up to a new hope.

Remember our brothers and sisters (N. and N.),
who have fallen asleep in the peace of your Christ,
and all the dead, whose faith you alone have known.
Admit them to rejoice in the light of your face,
and in the resurrection give them the fullness of life.

---

*Mention may be made here of the Coadjutor Bishop, or Auxiliary Bishops, as noted in the *General Instruction of the Roman Missal*, no. 149.

The Order of Mass

Grant also to us,
when our earthly pilgrimage is done,
that we may come to an eternal dwelling place
and live with you for ever;
there, in communion with the Blessed Virgin Mary, Mother of God,
with the Apostles and Martyrs,
(with Saint N.: the Saint of the day or Patron)
and with all the Saints,
we shall praise and exalt you

He joins his hands.

through Jesus Christ, your Son.

He takes the chalice and the paten with the host and, raising both, he says:

Through him, and with him, and in him,
O God, almighty Father,
in the unity of the Holy Spirit,
all glory and honour is yours,
for ever and ever.

The people acclaim:

Amen.

Then follows the Communion Rite, p.85.

LATIN TEXTS
for the People's parts of the Ordinary of the Mass

Introductory Rites
In nómine Patris, et Fílii, et Spíritus Sancti.
Amen.
or
Dóminus vobíscum
(or another greeting)
Et cum spíritu tuo.

Confiteor
**Confiteor Deo omnipoténti et vobis, fratres,
quia peccávi nimis
cogitatióne, verbo, ópere et omissióne:
mea culpa, mea culpa, mea máxima culpa.
Ideo precor beátam Maríam semper Vírginem,
omnes Angelos et Sanctos,
et vos, fratres, oráre pro me
ad Dóminum Deum nostrum.**

Kyrie
C Kyrie, eléison.
P **Kyrie, eléison.**
C Christe, eléison.
P **Christe, eléison.**
C Kyrie, eléison.
P **Kyrie, eléison.**

Gloria
**Gloria in excélsis Deo
et in terra pax homínibus bonæ voluntátis.**

**Laudámus te,
benedícimus te,
adorámus te,
glorificámus te,
grátias ágimus tibi propter magnam glóriam tuam,**

**Dómine Deus, Rex cæléstis,
Deus Pater omnípotens.
Dómine Fili unigenite, Iesu Christe,
Dómine Deus, Agnus Dei, Fílius Patris,
qui tollis peccáta mundi, miserére nobis;
qui tollis peccáta mundi,
súscipe deprecatiónem nostram.
Qui sedes ad déxteram Patris, miserére nobis.**

Quóniam tu solus Sanctus, tu solus Dóminus,
    tu solus Altíssimus,
Iesu Christe, cum Sancto Spíritu: in gloria Dei Patris.
Amen.

After the first and second readings
Deo grátias.

Before the Gospel
C Dóminus vobíscum.
P **Et cum spíritu tuo.**
C Léctio sancti Evangélii secundúm N.
P **Glória tibi, Dómine.**

At the end of the Gospel
C Verbum Dómini.
P **Laus tibi, Christe.**

Creed
**Credo in unum Deum,
Patrem omnipoténtem,
factórem cæli et terræ,
visibílium ómnium et invisibílium.**

**Et in unum Dóminum Iesum Christum,
Fílium Dei unigénitum,
et ex Patre natum ante ómnia sæcula.
Deum de Deo, lumen de lúmine,
    Deum verum de Deo vero,
génitum, non factum, consubstantiálem Patrí:
per quem ómnia facta sunt.
Qui propter nos hómines et propter nostram
salútem descéndit de cælis.
Et incarnátus est de Spíritu Sancto
ex María Vírgine, et homo factus est.
Crucifíxus étiam pro nobis sub Póntio Piláto;
    passus et sepúltus est,
et resurréxit tértia die, secúndum Scriptúras,
et ascéndit in cælum, sedet ad déxteram Patris.
Et íterum ventúrus est cum glória,
    iudicáre vivos et mórtuos,
cuius regni non erit finis.**

**Et in Spíritum Sanctum, Dóminum et vivificántem:
qui ex Patre Filióque procédit.
Qui cum Patre et Fílio simul adorátur**

et conglorificátur:
qui locútus est per prophétas.

Et unam, sanctam,
cathólicam et apostólicam Ecclésiam.
Confíteor unum baptísma in remissiónem peccatórum.
Et exspécto resurrectiónem mortuórum,
et vítam ventúri sǽculi. Amen.

Response to offertory prayers
Benedíctus Deus in sǽcula.

Response to the Orate Fratres
Suscípiat Dóminus sacrifícum de mánibus tuis
ad laudem et glóriam nóminis sui,
ad utilitátem quoque nostram
totiúsque Ecclésiæ suæ sanctæ.

Dialogue before the Preface
C Dóminus vobíscum.
P Et cum spíritu tuo.
C Sursum corda.
P Habémus ad Dóminum.
C Grátias agámus Dómino Deo nostro.
P Dignum et iustum est.

Holy, holy, holy . . .
Sanctus, Sanctus, Sanctus Dóminus Deus Sabaoth.
Pleni sunt cæli et terra glória tua.
Hosánna in excélsis.
Benedíctus qui venit in nómine Dómini.
Hosanna in excelsis.

Acclamation after the Consecration
<1 Mortem tuam annuntiámus, Dómine,
et tuam resurrectiónem confitémur, donec vénias.

<2 Quotiescúmque manducámus panem hunc
et cálicem bíbimus,
mortem tuam annuntiámus, Dómine, donec vénias.

<3 Salvátor mundi, salva nos,
qui per crucem et resurrectiónem tuam liberásti nos.

Our Father
C Præcéptis salutáribus móniti,
   et divína institutióne formáti,
   audémus dicere:

All **Pater noster, qui es in cælis:**
sanctificétur nomen tuum;
advéniat regnum tuum;
fiat volúntas tua, sicut in cælo, et in terra.
Panem nostrum cotidiánum da nobis hódie;
et dimítte nobis débita nostra,
sicut et nos dimíttimus debitóribus nostris;
et ne nos indúcas in tentatiónem;
sed líbera nos a malo.

Acclamation after the Our Father
Quia tuum est regnum,
et potéstas, et glória
in sǽcula.

At the Pax
C Pax Dómini sit semper vobíscum.
P **Et cum spíritu tuo.**

Lamb of God
Agnus Dei, qui tollis peccáta mundi:
  miserére nobis.
Agnus Dei, qui tollis peccáta mundi:
  miserére nobis.
Agnus Dei, qui tollis peccáta mundi:
  dona nobis pacem.

Lord, I am not worthy
Domine, non sum dignus ut intres sub tectum meum;
sed tantum dic verbo, et sanabitur anima mea.

At the Prayer after Communion
C Dóminus vobíscum.
P **Et cum spíritu tuo.**
Oremus.
At the conclusion of the Prayer:
P **Amen.**

At the Conclusion
C Dóminus vobíscum.
P **Et cum spíritu tuo.**
C Benedícat vos omnípotens Deus,
Pater, et Fílius, ✠ et Spíritus Sanctus.
P **Amen.**
C Ite, missa est.
P **Deo grátias.**

PRAYERS:
THANKSGIVING AFTER MASS

With gratitude in your hearts sing psalms and hymns and inspired songs to God. *Colossians 3:16*

Go on singing and chanting to the Lord in your hearts, so that always and everywhere you are giving thanks to God who is our Father in the name of our Lord Jesus Christ. *Ephesians 5:19–20*

Pray constantly, and for all things give thanks to God, because this is what God expects you to do in Christ Jesus.
1 Thessalonians 5:18

From the Didache
As regards the Eucharist, give thanks first, for the cup:
We thank you, Father,
for the holy vine of David, your servant,
which you have made known to us
through your servant, Jesus.
To you be glory for ever!

And for the broken bread:
We thank you, Father,
for the life and knowledge
which you have made known to us
through your servant, Jesus.
To you be glory for ever!

In the same way that this bread which is now broken
was scattered upon the mountains,
and was gathered up again, to become one,
so may your Church be gathered together
from the ends of the earth into your kingdom,
for yours is the glory and the power
through Jesus Christ for ever.

And, after you are filled, give thanks in this manner:
We thank you, Holy Father, for your holy name,
which you have made to dwell in our hearts,
and for the knowledge, faith and immortality
which you have made known to us
through your servant, Jesus.
To you be glory for ever! *1st or 2nd century*

Prayer of St Thomas Aquinas

I give you thanks,
Lord, holy Father, everlasting God.
In your great mercy,
you have fed me, a sinner and your unworthy servant,
with the precious Body and Blood of your Son,
our Lord Jesus Christ.
I pray that this holy communion
may not serve as my judgement and condemnation,
but as my forgiveness and salvation.
May it be my armour of faith
and shield of good purpose.
May it root out in me all vice and evil desires,
increase my love and patience,
humility and obedience,
and every virtue.
Make it a firm defence
against the wiles of all my enemies, seen and unseen,
while restraining all evil impulses of flesh and spirit.
May it help me to cleave to you, the one true God,
and bring me a blessed death when you call.
I beseech you to bring me, a sinner,
to that great feast where,
with your Son and the Holy Spirit,
you are the true light of your holy ones,
their flawless blessedness,
everlasting joy,
and perfect happiness.
Through Christ our Lord. Amen.

Anima Christi

Soul of Christ, sanctify me,
Body of Christ, save me,
Blood of Christ, inebriate me,
Water from the side of Christ, wash me,
Passion of Christ, strengthen me.
O good Jesus, hear me.
Within your wounds hide me.
Let me not be separated from you,
From the malicious enemy defend me,
In the hour of my death call me
And bid me come to you,

That with your saints I may praise you
For ever and ever. Amen.

O Sacrum Convivium
At this sacred banquet in which Christ is received,
the memory of his passion is renewed,
our lives are filled with grace
and a promise of future glory is given to us.

Adoro Te
Godhead here in hiding, whom I do adore
Masked by these bare shadows, shape and nothing more,
See, Lord, at thy service low lies here a heart
Lost, all lost in wonder at the God thou art.

Seeing, touching, tasting are in thee deceived;
How says trusty hearing? That shall be believed;
What God's Son has told me, take for truth I do;
Truth himself speaks truly or there's nothing true.

On the cross thy godhead made no sign to men;
Here thy very manhood steals from human ken:
Both are my confession, both are my belief,
And I pray the prayer of the dying thief.

O thou our reminder of Christ crucified,
Living Bread, the life of us for whom he died,
Lend this life to me then: feed and feast my mind,
There be thou the sweetness man was meant to find.

Jesus whom I look at shrouded here below,
I beseech thee send me what I thirst for so,
Some day to gaze on thee face to face in light
And be blest for ever with thy glory's sight.

Tr. Gerard Manley Hopkins

For prayers of preparation for Mass, turn to pp.xxiiff.
For other prayers, turn to pp.1157ff.

SUNDAY MASSES

Year A

SUNDAY MASSES

Year A

THE SEASON OF ADVENT

FIRST SUNDAY OF ADVENT   A

The Day of the Lord

Today we rejoice that the night of our long pilgrimage to God's eternal city, the new Jerusalem, will soon be over. The Lord's unending Day is dawning. Already, in the words of Isaiah, we see 'the mountain of the Temple of the Lord' etched against the eastern sky. Let us wake up and stand ready.

Entrance Antiphon   Cf. Ps 24:1-3
To you, I lift up my soul, O my God.
In you, I have trusted; let me not be put to shame.
Nor let my enemies exult over me;
and let none who hope in you be put to shame.

The Gloria in excelsis (Glory to God in the highest) is not said.

Collect
Grant your faithful, we pray, almighty God,
the resolve to run forth to meet your Christ
with righteous deeds at his coming,
so that, gathered at his right hand,
they may be worthy to possess the heavenly kingdom.
Through our Lord Jesus Christ, your Son,
who lives and reigns with you in the unity of the Holy Spirit,
one God, for ever and ever.
Amen.

First Sunday of Advent, Year A

FIRST READING

A reading from the prophet Isaiah 2:1-5

The vision of Isaiah son of Amoz, concerning Judah and Jerusalem.

In the days to come
the mountain of the Temple of the Lord
shall tower above the mountains
and be lifted higher than the hills.
All the nations will stream to it,
peoples without number will come to it; and they will say:

> 'Come, let us go up to the mountain of the Lord,
> to the Temple of the God of Jacob
> that he may teach us his ways
> so that we may walk in his paths;
> since the Law will go out from Zion,
> and the oracle of the Lord from Jerusalem.'

He will wield authority over the nations
and adjudicate between many peoples;
these will hammer their swords into ploughshares,
their spears into sickles.
Nation will not lift sword against nation,
there will be no more training for war.
O House of Jacob, come,
let us walk in the light of the Lord.

The word of the Lord.

Responsorial Psalm Ps 121:1-2.4-5. 6-9. ℟ cf. v.1

℟ **I rejoiced when I heard them say:**
'Let us go to God's house.'

1. I rejoiced when I heard them say:
   'Let us go to God's house.'
   And now our feet are standing
   within your gates, O Jerusalem. ℟

2. It is there that the tribes go up,
   the tribes of the Lord.
   For Israel's law it is,
   there to praise the Lord's name.
   There were set the thrones of judgement
   of the house of David. ℟

First Sunday of Advent, Year A

3   For the peace of Jerusalem pray:
    'Peace be to your homes!
    May peace reign in your walls,
    in your palaces, peace!'   ℟

4   For love of my brethren and friends
    I say: 'Peace upon you!'
    For love of the house of the Lord
    I will ask for your good.   ℟

SECOND READING
A reading from the letter of St Paul to the Romans   13:11-14

You know 'the time' has come: you must wake up now: our salvation is even nearer than it was when we were converted. The night is almost over, it will be daylight soon – let us give up all the things we prefer to do under cover of the dark; let us arm ourselves and appear in the light. Let us live decently as people do in the daytime: no drunken orgies, no promiscuity or licentiousness, and no wrangling or jealousy. Let your armour be the Lord Jesus Christ.

The word of the Lord.

Gospel Acclamation   Ps 84:8
Alleluia, alleluia!
Let us see, O Lord, your mercy
and give us your saving help.
Alleluia!

GOSPEL
A reading from the holy Gospel according to Matthew   24:37-44

Jesus said to his disciples: 'As it was in Noah's day, so will it be when the Son of Man comes. For in those days before the Flood people were eating, drinking, taking wives, taking husbands, right up to the day Noah went into the ark, and they suspected nothing till the Flood came and swept all away. It will be like this when the Son of Man comes. Then of two men in the fields one is taken, one left; of two women at the millstone grinding, one is taken, one left.

'So stay awake, because you do not know the day when your master is coming. You may be quite sure of this that if the householder had known at what time of the night the burglar would come, he would have stayed awake and would not have allowed anyone to break through the wall of his house. Therefore, you too must stand ready because the Son of Man is coming at an hour you do not expect.'

The Gospel of the Lord.

The Creed is said.

Prayer over the Offerings
Accept, we pray, O Lord, these offerings we make,
gathered from among your gifts to us,
and may what you grant us to celebrate devoutly here below
gain for us the prize of eternal redemption.
Through Christ our Lord.
Amen.

Preface I of Advent, p.19.

Communion Antiphon Ps 84:13
The Lord will bestow his bounty, and our earth shall yield its increase.

Prayer after Communion
May these mysteries, O Lord,
in which we have participated,
profit us, we pray,
for even now, as we walk amid passing things,
you teach us by them to love the things of heaven
and hold fast to what endures.
Through Christ our Lord.
Amen.

A formula of Solemn Blessing, pp.94-5, may be used.

SECOND SUNDAY OF ADVENT — A

Our Baptism with the Holy Spirit and Fire

May the Lord who gave us this baptism purify us in our celebration today; for though he does not judge by appearances or hearsay, he demands of us nothing less than integrity and truth. Then, through the Spirit of our baptism, united in heart and voice, we will be able to give glory to the God and Father of our Lord Jesus Christ.

Entrance Antiphon
Cf. Is 30:19. 30

O people of Sion, behold,
the Lord will come to save the nations,
and the Lord will make the glory of his voice heard
in the joy of your heart.

The Gloria in excelsis (Glory to God in the highest) is not said.

Collect

Almighty and merciful God,
may no earthly undertaking hinder those
who set out in haste to meet your Son,
but may our learning of heavenly wisdom
gain us admittance to his company.
Who lives and reigns with you in the unity of the Holy Spirit,
one God, for ever and ever.
Amen.

FIRST READING

A reading from the prophet Isaiah
11:1-10

A shoot springs from the stock of Jesse,
a scion thrusts from his roots:
on him the spirit of the Lord rests,
a spirit of wisdom and insight,
a spirit of counsel and power,
a spirit of knowledge and of the fear of the Lord.
(The fear of the Lord is his breath.)
He does not judge by appearances,
he gives no verdict on hearsay,
but judges the wretched with integrity,
and with equity gives a verdict for the poor of the land.
His word is a rod that strikes the ruthless;
his sentences bring death to the wicked.

Integrity is the loincloth round his waist,
faithfulness the belt about his hips.

The wolf lives with the lamb,
the panther lies down with the kid,
calf and lion cub feed together
with a little boy to lead them.
The cow and the bear make friends,
their young lie down together.
The lion eats straw like the ox.
The infant plays over the cobra's hole;
into the viper's lair
the young child puts his hand.
They do no hurt, no harm,
on all my holy mountain,
for the country is filled with the knowledge of the Lord
as the waters swell the sea.
That day, the root of Jesse
shall stand as a signal to the peoples.
It will be sought out by the nations
and its home will be glorious.

    The word of the Lord.

Responsorial Psalm
Ps 71:1-2. 7-8. 12-13. 17. ℟ cf. v.7

℟ **In his days justice shall flourish
and peace till the moon fails.**

1   O God, give your judgement to the king,
to a king's son your justice,
that he may judge your people in justice
and your poor in right judgement. ℟

2   In his days justice shall flourish
and peace till the moon fails.
He shall rule from sea to sea,
from the Great River to earth's bounds. ℟

3   For he shall save the poor when they cry
and the needy who are helpless.
He will have pity on the weak
and save the lives of the poor. ℟

4   May his name be blessed for ever
and endure like the sun.
Every tribe shall be blessed in him,
all nations bless his name. ℟

Second Sunday of Advent, Year A

SECOND READING
A reading from the letter of St Paul to the Romans 15:4-9

Everything that was written long ago in the scriptures was meant to teach us something about hope from the examples scripture gives of how people who did not give up were helped by God. And may he who helps us when we refuse to give up, help you all to be tolerant with each other, following the example of Christ Jesus, so that united in mind and voice you may give glory to the God and Father of our Lord Jesus Christ.

It can only be to God's glory, then, for you to treat each other in the same friendly way as Christ treated you. The reason Christ became the servant of circumcised Jews was not only so that God could faithfully carry out the promises made to the patriarchs, it was also to get the pagans to give glory to God for his mercy, as scripture says in one place: For this I shall praise you among the pagans and sing your name.

The word of the Lord.

Gospel Acclamation Lk 3:4. 6
Alleluia, alleluia!
Prepare a way for the Lord,
make his paths straight,
and all mankind shall see the salvation of God.
Alleluia!

GOSPEL
A reading from the holy Gospel according to Matthew 3:1-12

In due course John the Baptist appeared; he preached in the wilderness of Judaea and this was his message: 'Repent, for the kingdom of heaven is close at hand.' This was the man the prophet Isaiah spoke of when he said:

A voice cries in the wilderness:
Prepare a way for the Lord,
make his paths straight.

This man John wore a garment made of camel-hair with a leather belt round his waist, and his food was locusts and wild honey. Then Jerusalem and all Judaea and the whole Jordan district made their way to him, and as they were baptised by him in the river Jordan they confessed their sins. But when he saw a number of Pharisees and Sadducees coming for baptism he said to them, 'Brood of vipers, who warned you to fly from the retribution that is coming? But if you are repentant, produce the appropriate fruit, and do not presume to tell yourselves, "We have Abraham for our father," because, I tell you, God can raise children for Abraham from these stones. Even now the axe is laid to the roots of the trees, so that any tree which fails to produce good fruit will be cut down and thrown on the fire. I baptise you in water for repentance, but the one who follows me is more powerful than I am, and I am not fit to carry his sandals; he will baptise you with the Holy Spirit and fire. His winnowing-fan is in his hand; he will clear his threshing-floor and gather his wheat into the barn; but the chaff he will burn in a fire that will never go out.'

The Gospel of the Lord.

The Creed is said.

Prayer over the Offerings
Be pleased, O Lord, with our humble prayers and offerings,
and, since we have no merits to plead our cause,
come, we pray, to our rescue
with the protection of your mercy.
Through Christ our Lord.
Amen.

Preface I of Advent, p.19.

Communion Antiphon   Bar 5:5; 4:36
Jerusalem, arise and stand upon the heights,
and behold the joy which comes to you from God.

Prayer after Communion
Replenished by the food of spiritual nourishment,
we humbly beseech you, O Lord,
that, through our partaking in this mystery,
you may teach us to judge wisely the things of earth
and hold firm to the things of heaven.
Through Christ our Lord.
Amen.

A formula of Solemn Blessing, pp.94-5, may be used.

THIRD SUNDAY OF ADVENT   A

The Joy of Expectancy

At his coming Christ fulfilled the expectations of the prophets. He made the blind see again, the lame walk, and the lepers clean. We must not lose heart in face of all the evils of the world, for we too have a glorious expectation to see the glory and splendour of the Lord. Maranatha! Come, Lord Jesus, and save us.

In this Mass the colour violet or rose is used.

Entrance Antiphon   Phil 4:4-5
Rejoice in the Lord always; again I say, rejoice.
Indeed, the Lord is near.

The Gloria in excelsis (Glory to God in the highest) is not said.

Collect
O God, who see how your people
faithfully await the feast of the Lord's Nativity,
enable us, we pray,
to attain the joys of so great a salvation
and to celebrate them always
with solemn worship and glad rejoicing.
Through our Lord Jesus Christ, your Son,
who lives and reigns with you in the unity of the Holy Spirit,
one God, for ever and ever.
Amen.

FIRST READING
A reading from the prophet Isaiah   35:1-6. 10

Let the wilderness and the dry-lands exult,
let the wasteland rejoice and bloom,
let it bring forth flowers like the jonquil,
let it rejoice and sing for joy.

The glory of Lebanon is bestowed on it,
the splendour of Carmel and Sharon;
they shall see the glory of the Lord,
the splendour of our God.

Strengthen all weary hands,
steady all trembling knees
and say to all faint hearts,
'Courage! Do not be afraid.

'Look your God is coming,
vengeance is coming,
the retribution of God;
he is coming to save you.'

Then the eyes of the blind shall be opened,
the ears of the deaf unsealed,
then the lame shall leap like a deer
and the tongues of the dumb sing for joy,
for those the Lord has ransomed shall return.

They will come to Zion shouting for joy,
everlasting joy on their faces;
joy and gladness will go with them
and sorrow and lament be ended.

The word of the Lord.

Responsorial Psalm   Ps 145:6-10. ℟ cf. Is 35:4
   ℟   **Come, Lord, and save us.**

or

   ℟   **Alleluia!**

1   It is the Lord who keeps faith for ever,
    who is just to those who are oppressed.
    It is he who gives bread to the hungry,
    the Lord, who sets prisoners free.   ℟

2   It is the Lord who gives sight to the blind,
    who raises up those who are bowed down,
    the Lord, who protects the stranger
    and upholds the widow and orphan.   ℟

3   It is the Lord who loves the just
    but thwarts the path of the wicked.
    The Lord will reign for ever,
    Zion's God, from age to age.   ℟

SECOND READING

A reading from the letter of St James   5:7-10

Be patient, brothers, until the Lord's coming. Think of a farmer: how patiently he waits for the precious fruit of the ground until it has had the autumn rains and the spring rains! You too have to be patient; do not lose heart, because the Lord's coming will be soon. Do not make complaints against one another, brothers, so as not to be brought to judgement yourselves; the Judge is already to be seen waiting at the gates. For your example, brothers, in submitting with patience, take the prophets who spoke in the name of the Lord.

The word of the Lord.

Gospel Acclamation   Is 61:1 (Lk 4:18)
Alleluia, alleluia!
The spirit of the Lord has been given to me.
He has sent me to bring good news to the poor.
Alleluia!

GOSPEL

A reading from the holy Gospel according to Matthew   11:2-11

John in his prison had heard what Christ was doing and he sent his disciples to ask him, 'Are you the one who is to come, or have we got to wait for someone else?' Jesus answered, 'Go back and tell John what you hear and see; the blind see again, and the lame walk, lepers are cleansed, and the deaf hear, and the dead are raised to life and the Good News is proclaimed to the poor; and happy is the man who does not lose faith in me.'

As the messengers were leaving, Jesus began to talk to the people about John: 'What did you go out into the wilderness to see? A reed swaying in the breeze? No? Then what did you go out to see? A man wearing fine clothes? Oh no, those who wear fine clothes are to be found in palaces. Then what did you go out for? To see a prophet? Yes, I tell you, and much more than a prophet: he is the one of whom scripture says: Look, I am going to send my messenger before you; he will prepare your way before you. I tell you solemnly, of all the children born of women, a greater than John the Baptist has never been seen; yet the least in the kingdom of heaven is greater than he is.'

The Gospel of the Lord.

The Creed is said.

Prayer over the Offerings
May the sacrifice of our worship, Lord, we pray,
be offered to you unceasingly,
to complete what was begun in sacred mystery
and powerfully accomplish for us your saving work.
Through Christ our Lord.
Amen.

Preface I or II of Advent, pp.19-20.

Communion Antiphon
Cf. Is 35:4
Say to the faint of heart: Be strong and do not fear.
Behold, our God will come, and he will save us.

Prayer after Communion
We implore your mercy, Lord,
that this divine sustenance may cleanse us of our faults
and prepare us for the coming feasts.
Through Christ our Lord.
Amen.

A formula of Solemn Blessing, pp.94-5, may be used.

FOURTH SUNDAY OF ADVENT — A

Mary's Child: The Emmanuel

God's choice rested on the House of David which was to bring forth the Emmanuel, the God-with-us. But Mary's Child was to belong to all the nations. We are one of those nations who, by God's call, belong to Jesus Christ, God's beloved ones, called to be saints!

Entrance Antiphon
Cf. Is 45:8
Drop down dew from above, you heavens,
and let the clouds rain down the Just One;
let the earth be opened and bring forth a Saviour.

The Gloria in excelsis (Glory to God in the highest) is not said.

Collect
Pour forth, we beseech you, O Lord,
your grace into our hearts,
that we, to whom the Incarnation of Christ your Son
was made known by the message of an Angel,
may by his Passion and Cross
be brought to the glory of his Resurrection.
Who lives and reigns with you in the unity of the Holy Spirit,
one God, for ever and ever.
Amen.

FIRST READING
A reading from the prophet Isaiah
7:10-14

The Lord spoke to Ahaz and said, 'Ask the Lord your God for a sign for yourself coming either from the depths of Sheol or from

the heights above.' 'No,' Ahaz answered 'I will not put the Lord to the test.'
Then Isaiah said:

'Listen now, House of David:
are you not satisfied with trying the patience of men
without trying the patience of my God, too?
The Lord himself, therefore,
will give you a sign.
It is this: the maiden is with child
and will soon give birth to a son
whom she will call Emmanuel,
a name which means "God-is-with-us".'

The word of the Lord.

Responsional Psalm   Ps 23:1-6. ℟ cf. vv.7. 10

℟ **Let the Lord enter!**
He is the king of glory.

1 The Lord's is the earth and its fullness,
   the world and all its peoples.
   It is he who set it on the seas;
   on the waters he made it firm.   ℟

2 Who shall climb the mountain of the Lord?
   Who shall stand in his holy place?
   The man with clean hands and pure heart,
   who desires not worthless things.   ℟

3 He shall receive blessings from the Lord
   and reward from the God who saves him.
   Such are the men who seek him,
   seek the face of the God of Jacob.   ℟

SECOND READING
A reading from the letter of St Paul to the Romans   1:1-7

From Paul, a servant of Christ Jesus who has been called to be an apostle, and specially chosen to preach the Good News that God promised long ago through his prophets in the scriptures.
This news is about the Son of God, who, according to the human nature he took, was a descendant of David: it is about Jesus Christ our Lord who, in the order of the spirit, the spirit of holiness that was in him, was proclaimed Son of God in all his power through his resurrrection from the dead. Through him we received grace

and our apostolic mission to preach the obedience of faith to all pagan nations in honour of his name. You are one of these nations, and by his call belong to Jesus Christ. To you all, then, who are God's beloved in Rome, called to be saints, may God our Father and the Lord Jesus Christ send grace and peace.

The word of the Lord.

Gospel Acclamation Mt 1:23
Alleluia, alleluia!
The virgin will conceive and give birth to a son
and they will call him Emmanuel,
a name which means 'God-is-with-us'.
Alleluia!

GOSPEL
A reading from the holy Gospel according to Matthew 1:18-24

This is how Jesus Christ came to be born. His mother Mary was betrothed to Joseph; but before they came to live together she was found to be with child through the Holy Spirit. Her husband Joseph, being a man of honour and wanting to spare her publicity, decided to divorce her informally. He had made up his mind to do this when the angel of the Lord appeared to him in a dream, and said 'Joseph son of David, do not be afraid to take Mary home as your wife, because she has conceived what is in her by the Holy Spirit. She will give birth to a son and you must name him Jesus, because he is the one who is to save his people from their sins.' Now all this took place to fulfil the words spoken by the Lord through the prophet:

The virgin will conceive and give birth to a son
and they will call him Emmanuel,

a name which means 'God-is-with-us'. When Joseph woke up he did what the angel of the Lord had told him to do: he took his wife to his home.

The Gospel of the Lord.

The Creed is said.

Prayer over the Offerings
May the Holy Spirit, O Lord,
sanctify these gifts laid upon your altar,

just as he filled with his power the womb of the Blessed Virgin Mary.
Through Christ our Lord.
Amen.

Preface II of Advent, pp.19-20.

Communion Antiphon Is 7:14
Behold, a Virgin shall conceive and bear a son;
and his name will be called Emmanuel.

Prayer after Communion
Having received this pledge of eternal redemption,
we pray, almighty God,
that, as the feast day of our salvation draws ever nearer,
so we may press forward all the more eagerly
to the worthy celebration of the mystery of your Son's Nativity.
Who lives and reigns for ever and ever.
Amen.

A formula of Solemn Blessing, pp.94-5, may be used.

CHRISTMAS TIME

25 December

THE NATIVITY OF THE LORD   A, B, C
Solemnity
At the Vigil Mass

This Mass is used on the evening of 24 December, either before or after First Vespers (Evening Prayer I) of the Nativity.

Jesus, Son of David

God prepared the people of Israel to receive his Son. May we too be ready to welcome him.

Entrance Antiphon   Cf. Ex 16:6-7

Today you will know that the Lord will come, and he will save us, and in the morning you will see his glory.

The Gloria in excelsis (Glory to God in the highest) is said.

Collect
O God, who gladden us year by year
as we wait in hope for our redemption,
grant that, just as we joyfully welcome
your Only Begotten Son as our Redeemer,
we may also merit to face him confidently
when he comes again as our Judge.
Who lives and reigns with you in the unity of the Holy Spirit,
one God, for ever and ever.
Amen.

The Nativity of the Lord, At the Vigil Mass

FIRST READING
A reading from the prophet Isaiah 62:1-5

About Zion I will not be silent,
about Jerusalem I will not grow weary,
until her integrity shines out like the dawn
and her salvation flames like a torch.
The nations then will see your integrity,
all the kings your glory,
and you will be called by a new name,
one which the mouth of the Lord will confer.
You are to be a crown of splendour in the hand of the Lord,
a princely diadem in the hand of your God;
no longer are you to be named 'Forsaken',
nor your land 'Abandoned',
but you shall be called 'My Delight'
and your land 'The Wedded';
for the Lord takes delight in you
and your land will have its wedding.
Like a young man marrying a virgin,
so will the one who built you wed you,
and as the bridegroom rejoices in his bride,
so will your God rejoice in you.

The word of the Lord.

Responsional Psalm Ps 88:4-5. 16-17. 27. 29. ℟ cf. v.2
℟ **I will sing for ever of your love, O Lord.**

1 'I have made a covenant with my chosen one;
 I have sworn to David my servant:
 I will establish your dynasty for ever
 and set up your throne through all ages.' ℟

2 Happy the people who acclaim such a king,
 who walk, O Lord, in the light of your face,
 who find their joy every day in your name,
 who make your justice the source of their bliss. ℟

3 'He will say to me: "You are my father,
 my God, the rock who saves me."
 I will keep my love for him always;
 for him my covenant shall endure.' ℟

SECOND READING

A reading from the Acts of the Apostles　　　　　13:16-17. 22-25

When Paul reached Antioch in Pisidia, he stood up in the synagogue, held up a hand for silence and began to speak:

'Men of Israel, and fearers of God, listen! The God of our nation Israel chose our ancestors, and made our people great when they were living as foreigners in Egypt; then by divine power he led them out.

'Then he made David their king, of whom he approved in these words, "I have selected David son of Jesse, a man after my own heart, who will carry out my whole purpose". To keep his promise, God has raised up for Israel one of David's descendants, Jesus, as Saviour, whose coming was heralded by John when he proclaimed a baptism of repentance for the whole people of Israel. Before John ended his career he said, "I am not the one you imagine me to be; that one is coming after me and I am not fit to undo his sandal".'

The word of the Lord.

Gospel Acclamation

Alleluia, alleluia!
Tomorrow there will be an end to the sin of the world
and the saviour of the world will be our king.
Alleluia!

GOSPEL

A reading from the holy Gospel according to Matthew　　　1:1-25

A genealogy of Jesus Christ, son of David, son of Abraham:
Abraham was the father of Isaac,
Isaac the father of Jacob,
Jacob was the father of Judah and his brothers,
Judah was the father of Perez and Zerah, Tamar being their
　　mother,
Perez was the father of Hezron,
Hezron the father of Ram,
Ram was the father of Amminadab,
Amminadab the father of Nahshon,
Nahshon the father of Salmon,
Salmon was the father of Boaz, Rahab being his mother,
Boaz was the father of Obed, Ruth being his mother,
Obed was the father of Jesse;
and Jesse was the father of King David.

The Nativity of the Lord, At the Vigil Mass

David was the father of Solomon, whose mother had been Uriah's wife,
Solomon was the father of Rehoboam,
Rehoboam the father of Abijah,
Abijah the father of Asa,
Asa was the father of Jehoshaphat,
Jehoshaphat the father of Joram,
Joram the father of Azariah,
Azariah was the father of Jotham,
Jotham the father of Ahaz,
Ahaz the father of Hezekiah,
Hezekiah was the father of Manasseh,
Manasseh the father of Amon,
Amon the father of Josiah;
and Josiah was the father of Jechoniah and his brothers.
Then the deportation to Babylon took place.

After the deportation to Babylon:
Jechoniah was the father to Shealtiel,
Shealtiel the father of Zerubbabel,
Zerubbabel was the father of Abiud,
Abiud the father of Eliakim,
Eliakim the father of Azor,
Azor was the father of Zadok,
Zadok the father of Achim,
Achim the father of Eliud,
Eliud was the father of Eleazar,
Eleazar the father of Matthan,
Matthan the father of Jacob;
and Jacob was the father of Joseph the husband of Mary; of her was born Jesus who is called Christ.

The sum of generations is therefore: fourteen from Abraham to David; fourteen from David to the Babylonian deportation; and fourteen from the Babylonian deportation to Christ.

*This is how Jesus Christ came to be born. His mother Mary was betrothed to Joseph; but before they came to live together she was found to be with child through the Holy Spirit. Her husband Joseph, being a man of honour and wanting to spare her publicity, decided to divorce her informally. He had made up his mind to do this when the angel of the Lord appeared to him in a dream and said, 'Joseph son of David, do not be afraid to take Mary home as your wife, because she has conceived what is in her by the Holy Spirit. She will give birth to a son and you must name him Jesus, because he is the one who is to save his people from their sins.' Now all this took place to fulfil the words spoken by the Lord through the prophet:

> The Virgin will conceive and give birth to a son
> and they will call him Emmanuel,

a name which means 'God-is-with-us'. When Joseph woke up he did what the angel of the Lord had told him to do: he took his wife to his home and, though he had not had intercourse with her, she gave birth to a son; and he named him Jesus.

The Gospel of the Lord.*

Shorter form, verses 18-25. Read between

The Creed is said. At the words and by the Holy Spirit was incarnate of the Virgin Mary and became man all kneel.

Prayer over the Offerings
As we look forward, O Lord,
to the coming festivities,
may we serve you all the more eagerly
for knowing that in them
you make manifest the beginnings of our redemption.
Through Christ our Lord.
Amen.

Preface I, II or III of the Nativity of the Lord, pp.20-21.

When the Roman Canon is used, the proper form of the Communicantes (In communion with those) is said.

Communion Antiphon
Cf. Is 40:5
The glory of the Lord will be revealed,
and all flesh will see the salvation of our God.

Prayer after Communion
Grant, O Lord, we pray,
that we may draw new vigour
from celebrating the Nativity of your Only Begotten Son,
by whose heavenly mystery we receive both food and drink.
Who lives and reigns for ever and ever.
Amen.

A formula of Solemn Blessing, p.95, may be used.

At the Mass during the Night

A Saviour Is Born for Us

Tonight we celebrate the birth of a Child who was to bring the joy of God's saving love to the whole world. And we make our own the jubilant cry of the angels: 'Glory to God in the highest heaven and peace to all who enjoy God's favour.'

On the Nativity of the Lord all Priests may celebrate or concelebrate three Masses, provided the Masses are celebrated at their proper times.

Entrance Antiphon   Ps 2:7
The Lord said to me: You are my Son.
It is I who have begotten you this day.

or

Let us all rejoice in the Lord, for our Saviour has been born in the world.
Today true peace has come down to us from heaven.

The Gloria in excelsis (Glory to God in the highest) is said.

Collect
O God, who have made this most sacred night
radiant with the splendour of the true light,
grant, we pray, that we, who have known the mysteries of his light on earth,
may also delight in his gladness in heaven.
Who lives and reigns with you in the unity of the Holy Spirit,
one God, for ever and ever.
Amen.

FIRST READING
A reading from the prophet Isaiah   9:1-7

The people that walked in darkness
have seen a great light;
on those who live in a land of deep shadow
a light has shone.
You have made their gladness greater,
you have made their joy increase;
they rejoice in your presence
as men rejoice at harvest time,
as men are happy when they are dividing the spoils.
For the yoke that was weighing on him,

the bar across his shoulders,
the rod of his oppressor,
these you break as on the day of Midian.
For all the footgear of battle,
every cloak rolled in blood,
is burnt
and consumed by fire.
For there is a child born for us,
a son given to us
and dominion is laid on his shoulders;
and this is the name they give him:
Wonder-Counsellor, Mighty-God,
Eternal-Father, Prince-of-Peace.
Wide is his dominion
in a peace that has no end,
for the throne of David
and for his royal power,
which he establishes and makes secure
in justice and integrity.
From this time onwards and for ever,
the jealous love of the Lord of hosts will do this.

The word of the Lord.

Responsorial Psalm   Ps 95:1-3. 11-13. ℟ Lk 2:11

℟ **Today a saviour has been born to us;
he is Christ the Lord.**

1. O sing a new song to the Lord,
   sing to the Lord all the earth.
   O sing to the Lord, bless his name.   ℟

2. Proclaim his help day by day,
   tell among the nations his glory
   and his wonders among all the peoples.   ℟

3. Let the heavens rejoice and earth be glad,
   let the sea and all within it thunder praise,
   let the land and all it bears rejoice,
   all the trees of the wood shout for joy
   at the presence of the Lord for he comes,
   he comes to rule the earth.   ℟

4. With justice he will rule the world,
   he will judge the peoples with his truth.   ℟

The Nativity of the Lord, At the Mass during the Night

SECOND READING
A reading from the letter of St Paul to Titus   2:11-14

God's grace has been revealed, and it has made salvation possible for the whole human race and taught us that what we have to do is to give up everything that does not lead to God, and all our worldly ambitions; we must be self-restrained and live good and religious lives here in this present world, while we are waiting in hope for the blessing which will come with the Appearing of the glory of our great God and saviour Christ Jesus. He sacrificed himself for us in order to set us free from all wickedness and to purify a people so that it could be his very own and would have no ambition except to do good.

The word of the Lord.

Gospel Acclamation   Lk 2:10-11
Alleluia, alleluia!
I bring you news of great joy:
today a saviour has been born to us, Christ the Lord.
Alleluia!

GOSPEL
A reading from the holy Gospel according to Luke   2:1-14

Caesar Augustus issued a decree for a census of the whole world to be taken. This census – the first – took place while Quirinius was governor of Syria, and everyone went to his own town to be registered. So Joseph set out from the town of Nazareth in Galilee and travelled up to Judaea, to the town of David called Bethlehem, since he was of David's House and line, in order to be registered together with Mary, his betrothed, who was with child. While they were there the time came for her to have her child, and she gave birth to a son, her first-born. She wrapped him in swaddling clothes, and laid him in a manger because there was no room for them at the inn. In the countryside close by there were shepherds who lived in the fields and took it in turns to watch their flocks during the night. The angel of the Lord appeared to them and the glory of the Lord shone round them. They were terrified, but the angel said, 'Do not be afraid. Listen, I bring you news of great joy, a joy to be shared by the whole people. Today in the town of David a saviour has been born to you; he is Christ the Lord. And here is a sign for you: you will find a baby wrapped in swaddling clothes and lying in a manger.' And suddenly with the angel there was a great throng of the heavenly host, praising God and singing:

'Glory to God in the highest heaven,
and peace to men who enjoy his favour'.

The Gospel of the Lord.

The Creed is said. At the words and by the Holy Spirit was incarnate of the Virgin Mary and became man all kneel.

Prayer over the Offerings
May the oblation of this day's feast
be pleasing to you, O Lord, we pray,
that through this most holy exchange
we may be found in the likeness of Christ,
in whom our nature is united to you.
Who lives and reigns for ever and ever.
Amen.

Preface I, II or III of the Nativity of the Lord, pp.20-21.

When the Roman Canon is used, the proper form of the Communicantes (In communion with those) is said.

Communion Antiphon Jn 1:14
The Word became flesh, and we have seen his glory.

Prayer after Communion
Grant us, we pray, O Lord our God,
that we, who are gladdened by participation
in the feast of our Redeemer's Nativity,
may through an honourable way of life become worthy of union
 with him.
Who lives and reigns for ever and ever.
Amen.

A formula of Solemn Blessing, p.95, may be used.

At the Mass at Dawn

The First Dawn of a New Age

Radiant with the dawning light, we celebrate the marvellous events of the first morning of a new world, when the kindness and love of God our Saviour made us his holy people, the Lord's Redeemed, his 'sought-after', and his 'city-not-forsaken'.

Entrance Antiphon Cf. Is 9:1, 5; Lk 1:33
Today a light will shine upon us, for the Lord is born for us;
and he will be called Wondrous God,

The Nativity of the Lord, At the Mass at Dawn 217

Prince of peace, Father of future ages:
and his reign will be without end.

The Gloria in excelsis (Glory to God in the highest) is said.

Collect
Grant, we pray, almighty God,
that, as we are bathed in the new radiance of your incarnate Word,
the light of faith, which illumines our minds,
may also shine through in our deeds.
Through our Lord Jesus Christ, your Son,
who lives and reigns with you in the unity of the Holy Spirit,
one God, for ever and ever.
Amen.

FIRST READING
A reading from the prophet Isaiah   62:11-12

This the Lord proclaims
to the ends of the earth:

> Say to the daughter of Zion, 'Look,
> your saviour comes,
> the prize of his victory with him,
> his trophies before him'.
> They shall be called 'The Holy People',
> 'The Lord's Redeemed'.
> And you shall be called 'The-sought-after',
> 'City-not-forsaken'.

The word of the Lord.

Responsorial Psalm   Ps 96:1. 6. 11-12
℟ **This day new light will shine upon the earth:
the Lord is born for us.**

1   The Lord is king, let earth rejoice,
    the many coastlands be glad.
    The skies proclaim his justice;
    all peoples see his glory. ℟

2   Light shines forth for the just
    and joy for the upright of heart.
    Rejoice, you just, in the Lord;
    give glory to his holy name. ℟

SECOND READING

A reading from the letter of St Paul to Titus   3:4-7

When the kindness and love of God our saviour for mankind were revealed, it was not because he was concerned with any righteous actions we might have done ourselves; it was for no reason except his own compassion that he saved us, by means of the cleansing water of rebirth and by renewing us with the Holy Spirit which he has so generously poured over us through Jesus Christ our saviour. He did this so that we should be justified by his grace, to become heirs looking forward to inheriting eternal life.

> The word of the Lord.

Gospel Acclamation   Lk 2:14
> Alleluia, alleluia!
> Glory to God in the highest heaven,
> and peace to men who enjoy his favour.
> Alleluia!

GOSPEL

A reading from the holy Gospel according to Luke   2:15-20

Now when the angels had gone from them into heaven, the shepherds said to one another, 'Let us go to Bethlehem and see this thing that has happened which the Lord has made known to us.' So they hurried away and found Mary and Joseph, and the baby lying in the manger. When they saw the child they repeated what they had been told about him, and everyone who heard it was astonished at what the shepherds had to say. As for Mary, she treasured all these things and pondered them in her heart. And the shepherds went back glorifying and praising God for all they had heard and seen; it was exactly as they had been told.

> The Gospel of the Lord.

The Creed is said. At the words and by the Holy Spirit was incarnate of the Virgin Mary and became man all kneel.

Prayer over the Offerings
May our offerings be worthy, we pray, O Lord,
of the mysteries of the Nativity this day,
that, just as Christ was born a man and also shone forth as God,
so these earthly gifts may confer on us what is divine.
Through Christ our Lord.
Amen.

Preface I, II or III of the Nativity of the Lord, pp.20-21.

When the Roman Canon is used, the proper form of the Communicantes (In communion with those) is said.

Communion Antiphon Cf. Zec 9:9
Rejoice, O Daughter Sion; lift up praise, Daughter Jerusalem:
Behold, your King will come, the Holy One and Saviour of the world.

Prayer after Communion
Grant us, Lord, as we honour with joyful devotion
the Nativity of your Son,
that we may come to know with fullness of faith
the hidden depths of this mystery
and to love them ever more and more.
Through Christ our Lord.
Amen.

A formula of Solemn Blessing, p.95, may be used.

At the Mass during the Day

The Word Made Flesh

For us the Word of God is no longer the message spoken by prophets, but the messenger of God in person, the eternal Word begotten of the Father before time began, who brings the good news of salvation.

Entrance Antiphon Cf. Is 9:5
A child is born for us, and a son is given to us;
his sceptre of power rests upon his shoulder,
and his name will be called Messenger of great counsel.

The Gloria in excelsis (Glory to God in the highest) is said.

Collect
O God, who wonderfully created the dignity of human nature
and still more wonderfully restored it,
grant, we pray,
that we may share in the divinity of Christ,
who humbled himself to share in our humanity.
Who lives and reigns with you in the unity of the Holy Spirit,
one God, for ever and ever.
Amen.

The Nativity of the Lord, At the Mass during the Day

FIRST READING
A reading from the prophet Isaiah 52:7-10

How beautiful on the mountains,
are the feet of one who brings good news,
who heralds peace, brings happiness,
proclaims salvation,
and tells Zion,
'Your God is king!'
Listen! Your watchmen raise their voices,
they shout for joy together,
for they see the Lord face to face,
as he returns to Zion.
Break into shouts of joy together,
you ruins of Jerusalem;
for the Lord is consoling his people,
redeeming Jerusalem.
The Lord bares his holy arm
in the sight of all the nations,
and all the ends of the earth shall see
the salvation of our God.

The word of the Lord.

Responsorial Psalm   Ps 97:1-6. ℟ v.3

℟ **All the ends of the earth have seen
the salvation of our God.**

1 Sing a new song to the Lord
   for he has worked wonders.
   His right hand and his holy arm
   have brought salvation. ℟

2 The Lord has made known his salvation;
   has shown his justice to the nations.
   He has remembered his truth and love
   for the house of Israel. ℟

3 All the ends of the earth have seen
   the salvation of our God.
   Shout to the Lord all the earth,
   ring out your joy. ℟

4 Sing psalms to the Lord with the harp,
   with the sound of music.

With trumpets and the sound of the horn
acclaim the King, the Lord. ℟

SECOND READING

A reading from the letter to the Hebrews 1:1-6

At various times in the past and in various different ways, God spoke to our ancestors through the prophets; but in our own time, the last days, he has spoken to us through his Son, the Son that he has appointed to inherit everything and through whom he made everything there is. He is the radiant light of God's glory and the perfect copy of his nature, sustaining the universe by his powerful command; and now that he has destroyed the defilement of sin, he has gone to take his place in heaven at the right hand of divine Majesty. So he is now as far above the angels as the title which he has inherited is higher than their own name.

God has never said to any angel: You are my Son, today I have become your father, or: I will be a father to him and he a son to me. Again, when he brings the First-born into the world, he says: Let all the angels of God worship him.

The word of the Lord.

Gospel Acclamation
Alleluia, alleluia!
A hallowed day has dawned upon us.
Come, you nations, worship the Lord,
for today a great light has shone down upon the earth.
Alleluia!

GOSPEL

A reading from the holy Gospel according to John 1:1-18

*In the beginning was the Word:
the Word was with God
and the Word was God.
He was with God in the beginning.
Through him all things came to be,
not one thing had its being but through him.
All that came to be had life in him
and that life was the light of men,
a light that shines in the dark,
a light that darkness could not overpower.*

The Nativity of the Lord, At the Mass during the Day

A man came, sent by God.
His name was John.
He came as a witness,
as a witness to speak for the light,
so that everyone might believe through him.
He was not the light,
only a witness to speak for the light.

*The Word was the true light
that enlightens all men;
and he was coming into the world.
He was in the world
that had its being through him,
and the world did not know him.
He came to his own domain
and his own people did not accept him.
But to all who did accept him
he gave power to become children of God,
to all who believe in the name of him
who was born not out of human stock
or urge of the flesh
or will of man
but of God himself.
The Word was made flesh,
he lived among us,
and we saw his glory,
the glory that is his as the only Son of the Father,
full of grace and truth.*

John appears as his witness. He proclaims:
'This is the one of whom I said:
He who comes after me
ranks before me
because he existed before me.'

Indeed, from his fullness we have, all of us, received—
yes, grace in return for grace,
since, though the Law was given through Moses,
grace and truth have come through Jesus Christ.
No one has ever seen God;

The Nativity of the Lord, At the Mass during the Day

it is the only Son, who is nearest to the Father's heart,
who has made him known.

The Gospel of the Lord.

Shorter Form, verses 1-5. 9-14. Read between

The Creed is said. At the words and by the Holy Spirit was incarnate of the Virgin Mary and became man all kneel.

Prayer over the Offerings
Make acceptable, O Lord, our oblation on this solemn day,
when you manifested the reconciliation
that makes us wholly pleasing in your sight
and inaugurated for us the fullness of divine worship.
Through Christ our Lord.
Amen.

Preface I, II or III of the Nativity of the Lord, pp.20-21.

When the Roman Canon is used, the proper form of the Communicantes (In communion with those) is said.

Communion Antiphon   Cf. Ps 97:3
All the ends of the earth have seen the salvation of our God.

Prayer after Communion
Grant, O merciful God,
that, just as the Saviour of the world, born this day,
is the author of divine generation for us,
so he may be the giver even of immortality.
Who lives and reigns for ever and ever.
Amen.

A formula of Solemn Blessing, p.95, may be used.

The Holy Family of Jesus, Mary and Joseph, Year A

The Sunday within the Octave of the Nativity of the Lord

THE HOLY FAMILY OF JESUS, MARY AND JOSEPH — A

Feast

Where there is no Sunday occurring between 25 December and 1 January, this feast is celebrated on 30 December, with one reading only before the Gospel.

The Holy Family

We celebrate that Holy Family of Nazareth, which is the model for all who fear the Lord and walk in his way, so that the message of Christ may find its home in us.

Entrance Antiphon Lk 2:16
The shepherds went in haste,
and found Mary and Joseph and the Infant lying in a manger.

The Gloria in excelsis (Glory to God in the highest) is said.

Collect
O God, who were pleased to give us
the shining example of the Holy Family,
graciously grant that we may imitate them
in practising the virtues of family life and in the bonds of charity,
and so, in the joy of your house,
delight one day in eternal rewards.
Through our Lord Jesus Christ, your Son,
who lives and reigns with you in the unity of the Holy Spirit,
one God, for ever and ever.
Amen.

FIRST READING
A reading from the Book of Ecclesiasticus 3:2-6. 12-14

The Lord honours the father in his children,
and upholds the rights of a mother over her sons.
Whoever respects his father is atoning for his sins,
he who honours his mother is like someone amassing a fortune.
Whoever respects his father will be happy with children of his own,
he shall be heard on the day when he prays.
Long life comes to him who honours his father,

The Holy Family of Jesus, Mary and Joseph, Year A

he who sets his mother at ease is showing obedience to the Lord.
My son, support your father in his old age,
do not grieve him during his life.
Even if his mind should fail, show him sympathy,
do not despise him in your health and strength;
for kindness to a father shall not be forgotten
but will serve as reparation for your sins.

The word of the Lord.

Responsorial Psalm   Ps 127:1-5. R/ cf. v.1

R/ **O blessed are those who fear the Lord
and walk in his ways!**

1   O blessed are those who fear the Lord
    and walk in his ways!
    By the labour of your hands you shall eat.
    You will be happy and prosper. R/

2   Your wife like a fruitful vine
    in the heart of your house;
    your children like shoots of the olive,
    around your table. R/

3   Indeed thus shall be blessed
    the man who fears the Lord.
    May the Lord bless you from Zion
    all the days of your life! R/

SECOND READING
A reading from the letter of St Paul to the Colossians   3:12-21

You are God's chosen race, his saints; he loves you and you should be clothed in sincere compassion, in kindness and humility, gentleness and patience. Bear with one another; forgive each other as soon as a quarrel begins. The Lord has forgiven you; now you must do the same. Over all these clothes, to keep them together and complete them, put on love. And may the peace of Christ reign in your hearts, because it is for this that you were called together as parts of one body. Always be thankful.

Let the message of Christ, in all its richness, find a home with you. Teach each other, and advise each other, in all wisdom. With gratitude in your hearts sing psalms and hymns and inspired songs to God; and never say or do anything except in the name of the Lord Jesus, giving thanks to God the Father through him.

Wives, give way to your husbands, as you should in the Lord. Husbands, love your wives and treat them with gentleness. Children, be obedient to your parents always, because that is what will please the Lord. Parents, never drive your children to resentment or you will make them feel frustrated.

The word of the Lord.

Gospel Acclamation Col. 3:15. 16
Alleluia, alleluia!
May the peace of Christ reign in your hearts;
let the message of Christ find a home with you.
Alleluia!

GOSPEL
A reading from the holy Gospel according to Matthew

2:13-15. 19-23

After the wise men had left, the angel of the Lord appeared to Joseph in a dream and said, 'Get up, take the child and his mother with you, and escape into Egypt, and stay there until I tell you, because Herod intends to search for the child and do away with him.' So Joseph got up and, taking the child and his mother with him, left that night for Egypt, where he stayed until Herod was dead. This was to fulfil what the Lord had spoken through the prophet:

I called my son out of Egypt.

After Herod's death, the angel of the Lord appeared in a dream to Joseph in Egypt and said, 'Get up, take the child and his mother with you and go back to the land of Israel, for those who wanted to kill the child are dead'. So Joseph got up and, taking the child and his mother with him, went back to the land of Israel. But when he learnt that Archelaus had succeeded his father Herod as ruler of Judaea he was afraid to go there, and being warned in a dream he left for the region of Galilee. There he settled in a town called Nazareth. In this way the words spoken through the prophets were to be fulfilled:

He will be called a Nazarene.

The Gospel of the Lord.

When this Feast is celebrated on Sunday, the Creed is said.

Solemnity of Mary, the Holy Mother of God

Prayer over the Offerings
We offer you, Lord, the sacrifice of conciliation,
humbly asking that,
through the intercession of the Virgin Mother of God and Saint Joseph,
you may establish our families firmly in your grace and your peace.
Through Christ our Lord.
Amen.

Preface I, II or III of the Nativity of the Lord, pp.20-21.

When the Roman Canon is used, the proper form of the Communicantes (In communion with those) is said.

Communion Antiphon   Bar 3:38
Our God has appeared on the earth, and lived among us.

Prayer after Communion
Bring those you refresh with this heavenly Sacrament,
most merciful Father,
to imitate constantly the example of the Holy Family,
so that, after the trials of this world,
we may share their company for ever.
Through Christ our Lord.
Amen.

1 January
The Octave Day of the Nativity of the Lord

SOLEMNITY OF MARY, THE HOLY MOTHER OF GOD   A, B, C

Mary, Through Whom the World Would Be Blessed

We too bless God for Mary, who bore for us the Child she named Jesus, the Saviour.

Entrance Antiphon
Hail, Holy Mother, who gave birth to the King,
who rules heaven and earth for ever.

or   Cf. Is 9:1. 5; Lk 1:33

Today a light will shine upon us, for the Lord is born for us;
and he will be called Wondrous God,
Prince of peace, Father of future ages:
and his reign will be without end.

Solemnity of Mary, the Holy Mother of God

The Gloria in excelsis (Glory to God in the highest) is said.

Collect
O God, who through the fruitful virginity of Blessed Mary
bestowed on the human race
the grace of eternal salvation,
grant, we pray,
that we may experience the intercession of her,
through whom we were found worthy
to receive the author of life,
our Lord Jesus Christ, your Son.
Who lives and reigns with you in the unity of the Holy Spirit,
one God, for ever and ever.
Amen.

FIRST READING
A reading from the book of Numbers   6:22-27

The Lord spoke to Moses and said, 'Say this to Aaron and his sons: "This is how you are to bless the sons of Israel. You shall say to them:

> May the Lord bless you and keep you.
> May the Lord let his face shine on you and be gracious to you.
> May the Lord uncover his face to you and bring you peace."

This is how they are to call down my name on the sons of Israel, and I will bless them.'

The word of the Lord.

Responsorial Psalm   Ps 66:2-3. 5. 6. 8. ℟ v.2
   ℟   **O God, be gracious and bless us.**

1   God, be gracious and bless us
     and let your face shed its light upon us.
     So will your ways be known upon earth
     and all nations learn your saving help.   ℟

2   Let the nations be glad and exult
     for you rule the world with justice.
     With fairness you rule the peoples.
     You guide the nations on earth.   ℟

3   Let the peoples praise you, O God;
     let all the peoples praise you.
     May God still give us his blessing
     till the ends of the earth revere him.   ℟

SECOND READING
A reading from the letter of St Paul to the Galatians   4:4-7

When the appointed time came, God sent his Son, born of a woman, born a subject of the Law, to redeem the subjects of the Law and to enable us to be adopted as sons. The proof that you are sons is that God has sent the Spirit of his Son into our hearts: the Spirit that cries, 'Abba, Father', and it is this that makes you a son, you are not a slave any more; and if God has made you son, then he has made you heir.

The word of the Lord.

Gospel Acclamation   Heb 1:1-2
Alleluia, alleluia!
At various times in the past
and in various different ways,
God spoke to our ancestors through the prophets;
but in our own time, the last days,
he has spoken to us through his Son.
Alleluia!

GOSPEL
A reading from the holy Gospel according to Luke   2:16-21

The shepherds hurried away to Bethlehem and found Mary and Joseph, and the baby lying in the manger. When they saw the child they repeated what they had been told about him, and everyone who heard it was astonished at what the shepherds had to say. As for Mary, she treasured all these things and pondered them in her heart. And the shepherds went back glorifying and praising God for all they had heard and seen; it was exactly as they had been told. When the eighth day came and the child was to be circumcised, they gave him the name Jesus, the name the angel had given him before his conception.

The Gospel of the Lord.

The Creed is said.

Prayer over the Offerings
O God, who in your kindness begin all good things
and bring them to fulfilment,
grant to us, who find joy in the Solemnity of the holy Mother of
   God,

that, just as we glory in the beginnings of your grace,
so one day we may rejoice in its completion.
Through Christ our Lord.
Amen.

Preface I of the Blessed Virgin Mary (on the Solemnity of the Motherhood), p.42.

When the Roman Canon is used, the proper form of the Communicantes (In communion with those) is said.

Communion Antiphon Heb 13:8
Jesus Christ is the same yesterday, today, and for ever.

Prayer after Communion
We have received this heavenly Sacrament with joy, O Lord:
grant, we pray,
that it may lead us to eternal life,
for we rejoice to proclaim the blessed ever-Virgin Mary
Mother of your Son and Mother of the Church.
Through Christ our Lord.
Amen.

A formula of Solemn Blessing, p.101, may be used.

SECOND SUNDAY AFTER THE NATIVITY   A, B, C

Christ, the Wisdom of God

We celebrate Christ, the incarnate wisdom of God who has come to dwell in our midst, the true light that overcomes the darkness and enlightens all peoples.

Entrance Antiphon Wis 18:14-15
When a profound silence covered all things
and night was in the middle of its course,
your all-powerful Word, O Lord,
bounded from heaven's royal throne.

The Gloria in excelsis (Glory to God in the highest) is said.

Collect
Almighty ever-living God,
splendour of faithful souls,

Second Sunday after the Nativity

graciously be pleased to fill the world with your glory,
and show yourself to all peoples by the radiance of your light.
Through our Lord Jesus Christ, your Son,
who lives and reigns with you in the unity of the Holy Spirit,
one God, for ever and ever.
Amen.

FIRST READING
A reading from the book of Ecclesiasticus   24:1-2. 8-12

Wisdom speaks her own praises,
in the midst of her people she glories in herself.
She opens her mouth in the assembly of the Most High,
she glories in herself in the presence of the Mighty One;

> 'Then the creator of all things instructed me,
> and he who created me fixed a place for my tent.
> He said, "Pitch your tent in Jacob,
> make Israel your inheritance."
> From eternity, in the beginning, he created me,
> and for eternity I shall remain.
> I ministered before him in the holy tabernacle,
> and thus was I established on Zion.
> In the beloved city he has given me rest,
> and in Jerusalem I wield my authority.
> I have taken root in a privileged people
> in the Lord's property, in his inheritance.'

The word of the Lord.

Responsorial Psalm   Ps 147:12-15. 19-20. ℟ Jn 1:14

> ℟ **The Word was made flesh,
> and lived among us.**

or

> ℟ **Alleluia!**

1   O praise the Lord, Jerusalem!
    Zion, praise your God!
    He has strengthened the bars of your gates,
    he has blessed the children within you. ℟

2 He established peace on your borders,
  he feeds you with finest wheat.
  He sends out his word to the earth
  and swiftly runs his command. ℟

3 He makes his word known to Jacob,
  to Israel his laws and decrees.
  He has not dealt thus with other nations;
  he has not taught them his decrees. ℟

SECOND READING
A reading from the letter of St Paul to the Ephesians 1:3-6. 15-18

Blessed be God the Father of our Lord Jesus Christ, who has blessed us with all the spiritual blessings of heaven in Christ. Before the world was made, he chose us, chose us in Christ, to be holy and spotless, and to live through love in his presence, determining that we should become his adopted sons, through Jesus Christ, for his own kind purposes, to make us praise the glory of his grace, his free gift to us in the Beloved.

That will explain why I, having once heard about your faith in the Lord Jesus, and the love that you show towards all the saints, have never failed to remember you in my prayers and to thank God for you. May the God of our Lord Jesus Christ, the Father of glory, give you a spirit of wisdom and perception of what is revealed, to bring you to full knowledge of him. May he enlighten the eyes of your mind so that you can see what hope his call holds for you, what rich glories he has promised the saints will inherit.

The word of the Lord.

Gospel Acclamation   Cf. 1 Tim 3:16
  Alleluia, alleluia!
  Glory be to you, O Christ, proclaimed to the pagans;
  Glory be to you, O Christ, believed in by the world.
  Alleluia!

GOSPEL
A reading from the holy Gospel according to John 1:1-18

*In the beginning was the Word:
the Word was with God
and the Word was God.
He was with God in the beginning.
Through him all things came to be,
not one thing had its being but through him.

All that came to be had life in him
and that life was the light of men,
a light that shines in the dark,
a light that darkness could not overpower.*

A man came, sent by God.
His name was John.
He came as a witness,
as a witness to speak for the light,
so that everyone might believe through him.
He was not the light,
only a witness to speak for the light.

*The Word was the true light
that enlightens all men;
and he was coming into the world.
He was in the world
that had its being through him,
and the world did not know him.
He came to his own domain
and his own people did not accept him.
But to all who did accept him
he gave power to become children of God,
to all who believe in the name of him
who was born not out of human stock
or urge of the flesh
or will of man
but of God himself.
The Word was made flesh,
he lived among us,
and we saw his glory,
the glory that is his as the only Son of the Father,
full of grace and truth.*

John appears as his witness. He proclaims:
'This is the one of whom I said:
He who comes after me
ranks before me
because he existed before me.'

Indeed, from his fullness we have, all of us, received –
yes, grace in return for grace,
since though the Law was given through Moses,
grace and truth have come through Jesus Christ.
No one has ever seen God;

it is the only Son, who is nearest to the Father's heart,
who has made him known.

| *The Gospel of the Lord.*

Shorter Form, verses 1-5. 9-14. Read between

The Creed is said.

Prayer over the Offerings
Sanctify, O Lord, the offerings we make
on the Nativity of your Only Begotten Son,
for by it you show us the way of truth
and promise the life of the heavenly Kingdom.
Through Christ our Lord.
Amen.

Preface I, II or III of the Nativity of the Lord, pp.20-21.

Communion Antiphon Cf. Jn 1:12
To all who would accept him,
he gave the power to become children of God.

Prayer after Communion
Lord our God, we humbly ask you,
that, through the working of this mystery,
our offences may be cleansed
and our just desires fulfilled.
Through Christ our Lord.
Amen.

A formula of Solemn Blessing, p.95, may be used.

6 January

THE EPIPHANY OF THE LORD   A, B, C
Solemnity

The Revelation of Christ to the World

From the rising of the sun to its setting we join all the people of the world in worshipping the infant King of the Jews.

Where the Solemnity of the Epiphany is not to be observed as a Holyday of Obligation, it is assigned to the Sunday occurring between 2 and 8 January as its proper day.

The Epiphany of the Lord

At the Vigil Mass

This Mass is used on the evening of the day before the Solemnity, either before or after First Vespers (Evening Prayer I) of the Epiphany.

Entrance Antiphon Cf. Bar 5:5
Arise, Jerusalem, and look to the East
and see your children gathered from the rising to the setting of the sun.

The Gloria in excelsis (Glory to God in the highest) is said

Collect
May the splendour of your majesty, O Lord, we pray,
shed its light upon our hearts,
that we may pass through the shadows of this world
and reach the brightness of our eternal home.
Through our Lord Jesus Christ, your Son,
who lives and reigns with you in the unity of the Holy Spirit,
one God, for ever and ever.
Amen.

For the Readings, Gospel Acclamation and Gospel, see the Mass during the Day (pp.236-9).

The Creed is said.

Prayer over the Offerings
Accept we pray, O Lord, our offerings,
in honour of the appearing of your Only Begotten Son
and the first fruits of the nations,
that to you praise may be rendered
and eternal salvation be ours.
Through Christ our Lord.
Amen.

Preface of the Epiphany of the Lord, p.21.

Communion Antiphon Cf. Rv 21:23
The brightness of God illumined the holy city Jerusalem,
and the nations will walk by its light.

Prayer after Communion
Renewed by sacred nourishment,
we implore your mercy, O Lord,
that the star of your justice
may shine always bright in our minds
and that our true treasure may ever consist in our confession of you.

Through Christ our Lord.
Amen.

A formula of Solemn Blessing, p.96, may be used.

At the Mass during the Day

Entrance Antiphon   Cf. Mal 3:1; 1 Chr 29:12
Behold, the Lord, the Mighty One, has come;
and kingship is in his grasp, and power and dominion.

The Gloria in excelsis (Glory to God in the highest) is said.

Collect
O God, who on this day
revealed your Only Begotten Son to the nations
by the guidance of a star,
grant in your mercy,
that we, who know you already by faith,
may be brought to behold the beauty of your sublime glory.
Through our Lord Jesus Christ, your Son,
who lives and reigns with you in the unity of the Holy Spirit,
one God, for ever and ever.
Amen.

FIRST READING
A reading from the prophet Isaiah   60:1-6

Arise, shine out Jerusalem, for your light has come,
the glory of the Lord is rising on you,
though night still covers the earth
and darkness the peoples.
Above you the Lord now rises
and above you his glory appears.
The nations come to your light
and kings to your dawning brightness.

Lift up your eyes and look round:
all are assembling and coming towards you,
your sons from far away
and daughters being tenderly carried.

At this sight you will grow radiant,
your heart throbbing and full;
since the riches of the sea will flow to you;
the wealth of the nations come to you;

camels in throngs will cover you,
and dromedaries of Midian and Ephah;

everyone in Sheba will come,
bringing gold and incense
and singing the praise of the Lord.

    The word of the Lord.

Responsional Psalm   Ps 71:1-2. 7-8. 10-13. ℟ cf. v.11
    ℟   **All nations shall fall prostrate before you, O Lord.**

1   O God, give your judgement to the king,
     to a king's son your justice,
     that he may judge your people in justice
     and your poor in right judgement. ℟

2   In his days justice shall flourish
     and peace till the moon fails.
     He shall rule from sea to sea,
     from the Great River to earth's bounds. ℟

3   The kings of Tarshish and the sea coasts
     shall pay him tribute.
     The kings of Sheba and Seba
     shall bring him gifts.
     Before him all kings shall fall prostrate,
     all nations shall serve him. ℟

4   For he shall save the poor when they cry
     and the needy who are helpless.
     He will have pity on the weak
     and save the lives of the poor. ℟

SECOND READING
A reading from the letter of St Paul to the Ephesians   3:2-3. 5-6

You have probably heard how I have been entrusted by God with the grace he meant for you, and that it was by a revelation that I was given the knowledge of the mystery. This mystery that has now been revealed through the Spirit to his holy apostles and prophets was unknown to any men in past generations; it means that pagans now share the same inheritance, that they are parts of the same body, and that the same promise has been made to them, in Christ Jesus, through the gospel.

    The word of the Lord.

Gospel Acclamation Mt 2:2

Alleluia, alleluia!
We saw his star as it rose
and have come to do the Lord homage.
Alleluia!

GOSPEL

A reading from the holy Gospel according to Matthew 2:1-12

After Jesus had been born at Bethlehem in Judaea during the reign of King Herod, some wise men came to Jerusalem from the east. 'Where is the infant king of the Jews?' they asked. 'We saw his star as it rose and have come to do him homage.' When King Herod heard this he was perturbed, and so was the whole of Jerusalem. He called together all the chief priests and the scribes of the people, and enquired of them where the Christ was to be born. 'At Bethlehem in Judaea,' they told him 'for this is what the prophet wrote:

> And you, Bethlehem, in the land of Judah
> you are by no means least among the leaders of Judah,
> for out of you will come a leader
> who will shepherd my people Israel.'

Then Herod summoned the wise men to see him privately. He asked them the exact date on which the star had appeared, and sent them on to Bethlehem. 'Go and find out all about the child,' he said 'and when you have found him, let me know, so that I too may go and do him homage.' Having listened to what the king had to say, they set out. And there in front of them was the star they had seen rising; it went forward and halted over the place where the child was. The sight of the star filled them with delight, and going into the house they saw the child with his mother Mary, and falling to their knees they did him homage. Then, opening their treasures, they offered him gifts of gold and frankincense and myrrh. But they were warned in a dream not to go back to Herod, and returned to their own country by a different way.

The Gospel of the Lord.

Where it is the practice, if appropriate, the moveable Feasts of the current year may be proclaimed after the Gospel.

The Creed is said.

Prayer over the Offerings
Look with favour, Lord, we pray,
on these gifts of your Church,
in which are offered now not gold or frankincense or myrrh,
but he who by them is proclaimed,
sacrificed and received, Jesus Christ.
Who lives and reigns for ever and ever.
Amen.

Preface of the Epiphany of the Lord, p.21.

When the Roman Canon is used, the proper form of the Communicantes (In communion with those) is said.

Communion Antiphon Cf. Mt 2:2
We have seen his star in the East,
and have come with gifts to adore the Lord.

Prayer after Communion
Go before us with heavenly light, O Lord,
always and everywhere,
that we may perceive with clear sight
and revere with true affection
the mystery in which you have willed us to participate.
Through Christ our Lord.
Amen.

A formula of Solemn Blessing, p.96, may be used.

Sunday after 6 January
THE BAPTISM OF THE LORD   A
Feast

Where the Solemnity of the Epiphany is transferred to Sunday, if this Sunday occurs on 7 or 8 January, the Feast of the Baptism of the Lord is celebrated on the following Monday.

The Baptism of the Lord

At his baptism in the Jordan by John, the Father anointed his beloved son, Jesus, with the Holy Spirit and with power, to bring healing and peace to all the nations.

Entrance Antiphon Cf. Mt 3:16-17
After the Lord was baptized, the heavens were opened,
and the Spirit descended upon him like a dove,
and the voice of the Father thundered:
This is my beloved Son, with whom I am well pleased.

The Baptism of the Lord, Year A

The Gloria in excelsis (Glory to God in the highest) is said.

Collect
Almighty ever-living God,
who, when Christ had been baptized in the River Jordan
and as the Holy Spirit descended upon him,
solemnly declared him your beloved Son,
grant that your children by adoption,
reborn of water and the Holy Spirit,
may always be well pleasing to you.
Through our Lord Jesus Christ, your Son,
who lives and reigns with you in the unity of the Holy Spirit,
one God, for ever and ever.
Amen.

or

O God, whose Only Begotten Son
has appeared in our very flesh,
grant, we pray, that we may be inwardly transformed
through him whom we recognize as outwardly like ourselves.
Who lives and reigns with you in the unity of the Holy Spirit,
one God, for ever and ever.
Amen.

FIRST READING
A reading from the prophet Isaiah 42:1-4. 6-7

Thus says the Lord:

> Here is my servant whom I uphold,
> my chosen one in whom my soul delights.
> I have endowed him with my spirit
> that he may bring true justice to the nations.
>
> He does not cry out or shout aloud,
> or make his voice heard in the streets.
> He does not break the crushed reed,
> nor quench the wavering flame.
>
> Faithfully he brings true justice;
> he will neither waver, nor be crushed
> until true justice is established on earth,
> for the islands are awaiting his law.
>
> I, the Lord, have called you to serve the cause of right;
> I have taken you by the hand and formed you;
> I have appointed you as covenant of the people and light of

the nations,
to open the eyes of the blind,
to free captives from prison,
and those who live in darkness from the dungeon.

The word of the Lord.

Responsorial Psalm   Ps 28:1-4. 9-10. R/ v.11
R/ **The Lord will bless his people with peace.**

1. O give the Lord you sons of God,
   give the Lord glory and power;
   give the Lord the glory of his name.
   Adore the Lord in his holy court. R/

2. The Lord's voice resounding on the waters,
   the Lord on the immensity of waters;
   the voice of the Lord, full of power,
   the voice of the Lord, full of splendour. R/

3. The God of glory thunders.
   In his temple they all cry: 'Glory!'
   The Lord sat enthroned over the flood;
   the Lord sits as king for ever. R/

SECOND READING
A reading from the Acts of the Apostles   10:34-38

Peter addressed Cornelius and his household: 'The truth I have now come to realise' he said 'is that God does not have favourites, but that anybody of any nationality who fears God and does what is right is acceptable to him.

'It is true, God sent his word to the people of Israel, and it was to them that the good news of peace was brought by Jesus Christ – but Jesus Christ is Lord of all men. You must have heard about the recent happenings in Judaea; about Jesus of Nazareth and how he began in Galilee, after John had been preaching baptism. God had anointed him with the Holy Spirit and with power, and because God was with him, Jesus went about doing good and curing all who had fallen into the power of the devil.'

The word of the Lord.

Gospel Acclamation   Cf. Mk 9:8
Alleluia, alleluia!
The heavens opened and the Father's voice resounded:

'This is my Son, the Beloved. Listen to him.'
Alleluia!

GOSPEL
A reading from the holy Gospel according to Matthew 3:13-17

Jesus came from Galilee to the Jordan to be baptised by John. John tried to dissuade him. 'It is I who need baptism from you,' he said 'and yet you come to me!' But Jesus replied, 'Leave it like this for the time being; it is fitting that we should, in this way, do all that righteousness demands.' At this, John gave in to him. As soon as Jesus was baptised he came up from the water, and suddenly the heavens opened and he saw the Spirit of God descending like a dove and coming down on him. And a voice spoke from heaven, 'This is my Son, the Beloved; my favour rests on him.'

The Gospel of the Lord.

The Creed is said.

Prayer over the Offerings
Accept, O Lord, the offerings
we have brought to honour the revealing of your beloved Son,
so that the oblation of your faithful
may be transformed into the sacrifice of him
who willed in his compassion
to wash away the sins of the world.
Who lives and reigns for ever and ever.
Amen.

Preface of the Baptism of the Lord, p.22.

Communion Antiphon   Jn 1:32. 34
Behold the One of whom John said:
I have seen and testified that this is the Son of God.

Prayer after Communion
Nourished with these sacred gifts,
we humbly entreat your mercy, O Lord,
that, faithfully listening to your Only Begotten Son,
we may be your children in name and in truth.
Through Christ our Lord.
Amen.

Ordinary Time lasts from the Monday after this Sunday to the Tuesday before Lent. For Sunday Masses the texts given below on pp.487ff. are used.

THE SEASON OF LENT

PREPARATION FOR BAPTISM

Lent is a period of purification and enlightenment or illumination, the final stage of preparation for those catechumens who are to be baptised during the Easter Vigil.

The stages in the final process of becoming a Christian are:

1) *Election*, that is the choice and admission of those judged worthy to receive the sacraments of Christian initiation. This takes place, properly, during Mass of the First Sunday of Lent.

2) *Scrutinies*, the intention of which is to free the newly 'elect' from sin and the devil, and to give them strength in Christ. These take place during Mass on the Third, Fourth and Fifth Sundays of Lent.

3) *Presentation of the Creed and the Lord's Prayer* – usually on a weekday.

The election and the scrutinies take place after the homily at Sunday Mass. When these rites take place, the readings at the Mass are always taken from *Year A*. The elect should be dismissed before the offertory rite of the Mass begins. When the elect have gone out the General Intercessions and the Profession of Faith are said. For pastoral reasons both of these may be omitted.

If these rites are celebrated on weekdays there are special Mass formulae.

*In this missal the rites are given at the end of the particular Sundays of Year A. As a general rule only one formula for a particular prayer or section is given.

It is strongly recommended that the tradition of gathering the local Church after the fashion of the Roman 'stations' be kept and promoted, especially during Lent and at least in larger towns and cities, in a way best suited to individual places.

Such gatherings of the faithful can take place, especially with the chief Pastor of the diocese presiding, on Sundays or on other more convenient days during the week, either at the tombs of the Saints, or in the principal churches or shrines of a city, or even in the more frequently visited places of pilgrimage in the diocese.

If a procession precedes a Mass celebrated for such a gathering, according to circumstances and local conditions, the faithful gather at a smaller church or some other suitable place other than in the church to which the procession will head.

After greeting the people, the Priest says a Collect of the mystery of the Holy Cross, for the remission of sins, or for the Church, especially the local Church, or one of the Prayers over the People. Then the procession makes its way to the church in which Mass will be celebrated and meanwhile the Litany of the Saints is sung. Invocations to the Patron Saint or the Founder Saint and to the Saints of the local Church may be inserted at the appropriate point in the Litany.

When the procession reaches the church, the Priest venerates the altar and, if appopriate, incenses it. Afterwards, omitting the Introductory Rites and, if appropriate, the Kyrie, he says the Collect of the Mass, and then continues the Mass in the usual way.

At these gatherings, instead of Mass, some celebration of the Word of God may also take place, especially in the form of the penitential celebrations given in the Roman Ritual for Lent.

On weekdays of Lent, at the end of Mass and before the final blessing, the Prayer over the People indicated for each day may appropriately be used.

During Lent, it is not permitted to decorate the altar with flowers, and the use of musical instruments is allowed only so as to support the singing. Nevertheless, Laetare Sunday (the Fourth Sunday of Lent), Solemnities, and Feasts are exceptions to this rule.

ASH WEDNESDAY   A, B, C

Penitence is an essential part of the Christian life, for none of us can measure up to the tremendous vocation that is ours as Christians. We are in constant need of the mercy and forgiveness of God. Today we express this by taking part in an impressive corporate act of penitence and reconciliation, beseeching God for the grace to use with profit the 'favourable time' of preparation for the celebration of Christ's Passover feast.

In the course of today's Mass, ashes are blessed and distributed. These are made from the olive branches or branches of other trees that were blessed the previous year.

INTRODUCTORY RITES AND LITURGY OF THE WORD

Entrance Antiphon   Wis 11:24-25. 27
You are merciful to all, O Lord,
and despise nothing that you have made.
You overlook people's sins, to bring them to repentance,
and you spare them, for you are the Lord our God.

The Penitential Act is omitted, and the Distribution of Ashes takes its place.

Collect
Grant, O Lord, that we may begin with holy fasting
this campaign of Christian service,
so that, as we take up battle against spiritual evils,
we may be armed with weapons of self-restraint.
Through our Lord Jesus Christ, your Son,
who lives and reigns with you in the unity of the Holy Spirit,
one God, for ever and ever.
Amen.

FIRST READING

A reading from the prophet Joel   2:12-18

'Now, now – it is the Lord who speaks –
come back to me with all your heart,
fasting, weeping, mourning.'
Let your hearts be broken not your garments torn,
turn to the Lord your God again,
for he is all tenderness and compassion,
slow to anger, rich in graciousness,
and ready to relent.

Who knows if he will not turn again, will not relent,
will not leave a blessing as he passes,
oblation and libation
for the Lord your God?
Sound the trumpet in Zion!
Order a fast,
proclaim a solemn assembly,
call the people together,
summon the community,
assemble the elders,
gather the children,
even the infants at the breast.
Let the bridegroom leave his bedroom
and the bride her alcove.
Between vestibule and altar let the priests,
the ministers of the Lord, lament.
Let them say,
'Spare your people, Lord!
Do not make your heritage a thing of shame,
a byword for the nations.
Why should it be said among the nations,
"Where is their God?" '
Then the Lord, jealous on behalf of his land,
took pity on his people.

   The word of the Lord.

Responsorial Psalm   Ps 50:3-6. 12-14. 17. ℟ v.3

℟ **Have mercy on us, O Lord, for we have sinned.**

1 Have mercy on me, God, in your kindness.
   In your compassion blot out my offence.
   O wash me more and more from my guilt
   and cleanse me from my sin. ℟

2 My offences truly I know them;
   my sin is always before me.
   Against you, you alone, have I sinned:
   what is evil in your sight I have done. ℟

3 A pure heart create for me, O God,
   put a steadfast spirit within me.
   Do not cast me away from your presence,
   nor deprive me of your holy spirit. ℟

4   Give me again the joy of your help;
    with a spirit of fervour sustain me.
    O Lord, open my lips
    and my mouth shall declare your praise.   ℟

SECOND READING
A reading from the second letter of St Paul   5:20 – 6:2
to the Corinthians

We are ambassadors for Christ; it is as though God were appealing through us, and the appeal that we make in Christ's name is: be reconciled to God. For our sake God made the sinless one into sin, so that in him we might become the goodness of God. As his fellow workers, we beg you once again not to neglect the grace of God that you have received. For he says: At the favourable time, I have listened to you; on the day of salvation I came to your help. Well, now is the favourable time; this is the day of salvation.

The word of the Lord.

Gospel Acclamation   Ps 50:12. 14
    Praise to you, O Christ, king of eternal glory!
    A pure heart create for me, O God,
    and give me again the joy of your help.
    Praise to you, O Christ, king of eternal glory!

or   Cf. Ps 94:8
    Praise to you, O Christ, king of eternal glory!
    Harden not your hearts today,
    but listen to the voice of the Lord.
    Praise to you, O Christ, king of eternal glory!

GOSPEL
A reading from the holy Gospel according to Matthew   6:1-6. 16-18

Jesus said to his disciples:
    'Be careful not to parade your good deeds before men to attract their notice; by doing this you will lose all reward from your Father in heaven. So when you give alms, do not have it trumpeted before you; this is what the hypocrites do in the synagogues and in the streets to win men's admiration. I tell you solemnly, they have had their reward. But when you give alms, your left hand must not know what your right is doing; your almsgiving must be secret, and your Father who sees all that is done in secret will reward you.
    'And when you pray, do not imitate the hypocrites: they love to say their prayers standing up in the synagogues and at the street

corners for people to see them. I tell you solemnly, they have had their reward. But when you pray go to your private room and, when you have shut your door, pray to your Father who is in that secret place, and your Father who sees all that is done in secret will reward you.

'When you fast do not put on a gloomy look as the hypocrites do: they pull long faces to let men know they are fasting. I tell you solemnly, they have had their reward. But when you fast, put oil on your head and wash your face, so that no one will know you are fasting except your Father who sees all that is done in secret; and your Father who sees all that is done in secret will reward you.'

The Gospel of the Lord.

BLESSING AND DISTRIBUTION OF ASHES

After the Homily, the Priest, standing with hands joined, says:
Dear brethren (brothers and sisters), let us humbly ask God our Father
that he be pleased to bless with the abundance of his grace these ashes, which we will put on our heads in penitence.

After a brief prayer in silence, and with hands extended he continues:
O God, who are moved by acts of humility
and respond with forgiveness to works of penance,
lend your merciful ear to our prayers
and in your kindness pour out the grace of your ✚ blessing
on your servants who are marked with these ashes,
that, as they follow the Lenten observances,
they may be worthy to come with minds made pure
to celebrate the Paschal Mystery of your Son.
Through Christ our Lord.
Amen.

or

O God, who desire not the death of sinners,
but their conversion,
mercifully hear our prayers
and in your kindness be pleased to bless ✚ these ashes,
which we intend to receive upon our heads,
that, we, who acknowledge we are but ashes
and shall return to dust,
may, through a steadfast observance of Lent,

Ash Wednesday

gain pardon for sins and newness of life
after the likeness of your Risen Son.
Who lives and reigns for ever and ever.
Amen.

He sprinkles the ashes with holy water, without saying anything. Then the Priest places ashes on the head of all those present who come to him, and says to each one:

Repent, and believe in the Gospel.

or

Remember that you are dust, and to dust you shall return.

Meanwhile, the following are sung:

Antiphon 1
Let us change our garments to sackcloth and ashes,
let us fast and weep before the Lord,
that our God, rich in mercy, might forgive us our sins.

Antiphon 2   Cf. Jl 2:17; Est 4:17
Let the priests, the ministers of the Lord,
stand between the porch and the altar and weep and cry out:
Spare, O Lord, spare your people;
do not close the mouths of those who sing your praise, O Lord.

Antiphon 3   Ps 50:3
Blot out my transgressions, O Lord.

This may be repeated after each verse of Psalm 50 (Have mercy on me, O God).

Responsory   Cf. Bar 3:2; Ps 78:9
℣ Let us correct our faults which we have committed in ignorance, let us not be taken unawares by the day of our death, looking in vain for leisure to repent.
℟ **Hear us, O Lord, and show us your mercy, for we have sinned against you.**
℣ Help us, O God our Saviour; for the sake of your name, O Lord, set us free.
℟ **Hear us, O Lord ..**

Another appropriate chant may also be sung. After the distribution of ashes, the Priest washes his hands and proceeds to the Universal Prayer, and continues the Mass in the usual way.

The Creed is not said.

THE LITURGY OF THE EUCHARIST

Prayer over the Offerings
As we solemnly offer
the annual sacrifice for the beginning of Lent,
we entreat you, O Lord,
that, through works of penance and charity,
we may turn away from harmful pleasures
and, cleansed from our sins, may become worthy
to celebrate devoutly the Passion of your Son.
Who lives and reigns for ever and ever.
Amen.

Preface III or IV of Lent, p.23.

Communion Antiphon   Cf. Ps 1:2-3
He who ponders the law of the Lord day and night
will yield fruit in due season.

Prayer after Communion
May the Sacrament we have received sustain us, O Lord,
that our Lenten fast may be pleasing to you
and be for us a healing remedy.
Through Christ our Lord.
Amen.

Prayer over the People
For the dismissal, the Priest stands facing the people and, extending his hands over them, says this prayer:

Pour out a spirit of compunction, O God,
on those who bow before your majesty,
and by your mercy may they merit the rewards you promise
to those who do penance.
Through Christ our Lord.
Amen.

The blessing and distribution of ashes may also take place outside Mass. In this case, the rite is preceded by a Liturgy of the Word, with the Entrance Antiphon, the Collect, and the readings with their chants as at Mass. Then there follow the Homily and the blessing and distribution of ashes. The rite is concluded with the Universal Prayer, the Blessing, and the Dismissal of the Faithful.

First Sunday of Lent, Year A

FIRST SUNDAY OF LENT A

Christ, The Second Adam

Today we celebrate Christ, the Second Adam, who overcame temptation and sin, and by his obedience won back the world to God.

On this Sunday is celebrated the rite of 'election' or 'enrolment of names' for the catechumens who are to be admitted to the Sacraments of Christian Initiation at the Easter Vigil, using the proper prayers and intercessions.

Entrance Antiphon Cf. Ps 90:15-16
When he calls on me, I will answer him;
I will deliver him and give him glory,
I will grant him length of days.

The Gloria in excelsis (Glory to God in the highest) is not said.

Collect
Grant, almighty God,
through the yearly observances of holy Lent,
that we may grow in understanding
of the riches hidden in Christ
and by worthy conduct pursue their effects.
Through our Lord Jesus Christ, your Son,
who lives and reigns with you in the unity of the Holy Spirit,
one God, for ever and ever.
Amen.

FIRST READING
A reading from the book of Genesis 2:7-9. 3:1-7

The Lord God fashioned man of dust from the soil. Then he breathed into his nostrils a breath of life, and thus man became a living being.
 The Lord God planted a garden in Eden which is in the east, and there he put the man he had fashioned. The Lord God caused to spring up from the soil every kind of tree, enticing to look at and good to eat, with the tree of life and the tree of the knowledge of good and evil in the middle of the garden.
 The serpent was the most subtle of all the wild beasts that the Lord God had made. It asked the woman, 'Did God really say you were not to eat from any of the trees in the garden?' The woman answered the serpent, 'We may eat the fruit of the trees in the garden. But of the fruit of the tree in the middle of the garden God

said, "You must not eat it, nor touch it, under pain of death".' Then the serpent said to the woman, 'No! You will not die! God knows in fact that on the day you eat it your eyes will be opened and you will be like gods, knowing good and evil.' The woman saw that the tree was good to eat and pleasing to the eye, and that it was desirable for the knowledge that it could give. So she took some of its fruit and ate it. She gave some also to her husband who was with her, and he ate it. Then the eyes of both of them were opened and they realised that they were naked. So they sewed fig-leaves together to make themselves loin-cloths.

The word of the Lord.

Responsorial Psalm Ps 50:3-6. 12-14. 17. R/ cf. v.3

R/ **Have mercy on us, O Lord, for we have sinned.**

1 Have mercy on me, God, in your kindness.
In your compassion blot out my offence.
O wash me more and more from my guilt
and cleanse me from my sin. R/

2 My offences truly I know them;
my sin is always before me.
Against you, you alone, have I sinned;
what is evil in your sight I have done. R/

3 A pure heart create for me, O God,
put a steadfast spirit within me.
Do not cast me away from your presence,
nor deprive me of your holy spirit. R/

4 Give me again the joy of your help;
with a spirit of fervour sustain me.
O Lord, open my lips
and my mouth shall declare your praise. R/

SECOND READING
A reading from the letter of St Paul to the Romans 5:12-19

Sin entered the world through one man, and through sin death, and thus death has spread through the whole human race because everyone has sinned. Sin existed in the world long before the Law was given. There was no law and so no one could be accused of the sin of 'law breaking', yet death reigned over all from Adam to Moses, even though their sin, unlike that of Adam, was not a matter of breaking a law.

First Sunday of Lent, Year A

Adam prefigured the One to come, but the gift itself considerably outweighed the fall. If it is certain that through one man's fall so many died, it is even more certain that divine grace, coming through the one man, Jesus Christ, came to so many as an abundant free gift. The results of the gift also outweigh the results of one man's sin: for after one single fall came judgement with a verdict of condemnation, now after many falls comes grace with its verdict of acquittal. *If it is certain that death reigned over everyone as the consequence of one man's fall, it is even more certain that one man, Jesus Christ, will cause everyone to reign in life who receives the free gift that he does not deserve, of being made righteous. Again, as one man's fall brought condemnation on everyone, so the good act of one man brings everyone life and makes them justified. As by one man's disobedience many were made sinners, so by one man's obedience many will be made righteous.

The word of the Lord.*

Shorter Form, verses 12. 17-19. Read between

Gospel Acclamation   Mt 4:4

Praise to you, O Christ, king of eternal glory!
Man does not live on bread alone
but on every word that comes from the mouth of God.
Praise to you, O Christ, king of eternal glory!

GOSPEL
A reading from the holy Gospel according to Matthew   4:1-11

Jesus was led by the Spirit out into the wilderness to be tempted by the devil. He fasted for forty days and forty nights, after which he was very hungry, and the tempter came and said to him, 'If you are the Son of God, tell these stones to turn into loaves.' But he replied, 'Scripture says:

> Man does not live on bread alone but on every word that comes from the mouth of God.'

The devil then took him to the holy city and made him stand on the parapet of the Temple. 'If you are the Son of God' he said 'throw yourself down; for scripture says:

> He will put you in his angels' charge, and they will support you on their hands in case you hurt your foot against a stone.'

Jesus said to him, 'Scripture also says:

> You must not put the Lord your God to the test.'

Next, taking him to a very high mountain, the devil showed him all the kingdoms of the world and their splendour. 'I will give you all these' he said, 'if you fall at my feet and worship me.' Then Jesus replied, 'Be off, Satan! For scripture says: You must worship the Lord your God, and serve him alone.' Then the devil left him, and angels appeared and looked after him.

> The Gospel of the Lord.

After the homily, the Election or Enrolment of candidates for baptism may follow.

If there is no Election or Enrolment of candidates for baptism, the Creed is said.

Prayer over the Offerings
Give us the right dispositions, O Lord, we pray,
to make these offerings,
for with them we celebrate the beginning
of this venerable and sacred time.
Through Christ our Lord.
Amen.

Preface of the Temptation of the Lord, p.24.

Communion Antiphon   Mt 4:4
One does not live by bread alone,
but by every word that comes forth from the mouth of God.

or   Cf. Ps 90:4

The Lord will conceal you with his pinions,
and under his wings you will trust.

Prayer after Communion
Renewed now with heavenly bread,
by which faith is nourished, hope increased,
and charity strengthened,
we pray, O Lord,
that we may learn to hunger for Christ,
the true and living Bread,
and strive to live by every word
which proceeds from your mouth.
Through Christ our Lord.
Amen.

Prayer over the People
May bountiful blessing, O Lord, we pray,
come down upon your people,
that hope may grow in tribulation,
virtue be strengthened in temptation,
and eternal redemption be assured.
Through Christ our Lord.
Amen.

SECOND SUNDAY OF LENT — A

Our Transfigured Lord

Our natural inclination is to stay where we are, to make a tent and settle comfortably. But God is continually urging us on to a land he will show us. We follow our transfigured Lord in faith, putting our trust in him and bearing his hardships for the sake of the good news he has brought us.

Entrance Antiphon — Cf. Ps 26:8-9
Of you my heart has spoken: Seek his face.
It is your face, O Lord, that I seek;
hide not your face from me.

or — Cf. Ps 24:6. 2. 22

Remember your compassion, O Lord,
and your merciful love, for they are from of old.
Let not our enemies exult over us.
Redeem us, O God of Israel, from all our distress.

The Gloria in excelsis (Glory to God in the highest) is not said.

Collect
O God, who have commanded us
to listen to your beloved Son,
be pleased, we pray,
to nourish us inwardly by your word,
that, with spiritual sight made pure,
we may rejoice to behold your glory.
Through our Lord Jesus Christ, your Son,
who lives and reigns with you in the unity of the Holy Spirit,
one God, for ever and ever.
Amen.

FIRST READING

A reading from the book of Genesis 12:1-4

The Lord said to Abram, 'Leave your country, your family and your father's house, for the land I will show you. I will make you a great nation; I will bless you and make your name so famous that it will be used as a blessing.

> 'I will bless those who bless you:
> I will curse those who slight you.
> All the tribes of the earth
> shall bless themselves by you.'

So Abram went as the Lord told him.

The word of the Lord.

Responsorial Psalm Ps 32:4-5. 18-20. 22. ℟ v.22

℟ **May your love be upon us, O Lord,**
   as we place all our hope in you.

1 The word of the Lord is faithful
   and all his works to be trusted.
   The Lord loves justice and right
   and fills the earth with his love. ℟

2 The Lord looks on those who revere him,
   on those who hope in his love,
   to rescue their souls from death,
   to keep them alive in famine. ℟

3 Our soul is waiting for the Lord.
   The Lord is our help and our shield.
   May your love be upon us, O Lord,
   as we place all our hope in you. ℟

SECOND READING

A reading from the second letter of St Paul to Timothy 1:8-10

With me, bear the hardships for the sake of the Good News, relying on the power of God who has saved us and called us to be holy – not because of anything we ourselves have done but for his own purpose and by his own grace. This grace had already been granted to us, in Christ Jesus, before the beginning of time, but it has only been revealed by the Appearing of our saviour Christ Jesus. He abolished death, and he has proclaimed life and immortality through the Good News.

The word of the Lord.

Second Sunday of Lent, Year A

Gospel Acclamation — Mt 17:5
Glory and praise to you, O Christ!
From the bright cloud the Father's voice was heard:
'This is my Son, the Beloved. Listen to him.'
Glory and praise to you, O Christ!

GOSPEL
A reading from the holy Gospel according to Matthew — 17:1-9

Jesus took with him Peter and James and his brother John and led them up a high mountain where they could be alone. There in their presence he was transfigured; his face shone like the sun and his clothes became as white as the light. Suddenly Moses and Elijah appeared to them; they were talking with him. Then Peter spoke to Jesus. 'Lord,' he said 'it is wonderful for us to be here; if you wish, I will make three tents here, one for you, one for Moses and one for Elijah.' He was still speaking when suddenly a bright cloud covered them with shadow, and from the cloud there came a voice which said, 'This is my Son, the Beloved; he enjoys my favour. Listen to him'. When they heard this, the disciples fell on their faces, overcome with fear. But Jesus came up and touched them. 'Stand up,' he said 'do not be afraid.' And when they raised their eyes they saw no one but only Jesus.

As they came down from the mountain Jesus gave them this order. 'Tell no one about the vision until the Son of Man has risen from the dead.'

The Gospel of the Lord.

The Creed is said.

Prayer over the Offerings
May this sacrifice, O Lord, we pray,
cleanse us of our faults
and sanctify your faithful in body and mind
for the celebration of the paschal festivities.
Through Christ our Lord.
Amen.

Preface of the Transfiguration of the Lord, pp.24-5.

Communion Antiphon — Mt 17:5
This is my beloved Son, with whom I am well pleased;
listen to him.

Prayer after Communion
As we receive these glorious mysteries,
we make thanksgiving to you, O Lord,
for allowing us while still on earth
to be partakers even now of the things of heaven.
Through Christ our Lord.
Amen.

Prayer over the People
Bless your faithful, we pray, O Lord,
with a blessing that endures for ever,
and keep them faithful
to the Gospel of your Only Begotten Son,
so that they may always desire and at last attain
that glory whose beauty he showed in his own Body,
to the amazement of his Apostles.
Through Christ our Lord.
Amen.

THIRD SUNDAY OF LENT   A

On this Sunday is celebrated the First Scrutiny in preparation for the Baptism of the catechumens who are to be admitted to the Sacraments of Christian Initiation at the Easter Vigil, using the proper prayers and intercessions as given below, pp.263-8.

Entrance Antiphon   Cf. Ps 24:15-16
My eyes are always on the Lord,
for he rescues my feet from the snare.
Turn to me and have mercy on me,
for I am alone and poor.

or   Cf. Ez 36:23-26

When I prove my holiness among you,
I will gather you from all the foreign lands;
and I will pour clean water upon you
and cleanse you from all your impurities,
and I will give you a new spirit, says the Lord.

The Gloria in excelsis (Glory to God in the highest) is not said.

Collect
O God, author of every mercy and of all goodness,
who in fasting, prayer and almsgiving
have shown us a remedy for sin,
look graciously on this confession of our lowliness,

Third Sunday of Lent, Year A 259

that we, who are bowed down by our conscience,
may always be lifted up by your mercy.
Through our Lord Jesus Christ, your Son,
who lives and reigns with you in the unity of the Holy Spirit,
one God, for ever and ever.
Amen.

FIRST READING
A reading from the book of Exodus 17:3-7

Tormented by thirst, the people complained against Moses. 'Why did you bring us out of Egypt?' they said. 'Was it so that I should die of thirst, my children too, and my cattle?' Moses appealed to the Lord. 'How am I to deal with this people?' he said. 'A little more and they will stone me!' The Lord said to Moses, 'Take with you some of the elders of Israel and move on to the forefront of the people; take in your hand the staff with which you struck the river, and go. I shall be standing before you there on the rock, at Horeb. You must strike the rock, and water will flow from it for the people to drink.' This is what Moses did, in the sight of the elders of Israel. The place was named Massah and Meribah because of the grumbling of the sons of Israel and because they put the Lord to the test by saying, 'Is the Lord with us, or not?'

The word of the Lord.

Responsorial Psalm Ps 94:1-2. 6-9. ℟ v.8
℟ **O that today you would listen to his voice:
'Harden not your hearts.'**

1   Come, ring out our joy to the Lord;
    hail the rock who saves us.
    Let us come before him, giving thanks,
    with songs let us hail the Lord.   ℟

2   Come in; let us bow and bend low;
    let us kneel before the God who made us
    for he is our God and we
    the people who belong to his pasture,
    the flock that is led by his hand.   ℟

3   O that today you would listen to his voice!
    'Harden not your hearts as at Meribah,
    as on that day at Massah in the desert
    when your fathers put me to the test;
    when they tried me, though they saw my work.'   ℟

SECOND READING

A reading from the letter of St Paul to the Romans   5:1-2. 5-8

Through our Lord Jesus Christ by faith we are judged righteous and at peace with God, since it is by faith and through Jesus that we have entered this state of grace in which we can boast about looking forward to God's glory. This hope is not deceptive, because the love of God has been poured into our hearts by the Holy Spirit which has been given us. We were still helpless when at his appointed moment Christ died for sinful men. It is not easy to die even for a good man – though of course for someone really worthy, a man might be prepared to die – but what proves that God loves us is that Christ died for us while we were still sinners.

The word of the Lord.

Gospel Acclamation   Cf. Jn 4:42.15
Glory to you, O Christ, you are the Word of God!
Lord, you are really the saviour of the world;
give me the living water, so that I may never get thirsty.
Glory to you, O Christ, you are the Word of God!

GOSPEL

A reading from the holy Gospel according to John   4:5-42

*Jesus came to the Samaritan town called Sychar, near the land that Jacob gave to his son Joseph. Jacob's well is there and Jesus, tired by the journey, sat straight down by the well. It was about the sixth hour. When a Samaritan woman came to draw water, Jesus said to her, 'Give me a drink.' His disciples had gone into the town to buy food. The Samaritan woman said to him, 'What? You are a Jew and you ask me, a Samaritan, for a drink?' – Jews, in fact, do not associate with Samaritans. Jesus replied:

'If you only knew what God is offering
and who it is that is saying to you:
Give me a drink,
you would have been the one to ask,
and he would have given you living water.'

'You have no bucket, sir,' she answered 'and the well is deep: how could you get this living water? Are you a greater man than our father Jacob who gave us this well and drank from it himself with his sons and his cattle?' Jesus replied:

> 'Whoever drinks this water
> will get thirsty again;
> but anyone who drinks the water that I shall give
> will never be thirsty again:
> the water that I shall give
> will turn into a spring inside him, welling up to eternal life.'

'Sir,' said the woman 'give me some of that water, so that I may never get thirsty and never have to come here again to draw water.'*
'Go and call your husband' said Jesus to her 'and come back here.' The woman answered, 'I have no husband.' He said to her, 'You are right to say, "I have no husband"; for although you have had five, the one you have now is not your husband. You spoke the truth there.' *'I see you are a prophet, sir' said the woman. 'Our fathers worshipped on this mountain, while you say that Jerusalem is the place where one ought to worship.' Jesus said:

> 'Believe me, woman, the hour is coming
> when you will worship the Father
> neither on this mountain nor in Jerusalem.
> You worship what you do not know;
> we worship what we do know;
> for salvation comes from the Jews.
> But the hour will come – in fact it is here already –
> when true worshippers will worship the Father in spirit and truth:
> that is the kind of worshipper
> the Father wants.
> God is spirit,
> and those who worship
> must worship in spirit and truth.'

The woman said to him, 'I know that Messiah – that is, Christ – is coming; and when he comes he will tell us everything.' 'I who am speaking to you,' said Jesus 'I am he.'*

At this point his disciples returned, and were surprised to find him speaking to a woman, though none of them asked, 'What do you want from her?' or, 'Why are you talking to her?' The woman put down her water jar and hurried back to the town to tell the people, 'Come and see a man who has told me everything I ever did; I wonder if he is the Christ?' This brought people out of the town and they started walking towards him.

Meanwhile, the disciples were urging him, 'Rabbi, do have something to eat;' but he said, 'I have food to eat that you do not know about.' So the disciples asked one another, 'Has someone been bringing him food?' But Jesus said:

'My food
is to do the will of the one who sent me,
and to complete his work.
Have you not got a saying:
Four months and then the harvest?
Well, I tell you:
Look around you, look at the fields;
already they are white, ready for harvest!
Already the reaper is being paid his wages,
already he is bringing in the grain for eternal life,
and thus sower and reaper rejoice together.
For here the proverb holds good:
one sows, another reaps;
I sent you to reap
a harvest you had not worked for.
Others worked for it;
and you have come into the rewards of their trouble.'

*Many Samaritans of that town had believed in him on the strength of the woman's testimony when she said, 'He told me all I have ever done,' so, when the Samaritans came up to him, they begged him to stay with them. He stayed for two days, and when he spoke to them many more came to believe; and they said to the woman, 'Now we no longer believe because of what you told us; we have heard him ourselves and we know that he really is the saviour of the world.'

The Gospel of the Lord*

Shorter Form, verses 5-15. 19-26. 39-42. Read between

After the homily the First Scrutiny of the candidates for baptism may take place. The texts are given below, pp.263-8.

If there is no Scrutiny, the Creed is said.

Prayer over the Offerings
Be pleased, O Lord, with these sacrificial offerings,
and grant that we who beseech pardon for our own sins,
may take care to forgive our neighbour.
Through Christ our Lord.
Amen.

Third Sunday of Lent, Year A 263

Preface of the Samaritan Woman, p.25.

Communion Antiphon Jn 4:13-14
For anyone who drinks it, says the Lord,
the water I shall give will become in him
a spring welling up to eternal life.

Prayer after Communion
As we receive the pledge
of things yet hidden in heaven
and are nourished while still on earth
with the Bread that comes from on high,
we humbly entreat you, O Lord,
that what is being brought about in us in mystery
may come to true completion.
Through Christ our Lord.
Amen.

Prayer over the People
Direct, O Lord, we pray, the hearts of your faithful,
and in your kindness grant your servants this grace:
that, abiding in the love of you and their neighbour,
they may fulfil the whole of your commands.
Through Christ our Lord.
Amen.

FIRST SCRUTINY

After the homily, the elect with their godparents come forward and stand before the celebrant.

The celebrant first addresses the assembly of the faithful, inviting them to pray in silence and to ask that the elect will be given a spirit of repentance, a sense of sin, and the true freedom of the children of God.

The celebrant then addresses the elect, inviting them also to pray in silence and suggesting that as a sign of their inner spirit of repentance they bow their heads or kneel; he concludes his remarks with the following or similar words.

Elect of God, bow your heads [kneel down] and pray.

The elect bow their heads or kneel, and all pray for some time in silence. After the period of silent prayer, the community and the elect stand for the intercessions.

Intercessions for the Elect

Either of the following formularies, options A or B, may be used for the intercessions for the elect and both the introduction and the intentions may be adapted to fit various circumstances. During the intercessions the godparents stand with their right hand on the shoulder of the elect.

[If it is decided that after the dismissal of the elect the usual general intercessions of the Mass are to be omitted and that the Liturgy of the Eucharist is to begin immediately, intentions for the Church and the whole world are to be added to the following intentions for the elect.]

Celebrant: Let us pray for these elect whom the Church has confidently chosen. May they successfully complete their long preparation and at the paschal feast find Christ in his sacraments.

A

Assisting minister: That they may ponder the word of God in their hearts and savour its meaning more fully day by day, let us pray to the Lord:
Lord, hear our prayer.

Assisting minister: That they may learn to know Christ, who came to save what was lost, let us pray to the Lord:
Lord, hear our prayer.

Assisting minister: That they may humbly confess themselves to be sinners, let us pray to the Lord:
Lord, hear our prayer.

Assisting minister: That they may sincerely reject everything in their lives that is displeasing and contrary to Christ, let us pray to the Lord:
Lord, hear our prayer.

Assisting minister: That the Holy Spirit, who searches every heart, may help them to overcome their weakness through his power, let us pray to the Lord:
Lord, hear our prayer.

Assisting minister: That the same Holy Spirit may teach them to know the things of God and how to please him, let us pray to the Lord:
Lord, hear our prayer.

Assisting minister: That their families also may put their hope in Christ and find peace and holiness in him, let us pray to the Lord:
Lord, hear our prayer.

Assisting minister: That we ourselves in preparation for the Easter feast may seek a change of heart, give ourselves to prayer, and persevere in our good works, let us pray to the Lord:
Lord, hear our prayer.

Assisting minister: That throughout the whole world whatever is weak may be strengthened, whatever is broken restored, whatever is lost found, and what is found redeemed, let us pray to the Lord:
Lord, hear our prayer.

B

Assisting minister: That, like the woman of Samaria, our elect may review their lives before Christ and acknowledge their sins, let us pray to the Lord:
Lord, hear our prayer.

Assisting minister: That they may be freed from the spirit of mistrust that deters people from following Christ, let us pray to the Lord:
Lord, hear our prayer.

Assisting ministers: That while awaiting the gift of God, they may long with all their hearts for the living water that brings eternal life, let us pray to the Lord:
Lord, hear our prayer.

Assisting minister: That by accepting the Son of God as their teacher, they may become true worshippers of the Father in spirit and in truth, let us pray to the Lord:
Lord, hear our prayer.

Assisting minister: That they may share with their friends and neighbours the wonder of their own meeting with Christ, let us pray to the Lord:
Lord, hear our prayer.

Assisting minister: That those whose lives are empty for want of the word of God may come to the Gospel of Christ, let us pray to the Lord:
Lord, hear our prayer.

Assisting minister: That all of us may learn from Christ to do the Father's will in love, let us pray to the Lord:
Lord, hear our prayer.

Third Sunday of Lent, Year A

Exorcism
After the intercessions, the rite continues with one of the following exorcisms.

A

The celebrant faces the elect and, with hands joined, says:

God of power,
you sent your Son to be our Saviour.
Grant that these catechumens,
who, like the woman of Samaria, thirst for living water,
may turn to the Lord as they hear his word
and acknowledge the sins and weaknesses
   that weigh them down.

Protect them from vain reliance on self
and defend them from the power of Satan.

Free them from the spirit of deceit,
so that, admitting the wrong they have done,
they may attain purity of heart
and advance on the way to salvation.

We ask this through Christ our Lord.
Amen.

Here, if this can be done conveniently, the celebrant lays hands on each one of the elect.

Then, with hands outstretched over all the elect, he continues:

Lord Jesus,
you are the fountain for which they thirst,
you are the Master whom they seek.
In your presence
they dare not claim to be without sin,
for you alone are the Holy One of God.

They open their hearts to you in faith,
they confess their faults
and lay bare their hidden wounds.
In your love free them from their infirmities,
heal their sickness,
quench their thirst, and give them peace.

In the power of your name,
which we call upon in faith,

Third Sunday of Lent, Year A 267

stand by them now and heal them.
Rule over that spirit of evil,
conquered by your rising from the dead.

Show your elect the way of salvation in the Holy Spirit,
that they may come to worship the Father in truth,
for you live and reign for ever and ever.
Amen.

B

The celebrant faces the elect and, with hands joined, says:

All-merciful Father,
through your Son you revealed your mercy
to the woman of Samaria;
and moved by that same care
you have offered salvation to all sinners.

Look favourably on these elect,
who desire to become your adopted children
through the power of your sacraments.

Free them from the slavery of sin,
and for Satan's crushing yoke
exchange the gentle yoke of Jesus.

Protect them in every danger,
that they may serve you faithfully in peace and joy
and render you thanks for ever.
Amen.

Here, if this can be done conveniently, the celebrant lays hands on each one of the elect.

Then, with hands outstretched over all the elect, he continues:

Lord Jesus,
in your merciful wisdom
you touched the heart of the sinful woman
and taught her to worship the Father
in spirit and in truth.

Now, by your power,
free these elect from the cunning of Satan,
as they draw near to the fountain of living water.

Touch their hearts with the power of the Holy Spirit,
that they may come to know the Father

in true faith, which expresses itself in love,
for you live and reign for ever and ever.
Amen.

An appropriate song may be sung, for example, Psalm 6, 25(26), 31(32), 37(38), 38(39), 39(40), 50(51), 115(116):1-9, 129(130), 138(139), or 141(142).

Dismissal of the Elect
If the Eucharist is to be celebrated, the elect are normally dismissed at this point by use of option A; if the elect are to stay for the celebration of the eucharist, option B is used; if the eucharist is not to be celebrated, the entire assembly is dismissed by use of option C.

A

The celebrant dismisses the elect in these or similar words.

Dear elect, go in peace,
and join us again at the next scrutiny.
May the Lord remain with you always.

Elect: **Amen.**

B

If for serious reasons the elect cannot leave and must remain with the baptised, they are to be instructed that though they are present at the eucharist, they cannot take part in it as the baptised do. They may be reminded of this by the celebrant in these or similar words.

Although you cannot yet participate fully in the Lord's eucharist, stay with us as a sign of our hope that all God's children will eat and drink with the Lord and work with his Spirit to re-create the face of the earth.

C

The celebrant dismisses those present, using these or similar words.

Go in peace,
and may the Lord remain with you always.

All: **Thanks be to God.**

An appropriate song may conclude the celebration.

Fourth Sunday of Lent, Year A

FOURTH SUNDAY OF LENT A

Our Shepherd-King in This Valley of Darkness

We walk in the darkness of this world, often assailed by fear and misgiving. But Christ, the Shepherd-King, the second David, lights up our way for us and cures our congenital blindness as he leads us to his kingdom.

In this Mass, the colour violet or rose is used. Instrumental music is permitted, and the altar may be decorated with flowers.

On this Sunday is celebrated the Second Scrutiny in preparation for the Baptism of the catechumens who are to be admitted to the Sacraments of Christian Initiation at the Easter Vigil, using the proper prayers and intercessions as given below, pp.274-9.

Entrance Antiphon Cf. Is 66:10-11
Rejoice, Jerusalem, and all who love her.
Be joyful, all who were in mourning;
exult and be satisfied at her consoling breast.

The Gloria in excelsis (Glory to God in the highest) is not said.

Collect
O God, who through your Word
reconcile the human race to yourself in a wonderful way,
grant, we pray,
that with prompt devotion and eager faith
the Christian people may hasten
toward the solemn celebrations to come.
Through our Lord Jesus Christ, your Son,
who lives and reigns with you in the unity of the Holy Spirit,
one God, for ever and ever.
Amen.

FIRST READING
A reading from the first book of Samuel 16:1. 6-7. 10-13

The Lord said to Samuel, 'Fill your horn with oil and go. I am sending you to Jesse of Bethlehem, for I have chosen myself a king among his sons.' When Samuel arrived, he caught sight of Eliab and thought, 'Surely the Lord's anointed one stands there before him,' but the Lord said to Samuel, 'Take no notice of his appearance or his height for I have rejected him; God does not see as man sees; man looks at appearances but the Lord looks at the heart.' Jesse presented his seven sons to Samuel, but Samuel said to Jesse, 'The Lord has not chosen these.' He then asked Jesse, 'Are these all the sons you have?' He answered, 'There is still one left, the youngest; he is out looking after the sheep.' Then Samuel said to Jesse, 'Send for him; we will not sit down to eat until he comes.' Jesse had him sent for, a boy of fresh complexion, with fine eyes and pleasant bearing. The Lord said, 'Come, anoint him, for this is the one.' At this, Samuel took the horn of oil and anointed him where he stood with his brothers; and the spirit of the Lord seized on David and stayed with him from that day on.

The word of the Lord.

Responsorial Psalm Ps 22. ℟ v.1
℟ **The Lord is my shepherd;**
there is nothing I shall want.

1 The Lord is my shepherd;
 there is nothing I shall want.
 Fresh and green are the pastures
 where he gives me repose.
 Near restful waters he leads me,
 to revive my drooping spirit. ℟

2 He guides me along the right path;
 he is true to his name.
 If I should walk in the valley of darkness
 no evil would I fear.
 You are there with your crook and your staff;
 with these you give me comfort. ℟

3 You have prepared a banquet for me
 in the sight of my foes.
 My head you have anointed with oil;
 my cup is overflowing. ℟

4 Surely goodness and kindness shall follow me
 all the days of my life.
 In the Lord's own house shall I dwell
 for ever and ever. ℟

Fourth Sunday of Lent, Year A

SECOND READING
A reading from the letter of St Paul to the Ephesians 5:8-14

You were darkness once, but now you are light in the Lord; be like children of light, for the effects of the light are seen in complete goodness and right living and truth. Try to discover what the Lord wants of you, having nothing to do with the futile works of darkness but exposing them by contrast. The things which are done in secret are things that people are ashamed even to speak of; but anything exposed by the light will be illuminated and anything illuminated turns into light. That is why it is said: Wake up from your sleep, rise from the dead, and Christ will shine on you.

The word of the Lord.

Gospel Acclamation Jn 8:12
Glory to you, O Christ, you are the Word of God!
I am the light of the world, says the Lord;
anyone who follows me will have the light of life.
Glory to you, O Christ, you are the Word of God!

GOSPEL
A reading from the holy Gospel according to John 9:1-41

As Jesus went along, he saw a man who had been blind from birth. His disciples asked him, 'Rabbi, who sinned, this man or his parents, for him to have been born blind?' 'Neither he nor his parents sinned,' Jesus answered 'he was born blind so that the works of God might be displayed in him.

'As long as the day lasts
I must carry out the work of the one who sent me;
the night will soon be here when no one can work.
As long as I am in the world
I am the light of the world.'

Having said this, *he spat on the ground, made a paste with the spittle, put this over the eyes of the blind man and said to him, 'Go and wash in the Pool of Siloam' (a name that means 'sent'). So the blind man went off and washed himself, and came away with his sight restored.

His neighbours and people who earlier had seen him begging said, 'Isn't this the man who used to sit and beg?' Some said, 'Yes, it is the same one.' Others said, 'No, he only looks like him.' The man himself said, 'I am the man.'* So they said to him, 'Then how do your eyes come to be open?' 'The man called Jesus' he answered 'made a paste, daubed my eyes with it and said to me, "Go and wash at Siloam"; so I went, and when I washed I could see.' They asked, 'Where is he?' 'I don't know' he answered.

They brought the man who had been blind to the Pharisees. It had been a sabbath day when Jesus made the paste and opened the man's eyes, so when the Pharisees asked him how he had come to see, he said, 'He put a paste on my eyes, and I washed, and I can see.' Then some of the Pharisees said, 'This man cannot be from God: he does not keep the sabbath.' Others said, 'How could a sinner produce signs like this?' And there was disagreement among them, So they spoke to the blind man again, 'What have you to say about him yourself, now that he has opened your eyes?' 'He is a prophet' replied the man.

However, the Jews would not believe that the man had been blind and had gained his sight, without first sending for his parents and asking them, 'Is this man really your son who you say was born blind? If so how is it that he is now able to see?' His parents answered, 'We know he is our son and we know he was born blind, but we don't know how it is that he can see now, or who opened his eyes. He is old enough: let him speak for himself.' His parents spoke like this out of fear of the Jews, who had already agreed to expel from the synagogue anyone who should acknowledge Jesus as the Christ. This was why his parents said, 'He is old enough; ask him.'

So the Jews again sent for the man and said to him, 'Give glory to God! For our part, we know that this man is a sinner.' The man answered, 'I don't know if he is a sinner; I only know that I was blind and now I can see.' They said to him, 'What did he do to you? How did he open your eyes?' He replied, 'I have told you once and you wouldn't listen. Why do you want to hear it all again? Do you want to become his disciples too?' At this they hurled abuse at him: 'You can be his disciple,' they said 'we are disciples of Moses: we know that God spoke to Moses, but as for this man, we don't know where he comes from.' The man replied, 'Now here is an astonishing thing! He has opened my eyes and you don't know where he comes from! We know that God doesn't listen to sinners, but God does listen to men who are devout and do his will. Ever since the world began it is unheard of for anyone to open the eyes

Fourth Sunday of Lent, Year A

of a man who was born blind; if this man were not from God, he couldn't do a thing.' *'Are you trying to teach us,' they replied 'and you a sinner through and through, since you were born!' And they drove him away.

Jesus heard they had driven him away, and when he found him he said to him, 'Do you believe in the Son of Man?' 'Sir,' the man replied 'tell me who he is so that I may believe in him.' Jesus said, 'You are looking at him; he is speaking to you.' The man said, 'Lord, I believe', and worshipped him.*

Jesus said:

'It is for judgement
that I have come into this world,
so that those without sight may see
and those with sight turn blind.'

Hearing this, some Pharisees who were present said to him, 'We are not blind, surely?' Jesus replied:

'Blind? If you were,
you would not be guilty,
but since you say, "We see",
your guilt remains.'

The Gospel of the Lord.

Shorter Form, verses 1. 6-9. 13-17. 34-38. Read between

After the homily the Second Scrutiny of the candidates for baptism may take place. The texts are given below, pp.274-9.

If there is no Scrutiny, the Creed is said.

Prayer over the Offerings
We place before you with joy these offerings,
which bring eternal remedy, O Lord,
praying that we may both faithfully revere them
and present them to you, as is fitting,
for the salvation of all the world.
Through Christ our Lord.
Amen.

Preface of the Man Born Blind, p.25.

Communion Antiphon   Cf. Jn 9:11. 38
The Lord anointed my eyes: I went, I washed,
I saw and I believed in God.

Prayer after Communion
O God, who enlighten everyone who comes into this world,
illuminate our hearts, we pray,
with the splendour of your grace,
that we may always ponder
what is worthy and pleasing to your majesty
and love you in all sincerity.
Through Christ our Lord.
Amen.

Prayer over the People
Look upon those who call to you, O Lord,
and sustain the weak;
give life by your unfailing light
to those who walk in the shadow of death,
and bring those rescued by your mercy from every evil
to reach the highest good.
Through Christ our Lord.
Amen.

SECOND SCRUTINY

After the homily, the elect with their godparents come forward and stand before the celebrant.

The celebrant first addresses the assembly of the faithful, inviting them to pray in silence and to ask that the elect will be given a spirit of repentance, a sense of sin, and the true freedom of the children of God.

The celebrant then addresses the elect, inviting them also to pray in silence and suggesting that as a sign of their inner spirit of repentance they bow their heads or kneel; he concludes his remarks with the following or similar words.

Elect of God, bow your heads [kneel down] and pray.

The elect bow their heads or kneel, and all pray for some time in silence. After the period of silent prayer, the community and the elect stand for the intercessions.

Fourth Sunday of Lent, Year A

Intercessions for the Elect
Either of the following formularies, options A or B, may be used for the intercessions for the elect and both the introduction and the intentions may be adapted to fit various circumstances. During the intercessions the godparents stand with their right hand on the shoulder of the elect.

[If it is decided that after the dismissal of the elect the usual general intercessions of the Mass are to be omitted and that the liturgy of the eucharist is to begin immediately, intentions for the Church and the whole world are to be added to the following intentions for the elect.]

Celebrant: Let us pray for these elect whom God has called, that they may remain faithful to him and boldly give witness to the words of eternal life.

A

Assisting minister: That, trusting in the truth of Christ, they may find freedom of mind and heart and preserve it always, let us pray to the Lord:
Lord, hear our prayer.

Assisting minister: That, preferring the folly of the cross to the wisdom of the world, they may glory in God alone, let us pray to the Lord:
Lord, hear our prayer.

Assisting minister: That, freed by the power of the Spirit, they may put all fear behind them and press forward with confidence, let us pray to the Lord:

Lord, hear our prayer.

Assisting minister: That, transformed in the Spirit, they may seek those things that are holy and just, let us pray to the Lord:
Lord, hear our prayer.

Assisting minister: That all who suffer persecution for Christ's name may find their strength in him, let us pray to the Lord:
Lord, hear our prayer.

Assisting minister: That those families and nations prevented from embracing the faith may be granted freedom to believe the Gospel, let us pray to the Lord:
Lord, hear our prayer.

Assisting minister: That we who are faced with the values of the world may remain faithful to the spirit of the Gospel, let us pray to the Lord:
Lord, hear our prayer.

Assisting minister: That the whole world, which the Father so loves, may attain in the Church complete spiritual freedom, let us pray to the Lord:
Lord, hear our prayer.

B

Assisting minister: That God may dispel darkness and be the light that shines in the hearts of our elect, let us pray to the Lord:
Lord, hear our prayer.

Assisting minister: That he may gently lead them to Christ, the light of the world, let us pray to the Lord:
Lord, hear our prayer.

Assisting minister: That our elect may open their hearts to God and acknowledge him as the source of light and the witness of truth, let us pray to the Lord:
Lord, hear our prayer.

Assisting minister: That he may heal them and preserve them from the unbelief of this world, let us pray to the Lord:
Lord, hear our prayer.

Assisting minister: That, saved by him who takes away the sin of the world, they may be freed from the contagion and forces of sin, let us pray to the Lord:
Lord, hear our prayer.

Assisting minister: That, enlightened by the Holy Spirit, they may never fail to profess the Good News of salvation and share it with others, let us pray to the Lord:
Lord, hear our prayer.

Assisting minister: That all of us, by the example of our lives, may become in Christ the light of the world, let us pray to the Lord:
Lord, hear our prayer.

Fourth Sunday of Lent, Year A

Assisting minister: That every inhabitant of the earth may acknowledge the true God, the Creator of all things, who bestows upon us the gift of Spirit and life, let us pray to the Lord:
Lord, hear our prayer.

Exorcism
After the intercessions, the rite continues with one of the following exorcisms.

A

The celebrant faces the elect and, with hands joined, says:

Father of mercy,
you led the man born blind
to the kingdom of light
through the gift of faith in your Son.

Free these elect
from the false values that surround and blind them.
Set them firmly in your truth,
children of the light for ever.

We ask this through Christ our Lord.
Amen.

Here, if this can be done conveniently, the celebrant lays hands on each one of the elect.

Then, with hands outstretched over all the elect, he continues:

Lord Jesus,
you are the true light that enlightens the world.
Through your Spirit of truth
free those who are enslaved by the father of lies.

Stir up the desire for good in these elect,
whom you have chosen for your sacraments.

Let them rejoice in your light, that they may see,
and, like the man born blind whose sight you restored,
let them prove to be staunch and fearless witnesses to the faith,
for you are Lord for ever and ever.
Amen.

B

The celebrant faces the elect and, with hands joined, says:

Lord God,
source of unfailing light,
by the death and resurrection of Christ
you have cast out the darkness of hatred and lies
and poured forth the light of truth and love
upon the human family.

Hear our prayers for these elect,
whom you have called to be your adopted children.

Enable them to pass from darkness to light
and, delivered from the prince of darkness,
to live always as children of the light.

We ask this through Christ our Lord.
Amen.

Here, if this can be done conveniently, the celebrant lays hands on each one of the elect.

Then, with hands outstretched over all the elect, he continues:

Lord Jesus,
at your own baptism
the heavens were opened
and you received the Holy Spirit
to empower you to proclaim the Good News to the poor
and restore sight to the blind.

Pour out the same Holy Spirit on these elect,
who long for your sacraments.
Guide them along the paths of right faith,
safe from error, doubt, and unbelief,
so that with eyes unsealed
they may come to see you face to face,
for you live and reign for ever and ever.
Amen.

An appropriate song may be sung, for example, Psalm 6, 25(26), 31(32), 37(38), 38(39), 39(40), 50(51), 115(116):1-9, 129(130), 138(139), or 141(142).

Fourth Sunday of Lent, Year A

Dismissal of the Elect

If the eucharist is to be celebrated, the elect are normally dismissed at this point by use of option A; if the elect are to stay for the celebration of the eucharist, option B is used; if the eucharist is not to be celebrated, the entire assembly is dismissed by use of option C.

A

The celebrant dismisses the elect in these or similar words.

Dear elect, go in peace,
and join us again at the next scrutiny.
May the Lord remain with you always.

Elect: **Amen.**

If for serious reasons the elect cannot leave and must remain with the baptised, they are to be instructed that though they are present at the eucharist, they cannot take part in it as the baptised do. They may be reminded of this by the celebrant in these or similar words.

Although you cannot yet participate fully in the Lord's eucharist, stay with us as a sign of our hope that all God's children will eat and drink with the Lord and work with his Spirit to re-create the face of the earth.

C

The celebrant dismisses those present, using these or similar words.

Go in peace,
and may the Lord remain with you always.

All: **Thanks be to God.**

An appropriate song may conclude the celebration.

FIFTH SUNDAY OF LENT A

Christ Breathes Into Us His Living Spirit

Today we open ourselves to Christ's life-giving Spirit. We pray for all people but especially for those who are to be given the new life of the Spirit in baptism this Easter.

The practice of covering crosses and images throughout the church from this Sunday may be observed, if the Conference of Bishops so decides. Crosses remain covered until the end of the celebration of the Lord's Passion on Good Friday, but images remain covered until the beginning of the Easter Vigil.

On this Sunday is celebrated the Third Scrutiny in preparation for the Baptism of the catechumens who are to be admitted to the Sacraments of Christian Initiation at the Easter Vigil, using the proper prayers and intercessions as given below, pp.285-9.

Entrance Antiphon Cf. Ps 42:1-2
Give me justice, O God,
and plead my cause against a nation that is faithless.
From the deceitful and cunning rescue me,
for you, O God, are my strength.

The Gloria in excelsis (Glory to God in the highest) is not said.

Collect
By your help, we beseech you, Lord our God,
may we walk eagerly in that same charity
with which, out of love for the world,
your Son handed himself over to death.
Through our Lord Jesus Christ, your Son,
who lives and reigns with you in the unity of the Holy Spirit,
one God, for ever and ever.
Amen.

FIRST READING
A reading from the prophet Ezekiel 37:12-14

The Lord says this: I am now going to open your graves; I mean to raise you from your graves, my people, and lead you back to the soil of Israel. And you will know that I am the Lord, when I open your graves and raise you from your graves, my people. And I shall put my spirit in you, and you will live, and I shall resettle

Fifth Sunday of Lent, Year A

you on your own soil; and you will know that I, the Lord, have said and done this – it is the Lord who speaks.

The word of the Lord.

Responsorial Psalm Ps 129. ℟ v.7
℟ **With the Lord there is mercy
and fullness of redemption.**

1 Out of the depths I cry to you, O Lord,
Lord, hear my voice!
O let your ears be attentive
to the voice of my pleading. ℟

2 If you, O Lord, should mark our guilt,
Lord, who would survive?
But with you is found forgiveness:
for this we revere you. ℟

3 My soul is waiting for the Lord,
I count on his word.
My soul is longing for the Lord
more than watchman for daybreak.
(Let the watchman count on daybreak
and Israel on the Lord.) ℟

4 Because with the Lord there is mercy
and fullness of redemption,
Israel indeed he will redeem
from all its iniquity. ℟

SECOND READING
A reading from the letter of St Paul to the Romans 8:8-11

People who are interested only in unspiritual things can never be pleasing to God. Your interests, however, are not in the unspiritual, but in the spiritual, since the Spirit of God has made his home in you. In fact, unless you possessed the Spirit of Christ you would not belong to him. Though your body may be dead it is because of sin, but if Christ is in you then your spirit is life itself because you have been justified; and if the Spirit of him who raised Jesus from the dead is living in you, then he who raised Jesus from the dead will give life to your own mortal bodies through his Spirit living in you.

The word of the Lord.

Gospel Acclamation Jn 11:25-26
    Glory and praise to you, O Christ!
    I am the resurrection and the life, says the Lord;
    who ever believes in me will never die.
    Glory and praise to you, O Christ!

GOSPEL
A reading from the holy Gospel according to John 11:1-45

There was a man named Lazarus who lived in the village of Bethany with the two sisters, Mary and Martha, and he was ill. – It was the same Mary, the sister of the sick man Lazarus, who anointed the Lord with ointment and wiped his feet with her hair. *The sisters sent this message to Jesus, 'Lord, the man you love is ill.' On receiving the message, Jesus said, 'This sickness will end not in death but in God's glory, and through it the Son of God will be glorified.' Jesus loved Martha and her sister and Lazarus, yet when he heard that Lazarus was ill he stayed where he was for two more days before saying to the disciples, 'Let us go to Judaea.'* The disciples said, 'Rabbi, it is not long since the Jews wanted to stone you; are you going back again?' Jesus replied:

'Are there not twelve hours in the day?
A man can walk in the daytime without stumbling
because he has the light of this world to see by;
but if he walks at night he stumbles,
because there is no light to guide him'.

He said that and then added, 'Our friend Lazarus is resting, I am going to wake him.' The disciples said to him 'Lord, if he is able to rest he is sure to get better.' The phrase Jesus used referred to the death of Lazarus, but they thought that by 'rest' he meant 'sleep', so Jesus put it plainly, 'Lazarus is dead, and for your sake I am glad I was not there because now you will believe. But let us go to him.' Then Thomas – known as the Twin - said to the other disciples, 'Let us go too, and die with him.'

On arriving, Jesus found that Lazarus had been in the tomb for four days already. Bethany is only about two miles from Jerusalem, and many Jews had come to Martha and Mary to sympathise with them over their brother. *When Martha heard that Jesus had come she went to meet him. Mary remained sitting in the house. Martha said to Jesus, 'If you had been here, my brother would not have died, but I know that, even now, whatever you ask of God, he will grant you.' 'Your brother' said Jesus to her 'will rise again.' Martha said, 'I know he will rise again at the resurrection on the last day.' Jesus said:

Fifth Sunday of Lent, Year A

'I am the resurrection and the life.
If anyone believes in me, even though he dies he will live,
and whoever lives and believes in me
will never die.
Do you believe this?'

'Yes Lord,' she said 'I believe that you are the Christ, the Son of God, the one who was to come into this world.'*
When she had said this, she went and called her sister Mary, saying in a low voice, 'The Master is here and wants to see you.' Hearing this, Mary got up quickly and went to him. Jesus had not yet come into the village; he was still at the place where Martha had met him. When the Jews who were in the house sympathising with Mary saw her get up so quickly and go out, they followed her, thinking that she was going to the tomb to weep there.

Mary went to Jesus, and as soon as she saw him she threw herself at his feet, saying, 'Lord if you had been here, my brother would not have died.' At the sight of her tears, and those of the Jews who followed her, *Jesus said in great distress, with a sigh that came straight from the heart, 'Where have you put him?' They said, 'Lord, come and see.' Jesus wept; and the Jews said, 'See how much he loved him!' But there were some who remarked, 'He opened the eyes of the blind man, could he not have prevented this man's death?' Still sighing, Jesus reached the tomb: it was a cave with a stone to close the opening. Jesus said, 'Take the stone away.' Martha said to him 'Lord by now he will smell; this is the fourth day.' Jesus replied 'Have I not told you that if you believe you will see the glory of God?' So they took away the stone. Then Jesus lifted up his eyes and said:

'Father, I thank you for hearing my prayer.
I knew indeed that you always hear me.
But I speak
for the sake of all these who stand round me,
so that they may believe it was you who sent me.'

When he had said this, he cried in a loud voice, 'Lazarus, here! Come out!' The dead man came out, his feet and hands bound with bands of stuff and a cloth round his face. Jesus said to them, 'Unbind him, let him go free.' Many of the Jews who had come to visit Mary and had seen what he did believed in him.

The Gospel of the Lord.*

Shorter Form, verses 3-7. 17. 20-27. 33-45. Read between

After the homily the Third Scrutiny of candidates for baptism may take place. The texts are given below pp.285-9.

If there is no Scrutiny, the Creed is said.

Prayer over the Offerings
Hear us, almighty God,
and, having instilled in your servants
the teachings of the Christian faith,
graciously purify them
by the working of this sacrifice.
Through Christ our Lord.
Amen.

Preface of Lazarus, p.26.

Communion Antiphon
Cf. Jn 11:26
Everyone who lives and believes in me
will not die for ever, says the Lord.

Prayer after Communion
We pray, almighty God,
that we may always be counted among the members of Christ,
in whose Body and Blood we have communion.
Who lives and reigns for ever and ever.
Amen.

Prayer over the People
Bless, O Lord, your people,
who long for the gift of your mercy,
and grant that what, at your prompting, they desire
they may receive by your generous gift.
Through Christ our Lord.
Amen.

Fifth Sunday of Lent, Year A

THIRD SCRUTINY

After the homily, the elect with their godparents come forward and stand before the celebrant.

The celebrant first addresses the assembly of the faithful, inviting them to pray in silence and to ask that the elect will be given a spirit of repentance, a sense of sin, and the true freedom of the children of God.

The celebrant then addresses the elect, inviting them also to pray in silence and suggesting that as a sign of their inner spirit of repentance they bow their heads or kneel; he concludes his remarks with the following or similar words.

Elect of God, bow your heads [kneel down] and pray.

The elect bow their heads or kneel, and all pray for some time in silence. After the period of silent prayer, the community and the elect stand for the intercessions.

Intercessions for the Elect

Either of the following formularies, options A or B, may be used for the intercessions for the elect and both the introduction and the intentions may be adapted to fit various circumstances. During the intercessions the godparents stand with their right hand on the shoulder of the elect.
[If it is decided that after the dismissal of the elect the usual general intercessions of the Mass are to be omitted and that the liturgy of the eucharist is to begin immediately, intentions for the Church and the whole world are to be added to the following intentions for the elect.]

Celebrant: Let us pray for these elect whom God has chosen. May the grace of the sacraments conform them to Christ in his passion and resurrection and enable them to triumph over the bitter fate of death.

A

Assisting minister: That faith may strengthen them against worldly deceits of every kind, let us pray to the Lord:
Lord, hear our prayer.

Assisting minister: That they may always thank God, who has chosen to rescue them from their ignorance of eternal life and to set them on the way of salvation, let us pray to the Lord:
Lord, hear our prayer.

Assisting minister: That the example and prayers of catechumens who have shed their blood for Christ may encourage these elect in their hope of eternal life, let us pray to the Lord:
Lord, hear our prayer.

Assisting minister: That they may all have a horror of sin, which distorts life, let us pray to the Lord:
Lord, hear our prayer.

Assisting minister: That those who are saddened by the death of family or friends may find comfort in Christ, let us pray to the Lord:
Lord, hear our prayer.

Assisting minister: That we too at Easter may again be confirmed in our hope of rising to life with Christ, let us pray to the Lord:
Lord, hear our prayer.

Assisting minister: That the whole world, which God has created in love, may flower in faith and charity and so receive new life, let us pray to the Lord:
Lord, hear our prayer.

B

Assisting minister: That these elect may be given the faith to acknowledge Christ as the resurrection and the life, we pray to the Lord:
Lord, hear our prayer.

Assisting minister: That they may be freed from sin and grow in the holiness that leads to eternal life, we pray to the Lord:
Lord, hear our prayer.

Assisting minister: That liberated by repentance from the shackles of sin they may become like Christ by baptism, dead to sin and alive for ever in God's sight, we pray to the Lord:
Lord, hear our prayer.

Assisting minister: That they may be filled with the hope of the life-giving Spirit and prepare themselves thoroughly for their birth to new life, we pray to the Lord:
Lord, hear our prayer.

Assisting minister: That the eucharistic food, which they are soon to receive, may make them one with Christ, the source of life and of resurrection, we pray to the Lord:
Lord, hear our prayer.

Assisting minister: That all of us may walk in newness of life and show to the world the power of the risen Christ, we pray to the Lord:
Lord, hear our prayer.

Assisting minister: That all the world may find Christ and acknowledge in him the promises of eternal life, we pray to the Lord:
Lord, hear our prayer.

Exorcism
After the intercessions, the rite continues with one of the following exorcisms.

A

The celebrant faces the elect and, with hands joined, says:

Father of life and God not of the dead but of the living,
you sent your Son to proclaim life,
to snatch us from the realm of death,
and to lead us to the resurrection.

Free these elect
from the death-dealing power of the spirit of evil,
so that they may bear witness
to their new life in the risen Christ,
for he lives and reigns for ever and ever.
Amen.

Here, if this can be done conveniently, the celebrant lays hands on each one of the elect.

Then, with hands outstretched over all the elect, he continues:

Lord Jesus,
by raising Lazarus from the dead
you showed that you came that we might have life
and have it more abundantly.

Free from the grasp of death
those who await your life-giving sacraments
and deliver them from the spirit of corruption.

Through your Spirit, who gives life,
fill them with faith, hope, and charity,

that they may live with you always
in the glory of your resurrection,
for you are Lord for ever and ever.
Amen.

B

The celebrant faces the elect and, with hands joined, says:

Father,
source of all life,
in giving life to the living you seek out the image of your glory
and in raising the dead you reveal your unbounded power.

Rescue these elect from the tyranny of death,
for they long for new life through baptism.

Free them from the slavery of Satan,
the source of sin and death,
who seeks to corrupt the world you created
and saw to be good.

Place them under the reign of your beloved Son,
that they may share in the power of his resurrection
and give witness to your glory before all.

We ask this through Christ our Lord.
Amen.

Here, if this can be done conveniently, the celebrant lays hands on each one of the elect.

Then, with hands outstretched over all the elect, he continues:

Lord Jesus Christ,
you commanded Lazarus to step forth alive from his tomb
and by your own resurrection freed all people from death.

We pray for these your servants,
who eagerly approach the waters of new birth
and hunger for the banquet of life.

Do not let the power of death hold them back,
for, by their faith,
they will share in the triumph of your resurrection,
for you live and reign for ever and ever.
Amen.

Fifth Sunday of Lent, Year A

An appropriate song may be sung, for example, Psalm 6, 25(26), 31(32), 37(38), 38(39), 39(40), 50(51), 115(116):1-9, 129(130), 138(139), or 141(142).

Dismissal of the Elect
If the eucharist is to be celebrated, the elect are normally dismissed at this point by use of option A; if the elect are to stay for the celebration of the eucharist, option B is used; if the eucharist is not to be celebrated, the entire assembly is dismissed by use of option C.

A

The celebrant dismisses the elect in these or similar words.

Dear elect, go in peace,
and may the Lord remain with you always.

Elect: **Amen.**

B

If for serious reasons the elect cannot leave and must remain with the baptised, they are to be instructed that though they are present at the eucharist, they cannot take part in it as the baptised do. They may be reminded of this by the celebrant in these or similar words.

Although you cannot yet participate fully in the Lord's eucharist, stay with us as a sign of our hope that all God's children will eat and drink with the Lord and work with his Spirit to re-create the face of the earth.

C

The celebrant dismisses those present, using these or similar words.

Go in peace,
and may the Lord remain with you always.

All: **Thanks be to God.**

An appropriate song may conclude the celebration.

HOLY WEEK

PALM SUNDAY OF THE PASSION OF THE LORD

A, B, C

On this day the Church recalls the entrance of Christ the Lord into Jerusalem to accomplish his Paschal Mystery. Accordingly, the memorial of this entrance of the Lord takes place at all Masses, by means of the Procession or the Solemn Entrance before the principal Mass or the Simple Entrance before other Masses. The Solemn Entrance, but not the Procession, may be repeated before other Masses that are usually celebrated with a large gathering of people.

It is desirable that, where neither the Procession nor the Solemn Entrance can take place, there be a sacred celebration of the Word of God on the messianic entrance and on the Passion of the Lord, either on Saturday evening or on Sunday at a convenient time.

THE COMMEMORATION OF THE LORD'S ENTRANCE INTO JERUSALEM

First Form: The Procession

At an appropriate hour, a gathering takes place at a smaller church or other suitable place other than inside the church to which the procession will go. The faithful hold branches in their hands.

Wearing the red sacred vestments as for Mass, the Priest and the Deacon, accompanied by other ministers, approach the place where the people are gathered. Instead of the chasuble, the Priest may wear a cope, which he leaves aside when the procession is over, and puts on a chasuble.

Meanwhile, the following antiphon or another appropriate chant is sung.

Palm Sunday of the Passion of the Lord

Ant. *Mt 21:9*

Ho-san-na to the Son of Da-vid; bless-ed is he who comes in the name of the Lord, the King of Is-ra-el. Ho-san-na in the high-est.

or

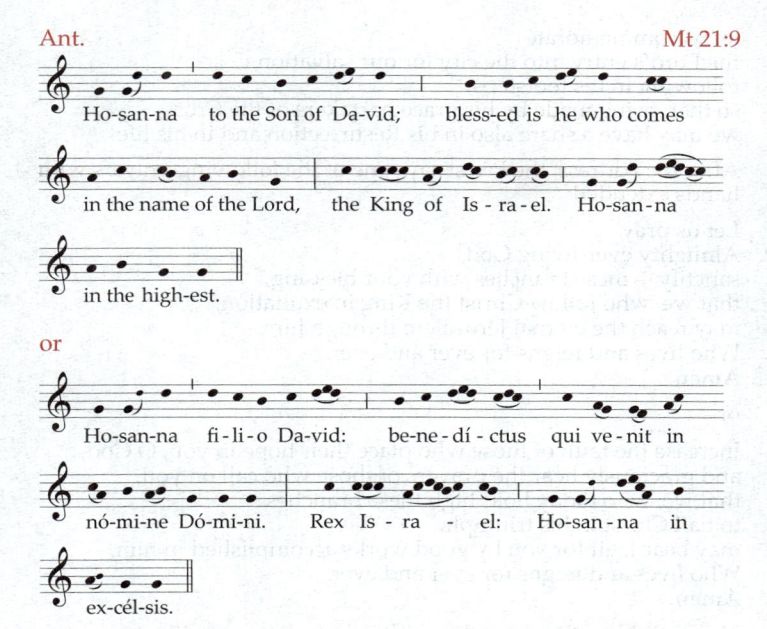

Ho-san-na fi-li-o David: be-ne-dí-ctus qui ve-nit in nó-mi-ne Dó-mi-ni. Rex Is-ra-el: Ho-san-na in ex-cél-sis.

After this, the Priest and people sign themselves, while the Priest says: In the name of the Father, and of the Son, and of the Holy Spirit. *Then he greets the people in the usual way. A brief address is given, in which the faithful are invited to participate actively and consciously in the celebration of this day, in these or similar words:*

Dear brethren (brothers and sisters),
since the beginning of Lent until now
we have prepared our hearts by penance and charitable works.
Today we gather together to herald with the whole Church
the beginning of the celebration
of our Lord's Paschal Mystery,
that is to say, of his Passion and Resurrection.
For it was to accomplish this mystery
that he entered his own city of Jerusalem.
Therefore, with all faith and devotion,

Palm Sunday of the Passion of the Lord

let us commemorate
the Lord's entry into the city for our salvation,
following in his footsteps,
so that, being made by his grace partakers of the Cross,
we may have a share also in his Resurrection and in his life.

After the address, the Priest says one of the following prayers with hands extended:

Let us pray.
Almighty ever-living God,
sanctify ✚ these branches with your blessing,
that we, who follow Christ the King in exultation,
may reach the eternal Jerusalem through him.
Who lives and reigns for ever and ever.
Amen.

or

Increase the faith of those who place their hope in you, O God,
and graciously hear the prayers of those who call on you,
that we, who today hold high these branches
to hail Christ in his triumph,
may bear fruit for you by good works accomplished in him.
Who lives and reigns for ever and ever.
Amen.

He sprinkles the branches with holy water without saying anything.

Then a Deacon or, if there is no Deacon, a Priest, proclaims in the usual way the Gospel concerning the Lord's entrance, Blessed is he who comes in the name of the Lord, *according to one of the four Gospels. If appropriate, incense may be used.*

Year A

✚ A reading from the holy Gospel according to Matthew.   21:1-11

1   When they drew near to Jerusalem
    and came to Bethphage, to the Mount of Olives,
    Jesus sent two disciples, saying to them,

2   'Go into the village opposite you,
    and immediately you will find an ass tied,
    and a colt with her; untie them and bring them to me.

Palm Sunday of the Passion of the Lord 293

3   If anyone says anything to you, you shall say,
    "The Lord has need of them,"
    and he will send them immediately'.

4   This took place to fulfil
    what was spoken by the prophet, saying,

5   'Tell the daughter of Sion,
    Behold, your king is coming to you,
    humble, and mounted on an ass,
    and on a colt, the foal of an ass'.

6   The disciples went and did as Jesus had directed them;

7   they brought the ass and the colt,
    and put their garments on them, and he sat thereon.

8   Most of the crowd spread their garments on the road,
    and others cut branches from the trees
    and spread them on the road.

9   And the crowds that went before him
    and that followed him shouted,
    'Hosanna to the Son of David!
    Blessed is he who comes in the name of the Lord!
    Hosanna in the highest!'

10 And when he entered Jerusalem
    all the city was stirred, saying, 'Who is this?'

11 And the crowds said,
    'This is the prophet Jesus from Nazareth of Galilee'.

    The Gospel of the Lord.

Year B

✚ A reading from the holy Gospel according to Mark.   11:1-10

1   When they drew near to Jerusalem,
    to Bethphage and Bethany
    at the Mount of Olives,
    Jesus sent two of his disciples, and said to them,

2   'Go into the village opposite you,
    and immediately as you enter it
    you will find a colt tied, on which no one has ever sat;
    untie it and bring it.

3 If anyone says to you,
 "Why are you doing this?" say,
 "The Lord has need of it
 and will send it back here immediately"'.

4 And they went away,
 and found a colt tied at the door out in the open street;
 and they untied it.

5 And those who stood there said to them,
 'What are you doing, untying the colt?'

6 And they told them what Jesus had said;
 and they let them go.

7 And they brought the colt to Jesus
 and threw their garments on it;
 and he sat upon it.

8 And many spread their garments on the road,
 and others spread leafy branches
 which they had cut from the fields.

9 And those who went before
 and those who followed cried out,
 'Hosanna!
 Blessed is he who comes in the name of the Lord!

10 Blessed is the kingdom of our father David that is coming!
 Hosanna in the highest!'

The Gospel of the Lord.

or

✝ A reading from the holy Gospel according to John.   12:12-16

12 A great crowd who had come to the feast
 heard that Jesus was coming to Jerusalem.

13 So they took branches of palm trees
 and went out to meet him, crying,
 'Hosanna!
 Blessed is he who comes in the name of the Lord,
 even *the* king of Israel!'

14 And Jesus found a young ass and sat upon it; as is written:

15 'Fear not, daughter Zion;
 behold, your king is coming,
 sitting on an ass's colt!'

16 His disciples did not understand this at first;
    but when Jesus was glorified,
    then they remembered that this had been written of him
    and had been done to him.

The Gospel of the Lord.

Year C

☩ A reading from the holy Gospel according to Luke.   19:28-40

28 Jesus went on ahead, going up to Jerusalem.

29 When he drew near to Bethphage and Bethany
    at the place called the mount that is called Olivet,
    he sent two disciples,

30 saying, 'Go into the village opposite,
    where on entering you will find a colt tied,
    on which no one has ever yet sat;
    untie it and bring it here.

31 If anyone asks you,
    "Why are you untying it?"
    you shall say this,
    "The Lord has need of it"'.

32 So those who were sent
    went away and found it as he had told them.

33 And as they were untying the colt,
    its owners said to them,
    'Why are you untying the colt?'

34 And they said,
    'The Lord has need of it'.

35 And they brought it to Jesus,
    and throwing their garments on the colt
    they set Jesus upon it.

36 And as he rode along,
    they spread their garments on the road.

37 As he was drawing near,
    at the descent of the Mount of Olives,
    the whole multitude of the disciples
    began to rejoice and praise God with a loud voice
    for all the mighty works that they had seen,

38 saying,
> 'Blessed is the King who comes in the name of the Lord!
39 Peace in heaven and glory in the highest!'
> And some of the Pharisees in the multitude said to him,
> 'Teacher, rebuke your disciples'.
40 He answered,
> 'I tell you, if these were silent,
> the very stones would cry out'.

The Gospel of the Lord.

After the Gospel, a brief homily may be given. Then, to begin the Procession, an invitation may be given by a Priest or a Deacon or a lay minister, in these or similar words (a musical setting may be found on p.598):

Dear brethren (brothers and sisters),
like the crowds who acclaimed Jesus in Jerusalem,
let us go forth in peace.

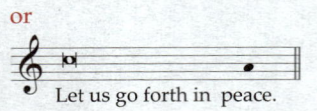

or

Let us go forth in peace.

In this latter case, all respond:

In the name of Christ. A-men.

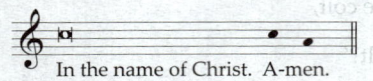

The Procession to the church where Mass will be celebrated then sets off in the usual way. If incense is used, the thurifer goes first, carrying a thurible with burning incense, then an acolyte or another minister, carrying a cross decorated with palm branches according to local custom, between two ministers with lighted candles. Then follow the Deacon carrying the Book of the Gospels, the Priest with the ministers, and, after them, all the faithful carrying branches.

As the Procession moves forward, the following or other suitable chants in honour of Christ the King are sung by the choir and people.

Antiphon 1
The children of the Hebrews, carrying olive branches,
went to meet the Lord, crying out and saying:
Hosanna in the highest.

If appropriate, this antiphon is repeated between the strophes of
the following Psalm.

Psalm 23
The Lord's is the earth and its fullness,*
the world, and those who dwell in it.
It is he who set it on the seas;*
on the rivers he made it firm.
(The antiphon is repeated.)
Who shall climb the mountain of the Lord?*
The clean of hands and pure of heart,
whose soul is not set on vain things, †
who has not sworn deceitful words.*
(The antiphon is repeated.)
Blessings from the Lord shall he receive,*
and right reward from the God who saves him.
Such are the people who seek him,*
who seek the face of the God of Jacob.
(The antiphon is repeated.)
O gates, lift high your heads, †
grow higher, ancient doors.*
Let him enter, the king of glory!
Who is this king of glory?*
The Lord, the mighty, the valiant;
the Lord, the valiant in war.
(The antiphon is repeated.)
O gates, lift high your heads; †
grow higher, ancient doors.*
Let him enter, the king of glory!
Who is this king of glory?*
He, the LORD of hosts,
he is the king of glory.
(The antiphon is repeated.)

Antiphon 2
The children of the Hebrews spread their garments on the road,
crying out and saying: Hosanna to the Son of David;
blesssed is he who comes in the name of the Lord.
If appropriate, this antiphon is repeated between the strophes of
the following Psalm.

Psalm 46
All peoples, clap your hands.*
Cry to God with shouts of joy!

For the Lord, the Most high, is awesome,*
the great king over all the earth.
(The antiphon is repeated.)
He humbles peoples under us*
and nations under our feet.
Our heritage he chose for us,*
the pride of Jacob whom he loves.
God goes up with shouts of joy.*
The Lord goes up with trumpet blast.
(The antiphon is repeated.)
Sing praise for God; sing praise!*
Sing praise to our king; sing praise!
God is king of all earth.*
Sing praise with all your skill.
(The antiphon is repeated.)
God reigns over the nations.*
God sits upon his holy throne.
The princes of the peoples are assembled
with the people of the God of Abraham. †
The rulers of the earth belong to God,*
who is greatly exalted.
(The antiphon is repeated.)

Hymn to Christ the King

Chorus:
Glory and honour and praise be to you, Christ, King and Redeemer,
to whom young children cried out loving Hosannas with joy.
All repeat: **Glory and honour ...**

Chorus:
Israel's King are you, King David's magnificent offspring;
you are the ruler who come blest in the name of the Lord.
All repeat: **Glory and honour ...**

Chorus:
Heavenly hosts on high unite in singing your praises;
men and women on earth and all creation join in.
All repeat: **Glory and honour ...**

Chorus:
Bearing branches of palm, Hebrews came crowding to greet you;
see how with prayers and hymns we come to pay you our vows.
All repeat: **Glory and honour ...**

Chorus:
They offered gifts of praise to you, so near to your Passion;
see how we sing this song now to you reigning on high.
All repeat: **Glory and honour . . .**

Chorus:
Those you were pleased to accept; now accept our gifts of devotion,
good and merciful King, lover of all that is good.
All repeat: **Glory and honour . . .**

As the procession enters the church, there is sung the following responsory or another chant, which should speak of the Lord's entrance.

℣ As the Lord entered the holy city, the children of the Hebrews proclaimed the resurrection of life.

℟ **Waving their branches of palm, they cried: Hosanna in the Highest.**

℣ When the people heard that Jesus was coming to Jerusalem, they went out to meet him.*

℟ **Waving their branches . . .**

When the Priest arrives at the altar, he venerates it and, if appropriate, incenses it. Then he goes to the chair, where he puts aside the cope, if he has worn one, and puts on the chasuble. Omitting the other Introductory Rites of the Mass and, if appropriate, the Kyrie (Lord, have mercy), he says the Collect of the Mass, and then continues the Mass in the usual way.

Second Form: The Solemn Entrance

When a procession outside the church cannot take place, the entrance of the Lord is celebrated inside the church by means of a Solemn Entrance before the principal Mass.

Holding branches in their hands, the faithful gather either outside, in front of the church door, or inside the church itself. The Priest and ministers and a representative group of the faithful go to a suitable place in the church outside the sanctuary, where at least the greater part of the faithful can see the rite.

While the Priest approaches the appointed place, the antiphon Hosanna or another appropriate chant is sung. Then the blessing of branches and the proclamation of the Gospel of the Lord's entrance into Jerusalem take place as above. After the Gospel, the Priest processes solemnly with the ministers and the representative group of the faithful through the church to the sanctuary, while the responsory As the Lord entered (see above) or another appropriate chant is sung.

Arriving at the altar, the Priest venerates it. He then goes to the chair and, omitting the Introductory Rites of the Mass and, if appropriate, the Kyrie (Lord, have mercy), he says the Collect of the Mass, and then continues the Mass in the usual way.

Third Form: The Simple Entrance

At all other Masses of this Sunday at which the Solemn Entrance is not held, the memorial of the Lord's entrance into Jerusalem takes place by means of a Simple Entrance.

While the Priest proceeds to the altar, the Entrance Antiphon with its Psalm or another chant on the same theme is sung. Arriving at the altar, the Priest venerates it and goes to the chair. After the Sign of the Cross, he greets the people and continues the Mass in the usual way.

At other Masses, in which singing at the entrance cannot take place, the Priest, as soon as he has arrived at the altar and venerated it, greets the people, reads the Entrance Antiphon, and continues the Mass in the usual way.

Entrance Antiphon   Cf. Jn 12:1. 12-13; Ps 23:9-10
Six days before the Passover,
when the Lord came into the city of Jerusalem,
the children ran to meet him;
in their hands they carried palm branches
and with a loud voice cried out:
* Hosanna in the highest!

Blessed are you, who have come in your abundant mercy!
O gates, lift high your heads;
grow higher, ancient doors.
Let him enter, the king of glory!
Who is this king of glory?
He, the Lord of hosts, he is the king of glory.
* Hosanna in the highest!

Blessed are you, who have come in your abundant mercy!

At the Mass

Collect
Almighty ever-living God,
who as an example of humility for the human race to follow
caused our Saviour to take flesh and submit to the Cross,
graciously grant that we may heed his lesson of patient suffering
and so merit a share in his Resurrection.
Who lives and reigns with you in the unity of the Holy Spirit,
one God, for ever and ever.
Amen.

The narrative of the Lord's Passion is read without candles and without incense, with no greeting or signing of the book. It is read by a Deacon or, if there is no Deacon, by a Priest. It may also be read by readers, with the part of Christ, if possible, reserved to a Priest.

    Deacons, but not others, ask for the blessing of the Priest before singing the Passion, as at other times before the Gospel.

After the narrative of the Passion, a brief homily should take place, if appropriate. A period of silence may also be observed.
The Creed is said, and the Universal Prayer takes place.

FIRST READING

A reading from the prophet Isaiah   50:4-7

The Lord has given me
a disciple's tongue.
So that I may know how to reply to the wearied
he provides me with speech.
Each morning he wakes me to hear,
to listen like a disciple.
The Lord has opened my ear.
For my part, I made no resistance,
neither did I turn away.
I offered my back to those who struck me,
my cheeks to those who tore at my beard;
I did not cover my face
against insult and spittle.
The Lord comes to my help,
so that I am untouched by the insults.

So, too, I set my face like flint;
I know I shall not be shamed.

    The word of the Lord.

Responsorial Psalm　　　　　　　　Ps 21:8-9. 17-20. 23-24. ℟ v.2

    ℟ **My God, my God, why have you forsaken me?**

1. All who see me deride me.
   They curl their lips, they toss their heads.
   'He trusted in the Lord, let him save him;
   let him release him if this is his friend.' ℟

2. Many dogs have surrounded me,
   a band of the wicked beset me.
   They tear holes in my hands and my feet.
   I can count every one of my bones. ℟

3. They divide my clothing among them.
   They cast lots for my robe.
   O Lord, do not leave me alone,
   my strength, make haste to help me! ℟

4. I will tell of your name to my brethren
   and praise you where they are assembled.
   'You who fear the Lord give him praise;
   all sons of Jacob, give him glory.
   Revere him, Israel's sons.' ℟

SECOND READING

A reading from the letter of St Paul to the Philippians　　　2:6-11

His state was divine,
yet Christ Jesus did not cling
to his equality with God
but emptied himself
to assume the condition of a slave,
and became as men are,
and being as all men are,
he was humbler yet,
even to accepting death,
death on a cross.
But God raised him high
and gave him the name
which is above all other names

so that all beings
in the heavens, on earth and in the underworld,
should bend the knee at the name of Jesus
and that every tongue should acclaim
Jesus Christ as Lord,
to the glory of God the Father.

The word of the Lord.

Gospel Acclamation Phil 2:8-9
Praise to you, O Christ, king of eternal glory:
Christ was humbler yet,
even to accepting death, death on a cross.
But God raised him high
and gave him the name which is above all names.
Praise to you, O Christ, king of eternal glory.

GOSPEL

Year A

N Narrator. J Jesus. O Other single speaker. C Crowd, or more than one other speaker.

The passion of our Lord Jesus Christ according
to Matthew 26:14 – 27:66

N One of the Twelve, the man called Judas Iscariot, went to the chief priests and said:
O What are you prepared to give me if I hand him over to you?
N They paid him thirty silver pieces, and from that moment he looked for an opportunity to betray him.
Now on the first day of Unleavened Bread the disciples came to Jesus to say,
C Where do you want us to make the preparations for you to eat the passover?
N He replied:
J Go to so-and-so in the city and say to him, 'The Master says: My time is near. It is at your house that I am keeping Passover with my disciples'.
N The disciples did what Jesus told them and prepared the Passover. When the evening came he was at table with the twelve disciples. And while they were eating he said:
J I tell you solemnly, one of you is about to betray me.
N They were greatly distressed and started asking him in turn,

C Not I, Lord, surely?
N He answered:
J Someone who has dipped his hand into the dish with me, will betray me. The Son of Man is going to his fate, as the scriptures say he will, but alas for that man by whom the Son of Man is betrayed! Better for that man if he had never been born!
N Judas, who was to betray him, asked in his turn,
O Not I, Rabbi, surely?
N Jesus answered:
J They are your own words.
N Now as they were eating, Jesus took some bread, and when he had said the blessing he broke it and gave it to the disciples and said:
J Take it and eat; this is my body.
N Then he took a cup, and when he had returned thanks he gave it to them saying:
J Drink all of you from this, for this is my blood, the blood of the covenant, which is to be poured out for many for the forgiveness of sins. From now on, I tell you, I shall not drink wine until the day I drink the new wine with you in the kingdom of my Father.
N After psalms had been sung they left for the Mount of Olives. Then Jesus said to them,
J You will all lose faith in me this night, for the scripture says: I shall strike the shepherd and the sheep of the flock will be scattered. But after my resurrection I shall go before you to Galilee.
N At this, Peter said:
O Though all lose faith in you, I will never lose faith.
N Jesus answered him,
J I tell you solemnly, this very night, before the cock crows, you will have disowned me three times.
N Peter said to him,
O Even if I have to die with you, I will never disown you.
N And all the disciples said the same. Then Jesus came with them to a small estate called Gethsemane; and he said to his disciples,
J *Stay here while I go over there to pray.*
N He took Peter and the two sons of Zebedee with him. And sadness came over him, and great distress. Then he said to them:
J My soul is sorrowful to the point of death. Wait here and keep awake with me.

N And going on a little further he fell on his face and prayed:
J My Father, if it is possible let this cup pass me by. Nevertheless, let it be as you, not I, would have it.
N He came back to the disciples and found them sleeping, and he said to Peter:
J So you had not the strength to keep awake with me one hour? You should be awake, and praying not to be put to the test. The spirit is willing, but the flesh is weak.
N Again, a second time, he went away and prayed:
J My father, if this cup cannot pass by without my drinking it, your will be done!
N And he came again back and found them sleeping, their eyes were so heavy. Leaving them there, he went away again and prayed for the third time, repeating the same words. Then he came back to the disciples and said to them,
J You can sleep on now and take your rest. Now the hour has come when the Son of Man is to be betrayed into the hands of sinners. Get up! Let us go! My betrayer is already close at hand.
N He was still speaking when Judas, one of the Twelve, appeared, and with him a large number of men armed with swords and clubs, sent by the chief priests and elders of the people. Now the traitor had arranged a sign with them. He had said:
O 'The one I kiss, he is the man. Take him in charge.'
N So he went straight up to Jesus and said:
O Greetings, Rabbi,
N and kissed him. Jesus said to him,
J My friend, do what you are here for.
N Then they came forward, seized Jesus and took him in charge. At that, one of the followers of Jesus grasped his sword and drew it; he struck out at the high priest's servant, and cut off his ear. Jesus then said:
J Put your sword back, for all who draw the sword will die by the sword. Or do you think that I cannot appeal to my Father who would promptly send more than twelve legions of angels to my defence? But then, how would the scriptures be fulfilled that say this is the way it must be?
N It was at this time that Jesus said to the crowds:
J Am I a brigand, that you had to set out to capture me with swords and clubs? I sat teaching in the Temple day after day and you never laid hands on me.
N Now all this happened to fulfil the prophecies in scripture. Then all the disciples deserted him and ran away.

> The men who had arrested Jesus led him off to Caiaphas the high priest, where the scribes and the elders were assembled. Peter followed him at a distance, and when he reached the high priest's palace, he went in and sat down with the attendants to see what the end would be.
>
> The chief priests and the whole Sanhedrin were looking for evidence against Jesus, however false, on which they might pass the death-sentence. But they could not find any, though several lying witnesses came forward. Eventually two stepped forward and made a statement,

O This man said: 'I have power to destroy the Temple of God and in three days build it up'.

N The high priest then stood up and said to him:

O Have you no answer to that? What is this evidence these men are bringing against you?

N But Jesus was silent. And the high priest said to him:

O I put you on oath by the living God to tell us if you are the Christ, the Son of God.

N Jesus answered:

J The words are your own. Moreover, I tell you that from this time onward you will see the Son of Man seated at the right hand of the Power and coming on the clouds of heaven.

N At this, the high priest tore his clothes and said:

O He has blasphemed. What need of witnesses have we now? There! You have just heard the blasphemy. What is your opinion?

N They answered:

C He deserves to die.

N Then they spat in his face and hit him with their fists; others said as they struck him:

C Play the prophet, Christ! Who hit you then?

N Meanwhile Peter was sitting outside in the courtyard, and a servant-girl came up to him and said:

O You too were with Jesus the Galilean.

N But he denied it in front of them all, saying:

O I do not know what you are talking about.

N When he went out to the gateway another servant-girl saw him and said to the people there:

O This man was with Jesus the Nazarene.

N And again, with an oath, he denied it,

O I do not know the man.

N A little later the bystanders came up and said to Peter:

C You are one of them for sure! Why, your accent gives you away.

N Then he started calling down curses on himself and swearing:
O I do not know the man.
N At that moment the cock crew, and Peter remembered what Jesus had said, 'Before the cock crows you will have disowned me three times.' And he went outside and wept bitterly.

When morning came, all the chief priests and the elders of the people met in council to bring about the death of Jesus. They had him bound, and led him away to hand him over to Pilate, the governor. When he found that Jesus had been condemned, Judas his betrayer was filled with remorse and took the thirty pieces of silver back to the chief priests and elders, saying:
O I have sinned. I have betrayed innocent blood.
N They replied:
C What is that to us? That is your concern.
N And flinging down the silver pieces in the sanctuary he made off, and went and hanged himself. The chief priests picked up the silver pieces and said:
C It is against the Law to put this into the treasury; it is blood money.
N So they discussed the matter and bought the potter's field with it as a graveyard for foreigners, and this is why the field is called the Field of Blood today. The words of the prophet Jeremiah were then fulfilled: And they took the thirty silver pieces, the sum at which the precious One was priced by children of Israel, and they gave them for the potter's field, just as the Lord directed me.

Jesus, then, was brought before the governor, and the governor put to him this question:
O Are you the king of the Jews?
N Jesus replied:
J It is you who say it.
N But when he was accused by the chief priests and the elders he refused to answer at all. Pilate then said to him:
O Do you not hear how many charges they have brought against you?
N But to the governor's complete amazement, he offered no reply to any of the charges.

At festival time it was the governor's practice to release a prisoner for the people, anyone they chose. Now there was at that time a notorious prisoner whose name was Barabbas. So when the crowd gathered, Pilate said to them,
O Which do you want me to release for you: Barabbas or Jesus who is called Christ?

N For Pilate knew it was out of jealousy that they had handed him over. Now as he was seated in the chair of judgement, his wife sent him a message,

O Have nothing to do with that man; I have been upset all day by a dream I had about him.

N The chief priests and the elders, however, had persuaded the crowd to demand the release of Barabbas and the execution of Jesus. So when the governor spoke and asked them:

O Which of the two do you want me to release for you?

N They said:

C Barabbas.

N Pilate said to them:

O What am I to do with Jesus who is called Christ?

N They all said:

C Let him be crucified!

N Pilate asked:

O Why? What harm has he done?

N But they shouted all the louder,

C Let him be crucified!

N Then Pilate saw that he was making no impression, that in fact a riot was imminent. So he took some water, washed his hands in front of the crowd and said:

O I am innocent of this man's blood. It is your concern.

N And the people, to a man, shouted back:

C His blood be on us and on our children.

N Then he released Barabbas for them. He ordered Jesus to be first scourged and then handed over to be crucified.

The governor's soldiers took Jesus with them into the Praetorium and collected the whole cohort round him. Then they stripped him and made him wear a scarlet cloak, and having twisted some thorns into a crown they put this on his head and placed a reed in his right hand. To make fun of him they knelt to him saying:

C Hail, king of the Jews!

N And they spat on him and took the reed and struck him on the head with it. And when they had finished making fun of him, they took off the cloak and dressed him in his own clothes and led him away to crucify him.

On their way out, they came across a man from Cyrene, Simon by name, and enlisted him to carry his cross. When they had reached a place called Golgotha, that is, the place of the skull, they gave him wine to drink. When they had finished crucifying him they shared out his clothing by casting lots, and

Palm Sunday of the Passion of the Lord

then sat down and stayed there keeping guard over him. Above his head was placed the charge against him; it read: 'This is Jesus, the King of the Jews'. At the same time two robbers were crucified with him, one on the right and one on the left. The passers-by jeered at him; they shook their heads and said:

C So you would destroy the Temple and rebuild it in three days! Then save yourself! If you are God's son, come down from the cross!

N The chief priests with the scribes and elders mocked him in the same way, saying:

C He saved others; he cannot save himself. He is the King of Israel; let him come down from the cross now, and we will believe in him. He put his trust in God; now let God rescue him if he wants him. For he did say, 'I am the son of God'.

N Even the robbers who were crucified with him taunted him in the same way.

From the sixth hour there was darkness over all the land until the ninth hour. And about the ninth hour, Jesus cried out in a loud voice:

J Eli, Eli, lama sabachthani?

N That is: 'My God, my God, why have you deserted me?' When some of those who stood there heard this, they said:

C The man is calling on Elijah,

N and one of them quickly ran to get a sponge which he dipped in vinegar and, putting it on a reed, gave it him to drink. The rest of them said:

C Wait! See if Elijah will come to save him.

N But Jesus, again crying out in a loud voice, yielded up his spirit.

All kneel and pause a moment.

N At that, the veil of the Temple was torn in two from top to bottom; the earth quaked; the rocks were split; the tombs opened and the bodies of many holy men rose from the dead, and these, after his resurrection, came out of the tombs, entered the Holy City and appeared to a number of people.

Meanwhile the centurion, together with the others guarding Jesus, had seen the earthquake and all that was taking place, and they were terrified and said:

C In truth this was a son of God.

N And many women were there, watching from a distance, the same women who had followed Jesus from Galilee and looked after him. Among them were Mary of Magdala, Mary the mother of James and Joseph, and the mother of Zebedee's sons.

When it was evening, there came a rich man of Arimathaea called Joseph, who had himself become a disciple of Jesus. This man went to Pilate and asked for the body of Jesus. Pilate thereupon ordered it to be handed over. So Joseph took the body, wrapped it in a clean shroud and put it in his own new tomb which he had hewn out of the rock. He then rolled a large stone across the entrance of the tomb and went away. Now Mary of Magdala and the other Mary were there, sitting opposite the sepulchre.

Next day, that is, when Preparation Day was over, the chief priests and the Pharisees went in a body to Pilate and said to him,

C Your Excellency, we recall that this impostor said, while he was still alive, 'After three days I shall rise again'. Therefore give the order to have the sepulchre kept secure until the third day, for fear his disciples come and steal him away and tell the people, 'He has risen from the dead'. This last piece of fraud would be worse than what went before.

N Pilate said to them:

O You may have your guards. Go and make all as secure as you know how.

N So they went and made the sepulchre secure, putting seals on the stone and mounting a guard.

Shorter form

The passion of our Lord Jesus Christ
according to Matthew   27:11-54

Jesus was brought before Pontius Pilate, the governor, and the governor put to him this question, 'Are you the king of the Jews?' Jesus replied, 'It is you who say it.' But when he was accused by the chief priests and the elders he refused to answer at all. Pilate then said to him, 'Do you not hear how many charges they have brought against you?' But to the governor's complete amazement, he offered no reply to any of the charges.

At festival time it was the governor's practice to release a prisoner for the people, anyone they chose. Now there was at that *time a notorious prisoner* whose name was Barabbas. So when the crowd gathered, Pilate said to them, 'Which do you want me to release for you: Barabbas, or Jesus who is called Christ?' For Pilate knew it was out of jealousy that they had handed him over.

Now as he was seated in the chair of judgement, his wife sent him a message, 'Have nothing to do with that man; I have been upset all day by a dream I had about him.'

Palm Sunday of the Passion of the Lord

The chief priests and the elders, however, had persuaded the crowd to demand the release of Barabbas and the execution of Jesus. So when the governor spoke and asked them, 'Which of the two do you want me to release for you?' they said 'Barabbas'. 'But in that case,' Pilate said to them 'what am I to do with Jesus who is called Christ?' They all said, 'Let him be crucified!' 'Why?' he asked 'What harm has he done?' But they shouted all the louder, 'Let him be crucified!' Then Pilate saw that he was making no impression, that in fact a riot was imminent. So he took some water, washed his hands in front of the crowd and said, 'I am innocent of this man's blood. It is your concern.' And the people, to a man, shouted back, 'His blood be on us and on our children!' Then he released Barabbas for them. He ordered Jesus to be first scourged and then handed over to be crucified.

The governor's soldiers took Jesus with them into the Praetorium and collected the whole cohort round him. Then they stripped him and made him wear a scarlet cloak, and having twisted some thorns into a crown they put this on his head and placed a reed in his right hand. To make fun of him they knelt to him saying, 'Hail, king of the Jews!' And they spat on him and took the reed and struck him on the head with it. And when they had finished making fun of him, they took off the cloak and dressed him in his own clothes and led him away to crucify him.

On their way out, they came across a man from Cyrene, Simon by name, and enlisted him to carry his cross. When they had reached a place called Golgotha, that is, the place of the skull, they gave him wine to drink mixed with gall, which he tasted but refused to drink. When they had finished crucifying him they shared out his clothing by casting lots, and then sat down and stayed there keeping guard over him.

Above his head was placed the charge against him; it read: 'This is Jesus, the King of the Jews.' At the same time two robbers were crucified with him, one on the right and one on the left.

The passers-by jeered at him; they shook their heads and said 'So you would destroy the Temple and rebuild it in three days! Then save yourself! If you are God's son, come down from the cross!' The chief priests with the scribes and elders mocked him in the same way. 'He saved others,' they said 'he cannot save himself. He is the king of Israel; let him come down from the cross now, and we will believe in him. He put his trust in God; now let God rescue him if he wants him. For he did say, "I am the son of God." ' Even the robbers who were crucified with him taunted him in the same way.

From the sixth hour there was darkness over all the land until the ninth hour. And about the ninth hour, Jesus cried out in a loud voice, 'Eli, Eli, lama sabachthani?' that is, 'My God, my God, why have you deserted me?' When some of those who stood there heard this, they said, 'The man is calling on Elijah,' and one of them quickly ran to get a sponge which he dipped in vinegar and putting it on a reed, gave it him to drink. 'Wait!' said the rest of them 'and see if Elijah will come to save him.' But Jesus again crying out in a loud voice, yielded up his spirit.

All kneel and pause a moment.

At that, the veil of the Temple was torn in two from top to bottom; the earth quaked; the rocks were split; the tombs opened and the bodies of many holy men rose from the dead, and these, after his resurrection, came out of the tombs, entered the Holy City and appeared to a number of people. Meanwhile the centurion, together with the others guarding Jesus, had seen the earthquake and all that was taking place, and they were terrified and said, 'In truth this was a son of God.'

Year B

N Narrator. J Jesus. O Other single speaker. C Crowd, or more than one other speaker.

The passion of our Lord Jesus Christ according to Mark   14:1 – 15:47

N It was two days before the Passover and the feast of Unleavened Bread, and the chief priests and scribes were looking for a way to arrest Jesus by some trick and have him put to death. For they said,

C It must not be during the festivities, or there will be a disturbance among the people.

N Jesus was at Bethany in the house of Simon the leper; he was at dinner when a woman came in with an alabaster jar of very costly ointment, pure nard. She broke the jar and poured the ointment on his head. Some who were there said to one another indignantly,

C Why this waste of ointment? Ointment like this could have been sold for over three hundred denarii and the money given to the poor;

N and they were angry with her. But Jesus said,
J Leave her alone. Why are you upsetting her? What she has done for me is one of the good works. You have the poor with you always and you can be kind to them whenever you wish, but you will not always have me. She has done what was in her power to do; she has anointed my body beforehand for its burial. I tell you solemnly, wherever throughout all the world the Good News is proclaimed, what she has done will be told also, in remembrance of her.
N Judas Iscariot, one of the Twelve, approached the chief priests with an offer to hand Jesus over to them. They were delighted to hear it, and promised to give him money; and he looked for a way of betraying him when the opportunity should occur.

On the first day of Unleavened Bread, when the Passover lamb was sacrificed, his disciples said to him,
C Where do you want us to go and make the preparations for you to eat the passover?
N So he sent two of his disciples, saying to them,
J Go into the city and you will meet a man carrying a pitcher of water. Follow him, and say to the owner of the house which he enters, 'The Master says: Where is my dining room in which I can eat the passover with my disciples?' He will show you a large upper room furnished with couches, all prepared. Make the preparations for us there.
N The disciples set out and went to the city and found everything as he had told them, and prepared the Passover.

When evening came he arrived with the Twelve. And while they were at table eating, Jesus said,
J I tell you solemnly, one of you is about to betray me, one of you eating with me.
N They were distressed and asked him, one after another,
O Not I, surely?
N He said to them,
J It is one of the Twelve, one who is dipping into the same dish with me. Yes, the Son of Man is going to his fate, as the scriptures say he will, but alas for that man by whom the Son of Man is betrayed! Better for that man if he had never been born!
N And as they were eating he took some bread, and when he had said the blessing he broke it and gave it to them, saying,
J Take it; this is my body.
N Then he took a cup, and when he had returned thanks he gave it to them, and all drank from it, and he said to them,

J This is my blood, the blood of the covenant, which is to be poured out for many. I tell you solemnly, I shall not drink any more wine until the day I drink the new wine in the kingdom of God.

N After psalms had been sung they left for the Mount of Olives. And Jesus said to them,

J You will all lose faith, for the scripture says, 'I shall strike the shepherd and the sheep will be scattered'. However after my resurrection I shall go before you to Galilee.

N Peter said,

O Even if all lose faith, I will not.

N And Jesus said to him,

J I tell you solemnly, this day, this very night, before the cock crows twice, you will have disowned me three times.

N But he repeated still more earnestly,

O If I have to die with you, I will never disown you.

N And they all said the same.

They came to a small estate called Gethsemane, and Jesus said to his disciples,

J Stay here while I pray.

N Then he took Peter and James and John with him. And a sudden fear came over him, and great distress. And he said to them,

J My soul is sorrowful to the point of death. Wait here, and keep awake.

N And going on a little further he threw himself on the ground and prayed that, if it were possible, this hour might pass him by. He said,

J Abba (Father)! Everything is possible for you. Take this cup away from me. But let it be as you, not I, would have it.

N He came back and found them sleeping, and he said to Peter,

J Simon, are you asleep? Had you not the strength to keep awake one hour? You should be awake, and praying not to be put to the test. The spirit is willing but the flesh is weak.

N Again he went away and prayed, saying the same words. And once more he came back and found them sleeping, their eyes were so heavy; and they could find no answer for him. He came back a third time and said to them,

J You can sleep on now and take your rest. It is all over. The hour has come. Now the Son of Man is to be betrayed into the hands of sinners. Get up! Let us go! My betrayer is close at hand already.

N Even while he was still speaking, Judas, one of the Twelve, came up with a number of men armed with swords and clubs, sent by

Palm Sunday of the Passion of the Lord

    the chief priests and the scribes and the elders. Now the traitor had arranged a signal with them. He had said,

O 'The one I kiss, he is the man. Take him in charge, and see he is well guarded when you lead him away.'

N So when the traitor came, he went straight up to Jesus and said,

O Rabbi!

N and kissed him. The others seized him and took him in charge. Then one of the bystanders drew his sword and struck out at the high priest's servant, and cut off his ear. Then Jesus spoke,

J Am I a brigand that you had to set out to capture me with swords and clubs? I was among you teaching in the Temple day after day and you never laid hands on me. But this is to fulfil the scriptures.

N And they all deserted him and ran away. A young man who followed him had nothing on but a linen cloth. They caught hold of him, but he left the cloth in their hands and ran away naked.

    They led Jesus off to the high priest; and all the chief priests and the elders and the scribes assembled there. Peter had followed him at a distance, right into the high priest's palace, and was sitting with the attendants warming himself at the fire. The chief priests and the whole Sanhedrin were looking for evidence against Jesus on which they might pass the death-sentence. But they could not find any. Several, indeed, brought false evidence against him, but their evidence was conflicting. Some stood up and submitted this false evidence against him,

C We heard him say, 'I am going to destroy this Temple made by human hands, and in three days build another, not made by human hands'.

N But even on this point their evidence was conflicting. The high priest then stood up before the whole assembly and put this question to Jesus,

O Have you no answer to that? What is this evidence these men are bringing against you?

N But he was silent and made no answer at all. The high priest put a second question to him,

O Are you the Christ the Son of the Blessed One?

N Jesus said,

J I am, and you will see the Son of Man seated at the right hand of the Power and coming with the clouds of heaven.

N The high priest tore his robes, and said,

O What need of witnesses have we now? You heard the blasphemy. What is your finding?

N And they all gave their verdict: he deserved to die. Some of them started spitting at him and, blindfolding him, began hitting him with their fists and shouting,
C Play the prophet!
N And the attendants rained blows on him.

While Peter was down below in the courtyard, one of the high-priest's servant-girls came up. She saw Peter warming himself there, stared at him and said,
O You too were with Jesus, the man from Nazareth.
N But he denied it, saying
O I do not know, I do not understand what you are talking about.
N And he went out into the forecourt. The servant-girl saw him and again started telling the bystanders,
O This fellow is one of them.
N But he again denied it. A little later the bystanders themselves said to Peter,
C You are one of them for sure! Why, you are a Galilean.
N But he started calling curses on himself and swearing,
O I do not know the man you speak of.
N At that moment the cock crew for the second time, and Peter recalled how Jesus had said to him, 'Before the cock crows twice, you will have disowned me three times'. And he burst into tears.

First thing in the morning, the chief priest together with the elders and scribes, in short the whole Sanhedrin, had their plan ready. They had Jesus bound and took him away and handed him over to Pilate.

Pilate questioned him,
O Are you the king of the Jews?
N He answered,
J It is you who say it.
N And the chief priests brought many accusations against him. Pilate questioned him again,
O Have you no reply at all? See how many accusations they are bringing against you!
N But to Pilate's amazement, Jesus made no further reply.

At festival time Pilate used to release a prisoner for them, anyone they asked for. Now a man called Barabbas was then in prison with the rioters who had committed murder during the uprising. When the crowd went up and began to ask Pilate the customary favour, Pilate answered them,
O Do you want me to release for you the king of the Jews?
N For he realised it was out of jealousy that the chief priests had handed Jesus over. The chief priests, however, had incited the

Palm Sunday of the Passion of the Lord

    crowd to demand that he should release Barabbas for them instead. Then Pilate spoke again.
O But in that case, what am I to do with the man you call king of the Jews?
N They shouted back,
C Crucify him!
N Pilate asked them,
O Why? What harm has he done?
N But they shouted all the louder,
C Crucify him!
N So Pilate, anxious to placate the crowd, released Barabbas for them and, having ordered Jesus to be scourged, handed him over to be crucified.

    The soldiers led him away to the inner part of the palace, that is, the Praetorium, and called the whole cohort together. They dressed him up in purple, twisted some thorns into a crown and put it on him. And they began saluting him,
C Hail, king of the Jews!
N They struck his head with a reed and spat on him; and they went down on their knees to do him homage. And when they had finished making fun of him, they took off the purple and dressed him in his own clothes.

    They led him out to crucify him. They enlisted a passer-by, Simon of Cyrene, father of Alexander and Rufus, who was coming in from the country, to carry his cross. They brought Jesus to the place called Golgotha, which means the place of the skull.

    They offered him wine mixed with myrrh, but he refused it. Then they crucified him, and shared out his clothing, casting lots to decide what each should get. It was the third hour when they crucified him. The inscription giving the charge against him read: 'The King of the Jews.' And they crucified two robbers with him, one on his right and one on his left.

The passers-by jeered at him; they shook their heads and said,
C Aha! So you would destroy the Temple and rebuild it in three days! Then save yourself: come down from the cross!
N The chief priests and the scribes mocked him among themselves in the same way. They said,
C He saved others, he cannot save himself. Let the Christ, the king of Israel, come down from the cross now, for us to see it and believe.
N Even those who were crucified with him taunted him.

When the sixth hour came there was darkness over the whole land until the ninth hour. And at the ninth hour Jesus cried out in a loud voice,

J Eloi, Eloi, lama sabachthani?
N This means 'My God, my God, why have you deserted me?' When some of those who stood by heard this, they said,
C Listen, he is calling on Elijah.
N Someone ran and soaked a sponge in vinegar and, putting it on a reed, gave it him to drink, saying,
O Wait and see if Elijah will come to take him down.
N But Jesus gave a loud cry and breathed his last.

All kneel and pause a moment.

N And the veil of the Temple was torn in two from top to bottom. The centurion, who was standing in front of him, had seen how he had died, and he said,
O In truth this man was a son of God.
N There were some women watching from a distance. Among them were Mary of Magdala, Mary who was the mother of James the younger, and Joset, and Salome. These used to follow him and look after him when he was in Galilee. And there were many other women there who had come up to Jerusalem with him.

It was now evening, and since it was Preparation Day (that is the vigil of the sabbath), there came Joseph of Arimathaea, a prominent member of the Council, who himself lived in the hope of seeing the kingdom of God, and he boldly went to Pilate and asked for the body of Jesus. Pilate, astonished that he should have died so soon, summoned the centurion and enquired if he was already dead. Having been assured of this by the centurion, he granted the corpse to Joseph who brought a shroud, took Jesus down from the cross, wrapped him in the shroud and laid him in a tomb which had been hewn out of the rock. He then rolled a stone against the entrance to the tomb. Mary of Magdala and Mary the mother of Joset were watching and took note of where he was laid.

Shorter form

The passion of our Lord Jesus Christ according to Mark   15:1-39

First thing in the morning, the chief priests together with the elders and scribes, in short the whole Sanhedrin, had their plan ready.

They had Jesus bound and took him away and handed him over to Pilate.

Pilate questioned him, 'Are you the king of the Jews?' 'It is you who say it' he answered. And the chief priests brought many accusations against him. Pilate questioned him again, 'Have you no reply at all? See how many accusations they are bringing against you!' But to Pilate's amazement, Jesus made no further reply.

At festival time Pilate used to release a prisoner for them, anyone they asked for. Now a man called Barabbas was then in prison with the rioters who had committed murder during the uprising. When the crowd went up and began to ask Pilate the customary favour, Pilate answered them, 'Do you want me to release for you the king of the Jews?' For he realised it was out of jealousy that the chief priests had handed Jesus over. The chief priests, however, had incited the crowd to demand that he should release Barabbas for them instead. Then Pilate spoke again. 'But in that case,' he said to them 'what am I to do with the man you call king of the Jews?' They shouted back, 'Crucify him!' 'Why?' Pilate asked them 'What harm has he done?' But they shouted all the louder, 'Crucify him!' So Pilate, anxious to placate the crowd, released Barabbas for them and, having ordered Jesus to be scourged, handed him over to be crucified.

The soldiers led him away to the inner part of the palace, that is, the Praetorium, and called the whole cohort together. They dressed him up in purple, twisted some thorns into a crown and put it on him. And they began saluting him, 'Hail, king of the Jews!' They struck his head with a reed and spat on him; and they went down on their knees to do him homage. And when they had finished making fun of him, they took off the purple and dressed him in his own clothes.

They led him out to crucify him. They enlisted a passer-by, Simon of Cyrene, father of Alexander and Rufus, who was coming in from the country, to carry his cross. They brought Jesus to the place called Golgotha, which means the place of the skull.

They offered him wine mixed with myrrh, but he refused it. Then they crucified him, and shared out his clothing, casting lots to decide what each should get. It was the third hour when they crucified him. The inscription giving the charge against him read: 'The King of the Jews'. And they crucified two robbers with him, one on his right and one on his left.

The passers-by jeered at him; they shook their heads and said, 'Aha! So you would destroy the Temple and rebuild it in three days! Then save yourself: come down from the cross!' The chief priests and the scribes mocked him among themselves in the same way. 'He saved others,' they said 'he cannot save himself. Let the Christ, the king of Israel, come down from the cross now, for us to see it and believe.' Even those who were crucified with him taunted him.

When the sixth hour came there was darkness over the whole land until the ninth hour. And at the ninth hour Jesus cried out in a loud voice, 'Eloi, Eloi, lama sabachthani?' which means, 'My God, my God, why have you deserted me?' When some of those who stood by heard this, they said, 'Listen he is calling on Elijah'. Someone ran and soaked a sponge in vinegar and, putting it on a reed, gave it him to drink saying, 'Wait and see if Elijah will come to take him down.' But Jesus gave a loud cry and breathed his last.

All kneel and pause a moment.

And the veil of the Temple was torn in two from top to bottom. The centurion, who was standing in front of him, had seen how he had died, and he said, 'In truth this man was a son of God.'

Year C

N Narrator. J Jesus. O Other single speaker. C Crowd, or more than one other speaker.

The passion of our Lord Jesus Christ   22:14 – 23:56
according to Luke

N When the hour came Jesus took his place at table, and the apostles with him. And he said to them,

J I have longed to eat this passover with you before I suffer; because, I tell you, I shall not eat it again until it is fulfilled in the kingdom of God.

N Then, taking a cup, he gave thanks and said,

J Take this and share it among you, because from now on, I tell you, I shall not drink wine until the kingdom of God comes.

N Then he took some bread, and when he had given thanks, broke it and gave it to them, saying,

J This is my body which will be given for you; do this as a memorial of me.

N He did the same with the cup after supper, and said,

J This cup is the new covenant in my blood which will be poured out for you. And yet, here with me on the table is the hand of the man who betrays me. The Son of Man does indeed go to his fate even as it has been decreed, but alas for that man by whom he is betrayed!

N And they began to ask one another which of them it could be who was to do this thing.

   A dispute arose also between them about which should be reckoned the greatest, but he said to them,

J Among pagans it is the kings who lord it over them, and those who have authority over them are given the title Benefactor. This must not happen with you. No; the greatest among you must behave as if he were the youngest, the leader as if he were the one who serves. For who is the greater: the one at table or the one who serves? The one at table, surely? Yet here I am among you as one who serves!

   You are the men who have stood by me faithfully in my trials; and now I confer a kingdom on you, just as my Father conferred one on me: you will eat and drink at my table in my kingdom, and you will sit on thrones to judge the twelve tribes of Israel.

   Simon, Simon! Satan, you must know, has got his wish to sift you all like wheat; but I have prayed for you, Simon, that your faith may not fail, and once you have recovered, you in your turn must strengthen your brothers.

N He answered,

O Lord, I would be ready to go to prison with you, and to death.

N Jesus replied,

J I tell you, Peter, by the time the cock crows today you will have denied three times that you know me.

N He said to them,

J When I sent you out without purse or haversack or sandals, were you short of anything?

N They answered,

C No.

N He said to them,

J But now if you have a purse, take it: if you have a haversack, do the same; if you have no sword, sell your cloak and buy one, because I tell you these words of scripture have to be fulfilled in me: He let himself be taken for a criminal. Yes, what scripture says about me is even now reaching its fulfilment.

N They said,

C Lord, there are two swords here now.

N He said to them,
J That is enough!
N He then left the upper room to make his way as usual to the Mount of Olives, with the disciples following. When they reached the place he said to them,
J Pray not to be put to the test.
N Then he withdrew from them, about a stone's throw away, and knelt down and prayed, saying,
J Father, if you are willing, take this cup away from me. Nevertheless, let your will be done, not mine.
N Then an angel appeared to him coming from heaven to give him strength. In his anguish he prayed even more earnestly, and his sweat fell to the ground like great drops of blood.

  When he rose from prayer he went to the disciples and found them sleeping for sheer grief. He said to them,
J Why are you asleep? Get up and pray not to be put to the test.
N He was still speaking when a number of men appeared, and at the head of them the man called Judas, one of the Twelve, who went up to Jesus to kiss him. Jesus said,
J Judas, are you betraying the Son of Man with a kiss?
N His followers, seeing what was happening, said,
C Lord, shall we use our swords?
N And one of them struck out at the high priest's servant, and cut off his right ear. But at this Jesus spoke,
J Leave off! That will do!
N And touching the man's ear he healed him. Then Jesus spoke to the chief priests and captains of the Temple guard and elders who had come for him. He said,
J Am I a brigand that you had to set out with swords and clubs? When I was among you in the Temple day after day you never moved to lay hands on me. But this is your hour; this is the reign of darkness.
N They seized him then and led him away, and they took him to the high priest's house. Peter followed at a distance. They had lit a fire in the middle of the courtyard and Peter sat down among them, and as he was sitting there by the blaze a servant-girl saw him, peered at him and said,
O This person was with him too.
N But he denied it, saying,
O Woman, I do not know him.
N Shortly afterwards, someone else saw him and said,
O You are another of them.
N But Peter replied,

Palm Sunday of the Passion of the Lord 323

O I am not, my friend.
N About an hour later, another man insisted, saying,
O This fellow was certainly with him. Why, he is a Galilean.
N Peter said,
O My friend, I do not know what you are talking about.
N At that instant, while he was still speaking, the cock crew, and the Lord turned and looked straight at Peter, and Peter remembered what the Lord had said to him, 'Before the cock crows today, you will have disowned me three times'. And he went outside and wept bitterly.

 Meanwhile the men who guarded Jesus were mocking and beating him. They blindfolded him and questioned him, saying,
C Play the prophet. Who hit you then?
N And they continued heaping insults on him.

 When day broke there was a meeting of the elders of the people, attended by the chief priests and scribes. He was brought before their council, and they said to him,
C If you are the Christ, tell us.
N He replied,
J If I tell you, you will not believe me, and if I question you, you will not answer. But from now on, the Son of Man will be seated at the right hand of the Power of God.
N Then they all said,
C So you are the Son of God then?
N He answered,
J It is you who say I am.
N They said,
C What need of witnesses have we now? We have heard it for ourselves from his own lips.
N The whole assembly then rose, and they brought him before Pilate.

 They began their accusation by saying,
C We found this man inciting our people to revolt, opposing payment of tribute to Caesar, and claiming to be Christ, a king.
N Pilate put to him this question,
O Are you the king of the Jews?
N He replied,
J It is you who say it.
N Pilate then said to the chief priests and the crowd,
O I find no case against this man.
N But they persisted,

C He is inflaming the people with his teaching all over Judaea; it has come all the way from Galilee, where he started, down to here.

N When Pilate heard this, he asked if the man were a Galilean; and finding that he came under Herod's jurisdiction he passed him over to Herod who was also in Jerusalem at that time.

Herod was delighted to see Jesus; he had heard about him and had been wanting for a long time to set eyes on him; moreover, he was hoping to see some miracle worked by him. So he questioned him at some length; but without getting any reply. Meanwhile the chief priests and the scribes were there, violently pressing their accusations. Then Herod, together with his guards, treated him with contempt and made fun of him; he put a rich cloak on him and sent him back to Pilate. And though Herod and Pilate had been enemies before, they were reconciled that same day.

Pilate then summoned the chief priests and the leading men and the people. He said,

O You brought this man before me as a political agitator. Now I have gone into the matter myself in your presence and found no case against him. Nor has Herod either, since he has sent him back to us. As you can see, the man has done nothing that deserves death, so I shall have him flogged and then let him go.

N But as one man they howled,

C Away with him! Give us Barabbas!

N This man had been thrown into prison for causing a riot in the city and for murder.

Pilate was anxious to set Jesus free and addressed them again, but they shouted back.

C Crucify him! Crucify him!

N And for the third time he spoke to them,

O Why? What harm has this man done? I have found no case against him that deserves death, so I shall have him punished and let him go.

N But they kept on shouting at the top of their voices, demanding that he should be crucified, and their shouts were growing louder.

Pilate then gave his verdict: their demand was to be granted. He released the man they asked for, who had been imprisoned for rioting and murder, and handed Jesus over to them to deal with as they pleased.

As they were leading him away they seized on a man, Simon from Cyrene, who was coming in from the country, and made him shoulder the cross and carry it behind Jesus. Large numbers of people followed him, and of women too who mourned and lamented for him. But Jesus turned to them and said,

J Daughters of Jerusalem, do not weep for me; weep rather for yourselves and for your children. For the days will surely come when people will say, 'Happy are those who are barren, the wombs that have never borne, the breasts that have never suckled!' Then they will begin to say to the mountains, 'Fall on us!'; to the hills, 'Cover us!' For if men use the green wood like this, what will happen when it is dry?

N Now with him they were also leading out two other criminals to be executed.

When they reached the place called The Skull, they crucified him there and the criminals also, one on the right, the other on the left. Jesus said,

J Father, forgive them; they do not know what they are doing.

N Then they cast lots to share out his clothing. The people stayed there watching him. As for the leaders, they jeered at him, saying,

C He saved others; let him save himself if he is the Christ of God, the Chosen One.

N The soldiers mocked him too, and when they approached to offer him vinegar they said,

C If you are the king of the Jews, save yourself.

N Above him there was an inscription: 'This is the King of the Jews.' One of the criminals hanging there abused him, saying,

O Are you not the Christ? Save yourself and us as well.

N But the other spoke up and rebuked him,

O Have you no fear of God at all? You got the same sentence as he did, but in our case we deserved it: we are paying for what we did. But this man has done nothing wrong. Jesus, remember me when you come into your kingdom.

N He replied,

J Indeed, I promise you, today you will be with me in paradise.

N It was now about the sixth hour and, with the sun eclipsed, a darkness came over the whole land until the ninth hour. The veil of the Temple was torn right down the middle; and when Jesus had cried out in a loud voice, he said,

J Father, into your hands I commit my spirit.

N With these words he breathed his last.

All kneel and pause a moment.

When the centurion saw what had taken place, he gave praise to God and said,

O This was a great and good man.
N And when all the people who had gathered for the spectacle saw what had happened, they went home beating their breasts.

All his friends stood at a distance; so also did the women who had accompanied him from Galilee, and they saw all this happen.

Then a member of the council arrived, an upright and virtuous man named Joseph. He had not consented to what the others had planned and carried out. He came from Arimathaea, a Jewish town, and he lived in the hope of seeing the kingdom of God. This man went to Pilate and asked for the body of Jesus. He then took it down, wrapped it in a shroud and put him in a tomb which was hewn in stone in which no one had yet been laid. It was Preparation Day and the sabbath was imminent.

Meanwhile the women who had come from Galilee with Jesus were following behind. They took note of the tomb and of the position of the body. Then they returned and prepared spices and ointments. And on the sabbath day they rested, as the law required.

Shorter form

The passion of our Lord Jesus Christ 23:1-49
according to Luke

The elders of the people and the chief priests and scribes rose, and they brought Jesus before Pilate.

They began their accusation by saying, 'We found this man inciting our people to revolt, opposing payment of tribute to Caesar, and claiming to be Christ, a king.' Pilate put to him this question, 'Are you the king of the Jews?' 'It is you who say it' he replied. Pilate then said to the chief priests and the crowd, 'I find no case against this man.' But they persisted, 'He is inflaming the people with his teaching all over Judaea; it has come all the way from Galilee, where he started, down to here.' When Pilate heard this, he asked if the man were a Galilean; and finding that he came under Herod's jurisdiction he passed him over to Herod who was also in Jerusalem at that time.

Herod was delighted to see Jesus; he had heard about him and had been wanting for a long time to set eyes on him; moreover, he was hoping to see some miracle worked by him. So he questioned him at some length; but without getting any reply. Meanwhile the chief priests and the scribes were there, violently pressing their accusations. Then Herod, together with his guards, treated him with contempt and made fun of him; he put a rich cloak on him and sent him back to Pilate. And though Herod and Pilate had been enemies before, they were reconciled that same day. Pilate then summoned the chief priests and the leading men and the people. 'You brought this man before me' he said 'as a political agitator. Now I have gone into the matter myself in your presence and found no case against the man in respect of all the charges you bring against him. Nor has Herod either, since he has sent him back to us. As you can see, the man has done nothing that deserves death, so I shall have him flogged and then let him go.' But as one man they howled, 'Away with him! Give us Barabbas!' (This man had been thrown into prison for causing a riot in the city and for murder.)

Pilate was anxious to set Jesus free and addressed them again, but they shouted back, 'Crucify him! Crucify him!' And for the third time he spoke to them, 'Why? What harm has this man done? I have found no case against him that deserves death, so I shall have him punished and then let him go.' But they kept on shouting at the top of their voices, demanding that he should be crucified. And their shouts were growing louder.

Pilate then gave his verdict: their demand was to be granted. He released the man they asked for, who had been imprisoned for rioting and murder, and handed Jesus over to them to deal with as they pleased.

As they were leading him away they seized on a man, Simon from Cyrene, who was coming in from the country, and made him shoulder the cross and carry it behind Jesus. Large numbers of people followed him, and of women too, who mourned and lamented for him. But Jesus turned to them and said, 'Daughters of Jerusalem, do not weep for me; weep rather for yourselves and for your children. For the days will surely come when people will say, "Happy are those who are barren, the wombs that have never borne, the breasts that have never suckled!" Then they will begin to say to the mountains, "Fall on us!"; to the hills, "Cover us!" For if men use the green wood like this, what will happen when it is dry?' Now with him they were also leading out two other criminals to be executed.

When they reached the place called The Skull, they crucified him there and the two criminals also, one on the right, the other on the left. Jesus said, 'Father forgive them; they do not know what they are doing.' Then they cast lots to share out his clothing.

The people stayed there watching him. As for the leaders, they jeered at him. 'He saved others,' they said 'let him save himself if he is the Christ of God, the Chosen One.' The soldiers mocked him too and when they approached to offer him vinegar they said, 'If you are the king of the Jews, save yourself.' Above him there was an inscription: 'This is the King of the Jews.'

One of the criminals hanging there abused him. 'Are you not the Christ?' he said. 'Save yourself and us as well.' But the other spoke up and rebuked him. 'Have you no fear of God at all?' he said. 'You got the same sentence as he did, but in our case we deserved it; we are paying for what we did. But this man has done nothing wrong. Jesus,' he said 'remember me when you come into your kingdom.' 'Indeed, I promise you,' he replied 'today you will be with me in paradise.'

It was now about the sixth hour and, with the sun eclipsed, a darkness came over the whole land until the ninth hour. The veil of the Temple was torn right down the middle; and when Jesus had cried out in a loud voice, he said, 'Father, into your hands I commit my spirit.' With these words he breathed his last.

All kneel and pause a moment.

When the centurion saw what had taken place, he gave praise to God and said, 'This was a great and good man.' And when all the people who had gathered for the spectacle saw what had happened, they went home beating their breasts. All his friends stood at a distance; so also did the women who had accompanied him from Galilee, and they saw all this happen.

Prayer over the Offerings
Through the Passion of your Only Begotten Son, O Lord,
may our reconciliation with you be near at hand,
so that, though we do not merit it by our own deeds,
yet by this sacrifice made once for all,
we may feel already the effects of your mercy.
Through Christ our Lord.
Amen.

Preface of the Passion of the Lord, p.27.

Communion Antiphon   Mt 26:42
Father, if this chalice cannot pass without my drinking it,
your will be done.

Prayer after Communion
Nourished with these sacred gifts,
we humbly beseech you, O Lord,
that, just as through the death of your Son

you have brought us to hope for what we believe,
so by his Resurrection
you may lead us to where you call.
Through Christ our Lord.
Amen.

Prayer over the People
Look, we pray, O Lord, on this your family,
for whom our Lord Jesus Christ
did not hesitate to be delivered into the hands of the wicked
and submit to the agony of the Cross.
Who lives and reigns for ever and ever.

THURSDAY OF HOLY WEEK

In accordance with a most ancient tradition of the Church, on this day all Masses without the people are forbidden.

The Chrism Mass

The blessing of the Oil of the Sick and of the Oil of Catechumens and the consecration of the Chrism are carried out by the Bishop, according to the Rite described in the Roman Pontifical, usually on this day, at a proper Mass to be celebrated during the morning.

If, however, it is very difficult for the clergy and the people to gather with the Bishop on this day, the Chrism Mass may be anticipated on another day, but near to Easter.

This Mass, which the Bishop concelebrates with his presbyterate, should be, as it were, a manifestation of the Priests' communion with their Bishop. Accordingly it is desirable that all the Priests participate in it, insofar as is possible, and during it receive Communion even under both kinds. To signify the unity of the presbyterate of the diocese, the Priests who concelebrate with the Bishop should be from different regions of the diocese.

In accord with traditional practice, the blessing of the Oil of the Sick takes place before the end of the Eucharistic Prayer, but the blessing of the Oil of Catechumens and the consecration of the Chrism take place after Communion. Nevertheless, for pastoral reasons, it is permitted for the entire rite of blessing to take place after the Liturgy of the Word.

Entrance Antiphon   Rv 1:6
Jesus Christ has made us into a kingdom, priests for his God and
  Father.

Thursday of Holy Week

To him be glory and power for ever and ever. Amen.

The Gloria in excelsis (Glory to God in the highest) is said.

Collect
O God, who anointed your Only Begotten Son with the Holy Spirit
and made him Christ and Lord,
graciously grant
that, being made sharers in his consecration,
we may bear witness to your Redemption in the world.
Through our Lord Jesus Christ, your Son,
who lives and reigns with you in the unity of the Holy Spirit,
one God, for ever and ever.
Amen.

FIRST READING
A reading from the prophet Isaiah   61:1-3. 6. 8-9

The spirit of the Lord has been given to me,
for the Lord has anointed me.
He has sent me to bring good news to the poor,
to bind up hearts that are broken;

to proclaim liberty to captives,
freedom to those in prison;
to proclaim a year of favour from the Lord,
a day of vengeance for our God;

to comfort all those who mourn and to give them
for ashes a garland;
for mourning robe the oil of gladness,
for despondency, praise.

But you, you will be named 'priests of the Lord',
they will call you 'ministers of our God'.
I reward them faithfully
and make an everlasting covenant with them.

Their race will be famous throughout the nations,
their descendants throughout the peoples.
All who see them will admit
that they are a race whom the Lord has blessed.

  The word of the Lord.

Responsorial Psalm
Ps 88:21-22. 25. 27. ℟ v.2

℟ **I will sing for ever of your love, O Lord.**

1 I have found David my servant
   and with my holy oil anointed him.
   My hand shall always be with him
   and my arm shall make him strong. ℟

2 My truth and my love shall be with him;
   by my name his might shall be exalted.
   He will say to me: 'You are my father,
   my God, the rock who saves me.' ℟

SECOND READING
A reading from the book of the Apocalypse
1:5-8

Grace and peace to you from Jesus Christ, the faithful witness, the First-born from the dead, the Ruler of the kings of the earth. He loves us and has washed away our sins with his blood, and made us a line of kings, priests to serve his God and Father; to him, then, be glory and power for ever and ever. Amen. It is he who is coming on the clouds; everyone will see him, even those who pierced him, and all the races of the earth will mourn over him. This is the truth. Amen. 'I am the Alpha and the Omega' says the Lord God, who is, who was, and who is to come, the Almighty.

The word of the Lord.

Gospel Acclamation
Is 61:1 (Lk 4:18)

Praise to you, O Christ, king of eternal glory!
The spirit of the Lord has been given to me;
he has sent me to bring the good news to the poor.
Praise to you, O Christ, king of eternal glory.

GOSPEL
A reading from the holy Gospel according to Luke
4:16-21

Jesus came to Nazara, where he had been brought up, and went into the synagogue on the sabbath day as he usually did. He stood up to read, and they handed him the scroll of the prophet Isaiah. Unrolling the scroll he found the place where it is written:

The spirit of the Lord has been given to me,
for he has anointed me.
He has sent me to bring the good news to the poor,

to proclaim liberty to captives
and to the blind new sight,
to set the downtrodden free,
to proclaim the Lord's year of favour.

He then rolled up the scroll, gave it back to the assistant and sat down. And all eyes in the synagogue were fixed on him. Then he began to speak to them, 'This text is being fulfilled today even as you listen.'

The Gospel of the Lord.

After the reading of the Gospel, the Bishop preaches the Homily in which, taking his starting point from the text of the readings proclaimed in the Liturgy of the Word, he speaks to the people and to his Priests about priestly anointing, urging the Priests to be faithful in their office and calling on them to renew publicly their priestly promises.

Renewal of Priestly Promises

After the Homily, the Bishop speaks with the Priests in these or similar words.

Beloved sons,
on the anniversary of that day
when Christ our Lord conferred his priesthood
on his Apostles and on us,
are you resolved to renew
in the presence of your Bishop and God's holy people,
the promises you once made?

The Priests, all together, respond: I am.

Are you resolved to be more united with the Lord Jesus
and more closely conformed to him,
denying yourselves and confirming those promises
about sacred duties towards Christ's Church
which, prompted by love of him,
you willingly and joyfully pledged
on the day of your priestly ordination?

Priests: I am.

Are you resolved to be faithful stewards of the mysteries of God
in the Holy Eucharist and the other liturgical rites
and to discharge faithfully the sacred office of teaching,

following Christ the Head and Shepherd,
not seeking any gain,
but moved only by zeal for souls?
Priests: I am.

Then, turned towards the people, the Bishop continues:
As for you, dearest sons and daughters,
pray for your Priests,
that the Lord may pour out his gifts abundantly upon them,
and keep them faithful as ministers of Christ, the High Priest,
so that they may lead you to him,
who is the source of salvation.

People: Christ, hear us. Christ, graciously hear us.

And pray also for me,
that I may be faithful to the apostolic office
entrusted to me in my lowliness
and that in your midst I may be made day by day
a living and more perfect image of Christ,
the Priest, the Good Shepherd,
the Teacher and the Servant of all.

People: Christ, hear us. Christ, graciously hear us.

May the Lord keep us all in his charity
and lead all of us,
shepherds and flock,
to eternal life.

All: **Amen.**

The Creed is not said.

Prayer over the Offerings
May the power of this sacrifice, O Lord, we pray,
mercifully wipe away what is old in us
and increase in us grace of salvation and newness of life.
Through Christ our Lord.
Amen.

Preface of the Priesthood of Christ and the Ministry of Priests, pp.27-8.

Communion Antiphon
Ps 88:2
I will sing for ever of your mercies, O Lord;
through all ages my mouth will proclaim your fidelity.

Prayer after Communion
We beseech you, almighty God,
that those you renew by your Sacraments
may merit to become the pleasing fragrance of Christ.
Who lives and reigns for ever and ever.
Amen.

The reception of the Holy Oils may take place in individual parishes either before the celebration of the Evening Mass of the Lord's Supper or at another time Blessing of Oils and Consecration of the Chrism that seems more appropriate.

Blessing of Oils and Consecration of the Chrism

The oils are brought in a solemn offertory procession to the bishop who places them on a table before the altar. The entire rite may take place immediately, or as detailed below. The Prayer over the Offerings of the Mass is on p.333 above.

Blessing of the Oil of the Sick
Before the conclusion of the eucharistic prayer the bishop blesses the oil held before him in a vessel:

Bishop: Lord God, loving Father,
you bring healing to the sick
through your Son Jesus Christ.
Hear us as we pray to you in faith,
and send the Holy Spirit, man's Helper and Friend,
upon this oil, which nature has provided
to serve the needs of men.
May your blessing ✛
come upon all who are anointed with this oil,
that they may be freed from pain and illness
and made well again in body, mind, and soul.
Father, may this oil be blessed for our use
in the name of our Lord Jesus Christ
(who lives and reigns with you for ever and
  ever.)   (**Amen.**)

The conclusion who lives and reigns with you is said only when this blessing takes place outside the Eucharistic Prayer.

Blessing of the Oil of Catechumens
After the Prayer after Communion, the bishop blesses the oils placed on a table in the centre of the sanctuary. The concelebrating priests stand on either side.

Bishop: Lord God,
protector of all who believe in you,
bless ✝ this oil
and give wisdom and strength
to all who are anointed with it
in preparation for their baptism.
Bring them to a deeper understanding of the gospel,
help them to accept the challenge of Christian living,
and lead them to the joy of new birth
in the family of your Church.
We ask this through Christ our Lord.
Amen.

Consecration of the Chrism
Then the bishop pours the balsam or perfume in the oil and mixes the chrism in silence, unless this was done beforehand.

After this he sings or says the invitation:

Let us pray
that God our almighty Father
will bless this oil
so that all who are anointed with it
may be inwardly transformed
and come to share in eternal salvation.

Then the bishop may breathe over the opening of the vessel of chrism. With his hands extended, he sings or says one of the following consecratory prayers.

Consecratory Prayer A
God our maker,
source of all growth in holiness
accept the joyful thanks and praise
we offer in the name of your Church.

In the beginning, at your command,
the earth produced fruit-bearing trees.
From the fruit of the olive tree
you have provided us with oil for holy chrism.
The prophet David sang of the life and joy
that the oil would bring us in the sacraments of your love.

After the avenging flood,
the dove returning to Noah with an olive branch
announced your gift of peace.
This was a sign of a greater gift to come.

Now the waters of baptism wash away the sins of men,
and by anointing with olive oil
you make us radiant with your joy.

At your command,
Aaron was washed with water,
and your servant Moses, his brother,
anointed him priest.
This too foreshadowed greater things to come.
After your Son, Jesus Christ our Lord,
asked John for baptism in the waters of Jordan,
you sent the Spirit upon him
in the form of a dove
and by the witness of your own voice
you declared him to be your only, well-beloved Son.
In this you clearly fulfilled the prophecy of David,
that Christ would be anointed with the oil of gladness
beyond his fellow men.

All the concelebrants extend their right hands towards the chrism, without saying anything, until the end of the prayer.

And so, Father, we ask you to bless ✠ this oil you have created.
Fill it with the power of your Holy Spirit
through Christ your Son.
It is from him that chrism takes its name
and with chrism you have anointed
for yourself priests and kings,
prophets and martyrs.

Make this chrism a sign of life and salvation
for those who are to be born again in the waters of baptism.
Wash away the evil they have inherited from sinful Adam,
and when they are anointed with this holy oil
make them temples of your glory,
radiant with the goodness of life
that has its source in you.

Through this sign of chrism
grant them royal, priestly, and prophetic honour,
and clothe them with incorruption.
Let this be indeed the chrism of salvation
for those who will be born again of water and the Holy Spirit.
May they come to share eternal life
in the glory of your kingdom.
We ask this through Christ our Lord.
Amen.

Alternative Consecratory Prayer B
Father,
we thank you for the gifts
you have given us in your love:
we thank you for life itself and for the sacraments
that strengthen it and give it fuller meaning.

In the Old Covenant you gave your people
a glimpse of the power of this holy oil
and when the fullness of time had come
you brought that mystery to perfection
in the life of our Lord Jesus Christ, your Son.

By his suffering, dying, and rising to life
he saved the human race.
He sent your Spirit to fill the Church
with every gift needed to complete your saving work.

From that time forward,
through the sign of holy chrism,
you dispense your life and love to men.
By anointing them with the Spirit,
you strengthen all who have been reborn in baptism.
Through that anointing
you transform them into the likeness of Christ your Son
and give them a share
in his royal, priestly, and prophetic work.

All the concelebrants extend their right hands towards the chrism, without saying anything, until the end of the prayer.

And so, Father, by the power of your love,
make this mixture of oil and perfume
a sign and source ✢ of your blessing.
Pour out the gifts of your Holy Spirit
on our brothers and sisters who will be anointed with it.
Let the splendour of holiness shine on the world
from every place and thing
signed with this oil.

Above all, Father, we pray
that through this sign of your anointing
you will grant increase to your Church
until it reaches the eternal glory
where you, Father, will be the all in all,

together with Christ your Son,
in the unity of the Holy Spirit,
for ever and ever.
Amen.

An appropriate Solemn Blessing or Prayer over the People may be used. See pp.96-7, 105-9. After the final blessing of the Mass, the bishop puts incense in the censer, and the procession to the sacristy is arranged.

The blessed oils are carried by the ministers immediately after the cross, and the choir and people sing some verses of the hymn *O Redeemer* or some other appropriate song. The faithful who receive communion at this Mass may receive communion again at the Mass of the Lord's Supper in the evening.

THE SACRED
PASCHAL TRIDUUM

THE SACRED
PASCHAL TRIDUUM

THE EASTER TRIDUUM

The Easter Triduum, *the three days that begin on Holy Thursday with the Mass of the Lord's Supper, celebrates the paschal event, and that newness of life which flows from the crucified, buried and risen Christ.*

In the Sacred Triduum, the Church solemnly celebrates the greatest mysteries of our redemption, keeping by means of special celebrations the memorial of her Lord, crucified, buried, and risen.

The Paschal Fast should also be kept sacred. It is to be celebrated everywhere on the Friday of the Lord's Passion and, where appropriate, prolonged also through Holy Saturday as a way of coming, with spirit uplifted, to the joys of the Lord's Resurrection.

For a fitting celebration of the Sacred Triduum, a sufficient number of lay ministers is required, who must be carefully instructed as to what they are to do.

The singing of the people, the ministers, and the Priest Celebrant has a special importance in the celebrations of these days, for when texts are sung, they have their proper impact.

Pastors should, therefore, not fail to explain to the Christian faithful, as best they can, the meaning and order of the celebrations and to prepare them for active and fruitful participation.

The celebrations of the Sacred Triduum are to be carried out in cathedral and parochial churches and only in those churches in which they can be performed with dignity, that is, with a good attendance of the faithful, an appropriate number of ministers, and the means to sing at least some of the parts.

Consequently, it is desirable that small communities, associations, and special groups of various kinds join together in these churches to carry out the sacred celebrations in a more noble manner.

THURSDAY OF THE LORD'S SUPPER

At the Evening Mass

Today we celebrate Christ's twofold giving of himself:
> *To his enemies, to die on the cross for the life of the world. He is the paschal victim, whose blood saves his people (see the Old Testament Reading).*
>
> *To his friends and disciples, his Church – that is, to us – in the sacrament of his body and blood (see the reading from St Paul).*

If we want to belong to Christ, we must follow his example of self-giving and of service – 'washing one another's feet' (see Gospel). We must be willing and ready to say with Christ, about our own selves:

'This is my body which is given up for you.'

The whole purpose of today's liturgy is to enable us to make this self-giving the real motivation for our lives.

THE INTRODUCTORY RITES AND LITURGY OF THE WORD

The Mass of the Lord's Supper is celebrated in the evening, at a convenient time, with the full participation of the whole local community and with all the Priests and ministers exercising their office.

All Priests may concelebrate even if they have already concelebrated the Chrism Mass on this day, or if they have to celebrate another Mass for the good of the Christian faithful.

Where a pastoral reason requires it, the local Ordinary may permit another Mass to be celebrated in churches and oratories in the evening and, in case of genuine necessity, even in the morning, but only for the faithful who are in no way able to participate in the evening Mass. Care should, nevertheless, be taken that celebrations of this sort do not take place for the advantage of private persons or special small groups, and do not prejudice the evening Mass.

Holy Communion may only be distributed to the faithful during Mass; but it may be brought to the sick at any hour of the day.

The altar may be decorated with flowers with a moderation that accords with the character of this day. The tabernacle should be entirely empty; but a sufficient amount of bread should be

Thursday of the Lord's Supper

consecrated in this Mass for the Communion of the clergy and the people on this and the following day.

Entrance Antiphon Cf. Gal 6:14
We should glory in the Cross of our Lord Jesus Christ,
in whom is our salvation, life and resurrection,
through whom we are saved and delivered.

The Gloria in excelsis (Glory to God in the highest) is said. While the hymn is being sung, bells are rung, and when it is finished, they remain silent until the Gloria in excelsis of the Easter Vigil, unless, if appropriate, the Diocesan Bishop has decided otherwise. Likewise, during this same period, the organ and other musical instruments may be used only so as to support the singing.

Collect
O God, who have called us to participate
in this most sacred Supper,
in which your Only Begotten Son,
when about to hand himself over to death,
entrusted to the Church a sacrifice new for all eternity,
the banquet of his love,
grant, we pray,
that we may draw from so great a mystery,
the fullness of charity and of life.
Through our Lord Jesus Christ, your Son,
who lives and reigns with you in the unity of the Holy Spirit,
one God, for ever and ever.
Amen.

FIRST READING
A reading from the book of Exodus 12:1-8. 11-14

The Lord said to Moses and Aaron in the land of Egypt, 'This month is to be the first of all the others for you, the first month of your year. Speak to the whole community of Israel and say, "On the tenth day of this month each man must take an animal from the flock, one for each family: one animal for each household. If the household is too small to eat the animal, a man must join with his neighbour, the nearest to his house, as the number of persons requires. You must take into account what each can eat in deciding the number for the animal. It must be an animal without blemish, a male one year old; you may take it from either sheep or goats. You must keep it till the fourteenth day of the month when the whole assembly of the community of Israel shall slaughter it between the two evenings. Some of the blood must then be taken and put on the two doorposts and the lintel of the houses where it is eaten. That night, the flesh is to be eaten, roasted over the fire; it must be eaten with unleavened bread and bitter herbs. You shall eat it like this: with a girdle round your waist, sandals on your feet, a staff in your hand. You shall eat it hastily; it is a passover in honour of the Lord. That night, I will go through the land of Egypt and strike down all the first-born in the land of Egypt, man and beast alike, and I shall deal out punishment to all the gods of Egypt, I am the Lord. The blood shall serve to mark the houses that you live in. When I see the blood I will pass over you and you shall escape the destroying plague when I strike the land of Egypt. This day is to be a day of remembrance for you, and you must celebrate it as a feast in the Lord's honour. For all generations you are to declare it a day of festival, for ever."'

The word of the Lord.

Responsorial Psalm Ps 115:12-13. 15-18. ℟ cf. 1 Cor 10:16

℟ **The blessing-cup that we bless
is a communion with the blood of Christ.**

1 How can I repay the Lord
for his goodness to me?
The cup of salvation I will raise;
I will call on the Lord's name. ℟

2 O precious in the eyes of the Lord
is the death of his faithful.
Your servant, Lord, your servant am I;
you have loosened my bonds. ℟

3 A thanksgiving sacrifice I make:
I will call on the Lord's name.
My vows to the Lord I will fulfil
before all his people. ℟

SECOND READING

A reading from the first letter of St Paul
to the Corinthians   11:23-26

This is what I received from the Lord, and in turn passed on to you: that on the same night that he was betrayed, the Lord Jesus took some bread, and thanked God for it and broke it, and he said, 'This is my body, which is for you; do this as a memorial of me.' In the same way he took the cup after supper, and said, 'This cup is

Thursday of the Lord's Supper

the new covenant in my blood. Whenever you drink it, do this as a memorial of me.' Until the Lord comes, therefore, every time you eat this bread and drink this cup, you are proclaiming his death.

The word of the Lord.

Gospel Acclamation Jn 13:34
Praise and honour to you, Lord Jesus!
I give you a new commandment:
love one another just as I have loved you, says the Lord.
Praise and honour to you, Lord Jesus!

GOSPEL
A reading from the holy Gospel according to John 13:1-15

It was before the festival of the Passover, and Jesus knew that the hour had come for him to pass from this world to the Father. He had always loved those who were his in the world, but now he showed how perfect his love was.

They were at supper, and the devil had already put it into the mind of Judas Iscariot son of Simon, to betray him. Jesus knew that the Father had put everything into his hands, and that he had come from God and was returning to God, and he got up from table, removed his outer garment and, taking a towel, wrapped it round his waist; he then poured water into a basin and began to wash the disciples' feet and to wipe them with the towel he was wearing.

He came to Simon Peter, who said to him, 'Lord, are you going to wash my feet?' Jesus answered, 'At the moment you do not know what I am doing, but later you will understand.' 'Never!' said Peter 'You shall never wash my feet.' Jesus replied, 'If I do not wash you, you can have nothing in common with me.' 'Then, Lord,' said Simon Peter 'not only my feet, but my hands and my head as well!' Jesus said, 'No one who has taken a bath needs washing, he is clean all over. You too are clean, though not all of you are.' He knew who was going to betray him, that was why he said, 'though not all of you are.'

When he had washed their feet and put on his clothes again he went back to the table. 'Do you understand' he said 'what I have done to you? You call me Master and Lord, and rightly; so I am. If I, then, the Lord and Master, have washed your feet, you should wash each other's feet. I have given you an example so that you may copy what I have done to you.'

The Gospel of the Lord.

After the proclamation of the Gospel, the Priest gives a homily in which light is shed on the principal mysteries that are commemorated in this Mass, namely, the institution of the Holy Eucharist and of the priestly Order, and the commandment of the Lord concerning fraternal charity.

THE WASHING OF FEET

After the Homily, where a pastoral reason suggests it, the Washing of Feet follows.

The men who have been chosen are led by the ministers to seats prepared in a suitable place. Then the Priest (removing his chasuble if necessary) goes to each one, and, with the help of the ministers, pours water over each one's feet and then dries them.

Meanwhile some of the following antiphons or other appropriate chants are sung:

Antiphon 1   Cf. Jn 13:4-5. 15
After the Lord had risen from supper,
he poured water into a basin
and began to wash the feet of his disciples:
he left them this example.

Antiphon 2   Cf. Jn 13:12-13. 15
The Lord Jesus, after eating supper with his disciples,
washed their feet and said to them:
Do you know what I, your Lord and Master, have done for you?
I have given you an example, that you should do likewise.

Antiphon 3   Jn 13:6-8
Lord, are you to wash my feet? Jesus said to him in answer:
If I do not wash your feet, you will have no share with me.
℣ So he came to Simon Peter and Peter said to him:
Lord . . .
℣ What I am doing, you do not know for now,
but later you will come to know.
Lord . . .

Antiphon 4   Cf. Jn 13:14
If I, your Lord and Master, have washed your feet,
how much more should you wash each other's feet?

Antiphon 5   Jn 13:35
This is how all will know that you are my disciples:
if you have love for one another.

℣ Jesus said to his disciples:
This is how ...

Antiphon 6   Jn 13:34
I give you a new commandment,
that you love one another
as I have loved you, says the Lord.

Antiphon 7   1 Cor 13:13
Let faith, hope and charity, these three, remain among you,
but the greatest of these is charity.
℣ Now faith, hope and charity, these three, remain;
but the greatest of these is charity.
Let ...

After the Washing of Feet, the Priest washes and dries his hands, puts the chasuble back on, and returns to the chair, and from there he directs the Universal Prayer.

The Creed is not said.

THE LITURGY OF THE EUCHARIST

At the beginning of the Liturgy of the Eucharist, there may be a procession of the faithful in which gifts for the poor may be presented with the bread and wine.

Meanwhile the following, or another appropriate chant, is sung.

Ant. Where true charity is dwelling, God is present there.
℣ By the love of Christ we have been brought together:
℣ let us find in him our gladness and our pleasure;
℣ may we love him and revere him, God the living,
℣ and in love respect each other with sincere hearts.
Ant. Where true charity is dwelling, God is present there.
℣ So when we as one are gathered all together,
℣ let us strive to keep our minds free of division;
℣ may there be an end to malice, strife and quarrels,
℣ and let Christ our God be dwelling here among us.
Ant. Where true charity is dwelling, God is present there.
℣ May your face thus be our vision, bright in glory,
℣ Christ our God, with all the blessed Saints in heaven:
℣ such delight is pure and faultless, joy unbounded,
℣ which endures through countless ages world without end.
Amen.

Prayer over the Offerings
Grant us, O Lord, we pray,
that we may participate worthily in these mysteries,
for whenever the memorial of this sacrifice is celebrated
the work of our redemption is accomplished.
Through Christ our Lord.
Amen.

Preface I of the Most Holy Eucharist, p.38.

When the Roman Canon is used, this special form of it is said, with proper formulas for the Communicantes (In communion with those), Hanc igitur (Therefore, Lord, we pray), and Qui pridie (On the day before he was to suffer).

The Priest, with hands extended, says:

To you, therefore, most merciful Father,
we make humble prayer and petition
through Jesus Christ, your Son, our Lord:

He joins his hands and says:

that you accept

He makes the Sign of the Cross once over the bread and chalice together, saying:

and bless ✜ these gifts, these offerings,
these holy and unblemished sacrifices,

With hands extended, he continues:

which we offer you firstly
for your holy catholic Church.
Be pleased to grant her peace,
to guard, unite and govern her
throughout the whole world,
together with your servant N. our Pope
and N. our Bishop,[1]
and all those who, holding to the truth,
hand on the catholic and apostolic faith.

Commemoration of the Living

Remember, Lord, your servants N. and N.

---

[1] Mention may be made here of the Coadjutor Bishop, or Auxiliary Bishops, as noted in the *General Instruction of the Roman Missal*, n. 149.

The Priest joins his hands and prays briefly for those for whom he intends to pray.

Then, with hands extended, he continues:

and all gathered here,
whose faith and devotion are known to you.
For them we offer you this sacrifice of praise
or they offer it for themselves
and all who are dear to them:
for the redemption of their souls,
in hope of health and well-being,
and paying their homage to you,
the eternal God, living and true.

Within the Action

Celebrating the most sacred day
on which our Lord Jesus Christ
was handed over for our sake,
and in communion with those whose memory we venerate,
especially the glorious ever-Virgin Mary,
Mother of our God and Lord, Jesus Christ,
and † blessed Joseph, her Spouse
your blessed Apostles and Martyrs,
Peter and Paul, Andrew,
(James, John,
Thomas, James, Philip,
Bartholomew, Matthew,
Simon and Jude;
Linus, Cletus, Clement, Sixtus,
Cornelius, Cyprian,
Lawrence, Chrysogonus,
John and Paul,
Cosmas and Damian)
and all your Saints;
we ask that through their merits and prayers,
in all things we may be defended
by your protecting help.
(Through Christ our Lord. Amen.)

With hands extended, the Priest continues:

Therefore, Lord, we pray:
graciously accept this oblation of our service,
that of your whole family,
which we make to you

as we observe the day
on which our Lord Jesus Christ
handed on the mysteries of his Body and Blood
for his disciples to celebrate;
order our days in your peace,
and command that we be delivered from eternal damnation
and counted among the flock of those you have chosen.

He joins his hands.

(Through Christ our Lord. Amen.)

Holding his hands extended over the offerings, he says:

Be pleased, O God, we pray,
to bless, acknowledge,
and approve this offering in every respect;
make it spiritual and acceptable,
so that it may become for us
the Body and Blood of your most beloved Son,
our Lord Jesus Christ.

He joins his hands.

In the formulas that follow, the words of the Lord should be pronounced clearly and distinctly, as the nature of these words requires.

On the day before he was to suffer
for our salvation and the salvation of all,
that is today,

He takes the bread and, holding it slightly raised above the altar, continues:

he took bread in his holy and venerable hands,

He raises his eyes.

and with eyes raised to heaven
to you, O God, his almighty Father,
giving you thanks, he said the blessing,
broke the bread
and gave it to his disciples, saying:

He bows slightly.

Take this, all of you, and eat of it,
for this is my Body,
which will be given up for you.

Thursday of the Lord's Supper

He shows the consecrated host to the people, places it again on the paten, and genuflects in adoration.

After this, the Priest continues:

In a similar way, when supper was ended,

He takes the chalice and, holding it slightly raised above the altar, continues:

he took this precious chalice
in his holy and venerable hands,
and once more giving you thanks, he said the blessing
and gave the chalice to his disciples, saying:

He bows slightly.

TAKE THIS, ALL OF YOU, AND DRINK FROM IT,
FOR THIS IS THE CHALICE OF MY BLOOD,
THE BLOOD OF THE NEW AND ETERNAL COVENANT,
WHICH WILL BE POURED OUT FOR YOU AND FOR MANY
FOR THE FORGIVENESS OF SINS.
DO THIS IN MEMORY OF ME.

He shows the chalice to the people, places it on the corporal, and genuflects in adoration.

Then he says:

The mystery of faith.

And the people continue, acclaiming:

We proclaim your Death, O Lord,
and profess your Resurrection
until you come again.

or

When we eat this Bread and drink this Cup,
we proclaim your Death, O Lord,
until you come again.

or

Save us, Saviour of the world,
for by your Cross and Resurrection
you have set us free.

Then the Priest, with hands extended, says:

Therefore, O Lord,
as we celebrate the memorial of the blessed Passion,
the Resurrection from the dead,

and the glorious Ascension into heaven
of Christ, your Son, our Lord,
we, your servants and your holy people,
offer to your glorious majesty
from the gifts that you have given us,
this pure victim,
this holy victim,
this spotless victim,
the holy Bread of eternal life
and the Chalice of everlasting salvation.

Be pleased to look upon these offerings
with a serene and kindly countenance,
and to accept them,
as once you were pleased to accept
the gifts of your servant Abel the just,
the sacrifice of Abraham, our father in faith,
and the offering of your high priest Melchizedek,
a holy sacrifice, a spotless victim.

Bowing, with hands joined, he continues:

In humble prayer we ask you, almighty God:
command that these gifts be borne
by the hands of your holy Angel
to your altar on high
in the sight of your divine majesty,
so that all of us, who through this participation at the altar
receive the most holy Body and Blood of your Son,

He stands upright and signs himself with the Sign of the Cross, saying:

may be filled with every grace and heavenly blessing.

He joins his hands.

(Through Christ our Lord. Amen.)

Commemoration of the Dead
With hands extended, the Priest says:

Remember also, Lord, your servants N. and N.,
who have gone before us with the sign of faith
and rest in the sleep of peace.

He joins his hands and prays briefly for those who have died and for whom he intends to pray.

Thursday of the Lord's Supper

Then, with hands extended he continues:

Grant them, O Lord, we pray,
and all who sleep in Christ,
a place of refreshment, light and peace.

He joins his hands.

(Through Christ our Lord. Amen.)

He strikes his breast with his right hand, saying:

To us, also, your servants, who, though sinners,

And, with hands extended he continues:

hope in your abundant mercies,
graciously grant some share
and fellowship with your holy Apostles and Martyrs:
with John the Baptist, Stephen,
Matthias, Barnabas,
(Ignatius, Alexander,
Marcellinus, Peter,
Felicity, Perpetua,
Agatha, Lucy,
Agnes, Cecilia, Anastasia)
and all your Saints;
admit us, we beseech you,
into their company,
not weighing our merits,
but granting us your pardon,

He joins his hands.

through Christ our Lord.

And he continues:

Through whom
you continue to make all these good things, O Lord;
you sanctify them, fill them with life,
bless them, and bestow them upon us.

He takes the chalice and the paten with the host and, elevating both, he says:

Through him, and with him, and in him,
O God, almighty Father,

in the unity of the Holy Spirit,
all glory and honour is yours
for ever and ever.

The people acclaim:

Amen.

Then follows the Communion Rite, p.85.

At an appropriate moment during Communion, the Priest entrusts the Eucharist from the table of the altar to Deacons or acolytes or other extraordinary ministers, so that afterwards it may be brought to the sick who are to receive Holy Communion at home.

Communion Antiphon 1 Cor 11:24-25
This is the Body that will be given up for you;
this is the Chalice of the new covenant in my Blood, says the Lord;
do this, whenever you receive it, in memory of me.

After the distribution of Communion, a ciborium with hosts for Communion on the following day is left on the altar. The Priest, standing at the chair, says the Prayer after Communion.

Prayer after Communion
Grant, almighty God,
that, just as we are renewed
by the Supper of your Son in this present age,
so we may enjoy his banquet for all eternity.
Who lives and reigns for ever and ever.
Amen.

THE TRANSFER OF THE MOST BLESSED SACRAMENT

After the Prayer after Communion, the Priest puts incense in the thurible while standing, blesses it and then, kneeling, incenses the Blessed Sacrament three times. Then, having put on a white humeral veil, he rises, takes the ciborium, and covers it with the ends of the veil.

A procession is formed in which the Blessed Sacrament, accompanied by torches and incense, is carried through the church to a place of repose prepared in a part of the church or in a chapel suitably decorated. A lay minister with a cross, standing between two other ministers with lighted candles leads off. Others carrying lighted candles follow. Before the Priest carrying the Blessed

Sacrament comes the thurifer with a smoking thurible. Meanwhile, the hymn **Pange, lingua** (exclusive of the last two stanzas) or another eucharistic chant is sung.

When the procession reaches the place of repose, the Priest, with the help of the Deacon if necessary, places the ciborium in the tabernacle, the door of which remains open. Then he puts incense in the thurible and, kneeling, incenses the Blessed Sacrament, while **Tantum ergo Sacraméntum** or another eucharistic chant is sung. Then the Deacon or the Priest himself places the Sacrament in the tabernacle and closes the door.

After a period of adoration in silence, the Priest and ministers genuflect and return to the sacristy.

At an appropriate time, the altar is stripped and, if possible, the crosses are removed from the church. It is expedient that any crosses which remain in the church be veiled.

Vespers (Evening Prayer) is not celebrated by those who have attended the Mass of the Lord's Supper.

The faithful are invited to continue adoration before the Blessed Sacrament for a suitable length of time during the night, according to local circumstances, but after midnight the adoration should take place without solemnity.

If the celebration of the Passion of the Lord on the following Friday does not take place in the same church, the Mass is concluded in the usual way and the Blessed Sacrament is placed in the tabernacle.

FRIDAY OF THE PASSION OF THE LORD

On this and the following day, by a most ancient tradition, the Church does not celebrate the Sacraments at all, except for Penance and the Anointing of the Sick.

On this day, Holy Communion is distributed to the faithful only within the celebration of the Lord's Passion; but it may be brought at any hour of the day to the sick who cannot participate in this celebration.

The altar should be completely bare: without a cross, without candles and without cloths.

The Celebration of the Passion of the Lord
On the afternoon of this day, about three o'clock (unless a later hour is chosen for a pastoral reason), there takes place the celebration of

the Lord's Passion consisting of three parts, namely, the Liturgy of the Word, the Adoration of the Cross, and Holy Communion.

The Priest and the Deacon, if a Deacon is present, wearing red vestments as for Mass, go to the altar in silence and, after making a reverence to the altar, prostrate themselves or, if appropriate, kneel and pray in silence for a while. All others kneel.

Then the Priest, with the ministers, goes to the chair where, facing the people, who are standing, he says, with hands extended, one of the following prayers, omitting the invitation Let us pray:

Prayer
Remember your mercies, O Lord,
and with your eternal protection sanctify your servants,
for whom Christ your Son,
by the shedding of his Blood,
established the Paschal Mystery.
Who lives and reigns for ever and ever.

or

O God, who by the Passion of Christ your Son, our Lord,
abolished the death inherited from ancient sin
by every succeeding generation,
grant that just as, being conformed to him,
we have borne by the law of nature
the image of the man of earth,
so by the sanctification of grace
we may bear the image of the Man of heaven.
Through Christ our Lord.
Amen.

FIRST PART:
LITURGY OF THE WORD

Then all sit and the First Reading, from the Book of the Prophet Isaiah (52:13–53:12), is read with its Psalm.

The Second Reading, from the Letter to the Hebrews (4:14-16; 5: 7-9), follows, and then the chant before the Gospel.

Then the narrative of the Lord's Passion according to John (18: 1–19:42) is read in the same way as on the preceding Sunday.

After the reading of the Lord's Passion, the Priest gives a brief homily and, at its end, the faithful may be invited to spend a short time in prayer.

Friday of the Passion of the Lord

FIRST READING
A reading from the prophet Isaiah 52:13 – 53:12

See, my servant will prosper,
he shall be lifted up, exalted, rise to great heights.

As the crowds were appalled on seeing him
– so disfigured did he look
that he seemed no longer human –
so will the crowds be astonished at him,
and kings stand speechless before him;
for they shall see something never told
and witness something never heard before:
'Who could believe what we have heard,
and to whom has the power of the Lord been revealed?'

Like a sapling he grew up in front of us,
like a root in arid ground.
Without beauty, without majesty (we saw him),
no looks to attract our eyes;
a thing despised and rejected by men,
a man of sorrows and familiar with suffering,
a man to make people screen their faces;
he was despised and we took no account of him.

And yet ours were the sufferings he bore,
ours the sorrows he carried.
But we, we thought of him as someone punished,
struck by God, and brought low.
Yet he was pierced through for our faults,
crushed for our sins.
On him lies a punishment that brings us peace,
and through his wounds we are healed.
We had all gone astray like sheep,
each taking his own way,
and the Lord burdened him
with the sins of all of us.
Harshly dealt with, he bore it humbly,
he never opened his mouth,
like a lamb that is led to the slaughter-house,
like a sheep that is dumb before its shearers
never opening its mouth.
By force and by law he was taken;
would anyone plead his cause?
Yes, he was torn away from the land of the living;

for our faults struck down in death.
They gave him a grave with the wicked,
a tomb with the rich,
though he had done no wrong
and there had been no perjury in his mouth.
The Lord has been pleased to crush him with suffering.
If he offers his life in atonement,
he shall see his heirs, he shall have a long life
and through him what the Lord wishes will be done.
His soul's anguish over
he shall see the light and be content.
By his sufferings shall my servant justify many,
taking their faults on himself.
Hence I will grant whole hordes for his tribute,
he shall divide the spoil with the mighty,
for surrendering himself to death
and letting himself be taken for a sinner,
while he was bearing the faults of many
and praying all the time for sinners.

The word of the Lord.

Responsorial Psalm   Ps 30:2. 6. 12-13. 15-17. 25. ℟ Lk 23:46

℟ **Father, into your hands I commend my spirit.**

1   In you, O Lord, I take refuge.
     Let me never be put to shame.
     In your justice, set me free.
     Into your hands I commend my spirit.
     It is you who will redeem me, Lord. ℟

2   In the face of all my foes
     I am a reproach,
     an object of scorn to my neighbours
     and of fear to my friends. ℟

3   Those who see me in the street
     run far away from me.
     I am like a dead man, forgotten in men's hearts,
     like a thing thrown away. ℟

4   But as for me, I trust in you, Lord,
     I say: 'You are my God.'
     My life is in your hands, deliver me
     from the hands of those who hate me. ℟

5   Let your face shine on your servant.
Save me in your love.
Be strong, let your heart take courage,
all who hope in the Lord. ℟

SECOND READING
A reading from the letter to the Hebrews   4:14-16; 5:7-9

Since in Jesus, the Son of God, we have the supreme high priest who has gone through to the highest heaven, we must never let go of the faith that we have professed. For it is not as if we had a high priest who was incapable of feeling our weaknesses with us; but we have one who has been tempted in every way that we are, though he is without sin. Let us be confident, then, in approaching the throne of grace, that we shall have mercy from him and find grace when we are in need of help.

During his life on earth, he offered up prayer and entreaty, aloud and in silent tears, to the one who had the power to save him out of death, and he submitted so humbly that his prayer was heard. Although he was Son, he learnt to obey through suffering; but having been made perfect, he became for all who obey him the source of eternal salvation.

The word of the Lord.

Gospel Acclamation   Phil 2:8-9
Glory and praise to you, O Christ!
Christ was humbler yet,
even to accepting death, death on a cross.
But God raised him high
and gave him the name which is above all names.
Glory and praise to you, O Christ!

GOSPEL
The passion of our Lord Jesus Christ
according to John   18:1 – 19:42
N Narrator. J Jesus. O Other single speaker. C Crowd, or more than one other speaker.

N Jesus left with his disciples and crossed the Kedron valley. There was a garden there, and he went into it with his disciples. Judas the traitor knew the place well, since Jesus had often met his disciples there, and he brought the cohort to this place together with a detachment of guards sent by the chief priests and the Pharisees, all with lanterns and torches and weapons. Knowing everything that was going to happen to him, Jesus then came forward and said,

J Who are you looking for?
N They answered,
C Jesus the Nazarene.
N He said,
J I am he.
N Now Judas the traitor was standing among them. When Jesus said, 'I am he', they moved back and fell to the ground. He asked them a second time,
J Who are you looking for?
N They said,
C Jesus the Nazarene.
N Jesus replied,
J I have told you that I am he. If I am the one you are looking for, let these others go.
N This was to fulfil the words he had spoken: 'Not one of those you gave me have I lost'.

Simon Peter, who carried a sword, drew it and wounded the high priest's servant, cutting off his right ear. The servant's name was Malchus. Jesus said to Peter,

J Put your sword back in its scabbard; am I not to drink the cup that the Father has given me?
N The cohort and its captain and the Jewish guards seized Jesus and bound him. They took him first to Annas, because Annas was the father-in-law of Caiaphas, who was high priest that year. It was Caiaphas who had suggested to the Jews, 'It is better for one man to die for the people'.

Simon Peter, with another disciple, followed Jesus. This disciple, who was known to the high priest, went with Jesus into the high priest's palace, but Peter stayed outside the door. So the other disciple, the one known to the high priest, went out, spoke to the woman who was keeping the door and brought Peter in. The maid on duty at the door said to Peter,

O Aren't you another of that man's disciples?
N He answered,
O I am not.
N Now it *was cold,* and the servants and guards had lit a charcoal fire and were standing there warming themselves; so Peter stood there too, warming himself with the others.

The high priest questioned Jesus about his disciples and his teaching. Jesus answered,

Friday of the Passion of the Lord

J I have spoken openly for all the world to hear; I have always taught in the synagogue and in the Temple where all the Jews meet together: I have said nothing in secret. But why ask me? Ask my hearers what I taught: they know what I said.

N At these words, one of the guards standing by gave Jesus a slap in the face, saying,

O Is that the way to answer the high priest?

N Jesus replied,

J If there is something wrong in what I said, point it out; but if there is no offence in it, why do you strike me?

N Then Annas sent him, still bound, to Caiaphas, the high priest.

As Simon Peter stood there warming himself, someone said to him,

O Aren't you another of his disciples?

N He denied it saying,

O I am not.

N One of the high priest's servants, a relation of the man whose ear Peter had cut off, said,

O Didn't I see you in the garden with him?

N Again Peter denied it; and at once a cock crew.

They then led Jesus from the house of Caiaphas to the Praetorium. It was now morning. They did not go into the Praetorium themselves or they would be defiled and unable to eat the passover. So Pilate came outside to them and said,

O What charge do you bring against this man?

N They replied,

C If he were not a criminal, we should not be handing him over to you.

N Pilate said,

O Take him yourselves, and try him by your own Law.

N The Jews answered,

C We are not allowed to put a man to death.

N This was to fulfil the words Jesus had spoken indicating the way he was going to die.

So Pilate went back into the Praetorium and called Jesus to him, and asked,

O Are you the king of the Jews?

N Jesus replied,

J Do you ask this of your own accord, or have others spoken to you about me?

N Pilate answered,

O Am I a Jew? It is your own people and the chief priests who have handed you over to me: what have you done?

N Jesus replied,
J Mine is not a kingdom of this world; if my kingdom were of this world, my men would have fought to prevent me being surrendered to the Jews. But my kingdom is not of this kind.
N Pilate said,
O So you are a king then?
N Jesus answered,
J It is you who say it. Yes, I am a king. I was born for this, I came into the world for this; to bear witness to the truth, and all who are on the side of truth listen to my voice.
N Pilate said,
O Truth? What is that?
N And with that he went out again to the Jews and said,
O I find no case against him. But according to a custom of yours I should release one prisoner at the Passover; would you like me, then, to release the king of the Jews?
N At this they shouted:
C Not this man, but Barabbas.
N Barabbas was a brigand.

Pilate then had Jesus taken away and scourged; and after this, the soldiers twisted some thorns into a crown and put it on his head, and dressed him in a purple robe. They kept coming up to him and saying,
C Hail, king of the Jews!
N and they slapped him in the face.

Pilate came outside again and said to them,
O Look, I am going to bring him out to you to let you see that I find no case.
N Jesus then came out wearing the crown of thorns and the purple robe. Pilate said,
O Here is the man.
N When they saw him the chief priests and the guards shouted,
C Crucify him! Crucify him!
N Pilate said,
O Take him yourselves and crucify him: I can find no case against him.
N The Jews replied,
C We have a Law, and according to the Law he ought to die, because he has claimed to be the son of God.
N When Pilate heard them say this his fears increased. Reentering the Praetorium, he said to Jesus,
O Where do you come from?

Friday of the Passion of the Lord

N But Jesus made no answer. Pilate then said to him,
O Are you refusing to speak to me? Surely you know I have power to release you and I have power to crucify you?
N Jesus replied
J You would have no power over me if it had not been given you from above; that is why the one who handed me over to you has the greater guilt.
N From that moment Pilate was anxious to set him free, but the Jews shouted,
C If you set him free you are no friend of Caesar's; anyone who makes himself king is defying Caesar.
N Hearing these words, Pilate had Jesus brought out, and seated himself on the chair of judgement at a place called the Pavement, in Hebrew Gabbatha. It was Passover Preparation Day, about the sixth hour. Pilate said to the Jews,
O Here is your king.
N They said,
C Take him away, take him away. Crucify him!
N Pilate said,
O Do you want me to crucify your king?
N The chief priests answered,
C We have no king except Caesar.
N So in the end Pilate handed him over to them to be crucified.

They then took charge of Jesus, and carrying his own cross he went out of the city to the place of the skull, or, as it was called in Hebrew, Golgotha, where they crucified him with two others, one on either side with Jesus in the middle. Pilate wrote out a notice and had it fixed to the cross; it ran: 'Jesus the Nazarene, King of the Jews.' This notice was read by many of the Jews, because the place where Jesus was crucified was not far from the city, and the writing was in Hebrew, Latin and Greek. So the Jewish chief priests said to Pilate,

C You should not write 'King of the Jews', but this man said: I am King of the Jews'.
N Pilate answered,
O What I have written, I have written.
N When the soldiers had finished crucifying Jesus they took his clothing and divided it into four shares, one for each soldier. His undergarment was seamless, woven in one piece from neck to hem; so they said to one another,
C Instead of tearing it, let's throw dice to decide who is to have it.

N In this way the words of scripture were fulfilled:

> They shared out my clothing among them.
> They cast lots for my clothes.
> This is exactly what the soldiers did.

Near the cross of Jesus stood his mother and his mother's sister, Mary the wife of Clopas, and Mary of Magdala. Seeing his mother and the disciple he loved standing near her, Jesus said to his mother,

J Woman, this is your son.
N Then to the disciple he said,
J This is your mother.
N And from that moment the disciple made a place for her in his home.

After this, Jesus knew that everything had now been completed, and to fulfil the scripture perfectly he said:

J I am thirsty.
N A jar full of vinegar stood there, so putting a sponge soaked in vinegar on a hyssop stick they held it up to his mouth. After Jesus had taken the vinegar he said,
J It is accomplished;
N and bowing his head he gave up the spirit.

All kneel and pause a moment.

N It was Preparation Day, and to prevent the bodies remaining on the cross during the sabbath – since that sabbath was a day of special solemnity – the Jews asked Pilate to have the legs broken and the bodies taken away. Consequently the soldiers came and broke the legs of the first man who had been crucified with him and then of the other. When they came to Jesus, they found that he was already dead, and so instead of breaking his legs one of the soldiers pierced his side with a lance; and immediately there came out blood and water. This is the evidence of one who saw it – trustworthy evidence, and he knows he speaks the truth – and he gives it so that you may believe as well. Because all this happened to fulfil the words of scripture:

> Not one bone of his will be broken,

and again, in another place scripture says:

> They will look on the one whom they have pierced.

After this, Joseph of Arimathaea, who was a disciple of Jesus – though a secret one because he was afraid of the Jews – asked Pilate to let him remove the body of Jesus. Pilate gave

permission, so they came and took it away. Nicodemus came as
well – the same one who had first come to Jesus at night-time –
and he brought a mixture of myrrh and aloes, weighing about
a hundred pounds. They took the body of Jesus and wrapped
it with the spices in linen cloths, following the Jewish burial
custom. At the place where he had been crucified there was a
garden, and in the garden a new tomb in which no one had yet
been buried. Since it was the Jewish Day of Preparation and the
tomb was near at hand, they laid Jesus there.

The Solemn Intercessions

The Liturgy of the Word concludes with the Solemn Intercessions, which take place in this way: the Deacon, if a Deacon is present, or if he is not, a lay minister, stands at the ambo, and sings or says the invitation in which the intention is expressed. Then all pray in silence for a while, and afterwards the Priest, standing at the chair or, if appropriate, at the altar, with hands extended, sings or says the prayer.

The faithful may remain either kneeling or standing throughout the entire period of the prayers.

Before the Priest's prayer, in accord with tradition, it is permissible to use the Deacon's invitations Let us kneel — Let us stand, with all kneeling for silent prayer.

Let us kneel.   Let us stand.

The Conferences of Bishops may provide other invitations to introduce the prayer of the Priest.

In a situation of grave public need, the Diocesan Bishop may permit or order the addition of a special intention.

I. For Holy Church

The prayer is sung in the simple tone or, if the invitations Let us kneel — Let us stand are used, in the solemn tone.

Let us pray, dearly beloved, for the holy Church of God,
that our God and Lord be pleased to give her peace,
to guard her and to unite her throughout the whole world
and grant that, leading our life in tranquillity and quiet,
we may glorify God the Father almighty.

Prayer in silence. Then the Priest says:

Almighty ever-living God,
who in Christ revealed your glory to all the nations,
watch over the works of your mercy,
that your Church, spread throughout all the world,
may persevere with steadfast faith in confessing your name.
Through Christ our Lord.
Amen.

II. For the Pope
Let us pray also for our most Holy Father Pope N.,
that our God and Lord,
who chose him for the Order of Bishops,
may keep him safe and unharmed for the Lord's holy Church,
to govern the holy People of God.

Prayer in silence. Then the Priest says:

Almighty ever-living God,
by whose decree all things are founded,
look with favour on our prayers
and in your kindness protect the Pope chosen for us,
that, under him, the Christian people,
governed by you their maker,
may grow in merit by reason of their faith.
Through Christ our Lord.
Amen.

III. For all orders and degrees of the faithful
Let us pray also for our Bishop N.,*
for all Bishops, Priests, and Deacons of the Church
and for the whole of the faithful people.

Prayer in silence. Then the Priest says:

Almighty ever-living God,
by whose Spirit the whole body of the Church
is sanctified and governed,
hear our humble prayer for your ministers,
that, by the gift of your grace,
all may serve you faithfully.

---

* Mention may be made here of the Coadjutor Bishop, or Auxiliary Bishops, as noted in the *General Instruction of the Roman Missal*, no. 149.

Through Christ our Lord.
Amen.

IV. **For catechumens**
Let us pray also for (our) catechumens,
that our God and Lord
may open wide the ears of their inmost hearts
and unlock the gates of his mercy,
that, having received forgiveness of all their sins
through the waters of rebirth,
they, too, may be one with Christ Jesus our Lord.

Prayer in silence. Then the Priest says:

Almighty ever-living God,
who make your Church ever fruitful with new offspring,
increase the faith and understanding of (our) catechumens,
that, reborn in the font of Baptism,
they may be added to the number of your adopted children.
Through Christ our Lord.
Amen.

V. **For the unity of Christians**
Let us pray also for all our brothers and sisters who believe in Christ,
that our God and Lord may be pleased,
as they live the truth,
to gather them together and keep them in his one Church.

Prayer in silence. Then the Priest says:

Almighty ever-living God,
who gather what is scattered
and keep together what you have gathered,
look kindly on the flock of your Son,
that those whom one Baptism has consecrated
may be joined together by integrity of faith
and united in the bond of charity.
Through Christ our Lord.
Amen.

VI. **For the Jewish people**
Let us pray also for the Jewish people,
to whom the Lord our God spoke first,
that he may grant them to advance in love of his name
and in faithfulness to his covenant.

Prayer in silence. Then the Priest says:

Almighty ever-living God,
who bestowed your promises on Abraham and his descendants,
graciously hear the prayers of your Church,
that the people you first made your own
may attain the fullness of redemption.
Through Christ our Lord.
Amen.

VII.   For those who do not believe in Christ
Let us pray also for those who do not believe in Christ,
that, enlightened by the Holy Spirit,
they, too, may enter on the way of salvation.

Prayer in silence. Then the Priest says:

Almighty ever-living God,
grant to those who do not confess Christ
that, by walking before you with a sincere heart,
they may find the truth
and that we ourselves, being constant in mutual love
and striving to understand more fully the mystery of your life,
may be made more perfect witnesses to your love in the world.
Through Christ our Lord.
Amen.

VIII.   For those who do not believe in God
Let us pray also for those who do not acknowledge God,
that, following what is right in sincerity of heart,
they may find the way to God himself.

Prayer in silence. Then the Priest says:

Almighty ever-living God,
who created all people
to seek you always by desiring you
and, by finding you, come to rest,
grant, we pray,
that, despite every harmful obstacle,
all may recognize the signs of your fatherly love
and the witness of the good works
done by those who believe in you,
and so in gladness confess you,
the one true God and Father of our human race.
Through Christ our Lord.
Amen.

Friday of the Passion of the Lord

IX. For those in public office
Let us pray also for those in public office,
that our God and Lord
may direct their minds and hearts according to his will
for the true peace and freedom of all.

Prayer in silence. Then the Priest says:

Almighty ever-living God,
in whose hand lies every human heart
and the rights of peoples,
look with favour, we pray,
on those who govern with authority over us,
that throughout the whole world,
the prosperity of peoples,
the assurance of peace,
and freedom of religion
may through your gift be made secure.
Through Christ our Lord.
Amen.

X. For those in tribulation
Let us pray, dearly beloved,
to God the Father almighty,
that he may cleanse the world of all errors,
banish disease, drive out hunger,
unlock prisons, loosen fetters,
granting to travellers safety, to pilgrims return,
health to the sick, and salvation to the dying.

Prayer in silence. Then the Priest says:

Almighty ever-living God,
comfort of mourners, strength of all who toil,
may the prayers of those who cry out in any tribulation
come before you,
that all may rejoice,
because in their hour of need
your mercy was at hand.
Through Christ our Lord.
Amen.

Friday of the Passion of the Lord

SECOND PART:

THE ADORATION OF THE HOLY CROSS

After the Solemn Intercessions, the solemn Adoration of the Holy Cross takes place. Of the two forms of the showing of the Cross presented here, the more appropriate one, according to pastoral needs, should be chosen.

The Showing of the Holy Cross

First Form
The Deacon accompanied by ministers, or another suitable minister, goes to the sacristy, from which, in procession, accompanied by two ministers with lighted candles, he carries the Cross, covered with a violet veil, through the church to the middle of the sanctuary.

The Priest, standing before the altar and facing the people, receives the Cross, uncovers a little of its upper part and elevates it while beginning the Ecce lignum Crucis (Behold the wood of the Cross). (Alternative musical settings for this may be found on p.590). He is assisted in singing by the Deacon or, if need be, by the choir. All respond, Come, let us adore. At the end of the singing, all kneel and for a brief moment adore in silence, while the Priest stands and holds the Cross raised.

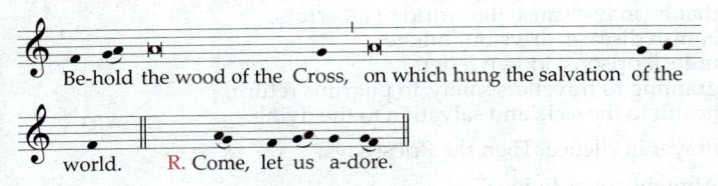

Be-hold the wood of the Cross, on which hung the salvation of the world. R. Come, let us a-dore.

Then the Priest uncovers the right arm of the Cross and again, raising up the Cross, begins, Behold the wood of the Cross and everything takes place as above.

Finally, he uncovers the Cross entirely and, raising it up, he begins the invitation Behold the wood of the Cross a third time and everything takes place like the first time.

Second Form
The Priest or the Deacon accompanied by ministers, or another suitable minister, goes to the door of the church, where he receives the unveiled Cross, and the ministers take lighted candles; then the procession sets off through the church to the sanctuary. Near

the door, in the middle of the church and before the entrance of the sanctuary, the one who carries the Cross elevates it, singing, **Behold the wood of the Cross**, to which all respond, **Come, let us adore**. *After each response all kneel and for a brief moment adore in silence, as above.*

The Adoration of the Holy Cross

Then, accompanied by two ministers with lighted candles, the Priest or the Deacon carries the Cross to the entrance of the sanctuary or to another suitable place and there puts it down or hands it over to the ministers to hold. Candles are placed on the right and left sides of the Cross.

For the Adoration of the Cross, first the Priest Celebrant alone approaches, with the chasuble and his shoes removed, if appropriate. Then the clergy, the lay ministers, and the faithful approach, moving as if in procession, and showing reverence to the Cross by a simple genuflection or by some other sign appropriate to the usage of the region, for example, by kissing the Cross.

Only one Cross should be offered for adoration. If, because of the large number of people, it is not possible for all to approach individually, the Priest, after some of the clergy and faithful have adored, takes the Cross and, standing in the middle before the altar, invites the people in a few words to adore the Holy Cross and afterwards holds the Cross elevated higher for a brief time, for the faithful to adore it in silence.

While the adoration of the Holy Cross is taking place, the antiphon **Crucem tuam adoramus** (We adore your Cross, O Lord), *the Reproaches, the hymn* **Crux fidelis** (Faithful Cross) *or other suitable chants are sung, during which all who have already adored the Cross remain seated.*

Chants to Be Sung during the Adoration of the Holy Cross

Ant. We adore your Cross, O Lord,
we praise and glorify your holy Resurrection,
for behold, because of the wood of a tree
joy has come to the whole world.

May God have mercy on us and bless us;   Cf. Ps 66:2
may he let his face shed its light upon us
and have mercy on us.
And the antiphon is repeated: We adore . . .

The Reproaches

Parts assigned to one of the two choirs separately are indicated by the numbers 1 (first choir) and 2 (second choir); parts sung by both choirs together are marked: 1 and 2. Some of the verses may also be sung by two cantors.

I

1 and 2	My people, what have I done to you? Or how have I grieved you? Answer me!
1	Because I led you out of the land of Egypt, you have prepared a Cross for your Saviour.
1	Hagios o Theos,
2	Holy is God,
1	Hagios Ischyros,
2	Holy and Mighty,
1	Hagios Athanatos, eleison himas.
2	Holy and Immortal One, have mercy on us.
1 and 2	Because I led you out through the desert forty years and fed you with manna and brought you into a land of plenty, you have prepared a Cross for your Saviour.
1	Hagios o Theos,
2	Holy is God,
1	Hagios Ischyros,
2	Holy and Mighty,
1	Hagios Athanatos, eleison himas.
2	Holy and Immortal One, have mercy on us.
1 and 2	What more should I have done for you and have not done? Indeed, I planted you as my most beautiful chosen vine and you have turned very bitter for me, for in my thirst you gave me vinegar to drink and with a lance you pierced your Saviour's side.
1	Hagios o Theos,
2	Holy is God,
1	Hagios Ischyros,
2	Holy and Mighty,
1	Hagios Athanatos, eleison himas.
2	Holy and Immortal One, have mercy on us.

II

Cantors:
I scourged Egypt for your sake with its firstborn sons,
and you scourged me and handed me over.

1 and 2 repeat:
My people, what have I done to you?
Or how have I grieved you? Answer me!

Cantors:
I led you out from Egypt as Pharoah lay sunk in the Red Sea,
and you handed me over to the chief priests.

1 and 2 repeat:
My people . . .

Cantors:
I opened up the sea before you,
and you opened my side with a lance.

1 and 2 repeat:
My people . . .

Cantors:
I went before you in a pillar of cloud,
and you led me into Pilate's palace.

1 and 2 repeat:
My people . . .

Cantors:
I fed you with manna in the desert,
and on me you rained blows and lashes.

1 and 2 repeat:
My people . . .

Cantors:
I gave you saving water from the rock to drink,
and for drink you gave me gall and vinegar.

1 and 2 repeat:
My people . . .

Cantors:
I struck down for you the kings of the Canaanites,
and you struck my head with a reed.

Friday of the Passion of the Lord

1 and 2 repeat:
My people . . .

Cantors:
I put in your hand a royal sceptre,
and you put on my head a crown of thorns.

1 and 2 repeat:
My people . . .

Cantors:
I exalted you with great power,
and you hung me on the scaffold of the Cross.

1 and 2 repeat:
My people . . .

Hymn
All:
Faithful Cross the Saints rely on,
Noble tree beyond compare!
Never was there such a scion,
Never leaf or flower so rare.
Sweet the timber, sweet the iron,
Sweet the burden that they bear!

Cantors:
Sing, my tongue, in exultation
Of our banner and device!
Make a solemn proclamation
Of a triumph and its price:
How the Saviour of creation
Conquered by his sacrifice!

All:
Faithful Cross the Saints rely on,
Noble tree beyond compare!
Never was there such a scion,
Never leaf or flower so rare.

Cantors:
For, when Adam first offended,
Eating that forbidden fruit,
Not all hopes of glory ended
With the serpent at the root:

Broken nature would be mended
By a second tree and shoot.

All:
Sweet the timber, sweet the iron,
Sweet the burden that they bear!

Cantors:
Thus the tempter was outwitted
By a wisdom deeper still:
Remedy and ailment fitted,
Means to cure and means to kill;
That the world might be acquitted,
Christ would do his Father's will.

All:
Faithful Cross the Saints rely on,
Noble tree beyond compare!
Never was there such a scion,
Never leaf or flower so rare.

Cantors:
So the Father, out of pity
For our self-inflicted doom,
Sent him from the heavenly city
When the holy time had come:
He, the Son and the Almighty,
Took our flesh in Mary's womb.

All:
Sweet the timber, sweet the iron,
Sweet the burden that they bear!

Cantors:
Hear a tiny baby crying,
Founder of the seas and strands;
See his virgin Mother tying
Cloth around his feet and hands;
Find him in a manger lying
Tightly wrapped in swaddling-bands!

All:
Faithful Cross the Saints rely on,
Noble tree beyond compare!
Never was there such a scion,
Never leaf or flower so rare.

Cantors:
So he came, the long-expected,
Not in glory, not to reign;
Only born to be rejected,
Choosing hunger, toil and pain,
Till the scaffold was erected
And the Paschal Lamb was slain.

All:
Sweet the timber, sweet the iron,
Sweet the burden that they bear!

Cantors:
No disgrace was too abhorrent:
Nailed and mocked and parched he died;
Blood and water, double warrant,
Issue from his wounded side,
Washing in a mighty torrent
Earth and stars and oceantide.

All:
Faithful Cross the Saints rely on,
Noble tree beyond compare!
Never was there such a scion,
Never leaf or flower so rare.

Cantors:
Lofty timber, smooth your roughness,
Flex your boughs for blossoming;
Let your fibres lose their toughness,
Gently let your tendrils cling;
Lay aside your native gruffness,
Clasp the body of your King!

All:
Sweet the timber, sweet the iron,
Sweet the burden that they bear!

Cantors:
Noblest tree of all created,
Richly jeweled and embossed:
Post by Lamb's blood consecrated;
Spar that saves the tempest-tossed;
Scaffold-beam which, elevated,
Carries what the world has cost!

All:
Faithful Cross the Saints rely on,
Noble tree beyond compare!
Never was there such a scion,
Never leaf or flower so rare.

The following conclusion is never to be omitted:

All:
Wisdom, power, and adoration
To the blessed Trinity
For redemption and salvation
Through the Paschal Mystery,
Now, in every generation,
And for all eternity. Amen.

In accordance with local circumstances or popular traditions and if it is pastorally appropriate, the Stabat Mater may be sung, as found in the Graduale Romanum, or another suitable chant in memory of the compassion of the Blessed Virgin Mary.

When the adoration has been concluded, the Cross is carried by the Deacon or a minister to its place at the altar. Lighted candles are placed around or on the altar or near the Cross.

THIRD PART:

HOLY COMMUNION

A cloth is spread on the altar, and a corporal and the Missal put in place. Meanwhile the Deacon or, if there is no Deacon, the Priest himself, putting on a humeral veil, brings the Blessed Sacrament back from the place of repose to the altar by a shorter route, while all stand in silence. Two ministers with lighted candles accompany the Blessed Sacrament and place their candlesticks around or upon the altar.

When the Deacon, if a Deacon is present, has placed the Blessed Sacrament upon the altar and uncovered the ciborium, the Priest goes to the altar and genuflects.

Then the Priest, with hands joined, says aloud:

At the Saviour's command
and formed by divine teaching,
we dare to say:

The Priest, with hands extended says, and all present continue:

Our Father, who art in heaven,
hallowed be thy name;
thy kingdom come,
thy will be done
on earth as it is in heaven.
Give us this day our daily bread,
and forgive us our trespasses,
as we forgive those who trespass against us;
and lead us not into temptation,
but deliver us from evil.

(Musical settings for the Lord's Prayer may be found on pp.85 and 153.)

With hands extended, the Priest continues alone:

Deliver us, Lord, we pray, from every evil,
graciously grant peace in our days,
that, by the help of your mercy,
we may be always free from sin
and safe from all distress,
as we await the blessed hope
and the coming of our Saviour, Jesus Christ.

He joins his hands.

The people conclude the prayer, acclaiming:

For the kingdom,
the power and the glory are yours
now and for ever.

Then the Priest, with hands joined, says quietly:

May the receiving of your Body and Blood,
Lord Jesus Christ,
not bring me to judgement and condemnation,
but through your loving mercy
be for me protection in mind and body
and a healing remedy.

The Priest then genuflects, takes a particle, and, holding it slightly raised over the ciborium, while facing the people, says aloud:

Behold the Lamb of God,
behold him who takes away the sins of the world.
Blessed are those called to the supper of the Lamb.

And together with the people he adds once:

Lord, I am not worthy
that you should enter under my roof,
but only say the word
and my soul shall be healed.

And facing the altar, he reverently consumes the Body of Christ, saying quietly: May the Body of Christ keep me safe for eternal life.

He then proceeds to distribute Communion to the faithful. During Communion, Psalm 21 or another appropriate chant may be sung.

When the distribution of Communion has been completed, the ciborium is taken by the Deacon or another suitable minister to a place prepared outside the church or, if circumstances so require, it is placed in the tabernacle.

Then the Priest says: Let us pray, *and, after a period of sacred silence, if circumstances so suggest, has been observed, he says the Prayer after Communion.*

Almighty ever-living God,
who have restored us to life
by the blessed Death and Resurrection of your Christ,
preserve in us the work of your mercy,
that, by partaking of this mystery,
we may have a life unceasingly devoted to you.
Through Christ our Lord.
Amen.

For the Dismissal the Deacon or, if there is no Deacon, the Priest himself, may say the invitation Bow down for the blessing.

Then the Priest, standing facing the people and extending his hands over them, says this Prayer over the People:

May abundant blessing, O Lord, we pray,
descend upon your people,
who have honoured the Death of your Son
in the hope of their resurrection:
may pardon come,
comfort be given,
holy faith increase,
and everlasting redemption be made secure.
Through Christ our Lord.
Amen.

And all, after genuflecting to the Cross, depart in silence.

After the celebration, the altar is stripped, but the Cross remains on the altar with two or four candlesticks.
Vespers (Evening Prayer) is not celebrated by those who have been present at the solemn afternoon liturgical celebration.

HOLY SATURDAY

On Holy Saturday the Church waits at the Lord's tomb in prayer and fasting, meditating on his Passion and Death and on his Descent into Hell, and awaiting his Resurrection.

The Church abstains from the Sacrifice of the Mass, with the sacred table left bare, until after the solemn Vigil, that is, the anticipation by night of the Resurrection, when the time comes for paschal joys, the abundance of which overflows to occupy fifty days.

Holy Communion may only be given on this day as Viaticum.

EASTER TIME

EASTERTIME

EASTER SUNDAY OF THE RESURRECTION OF THE LORD

THE EASTER VIGIL IN THE HOLY NIGHT

By most ancient tradition, this is the night of keeping vigil for the Lord (Ex 12:42), in which, following the Gospel admonition (Lk 12:35-37), the faithful, carrying lighted lamps in their hands, should be like those looking for the Lord when he returns, so that at his coming he may find them awake and have them sit at his table.

Of this night's Vigil, which is the greatest and most noble of all solemnities, there is to be only one celebration in each church. It is arranged, moreover, in such a way that after the Lucernarium and Easter Proclamation (which constitutes the first part of this Vigil), Holy Church meditates on the wonders the Lord God has done for his people from the beginning, trusting in his word and promise (the second part, that is, the Liturgy of the Word) until, as day approaches, with new members reborn in Baptism (the third part), the Church is called to the table the Lord has prepared for his people, the memorial of his Death and Resurrection until he comes again (the fourth part).

The entire celebration of the Easter Vigil must take place during the night, so that it begins after nightfall and ends before daybreak on the Sunday.

The Mass of the Vigil, even if it is celebrated before midnight, is a paschal Mass of the Sunday of the Resurrection.

Anyone who participates in the Mass of the night may receive Communion again at Mass during the day. A Priest who celebrates or concelebrates the Mass of the night may again celebrate or concelebrate Mass during the day.

The Easter Vigil takes the place of the Office of Readings.

The Priest is usually assisted by a Deacon. If, however, there is no Deacon, the duties of his Order, except those indicated below, are assumed by the Priest Celebrant or by a concelebrant.

The Priest and Deacon vest as at Mass, in white vestments. Candles should be prepared for all who participate in the Vigil. The lights of the church are extinguished.

FIRST PART:

THE SOLEMN BEGINNING OF THE VIGIL OR LUCERNARIUM

The Blessing of the Fire and Preparation of the Candle

A blazing fire is prepared in a suitable place outside the church. When the people are gathered there, the Priest approaches with the ministers, one of whom carries the paschal candle. The processional cross and candles are not carried.

The Priest and faithful sign themselves while the Priest says: In the name of the Father, and of the Son, and of the Holy Spirit, and then he greets the assembled people in the usual way and briefly instructs them about the night vigil in these or similar words:

Dear brethren (brothers and sisters),
on this most sacred night,
in which our Lord Jesus Christ
passed over from death to life,
the Church calls upon her sons and daughters,
scattered throughout the world,
to come together to watch and pray.
If we keep the memorial
of the Lord's paschal solemnity in this way,
listening to his word and celebrating his mysteries,
then we shall have the sure hope
of sharing his triumph over death
and living with him in God.

Then the Priest blesses the fire, saying with hands extended:

Let us pray.
O God, who through your Son
bestowed upon the faithful the fire of your glory,
sanctify ✢ this new fire, we pray,
and grant that,
by these paschal celebrations,
we may be so inflamed with heavenly desires,
that with minds made pure
we may attain festivities of unending splendour.
Through Christ our Lord.
Amen.

The Easter Vigil

After the blessing of the new fire, one of the ministers brings the paschal candle to the Priest, who cuts a cross into the candle with a stylus. Then he makes the Greek letter Alpha above the cross, the letter Omega below, and the four numerals of the current year between the arms of the cross, saying meanwhile:

1. Christ yesterday and today (he cuts a vertical line);
2. the Beginning and the End (he cuts a horizontal line);
3. the Alpha (he cuts the letter Alpha above the vertical line);
4. and the Omega (he cuts the letter Omega below the vertical line).
5. All time belongs to him (he cuts the first numeral of the current year in the upper left corner of the cross);
6. and all the ages (he cuts the second numeral of the current year in the upper right corner of the cross).
7. To him be glory and power (he cuts the third numeral of the current year in the lower left corner of the cross);
8. through every age and for ever. Amen (he cuts the fourth numeral of the current year in the lower right corner of the cross).

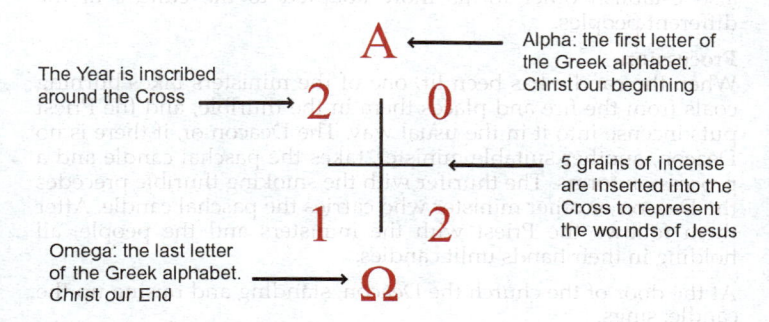

Alpha: the first letter of the Greek alphabet. Christ our beginning

The Year is inscribed around the Cross

5 grains of incense are inserted into the Cross to represent the wounds of Jesus

Omega: the last letter of the Greek alphabet. Christ our End

When the cutting of the cross and of the other signs has been completed, the Priest may insert five grains of incense into the candle in the form of a cross, meanwhile saying:

1. By his holy
2. and glorious wounds,
3. may Christ the Lord
4. guard us
5. and protect us. **Amen.**

Where, because of difficulties that may occur, a fire is not lit, the blessing of fire is adapted to the circumstances. When the people are gathered in the church as on other occasions, the Priest comes to the door of the church, along with the ministers carrying the paschal candle. The people, insofar as is possible, turn to face the Priest.

The greeting and address take place as above; then the fire is blessed and the candle is prepared, as above.

The Priest lights the paschal candle from the new fire, saying:

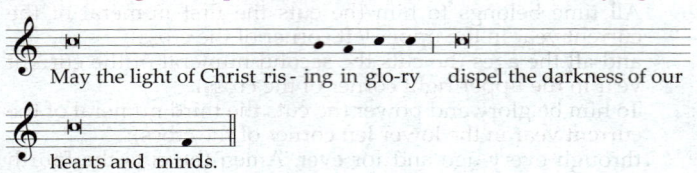

May the light of Christ ris-ing in glo-ry dispel the darkness of our hearts and minds.

As regards the preceding elements, Conferences of Bishops may also establish other forms more adapted to the culture of the different peoples.

Procession

When the candle has been lit, one of the ministers takes burning coals from the fire and places them in the thurible, and the Priest puts incense into it in the usual way. The Deacon or, if there is no Deacon, another suitable minister, takes the paschal candle and a procession forms. The thurifer with the smoking thurible precedes the Deacon or other minister who carries the paschal candle. After them follows the Priest with the ministers and the people, all holding in their hands unlit candles.

At the door of the church the Deacon, standing and raising up the candle, sings:

The Light of Christ.

And all reply:

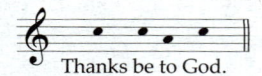

Thanks be to God.

(See p.598 for an alternative musical setting.)

or

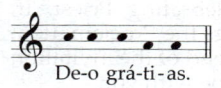

De-o grá-ti-as.

The Priest lights his candle from the flame of the paschal candle.

Then the Deacon moves forward to the middle of the church and, standing and raising up the candle, sings a second time:

The Light of Christ.

And all reply:

Thanks be to God.

All light their candles from the flame of the paschal candle and continue in procession.
When the Deacon arrives before the altar, he stands facing the people, raises up the candle and sings a third time:

The Light of Christ.

And all reply:

Thanks be to God.

Then the Deacon places the paschal candle on a large candle stand prepared next to the ambo or in the middle of the sanctuary, and lights are lit throughout the church, except for the altar candles.

The Easter Proclamation (Exsultet)
Arriving at the altar, the Priest goes to his chair, gives his candle to a minister, puts incense into the thurible and blesses the incense as at the Gospel at Mass. The Deacon goes to the Priest and saying, Your blessing, Father, asks for and receives a blessing from the Priest, who says in a low voice:

May the Lord be in your heart and on your lips,
that you may proclaim his paschal praise worthily and well,
in the name of the Father and of the Son, ✠ and of the Holy Spirit.

The Deacon replies: Amen.

This blessing is omitted if the Proclamation is made by someone who is not a Deacon.

The Deacon, after incensing the book and the candle, proclaims the Easter Proclamation (Exsultet) at the ambo or at a lectern, with all standing and holding lighted candles in their hands.

The Easter Vigil

The Easter Proclamation may be made, in the absence of a Deacon, by the Priest himself or by another concelebrating Priest. If, however, because of necessity, a lay cantor sings the Proclamation, the words Therefore, dearest friends up to the end of the invitation are omitted, along with the greeting The Lord be with you.

The Proclamation may also be sung in the shorter form.

Longer Form of the Easter Proclamation
(A musical setting may be found on pp.599-604.)

Exult, let them exult, the hosts of heaven,
exult, let Angel ministers of God exult,
let the trumpet of salvation
sound aloud our mighty King's triumph!
Be glad, let earth be glad, as glory floods her,
ablaze with light from her eternal King,
let all corners of the earth be glad,
knowing an end to gloom and darkness.
Rejoice, let Mother Church also rejoice,
arrayed with the lightning of his glory,
let this holy building shake with joy,
filled with the mighty voices of the peoples.

(Therefore, dearest friends,
standing in the awesome glory of this holy light,
invoke with me, I ask you,
the mercy of God almighty,
that he, who has been pleased to number me,
though unworthy, among the Levites,
may pour into me his light unshadowed,
that I may sing this candle's perfect praises).

℣ The Lord be with you.
℟ **And with your spirit.)**
℣ Lift up your hearts.
℟ **We lift them up to the Lord.**
℣ Let us give thanks to the Lord our God.
℟ **It is right and just.**

It is truly right and just,
with ardent love of mind and heart
and with devoted service of our voice,
to acclaim our God invisible, the almighty Father,
and Jesus Christ, our Lord, his Son, his Only Begotten.

The Easter Vigil

Who for our sake paid Adam's debt to the eternal Father,
and, pouring out his own dear Blood,
wiped clean the record of our ancient sinfulness.

These, then, are the feasts of Passover,
in which is slain the Lamb, the one true Lamb,
whose Blood anoints the doorposts of believers.

This is the night,
when once you led our forebears, Israel's children,
from slavery in Egypt
and made them pass dry-shod through the Red Sea.

This is the night
that with a pillar of fire
banished the darkness of sin.

This is the night
that even now, throughout the world,
sets Christian believers apart from worldly vices
and from the gloom of sin,
leading them to grace
and joining them to his holy ones.

This is the night,
when Christ broke the prison-bars of death
and rose victorious from the underworld.

Our birth would have been no gain,
had we not been redeemed.
O wonder of your humble care for us!
O love, O charity beyond all telling,
to ransom a slave you gave away your Son!

O truly necessary sin of Adam,
destroyed completely by the Death of Christ!

O happy fault
that earned so great, so glorious a Redeemer!

O truly blessed night,
worthy alone to know the time and hour
when Christ rose from the underworld!

This is the night
of which it is written:
The night shall be as bright as day,
dazzling is the night for me,
and full of gladness.

The sanctifying power of this night
dispels wickedness, washes faults away,
restores innocence to the fallen, and joy to mourners,
drives out hatred, fosters concord, and brings down the mighty.

On this, your night of grace, O holy Father,
accept this candle, a solemn offering,
the work of bees and of your servants' hands,
an evening sacrifice of praise,
this gift from your most holy Church.

But now we know the praises of this pillar,
which glowing fire ignites for God's honour,
a fire into many flames divided,
yet never dimmed by sharing of its light,
for it is fed by melting wax,
drawn out by mother bees
to build a torch so precious.

O truly blessed night,
when things of heaven are wed to those of earth,
and divine to the human.

Therefore, O Lord,
we pray you that this candle,
hallowed to the honour of your name,
may persevere undimmed,
to overcome the darkness of this night.
Receive it as a pleasing fragrance,
and let it mingle with the lights of heaven.
May this flame be found still burning
by the Morning Star:
the one Morning Star who never sets,
Christ your Son,
who, coming back from death's domain,
has shed his peaceful light on humanity,
and lives and reigns for ever and ever.
Amen.

Shorter Form of the Easter Proclamation
(A musical setting may be found on pp.605-8.)

Exult, let them exult, the hosts of heaven,
exult, let Angel ministers of God exult,
let the trumpet of salvation
sound aloud our mighty King's triumph!

Be glad, let earth be glad, as glory floods her,
ablaze with light from her eternal King,
let all corners of the earth be glad,
knowing an end to gloom and darkness.
Rejoice, let Mother Church also rejoice,
arrayed with the lightning of his glory,
let this holy building shake with joy,
filled with the mighty voices of the peoples.

(℣ The Lord be with you.
℟ **And with your spirit.**)
℣ Lift up your hearts.
℟ **We lift them up to the Lord.**
℣ Let us give thanks to the Lord our God.
℟ **It is right and just.**

It is truly right and just,
with ardent love of mind and heart
and with devoted service of our voice,
to acclaim our God invisible, the almighty Father,
and Jesus Christ, our Lord, his Son, his Only Begotten.

Who for our sake paid Adam's debt to the eternal Father,
and, pouring out his own dear Blood,
wiped clean the record of our ancient sinfulness.

These then are the feasts of Passover,
in which is slain the Lamb, the one true Lamb,
whose Blood anoints the doorposts of believers.

This is the night,
when once you led our forebears, Israel's children,
from slavery in Egypt
and made them pass dry-shod through the Red Sea.

This is the night
that with a pillar of fire
banished the darkness of sin.

This is the night
that even now, throughout the world,
sets Christian believers apart from worldly vices
and from the gloom of sin,
leading them to grace
and joining them to his holy ones.

This is the night,
when Christ broke the prison-bars of death
and rose victorious from the underworld.

O wonder of your humble care for us!
O love, O charity beyond all telling,
to ransom a slave you gave away your Son!

O truly necessary sin of Adam,
destroyed completely by the Death of Christ!

O happy fault
that earned so great, so glorious a Redeemer!
The sanctifying power of this night
dispels wickedness, washes faults away,
restores innocence to the fallen, and joy to mourners.

O truly blessed night,
when things of heaven are wedded to those of earth
and divine to the human.

On this, your night of grace, O holy Father,
accept this candle, a solemn offering,
the work of bees and of your servants' hands,
an evening sacrifice of praise,
this gift from your most holy Church

Therefore, O Lord,
we pray you that this candle,
hallowed to the honour of your name,
may persevere undimmed,
to overcome the darkness of this night.
Receive it as a pleasing fragrance,
and let it mingle with the lights of heaven.
May this flame be found still burning
by the Morning Star:
the one Morning Star who never sets,
Christ your Son,
who, coming back from death's domain,
has shed his peaceful light on humanity,
and lives and reigns for ever and ever.
Amen.

SECOND PART:

THE LITURGY OF THE WORD

In this Vigil, the mother of all Vigils, nine readings are provided, namely seven from the Old Testament and two from the New (the Epistle and Gospel), all of which should be read whenever this can be done, so that the character of the Vigil, which demands an extended period of time, may be preserved.

Nevertheless, where more serious pastoral circumstances demand it, the number of readings from the Old Testament may be reduced, always bearing in mind that the reading of the Word of God is a fundamental part of this Easter Vigil. At least three readings should be read from the Old Testament, both from the Law and from the Prophets, and their respective Responsorial Psalms should be sung. Never, moreover, should the reading of chapter 14 of Exodus with its canticle be omitted.

After setting aside their candles, all sit. Before the readings begin, the Priest instructs the people in these or similar words:

Dear brethren (brothers and sisters),
now that we have begun our solemn Vigil,
let us listen with quiet hearts to the Word of God.
Let us meditate on how God in times past saved his people
and in these, the last days, has sent us his Son as our Redeemer.
Let us pray that our God may complete this paschal work of salvation
by the fullness of redemption.

Then the readings follow. A reader goes to the ambo and proclaims the reading. Afterwards a psalmist or a cantor sings or says the Psalm with the people making the response. Then all rise, the Priest says, Let us pray and, after all have prayed for a while in silence, he says the prayer corresponding to the reading. In place of the Responsorial Psalm a period of sacred silence may be observed, in which case the pause after Let us pray is omitted.

FIRST READING

A reading from the book of Genesis 1:1 – 2:2

| *In the beginning God created the heavens and the earth.* Now the earth was a formless void, there was darkness over the deep, and God's spirit hovered over the water.
God said, 'Let there be light', and there was light. God saw that light was good, and God divided light from darkness. God called light

'day', and darkness he called 'night'. Evening came and morning came: the first day.

God said, 'Let there be a vault in the waters to divide the waters in two.' And so it was. God made the vault, and it divided the waters above the vault from the waters under the vault. God called the vault 'heaven'. Evening came and morning came: the second day.

God said, 'Let the waters under heaven come together into a single mass, and let dry land appear.' And so it was. God called the dry land 'earth' and the mass of waters 'seas', and God saw that it was good.

God said, 'Let the earth produce vegetation: seed-bearing plants, and fruit trees bearing fruit with their seed inside, on the earth.' And so it was. The earth produced vegetation: plants bearing seed in their several kinds, and trees bearing fruit with their seed inside in their several kinds. God saw that it was good. Evening came and morning came: the third day.

God said, 'Let there be lights in the vault of heaven to divide day from night, and let them indicate festivals, days and years. Let them be lights in the vault of heaven to shine on the earth.' And so it was. God made the two great lights: the greater light to govern the day, the smaller light to govern the night, and the stars. God set them in the vault of heaven to shine on the earth, to govern the day and the night and to divide light from darkness. God saw that it was good. Evening came and morning came: the fourth day.

God said, 'Let the waters teem with living creatures, and let birds fly above the earth within the vault of heaven.' And so it was. God created great sea-serpents and every kind of living creature with which the waters teem, and every kind of winged creature. God saw that it was good. God blessed them, saying 'Be fruitful, multiply, and fill the waters of the seas; and let the birds multiply upon the earth.' Evening came and morning came: the fifth day.

God said, 'Let the earth produce every kind of living creature: cattle, reptiles, and every kind of wild beast.' And so it was. God made every kind of wild beast, every kind of cattle, and every kind of land reptile. God saw that it was good.

*God said, 'Let us make man in our own image, in the likeness of ourselves, and let them be masters of the fish of the sea, the birds of heaven, the cattle, all the wild beasts and all the reptiles that crawl upon the earth.'

God created man in the image of himself,
in the image of God he created him,
male and female he created them.

God blessed them, saying to them, 'Be fruitful, multiply, fill the earth and conquer it. Be masters of the fish of the sea, the birds of heaven and all living animals on the earth.' God said, 'See, I give you all the seed-bearing plants that are upon the whole earth, and all the trees with seed-bearing fruit; this shall be your food. To all wild beasts, all birds of heaven and all living reptiles on the earth I give all the foliage of plants for food.' And so it was. God saw all he had made, and indeed it was very good. Evening came and morning came: the sixth day.

Thus heaven and earth were completed with all their array. On the seventh day God completed the work he had been doing. He rested on the seventh day after all the work he had been doing.

The word of the Lord.*

Shorter Form, verses 1. 26-31. Read between

Responsorial Psalm Ps 103:1-2. 5-6. 10. 12-14. 24. 35. ℟ cf. v.30

℟ **Send forth your spirit, O Lord,**
   and renew the face of the earth.

1 Bless the Lord, my soul!
   Lord God, how great you are,
   clothed in majesty and glory,
   wrapped in light as in a robe!   ℟

2 You founded the earth on its base,
   to stand firm from age to age.
   You wrapped it with the ocean like a cloak:
   the waters stood higher than the mountains.   ℟

3 You make springs gush forth in the valleys:
   they flow in between the hills.
   On their banks dwell the birds of heaven;
   from the branches they sing their song.   ℟

4 From your dwelling you water the hills;
   earth drinks its fill of your gift.
   You make the grass grow for the cattle
   and the plants to serve man's needs.   ℟

5 How many are your works, O Lord!
   In wisdom you have made them all.
   The earth is full of your riches.
   Bless the Lord, my soul!   ℟

Alternative Psalm   Ps 32:4-7. 12-13. 20. 22. v.5

℟ **The Lord fills the earth with his love.**

1. The word of the Lord is faithful
and all his works to be trusted.
The Lord loves justice and right
and fills the earth with his love. ℟

2. By his word the heavens were made,
by the breath of his mouth all the stars.
He collects the waves of the ocean;
he stores up the depths of the sea. ℟

3. They are happy, whose God is the Lord,
the people he has chosen as his own.
From the heavens the Lord looks forth,
he sees all the children of men. ℟

4. Our soul is waiting for the Lord.
The Lord is our help and our shield.
May your love be upon us, O Lord,
as we place all our hope in you. ℟

Prayer
Let us pray.
Almighty ever-living God,
who are wonderful in the ordering of all your works,
may those you have redeemed understand
that there exists nothing more marvellous
than the world's creation in the beginning
except that, at the end of the ages,
Christ our Passover has been sacrificed.
Who lives and reigns for ever and ever.
Amen.

or, On the creation of man:

O God, who wonderfully created human nature
and still more wonderfully redeemed it,
grant us, we pray,
to set our minds against the enticements of sin,
that we may merit to attain eternal joys.
Through Christ our Lord.
Amen.

SECOND READING
A reading from the book of Genesis   22:1-18

God put Abraham to the test. 'Abraham, Abraham,' he called. 'Here I am' he replied. 'Take your son,' God said 'your only child Isaac, whom you love, and go to the land of Moriah. There you shall offer him as a burnt offering, on a mountain I will point out to you.'

Rising early next morning Abraham saddled his ass and took with him two of his servants and his son Isaac. He chopped wood for the burnt offering and started on his journey to the place God had pointed out to him. On the third day Abraham looked up and saw the place in the distance. Then Abraham said to his servants, 'Stay here with the donkey. The boy and I will go over there; we will worship and come back to you.'

Abraham took the wood for the burnt offering, loaded it on Isaac, and carried in his own hands the fire and the knife. Then the two of them set out together. Isaac spoke to his father Abraham, 'Father' he said. 'Yes, my son" he replied. 'Look,' he said 'here are the fire and the wood, but where is the lamb for the burnt offering?' Abraham answered, 'My son, God himself will provide the lamb for the burnt offering.' Then the two of them went on together.

*When they arrived at the place God had pointed out to him, Abraham built an altar there, and arranged the wood. Then he bound his son Isaac and put him on the altar on top of the wood. Abraham stretched out his hand and seized the knife to kill his son.

But the angel of the Lord called to him from heaven, 'Abraham, Abraham' he said. 'I am here' he replied. 'Do not raise your hand against the boy' the angel said. 'Do not harm him, for now I know you fear God. You have not refused me your son, your only son.' Then looking up, Abraham saw a ram caught by its horns in a bush. Abraham took the ram and offered it as a burnt-offering in place of his son.*

Abraham called this place 'The Lord provides', and hence the saying today: On the mountain the Lord provides.

*The angel of the Lord called Abraham a second time from heaven. 'I swear by my own self – it is the Lord who speaks – because you have done this, because you have not refused me your son, your only son, I will shower blessings on you, I will make your descendants as many as the stars of heaven and the grains of sand on the seashore. Your descendants shall gain possession of the gates of their enemies. All the nations of the earth shall bless themselves by your descendants, as a reward for your obedience.'

The word of the Lord.

Shorter Form, verses 1-2. 9-13. 15-18. Read between

Responsorial Psalm
Ps 15:5. 8-11. ℟ v.1

℟ **Preserve me, God, I take refuge in you.**

1. O Lord, it is you who are my portion and cup;
   it is you yourself who are my prize.
   I keep the Lord ever in my sight:
   since he is at my right hand, I shall stand firm. ℟

2. And so my heart rejoices, my soul is glad;
   even my body shall rest in safety.
   For you will not leave my soul among the dead,
   nor let your beloved know decay. ℟

3. You will show me the path of life,
   the fullness of joy in your presence,
   at your right hand happiness for ever. ℟

Prayer
Let us pray.
O God, supreme Father of the faithful,
who increase the children of your promise
by pouring out the grace of adoption
throughout the whole world
and who through the Paschal Mystery
make your servant Abraham father of nations,
as once you swore,
grant, we pray,
that your peoples may enter worthily
into the grace to which you call them.
Through Christ our Lord.
Amen.

THIRD READING
A reading from the book of Exodus
14:15 – 15:1

The Lord said to Moses, 'Why do you cry to me so? Tell the sons of Israel to march on. For yourself, raise your staff and stretch out your hand over the sea and part it for the sons of Israel to walk through the sea on dry ground. I for my part will make the heart of the Egyptians so stubborn that they will follow them. So shall I win myself glory at the expense of Pharaoh, of all his army, his chariots, his horsemen. And when I have won glory for myself, at the expense of Pharaoh and his chariots and his army, the Egyptians will learn that I am the Lord.'

Then the angel of the Lord, who marched at the front of the army of Israel, changed station and moved to their rear. The pillar of cloud changed station from the front to the rear of them, and remained there. It came between the camp of the Egyptians and the camp of Israel. The cloud was dark, and the night passed without the armies drawing any closer the whole night long. Moses stretched out his hand over the sea. The Lord drove back the sea with a strong easterly wind all night, and he made dry land of the sea. The waters parted and the sons of Israel went on dry ground right into the sea, walls of water to right and to left of them. The Egyptians gave chase: after them they went, right into the sea, all Pharaoh's horses, his chariots, and his horsemen. In the morning watch, the Lord looked down on the army of the Egyptians from the pillar of fire and of cloud, and threw the army into confusion. He so clogged their chariot wheels that they could scarcely make headway. 'Let us flee from the Israelites,' the Egyptians cried 'the Lord is fighting for them against the Egyptians!' 'Stretch out your hand over the sea,' the Lord said to Moses 'that the waters may flow back on the Egyptians and their chariots and their horsemen.' Moses stretched out his hand over the sea and, as day broke, the sea returned to its bed. The fleeing Egyptians marched right into it, and the Lord overthrew the Egyptians in the very middle of the sea. The returning waters overwhelmed the chariots and the horsemen of Pharaoh's whole army, which had followed the Israelites into the sea; not a single one of them was left. But the sons of Israel had marched through the sea on dry ground, walls of water to right and to left of them. That day, the Lord rescued Israel from the Egyptians, and Israel saw the Egyptians lying dead on the shore. Israel witnessed the great act that the Lord had performed against the Egyptians, and the people venerated the Lord; they put their faith in the Lord and in Moses, his servant.

It was then that Moses and the sons of Israel sang this song in honour of the Lord:

The choir takes up the Responsorial Psalm immediately.

Responsorial Psalm   Ex 15:1-6. 17-18. ℟ v.1
℟   **I will sing to the Lord, glorious his triumph!**

1   I will sing to the Lord, glorious his triumph!
    Horse and rider he has thrown into the sea!
    The Lord is my strength, my song, my salvation.
    This is my God and I extol him,
    my father's God and I give him praise.   ℟

2   The Lord is a warrior! The Lord is his name.
    The chariots of Pharaoh he hurled into the sea,
    the flower of his army is drowned in the sea.
    The deeps hide them; they sank like a stone.   ℟

3   Your right hand, Lord, glorious in its power,
    your right hand, Lord, has shattered the enemy.
    In the greatness of your glory you crushed the foe.   ℟

4   You will lead your people and plant them on your mountain,
    the place, O Lord, where you have made your home,
    the sanctuary, Lord, which your hands have made.
    The Lord will reign for ever and ever.   ℟

Prayer
Let us pray.
O God, whose ancient wonders
remain undimmed in splendour even in our day,
for what you once bestowed on a single people,
freeing them from Pharaoh's persecution
by the power of your right hand
now you bring about as the salvation of the nations
through the waters of rebirth,
grant, we pray, that the whole world
may become children of Abraham
and inherit the dignity of Israel's birthright.
Through Christ our Lord.
Amen.

or

O God, who by the light of the New Testament
have unlocked the meaning
of wonders worked in former times,
so that the Red Sea prefigures the sacred font
and the nation delivered from slavery

The Easter Vigil

foreshadows the Christian people,
grant, we pray, that all nations,
obtaining the privilege of Israel by merit of faith,
may be reborn by partaking of your Spirit.
Through Christ our Lord.
Amen.

FOURTH READING

A reading from the prophet Isaiah 54:5-14

Thus says the Lord:

> Now your creator will be your husband,
> his name, the Lord of hosts;
> your redeemer will be the Holy One of Israel,
> he is called the God of the whole earth.
> Yes, like a forsaken wife, distressed in spirit,
> the Lord calls you back.
> Does a man cast off the wife of his youth?
> says your God.
>
> I did forsake you for a brief moment,
> but with great love will I take you back.
> In excess of anger, for a moment
> I hid my face from you.
> But with everlasting love I have taken pity on you,
> says the Lord, your redeemer.
>
> I am now as I was in the days of Noah
> when I swore that Noah's waters
> should never flood the world again.
> So now I swear concerning my anger with you
> and the threats I made against you;
>
> for the mountains may depart,
> the hills be shaken,
> but my love for you will never leave you
> and my covenant of peace with you will never be shaken,
> says the Lord who takes pity on you.
>
> Unhappy creature, storm-tossed, disconsolate,
> see, I will set your stones on carbuncles
> and your foundations on sapphires.
> I will make rubies your battlements,

your gates crystal,
and your entire wall precious stones.
Your sons will all be taught by the Lord.
The prosperity of your sons will be great.
You will be founded on integrity;
remote from oppression, you will have nothing to fear;
remote from terror, it will not approach you.

The word of the Lord.

Responsorial Psalm Ps 29:2. 4-6. 11-13. ℟ v.2

℟ **I will praise you, Lord, you have rescued me.**

1   I will praise you, Lord, you have rescued me
    and have not let my enemies rejoice over me.
    O Lord, you have raised my soul from the dead,
    restored me to life from those who sink into the grave.   ℟

2   Sing psalms to the Lord, you who love him,
    give thanks to his holy name.
    His anger lasts but a moment; his favour through life.
    At night there are tears, but joy comes with dawn.   ℟

3   The Lord listened and had pity.
    The Lord came to my help.
    For me you have changed my mourning into dancing,
    O Lord my God, I will thank you for ever.   ℟

Prayer
Let us pray.
Almighty ever-living God,
surpass, for the honour of your name,
what you pledged to the Patriarchs by reason of their faith,
and through sacred adoption increase the children of your promise,
so that what the Saints of old never doubted would come to pass
your Church may now see in great part fulfilled.
Through Christ our Lord.
Amen.

Alternatively, other prayers may be used from among those which follow the readings that have been omitted.

FIFTH READING

A reading from the prophet Isaiah 55:1-11

Thus says the Lord:

> Oh, come to the water all you who are thirsty;
> though you have no money, come!
> Buy corn without money, and eat,
> and, at no cost, wine and milk.
> Why spend money on what is not bread,
> your wages on what fails to satisfy?
> Listen, listen to me, and you will have good things to eat
> and rich food to enjoy.
> Pay attention, come to me;
> listen, and your soul will live.
>
> With you I will make an everlasting covenant
> out of the favours promised to David.
> See, I have made of you a witness to the peoples,
> a leader and a master of the nations.
> See, you will summon a nation you never knew,
> those unknown will come hurrying to you,
> for the sake of the Lord your God,
> of the Holy One of Israel who will glorify you.
>
> Seek the Lord while he is still to be found,
> call to him while he is still near.
> Let the wicked man abandon his way,
> the evil man his thoughts.
> Let him turn back to the Lord who will take pity on him,
> to our God who is rich in forgiving;
> for my thoughts are not your thoughts,
> my ways not your ways – it is the Lord who speaks.
> Yes, the heavens are as high above earth
> as my ways are above your ways,
> my thoughts above your thoughts.

Yes, as the rain and the snow come down from the heavens and do not return without watering the earth, making it yield and giving growth to provide seed for the sower and bread for the eating, so the word that goes from my mouth does not return to me empty, without carrying out my will and succeeding in what it was sent to do.

> The word of the Lord.

The Easter Vigil

Responsorial Psalm   Is 12:2-6. ℟ v.3

  ℟ **With joy you will draw water from the wells of salvation.**

1. Truly God is my salvation,
I trust, I shall not fear.
For the Lord is my strength, my song,
he became my saviour.
With joy you will draw water
from the wells of salvation. ℟

2. Give thanks to the Lord, give praise to his name!
Make his mighty deeds known to the peoples,
declare the greatness of his name. ℟

3. Sing a psalm to the Lord
for he has done glorious deeds,
make them known to all the earth!
People of Zion, sing and shout for joy
for great in your midst is the Holy One of Israel. ℟

Prayer
Let us pray.
Almighty ever-living God,
sole hope of the world,
who by the preaching of your Prophets
unveiled the mysteries of this present age,
graciously increase the longing of your people,
for only at the prompting of your grace
do the faithful progress in any kind of virtue.
Through Christ our Lord.
Amen.

SIXTH READING

A reading from the prophet Baruch   3:9-15. 32 – 4:4

Listen, Israel, to commands that bring life;
hear, and learn what knowledge means.
Why, Israel, why are you in the country of your enemies,
growing older and older in an alien land,
sharing defilement with the dead,
reckoned with those who go to Sheol?
Because you have forsaken the fountain of wisdom.

Had you walked in the way of God,
you would have lived in peace for ever.
Learn where knowledge is, where strength,
where understanding, and so learn
where length of days is, where life,
where the light of the eyes and where peace.
But who has found out where she lives,
who has entered her treasure house?

But the One who knows all knows her,
he has grasped her with his own intellect,
he has set the earth firm for ever
and filled it with four-footed beasts,
he sends the light – and it goes,
he recalls it – and trembling it obeys;
the stars shine joyfully at their set times:
when he calls them, they answer, 'Here we are';
they gladly shine for their creator.
It is he who is our God,
no other can compare with him.
He has grasped the whole way of knowledge,
and confided it to his servant Jacob,
to Israel his well-beloved;
so causing her to appear on earth
and move among men.

This is the book of the commandments of God,
the Law that stands for ever;
those who keep her live,
those who desert her die.
Turn back, Jacob, seize her,
in her radiance make your way to light:
do not yield your glory to another,
your privilege to a people not your own.
Israel, blessed are we:
what pleases God has been revealed to us.

    The word of the Lord.

Responsorial Psalm   Ps 18:8-11. ℟ Jn 6:69
  ℟ **You have the message of eternal life, O Lord.**

1   The law of the Lord is perfect,
      it revives the soul.
    The rule of the Lord is to be trusted,
      it gives wisdom to the simple.   ℟

2 The precepts of the Lord are right,
   they gladden the heart.
   The command of the Lord is clear,
   it gives light to the eyes. ℟

3 The fear of the Lord is holy,
   abiding for ever.
   The decrees of the Lord are truth
   and all of them just. ℟

4 They are more to be desired than gold,
   than the purest of gold
   and sweeter are they than honey,
   than honey from the comb. ℟

Prayer
Let us pray.
O God, who constantly increase your Church
by your call to the nations,
graciously grant
to those you wash clean in the waters of Baptism
the assurance of your unfailing protection.
Through Christ our Lord.
Amen.

SEVENTH READING
A reading from the prophet Ezekiel   36:16-28

The word of the Lord was addressed to me as follows: 'Son of man, the members of the House of Israel used to live in their own land, but they defiled it by their conduct and actions. I then discharged my fury at them because of the blood they shed in their land and the idols with which they defiled it. I scattered them among the nations and dispersed them in foreign countries. I sentenced them as their conduct and actions deserved. And now they have profaned my holy name among the nations where they have gone, so that people say of them, "These are the people of the Lord; they have been exiled from his land." But I have been concerned about my holy name, which the House of Israel has profaned among the nations *where they* have gone. And so, say to the House of Israel, "The Lord says this: I am not doing this for my sake, House of Israel, but for the sake of my holy name, which you have profaned among the nations where you have gone. I mean to display the holiness of my great name, which has been profaned among the nations, which you have profaned among them. And the nations will learn that I am the Lord – it is the Lord who speaks – when I display my holiness for your sake before their eyes. Then I am going to take you from among the nations and gather you together from all the foreign countries, and bring you home to your own land. I shall pour clean water over you and you will be cleansed; I shall cleanse you of all your defilement and all your idols. I shall give you a new heart, and put a new spirit in you; I shall remove the heart of stone from your bodies and give you a heart of flesh instead. I shall put my spirit in you, and make you keep my laws and sincerely respect my observances. You will live in the land which I gave your ancestors. You shall be my people and I will be your God."'

The word of the Lord.

Responsorial Psalm   Pss 41:3. 5; 42:3. 4. ℟ 41:2
> ℟ **Like the deer that yearns for running streams,**
> **so my soul is yearning for you, my God.**

1   My soul is thirsting for God.
    the God of my life;
    when can I enter and see
    the face of God?   ℟

2   These things will I remember
    as I pour out my soul:
    how I would lead the rejoicing crowd
    into the house of God,
    amid cries of gladness and thanksgiving,
    the throng wild with joy.   ℟

3   O send forth your light and your truth;
    let these be my guide.
    Let them bring me to your holy mountain
    to the place where you dwell.   ℟

4   And I will come to the altar of God,
    the God of my joy.
    My redeemer, I will thank you on the harp,
    O God, my God.   ℟

If a Baptism takes place the Responsorial Psalm which follows the Fifth reading above, p.404 is used, or Ps 50 as follows:

Responsorial Psalm Ps 50:12-15. 18. 19. ℟ v.12
℟ **A pure heart create for me, O God.**

1 A pure heart create for me, O God,
   put a steadfast spirit within me.
   Do not cast me away from your presence,
   nor deprive me of your holy spirit. ℟

2 Give me again the joy of your help;
   with a spirit of fervour sustain me,
   that I may teach transgressors your ways
   and sinners may return to you. ℟

3 For in sacrifice you take no delight,
   burnt offering from me you would refuse,
   my sacrifice, a contrite spirit.
   A humbled, contrite heart you will not spurn. ℟

Prayer
Let us pray.
O God of unchanging power and eternal light,
look with favour on the wondrous mystery of the whole Church
and serenely accomplish the work of human salvation,
which you planned from all eternity;
may the whole world know and see
that what was cast down is raised up,
what had become old is made new,
and all things are restored to integrity through Christ,
just as by him they came into being.
Who lives and reigns for ever and ever.
Amen.

or

O God, who by the pages of both Testaments
instruct and prepare us to celebrate the Paschal Mystery,
grant that we may comprehend your mercy,
so that the gifts we receive from you this night
may confirm our hope of the gifts to come.
Through Christ our Lord.
Amen.

After the last reading from the Old Testament with its Responsorial Psalm and its prayer, the altar candles are lit, and the Priest intones the hymn Gloria in excelsis Deo (Glory to God in the highest),

The Easter Vigil

which is taken up by all, while bells are rung, according to local custom. (A musical setting for the Gloria may be found on p.608.)

When the hymn is concluded, the Priest says the Collect in the usual way.

Let us pray.
O God, who make this most sacred night radiant
with the glory of the Lord's Resurrection,
stir up in your Church a spirit of adoption,
so that, renewed in body and mind,
we may render you undivided service.
Through our Lord Jesus Christ, your Son,
who lives and reigns with you in the unity of the Holy Spirit,
one God, for ever and ever.
Amen.

Then the reader proclaims the reading from the Apostle.

FIRST READING
A reading from the letter of St Paul to the Romans   6:3-11

When we were baptised in Christ Jesus we were baptised in his death; in other words, when we were baptised we went into the tomb with him and joined him in death, so that as Christ was raised from the dead by the Father's glory, we too might live a new life.

If in union with Christ we have imitated his death, we shall also imitate him in his resurrection. We must realise that our former selves have been crucified with him to destroy this sinful body and to free us from the slavery of sin. When a man dies, of course, he has finished with sin.

But we believe that having died with Christ we shall return to life with him: Christ, as we know, having been raised from the dead will never die again. Death has no power over him any more. When he died, he died, once for all, to sin, so his life now is life with God; and in that way, you too must consider yourselves to be dead to sin but alive for God in Christ Jesus.

The word of the Lord.

After the Epistle has been read, all rise, then the Priest solemnly intones the Alleluia three times, raising his voice by a step each time, with all repeating it. If necessary, the psalmist intones the Alleluia.

Al-le - lú - ia.

Then the psalmist or cantor proclaims Psalm 117 with the people responding Alleluia.

Responsorial Psalm   Ps 117:1-2. 16-17. 22-23

℟ **Alleluia, alleluia, alleluia!**

1. Give thanks to the Lord for he is good,
   for his love has no end.
   Let the sons of Israel say:
   'His love has no end.' ℟

2. The Lord's right hand has triumphed;
   his right hand raised me up.
   I shall not die, I shall live
   and recount his deeds. ℟

3. The stone which the builders rejected
   has become the corner stone.
   This is the work of the Lord,
   a marvel in our eyes. ℟

The Priest, in the usual way, puts incense in the thurible and blesses the Deacon. At the Gospel lights are not carried, but only incense.

GOSPEL

Year A

A reading from the holy Gospel according to Matthew   28:1-10

After the sabbath, and towards dawn on the first day of the week, Mary of Magdala and the other Mary went to visit the sepulchre. And all at once there was a violent earthquake, for the angel of the Lord, descending from heaven, came and rolled away the stone and sat on it. His face was like lightning, his robe white as snow. The guards were so shaken, so frightened of him, that they were like dead men. But the angel spoke; and he said to the women, 'There is no need for you to be afraid. I know you are looking for Jesus, who was crucified. He is not here, for he has risen, as he said he would. Come and see the place where he lay, then go quickly and tell his disciples, "He has risen from the dead and now he is going before you to Galilee; it is there you will see him." Now I have told you.'

Filled with awe and great joy the women came quickly away from the tomb and ran to tell the disciples. And there, coming to meet them, was Jesus. 'Greetings' he said. And the women came up to him and, falling down before him, clasped his feet. Then Jesus said to them, 'Do not be afraid; go and tell my brothers that they must leave for Galilee; they will see me there.'

The Gospel of the Lord.

Year B

A reading from the holy Gospel according to Mark   16:1-7

When the sabbath was over, Mary of Magdala, Mary the mother of James, and Salome, bought spices with which to go and anoint him. And very early in the morning on the first day of the week they went to the tomb, just as the sun was rising.

They had been saying to one another, 'Who will roll away the stone for us from the entrance to the tomb?' But when they looked they could see that the stone – which was very big – had already been rolled back. On entering the tomb they saw a young man in a white robe seated on the right-hand side, and they were struck with amazement. But he said to them, 'There is no need for alarm. You are looking for Jesus of Nazareth, who was crucified: he has risen, he is not here. See, here is the place where they laid him. But you must go and tell his disciples and Peter, "He is going before you to Galilee; it is there you will see him, just as he told you."'

The Gospel of the Lord.

Year C

A reading from the holy Gospel according to Luke   24:1-12

On the first day of the week, at the first sign of dawn, the women went to the tomb with the spices they had prepared. They found that the stone had been rolled away from the tomb, but on entering discovered that the body of the Lord Jesus was not there. As they stood there not knowing what to think, two men in brilliant clothes suddenly appeared at their side. Terrified, the women lowered their eyes. But the two men said to them, 'Why look among the dead for someone who is alive? He is not here; he has risen. Remember what he told you when he was still in Galilee: that the Son of Man had to be handed over into the power of sinful men and be crucified, and rise again on the third day?' And they remembered his words.

When the women returned from the tomb they told all this to the Eleven and to all the others. The women were Mary of Magdala, Joanna, and Mary the mother of James. The other women with them also told the apostles, but this story of theirs seemed pure nonsense, and they did not believe them.

Peter, however, went running to the tomb. He bent down and saw the binding cloths, but nothing else; he then went back home, amazed at what had happened.

The Gospel of the Lord.

Homily
After the Gospel, the Homily, even if brief, is not to be omitted.

THIRD PART:

BAPTISMAL LITURGY

After the Homily the Baptismal Liturgy begins. The Priest goes with the ministers to the baptismal font, if this can be seen by the faithful. Otherwise a vessel with water is placed in the sanctuary.

Catechumens, if there are any, are called forward and presented by their godparents in front of the assembled Church or, if they are small children, are carried by their parents and godparents.

Then, if there is to be a procession to the baptistery or to the font, it forms immediately. A minister with the paschal candle leads off, and those to be baptized follow him with their godparents, then the ministers, the Deacon, and the Priest. During the procession, the Litany is sung. When the Litany is completed, the Priest gives the address.

If, however, the Baptismal Liturgy takes place in the sanctuary, the Priest immediately makes an introductory statement in these or similar words. (Musical settings for these can be found on pp.608-9.)

If there are candidates to be baptized:

Dearly beloved,
with one heart and one soul, let us by our prayers
come to the aid of these our brothers and sisters in their blessed hope,
so that, as they approach the font of rebirth,
the almighty Father may bestow on them
all his merciful help.

The Easter Vigil

If the font is to be blessed, but no one is to be baptized:

Dearly beloved,
let us humbly invoke upon this font
the grace of God the almighty Father,
that those who from it are born anew
may be numbered among the children of adoption in Christ.

The Litany is sung by two cantors, with all standing (because it is Easter Time) and responding.

If, however, there is to be a procession of some length to the baptistery, the Litany is sung during the procession; in this case, those to be baptized are called forward before the procession begins, and the procession takes place led by the paschal candle, followed by the catechumens with their godparents, then the ministers, the Deacon, and the Priest. The address should occur before the Blessing of Water.

If no one is to be baptized and the font is not to be blessed, the Litany is omitted, and the Blessing of Water takes place at once.

In the Litany the names of some Saints may be added, especially the Titular Saint of the church and the Patron Saints of the place and of those to be baptized.

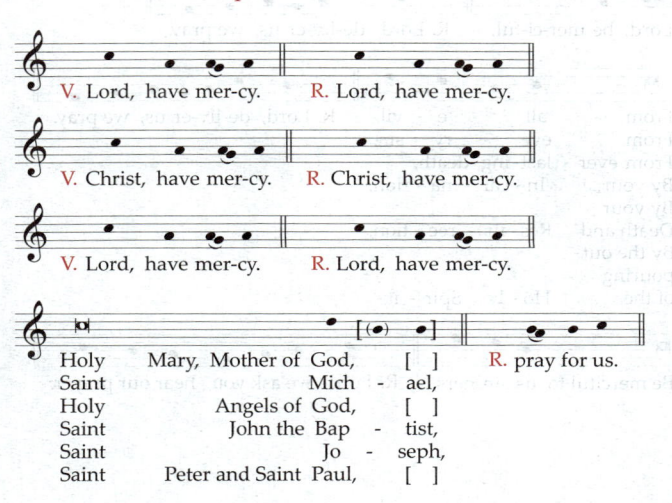

V. Lord, have mer-cy.   R. Lord, have mer-cy.

V. Christ, have mer-cy.   R. Christ, have mer-cy.

V. Lord, have mer-cy.   R. Lord, have mer-cy.

Holy	Mary, Mother of God,	[ ]	R. pray for us.
Saint	Mich - ael,		
Holy	Angels of God,	[ ]	
Saint	John the Bap - tist,		
Saint	Jo - seph,		
Saint	Peter and Saint Paul,	[ ]	

The Easter Vigil

Saint	An - drew,
Saint	John, [ ]
Saint	Mary Mag - da - lene,
Saint	Ste - phen,
Saint	Ignatius of An - ti - och,
Saint	Law - rence,
Saint Perpetua and Saint Fe - li - ci - ty,
Saint	Ag - nes,
Saint	Gre - go - ry,
Saint	Au - gus - tine,
Saint	Atha - na - sius,
Saint	Bas - il,
Saint	Mar - tin,
Saint	Ben - e - dict,
Saint Francis and Saint Dom - i - nic,
Saint	Francis Xa - vi - er,
Saint	John Vi - an - ney,
Saint	Catherine of Si - e - na,
Saint	Teresa of Je - sus,
All holy men and women, Saints of God, [ ]

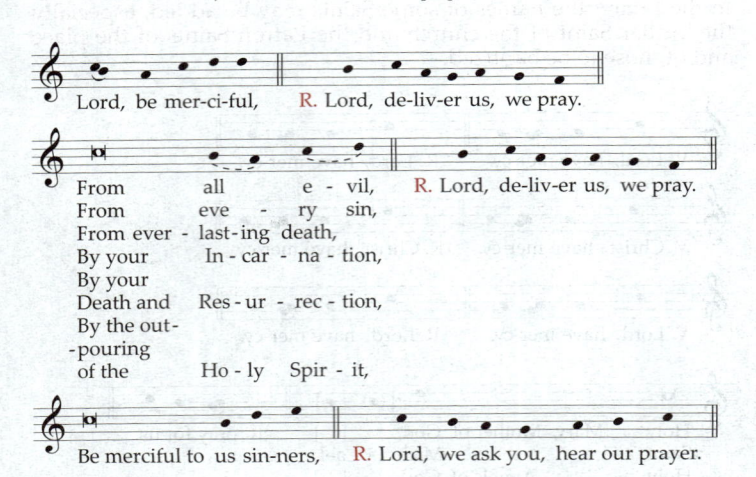

Lord, be mer-ci-ful, R. Lord, de-liv-er us, we pray.

From all e - vil, R. Lord, de-liv-er us, we pray.
From eve - ry sin,
From ever - last-ing death,
By your In - car - na - tion,
By your Death and Res - ur - rec - tion,
By the out- -pouring of the Ho - ly Spir - it,

Be merciful to us sin-ners, R. Lord, we ask you, hear our prayer.

If there are candidates to be baptized

Bring these chosen ones to new birth through the grace of Bap-tism,

R. Lord, we ask you, hear our prayer.

If there is no one to be baptized

Make this font holy by your grace for the new birth of your child-ren,

R. Lord, we ask you, hear our prayer.

Jesus, Son of the liv-ing God, R. Lord, we ask you, hear our prayer.

Christ, hear us. R. Christ, hear us.

Christ, gra-cious-ly hear us. R. Christ, gra-cious-ly hear us.

If there are candidates to be baptized, the Priest, with hands extended, says the following prayer:

Almighty ever-living God,
be present by the mysteries of your great love
and send forth the spirit of adoption
to create the new peoples
brought to birth for you in the font of Baptism,
so that what is to be carried out by our humble service
may be brought to fulfilment by your mighty power.
Through Christ our Lord.
Amen.

Blessing of Baptismal Water

The Priest then blesses the baptismal water, saying the following prayer with hands extended (musical settings for these prayers can be found on pp.609-12).

O God, who by invisible power
accomplish a wondrous effect
through sacramental signs
and who in many ways have prepared water, your creation,
to show forth the grace of Baptism;

O God, whose Spirit
in the first moments of the world's creation
hovered over the waters,
so that the very substance of water
would even then take to itself the power to sanctify;

O God, who by the outpouring of the flood
foreshadowed regeneration,
so that from the mystery of one and the same element of water
would come an end to vice and a beginning of virtue;

O God, who caused the children of Abraham
to pass dry-shod through the Red Sea,
so that the chosen people,
set free from slavery to Pharaoh,
would prefigure the people of the baptized;

O God, whose Son,
baptized by John in the waters of the Jordan,
was anointed with the Holy Spirit,
and, as he hung upon the Cross,
gave forth water from his side along with blood,
and after his Resurrection, commanded his disciples:
'Go forth, teach all nations, baptizing them
in the name of the Father and of the Son and of the Holy Spirit,'
look now, we pray, upon the face of your Church
and graciously unseal for her the fountain of Baptism.

May this water receive by the Holy Spirit
the grace of your Only Begotten Son,
so that human nature, created in your image
and washed clean through the Sacrament of Baptism
from all the squalor of the life of old,
may be found worthy to rise to the life of newborn children
through water and the Holy Spirit.

The Easter Vigil

And, if appropriate, lowering the paschal candle into the water either once or three times, he continues:

May the power of the Holy Spirt,
O Lord, we pray,
come down through your Son
into the fullness of this font,

and, holding the candle in the water, he continues:

that all who have been buried with Christ
by Baptism into death
may rise again to life with him.
Who lives and reigns with you in the unity of the Holy Spirit,
one God, for ever and ever.
Amen.

Then the candle is lifted out of the water, as the people acclaim:

**Springs of water, bless the Lord;
praise and exalt him above all for ever.**

After the blessing of baptismal water and the acclamation of the people, the Priest, standing, puts the prescribed questions to the adults and the parents or godparents of the children, as is set out in the respective Rites of the Roman Ritual, in order for them to make the required renunciation.

If the anointing of the adults with the Oil of Catechumens has not taken place beforehand, as part of the immediately preparatory rites, it occurs at this moment.

Then the Priest questions the adults individually about the faith and, if there are children to be baptized, he requests the triple profession of faith from all the parents and godparents together, as is indicated in the respective Rites.

Where many are to be baptized on this night, it is possible to arrange the rite so that, immediately after the response of those to be baptized and of the godparents and the parents, the Celebrant asks for and receives the renewal of baptismal promises of all present.

When the interrogation is concluded, the Priest baptizes the adult elect and the children.

After the Baptism, the Priest anoints the infants with chrism. A white garment is given to each, whether adults or children. Then the Priest or Deacon receives the paschal candle from the hand of the minister, and the candles of the newly baptized are lighted. For infants the rite of Ephphetha is omitted.

Afterwards, unless the baptismal washing and the other explanatory rites have occurred in the sanctuary, a procession returns to the sanctuary, formed as before, with the newly baptized or the godparents or parents carrying lighted candles. During this procession, the baptismal canticle **Vidi aquam** (I saw water) (see below, p.420) or another appropriate chant is sung.

If adults have been baptized, the Bishop or, in his absence, the Priest who has conferred Baptism, should at once administer the Sacrament of Confirmation to them in the sanctuary, as is indicated in the Roman Pontifical or Roman Ritual.

The Blessing of Water

If no one present is to be baptized and the font is not to be blessed, the Priest introduces the faithful to the blessing of water.

The Priest then blesses the baptismal water (a musical setting for this may be found on pp.612-13), saying the following prayer with hands extended:

Dear brothers and sisters,
let us humbly beseech the Lord our God
to bless this water he has created,
which will be sprinkled upon us
as a memorial of our Baptism.
May he graciously renew us,
that we may remain faithful to the Spirit
whom we have received.

And after a brief pause in silence, he proclaims the following prayer, with hands extended:

Lord our God,
in your mercy be present to your people
who keep vigil on this most sacred night,
and, for us who recall the wondrous work of our creation
and the still greater work of our redemption,
graciously bless this water.
For you created water to make the fields fruitful
and to refresh and cleanse our bodies.
You also made water the instrument of your mercy:
for through water you freed your people from slavery
and quenched their thirst in the desert;

through water the Prophets proclaimed the new covenant
you were to enter upon with the human race;
and last of all,
through water, which Christ made holy in the Jordan,
you have renewed our corrupted nature
in the bath of regeneration.
Therefore, may this water be for us
a memorial of the Baptism we have received,
and grant that we may share
in the gladness of our brothers and sisters,
who at Easter have received their Baptism.
Through Christ our Lord.
Amen.

The Renewal of Baptismal Promises

When the Rite of Baptism (and Confirmation) has been completed or, if this has not taken place, after the blessing of water, all stand, holding lighted candles in their hands, and renew the promise of baptismal faith, unless this has already been done together with those to be baptized.

The Priest addresses the faithful in these or similar words:

Dear brethren (brothers and sisters), through the Paschal Mystery
we have been buried with Christ in Baptism,
so that we may walk with him in newness of life.
And so, now that our Lenten observance is concluded,
let us renew the promises of Holy Baptism,
by which we once renounced Satan and his works
and promised to serve God in the holy Catholic Church.

And so I ask you:
Priest: Do you renounce Satan?
All: I do.
Priest: And all his works?
All: I do.
Priest: And all his empty show?
All: I do.

or

Priest: Do you renounce sin,
so as to live in the freedom of the children of God?
All: I do.
Priest: Do you renounce the lure of evil,
so that sin may have no mastery over you?

All: I do.
Priest: Do you renounce Satan,
the author and prince of sin?
All: I do.

If the situation warrants, this second formula may be adapted by Conferences of Bishops according to local needs.

Then the Priest continues:

Priest: Do you believe in God,
the Father almighty,
Creator of heaven and earth?
All: I do.
Priest: Do you believe in Jesus Christ, his only Son, our Lord,
who was born of the Virgin Mary,
suffered death and was buried,
rose again from the dead
and is seated at the right hand of the Father?
All: I do.
Priest: Do you believe in the Holy Spirit,
the holy Catholic Church,
the communion of saints,
the forgiveness of sins,
the resurrection of the body,
and life everlasting?
All: I do.

And the Priest concludes:

And may almighty God, the Father of our Lord Jesus Christ,
who has given us new birth by water and the Holy Spirit
and bestowed on us forgiveness of our sins,
keep us by his grace,
in Christ Jesus our Lord,
for eternal life.
All: **Amen.**

The Priest sprinkles the people with the blessed water, while all sing:

Antiphon

I saw water flowing from the Temple,
from its right-hand side, alleluia;
and all to whom this water came were saved
and shall say: Alleluia, alleluia.

(Musical settings and Latin text for this antiphon may be found on p.614.) Another chant that is baptismal in character may also be sung.

Meanwhile the newly baptized are led to their place among the faithful.

If the blessing of baptismal water has not taken place in the baptistery, the Deacon and the ministers reverently carry the vessel of water to the font.

If the blessing of the font has not occurred, the blessed water is put aside in an appropriate place.

After the sprinkling, the Priest returns to the chair where, omitting the Creed, he directs the Universal Prayer, in which the newly baptized participate for the first time.

FOURTH PART:
THE LITURGY OF THE EUCHARIST

The Priest goes to the altar and begins the Liturgy of the Eucharist in the usual way.

It is desirable that the bread and wine be brought forward by the newly baptized or, if they are children, by their parents or godparents.

Prayer over the Offerings
Accept, we ask, O Lord,
the prayers of your people
with the sacrificial offerings,
that what has begun in the paschal mysteries
may, by the working of your power,
bring us to the healing of eternity.
Through Christ our Lord.
Amen.

Preface I of Easter: The Paschal Mystery (. . . on this night above all . . .), p.28.

In the Eucharistic Prayer, a commemoration is made of the baptized and their godparents in accord with the formulas which are found in the Roman Missal and Roman Ritual for each of the Eucharistic Prayers.

Before the Ecce Agnus Dei (Behold the Lamb of God), the Priest may briefly address the newly baptized about receiving their first

Communion and about the excellence of this great mystery, which is the climax of Initiation and the centre of the whole of Christian life.

It is desirable that the newly baptized receive Holy Communion under both kinds, together with their godfathers, godmothers, and Catholic parents and spouses, as well as their lay catechists. It is even appropriate that, with the consent of the Diocesan Bishop, where the occasion suggests this, all the faithful be admitted to Holy Communion under both kinds.

Communion Antiphon
1 Cor 5:7-8

Christ our Passover has been sacrificed;
therefore let as keep the feast
with the unleavened bread of purity and truth, alleluia.
Psalm 117 may appropriately be sung.

Prayer after Communion
Pour out on us, O Lord, the Spirit of your love,
and in your kindness make those you have nourished
by this paschal Sacrament
one in mind and heart.
Through Christ our Lord.
Amen.

Solemn Blessing
May almighty God bless you
through today's Easter Solemnity
and, in his compassion,
defend you from every assault of sin.
Amen.

And may he, who restores you to eternal life
in the Resurrection of his Only Begotten,
endow you with the prize of immortality.
Amen.

Now that the days of the Lord's Passion have drawn to a close,
may you who celebrate the gladness of the Paschal Feast
come with Christ's help, and exulting in spirit,
to those feasts that are celebrated in eternal joy.
Amen.

And may the blessing of almighty God,
the Father, and the Son, ✢ and the Holy Spirit,
come down on you and remain with you for ever.
Amen.

The final blessing formula from the Rite of Baptism of Adults or of Children may also be used, according to circumstances.

To dismiss the people the Deacon or, if there is no Deacon, the Priest himself sings or says:

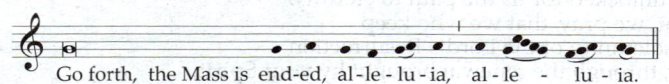

Go forth, the Mass is end-ed, al-le-lu-ia, al-le - lu - ia.

or

Go in peace, al-le-lu-ia, al-le - lu - ia.

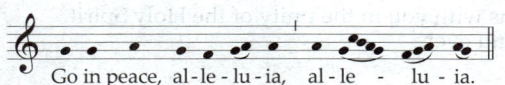

All reply:

Thanks be to God, al-le-lu-ia, al-le - lu - ia.

This practice is observed throughout the Octave of Easter.

The paschal candle is lit in all the more solemn liturgical celebrations of this period.

At Mass during the Day

Alleluia!

This Eucharist is our Alleluia; our song of thanksgiving and praise to the risen Christ who is our life and whose triumph over death we proclaim to all the world.

Entrance Antiphon   Cf. Ps 138:18. 5-6

I have risen, and I am with you still, alleluia.
You have laid your hand upon me, alleluia.
Too wonderful for me, this knowledge, alleluia, alleluia.

or   Lk 24:34; cf. ℟ v.1:6

The Lord is truly risen, alleluia.
To him be glory and power
for all the ages of eternity, alleluia, alleluia.

The Gloria in excelsis (Glory to God in the highest) *is said.*

Collect

O God, who on this day,
through your Only Begotten Son,
have conquered death
and unlocked for us the path to eternity,
grant, we pray, that we who keep
the solemnity of the Lord's Resurrection
may, through the renewal brought by your Spirit,
rise up in the light of life.
Through our Lord Jesus Christ, your Son,
who lives and reigns with you in the unity of the Holy Spirit,
one God, for ever and ever.
Amen.

FIRST READING

A reading from the Acts of the Apostles 10:34. 37-43

Peter addressed Cornelius and his household: 'You must have heard about the recent happenings in Judaea; about Jesus of Nazareth and how he began in Galilee, after John had been preaching baptism. God had anointed him with the Holy Spirit and with power, and because God was with him, Jesus went about doing good and curing all who had fallen into the power of the devil. Now I, and those with me, can witness to everything he did throughout the countryside of Judaea and in Jerusalem itself: and also to the fact that they killed him by hanging him on a tree, yet three days afterwards God raised him to life and allowed him to be seen, not by the whole people but only by certain witnesses God had chosen beforehand. Now we are those witnesses – we have eaten and drunk with him after his resurection from the dead – and he has ordered us to proclaim this to his people and to tell them that God has appointed him to judge everyone, alive or dead. It is to him that all the prophets bear this witness: that all who believe in Jesus will have their sins forgiven through his name.'

The word of the Lord.

Responsorial Psalm Ps 117:1-2. 16-17. 22-23. ℞ v.24

℞ **This day was made by the Lord;
we rejoice and are glad.**

or

Alleluia, alleluia, alleluia!

1 Give thanks to the Lord for he is good,
for his love has no end.

The Easter Vigil

Let the sons of Israel say:
'His love has no end.' ℟

2. The Lord's right hand has triumphed;
his right hand raised me up.
I shall not die, I shall live
and recount his deeds. ℟

3. The stone which the builders rejected
has become the corner stone.
This is the work of the Lord,
a marvel in our eyes. ℟

SECOND READING

A reading from the letter of St Paul to the Colossians 3:1-4

Since you have been brought back to true life with Christ, you must look for the things that are in heaven, where Christ is, sitting at God's right hand. Let your thoughts be on heavenly things, not on the things that are on the earth, because you have died, and now the life you have is hidden with Christ in God. But when Christ is revealed – and he is your life – you too will be revealed in all your glory with him.

The word of the Lord.

Alternative Reading

A reading from the first letter of St Paul 5:6-8
to the Corinthians

You must know how even a small amount of yeast is enough to leaven all the dough, so get rid of all the old yeast, and make yourselves into a completely new batch of bread, unleavened as you are meant to be. Christ, our passover, has been sacrificed; let us celebrate the feast, by getting rid of all the old yeast of evil and wickedness, having only the unleavened bread of sincerity and truth.

The word of the Lord.

The sequence is said or sung on this day.

SEQUENCE

Christians, to the Paschal Victim offer sacrifice and praise.
The sheep are ransomed by the Lamb;
and Christ, the undefiled,

hath sinners to his Father reconciled.
Death with life contended: combat strangely ended!
Life's own Champion, slain, yet lives to reign.
Tell us, Mary: say what thou didst see upon the way.
The tomb the Living did enclose;
I saw Christ's glory as he rose!
The angels there attesting;
shroud with grave-clothes resting.
Christ, my hope, has risen: he goes before you into Galilee.
That Christ is truly risen from the dead we know.
Victorious king, thy mercy show!

Gospel Acclamation 1 Cor 5:7-8

Alleluia, alleluia!
Christ, our passover, has been sacrificed;
let us celebrate the feast then, in the Lord.
Alleluia!

GOSPEL
A reading from the holy Gospel according to John 20:1-9

It was very early on the first day of the week and still dark, when Mary of Magdala came to the tomb. She saw that the stone had been moved away from the tomb and came running to Simon Peter and the other disciple, the one Jesus loved. 'They have taken the Lord out of the tomb' she said 'and we don't know where they have put him.'

So Peter set out with the other disciple to go to the tomb. They ran together, but the other disciple, running faster than Peter, reached the tomb first; he bent down and saw the linen cloths lying on the ground, but did not go in. Simon Peter who was following now came up, went right into the tomb, saw the linen cloths on the ground, and also the cloth that had been over his head; this was not with the linen cloths but rolled up in a place by itself. Then the other disciple who had reached the tomb first also went in; he saw and he believed. Till this moment they had failed to understand the teaching of scripture, that he must rise from the dead.

The Gospel of the Lord.

As an alternative, the Gospel of the Mass of Easter Night above, may be read. At an evening Mass, Luke 24:13-35 below, may be used as an alternative.

The Easter Vigil

Renewal of Baptismal Promises
In Easter Sunday Masses which are celebrated with a congregation, the rite of the renewal of baptismal promises may be repeated after the homily. See above, pp.419. When this is done, the Profession of Faith is omitted.

Prayer over the Offerings
Exultant with paschal gladness, O Lord,
we offer the sacrifice
by which your Church
is wondrously reborn and nourished.
Through Christ our Lord.
Amen.

Preface I of Easter, The Paschal Mystery, p.28.

When the Roman Canon is used, the proper forms of the Communicantes (In communion with those) and Hanc igitur (Therefore, Lord, we pray) are said.

Communion Antiphon 1 Cor 5:7-8
Christ our Passover has been sacrificed, alleluia;
therefore let us keep the feast with the unleavened bread
of purity and truth, alleluia, alleluia.

Prayer after Communion
Look upon your Church, O God,
with unfailing love and favour,
so that, renewed by the paschal mysteries,
she may come to the glory of the resurrection.
Through Christ our Lord.
Amen.

To impart the blessing at the end of Mass, the Priest may appropriately use the formula of Solemn Blessing for the Mass of the Easter Vigil.

For the dismissal of the people, there is sung (as above) or said:

Go forth, the Mass is ended, alleluia, alleluia.

or

Go in peace, alleluia, alleluia.
℟ **Thanks be to God, alleluia, alleluia.**

THE SEASON OF EASTER

SECOND SUNDAY OF EASTER   A
(or of Divine Mercy)

Our Easter Joy

Today as we hail Christ as our Lord and God we are filled with the joy of the disciples in seeing the risen Lord. In this season of renewed hope, we are like those early Christians who were 'already filled with a joy so glorious that it cannot be described.'

Entrance Antiphon   1 Pt 2:2
Like newborn infants, you must long for the pure, spiritual milk,
that in him you may grow to salvation, alleluia.

or   4 Esdr 2:36-37

Receive the joy of your glory, giving thanks to God,
who has called you into the heavenly kingdom, alleluia.

The Gloria in excelsis (Glory to God in the highest) is said.

Collect
God of everlasting mercy,
who, in the very recurrence of the paschal feast
kindle the faith of the people you have made your own,
increase, we pray, the grace you have bestowed,
that all may grasp and rightly understand
in what font they have been washed,
by whose Spirit they have been reborn,
by whose Blood they have been redeemed.
Through our Lord Jesus Christ, your Son,
who lives and reigns with you in the unity of the Holy Spirit,
one God, for ever and ever.
Amen.

Second Sunday of Easter, Year A

FIRST READING
A reading from the Acts of the Apostles   2:42-47

The whole community remained faithful to the teaching of the apostles, to the brotherhood, to the breaking of bread and to the prayers.

The many miracles and signs worked through the apostles made a deep impression on everyone.

The faithful all lived together and owned everything in common; they sold their goods and possessions and shared out the proceeds among themselves according to what each one needed.

They went as a body to the Temple every day but met in their houses for the breaking of bread; they shared their food gladly and generously; they praised God and were looked up to by everyone. Day by day the Lord added to their community those destined to be saved.

The word of the Lord.

Responsorial Psalm   Ps 117:2-4. 13-15. 22-24. ℟ v.1

℟ **Give thanks to the Lord for he is good,
for his love has no end.**

or

Alleluia, alleluia, alleluia!

1 Let the sons of Israel say:
'His love has no end.'
Let the sons of Aaron say:
'His love has no end,'
Let those who fear the Lord say:
'His love has no end.'   ℟

2 I was thrust, thrust down and falling
but the Lord was my helper.
The Lord is my strength and my song;
he was my saviour.
There are shouts of joy and victory
in the tents of the just.   ℟

3 The stone which the builders rejected
has become the corner stone.
This is the work of the Lord,
a marvel in our eyes.
This day was made by the Lord;
we rejoice and are glad.   ℟

SECOND READING

A reading from the first letter of St Peter   1:3-9

Blessed be God the Father of our Lord Jesus Christ, who in his great mercy has given us a new birth as his sons, by raising Jesus Christ from the dead, so that we have a sure hope and the promise of an inheritance that can never be spoilt or soiled and never fade away, because it is being kept for you in the heavens. Through your faith, God's power will guard you until the salvation which had been prepared is revealed at the end of time. This is a cause of great joy for you, even though you may for a short time have to bear being plagued by all sorts of trials; so that, when Jesus Christ is revealed, your faith will have been tested and proved like gold– only it is more precious than gold, which is corruptible even though it bears testing by fire – and then you will have praise and glory and honour. You did not see him, yet you love him; and still without seeing him, you are already filled with a joy so glorious that it cannot be described, because you believe; and you are sure of the end to which your faith looks forward, that is, the salvation of your souls.

The word of the Lord.

Gospel Acclamation   Jn 20:29
    Alleluia, alleluia!
    Jesus said: 'You believe because you can see me.
    Happy are those who have not seen and yet believe.'
    Alleluia!

GOSPEL

A reading from the holy Gospel according to John   20:19-31

In the evening of that same day, the first day of the week, the doors were closed in the room where the disciples were, for fear of the Jews. Jesus came and stood among them. He said to them, 'Peace be with you,' and showed them his hands and his side. The disciples were filled with joy when they saw the Lord, and he said to them again, 'Peace be with you.

    'As the Father sent me,
    so am I sending you.'

After saying this he breathed on them and said:

'Receive the Holy Spirit.
For those whose sins you forgive,
they are forgiven;
for those whose sins you retain,
they are retained.'

Thomas, called the Twin, who was one of the Twelve, was not with them when Jesus came. When the disciples said, 'We have seen the Lord,' he answered, 'Unless I see the holes that the nails made in his hands and can put my finger into the holes they made, and unless I can put my hand into his side, I refuse to believe.' Eight days later the disciples were in the house again and Thomas was with them. The doors were closed, but Jesus came in and stood among them. 'Peace be with you,' he said. Then he spoke to Thomas, 'Put your finger here; look, here are my hands. Give me your hand; put it into my side. Doubt no longer but believe.' Thomas replied,

'My Lord
and my God!'

Jesus said to him:

'You believe because you can see me.
Happy are those who have not seen and yet believe.'

There were many other signs that Jesus worked and the disciples saw, but they are not recorded in this book. These are recorded so that you may believe that Jesus is the Christ, the Son of God, and that believing this you may have life through his name.

The Gospel of the Lord.

The Creed is said.

Prayer over the Offerings
Accept, O Lord, we pray,
the oblations of your people
(and of those you have brought to new birth),
that, renewed by confession of your name and by Baptism,
they may attain unending happiness.
Through Christ our Lord.
Amen.

Preface I of Easter (. . . on this day above all . . .), p.28.

When the Roman Canon is used, the proper forms of the Communicantes (In communion with those) and Hanc igitur (Therefore, Lord, we pray) are said.

Communion Antiphon Cf. Jn 20:27
Bring your hand and feel the place of the nails,
and do not be unbelieving but believing, alleluia.

Prayer after Communion
Grant, we pray, almighty God,
that our reception of this paschal Sacrament
may have a continuing effect
in our minds and hearts.
Through Christ our Lord.
Amen.

A formula of Solemn Blessing, p.97, may be used.

For the dismissal of the people, there is sung (as above, p.423) or said: Go forth, the Mass is ended, alleluia, alleluia. Or Go in peace, alleluia, alleluia. The people respond: **Thanks be to God, alleluia, alleluia.**

THIRD SUNDAY OF EASTER A

Christ With Us on the Way of Life

Christ has made known to us the true way of life and restored us to glory. He fills us with gladness in his presence. He is with us today in the breaking of bread.

Entrance Antiphon Cf. Ps 65:1-2
Cry out with joy to God, all the earth;
O sing to the glory of his name.
O render him glorious praise, alleluia.

The Gloria in excelsis (Glory to God in the highest) is said.

Collect
May your people exult for ever, O God,
in renewed youthfulness of spirit,
so that, rejoicing now in the restored glory of our adoption,
we may look forward in confident hope
to the rejoicing of the day of resurrection.
Through our Lord Jesus Christ, your Son,
who lives and reigns with you in the unity of the Holy Spirit,
one God, for ever and ever.
Amen.

Third Sunday of Easter, Year A

FIRST READING
A reading from the Acts of the Apostles   2:14. 22-33

On the day of Pentecost Peter stood up with the Eleven and addressed the crowd in a loud voice: 'Men of Israel, listen to what I am going to say: Jesus the Nazarene was a man commended to you by God by the miracles and portents and signs that God worked through him when he was among you, as you all know. This man, who was put into your power by the deliberate intention and foreknowledge of God, you took and had crucified by men outside the Law. You killed him, but God raised him to life, freeing him from the pangs of Hades; for it was impossible for him to be held in its power since, as David says of him:

> "I saw the Lord before me always,
> for with him at my right hand nothing can shake me.
> So my heart was glad and my tongue cried out with joy:
> my body, too, will rest in the hope
> that you will not abandon my soul to Hades
> nor allow your holy one to experience corruption.
> You have made known the way of life to me,
> you will fill me with gladness through your presence."

'Brothers, no one can deny that the patriarch David himself is dead and buried: his tomb is still with us. But since he was a prophet, and knew that God had sworn him an oath to make one of his descendants succeed him on the throne, what he foresaw and spoke about was the resurrection of the Christ: he is the one who was not abandoned to Hades, and whose body did not experience corruption. God raised this man Jesus to life, and all of us are witnesses to that. Now raised to the heights by God's right hand, he has received from the Father the Holy Spirit, who was promised, and what you see and hear is the outpouring of that Spirit.'

The word of the Lord.

Responsional Psalm   Ps 15:1-2. 5. 7-11. R̷ v.11

  R̷   **Show us, Lord, the path of life.**

or

  R̷   **Alleluia!**

1   Preserve me, God, I take refuge in you.
    I say to the Lord: 'You are my God.
    O Lord, it is you who are my portion and cup;
    it is you yourself who are my prize.'   R̷

2 I will bless the Lord who gives me counsel,
 who even at night directs my heart.
 I keep the Lord ever in my sight:
 since he is at my right hand, I shall stand firm. ℟

3 And so my heart rejoices, my soul is glad;
 even my body shall rest in safety.
 For you will not leave my soul among the dead,
 nor let your beloved know decay. ℟

4 You will show me the path of life,
 the fullness of joy in your presence,
 at your right hand happiness for ever. ℟

SECOND READING
A reading from the first letter of St Peter 1:17-21

If you are acknowledging as your Father one who has no favourites and judges everyone according to what he has done, you must be scrupulously careful as long as you are living away from your home. Remember, the ransom that was paid to free you from the useless way of life your ancestors handed down was not paid in anything corruptible, neither in silver nor gold, but in the precious blood of a lamb without spot or stain, namely Christ; who, though known since before the world was made, has been revealed only in our time, the end of the ages, for your sake. Through him you now have faith in God, who raised him from the dead and gave him glory for that very reason – so that you would have faith and hope in God.

The word of the Lord.

Gospel Acclamation Cf. Lk 24:32
 Alleluia, alleluia!
 Lord Jesus, explain the scriptures to us.
 Make our hearts burn within us as you talk to us.
 Alleluia!

GOSPEL
A reading from the holy Gospel according to Luke 24:13-35

Two of the disciples of Jesus were on their way to a village called Emmaus, seven miles from Jerusalem, and they were talking together about all that had happened. Now as they talked this over, Jesus himself came up and walked by their side; but something prevented them from recognising him. He said to them, 'What matters are you discussing as you walk along?' They stopped short, their faces downcast.

Then one of them, called Cleopas answered him, 'You must be the only person staying in Jerusalem who does not know the things that have been happening there these last few days.' 'What things?' he asked. 'All about Jesus of Nazareth' they answered 'who proved he was a great prophet by the things he said and did in the sight of God and of the whole people; and how our chief priests and our leaders handed him over to be sentenced to death, and had him crucified. Our own hope had been that he would be the one to set Israel free. And this is not all: two whole days have gone by since it all happened; and some women from our group have astounded us: they went to the tomb in the early morning, and when they did not find the body, they came back to tell us they had seen a vision of angels who declared he was alive. Some of our friends went to the tomb and found everything exactly as the women had reported, but of him they saw nothing.'

Then he said to them, 'You foolish men! So slow to believe the full message of the prophets! Was it not ordained that the Christ should suffer and so enter into his glory?' Then, starting with Moses and going through all the prophets, he explained to them the passages throughout the scriptures that were about himself.

When they drew near to the village to which they were going, he made as if to go on; but they pressed him to stay with them. 'It is nearly evening' they said 'and the day is almost over.' So he went in to stay with them. Now while he was with them at the table, he took the bread and said the blessing; then he broke it and handed it to them. And their eyes were opened and they recognised him; but he had vanished from their sight. Then they said to each other, 'Did not our hearts burn within us as he talked to us on the road and explained the scriptures to us?'

They set out that instant and returned to Jerusalem. There they found the Eleven assembled together with their companions, who said to them, 'Yes, it is true. The Lord has risen and has appeared to Simon.' Then they told their story of what had happened on the road and how they had recognised him at the breaking of bread.

The Gospel of the Lord.

The Creed is said.

Prayer over the Offerings
Receive, O Lord, we pray,
these offerings of your exultant Church,
and, as you have given her cause for such great gladness,
grant also that the gifts we bring
may bear fruit in perpetual happiness.
Through Christ our Lord.
Amen.

An appropriate Preface of Easter, pp.28-30.

Communion Antiphon Lk 24:35
The disciples recognized the Lord Jesus
in the breaking of the bread, alleluia.

Prayer after Communion
Look with kindness upon your people, O Lord,
and grant, we pray,
that those you were pleased to renew by eternal mysteries
may attain in their flesh
the incorruptible glory of the resurrection.
Through Christ our Lord.
Amen.

A formula of Solemn Blessing, p.97, may be used.

FOURTH SUNDAY OF EASTER   A

The Shepherd and Guardian of Our Souls

Today we rejoice in the Lord, our Shepherd, who guides us along the right paths, to his own house where we shall dwell for ever and ever.

Entrance Antiphon Cf. Ps 32:5-6
The merciful love of the Lord fills the earth;
by the word of the Lord the heavens were made, alleluia.

The Gloria in excelsis (Glory to God in the highest) is said.

Fourth Sunday of Easter, Year A

Collect
Almighty ever-living God,
lead us to a share in the joys of heaven,
so that the humble flock may reach
where the brave Shepherd has gone before.
Who lives and reigns with you in the unity of the Holy Spirit,
one God, for ever and ever.
Amen.

FIRST READING
A reading from the Acts of the Apostles   2:14. 36-41

On the day of Pentecost Peter stood up with the Eleven and addressed the crowd with a loud voice: 'The whole House of Israel can be certain that God has made this Jesus whom you crucified both Lord and Christ.'

Hearing this, they were cut to the heart and said to Peter and the apostles, 'What must we do, brothers?' 'You must repent,' Peter answered 'and every one of you must be baptised in the name of Jesus Christ for the forgiveness of your sins, and you will receive the gift of the Holy Spirit. The promise that was made is for you and your children, and for all those who are far away, for all those whom the Lord our God will call to himself.' He spoke to them for a long time using many arguments, and he urged them, 'Save yourselves from this perverse generation.' They were convinced by his arguments, and they accepted what he said and were baptised. That very day about three thousand were added to their number.

The word of the Lord.

Responsorial Psalm   Ps 22:1-6. ℟ v.1

℟   **The Lord is my shepherd;
    there is nothing I shall want.**

or

    Alleluia!

1   The Lord is my shepherd;
    there is nothing I shall want.
    Fresh and green are the pastures
    where he gives me repose.
    Near restful waters he leads me,
    to revive my drooping spirit.   ℟

2   He guides me along the right path;
    he is true to his name.
    If I should walk in the valley of darkness
    no evil would I fear.
    You are there with your crook and your staff;
    with these you give me comfort. ℟

3   You have prepared a banquet for me
    in the sight of my foes.
    My head you have anointed with oil;
    my cup is overflowing. ℟

4   Surely goodness and kindness shall follow me
    all the days of my life.
    In the Lord's own house shall I dwell
    for ever and ever. ℟

SECOND READING

A reading from the first letter of St Peter   2:20-25

The merit, in the sight of God, is in bearing punishment patiently when you are punished after doing your duty. This, in fact, is what you were called to do, because Christ suffered for you and left an example for you to follow the way he took. He had not done anything wrong, and there had been no perjury in his mouth. He was insulted and did not retaliate with insults; when he was tortured he made no threats but he put his trust in the righteous judge. He was bearing our faults in his own body on the cross, so that we might die to our faults and live for holiness; through his wounds you have been healed. You had gone astray like sheep but now you have come back to the shepherd and guardian of your souls.

The word of the Lord.

Gospel Acclamation   Jn 10:14
Alleluia, alleluia!
I am the good shepherd, says the Lord;
I know my own sheep and my own know me.
Alleluia!

Fourth Sunday of Easter, Year A

GOSPEL
A reading from the holy Gospel according to John 10:1-10

Jesus said: 'I tell you most solemnly, anyone who does not enter the sheepfold through the gate, but gets in some other way is a thief and a brigand. The one who enters through the gate is the shepherd of the flock; the gatekeeper lets him in, the sheep hear his voice, one by one he calls his own sheep and leads them out. When he has brought out his flock, he goes ahead of them, and the sheep follow because they know his voice. They never follow a stranger but run away from him: they do not recognise the voice of strangers.'

Jesus told them this parable but they failed to understand what he meant by telling it to them.

So Jesus spoke to them again:

'I tell you most solemnly,
I am the gate of the sheepfold.
All others who have come
are thieves and brigands;
but the sheep took no notice of them.
I am the gate.
Anyone who enters through me will be safe:
he will go freely in and out
and be sure of finding pasture.
The thief comes
only to steal and kill and destroy.
I have come
so that they may have life
and have it to the full.'

The Gospel of the Lord.

The Creed is said.

Prayer over the Offerings
Grant, we pray, O Lord,
that we may always find delight in these paschal mysteries,
so that the renewal constantly at work within us
may be the cause of our unending joy.
Through Christ our Lord.
Amen.

An appropriate Preface of Easter, pp.28-30.

Communion Antiphon
The Good Shepherd has risen,
who laid down his life for his sheep
and willingly died for his flock, alleluia.

Prayer after Communion
Look upon your flock, kind Shepherd,
and be pleased to settle in eternal pastures
the sheep you have redeemed
by the Precious Blood of your Son.
Who lives and reigns for ever and ever.
Amen.

A formula of Solemn Blessing, p.97, may be used.

FIFTH SUNDAY OF EASTER   A

Our Royal Priesthood

We are assembled here today to exercise our royal priesthood and to offer the spiritual sacrifice which Jesus Christ has made acceptable to God our Father.

Entrance Antiphon   Cf. Ps 97:1-2
O sing a new song to the Lord,
for he has worked wonders;
in the sight of the nations
he has shown his deliverance, alleluia.

The Gloria in excelsis (Glory to God in the highest) is said.

Collect
Almighty ever-living God,
constantly accomplish the Paschal Mystery within us,
that those you were pleased to make new in Holy Baptism
may, under your protective care, bear much fruit
and come to the joys of life eternal.
Through our Lord Jesus Christ, your Son,
who lives and reigns with you in the unity of the Holy Spirit,
one God, for ever and ever.
Amen.

Fifth Sunday of Easter, Year A

FIRST READING
A reading from the Acts of the Apostles 6:1-7

About this time, when the number of disciples was increasing, the Hellenists made a complaint against the Hebrews: in the daily distribution their own widows were being overlooked. So the Twelve called a full meeting of the disciples and addressed them, 'It would not be right for us to neglect the word of God so as to give out food; you, brothers, must select from among yourselves seven men of good reputation, filled with the Spirit and with wisdom; we will hand over this duty to them, and continue to devote ourselves to prayer and to the service of the word.' The whole assembly approved of this proposal and elected Stephen, a man full of faith and of the Holy Spirit, together with Philip, Prochorus, Nicanor, Timon, Parmenas, and Nicolaus of Antioch, a convert to Judaism. They presented these to the apostles, who prayed and laid their hands on them.

The word of the Lord continued to spread: the number of disciples in Jerusalem was greatly increased, and a large group of priests made their submission to the faith.

The word of the Lord.

Responsorial Psalm Ps 32:1-2. 4-5. 18-19. ℟ v.22

℟ **May your love be upon us, O Lord,
as we place all our hope in you.**

or

℟ **Alleluia!**

1 Ring out your joy to the Lord, O you just;
   for praise is fitting for loyal hearts.
   Give thanks to the Lord upon the harp,
   with a ten-stringed lute sing him songs. ℟

2 For the word of the Lord is faithful
   and all his works to be trusted.
   The Lord loves justice and right
   and fills the earth with his love. ℟

3 The Lord looks on those who revere him,
   on those who hope in his love,
   to rescue their souls from death,
   to keep them alive in famine. ℟

Fifth Sunday of Easter, Year A

SECOND READING
A reading from the first letter of St Peter 2:4-9

The Lord is the living stone, rejected by men but chosen by God and precious to him; set yourselves close to him so that you too, the holy priesthood that offers the spiritual sacrifices which Jesus Christ has made acceptable to God, may be living stones making a spiritual house. As scripture says: See how I lay in Zion a precious cornerstone that I have chosen and the man who rests his trust on it will not be disappointed. That means that for you who are believers, it is precious; but for unbelievers, the stone rejected by the builders has proved to be the keystone, a stone to stumble over, a rock to bring men down. They stumble over it because they do not believe in the word; it was the fate in store for them. But you are a chosen race, a royal priesthood, a consecrated nation, a people set apart to sing the praises of God who called you out of the darkness into his wonderful light.

The word of the Lord.

Gospel Acclamation Jn 14:6
Alleluia, alleluia!
Jesus said: 'I am the Way, the Truth and the Life.
No one can come to the Father except through me.'
Alleluia!

GOSPEL
A reading from the holy Gospel according to John 14:1-12

Jesus said to his disciples:

'Do not let your hearts be troubled.
Trust in God still, and trust in me.
There are many rooms in my Father's house;
if there were not, I should have told you.
I am now going to prepare a place for you,
and after I have gone and prepared you a place,
I shall return to take you with me;
so that where I am
you may be too.
You know the way to the place where I am going.'

Thomas said, 'Lord, we do not know where you are going, so how can we know the way?' Jesus said:

'I am the Way, the Truth and the Life.
No one can come to the Father except through me.
If you know me, you know my Father too.
From this moment you know him and have seen him.'

Philip said, 'Lord, let us see the Father and then we shall be satisfied.' 'Have I been with you all this time, Philip,' said Jesus to him 'and you still do not know me?

'To have seen me is to have seen the Father,
so how can you say, "Let us see the Father"?
Do you not believe
that I am in the Father and the Father is in me?
The words I say to you I do not speak as from myself:
it is the Father, living in me, who is doing this work.
You must believe me when I say
that I am in the Father and the Father is in me;
believe it on the evidence of this work, if for no other reason.

'I tell you most solemnly,
whoever believes in me
will perform the same works as I do myself,
he will perform even greater works,
because I am going to the Father.'

The Gospel of the Lord.

Prayer over the Offerings
O God, who by the wonderful exchange effected in this sacrifice
have made us partakers of the one supreme Godhead,
grant, we pray,
that, as we have come to know your truth,
we may make it ours by a worthy way of life.
Through Christ our Lord.
Amen.

An appropriate Preface of Easter, pp.28-30.

Communion Antiphon   Cf. Jn 15:1, 5
I am the true vine and you are the branches, says the Lord.
Whoever remains in me, and I in him, bears fruit in plenty, alleluia!

Prayer after Communion
Graciously be present to your people, we pray, O Lord,
and lead those you have imbued with heavenly mysteries

to pass from former ways to newness of life.
Through Christ our Lord.
Amen.

A formula of Solemn Blessing, p.97, may be used.

SIXTH SUNDAY OF EASTER   A

The Spirit of Truth

We celebrate the coming of Christ's Spirit of truth on the Church a source of joy and praise, the source of the Churchs' proclamation of the good news to the world.

Entrance Antiphon   Cf. Is 48:20
Proclaim a joyful sound and let it be heard;
proclaim to the ends of the earth:
The Lord has freed his people, alleluia.
The Gloria in excelsis (Glory to God in the highest) is said.

Collect
Grant, almighty God,
that we may celebrate with heartfelt devotion these days of joy,
which we keep in honour of the risen Lord,
and that what we relive in remembrance
we may always hold to in what we do.
Through our Lord Jesus Christ, your Son,
who lives and reigns with you in the unity of the Holy Spirit,
one God, for ever and ever.
Amen.

FIRST READING
A reading from the Acts of the Apostles   8:5-8. 14-17

Philip went to a Samaritan town and proclaimed the Christ to them. The people united in welcoming the message Philip preached, either because they had heard of the miracles he worked or because they saw them for themselves. There were, for example, unclean spirits that came shrieking out of many who were possessed, and several paralytics and cripples were cured. As a result there was great rejoicing in that town.

When the apostles in Jerusalem heard that Samaria had accepted the word of God, they sent Peter and John to them, and they went down there, and prayed for the Samaritans to receive the Holy

Spirit, for as yet he had not come down on any of them: they had only been baptised in the name of the Lord Jesus. Then they laid hands on them, and they received the Holy Spirit.

The word of the Lord.

Responsorial Psalm   Ps 65:1-7. 16. 20. ℟ v.1

   ℟   **Cry out with joy to God all the earth.**

or

      ℟   **Alleluia!**

1 Cry out with joy to God all the earth,
   O sing to the glory of his name.
   O render him glorious praise.
   Say to God: 'How tremendous your deeds!' ℟

2 'Before you all the earth shall bow;
   shall sing to you, sing to your name!'
   Come and see the works of God,
   tremendous his deeds among men. ℟

3 He turned the sea into dry land,
   they passed through the river dry-shod.
   Let our joy then be in him;
   he rules for ever by his might. ℟

4 Come and hear, all who fear God.
   I will tell what he did for my soul:
   Blessed be God who did not reject my prayer
   nor withhold his love from me. ℟

SECOND READING

A reading from the first letter of St Peter   3:15-18

Reverence the Lord Christ in your hearts, and always have your answer ready for people who ask you the reason for the hope that you all have. But give it with courtesy and respect and with a clear conscience, so that those who slander you when you are living a good life in Christ may be proved wrong in the accusations that they bring. And if it is the will of God that you should suffer, it is better to suffer for doing right than for doing wrong.

    Why, Christ himself, innocent though he was, had died once for sins, died for the guilty, to lead us to God. In the body he was put to death, in the spirit he was raised to life.

The word of the Lord.

Gospel Acclamation   Jn 14:23
    Alleluia, alleluia!
    Jesus said: 'If anyone loves me he will keep my word,
    and my Father will love him, and we shall come to him.'
    Alleluia!

GOSPEL

A reading from the holy Gospel according to John   14:15-21

Jesus said to his disciples:

'If you love me you will keep my commandments.
I shall ask the Father,
and he will give you another Advocate
to be with you for ever,
that Spirit of truth
whom the world can never receive
since it neither sees nor knows him;
but you know him,
because he is with you, he is in you.
I will not leave you orphans;
I will come back to you.
In a short time the world will no longer see me;
but you will see me,
because I live and you will live.
On that day
you will understand that I am in my Father
and you in me and I in you.
Anybody who receives my commandments and keeps them
will be one who loves me;
and anybody who loves me will be loved by my Father,
and I shall love him and show myself to him.'

The Gospel of the Lord.

When the Ascension of the Lord is celebrated on the Seventh Sunday of Easter, the Second Reading and Gospel assigned to the Seventh Sunday (see below, pp.453-5.) may be read on the Sixth Sunday.

The Creed is said.

Prayer over the Offerings
May our prayers rise up to you, O Lord,
together with the sacrificial offerings,
so that, purified by your graciousness,

we may be conformed to the mysteries of your mighty love.
Through Christ our Lord.
Amen.

An appropriate Preface of Easter, pp.28-30.

Communion Antiphon   Jn 14:15-16
If you love me, keep my commandments, says the Lord,
and I will ask the Father and he will send you another Paraclete,
to abide with you for ever, alleluia.

Prayer after Communion
Almighty ever-living God,
who restore us to eternal life in the Resurrection of Christ,
increase in us, we pray, the fruits of this paschal Sacrament
and pour into our hearts the strength of this saving food.
Through Christ our Lord.
Amen.

A formula of Solemn Blessing, p.97, may be used.

THE ASCENSION OF THE LORD   A

Solemnity

Christ's Eternal Glory

We celebrate today Christ's ascension to his eternal glory in heaven and express our Christian hope that where he, our Head, has gone before us, we, his Body, will one day follow, to live for ever in the Kingdom of God.

Where the Solemnity of the Ascension is not to be observed as a Holyday of Obligation, it is assigned to the Seventh Sunday of Easter as its proper day.

At the Vigil Mass

This Mass is used on the evening of the day before the Solemnity, either before or after First Vespers (Evening Prayer I) of the Ascension.

Entrance Antiphon   Ps 67:33. 35
You kingdoms of the earth, sing to God;
praise the Lord, who ascends above the highest heavens;
his majesty and might are in the skies, alleluia.

The Gloria in excelsis (Glory to God in the highest) is said.

The Ascension of the Lord, Year A

Collect
O God, whose Son today ascended to the heavens
as the Apostles looked on,
grant, we pray, that, in accordance with his promise,
we may be worthy for him to live with us always on earth,
and we with him in heaven.
Who lives and reigns with you in the unity of the Holy Spirit,
one God, for ever and ever.
Amen.

For the Readings, Gospel Acclamation and Gospel, see the Mass during the Day (pp.449-51).

The Creed is said.

Prayer over the Offerings
O God, whose Only Begotten Son, our High Priest,
is seated ever-living at your right hand to intercede for us,
grant that we may approach with confidence the throne of grace
and there obtain your mercy.
Through Christ our Lord.
Amen.

Preface I or II of the Ascension, p.31.

When the Roman Canon is used, the proper form of the Communicantes (In communion with those) is said.

Communion Antiphon Cf. Heb 10:12
Christ, offering a single sacrifice for sins,
is seated for ever at God's right hand, alleluia.

Prayer after Communion
May the gifts we have received from your altar, Lord,
kindle in our hearts a longing for the heavenly homeland
and cause us to press forward, following in the Saviour's footsteps,
to the place where for our sake he entered before us.
Who lives and reigns for ever and ever.
Amen.

A formula of Solemn Blessing, pp.97-8, may be used.

At the Mass during the Day

Entrance Antiphon Acts 1:11
Men of Galilee, why gaze in wonder at the heavens?
This Jesus whom you saw ascending into heaven
will return as you saw him go, alleluia.

The Gloria in excelsis (Glory to God in the highest) is said.

Collect
Gladden us with holy joys, almighty God,
and make us rejoice with devout thanksgiving,
for the Ascension of Christ your Son
is our exaltation,
and, where the Head has gone before in glory,
the Body is called to follow in hope.
Through our Lord Jesus Christ, your Son,
who lives and reigns with you in the unity of the Holy Spirit,
one God, for ever and ever.
Amen.

or

Grant, we pray, almighty God,
that we, who believe that your Only Begotten Son, our Redeemer,
ascended this day to the heavens,
may in spirit dwell already in heavenly realms.
Who lives and reigns with you in the unity of the Holy Spirit,
one God, for ever and ever.
Amen.

FIRST READING
A reading from the Acts of the Apostles 1:1-11

In my earlier work, Theophilus, I dealt with everything Jesus had done and taught from the beginning until the day he gave his instructions to the apostles he had chosen through the Holy Spirit, and was taken up to heaven. He had shown himself alive to them after his Passion by many demonstrations: for forty days he had continued to appear to them and tell them about the kingdom of God. When he had been at table with them, he had told them not to leave Jerusalem, but to wait there for what the Father had promised. 'It is' he had said 'what you have heard me speak about: John baptised with water but you, not many days from now, will be baptised with the Holy Spirit.'

Now having met together, they asked him, 'Lord, has the time come? Are you going to restore the kingdom to Israel?' He replied, 'It is not for you to know times or dates that the Father has decided by his own authority, but you will receive power when the Holy Spirit comes on you, and then you will be my witnesses not only in Jerusalem but throughout Judaea and Samaria, and indeed to the ends of the earth.'

As he said this he was lifted up while they looked on, and a cloud took him from their sight. They were still staring into the sky when suddenly two men in white were standing near them and they said, 'Why are you men from Galilee standing here looking into the sky? Jesus who has been taken up from you into heaven, this same Jesus will come back in the same way as you have seen him go there.'

The word of the Lord.

Responsional Psalm   Ps 46:2-3. 6-9. R̸ v.6

   R̸ **God goes up with shouts of joy;**
      the Lord goes up with trumpet blast.

or

   R̸ **Alleluia!**

1   All peoples, clap your hands,
     cry to God with shouts of joy!
     For the Lord, the Most High, we must fear,
     great king over all the earth.   R̸

2   God goes up with shouts of joy;
     the Lord goes up with trumpet blast.
     Sing praise for God, sing praise,
     sing praise to our king, sing praise.   R̸

3   God is king of all the earth.
     Sing praise with all your skill.
     God is king over the nations;
     God reigns on his holy throne.   R̸

SECOND READING
A reading from the letter of St Paul to the Ephesians   1:17-23

May the God of our Lord Jesus Christ, the Father of glory, give you a spirit of wisdom and perception of what is revealed, to bring you to full knowledge of him. May he enlighten the eyes of your mind so that you can see what hope his call holds for you, what rich glories he has promised the saints will inherit and how infinitely great is the power that he has exercised for us believers. This you can tell from the strength of his power at work in Christ, when he used it to raise him from the dead and to make him sit at his right hand, in heaven, far above every Sovereignty, Authority, Power, or Domination, or any other name that can be named, not only in this age, but also in the age to come. He has put all things under his feet, and made him as the ruler of everything, the head of the Church; which is his body, the fullness of him who fills the whole creation.

The word of the Lord.

Gospel Acclamation Mt 28:19. 20
Alleluia, alleluia!
Go, make disciples of all the nations;
I am with you always; yes, to the end of time.
Alleluia!

GOSPEL
A reading from the holy Gospel according to Matthew 28:16-20

The eleven disciples set out for Galilee, to the mountain where Jesus had arranged to meet them. When they saw him they fell down before him, though some hesitated. Jesus came up and spoke to them. He said, 'All authority in heaven and on earth has been given to me. Go, therefore, make disciples of all the nations; baptise them in the name of the Father and of the Son and of the Holy Spirit, and teach them to observe all the commands I gave you. And know that I am with you always; yes, to the end of time.'

The Gospel of the Lord.

The Creed is said.

Prayer over the Offerings
We offer sacrifice now in supplication, O Lord,
to honour the wondrous Ascension of your Son:
grant, we pray,
that through this most holy exchange
we, too, may rise up to the heavenly realms.
Through Christ our Lord.
Amen.

Preface I or II of the Ascension of the Lord, p.31.

When the Roman Canon is used, the proper form of the Communicantes (In communion with those) is said.

Communion Antiphon — Mt 28:20
Behold, I am with you always,
even to the end of the age, alleluia.

Prayer after Communion
Almighty ever-living God,
who allow those on earth to celebrate divine mysteries,
grant, we pray,
that Christian hope may draw us onward
to where our nature is united with you.
Through Christ our Lord.
Amen.

A formula of Solemn Blessing, pp.97-8, may be used.

SEVENTH SUNDAY OF EASTER — A

Where the Ascension of the Lord is celebrated on this day, the readings given for Ascension, see above pp.442-4, are used.

The Spirit of Prayer and Praise

Christ prayed in the Spirit, and the Holy Spirit is the source of the prayer and praise of the whole Church. The Spirit of God is resting on us as we offer this sacrifice of praise today.

Entrance Antiphon — Cf. Ps 26:7-9
O Lord, hear my voice, for I have called to you;
of you my heart has spoken: Seek his face;
hide not your face from me, alleluia.

The Gloria in excelsis (Glory to God in the highest) is said.

Collect
Graciously hear our supplications, O Lord,
so that we, who believe that the Saviour of the human race
is with you in your glory,
may experience, as he promised,
until the end of the world,
his abiding presence among us.
Who lives and reigns with you in the unity of the Holy Spirit,
one God, for ever and ever.
Amen.

Seventh Sunday of Easter, Year A

FIRST READING
A reading from the Acts of the Apostles 1:12-14

After Jesus was taken up into heaven, the apostles went back from the Mount of Olives, as it is called, to Jerusalem, a short distance away, no more than a sabbath walk; and when they reached the city they went to the upper room where they were staying; there were Peter and John, James and Andrew, Philip and Thomas, Bartholomew and Matthew, James son of Alphaeus and Simon the Zealot, and Jude son of James. All these joined in continuous prayer, together with several women, including Mary the mother of Jesus, and with his brothers.

The word of the Lord.

Responsional Psalm
Ps 26:1. 4. 7-8. ℟ v.13

℟ **I am sure I shall see the Lord's goodness in the land of the living.**

or

℟ **Alleluia!**

1. The Lord is my light and my help;
whom shall I fear?
The Lord is the stronghold of my life;
before whom shall I shrink? ℟

2. There is one thing I ask of the Lord,
for this I long,
to live in the house of the Lord,
all the days of my life,
to savour the sweetness of the Lord,
to behold his temple. ℟

3. O Lord, hear my voice when I call;
have mercy and answer.
Of you my heart has spoken;
'Seek his face.' ℟

SECOND READING
A reading from the first letter of St Peter 4:13-16

If you can have some share in the sufferings of Christ, be glad, because you will enjoy a much greater gladness when his glory is revealed. It is a blessing for you when they insult you for bearing the name of Christ, because it means that you have the Spirit of glory, the Spirit of God resting on you. None of you should ever deserve to suffer for being a murderer, a thief, a criminal or an informer; but if anyone of you should suffer for being a Christian, then he is not to be ashamed of it; he should thank God that he has been called one.

The word of the Lord.

Gospel Acclamation Cf. Jn 14:18
Alleluia, alleluia!
I will not leave you orphans, says the Lord;
I will come back to you, and your hearts will be full of joy.
Alleluia!

GOSPEL

A reading from the holy Gospel according to John 17:1-11

Jesus raised his eyes to heaven and said:

'Father, the hour has come:
glorify your Son
so that your Son may glorify you;
and, through the power over all mankind that you have given him,
let him give eternal life to all those you have entrusted to him.
And eternal life is this:
to know you,
the only true God,
and Jesus Christ whom you have sent.
I have glorified you on earth
and finished the work
that you gave me to do.
Now, Father, it is time for you to glorify me
with that glory I had with you
before ever the world was.
I have made your name known
to the men you took from the world to give me.
They were yours and you gave them to me,
and they have kept your word.
Now at last they know
that all you have given me comes indeed from you;
for I have given them
the teaching you gave to me,
and they have truly accepted this, that I came from you,

and have believed that it was you who sent me.
I pray for them;
I am not praying for the world
but for those you have given me,
because they belong to you:
all I have is yours
and all you have is mine,
and in them I am glorified.
I am not in the world any longer,
but they are in the world,
and I am coming to you.'

The Gospel of the Lord.

Prayer over the Offerings
Accept, O Lord, the prayers of your faithful
with the sacrificial offerings,
that through these acts of devotedness
we may pass over to the glory of heaven.
Through Christ our Lord.
Amen.

An appropriate Preface of Easter, or of the Ascension, pp.28-31.

Communion Antiphon   Jn 17:22
Father, I pray that they may be one
as we also are one, alleluia.

Prayer after Communion
Hear us, O God our Saviour,
and grant us confidence,
that through these sacred mysteries
there will be accomplished in the body of the whole Church
what has already come to pass in Christ her Head.
Who lives and reigns for ever and ever.
Amen.

A formula of Solemn Blessing, p.97, may be used.

PENTECOST SUNDAY A, B, C

Solemnity

Vigil Mass
(Extended Form)

This Vigil Mass may be celebrated on the Saturday evening, either before or after First Vespers (Evening Prayer I) of Pentecost Sunday.

In churches where the Vigil Mass is celebrated in an extended form, this may be done as follows.

a) If First Vespers (Evening Prayer I) celebrated in choir or in common immediately precede Mass, the celebration may begin either from the introductory verse and the hymn (*Veni, creátor Spíritus*) or else from the singing of the Entrance Antiphon with the procession and greeting of the Priest; in either case the Penitential Act is omitted (cf. *General Instruction of the Liturgy of the Hours*, nos. 94 and 96).

Then the Psalmody prescribed for Vespers follows, up to but not including the Short Reading.

After the Psalmody, omitting the Penitential Act, and if appropriate, the Kyrie, (Lord, have mercy), the Priest says the prayer Grant, we pray, almighty God, that the splendour, as at the Vigil Mass.

b) If Mass is begun in the usual way, after the Kyrie (Lord, have mercy), the Priest says the prayer Grant, we pray, almighty God, that the splendour, as at the Vigil Mass.

Then the Priest may address the people in these or similar words:

Dear brethren (brothers and sisters),
we have now begun our Pentecost Vigil,
after the example of the Apostles and disciples,
who with Mary, the Mother of Jesus, persevered in prayer,
awaiting the Spirit promised by the Lord;
like them, let us, too, listen with quiet hearts to the Word of God.
Let us meditate on how many great deeds
God in times past did for his people
and let us pray that the Holy Spirit,
whom the Father sent as the first fruits for those who believe,
may bring to perfection his work in the world.

Then follow the readings proposed as options in the Lectionary. A reader goes to the ambo and proclaims the reading. Afterwards a psalmist or a cantor sings or says the Psalm with the people making the response. Then all rise, the Priest says, Let us pray and, after all have prayed for a while in silence, he says the prayer corresponding to the reading. In place of the Responsorial Psalm a period of sacred silence may be observed, in which case the pause after Let us pray is omitted.

Any of these readings from the Old Testament may be chosen.

FIRST READING
1

A reading from the book of Genesis 11:1-9

Throughout the earth men spoke the same language, with the same vocabulary. Now as they moved eastwards they found a plain in the land of Shinar where they settled. They said to one another, 'Come, let us make bricks and bake them in the fire.' – For stone they used bricks, and for mortar they used bitumen. – 'Come,' they said 'let us build ourselves a town and a tower with its top reaching heaven. Let us make a name for ourselves, so that we may not be scattered about the whole earth.'

Now the Lord came down to see the town and the tower that the sons of man had built. 'So they are all a single people with a single language!' said the Lord. 'This is but the start of their undertakings! There will be nothing too hard for them to do. Come, let us go down and confuse their language on the spot so that they can no longer understand one another.' The Lord scattered them thence over the whole face of the earth, and they stopped building the town. It was named Babel therefore, because there the Lord confused the language of the whole earth. It was from there that the Lord scattered them over the whole face of the earth.

The word of the Lord.

Responsorial Psalm 32:10-15 R͡ v.12b

R͡ **Happy the people the Lord has chosen as his own.**

1   He frustrates the designs of the nations,
    he defeats the plans of the peoples.
    His own designs shall stand for ever,
    the plans of his heart from age to age. R͡

2   They are happy, whose God is the Lord,
    the people he has chosen as his own.

From the heavens the Lord looks forth,
he sees all the children of men. ℟

3 From the place where he dwells he gazes
on all the dwellers on the earth,
he who shapes the hearts of them all
and considers all their deeds. ℟

Prayer
Let us pray.
Grant, we pray, almighty God,
that your Church may always remain that holy people,
formed as one by the unity of Father, Son and Holy Spirit,
which manifests to the world
the Sacrament of your holiness and unity
and leads it to the perfection of your charity.
Through Christ our Lord.
Amen.

2

A reading from the book of Exodus   19:3-8. 16-20

Moses went up to God, and the Lord called to him from the mountain, saying, 'Say this to the House of Jacob, declare this to the sons of Israel, "You yourselves have seen what I did with the Egyptians, how I carried you on eagle's wings and brought you to myself. From this you know that now, if you obey my voice and hold fast to my covenant, you of all the nations shall be my very own, for all the earth is mine. I will count you a kingdom of priests, a consecrated nation." Those are the words you are to speak to the sons of Israel.' So Moses went and summoned the elders of the people, putting before them all that the Lord had bidden him. Then all the people answered as one, 'All that the Lord has said, we will do.'

Now at daybreak on the third day there were peals of thunder on the mountain and lightning flashes, a dense cloud, and a loud trumpet blast, and inside the camp all the people trembled. Then Moses led the people out of the camp to meet God; and they stood at the bottom of the mountain. The mountain of Sinai was entirely wrapped in smoke, because the Lord had descended on it in the form of fire. Like smoke from a furnace the smoke went up, and the whole mountain shook violently. Louder and louder grew the sound of the trumpet. Moses spoke, and God answered him with peals of thunder. The Lord came down on the mountain of Sinai, on the mountain top, and the Lord called Moses to the top of the mountain.

The word of the Lord.

Canticle   Daniel: 3:52. 53. 54. 55. 56. ℟ v.52b

You are blest, Lord God of our fathers.
To you glory and praise for evermore.
Blest your glorious holy name.
To you glory and praise for evermore.

You are blest in the temple of your glory.
To you glory and praise for evermore.
You are blest on the throne of your kingdom.
To you glory and praise for evermore.

You are blest who gaze into the depths.
To you glory and praise for evermore.
You are blest in the firmament of heaven.
To you glory and praise for evermore.

or

Responsorial Psalm   18:8. 9. 10. 11. ℟ v.6:68c

    ℟   **You have the message of eternal life, O Lord.**

1   The law of the Lord is perfect,
     it revives the soul.
     The rule of the Lord is to be trusted,
     it gives wisdom to the simple.   ℟

2   The precepts of the Lord are right,
     they gladden the heart.
     The command of the Lord is clear,
     it gives light to the eyes.   ℟

3   The fear of the Lord is holy,
     abiding for ever.
     The decrees of the Lord are truth
     and all of them just.   ℟

4   They are more to be desired than gold,
     than the purest of gold
     and sweeter are they than honey,
     than honey from the comb.   ℟

Prayer
Let us pray.
O God, who in fire and lightning
gave the ancient Law to Moses on Mount Sinai
and on this day manifested the new covenant
in the fire of the Spirit,
grant, we pray,
that we may always be aflame with that same Spirit
whom you wondrously poured out on your Apostles,
and that the new Israel,
gathered from every people,
may receive with rejoicing
the eternal commandment of your love.
Through Christ our Lord.
Amen.

3

A reading from the prophet Ezekiel 37:1-14

The hand of the Lord was laid on me, and he carried me away by the spirit of the Lord and set me down in the middle of a valley, a valley full of bones. He made me walk up and down among them. There were vast quantities of these bones on the ground the whole length of the valley; and they were quite dried up. He said to me, 'Son of man, can these bones live?' I said, 'You know, Lord.' He said, 'Prophesy over these bones. Say, "Dry bones, hear the word of the Lord. The Lord says this to these bones: I am now going to make the breath enter you, and you will live. I shall put sinews on you, I shall make flesh grow on you, I shall cover you with skin and give you breath, and you will live; and you will learn that I am the Lord." ' I prophesied as I had been ordered. While I was prophesying, there was a noise, a sound of clattering; and the bones joined together. I looked, and saw that they were covered with sinews; flesh was growing on them and skin was covering them, but there was no breath in them. He said to me, 'Prophesy to the breath; prophesy, son of man. Say to the breath, "The Lord says this: Come from the four winds, breath; breathe on these dead; let them live!" ' I prophesied as he had ordered me, and the breath entered them; they came to life again and stood up on their feet, a great, an immense army.

Then he said, 'Son of man, these bones are the whole House of Israel. They keep saying, "Our bones are dried up, our hope has gone; we are as good as dead." So prophesy. Say to them, "The Lord says this: I am now going to open your graves; I mean to raise you from your graves, my people, and lead you back to the soil of Israel. And you will know that I am the Lord, when I open your graves and raise you from your graves, my people. And I shall put my spirit in you, and you will live, and I shall resettle you on your own soil; and you will know that I, the Lord, have said and done this – it is the Lord who speaks."

The word of the Lord.

Responsorial Psalm 106:2-9; ℟ v.1 or Alleluia

℟ **O give thanks to the Lord, for he is good;**
for his love has no end.

or

℟ **Alleluia!**

1 Let them say this, the Lord's redeemed,
whom he redeemed from the hand of the foe
and gathered from far-off lands,
from east and west, north and south. ℟

2 Some wandered in the desert, in the wilderness,
finding no way to a city they could dwell in.
Hungry they were and thirsty;
their soul was fainting within them. ℟

3 Then they cried to the Lord in their need
and he rescued them from their distress
and he led them along the right way,
to reach a city they could dwell in. ℟

4 Let them thank the Lord for his love,
for the wonders he does for men.
For he satisfies the thirsty soul;
he fills the hungry with good things. ℟

Prayer
Let us pray.
Lord, God of power,
who restore what has fallen
and preserve what you have restored,
increase, we pray, the peoples
to be renewed by the sanctification of your name,
that all who are washed clean by holy Baptism
may always be directed by your prompting.
Through Christ our Lord.
Amen.

or

O God, who have brought us to rebirth by the word of life,
pour out upon us your Holy Spirit,
that walking in oneness of faith,
we may attain in our flesh
the incorruptible glory of the resurrection.
Through Christ our Lord.
Amen.

or

May your people exult for ever, O God,
in renewed youthfulness of spirit,
so that, rejoicing now in the restored glory of our adoption,
we may look forward in confident hope
to the rejoicing of the day of resurrection.
Through Christ our Lord.
Amen.

4

A reading from the prophet Joel 3:1-5

Thus says the Lord:

> 'I will pour out my spirit on all mankind.
> Your sons and daughters shall prophesy,
> your old men shall dream dreams,
> and your young men see visions.
> Even on the slaves, men and women,
> will I pour out my spirit in those days.
> I will display portents in heaven and on earth.
> blood and fire and columns of smoke.'

The sun will be turned into darkness,
and the moon into blood,
before the day of the Lord dawns,
that great and terrible day.
All who call on the name of the Lord will be saved,
for on Mount Zion there will be some who have escaped,
as the Lord has said,
and in Jerusalem some survivors whom the Lord will call.

The word of the Lord.

Responsorial Psalm Ps 103:1-2. 24. 27-30. 35. ℟ cf. v.30

℟ **Send forth your Spirit, O Lord,
and renew the face of the earth.**

or
℟ **Alleluia!**

1 Bless the Lord, my soul!
 Lord God, how great you are,
 clothed in majesty and glory,
 wrapped in light as in a robe! ℟

2 How many are your works, O Lord!
 In wisdom you have made them all.
 The earth is full of your riches.
 Bless the Lord, my soul. ℟

3 All of these look to you
 to give them their food in due season.
 You give it, they gather it up:
 you open your hand, they have their fill. ℟

4 You take back your spirit, they die,
 returning to the dust from which they came.
 You send forth your spirit, they are created;
 and you renew the face of the earth. ℟

Prayer
Let us pray.
Fulfil for us your gracious promise,
O Lord, we pray, so that by his coming
the Holy Spirit may make us witnesses before the world
to the Gospel of our Lord Jesus Christ.
Who lives and reigns for ever and ever.
Amen.

Then the Priest intones the hymn Gloria in excelsis Deo (Glory to God in the highest). (A musical setting of the Gloria may be found on pp.8-9.)

When the hymn Gloria in excelsis is concluded, the Priest says the Collect in the usual way: Almighty ever-living God, who willed, (see below).

Then the reader proclaims the reading from the Apostle (Rm 8: 22-27) (see below) and Mass continues in the usual way.

If Vespers (Evening Prayer) are joined to Mass, after Communion with the Communion Antiphon (On the last day), the Magnificat is sung, with its Vespers antiphon (Veni, Sancte Spíritus); then the Prayer after Communion is said and the rest follows as usual.

It is appropriate that the formula of Solemn Blessing be used, p.98.

To dismiss the people the Deacon or, if there is no Deacon, the Priest himself sings (as above, p.423) or says:
Go forth, the Mass is ended, alleluia, alleluia.
or
Go in peace, alleluia, alleluia.

The people respond:
Thanks be to God, alleluia, alleluia.

SECOND READING
A reading from the letter of St Paul to the Romans   8:22-27

From the beginning till now the entire creation, as we know, has been groaning in one great act of giving birth; and not only creation, but all of us who possess the first-fruits of the Spirit, we too groan inwardly as we wait for our bodies to be set free. For we must be content to hope that we shall be saved – our salvation is not in sight, we should not have to be hoping for it if it were – but, as I say, we must hope to be saved since we are not saved yet – it is something we must wait for with patience.

    The Spirit too comes to help us in our weakness. For when we cannot choose words in order to pray properly, the Spirit himself expresses our plea in a way that could never be put into words, and God who knows everything in our hearts knows perfectly well what he means, and that the pleas of the saints expressed by the Spirit are according to the mind of God.

    The word of the Lord.

Gospel Acclamation
    Alleluia, alleluia!
    Come, Holy Spirit, fill the hearts of your faithful
    and kindle in them the fire of your love.
    Alleluia!

GOSPEL
A reading from the holy Gospel according to John   7:37-39

On the last day and greatest day of the festival, Jesus stood there and cried out:

'If any man is thirsty, let him come to me!
Let the man come and drink who believes in me!'

As scripture says: From his breast shall flow fountains of living water.

He was speaking of the Spirit which those who believed in him were to receive; for there was no Spirit as yet because Jesus had not yet been glorified.

The Gospel of the Lord.

At the Vigil Mass

(Simple form)

This Mass is used on the Saturday evening, either before or after First Vespers (Evening Prayer I) of Pentecost Sunday.

Entrance Antiphon   Rm 5:5; cf. 8:11
The love of God has been poured into our hearts
through the Spirit of God dwelling within us, alleluia.

The Gloria in excelsis (Glory to God in the highest) is said.

Collect
Almighty ever-living God,
who willed the Paschal Mystery
to be encompassed as a sign in fifty days,
grant that from out of the scattered nations
the confusion of many tongues
may be gathered by heavenly grace
into one great confession of your name.
Through our Lord Jesus Christ, your Son,
who lives and reigns with you in the unity of the Holy Spirit,
one God, for ever and ever.

or

Grant, we pray, almighty God,
that the splendour of your glory
may shine forth upon us
and that, by the bright rays of the Holy Spirit,
the light of your light may confirm the hearts
of those born again by your grace.
Through our Lord Jesus Christ, your Son,
who lives and reigns with you in the unity of the Holy Spirit,
one God, for ever and ever.

The Creed is said.

Prayer over the Offerings
Pour out upon these gifts the blessing of your Spirit,
we pray, O Lord,
so that through them your Church may be imbued with such love
that the truth of your saving mystery
may shine forth for the whole world.
Through Christ our Lord.

Preface of the Mystery of Pentecost, p.32.

When the Roman Canon is used, the proper form of the Communicantes (In communion with those) is said.

Communion Antiphon   Jn 7:37
On the last day of the festival, Jesus stood and cried out:
If anyone is thirsty, let him come to me and drink, alleluia.

Prayer after Communion
May these gifts we have consumed
benefit us, O Lord,
that we may always be aflame with the same Spirit,
whom you wondrously poured out on your Apostles.
Through Christ our Lord.
Amen.

A formula of Solemn Blessing, p.98, may be used.

To dismiss the people the Deacon or, if there is no Deacon, the Priest himself sings (as above p.423) or says:

Go forth, the Mass is ended, alleluia, alleluia.
or:
Go in peace, alleluia, alleluia.
Thanks be to God, alleluia, alleluia.

At the Mass during the Day

The Day of Pentecost

Today we celebrate the great day of Pentecost when Christ filled the Church with the power of his Spirit and sent it out into the world to bring his peace, joy and forgiveness to all mankind. Come Holy Spirit, fill the hearts of your faithful, and kindle in them the fire of your love.

Entrance Antiphon   Wis 1:7
The Spirit of the Lord has filled the whole world
and that which contains all things
understands what is said, alleluia.

or   Rm 5:5; cf. 8:11
The love of God has been poured into our hearts
through the Spirit of God dwelling within us, alleluia.

The Gloria in excelsis (Glory to God in the highest) is said.

Collect
O God, who by the mystery of today's great feast
sanctify your whole Church in every people and nation,
pour out, we pray, the gifts of the Holy Spirit
across the face of the earth
and, with the divine grace that was at work
when the Gospel was first proclaimed,
fill now once more the hearts of believers.
Through our Lord Jesus Christ, your Son,
who lives and reigns with you in the unity of the Holy Spirit,
one God, for ever and ever.
Amen.

FIRST READING
A reading from the Acts of the Apostles   2:1-11

When Pentecost day came round, the apostles had all met in one room, when suddenly they heard what sounded like a powerful wind from heaven, the noise of which filled the entire house in which they were sitting; and something appeared to them that seemed like tongues of fire; these separated and came to rest on the head of each of them. They were all filled with the Holy Spirit, and began to speak foreign languages as the Spirit gave them the gift of speech. Now there were devout men living in Jerusalem from every nation under heaven, and at this sound they all assembled, each one bewildered to hear these men speaking his own language. They were amazed and astonished. 'Surely' they said 'all these men speaking are Galileans? How does it happen that each of us hears them in his own native language? Parthians, Medes and Elamites; people from Mesopotamia, Judaea and Cappadocia, Pontus and Asia, Phrygia and Pamphylia, Egypt and the parts of Libya round Cyrene; as well as visitors from Rome – Jews and proselytes alike – Cretans and Arabs; we hear them preaching in our own language about the marvels of God.'

The word of the Lord.

Responsorial Psalm   Ps 103:1. 24. 29-31. 34. ℟ cf. v.30

℟ **Send forth your Spirit, O Lord,
and renew the face of the earth.**

or

℟ **Alleluia.**

1. Bless the Lord, my soul!
   Lord God, how great you are,
   How many are your works, O Lord!
   The earth is full of your riches.

2. You take back your spirit, they die,
   returning to the dust from which they came.
   You send forth your spirit, they are created;
   and you renew the face of the earth.

3. May the glory of the Lord last for ever!
   May the Lord rejoice in his works!
   May my thoughts be pleasing to him.
   I find my joy in the Lord.

SECOND READING

A reading from the first letter of St Paul   12:3-7. 12-13
to the Corinthians

No one can say, 'Jesus is Lord' unless he is under the influence of the Holy Spirit.

There is a variety of gifts but always the same Spirit; there are all sorts of service to be done, but always to the same Lord; working in all sorts of different ways in different people, it is the same God who is working in all of them. The particular way in which the Spirit is given to each person is for a good purpose. Just as a human body, though it is made up of many parts, is a single unit because all these parts, though many, make one body, so it is with Christ. In the one Spirit we were all baptised, Jews as well as Greeks, slaves as well as citizens, and one Spirit was given to us all to drink.

The word of the Lord.

SEQUENCE

The sequence may be said or sung.

Holy Spirit, Lord of light,
From the clear celestial height
Thy pure beaming radiance give.

Come, thou Father of the poor,
   Come with treasures which endure;
Come, thou light of all that live!

Thou, of all consolers best,
   Thou, the soul's delightful guest,
Dost refreshing peace bestow;

Thou in toil art comfort sweet;
   Pleasant coolness in the heat;
Solace in the midst of woe.

Light immortal, light divine,
   Visit thou these hearts of thine,
And our inmost being fill:

If thou take thy grace away,
   Nothing pure in man will stay;
All his good is turned to ill.

Heal our wounds, our strength renew;
   On our dryness pour thy dew;
Wash the stains of guilt away:

Bend the stubborn heart and will;
   Melt the frozen, warm the chill;
Guide the steps that go astray.

Thou, on us who evermore
   Thee confess and thee adore,
With thy sevenfold gifts descend:

Give us comfort when we die;
   Give us life with thee on high;
Give us joys that never end.

Gospel Acclamation
Alleluia, alleluia!
Come, Holy Spirit, fill the hearts of your faithful
and kindle in them the fire of your love.
Alleluia!

GOSPEL
A reading from the holy Gospel according to John   20:19-23

In the evening of the first day of the week, the doors were closed in the room where the disciples were, for fear of the Jews. Jesus came and stood among them. He said to them, 'Peace be with you,' and showed them his hands and his side. The disciples were filled with joy when they saw the Lord, and he said to them again, 'Peace be with you.

> 'As the Father sent me,
> so am I sending you.'

After saying this he breathed on them and said:

> 'Receive the Holy Spirit.
> For those whose sins you forgive,
> they are forgiven;
> for those whose sins you retain,
> they are retained.'

The Gospel of the Lord.

The Creed is said.

Prayer over the Offerings
Grant, we pray, O Lord,
that, as promised by your Son,
the Holy Spirit may reveal to us more abundantly
the hidden mystery of this sacrifice
and graciously lead us into all truth.
Through Christ our Lord.
Amen.

Preface of the Mystery of Pentecost, p.32.

When the Roman Canon is used, the proper form of the Communicantes (In communion with those) is said.

Communion Antiphon Acts 2:4, 11
They were all filled with the Holy Spirit
and spoke of the marvels of God, alleluia.

Prayer after Communion
O God, who bestow heavenly gifts upon your Church,
safeguard, we pray, the grace you have given,
that the gift of the Holy Spirit poured out upon her
may retain all its force
and that this spiritual food
may gain her abundance of eternal redemption.
Through Christ our Lord.
Amen.

A formula of Solemn Blessing, p.98, may be used.

Pentecost Sunday, At the Mass during the Day 471

To dismiss the people the Deacon or, if there is no Deacon, the Priest himself sings or says:

Go forth, the Mass is end-ed, al-le-lu-ia, al-le-lu-ia.

or

Go in peace, al-le-lu-ia, al-le-lu-ia.

Thanks be to God, al-le-lu-ia, al-le-lu-ia.

With Easter Time now concluded, the paschal candle is extinguished. It is desirable to keep the paschal candle in the baptistery with due honour so that it is lit at the celebration of Baptism and the candles of those baptized are lit from it.

Where the Monday or Tuesday after Pentecost are days on which the faithful are obliged or accustomed to attend Mass, the Mass of Pentecost Sunday may be repeated.

ORDINARY TIME

Ordinary Time contains thirty-three or thirty-four weeks. It begins on the Monday following the Sunday after 6 January and continues until the beginning of Lent; it begins again on the Monday after Pentecost Sunday and ends on the Saturday before the First Sunday of Advent.

The numbering of Sundays and weeks in Ordinary Time is calculated as follows:

a) The Sunday on which the Feast of the Baptism of the Lord occurs takes the place of the first Sunday in Ordinary Time; the week that follows is counted as the first week in Ordinary Time. The remaining Sundays and weeks are numbered in order until the beginning of Lent.

b) If there are thirty-four weeks in Ordinary Time, after Pentecost the series is resumed with the week that follows immediately the last week celebrated before Lent; it should be noted, however, that the Masses of Pentecost Sunday and of the Solemnity of the Most Holy Trinity take the place of the Sunday Masses. If, however, there are thirty-three weeks in Ordinary Time, the first week that would otherwise follow Pentecost is omitted.

Thus, in the Missal, thirty-four Masses for the Sundays and weekdays in Ordinary Time are found. They are used in this way:

a) On Sundays the Mass corresponding to the number of the Sunday in Ordinary Time is ordinarily used, unless there occurs a Solemnity or a Feast of the Lord which takes the place of the Sunday.

b) On weekdays, however, any of the thirty-four Masses may be used, provided the pastoral needs of the faithful are taken into consideration.

The Gloria in excelsis (Glory to God in the highest) and the Creed are said on Sundays; on weekdays, however, both are omitted.

Unless a Eucharistic Prayer is used that has a proper Preface, on Sundays one of the Prefaces for Sundays in Ordinary Time is said, pp.32-6; but on weekdays, a Common Preface is said, pp.50-53.

THE SOLEMNITIES OF THE LORD
DURING ORDINARY TIME

First Sunday after Pentecost
THE MOST HOLY TRINITY   A
Solemnity

The God of Love and Peace

Our celebration today is a song of praise to God who has taken us up to share in the very life of the Trinity. The grace of the Lord Jesus Christ, the love of God and the fellowship of the Holy Spirit is with us all.

Entrance Antiphon
Blest be God the Father,
and the Only Begotten Son of God,
and also the Holy Spirit,
for he has shown us his merciful love.

The Gloria in excelsis (Glory to God in the highest) is said.

Collect
God our Father, who by sending into the world
the Word of truth and the Spirit of sanctification
made known to the human race your wondrous mystery,
grant us, we pray, that in professing the true faith,
we may acknowledge the Trinity of eternal glory
and adore your Unity, powerful in majesty.
Through our Lord Jesus Christ, your Son,
who lives and reigns with you in the unity of the Holy Spirit,
one God, for ever and ever.
Amen.

FIRST READING
A reading from the book of Exodus   34:4-6. 8-9

With the two tablets of stone in his hands, Moses went up the mountain of Sinai in the early morning as the Lord had commanded him. And the Lord descended in the form of a cloud, and Moses stood with him there.

    He called on the name of the Lord. The Lord passed before him and proclaimed, 'Lord, Lord, a God of tenderness and compassion, slow to anger, rich in kindness and faithfulness.' And Moses bowed down to the ground at once and worshipped. 'If I have indeed won your favour, Lord,' he said 'let my Lord come with us, I beg. True, they are a headstrong people, but forgive us our faults and our sins, and adopt us as your heritage.'

The word of the Lord.

Responsorial Psalm   Dan 3:52-56. ℟ v.52

1. You are blest, Lord God of our fathers.
   To you glory and praise for evermore.
   Blest your glorious holy name.
   To you glory and praise for evermore.

2. You are blest in the temple of your glory.
   To you glory and praise for evermore.
   You are blest on the throne of your kingdom.
   To you glory and praise for evermore.

3. You are blest who gaze into the depths.
   To you glory and praise for evermore.
   You are blest in the firmament of heaven.
   To you glory and praise for evermore.

SECOND READING

A reading from the second letter of St Paul   13:11-13
to the Corinthians

Brothers, we wish you happiness; try to grow perfect; help one another. Be united; live in peace, and the God of love and peace will be with you.

Greet one another with the holy kiss. All the saints send you greetings.

The grace of the Lord Jesus Christ, the love of God and the fellowship of the Holy Spirit be with you all.

The word of the Lord.

Gospel Acclamation   Cf. Apoc 1:8
Alleluia, alleluia!
Glory be to the Father, and to the Son, and to the Holy Spirit,
the God who is, who was, and who is to come.
Alleluia!

GOSPEL

A reading from the holy Gospel according to John 3:16-18

Jesus said to Nicodemus,

> 'God loved the world so much
> that he gave his only Son,
> so that everyone who believes in him may not be lost
> but may have eternal life.
> For God sent his Son into the world
> not to condemn the world,
> but so that through him the world might be saved.
> No one who believes in him will be condemned;
> but whoever refuses to believe is condemned already,
> because he has refused to believe
> in the name of God's only Son.'

The Gospel of the Lord.

The Creed is said.

Prayer over the Offerings
Sanctify by the invocation of your name,
we pray, O Lord our God,
this oblation of our service,
and by it make of us an eternal offering to you.
Through Christ our Lord.
Amen.

Preface of the Mystery of the Most Holy Trinity, p.36.

Communion Antiphon
Gal 4:6
Since you are children of God,
God has sent into your hearts the Spirit of his Son,
the Spirit who cries out: Abba, Father.

Prayer after Communion
May receiving this Sacrament, O Lord our God,
bring us health of body and soul,
as we confess your eternal holy Trinity and undivided Unity.
Through Christ our Lord.
Amen.

The Most Holy Body and Blood of Christ, Year A

Thursday after the Most Holy Trinity
THE MOST HOLY BODY AND BLOOD OF CHRIST A
(CORPUS CHRISTI)
Solemnity

The Food and Drink of Eternal Life

God kept his people alive in the desert by giving them food and drink from heaven. The food and drink he gives us in this sacrament is the body and blood of his Son, given for the life of the world.

Where the Solemnity of the Most Holy Body and Blood of Christ is not a Holyday of Obligation, it is assigned to the Sunday after the Most Holy Trinity as its proper day.

Entrance Antiphon Cf. Ps 80:17
He fed them with the finest wheat
and satisfied them with honey from the rock.

The Gloria in excelsis (Glory to God in the highest) is said.

Collect
O God, who in this wonderful Sacrament
have left us a memorial of your Passion,
grant us, we pray,
so to revere the sacred mysteries of your Body and Blood
that we may always experience in ourselves
the fruits of your redemption.
Who live and reign with God the Father
in the unity of the Holy Spirit,
one God, for ever and ever.
Amen.

FIRST READING
A reading from the book of Deuteronomy 8:2-3. 14-16

Moses said to the people: 'Remember how the Lord your God led you for forty years in the wilderness, to humble you, to test you and know your inmost heart – whether you would keep his commandments or not. He humbled you, he made you feel hunger, he fed you with manna which neither you nor your fathers had known, to make you understand that man does not live on bread alone but that man lives on everything that comes from the mouth of the Lord.

'Do not then forget the Lord your God who brought you out of the land of Egypt, out of the house of slavery: who guided you through this vast and dreadful wilderness, a land of fiery serpents, scorpions, thirst; who in this waterless place brought you water from the hardest rock; who in this wilderness fed you with manna that your fathers had not known.'

The word of the Lord.

Responsional Psalm   Ps 147:12-15. 19-20. ℟ v.12

   ℟   **O praise the Lord, Jerusalem!**

or

   ℟   **Alleluia!**

1. O praise the Lord, Jerusalem!
Zion, praise your God!
He has strengthened the bars of your gates,
he has blessed the children within you. ℟

2. He established peace on your borders,
he feeds you with finest wheat.
He sends out his word to the earth
and swiftly runs his command. ℟

3. He makes his word known to Jacob,
to Israel his laws and decrees.
He has not dealt thus with other nations;
he has not taught them his decrees. ℟

SECOND READING

A reading from the first letter of St Paul   10:16-17
to the Corinthians

The blessing-cup that we bless is a communion with the blood of Christ, and the bread that we break is a communion with the body of Christ. The fact that there is only one loaf means that, though there are many of us, we form a single body because we all have a share in this one loaf.

The word of the Lord.

SEQUENCE
The sequence may be said or sung in full, or using the shorter form indicated by the asterisked verses.

Sing forth, O Zion, sweetly sing
The praises of thy Shepherd-King,
  In hymns and canticles divine;
Dare all thou canst, thou hast no song
Worthy his praises to prolong,
  So far surpassing powers like thine.

Today no theme of common praise
Forms the sweet burden of thy lays –
  The living, life-dispensing food –
That food which at the sacred board
Unto the brethren twelve our Lord
  His parting legacy bestowed.

Then be the anthem clear and strong,
Thy fullest note, thy sweetest song, –
  The very music of the breast:
For now shines forth the day sublime
That brings remembrance of the time
  When Jesus first his table blessed.

Within our new King's banquet-hall
They meet to keep the festival
  That closed the ancient paschal rite:
The old is by the new replaced;
The substance hath the shadow chased;
  And rising day dispels the night.

Christ willed what he himself had done
Should be renewed while time should run,
  In memory of his parting hour:
Thus, tutored in his school divine,
We consecrate the bread and wine;
  And lo – a Host of saving power.

This faith to Christian men is given –
Bread is made flesh by words from heaven:
  Into his blood the wine is turned:
What though it baffles nature's powers
Of sense and sight? This faith of ours
  Proves more than nature e'er discerned.

Concealed beneath the two-fold sign,
Meet symbols of the gifts divine,
  There lie the mysteries adored:
The living body is our food;

Our drink the ever-precious blood;
  In each, one undivided Lord.

Not he that eateth it divides
The sacred food, which whole abides
  Unbroken still, nor knows decay;
Be one, or be a thousand fed,
They eat alike that living bread
  Which, still received, ne'er wastes away.

The good, the guilty share therein,
  With sure increase of grace or sin,
The ghostly life, or ghostly death:
Death to the guilty; to the good
  Immortal life. See how one food
Man's joy or woe accomplisheth.

We break the Sacrament; but bold
And firm thy faith shall keep its hold;
  Deem not the whole doth more enfold
Than in the fractured part resides:
Deem not that Christ doth broken lie;
'Tis but the sign that meets the eye;
The hidden deep reality
  In all its fullness still abides.

*Behold the bread of angels, sent
For pilgrims in their banishment,
The bread for God's true children meant,
  That may not unto dogs be given:
Oft in the olden types foreshowed;
In Isaac on the altar bowed,
And in the ancient paschal food,
  And in the manna sent from heaven.

*Come then, good shepherd, bread divine,
Still show to us thy mercy sign;
  Oh, feed us still, still keep us thine;
So may we see thy glories shine
  In fields of immortality;

*O thou, the wisest, mightiest, best,
  Our present food, our future rest,
Come, make us each thy chosen guest,
Co-heirs of thine, and comrades blest
  With saints whose dwelling is with thee.

Gospel Acclamation   Jn 6:51-52
> Alleluia, alleluia!
> I am the living bread which has come down from heaven,
> says the Lord.
> Anyone who eats this bread will live for ever.
> Alleluia!

GOSPEL

A reading from the holy Gospel according to John   6:51-58

Jesus said to the Jews:

> 'I am the living bread which has come down from heaven.
> Anyone who eats this bread will live for ever;
> and the bread that I shall give
> is my flesh, for the life of the world.'

Then the Jews started arguing with one another: 'How can this man give us his flesh to eat?' they said. Jesus replied:

> 'I tell you most solemnly,
> if you do not eat the flesh of the Son of Man
> and drink his blood,
> you will not have life in you.
> Anyone who does eat my flesh and drink my blood
> has eternal life,
> and I shall raise him up on the last day.
> For my flesh is real food
> and my blood is real drink.
> He who eats my flesh and drinks my blood lives in me
> and I live in him.
> As I, who am sent by the living Father,
> myself draw life from the Father,
> so whoever eats me will draw life from me.
> This is the bread come down from heaven;
> not like the bread our ancestors ate:
> they are dead,
> but anyone who eats this bread will live for ever.'

The Gospel of the Lord.

The Creed is said.

Prayer over the Offerings
Grant your Church, O Lord, we pray,
the gifts of unity and peace,

whose signs are to be seen in mystery
in the offerings we here present.
Through Christ our Lord.
Amen.

Preface II or I of the Most Holy Eucharist, pp.38-9.

Communion Antiphon Jn 6:57
Whoever eats my flesh and drinks my blood
remains in me and I in him, says the Lord.

Prayer after Communion
Grant, O Lord, we pray,
that we may delight for all eternity
in that share in your divine life,
which is foreshadowed in the present age
by our reception of your precious Body and Blood.
Who live and reign for ever and ever.
Amen.

It is desirable that a procession take place after the Mass in which the Host to be carried in the procession is consecrated. However, nothing prohibits a procession from taking place even after a public and lengthy period of adoration following the Mass. If a procession takes place after Mass, when the Communion of the faithful is over, the monstrance in which the consecrated host has been placed is set on the altar. When the Prayer after Communion has been said, the Concluding Rites are omitted and the procession forms.

Friday after the Second Sunday after Pentecost

THE MOST SACRED HEART OF JESUS A
Solemnity

The Heart of Christ

God who is love has set his heart on his people and given us his Son, the gentle and humble at heart.

Entrance Antiphon Ps 32:11. 19
The designs of his Heart are from age to age,
to rescue their souls from death,
and to keep them alive in famine.

The Gloria in excelsis (Glory to God in the highest) is said.

Collect

Grant, we pray, almighty God,
that we, who glory in the Heart of your beloved Son
and recall the wonders of his love for us,
may be made worthy to receive
an overflowing measure of grace
from that fount of heavenly gifts.
Through our Lord Jesus Christ, your Son,
who lives and reigns with you in the unity of the Holy Spirit,
one God, for ever and ever.
Amen.

or

O God, who in the Heart of your Son,
wounded by our sins,
bestow on us in mercy
the boundless treasures of your love,
grant, we pray,
that, in paying him the homage of our devotion,
we may also offer worthy reparation.
Through our Lord Jesus Christ, your Son,
who lives and reigns with you in the unity of the Holy Spirit,
one God, for ever and ever.
Amen.

FIRST READING

A reading from the book of Deuteronomy 7:6-11

Moses said to the people: 'You are a people consecrated to the Lord your God; it is you that the Lord our God has chosen to be his very own people out of all the peoples on the earth.

'If the Lord set his heart on you and chose you, it was not because you outnumbered other peoples: you were the least of all peoples. It was for love of you and to keep the oath he swore to your fathers that the Lord brought you out with his mighty hand and redeemed you from the house of slavery, from the power of Pharaoh king of Egypt. Know then that the Lord your God is God indeed, the faithful God who is true to his covenant and his graciousness for a thousand generations towards those who love him and keep his commandments, but who punishes in their own persons those that hate him; he makes him work out his punishment in person. You are therefore to keep and observe the commandments and statutes and ordinances that I lay down for you today.'

The word of the Lord.

Responsorial Psalm   Ps 102:1-4. 6-8. 10. ℟ v.17

  ℟ **The love of the Lord is everlasting
upon those who hold him in fear.**

1. My soul, give thanks to the Lord,
all my being, bless his holy name.
My soul, give thanks to the Lord
and never forget all his blessings. ℟

2. It is he who forgives all your guilt,
who heals every one of your ills,
who redeems your life from the grave,
who crowns you with love and compassion. ℟

3. The Lord does deeds of justice,
gives judgement for all who are oppressed.
He made known his ways to Moses
and his deeds to Israel's sons. ℟

4. The Lord is compassion and love,
slow to anger and rich in mercy.
He does not treat us according to our sins
nor repay us according to our faults. ℟

SECOND READING

A reading from the first letter of St John   4:7-16

My dear people,
let us love one another
since love comes from God
and everyone who loves is begotten by God and knows God.
Anyone who fails to love can never have known God,
because God is love.
God's love for us was revealed
when God sent into the world his only Son
so that we could have life through him;
This is the love I mean:
not our love for God,
but God's love for us when he sent his Son
to be the sacrifice that takes our sins away.
My dear people,
since God has loved us so much,
we too should love one another.
No one has ever seen God;
but as long as we love one another

God will live in us
and his love will be complete in us.
We can know that we are living in him
and he is living in us
because he lets us share his Spirit.
We ourselves saw and we testify
that the Father sent his Son
as saviour of the world.
If anyone acknowledges that Jesus is the Son of God,
God lives in him, and he in God.
We ourselves have known and put our faith in
God's love towards ourselves.
God is love
and anyone who lives in love lives in God,
and God lives in him.

The word of the Lord.

Gospel Acclamation — Mt 11:29
Alleluia, alleluia!
Shoulder my yoke and learn from me,
for I am gentle and humble in heart.
Alleluia!

GOSPEL
A reading from the holy Gospel according to Matthew 11:25-30

Jesus exclaimed, 'I bless you, Father, Lord of heaven and of earth, for hiding these things from the learned and the clever and revealing them to mere children. Yes, Father, for that is what it pleased you to do. Everything has been entrusted to me by my Father; and no one knows the Son except the Father, just as no one knows the Father except the Son and those to whom the Son chooses to reveal him.

'Come to me, all you who labour and are overburdened, and I will give you rest. Shoulder my yoke and learn from me, for I am gentle and humble in heart, and you will find rest for your souls. Yes, my yoke is easy and my burden light.'

The Gospel of the Lord.

The Creed is said.

Prayer over the Offerings
Look, O Lord, we pray, on the surpassing charity
in the Heart of your beloved Son,

that what we offer may be a gift acceptable to you
and an expiation of our offences.
Through Christ our Lord.
Amen.

Preface of the Sacred Heart, p.37.

Communion Antiphon Cf. Jn 7:37-38
Thus says the Lord:
Let whoever is thirsty come to me and drink.
Streams of living water will flow
from within the one who believes in me.
or Jn 19:34
One of the soldiers opened his side with a lance,
and at once there came forth blood and water.

Prayer after Communion
May this sacrament of charity, O Lord,
make us fervent with the fire of holy love,
so that, drawn always to your Son,
we may learn to see him in our neighbour.
Through Christ our Lord.
Amen.

SUNDAYS IN ORDINARY TIME   A

The readings for the Sundays in Ordinary Time follow a three-year cycle.

The Masses for Year A are given in the following pages. The Masses for Year B begin on p.615, and for Year C on p.817. To know which cycle is being used in a particular calendar year, see the Table of Principal Celebrations, p.xxi.

The cycle of Sundays in Ordinary Time runs from the end of the Christmas Season to the beginning of Lent; it recommences after Trinity Sunday, and runs until the beginning of Advent. The number of Sundays in Ordinary Time before Lent, and between Trinity Sunday and Advent, varies: see the Table of Principal Celebrations.

The first week of Ordinary Time begins on the Monday following the Feast of the Baptism of the Lord. In Year A, the Gospel Readings are taken mainly from the Gospel According to St Matthew.

THE BAPTISM OF THE LORD
Feast
See above, pp.239-42.

SECOND SUNDAY IN ORDINARY TIME   A

The Lamb of God

We celebrate the Servant of God who came to do the Father's will in perfect obedience. Yet he was more than a servant. John the Baptist calls him the Lamb, the chosen one of God.

Entrance Antiphon   Ps 65:4
All the earth shall bow down before you, O God,
and shall sing to you,
shall sing to your name, O Most High!

The Gloria in excelsis (Glory to God in the highest) is said.

Collect
Almighty ever-living God,
who govern all things,
both in heaven and on earth,
mercifully hear the pleading of your people
and bestow your peace on our times.
Through our Lord Jesus Christ, your Son,
who lives and reigns with you in the unity of the Holy Spirit,
one God, for ever and ever.
Amen.

FIRST READING
A reading from the prophet Isaiah   49:3. 5-6

The Lord said to me, 'You are my servant, Israel,
in whom I shall be glorified';
I was honoured in the eyes of the Lord,
my God was my strength.
And now the Lord has spoken,
he who formed me in the womb to be his servant,
to bring Jacob back to him,
to gather Israel to him:

   'It is not enough for you to be my servant,

Second Sunday in Ordinary Time, Year A

to restore the tribes of Jacob and bring back the survivors of Israel;
I will make you the light of the nations
so that my salvation may reach to the ends of the earth.'

The word of the Lord.

Responsorial Psalm   Ps 39:2. 4. 7-10. ℟ vv.8. 9

℟ **Here I am, Lord!**
   I come to do your will.

1. I waited, I waited for the Lord
    and he stooped down to me;
    he heard my cry.
    He put a new song into my mouth,
    praise of our God. ℟

2. You do not ask for sacrifice and offerings,
    but an open ear.
    You do not ask for holocaust and victim.
    Instead, here am I. ℟

3. In the scroll of the book it stands written
    that I should do your will.
    My God, I delight in your law
    in the depth of my heart. ℟

4. Your justice I have proclaimed
    in the great assembly.
    My lips I have not sealed;
    you know it, O Lord. ℟

SECOND READING

A reading from the first letter of St Paul to the Corinthians   1:1-3

I, Paul, appointed by God to be an apostle, together with brother Sosthenes, send greetings to the church of God in Corinth, to the holy people of Jesus Christ, who are called to take their place among all the saints everywhere who pray to our Lord Jesus Christ; for he is their Lord no less than ours. May God our Father and the Lord Jesus Christ send you grace and peace.

The word of the Lord.

Gospel Acclamation
Alleluia, alleluia!
Blessings on the King who comes,
in the name of the Lord!
Peace in heaven
and glory in the highest heavens!
Alleluia!

or   Jn 1:14. 12

Alleluia, alleluia!
The Word was made flesh and lived among us;
to all who did accept him
he gave power to become children of God.
Alleluia!

GOSPEL
A reading from the holy Gospel according to John   1:29-34

Seeing Jesus coming towards him, John said, 'Look, there is the lamb of God that takes away the sin of the world. This is the one I spoke of when I said: A man is coming after me who ranks before me because he existed before me. I did not know him myself, and yet it was to reveal him to Israel that I came baptising with water.' John also declared, 'I saw the Spirit coming down on him from heaven like a dove and resting on him. I did not know him myself, but he who sent me to baptise with water had said to me, "The man on whom you see the Spirit come down and rest is the one who is going to baptise with the Holy Spirit." Yes, I have seen and I am the witness that he is the Chosen One of God.'

The Gospel of the Lord.

The Creed is said.

Prayer over the Offerings
Grant us, O Lord, we pray,
that we may participate worthily in these mysteries,
for whenever the memorial of this sacrifice is celebrated
the work of our redemption is accomplished.
Through Christ our Lord.
Amen.

Communion Antiphon   Cf. Ps 22:5
You have prepared a table before me,
and how precious is the chalice that quenches my thirst.

or 1 Jn 4:16
We have come to know and to believe
in the love that God has for us.

Prayer after Communion
Pour on us, O Lord, the Spirit of your love,
and in your kindness
make those you have nourished
by this one heavenly Bread
one in mind and heart.
Through Christ our Lord.
Amen.

THIRD SUNDAY IN ORDINARY TIME   A

Jesus, the Light of the World

The Good News we have heard is like a beacon whose light draws people irresistably to Christ. We must not be content with lesser lights.

Entrance Antiphon Cf. Ps 95:1. 6
O sing a new song to the Lord;
sing to the Lord, all the earth.
In his presence are majesty and splendour,
strength and honour in his holy place.

The Gloria in excelsis (Glory to God in the highest) is said.

Collect
Almighty ever-living God,
direct our actions according to your good pleasure,
that in the name of your beloved Son
we may abound in good works.
Through our Lord Jesus Christ, your Son,
who lives and reigns with you in the unity of the Holy Spirit,
one God, for ever and ever.
Amen.

FIRST READING
A reading from the prophet Isaiah 8:23 – 9:3

In days past the Lord humbled the land of Zebulun and the land of Naphtali, but in days to come he will confer glory on the Way of the Sea on the far side of Jordan, province of the nations.

The people that walked in darkness
has seen a great light;

on those who live in a land of deep shadow
a light has shone.
You have made their gladness greater,
you have made their joy increase;
they rejoice in your presence
as men rejoice at harvest time,
as men are happy when they are dividing the spoils.

For the yoke that was weighing on him,
the bar across his shoulders,
the rod of his oppressor,
these you break as on the day of Midian.

The word of the Lord.

Responsorial Psalm   Ps 26:1. 4. 13-14. ℟ v.1

   ℟ **The Lord is my light and my help.**

1   The Lord is my light and my help;
     whom shall I fear?
    The Lord is the stronghold of my life;
     before whom shall I shrink? ℟

2   There is one thing I ask of the Lord,
     for this I long,
    to live in the house of the Lord,
     all the days of my life,
    to savour the sweetness of the Lord,
     to behold his temple. ℟

3   I am sure I shall see the Lord's goodness
     in the land of the living.
    Hope in him, hold firm and take heart.
    Hope in the Lord! ℟

SECOND READING

A reading from the first letter of St Paul   1:10-13. 17
to the Corinthians

I appeal to you, brothers, for the sake of our Lord Jesus Christ, to make up the differences between you, and instead of disagreeing among yourselves, to be united again in your belief and practice. From what Chloe's people have been telling me, my dear brothers, it is clear that there are serious differences among you. What I mean are all these slogans that you have, like: 'I am for Paul,' 'I am for Apollos,' 'I am for Cephas,' 'I am for Christ.' Has Christ been

Third Sunday in Ordinary Time, Year A

parcelled out? Was it Paul that was crucified for you? Were you baptised in the name of Paul?

For Christ did not send me to baptise, but to preach the Good News, and not to preach that in the terms of philosophy in which the crucifixion of Christ cannot be expressed.

The word of the Lord.

Gospel Acclamation
Mt 4:23
Alleluia, alleluia!
Jesus proclaimed the Good News of the kingdom,
and cured all kinds of sickness among the people.
Alleluia!

GOSPEL
A reading from the holy Gospel according to Matthew 4:12-23

*Hearing that John had been arrested Jesus went back to Galilee, and leaving Nazareth he went and settled in Capernaum, a lakeside town on the borders of Zebulun and Naphtali. In this way the prophecy of Isaiah was to be fulfilled:

Land of Zebulun! Land of Naphtali!
Way of the sea on the far side of Jordan,
Galilee of the nations!
The people that lived in darkness
has seen a great light;
on those who dwell in the land and shadow of death
a light has dawned.

From that moment Jesus began his preaching with the message, 'Repent, for the kingdom of heaven is close at hand.'*

As he was walking by the Sea of Galilee he saw two brothers, Simon, who was called Peter, and his brother Andrew; they were making a cast in the lake with their net, for they were fishermen. And he said to them, 'Follow me and I will make you fishers of men.' And they left their nets at once and followed him.

Going on from there he saw another pair of brothers, James son of Zebedee and his brother John; they were in their boat with their father Zebedee, mending their nets, and he called them. At once, leaving the boat and their father, they followed him.

He went round the whole of Galilee teaching in their synagogues, proclaiming the Good News of the kingdom and curing all kinds of diseases and sickness among the people.

The Gospel of the Lord.

Shorter Form, verses 12-17. Read between

The Creed is said.

Prayer over the Offerings
Accept our offerings, O Lord, we pray,
and in sanctifying them
grant that they may profit us for salvation.
Through Christ our Lord.
Amen.

Communion Antiphon Cf. Ps 33:6
Look toward the Lord and be radiant;
let your faces not be abashed.
or Jn 8:12
I am the light of the world, says the Lord;
whoever follows me will not walk in darkness,
but will have the light of life.

Prayer after Communion
Grant, we pray, almighty God,
that, receiving the grace
by which you bring us to new life,
we may always glory in your gift.
Through Christ our Lord.
Amen.

FOURTH SUNDAY IN ORDINARY TIME   A

Our Nothingness

Yes, we can celebrate today our nothingness in the eyes of the world, because God has looked on our humility and lowliness and given us the wisdom, virtue and holiness of Christ. As St Paul says, let us boast about the Lord.

Entrance Antiphon Ps 105:47
Save us, O Lord our God!
And gather us from the nations,
to give thanks to your holy name,
and make it our glory to praise you.

The Gloria in excelsis (Glory to God in the highest) is said.

Collect
Grant us, Lord our God,
that we may honour you with all our mind,

and love everyone in truth of heart.
Through our Lord Jesus Christ, your Son,
who lives and reigns with you in the unity of the Holy Spirit,
one God, for ever and ever.
Amen.

FIRST READING
A reading from the prophet Zephaniah 2:3; 3:12-13

Seek the Lord
all you, the humble of the earth,
who obey his commands.
Seek integrity,
seek humility:
you may perhaps find shelter
on the day of the anger of the Lord.
In your midst I will leave
a humble and lowly people,
and those who are left in Israel will seek refuge in the name of the Lord.
They will do no wrong,
will tell no lies;
and the perjured tongue will no longer
be found in their mouths.
But they will be able to graze and rest
with no one to disturb them.

The word of the Lord.

Responsorial Psalm Ps 145:7-10. ℟ Mt 5:3

℟ **How happy are the poor in spirit;
theirs is the kingdom of heaven.**

or

℟ **Alleluia!**

1 It is the Lord who keeps faith for ever,
who is just to those who are oppressed.
It is he who gives bread to the hungry,
the Lord, who sets prisoners free. ℟

2 It is the Lord who gives sight to the blind,
who raises up those who are bowed down,
the Lord, who protects the stranger
and upholds the widow and orphan. ℟

3 It is the Lord who loves the just
   but thwarts the path of the wicked.
   The Lord will reign for ever,
   Zion's God, from age to age. ℟

SECOND READING

A reading from the first letter of St Paul
to the Corinthians   1:26-31

Take yourselves, brothers, at the time when you were called: how many of you were wise in the ordinary sense of the word, how many were influential people, or came from noble families? No, it was to shame the wise that God chose what is foolish by human reckoning, and to shame what is strong that he chose what is weak by human reckoning; those whom the world thinks common and contemptible are the ones that God has chosen – those who are nothing at all to show up those who are everything. The human race has nothing to boast about to God, but you, God has made members of Christ Jesus and by God's doing he has become our wisdom, and our virtue, and our holiness, and our freedom. As scripture says: if anyone wants to boast, let him boast about the Lord.

The word of the Lord.

Gospel Acclamation   Mt 11:25
   Alleluia, alleluia!
   Blessed are you, Father,
   Lord of heaven and earth,
   for revealing the mysteries of the kingdom
   to mere children.
   Alleluia!

or   Mt 5:12

   Alleluia, alleluia!
   Rejoice and be glad:
   your reward will be great in heaven.
   Alleluia!

GOSPEL

A reading from the holy Gospel according to Matthew   5:1-12

Seeing the crowds, Jesus went up the hill. There he sat down and was joined by his disciples. Then he began to speak. This is what he taught them:

Fourth Sunday in Ordinary Time, Year A

'How happy are the poor in spirit;
theirs is the kingdom of heaven.
Happy the gentle:
they shall have the earth for their heritage.
Happy those who mourn:
they shall be comforted.
Happy those who hunger and thirst for what is right:
they shall be satisfied.
Happy the merciful:
they shall have mercy shown them.
Happy the pure in heart:
they shall see God.
Happy the peacemakers:
they shall be called sons of God.
Happy those who are persecuted in the cause of right:
theirs is the kingdom of heaven.

'Happy are you when people abuse you and persecute you and speak all kinds of calumny against you on my account. Rejoice and be glad, for your reward will be great in heaven.'

The Gospel of the Lord.

The Creed is said.

Prayer over the Offerings
O Lord, we bring to your altar
these offerings of our service:
be pleased to receive them, we pray,
and transform them
into the Sacrament of our redemption.
Through Christ our Lord.
Amen.

Communion Antiphon   Cf. Ps 30:17-18
Let your face shine on your servant.
Save me in your merciful love.
O Lord, let me never be put to shame, for I call on you.
or   Mt 5:3-4
Blessed are the poor in spirit,
for theirs is the Kingdom of Heaven.
Blessed are the meek, for they shall possess the land.

Prayer after Communion
Nourished by these redeeming gifts,
we pray, O Lord,
that through this help to eternal salvation
true faith may ever increase.
Through Christ our Lord.
Amen.

FIFTH SUNDAY IN ORDINARY TIME A

Christ's Church: A Light In The Darkness

The Church is a light shining in the darkness of the world. But today's celebration is overshadowed by a great If. How much more brightly would that light shine if we who are Christians were really like Christ?

Entrance Antiphon Ps 94:6-7
O come, let us worship God
and bow low before the God who made us,
for he is the Lord our God.

The Gloria in excelsis (Glory to God in the highest) is said.

Collect
Keep your family safe, O Lord, with unfailing care,
that, relying solely on the hope of heavenly grace,
they may be defended always by your protection.
Through our Lord Jesus Christ, your Son,
who lives and reigns with you in the unity of the Holy Spirit,
one God, for ever and ever.
Amen.

FIRST READING
A reading from the prophet Isaiah 58:7-10

Thus says the Lord:

> Share your bread with the hungry,
> and shelter the homeless poor,
> clothe the man you see to be naked
> and turn not from your own kin.
> Then will your light shine like the dawn
> and your wound be quickly healed over.
>
> Your integrity will go before you
> and the glory of the Lord behind you.
> Cry, and the Lord will answer;

Fifth Sunday in Ordinary Time, Year A

call, and he will say, 'I am here.'
If you do away with the yoke,
the clenched fist, the wicked word,
if you give your bread to the hungry,
and relief to the oppressed,
your light will rise in the darkness,
and your shadows become like noon.

The word of the Lord.

Responsorial Psalm Ps 111:4-9. R℣ v.4

℟ **The good man is a light in the darkness for the upright.**

or

℟ **Alleluia!**

1 He is a light in the darkness for the upright:
   he is generous, merciful and just.
   The good man takes pity and lends,
   he conducts his affairs with honour.   ℟

2 The just man will never waver:
   he will be remembered for ever.
   He has no fear of evil news;
   with a firm heart he trusts in the Lord.   ℟

3 With a steadfast heart he will not fear;
   open-handed, he gives to the poor;
   his justice stands firm for ever.
   His head will be raised in glory.   ℟

SECOND READING

A reading from the first letter of St Paul to the Corinthians 2:1-5

When I came to you, brothers, it was not with any show of oratory or philosophy, but simply to tell you what God had guaranteed. During my stay with you, the only knowledge I claimed to have was about Jesus, and only about him as the crucified Christ. Far from relying on any power of my own, I came among you in great 'fear and trembling' and in my speeches and the sermons that I gave, there were none of the arguments that belong to philosophy; only a demonstration of the power of the Spirit. And I did this so that your faith should not depend on human philosophy but on the power of God.

The word of the Lord.

Gospel Acclamation
Jn 8:12

Alleluia, alleluia!
I am the light of the world, says the Lord,
anyone who follows me
will have the light of life.
Alleluia!

GOSPEL
A reading from the holy Gospel according to Matthew 5:13-16

Jesus said to his disciples: 'You are the salt of the earth. But if salt becomes tasteless, what can make it salty again? It is good for nothing, and can only be thrown out to be trampled underfoot by men.

'You are the light of the world. A city built on a hill-top cannot be hidden. No one lights a lamp to put it under a tub; they put it on the lamp-stand where it shines for everyone in the house. In the same way your light must shine in the sight of men, so that, seeing your good works, they may give the praise to your Father in heaven.'

The Gospel of the Lord.

The Creed is said.

Prayer over the Offerings
O Lord, our God,
who once established these created things
to sustain us in our frailty,
grant, we pray,
that they may become for us now
the Sacrament of eternal life.
Through Christ our Lord.
Amen.

Communion Antiphon
Cf. Ps 106:8-9

Let them thank the Lord for his mercy,
his wonders for the children of men,
for he satisfies the thirsty soul,
and the hungry he fills with good things.

or
Mt 5:5-6

Blessed are those who mourn, for they shall be consoled.
Blessed are those who hunger and thirst for righteousness,
for they shall have their fill.

Prayer after Communion
O God, who have willed that we be partakers
in the one Bread and the one Chalice,
grant us, we pray, so to live
that, made one in Christ,
we may joyfully bear fruit
for the salvation of the world.
Through Christ our Lord.
Amen.

SIXTH SUNDAY IN ORDINARY TIME   A

The Law of Christ

The law of Christ is unlike any human law; it contains the hidden wisdom of God. It is a law given by love, and can only be fulfilled by genuine love and true concern for others.

Entrance Antiphon   Cf. Ps 30:3-4
Be my protector, O God,
a mighty stronghold to save me.
For you are my rock, my stronghold!
Lead me, guide me, for the sake of your name.

The Gloria in excelsis (Glory to God in the highest) is said.

Collect
O God, who teach us that you abide
in hearts that are just and true,
grant that we may be so fashioned by your grace
as to become a dwelling pleasing to you.
Through our Lord Jesus Christ, your Son,
who lives and reigns with you in the unity of the Holy Spirit,
one God, for ever and ever.
Amen.

FIRST READING
A reading from the book of Ecclesiasticus   15:15-20

If you wish, you can keep the commandments,
to behave faithfully is within your power.
He has set fire and water before you;
put out your hand to whichever you prefer.
Man has life and death before him;
whichever a man likes better will be given him.
For vast is the wisdom of the Lord;

he is almighty and all-seeing.
His eyes are on those who fear him,
he notes every action of man.
He never commanded anyone to be godless,
he has given no one permission to sin.

The word of the Lord.

Responsorial Psalm   Ps 118:1-2. 4-5. 17-18. 33-34. ℟ v.1

℟   **They are happy who follow God's law!**

1. They are happy whose life is blameless,
who follow God's law!
They are happy those who do his will,
seeking him with all their hearts.   ℟

2. You have laid down your precepts
to be obeyed with care.
May my footsteps be firm
to obey your statutes.   ℟

3. Bless your servant and I shall live
and obey your word.
Open my eyes that I may consider
the wonders of your law.   ℟

4. Teach me the demands of your statutes
and I will keep them to the end.
Train me to observe your law,
to keep it with my heart.   ℟

SECOND READING

A reading from the first letter of St Paul to the Corinthians   2:6-10

We have a wisdom to offer those who have reached maturity: not a philosophy of our age, it is true, still less of the masters of our age, which are coming to their end. The hidden wisdom of God which we teach in our mysteries is the wisdom that God predestined to be for our glory before the ages began. It is a wisdom that none of the masters of this age have ever known, or they would not have crucified the Lord of Glory; we teach what scripture calls: the things that no eye has seen and no ear has heard, things beyond the mind of man, all that God has prepared for those who love him.

These are the very things that God has revealed to us through the Spirit, for the Spirit reaches the depths of everything, even the depths of God.

The word of the Lord.

Gospel Acclamation 1 Sam 3:9; Jn 6:68
  Alleluia, alleluia!
  Speak, Lord, your servant is listening:
  you have the message of eternal life.
  Alleluia!
or Cf. Mt 11:25
  Alleluia, alleluia!
  Blessed are you, Father,
  Lord of heaven and earth,
  for revealing the mysteries of the kingdom
  to mere children.
  Alleluia!

GOSPEL

A reading from the holy Gospel according to Matthew 5:17-37

Jesus said to his disciples: 'Do not imagine that I have come to abolish the Law or the Prophets. I have come not to abolish them but to complete them. I tell you solemnly, till heaven and earth disappear, not one dot, one little stroke, shall disappear from the Law until its purpose is achieved. Therefore, the man who infringes even one of the least of these commandments and teaches others to do the same will be considered the least in the kingdom of heaven; but the man who keeps them and teaches them will be considered great in the kingdom of heaven.

*'For I tell you, if your virtue goes no deeper than that of the scribes and Pharisees, you will never get into the kingdom of heaven.

'You have learnt how it was said to our ancestors: You must not kill; and if anyone does kill he must answer for it before the court. But I say this to you: anyone who is angry with his brother will answer for it before the court;* if a man calls his brother "Fool" he will answer for it before the Sanhedrin; and if a man calls him "Renegade" he will answer for it in hell fire. So then, if you are bringing your offering to the altar and there remember that your brother has something against you, leave your offering there before the altar, go and be reconciled with your brother first, and then come back and present your offering. Come to terms with your opponent in good time while you are still on the way to the court with him, or he may hand you over to the judge and the judge to the officer, and you will be thrown into prison. I tell you solemnly, you will not get out till you have paid the last penny.

'You have learnt how it was said: You must not commit adultery. But I say this to you: if a man looks at a woman lustfully, he has already committed adultery with her in his heart. If your right eye should cause you to sin, tear it out and throw it away; for it will do you less harm to lose one part of you than to have your whole body thrown into hell. And if your right hand should cause you to sin, cut it off and throw it away; for it will do you less harm to lose one part of you than to have your whole body go to hell.

'It has also been said: Anyone who divorces his wife must give her a writ of dismissal. But I say this to you: everyone who divorces his wife, except for the case of fornication, makes her an adulteress; and anyone who marries a divorced woman commits adultery.

'Again, you have learnt how it was said to our ancestors: You must not break your oath, but must fulfil your oaths to the Lord. But I say this to you: do not swear at all, either by heaven, since that is God's throne; or by the earth, since that is his footstool; or by Jerusalem, since that is the city of the great king. Do not swear by your own head either, since you cannot turn a single hair white or black. *All you need say is "Yes" if you mean yes, "No" if you mean no; anything more than this comes from the evil one.'

The Gospel of the Lord.*

Shorter Form, verses 20-22. 27-28. 33-34. 37. Read between

The Creed is said.

Prayer over the Offerings
May this oblation, O Lord, we pray,
cleanse and renew us
and may it become for those who do your will
the source of eternal reward.
Through Christ our Lord.
Amen.

Communion Antiphon Cf. Ps 77:29-30
They ate and had their fill,
and what they craved the Lord gave them;
they were not disappointed in what they craved.

or Jn 3:16

God so loved the world
that he gave his Only Begotten Son,
so that all who believe in him may not perish,
but may have eternal life.

Prayer after Communion
Having fed upon these heavenly delights,
we pray, O Lord,
that we may always long
for that food by which we truly live.
Through Christ our Lord.
Amen.

SEVENTH SUNDAY IN ORDINARY TIME   A

The Lord Is Compassion and Love

We cannot celebrate the Lord of love without resolving to be more like him; for we are built into him like stones into a living Temple erected to give glory to God. We belong to Christ.

Entrance Antiphon   Ps 12:6
O Lord, I trust in your merciful love.
My heart will rejoice in your salvation.
I will sing to the Lord who has been bountiful with me.

The Gloria in excelsis (Glory to God in the highest) is said.

Collect
Grant, we pray, almighty God,
that, always pondering spiritual things,
we may carry out in both word and deed
that which is pleasing to you.
Through our Lord Jesus Christ, your Son,
who lives and reigns with you in the unity of the Holy Spirit,
one God, for ever and ever.
Amen.

FIRST READING
A reading from the book of Leviticus   19:1-2. 17-18

The Lord spoke to Moses; he said: 'Speak to the whole community of the sons of Israel and say to them: "Be holy, for I, the Lord your God, am holy.

"You must not bear hatred for your brother in your heart. You must openly tell him, your neighbour, of his offence; this way you will not take a sin upon yourself. You must not exact vengeance, nor must you bear a grudge against the children of your people. You must love your neighbour as yourself. I am the Lord."'

The word of the Lord.

Responsorial Psalm   Ps 102:1-4. 8. 10. 12-13. ℟ v.8
    ℟ **The Lord is compassion and love.**

1. My soul, give thanks to the Lord,
   all my being, bless his holy name.
   My soul, give thanks to the Lord
   and never forget all his blessings. ℟

2. It is he who forgives all your guilt,
   who heals every one of your ills,
   who redeems your life from the grave,
   who crowns you with love and compassion. ℟

3. The Lord is compassion and love,
   slow to anger and rich in mercy. ℟
   He does not treat us according to our sins
   nor repay us according to our faults. ℟

4. As far as the east is from the west
   so far does he remove our sins.
   As a father has compassion on his sons,
   the Lord has pity on those who fear him. ℟

SECOND READING

A reading from the first letter of St Paul   3:16-23
to the Corinthians

Didn't you realise that you were God's temple and that the Spirit of God was living among you? If anybody should destroy the temple of God, God will destroy him, because the temple of God is sacred; and you are that temple.

    Make no mistake about it: if any one of you thinks of himself as wise, in the ordinary sense of the word, then he must learn to be a fool before he really can be wise. Why? Because the wisdom of this world is foolishness to God. As scripture says: The Lord knows wise men's thoughts: he knows how useless they are, or again: God is not convinced by the arguments of the wise. So there is nothing to boast about in anything human: Paul, Apollos, Cephas, the world, life and death, the present and the future, are all your servants; but you belong to Christ and Christ belongs to God.

The word of the Lord.

Gospel Acclamation   Jn 14:23
    Alleluia, alleluia!
    If anyone loves me he will keep my word,
    and my Father will love him,

and we shall come to him.
Alleluia!

or 1 Jn 2:5

Alleluia, alleluia!
When anyone obeys what Christ has said,
God's love comes to perfection in him.
Alleluia!

GOSPEL
A reading from the holy Gospel according to Matthew 5:38-48

Jesus said to his disciples: 'You have learnt how it was said: Eye for eye and tooth for tooth. But I say this to you: offer the wicked man no resistance. On the contrary, if anyone hits you on the right cheek, offer him the other as well; if a man takes you to law and would have your tunic, let him have your cloak as well. And if anyone orders you to go one mile, go two miles with him. Give to anyone who asks, and if anyone wants to borrow, do not turn away.

'You have learnt how it was said: You must love your neighbour and hate your enemy. But I say this to you: love your enemies and pray for those who persecute you; in this way you will be sons of your Father in heaven, for he causes his sun to rise on bad men as well as good, and his rain to fall on honest and dishonest men alike. For if you love those who love you, what right have you to claim any credit? Even the tax collectors do as much, do they not? And if you save your greetings for your brothers, are you doing anything exceptional? Even the pagans do as much, do they not? You must therefore be perfect just as your heavenly Father is perfect.'

The Gospel of the Lord.

The Creed is said.

Prayer over the Offerings
As we celebrate your mysteries, O Lord,
with the observance that is your due,
we humbly ask you,
that what we offer to the honour of your majesty
may profit us for salvation.
Through Christ our Lord.
Amen.

Communion Antiphon
Ps 9:2-3
I will recount all your wonders,
I will rejoice in you and be glad,
and sing psalms to your name, O Most High.

or   Jn 11:27
Lord, I have come to believe that you are the Christ,
the Son of the living God, who is coming into this world.

Prayer after Communion
Grant, we pray, almighty God,
that we may experience the effects of the salvation
which is pledged to us by these mysteries.
Through Christ our Lord.
Amen.

EIGHTH SUNDAY IN ORDINARY TIME   A

The Tremendous Love of God

We are cherished by the tremendous love of God, tender and forgiving above every human love. We pray that we may be able to surrender to this love in perfect trust.

Entrance Antiphon   Cf. Ps 17:19-20
The Lord became my protector.
He brought me out to a place of freedom;
he saved me because he delighted in me.

The Gloria in excelsis (Glory to God in the highest) is said.

Collect
Grant us, O Lord, we pray,
that the course of our world
may be directed by your peaceful rule
and that your Church may rejoice,
untroubled in her devotion.
Through our Lord Jesus Christ, your Son,
who lives and reigns with you in the unity of the Holy Spirit,
one God, for ever and ever.
Amen.

FIRST READING
A reading from the prophet Isaiah   49:14-15

Zion was saying, 'The Lord has abandoned me,
the Lord has forgotten me.'
Does a woman forget her baby at the breast,
or fail to cherish the son of her womb?

Eighth Sunday in Ordinary Time, Year A

Yet even if these forget,
I will never forget you.

The word of the Lord.

Responsorial Psalm
Ps 61:2-3. 6-9. ℟ v.6

℟ **In God alone is my soul at rest.**

1. In God alone is my soul at rest;
   my help comes from him.
   He alone is my rock, my stronghold,
   my fortress: I stand firm.   ℟

2. In God alone be at rest, my soul;
   for my hope comes from him.
   He alone is my rock, my stronghold,
   my fortress: I stand firm.   ℟

3. In God is my safety and glory,
   the rock of my strength.
   Take refuge in God all you people.
   Trust him at all times.
   Pour out your hearts before him.   ℟

SECOND READING
A reading from the first letter of St Paul to the Corinthians   4:1-5

People must think of us as Christ's servants, stewards entrusted with the mysteries of God. What is expected of stewards is that each one should be found worthy of his trust. Not that it makes the slightest difference to me whether you, or indeed any human tribunal, find me worthy or not. I will not even pass judgement on myself. True, my conscience does not reproach me at all, but that does not prove that I am acquitted; the Lord alone is my judge. There must be no passing of premature judgement. Leave that until the Lord comes: he will light up all that is hidden in the dark and reveal the secret intentions of men's hearts. Then will be the time for each one to have whatever praise he deserves, from God.

The word of the Lord.

Gospel Acclamation
Jn 17:17

Alleluia, alleluia!
Your word is truth, O Lord,
consecrate us in the truth.
Alleluia!

or   Heb 4:12
Alleluia, alleluia!
The word of God is something alive and active;
it can judge secret emotions and thoughts.
Alleluia!

GOSPEL
A reading from the holy Gospel according to Matthew   6:24-34

Jesus said to his disciples: 'No one can be the slave of two masters: he will either hate the first and love the second, or treat the first with respect and the second with scorn. You cannot be the slave both of God and of money.

'That is why I am telling you not to worry about your life and what you are to eat, nor about your body and how you are to clothe it. Surely life means more than food, and the body more than clothing! Look at the birds in the sky. They do not sow or reap or gather into barns; yet your heavenly Father feeds them. Are you not worth much more than they are? Can any of you, for all his worrying, add one single cubit to his span of life? And why worry about clothing? Think of the flowers growing in the fields; they never have to work or spin; yet I assure you that not even Solomon in all his regalia was robed like one of these. Now if that is how God clothes the grass in the field which is there today and thrown into the furnace tomorrow, will he not much more look after you, you men of little faith? So do not worry; do not say, "What are we to eat? What are we to drink? How are we to be clothed?" It is the pagans who set their hearts on all these things. Your heavenly Father knows you need them all. Set your hearts on his kingdom first, and on his righteousness, and all these other things will be given you as well. So do not worry about tomorrow; tomorrow will take care of itself. Each day has enough trouble of its own.'

The Gospel of the Lord.

The Creed is said.

Prayer over the Offerings
O God, who provide gifts to be offered to your name
and count our oblations as signs
of our desire to serve you with devotion,
we ask of your mercy
that what you grant as the source of merit
may also help us to attain merit's reward.
Through Christ our Lord.
Amen.

Communion Antiphon
Cf. Ps 12:6

I will sing to the Lord who has been bountiful with me,
sing psalms to the name of the Lord Most High.

or
Mt 28:20

Behold, I am with you always,
even to the end of the age, says the Lord.

Prayer after Communion
Nourished by your saving gifts,
we beseech your mercy, Lord,
that by this same Sacrament
with which you feed us in the present age,
you may make us partakers of life eternal.
Through Christ our Lord.
Amen.

NINTH SUNDAY IN ORDINARY TIME   A

Christ, Our Rock of Refuge

It is through Christ alone that we can keep our side of the covenant with him, which is to love God with all our heart and keep his commandments so as to gain his blessing.

Entrance Antiphon
Cf. Ps 24:16. 18

Turn to me and have mercy on me, O Lord,
for I am alone and poor.
See my lowliness and suffering
and take away all my sins, my God.

The Gloria in excelsis (Glory to God in the highest) is said.

Collect
O God, whose providence never fails in its design,
keep from us, we humbly beseech you,
all that might harm us
and grant all that works for our good.
Through our Lord Jesus Christ, your Son,
who lives and reigns with you in the unity of the Holy Spirit,
one God, for ever and ever.
Amen.

Ninth Sunday in Ordinary Time, Year A

FIRST READING
A reading from the book of Deuteronomy   11:18. 26-28. 32

Moses said to the people: 'Let these words of mine remain in your heart and in your soul; fasten them on your hand as a sign and on your forehead as a circlet.

'See, I set before you today a blessing and a curse: a blessing, if you obey the commandments of the Lord our God that I enjoin on you today; a curse, if you disobey the commandments of the Lord your God and leave the way I have marked out for you today, by going after other gods you have not known. You must keep and observe all the laws and customs that I set before you today.'

The word of the Lord.

Responsional Psalm   Ps 30:2-4. 17. 25. R̸ v.3

R̸ **Be a rock of refuge for me, O Lord.**

1. In you, O Lord, I take refuge.
   Let me never be put to shame.
   In your justice, set me free,
   hear me and speedily rescue me. R̸

2. Be a rock of refuge to me,
   a mighty stronghold to save me,
   for you are my rock, my stronghold.
   For your name's sake, lead me and guide me. R̸

3. Let your face shine on your servant.
   Save me in your love.
   Be strong, let your heart take courage,
   all who hope in the Lord. R̸

SECOND READING
A reading from the letter of St Paul to the Romans   3:21-25. 28

God's justice that was made known through the Law and the Prophets has now been revealed outside the Law, since it is the same justice of God that comes through faith to everyone, Jew and pagan alike, who believes in Jesus Christ. Both Jew and pagan sinned and forfeited God's glory, and both are justified through the free gift of his grace by being redeemed in Christ Jesus who was appointed by God to sacrifice his life so as to win reconciliation through faith since, as we see it, a man is justified by faith and not by doing something the Law tells him to do.

The word of the Lord.

Gospel Acclamation Jn 14:23
Alleluia, alleluia!
If anyone loves me he will keep my word,
and my Father will love him,
and we shall come to him.
Alleluia!

or Jn 15:5

Alleluia, alleluia!
I am the vine, you are the branches,
says the Lord.
Whoever remains in me, with me in him,
bears fruit in plenty.
Alleluia!

GOSPEL

A reading from the holy Gospel according to Matthew 7:21-27

Jesus said to his disciples: 'It is not those who say to me, "Lord, Lord", who will enter the kingdom of heaven, but the person who does the will of my Father in heaven. When the day comes many will say to me, "Lord, Lord, did we not prophesy in your name, cast out demons in your name, work many miracles in your name?" Then I shall tell them to their faces: I have never known you; away from me, you evil men!

'Therefore, everyone who listens to these words of mine and acts on them will be like a sensible man who built his house on rock. Rain came down, floods rose, gales blew and hurled themselves against that house, and it did not fall: it was founded on rock. But everyone who listens to these words of mine and does not act on them will be like a stupid man who built his house on sand. Rain came down, floods rose, gales blew and struck that house, and it fell; and what a fall it had!'

The Gospel of the Lord.

The Creed is said.

Prayer over the Offerings
Trusting in your compassion, O Lord,
we come eagerly with our offerings to your sacred altar,
that, through the purifying action of your grace,
we may be cleansed by the very mysteries we serve.
Through Christ our Lord.
Amen.

Communion Antiphon Cf. Ps 16:6
To you I call, for you will surely heed me, O God;
turn your ear to me; hear my words.
or Mk 11:23-24
Amen, I say to you: Whatever you ask for in prayer,
believe you will receive it,
and it will be yours, says the Lord.

Prayer after Communion
Govern by your Spirit, we pray, O Lord,
those you feed with the Body and Blood of your Son,
that, professing you not just in word or in speech,
but also in works and in truth,
we may merit to enter the Kingdom of Heaven.
Through Christ our Lord.
Amen.

TENTH SUNDAY IN ORDINARY TIME   A

Our Sacrifice of Praise and Thanksgiving

Our love of God is like the morning dew, it evaporates so quickly. We tend to reduce religion to a mere formality. Today we renew our love and, approaching God with the sincerity and faith of Abraham, we offer the one sacrifice of praise and thanksgiving which gives glory to God.

Entrance Antiphon Cf. Ps 26:1-2
The Lord is my light and my salvation; whom shall I fear?
The Lord is the stronghold of my life; whom should I dread?
When those who do evil draw near, they stumble and fall.

The Gloria in excelsis (Glory to God in the highest) is said.

Collect
O God, from whom all good things come,
grant that we, who call on you in our need,
may at your prompting discern what is right,
and by your guidance do it.
Through our Lord Jesus Christ, your Son,
who lives and reigns with you in the unity of the Holy Spirit,
one God, for ever and ever.
Amen.

FIRST READING
A reading from the prophet Hosea 6:3-6

Let us set ourselves to know the Lord;
that he will come is as certain as the dawn
his judgement will rise like the light,
he will come to us as showers come,
like spring rains watering the earth.

What am I to do with you, Ephraim?
What am I to do with you, Judah?
This love of yours is like a morning cloud,
like the dew that quickly disappears.
This is why I have torn them to pieces by the prophets,
why I slaughtered them with the words from my mouth,
since what I want is love, not sacrifice;
knowledge of God, not holocausts.

The word of the Lord.

Responsorial Psalm Ps 49:1. 8. 12-15. ℟ v.23

℟ **I will show God's salvation to the upright.**

1. The God of gods, the Lord,
has spoken and summoned the earth,
from the rising of the sun to its setting.
'I find no fault with your sacrifices,
your offerings are always before me. ℟

2. 'Were I hungry, I would not tell you,
for I own the world and all it holds.
Do you think I eat the flesh of bulls,
or drink the blood of goats? ℟

3. 'Pay your sacrifice of thanksgiving to God
and render him your votive offerings.
Call on me in the day of distress.
I will free you and you shall honour me.' ℟

SECOND READING
A reading from the letter of St Paul to the Romans 4:18-25

Though it seemed Abraham's hope could not be fulfilled, he hoped and he believed, and through doing so he did become the father of many nations exactly as he had been promised: Your descendants will be as many as the stars. Even the thought that his body was past fatherhood – he was about a hundred years old – and Sarah too old to become a mother, did not shake his belief. Since God had promised it, Abraham refused either to deny it or even to doubt it, but drew strength from faith and gave glory to God, convinced that God had power to do what he had promised. This is the faith that was 'considered as justifying him'. Scripture however does not refer only to him but to us as well when it says that his faith was thus 'considered'; our faith too will be 'considered' if we believe in him who raised Jesus our Lord from the dead, Jesus who was put to death for our sins and raised to life to justify us.

The word of the Lord.

Gospel Acclamation Cf. Acts 16:14
Alleluia, alleluia!
Open our heart, O Lord,
to accept the words of your Son.
Alleluia!

or Lk 4:18

Alleluia, alleluia!
The Lord has sent me to bring the good news to the poor,
to proclaim liberty to captives.
Alleluia!

GOSPEL
A reading from the holy Gospel according to Matthew 9:9-13

As Jesus was walking on he saw a man named Matthew sitting by the customs house, and he said to him, 'Follow me.' And he got up and followed him.

While he was at dinner in the house it happened that a number of tax collectors and sinners came to sit at the table with Jesus and his disciples. When the Pharisees saw this, they said to his disciples, 'Why does your master eat with tax collectors and sinners?' When he heard this he replied, 'It is not the healthy who need the doctor, but the sick. Go and learn the meaning of the words: What I want is mercy, not sacrifice. And indeed I did not come to call the virtuous, but sinners.'

The Gospel of the Lord.

The Creed is said.

Eleventh Sunday in Ordinary Time, Year A 517

Prayer over the Offerings
Look kindly upon our service, O Lord, we pray,
that what we offer
may be an acceptable oblation to you
and lead us to grow in charity.
Through Christ our Lord.
Amen.

Communion Antiphon
Ps 17:3
The Lord is my rock, my fortress, and my deliverer;
my God is my saving strength.

or   1 Jn 4:16

God is love, and whoever abides in love
abides in God, and God in him.

Prayer after Communion
May your healing work, O Lord,
free us, we pray, from doing evil
and lead us to what is right.
Through Christ our Lord.
Amen.

ELEVENTH SUNDAY IN ORDINARY TIME   A

Our Calling

God has made us his own. He reconciles us in Christ and calls each of us by name to be a people consecrated to him. As his priestly people we offer this sacrifice today, filled with joyful trust in him.

Entrance Antiphon
Cf. Ps 26:7. 9
O Lord, hear my voice, for I have called to you; be my help.
Do not abandon or forsake me, O God, my Saviour!

The Gloria in excelsis (Glory to God in the highest) is said.

Collect
O God, strength of those who hope in you,
graciously hear our pleas,
and, since without you mortal frailty can do nothing,
grant us always the help of your grace,
that in following your commands
we may please you by our resolve and our deeds.
Through our Lord Jesus Christ, your Son,
who lives and reigns with you in the unity of the Holy Spirit,
one God, for ever and ever.
Amen.

FIRST READING

A reading from the book of Exodus   19:2-6

From Rephidim the Israelites set out again; and when they reached the wilderness of Sinai, there in the wilderness they pitched their camp; there facing the mountain Israel pitched camp.

Moses then went up to God, and the Lord called to him from the mountain, saying, 'Say this to the House of Jacob, declare this to the sons of Israel, "You yourselves have seen what I did with the Egyptians, how I carried you on eagle's wings and brought you to myself. From this you know that now, if you obey my voice and hold fast to my covenant, you of all the nations shall be my very own, for all the earth is mine. I will count you a kingdom of priests, a consecrated nation." '

The word of the Lord.

Responsorial Psalm   Ps 99:2-3. 5. R̸ v.3

R̸ **We are his people:
the sheep of his flock.**

1 Cry out with joy to the Lord, all the earth.
Serve the Lord with gladness.
Come before him, singing for joy. R̸

2 Know that he, the Lord, is God.
He made us, we belong to him,
we are his people, the sheep of his flock. R̸

3 Indeed, how good is the Lord,
eternal his merciful love.
He is faithful from age to age. R̸

SECOND READING

A reading from the letter of St Paul to the Romans   5:6-11

We were still helpless when at his appointed moment Christ died for sinful men. It is not easy to die even for a good man – though of course for someone really worthy, a man might be prepared to die – but what proves that God loves us is that Christ died for us while we were still sinners. Having died to make us righteous, is it likely that he would now fail to save us from God's anger? When we were reconciled to God by the death of his Son, we were still enemies; now that we have been reconciled surely we may count on being saved by the life of his Son? Not merely because we have been reconciled but because we are filled with joyful trust in God through our Lord Jesus Christ, through whom we have already gained our reconciliation.

The word of the Lord.

Gospel Acclamation Jn 10:27
Alleluia, alleluia!
The sheep that belong to me listen to my voice,
says the Lord,
I know them and they follow me.
Alleluia!

or Mk 1:15
Alleluia, alleluia!
The kingdom of God is close at hand.
Repent, and believe the Good News.
Alleluia!

GOSPEL
A reading from the holy Gospel according to Matthew   9:36 – 10:8

When Jesus saw the crowds he felt sorry for them because they were harassed and dejected, like sheep without a shepherd. Then he said to his disciples, 'The harvest is rich but the labourers are few, so ask the Lord of the harvest to send labourers to his harvest.'

He summoned his twelve disciples, and gave them authority over unclean spirits with power to cast them out and to cure all kinds of diseases and sickness.

These are the names of the twelve apostles: first, Simon who is called Peter, and his brother Andrew; James the son of Zebedee, and his brother John; Philip and Bartholomew; Thomas, and Matthew the tax collector; James the son of Alphaeus, and Thaddaeus; Simon the Zealot and Judas Iscariot, the one who was to betray him. These twelve Jesus sent out, instructing them as follows:

'Do not turn your steps to pagan territory, and do not enter any Samaritan town; go rather to the lost sheep of the House of Israel. And as you go, proclaim that the kingdom of heaven is close at hand. Cure the sick, raise the dead, cleanse the lepers, cast out devils. You received without charge, give without charge.'

The Gospel of the Lord.

The Creed is said.

Prayer over the Offerings
O God, who in the offerings presented here
provide for the twofold needs of human nature,
nourishing us with food

and renewing us with your Sacrament,
grant, we pray,
that the sustenance they provide
may not fail us in body or in spirit.
Through Christ our Lord.
Amen.

Communion Antiphon   Ps 26:4
There is one thing I ask of the Lord, only this do I seek:
to live in the house of the Lord all the days of my life.
or   Jn 17:11
Holy Father, keep in your name those you have given me,
that they may be one as we are one, says the Lord.

Prayer after Communion
As this reception of your Holy Communion, O Lord,
foreshadows the union of the faithful in you,
so may it bring about unity in your Church.
Through Christ our Lord.
Amen.

TWELFTH SUNDAY IN ORDINARY TIME   A

The Lord at Our Side

Faced with all the evil in the world and the fearful consequences of sin, we might well be afraid did we not have Christ as a mighty hero at our side, the source of divine grace.

Entrance Antiphon   Cf. Ps 27:8-9
The Lord is the strength of his people,
a saving refuge for the one he has anointed.
Save your people, Lord, and bless your heritage,
and govern them for ever.

The Gloria in excelsis (Glory to God in the highest) is said.

Collect
Grant, O Lord,
that we may always revere and love your holy name,
for you never deprive of your guidance
those you set firm on the foundation of your love.
Through our Lord Jesus Christ, your Son,
who lives and reigns with you in the unity of the Holy Spirit,
one God, for ever and ever.
Amen.

Twelfth Sunday in Ordinary Time, Year A

FIRST READING
A reading from the prophet Jeremiah 20:10-13

Jeremiah said:

I hear so many disparaging me,
' "Terror from every side!"
Denounce him! Let us denounce him!'
All those who used to be my friends
watched for my downfall,
'Perhaps he will be seduced into error.
Then we will master him
and take our revenge!'
But the Lord is at my side, a mighty hero;
my opponents will stumble, mastered,
confounded by their failure;
everlasting, unforgettable disgrace will be theirs.
But you, Lord of Hosts, you who probe with justice,
who scrutinise the loins and heart,
let me see the vengeance you will take on them,
for I have committed my cause to you.
Sing to the Lord,
praise the Lord,
for he has delivered the soul of the needy
from the hands of evil men.

The word of the Lord.

Responsorial Psalm
Ps 68:8-10. 14. 17. 33-35. ℟ v.14

℟ **In your great love, answer me, O God.**

1 It is for you that I suffer taunts,
   that shame covers my face,
   that I have become a stranger to my brothers,
   an alien to my own mother's sons.
   I burn with zeal for your house
   and taunts against you fall on me. ℟

2 This is my prayer to you,
   my prayer for your favour.
   In your great love, answer me, O God,
   with your help that never fails:
   Lord, answer, for your love is kind;
   in your compassion, turn towards me. ℟

3   The poor when they see it will be glad
    and God-seeking hearts will revive;
    for the Lord listens to the needy
    and does not spurn his servants in their chains.
    Let the heavens and the earth give him praise,
    the sea and all its living creatures. ℟

SECOND READING

A reading from the letter of St Paul to the Romans   5:12-15

Sin entered the world through one man, and through sin death, and thus death has spread through the whole human race because everyone has sinned. Sin existed in the world long before the Law was given. There was no law and so no one could be accused of the sin of 'law- breaking', yet death reigned over all from Adam to Moses, even though their sin, unlike that of Adam, was not a matter of breaking a law.

Adam prefigured the One to come, but the gift itself considerably outweighed the fall. If it is certain that through one man's fall so many died, it is even more certain that divine grace, coming through the one man, Jesus Christ, came to so many as an abundant free gift.

The word of the Lord.

Gospel Acclamation   Jn 1:14. 12
Alleluia, alleluia!
The Word was made flesh and lived among us;
to all who did accept him
he gave power to become children of God.
Alleluia!

or   Jn 15:26. 27
Alleluia, alleluia!
The Spirit of truth will be my witness;
and you too will be my witnesses.
Alleluia!

GOSPEL

A reading from the holy Gospel according to Matthew   10:26-33

Jesus instructed the Twelve as follows: 'Do not be afraid. For everything that is now covered will be uncovered, and everything now hidden will be made clear. What I say to you in the dark, tell in the daylight; what you hear in whispers, proclaim from the house-tops.

'Do not be afraid of those who kill the body but cannot kill the soul; fear him rather who can destroy both body and soul in hell. Can you not buy two sparrows for a penny? And yet not one falls to the ground without your Father knowing. Why, every hair on your head has been counted. So there is no need to be afraid; you are worth more than hundreds of sparrows.

'So if anyone declares himself for me in the presence of men, I will declare myself for him in the presence of my Father in heaven. But the one who disowns me in the presence of men, I will disown in the presence of my Father in heaven.'

The Gospel of the Lord.

The Creed is said.

Prayer over the Offerings
Receive, O Lord, the sacrifice of conciliation and praise
and grant that, cleansed by its action,
we may make offering of a heart pleasing to you.
Through Christ our Lord.
Amen.

Communion Antiphon   Ps 144:15
The eyes of all look to you, Lord,
and you give them their food in due season.
or   Jn 10:11. 15
I am the Good Shepherd,
and I lay down my life for my sheep, says the Lord.

Prayer after Communion
Renewed and nourished
by the Sacred Body and Precious Blood of your Son,
we ask of your mercy, O Lord,
that what we celebrate with constant devotion
may be our sure pledge of redemption.
Through Christ our Lord.
Amen.

THIRTEENTH SUNDAY IN ORDINARY TIME   A

Welcoming Christ

We welcome Christ today as the woman of Shunem welcomed the prophet Elisha. But the Christ we welcome is the Christ who gave his life for others, and our celebration would be a mockery if we were not prepared to welcome him in one another, even in the least of his brothers and sisters.

Entrance Antiphon   Ps 46:2
All peoples, clap your hands.
Cry to God with shouts of joy!

The Gloria in excelsis (Glory to God in the highest) is said.

Collect
O God, who through the grace of adoption
chose us to be children of light,
grant, we pray,
that we may not be wrapped in the darkness of error
but always be seen to stand in the bright light of truth.
Through our Lord Jesus Christ, your Son,
who lives and reigns with you in the unity of the Holy Spirit,
one God, for ever and ever.
Amen.

FIRST READING
A reading from the second book of the Kings   4:8-11. 14-16

One day as Elisha was on his way to Shunem, a woman of rank who lived there pressed him to stay and eat there. After this he always broke his journey for a meal when he passed that way. She said to her husband, 'Look, I am sure the man who is constantly passing our way must be a holy man of God. Let us build him a small room on the roof, and put him a bed in it, and a table and chair and lamp; whenever he comes to us he can rest there.'

One day when he came, he retired to the upper room and lay down. 'What can be done for her?' he asked. Gehazi, his servant, answered, 'Well, she has no son and her husband is old.' Elisha said, 'Call her.' The servant called her and she stood at the door. 'This time next year,' Elisha said 'you will hold a son in your arms.'

The word of the Lord.

Thirteenth Sunday in Ordinary Time, Year A

Responsorial Psalm   Ps 88:2-3. 16-19. ℟ v.2

℟ **I will sing for ever of your love, O Lord.**

1. I will sing for ever of your love, O Lord;
   through all ages my mouth will proclaim your truth.
   Of this I am sure, that your love lasts for ever,
   that your truth is firmly established as the heavens. ℟

2. Happy the people who acclaim such a king,
   who walk, O Lord, in the light of your face,
   who find their joy every day in your name,
   who make your justice the source of their bliss. ℟

3. For it is you, O Lord, who are the glory of their strength;
   it is by your favour that our might is exalted:
   for our ruler is in the keeping of the Lord;
   our king in the keeping of the Holy One of Israel. ℟

SECOND READING

A reading from the letter of St Paul to the Romans   6:3-4. 8-11

When we were baptised in Christ Jesus we were baptised in his death; in other words, when we were baptised we went into the tomb with him and joined him in death, so that as Christ was raised from the dead by the Father's glory, we too might live a new life.

But we believe that having died with Christ we shall return to life with him: Christ, as we know, having been raised from the dead will never die again. Death has no power over him any more. When he died, he died, once for all, to sin, so his life now is life with God; and in that way, you too must consider yourselves to be dead to sin but alive for God in Christ Jesus.

The word of the Lord.

Gospel Acclamation   Cf. Acts 16:14

Alleluia, alleluia!
Open our heart, O Lord,
to accept the words of your Son.
Alleluia!

or   1 Peter 2:9

Alleluia, alleluia!
You are a chosen race, a royal priesthood, a people set apart
to sing the praises of God
who called you out of darkness into his wonderful light.
Alleluia!

GOSPEL

A reading from the holy Gospel according to Matthew 10:37-42

Jesus instructed the Twelve as follows: 'Anyone who prefers father or mother to me is not worthy of me. Anyone who prefers son or daughter to me is not worthy of me. Anyone who does not take his cross and follow in my footsteps is not worthy of me. Anyone who finds his life will lose it; anyone who loses his life for my sake will find it.

'Anyone who welcomes you welcomes me; and those who welcome me welcome the one who sent me.

'Anyone who welcomes a prophet because he is a prophet will have a prophet's reward; and anyone who welcomes a holy man because he is a holy man will have a holy man's reward. If anyone gives so much as a cup of cold water to one of these little ones because he is a disciple, then I tell you solemnly, he will most certainly not lose his reward.'

The Gospel of the Lord.

The Creed is said.

Prayer over the Offerings
O God, who graciously accomplish
the effects of your mysteries,
grant, we pray,
that the deeds by which we serve you
may be worthy of these sacred gifts.
Through Christ our Lord.
Amen.

Communion Antiphon   Cf. Ps 102:1
Bless the Lord, O my soul,
and all within me, his holy name.
or   Jn 17:20-21
O Father, I pray for them, that they may be one in us,
that the world may believe that you have sent me, says the Lord.

Prayer after Communion
May this divine sacrifice we have offered and received
fill us with life, O Lord, we pray,
so that, bound to you in lasting charity,
we may bear fruit that lasts for ever.
Through Christ our Lord.
Amen.

FOURTEENTH SUNDAY IN ORDINARY TIME   A

The Lord Who Is Kind and Full of Compassion

Our Lord has every claim to the title and majesty of kingship, and yet he comes to us in humility and gentleness. We pray that this spirit of Christ may also be in us.

Entrance Antiphon   Cf. Ps 47:10-11
Your merciful love, O God,
we have received in the midst of your temple.
Your praise, O God, like your name,
reaches the ends of the earth;
your right hand is filled with saving justice.

The Gloria in excelsis (Glory to God in the highest) is said.

Collect
O God, who in the abasement of your Son
have raised up a fallen world,
fill your faithful with holy joy,
for on those you have rescued from slavery to sin
you bestow eternal gladness.
Through our Lord Jesus Christ, your Son,
who lives and reigns with you in the unity of the Holy Spirit,
one God, for ever and ever.
Amen.

FIRST READING
A reading from the prophet Zechariah   9:9-10

The Lord says this:

'Rejoice heart and soul, daughter of Zion!
Shout with gladness, daughter of Jerusalem!
See now, your king comes to you;
he is victorious, he is triumphant,
humble and riding on a donkey,
on a colt, the foal of a donkey.
He will banish chariots from Ephraim
and horses from Jerusalem;
the bow of war will be banished.
He will proclaim peace for the nations.
His empire shall stretch from sea to sea,
from the River to the ends of the earth.'

The word of the Lord.

Responsorial Psalm   Ps 144:1-2. 8-11. 13-14. ℟ v.1

> ℟ **I will bless your name for ever,**
> **O God my King.**

or

> ℟ **Alleluia!**

1. I will give you glory, O God my King,
   I will bless your name for ever.
   I will bless you day after day
   and praise your name for ever. ℟

2. The Lord is kind and full of compassion,
   slow to anger, abounding in love.
   How good is the Lord to all,
   compassionate to all his creatures. ℟

3. All your creatures shall thank you, O Lord,
   and your friends shall repeat their blessing.
   They shall speak of the glory of your reign
   and declare your might, O God. ℟

4. The Lord is faithful in all his words
   and loving in all his deeds.
   The Lord supports all who fall
   and raises all who are bowed down. ℟

SECOND READING

A reading from the letter of St Paul to the Romans   8:9. 11-13

Your interests are not in the unspiritual, but in the spiritual, since the Spirit of God has made his home in you. In fact, unless you possessed the Spirit of Christ you would not belong to him, and if the Spirit of him who raised Jesus from the dead is living in you, then he who raised Jesus from the dead will give life to your own mortal bodies through his Spirit living in you.

So then, my brothers, there is no necessity for us to obey our unspiritual selves or to live unspiritual lives. If you do live in that way, you are doomed to die; but if by the Spirit you put an end to the misdeeds of the body you will live.

The word of the Lord.

Gospel Acclamation
Cf. Mt 11:25
Alleluia, alleluia!
Blessed are you, Father, Lord of heaven and earth,
for revealing the mysteries of the kingdom to mere children.
Alleluia!

GOSPEL
A reading from the holy Gospel according to Matthew   11:25-30

Jesus exclaimed, 'I bless you, Father, Lord of heaven and of earth, for hiding these things from the learned and the clever and revealing them to mere children. Yes, Father, for that is what it pleased you to do. Everything has been entrusted to me by my Father; and no one knows the Son except the Father, just as no one knows the Father except the Son and those to whom the Son chooses to reveal him.

'Come to me, all you who labour and are overburdened, and I will give you rest. Shoulder my yoke and learn from me, for I am gentle and humble in heart, and you will find rest for your souls. Yes, my yoke is easy and my burden light.'

The Gospel of the Lord.

The Creed is said.

Prayer over the Offerings
May this oblation dedicated to your name
purify us, O Lord,
and day by day bring our conduct
closer to the life of heaven.
Through Christ our Lord.
Amen.

Communion Antiphon
Ps 33:9
Taste and see that the Lord is good;
blessed the man who seeks refuge in him.

or   Mt 11:28

Come to me, all who labour and are burdened,
and I will refresh you, says the Lord.

Prayer after Communion
Grant, we pray, O Lord,
that, having been replenished by such great gifts,
we may gain the prize of salvation
and never cease to praise you.
Through Christ our Lord.
Amen.

FIFTEENTH SUNDAY IN ORDINARY TIME   A

Christ, the Sower

We celebrate Christ who came to sow the seed of God's word in the world, and we rejoice with him as we see everywhere around us the first-fruits of the Spirit and wait for the glory to be fulfilled.

Entrance Antiphon   Cf. Ps 16:15

As for me, in justice I shall behold your face;
I shall be filled with the vision of your glory.

The Gloria in excelsis (Glory to God in the highest) is said.

Collect

O God, who show the light of your truth
to those who go astray,
so that they may return to the right path,
give all who for the faith they profess
are accounted Christians
the grace to reject whatever is contrary to the name of Christ
and to strive after all that does it honour.
Through our Lord Jesus Christ, your Son,
who lives and reigns with you in the unity of the Holy Spirit,
one God, for ever and ever.
Amen.

FIRST READING

A reading from the prophet Isaiah   55:10-11

Thus says the Lord: 'As the rain and the snow come down from the heavens and do not return without watering the earth, making it yield and giving growth to provide seed for the sower and bread for the eating, so the word that goes from my mouth does not return to me empty, without carrying out my will and succeeding in what it was sent to do.'

The word of the Lord.

Responsorial Psalm   Ps 64:10-14. ℟ Lk 8:8

   ℟ **Some seed fell into rich soil
      and produced its crop.**

1   You care for the earth, give it water,
    you fill it with riches.
    Your river in heaven brims over
    to provide its grain.   ℟

Fifteenth Sunday in Ordinary Time, Year A

2   And thus you provide for the earth;
    you drench its furrows,
    you level it, soften it with showers,
    you bless its growth.   ℟

3   You crown the year with your goodness.
    Abundance flows in your steps,
    in the pastures of the wilderness it flows.   ℟

4   The hills are girded with joy,
    the meadows covered with flocks,
    the valleys are decked with wheat.
    They shout for joy, yes, they sing.   ℟

SECOND READING

A reading from the letter of St Paul to the Romans   8:18-23

I think that what we suffer in this life can never be compared to the glory, as yet unrevealed, which is waiting for us. The whole creation is eagerly waiting for God to reveal his sons. It was not for any fault on the part of creation that it was made unable to attain its purpose, it was made so by God; but creation still retains the hope of being freed, like us, from its slavery to decadence, to enjoy the same freedom and glory as the children of God. From the beginning till now the entire creation, as we know, has been groaning in one great act of giving birth; and not only creation, but all of us who possess the first-fruits of the Spirit, we too groan inwardly as we wait for our bodies to be set free.

The word of the Lord.

Gospel Acclamation   1 Sam 3:9; Jn 6:68
   Alleluia, alleluia!
   Speak, Lord, your servant is listening;
   you have the message of eternal life.
   Alleluia!

or

   Alleluia, alleluia!
   The seed is the word of God, Christ the sower;
   whoever finds this seed will remain for ever.
   Alleluia!

GOSPEL

A reading from the holy Gospel according to Matthew 13:1-23

*Jesus left the house and sat by the lakeside, but such crowds gathered round him that he got into a boat and sat there. The people all stood on the beach, and he told them many things in parables.

He said, 'Imagine a sower going out to sow. As he sowed, some seeds fell on the edge of the path, and the birds came and ate them up. Others fell on patches of rock where they found little soil and sprang up straight away, because there was no depth of earth; but as soon as the sun came up they were scorched and, not having any roots, they withered away. Others fell among thorns, and the thorns grew up and choked them. Others fell on rich soil and produced their crop, some a hundredfold, some sixty, some thirty. Listen, anyone who has ears!'*

Then the disciples went up to him and asked, 'Why do you talk to them in parables?' 'Because' he replied 'the mysteries of the kingdom of heaven are revealed to you, but they are not revealed to them. For anyone who has will be given more, and he will have more than enough; but from anyone who has not, even what he has will be taken away. The reason I talk to them in parables is that they look without seeing and listen without hearing or understanding. So in their case this prophecy of Isaiah is being fulfilled:

You will listen and listen again, but not understand,
see and see again, but not perceive.
For the heart of this nation has grown coarse,
their ears are dull of hearing, and they have shut their eyes,
for fear they should see with their eyes,
hear with their ears,
understand with their heart,
and be converted
and be healed by me.

'But happy are your eyes because they see, your ears because they hear! I tell you solemnly, many prophets and holy men longed to see what you see, and never saw it; to hear what you hear, and never heard it.

'You, therefore, are to hear the parable of the sower. When anyone hears the word of the kingdom without understanding, the evil one comes and carries off what was sown in his heart: this is the man who received the seed on the edge of the path. The one who received it on patches of rock is the man who hears the word and welcomes it at once with joy. But he has no root in him, he does not last; let some trial come, or some persecution on account of the word, and he falls away at once. The one who received the seed in thorns is the man who hears the word but the worries of this world and the lure of riches choke the word and so he produces nothing. And the one who received the seed in rich soil is the man who hears the word and understands it; he is the one who yields a harvest and produces now a hundredfold, now sixty, now thirty.'

The Gospel of the Lord.

Shorter Form, verses 1-9. Read between

The Creed is said.

Prayer over the Offerings
Look upon the offerings of the Church, O Lord,
as she makes her prayer to you,
and grant that, when consumed by those who believe,
they may bring ever greater holiness.
Through Christ our Lord.
Amen.

Communion Antiphon
Cf. Ps 83:4-5

The sparrow finds a home,
and the swallow a nest for her young:
by your altars, O Lord of hosts, my King and my God.
Blessed are they who dwell in your house,
for ever singing your praise.

or
Jn 6:57

Whoever eats my flesh and drinks my blood
remains in me and I in him, says the Lord.

Prayer after Communion
Having consumed these gifts, we pray, O Lord,
that, by our participation in this mystery,
its saving effects upon us may grow.
Through Christ our Lord.
Amen.

SIXTEENTH SUNDAY IN ORDINARY TIME   A

God our helper

There is no other God than the one who cares for us in love and forgiveness. May we always be attentive to his voice.

Entrance Antiphon   Ps 53:6. 8
See, I have God for my help.
The Lord sustains my soul.
I will sacrifice to you with willing heart,
and praise your name, O Lord, for it is good.

The Gloria in excelsis (Glory to God in the highest) is said.

Collect
Show favour, O Lord, to your servants
and mercifully increase the gifts of your grace,
that, made fervent in hope, faith and charity,
they may be ever watchful in keeping your commands.
Through our Lord Jesus Christ, your Son,
who lives and reigns with you in the unity of the Holy Spirit,
one God, for ever and ever.
Amen.

FIRST READING
A reading from the book of Wisdom   12:13. 16-19

There is no god, other than you, who cares for everything,
to whom you might have to prove that you never judged
    unjustly.
Your justice has its source in strength,
your sovereignty over all makes you lenient to all.
You show your strength when your sovereign power is
    questioned
and you expose the insolence of those who know it;
but, disposing of such strength, you are mild in judgement,
you govern us with great lenience,
for you have only to will, and your power is there.
By acting thus you have taught a lesson to your people
how the virtuous man must be kindly to his fellow men,
and you have given your sons the good hope
that after sin you will grant repentance.

   The word of the Lord.

Sixteenth Sunday in Ordinary Time, Year A

Responsorial Psalm   Ps 85:5-6. 9-10. 15-16. ℟ v.5
  ℟   **O Lord, you are good and forgiving.**

1.   O Lord, you are good and forgiving,
   full of love to all who call.
   Give heed, O Lord, to my prayer
   and attend to the sound of my voice. ℟

2.   All the nations shall come to adore you
   and glorify your name, O Lord:
   for you are great and do marvellous deeds,
   you who alone are God. ℟

3.   But you, God of mercy and compassion,
   slow to anger, O Lord,
   abounding in love and truth,
   turn and take pity on me. ℟

SECOND READING
A reading from the letter of St Paul to the Romans   8:26-27

The Spirit comes to help us in our weakness. For when we cannot choose words in order to pray properly, the Spirit himself expresses our plea in a way that could never be put into words, and God who knows everything in our hearts knows perfectly well what he means, and that the pleas of the saints expressed by the Spirit are according to the mind of God.

    The word of the Lord.

Gospel Acclamation   Cf. Eph 1:17. 18
    Alleluia, alleluia!
    May the Father of our Lord Jesus Christ
    enlighten the eyes of our mind,
    so that we can see what hope his call holds for us.
    Alleluia!

or   Cf. Mt 11:25
    Alleluia, alleluia!
    Blessed are you, Father,
    Lord of heaven and earth,
    for revealing the mysteries of the kingdom
    to mere children.
    Alleluia!

GOSPEL

A reading from the holy Gospel according to Matthew 13:24-43

Jesus put a parable before the crowds, 'The kingdom of heaven may be compared to a man who sowed good seed in his field. While everybody was asleep his enemy came, sowed darnel all among the wheat, and made off. When the new wheat sprouted and ripened, the darnel appeared as well. The owner's servants went to him and said, "Sir, was it not good seed that you sowed in your field? If so, where does the darnel come from?" "Some enemy has done this" he answered. And the servants said, "Do you want us to go and weed it out?" But he said, "No, because when you weed out the darnel you might pull up the wheat with it. Let them both grow till the harvest; and at harvest time I shall say to the reapers: First collect the darnel and tie it in bundles to be burnt, then gather the wheat into my barn."

He put another parable before them, 'The kingdom of heaven is like a mustard seed which a man took and sowed in his field. It is the smallest of all the seeds, but when it has grown it is the biggest shrub of all and becomes a tree so that the birds of the air come and shelter in its branches.'

He told them another parable, 'The kingdom of heaven is like the yeast a woman took and mixed in with three measures of flour till it was leavened all through.'

In all this Jesus spoke to the crowds in parables; indeed, he would never speak to them except in parables. This was to fulfill the prophecy:

I will speak to you in parables
and expound things hidden since the foundation of the world.

Then, leaving the crowds, he went to the house; and his disciples came to him and said, 'Explain the parable about the darnel in the field to us.' He said in reply, 'The sower of the good seed is the Son of Man. The field is the world; the good seed is the subjects of the kingdom; the darnel, the subjects of the evil one; the enemy who sowed them, the devil; the harvest is the end of the world; the reapers are the angels. Well then, just as the darnel is gathered up and burnt in the fire, so it will be at the end of time. The Son of Man will send his angels and they will gather out of his kingdom all things that provoke offences and all who do evil, and throw them into the blazing furnace, where there will be weeping and grinding of teeth. Then the virtuous will shine like the sun in the kingdom of their Father. Listen, anyone who has ears!'

The Gospel of the Lord.

Shorter Form, verses 24-30. Read between

The Creed is said.

Prayer over the Offerings
O God, who in the one perfect sacrifice
brought to completion varied offerings of the law,
accept, we pray, this sacrifice from your faithful servants
and make it holy, as you blessed the gifts of Abel,
so that what each has offered to the honour of your majesty
may benefit the salvation of all.
Through Christ our Lord.
Amen.

Communion Antiphon
Ps 110:4-5

The Lord, the gracious, the merciful,
has made a memorial of his wonders;
he gives food to those who fear him.

or
Rv 3:20

Behold, I stand at the door and knock, says the Lord.
If anyone hears my voice and opens the door to me,
I will enter his house and dine with him, and he with me.

Prayer after Communion
Graciously be present to your people, we pray, O Lord,
and lead those you have imbued with heavenly mysteries
to pass from former ways to newness of life.
Through Christ our Lord.
Amen.

SEVENTEENTH SUNDAY IN ORDINARY TIME   A

The Treasure We Have Found

Solomon prayed for the wisdom to discern the true value of things. We scarcely need the wisdom of Solomon to realise that in finding the love of God and the kingdom of God we have found a treasure beyond price. It is in the joy of this realisation that we hold our celebration today.

Entrance Antiphon
Cf. Ps 67:6-7. 36

God is in his holy place,
God who unites those who dwell in his house;
he himself gives might and strength to his people.

Collect

O God, protector of those who hope in you,
without whom nothing has firm foundation, nothing is holy,
bestow in abundance your mercy upon us
and grant that, with you as our ruler and guide,
we may use the good things that pass
in such a way as to hold fast even now
to those that ever endure.
Through our Lord Jesus Christ, your Son,
who lives and reigns with you in the unity of the Holy Spirit,
one God, for ever and ever.
Amen.

FIRST READING

A reading from the first book of the Kings   3:5. 7-12

The Lord appeared to Solomon in a dream and said, 'Ask what you would like me to give you.' Solomon replied, 'Lord, my God, you have made your servant king in succession to David my father. But I am a very young man, unskilled in leadership. Your servant finds himself in the midst of this people of yours that you have chosen, a people so many its numbers cannot be counted or reckoned. Give your servant a heart to understand how to discern between good and evil, for who could govern this people of yours that is so great?

It pleased the Lord that Solomon should have asked for this. 'Since you have asked for this' the Lord said 'and not asked for long life for yourself or riches or the lives of your enemies, but have asked for a discerning judgement for yourself, here and now I do what you ask. I give you a heart wise and shrewd as none before you has had and none will have after you.'

The word of the Lord.

Responsorial Psalm   Ps 118:57. 72. 76-77. 127-130. ℟ v.97

℟   **Lord how I love your law!**

1   My part, I have resolved, O Lord,
    is to obey your word.
    The law from your mouth means more to me
    than silver and gold.   ℟

2   Let your love be ready to console me
    by your promise to your servant.
    Let your love come to me and I shall live
    for your law is my delight.   ℟

3   That is why I love your commands
    more than finest gold.
    That is why I rule my life by your precepts:
    I hate false ways. ℟

4   Your will is wonderful indeed;
    therefore I obey it.
    The unfolding of your word gives light
    and teaches the simple. ℟

SECOND READING
A reading from the letter of St Paul to the Romans   8:28-30

We know that by turning everything to their good God cooperates with all those who love him, with all those that he has called according to his purpose. They are the ones he chose specially long ago and intended to become true images of his Son, so that his Son might be the eldest of many brothers. He called those he intended for this; those he called he justified, and with those he justified he shared his glory.

The word of the Lord

Gospel Acclamation　　　　　　　　　　　　　　　　　Jn 15:15
  Alleluia, alleluia!
  I call you friends, says the Lord,
  because I have made known to you
  everything I have learnt from my Father.
  Alleluia!

or　　　　　　　　　　　　　　　　　　　　　　　　　Cf. Mt 11:25
  Alleluia, alleluia!
  Blessed are you, Father,
  Lord of heaven and earth,
  for revealing the mysteries of the kingdom
  to mere children.
  Alleluia!

GOSPEL
A reading from the holy Gospel according to Matthew   13:44-52

*Jesus said to the crowds, 'The kingdom of heaven is like treasure hidden in a field which someone has found; he hides it again, goes off happy, sells everything he owns and buys the field.

'Again, the kingdom of heaven is like a merchant looking for fine pearls; when he finds one of great value he goes and sells everything he owns and buys it.*

'Again, the kingdom of heaven is like a dragnet cast into the sea that brings in a haul of all kinds. When it is full, the fishermen haul it ashore; then, sitting down, they collect the good ones in a basket and throw away those that are no use. This is how it will be at the end of time: the angels will appear and separate the wicked from the just to throw them into the blazing furnace where there will be weeping and grinding of teeth.

'Have you understood all this?' They said 'Yes.' And he said to them, 'Well then, every scribe who becomes a disciple of the kingdom of heaven is like a householder who brings out from his storeroom things both new and old.'

The Gospel of the Lord.

Shorter Form, verses 44-46. Read between

The Creed is said.

Prayer over the Offerings
Accept, O Lord, we pray, the offerings
which we bring from the abundance of your gifts,
that through the powerful working of your grace
these most sacred mysteries may sanctify our present way of life
and lead us to eternal gladness.
Through Christ our Lord.
Amen.

Communion Antiphon   Ps 102:2
Bless the Lord, O my soul,
and never forget all his benefits.

or   Mt 5:7-8

Blessed are the merciful, for they shall receive mercy.
Blessed are the clean of heart, for they shall see God.

Prayer after Communion
We have consumed, O Lord, this divine Sacrament,
the perpetual memorial of the Passion of your Son;
grant, we pray, that this gift,
which he himself gave us with love beyond all telling,
may profit us for salvation.
Through Christ our Lord.
Amen.

Eighteenth Sunday in Ordinary Time, Year A

EIGHTEENTH SUNDAY IN ORDINARY TIME   A

The Lord Who Feeds Us

Today we celebrate the great love of God that not only gives us life, but also sustains that life with the food of the eucharist, the love of God made visible in Christ our Lord.

Entrance Antiphon   Ps 69:2. 6
O God, come to my assistance;
O Lord, make haste to help me!
You are my rescuer, my help;
O Lord, do not delay.

The Gloria in excelsis (Glory to God in the highest) is said.

Collect
Draw near to your servants, O Lord,
and answer their prayers with unceasing kindness,
that, for those who glory in you as their Creator and guide,
you may restore what you have created
and keep safe what you have restored.
Through our Lord Jesus Christ, your Son,
who lives and reigns with you in the unity of the Holy Spirit,
one God, for ever and ever.
Amen.

FIRST READING
A reading from the prophet Isaiah   55:1-3

Thus says the Lord:

> Oh, come to the water all you who are thirsty;
> though you have no money, come!
> Buy corn without money, and eat,
> and, at no cost, wine and milk.
> Why spend money on what is not bread,
> your wages on what fails to satisfy?
> Listen, listen to me and you will have good things to eat
> and rich food to enjoy.
> Pay attention, come to me;
> listen, and your soul will live.
> With you I will make an everlasting covenant
> out of the favours promised to David.

The word of the Lord.

Eighteenth Sunday in Ordinary Time, Year A

Responsorial Psalm   Ps 144:8-9. 15-18. ℟ v.16

  ℟ **You open wide your hand, O Lord,
you grant our desires.**

1. The Lord is kind and full of compassion,
slow to anger, abounding in love.
How good is the Lord to all,
compassionate to all his creatures. ℟

2. The eyes of all creatures look to you
and you give them their food in due time.
You open wide your hand,
grant the desires of all who live. ℟

3. The Lord is just in all his ways
and loving in all his deeds.
He is close to all who call him,
call on him from their hearts. ℟

SECOND READING

A reading from the letter of St Paul to the Romans   8:35. 37-39

Nothing can come between us and the love of Christ, even if we are troubled or worried, or being persecuted, or lacking food or clothes, or being threatened or even attacked. These are the trials through which we triumph, by the power of him who loved us.

For I am certain of this: neither death nor life, no angel, no prince, nothing that exists, nothing still to come, not any power, or height or depth, nor any created thing, can ever come between us and the love of God made visible in Christ Jesus our Lord.

The word of the Lord.

Gospel Acclamation   Lk 19:38. 2:14

  Alleluia, alleluia!
Blessings on the King who comes,
in the name of the Lord!
Peace in heaven
and glory in the highest heavens!
Alleluia!

or   Mt 4:4

  Alleluia, alleluia!
Man does not live on bread alone,
but on every word that comes from the mouth of God.
Alleluia!

Eighteenth Sunday in Ordinary Time, Year A

GOSPEL
A reading from the holy Gospel according to Matthew 14:13-21

When Jesus received the news of John the Baptist's death he withdrew by boat to a lonely place where they could be by themselves. But the people heard of this and, leaving the towns, went after him on foot. So as he stepped ashore he saw a large crowd; and he took pity on them and healed their sick.

When evening came, the disciples went to him and said, 'This is a lonely place, and the time has slipped by; so send the people away, and they can go to the villages to buy themselves some food.' Jesus replied, 'There is no need for them to go: give them something to eat yourselves.' But they answered, 'All we have with us is five loaves and two fish.' 'Bring them here to me,' he said. He gave orders that the people were to sit down on the grass; then he took the five loaves and the two fish, raised his eyes to heaven and said the blessing. And breaking the loaves he handed them to his disciples who gave them to the crowds. They all ate as much as they wanted, and they collected the scraps remaining, twelve baskets full. Those who ate numbered about five thousand men, to say nothing of women and children.

The Gospel of the Lord.

The Creed is said.

Prayer over the Offerings
Graciously sanctify these gifts, O Lord, we pray,
and, accepting the oblation of this spiritual sacrifice,
make of us an eternal offering to you.
Through Christ our Lord.
Amen.

Communion Antiphon
Wis 16:20
You have given us, O Lord, bread from heaven,
endowed with all delights and sweetness in every taste.

or
Jn 6:35

I am the bread of life, says the Lord;
whoever comes to me will not hunger
and whoever believes in me will not thirst.

Prayer after Communion
Accompany with constant protection, O Lord,
those you renew with these heavenly gifts
and, in your never-failing care for them,

make them worthy of eternal redemption.
Through Christ our Lord.
Amen.

NINETEENTH SUNDAY IN ORDINARY TIME   A

His Voice That Speaks of Peace

In times of great anguish, such as St Paul himself experienced, Christ is always with us, calming the storm and bringing peace.

Entrance Antiphon Cf. Ps 73:20. 19. 22-23
Look to your covenant, O Lord,
and forget not the life of your poor ones for ever.
Arise, O God, and defend your cause,
and forget not the cries of those who seek you.

Collect
Almighty ever-living God,
whom, taught by the Holy Spirit,
we dare to call our Father,
bring, we pray, to perfection in our hearts
the spirit of adoption as your sons and daughters,
that we may merit to enter into the inheritance
which you have promised.
Through our Lord Jesus Christ, your Son,
who lives and reigns with you in the unity of the Holy Spirit,
one God, for ever and ever.
Amen.

FIRST READING
A reading from the first book of the Kings   19:9. 11-13

When Elijah reached Horeb, the mountain of God, he went into the cave and spent the night in it. Then he was told, 'Go out and stand on the mountain before the Lord.' Then the Lord himself went by. There came a mighty wind, so strong it tore the mountains and shattered the rocks before the Lord. But the Lord was not in the wind. After the wind came an earthquake. But the Lord was not in the earthquake. After the earthquake came a fire. But the Lord was not in the fire. And after the fire there came the sound of a gentle breeze. And when Elijah heard this, he covered his face with his cloak and went out and stood at the entrance of the cave.

The word of the Lord.

Nineteenth Sunday in Ordinary Time, Year A

Responsorial Psalm   Ps 84:9-14. ℟ v.8

℟   **Let us see, O Lord, your mercy
and give us your saving help.**

1. I will hear what the Lord God has to say,
a voice that speaks of peace.
His help is near for those who fear him
and his glory will dwell in our land. ℟

2. Mercy and faithfulness have met;
justice and peace have embraced.
Faithfulness shall spring from the earth
and justice look down from heaven. ℟

3. The Lord will make us prosper
and our earth shall yield its fruit.
Justice shall march before him
and peace shall follow his steps. ℟

SECOND READING

A reading from the letter of St Paul to the Romans   9:1-5

What I want to say is no pretence; I say it in union with Christ – it is the truth – my conscience in union with the Holy Spirit assures me of it too. What I want to say is this: my sorrow is so great, my mental anguish so endless, I would willingly be condemned and be cut off from Christ if it could help my brothers of Israel, my own flesh and blood. They were adopted as sons, they were given the glory and the covenants; the Law and the ritual were drawn up for them, and the promises were made to them. They are descended from the patriarchs and from their flesh and blood came Christ who is above all, God for ever blessed! Amen.

The word of the Lord.

Gospel Acclamation   Lk 19:38

Alleluia, alleluia!
Blessings on the King who comes, in the name of the Lord!
Peace in heaven and glory in the highest heavens!
Alleluia!

or   Ps 129:5

Alleluia, alleluia!
My soul is waiting for the Lord,
I count on his word.
Alleluia!

GOSPEL
A reading from the holy Gospel according to Matthew 14:22-33

Jesus made the disciples get into the boat and go on ahead to the other side while he would send the crowds away. After sending the crowds away he went up into the hills by himself to pray. When evening came, he was there alone, while the boat, by now far out on the lake, was battling with a heavy sea, for there was a headwind. In the fourth watch of the night he went towards them, walking on the lake, and when the disciples saw him walking on the lake they were terrified. 'It is a ghost' they said, and cried out in fear. But at once Jesus called out to them, saying, 'Courage! It is I! Do not be afraid.' It was Peter who answered. 'Lord ', he said 'if it is you, tell me to come to you across the water.' 'Come' said Jesus. Then Peter got out of the boat and started walking towards Jesus across the water, but as soon as he felt the force of the wind, he took fright and began to sink. 'Lord! Save me!' he cried. Jesus put out his hand at once and held him. 'Man of little faith,' he said 'why did you doubt?' And as they got into the boat the wind dropped. The men in the boat bowed down before him and said, 'Truly, you are the Son of God.'

The Gospel of the Lord.

The Creed is said.

Prayer over the Offerings
Be pleased, O Lord, to accept the offerings of your Church,
for in your mercy you have given them to be offered
and by your power you transform them
into the mystery of our salvation.
Through Christ our Lord.
Amen.

Communion Antiphon Ps 147:12. 14
O Jerusalem, glorify the Lord,
who gives you your fill of finest wheat.

or Cf. Jn 6:51

The bread that I will give, says the Lord,
is my flesh for the life of the world.

Prayer after Communion
May the communion in your Sacrament
that we have consumed, save us, O Lord,
and confirm us in the light of your truth.

Through Christ our Lord.
Amen.

TWENTIETH SUNDAY IN ORDINARY TIME   A

Mercy to All People

We tend to think of God as exclusively our own property. But he is God of all the world, of Christians and non-Christians alike; and today we celebrate his mercies to others who are not of our faith.

Entrance Antiphon   Ps 83:10-11
Turn your eyes, O God, our shield;
and look on the face of your anointed one;
one day within your courts
is better than a thousand elsewhere.

The Gloria in excelsis (Glory to God in the highest) is said.

Collect
O God, who have prepared for those who love you
good things which no eye can see,
fill our hearts, we pray, with the warmth of your love,
so that, loving you in all things and above all things,
we may attain your promises,
which surpass every human desire.
Through our Lord Jesus Christ, your Son,
who lives and reigns with you in the unity of the Holy Spirit,
one God, for ever and ever.
Amen.

FIRST READING
A reading from the prophet Isaiah   56:1. 6-7

Thus says the Lord: Have a care for justice, act with integrity, for soon my salvation will come and my integrity be manifest.

   Foreigners who have attached themselves to the Lord to serve him and to love his name and be his servants – all who observe the sabbath, not profaning it, and cling to my covenant – these I will bring to my holy mountain. I will make them joyful in my house of prayer. Their holocausts and their sacrifices will be accepted on my altar, for my house will be called a house of prayer for all the peoples.

   The word of the Lord.

Responsorial Psalm Ps 66:2-3. 5-6. 8. ℟ v.4
℟ **Let the peoples praise you, O God;**
   let all the peoples praise you.

1 O God, be gracious and bless us
   and let your face shed its light upon us.
   So will your ways be known upon earth
   and all nations learn your saving help. ℟

2 Let the nations be glad and exult
   for you rule the world with justice.
   With fairness you rule the peoples,
   you guide the nations on earth. ℟

3 Let the peoples praise you, O God;
   let all the peoples praise you.
   May God still give us his blessing
   till the ends of the earth revere him. ℟

SECOND READING

A reading from the letter of St Paul to the Romans 11:13-15. 29-32

Let me tell you pagans this: I have been sent to the pagans as their apostle, and I am proud of being sent, but the purpose of it is to make my own people envious of you, and in this way save some of them. Since their rejection meant the reconciliation of the world, do you know what their admission will mean? Nothing less than a resurrection from the dead! God never takes back his gifts or revokes his choice.

Just as you changed from being disobedient to God, and now enjoy mercy because of their disobedience, so those who are disobedient now – and only because of the mercy shown to you – will also enjoy mercy eventually. God has imprisoned all men in their own disobedience only to show mercy to all mankind.

The word of the Lord.

Gospel Acclamation Jn 10:27
Alleluia, alleluia!
The sheep that belong to me listen to my voice,
says the Lord,
I know them and they follow me.
Alleluia!

or   Cf. Mt 4:23
> Alleluia, alleluia!
> Jesus proclaimed the Good News of the kingdom,
> and cured all kinds of sickness among the people.
> Alleluia!

GOSPEL
A reading from the holy Gospel according to Matthew   15:21-28

Jesus left Gennesaret and withdrew to the region of Tyre and Sidon. Then out came a Canaanite woman from that district and started shouting, 'Sir, Son of David, take pity on me. My daughter is tormented by a devil.' But he answered her not a word. And his disciples went and pleaded with him. 'Give her what she wants,' they said 'because she is shouting after us.' He said in reply, 'I was sent only to the lost sheep of the House of Israel.' But the woman had come up and was kneeling at his feet. 'Lord,' she said 'help me.' He replied, 'It is not fair to take the children's food and throw it to the house-dogs.' She retorted, 'Ah yes, sir; but even house-dogs can eat the scraps that fall from their master's table.' Then Jesus answered her, 'Woman, you have great faith. Let your wish be granted.' And from that moment her daughter was well again.

The Gospel of the Lord.

The Creed is said.

Prayer over the Offerings
Receive our oblation, O Lord,
by which is brought about a glorious exchange,
that, by offering what you have given,
we may merit to receive your very self.
Through Christ our Lord.
Amen.

Communion Antiphon   Ps 129:7
With the Lord there is mercy;
in him is plentiful redemption.

or   Jn 6:51-52

I am the living bread that came down from heaven, says the Lord.
Whoever eats of this bread will live for ever.

Prayer after Communion
Made partakers of Christ through these Sacraments,
we humbly implore your mercy, Lord,
that, conformed to his image on earth,
we may merit also to be his coheirs in heaven.
Who lives and reigns for ever and ever.

TWENTY-FIRST SUNDAY IN ORDINARY TIME A

Peter the Rock

We rejoice today that Christ chose Peter in spite of his human failings to be the rock on which he built his Church. The reason for that choice lies in the unfathomable depth of God's wisdom. 'The Lord is high, yet he looks on the lowly.'

Entrance Antiphon Cf. Ps 85:1-3
Turn your ear, O Lord, and answer me;
save the servant who trusts in you, my God.
Have mercy on me, O Lord, for I cry to you all the day long.

The Gloria in excelsis (Glory to God in the highest) is said.

Collect
O God, who cause the minds of the faithful
to unite in a single purpose,
grant your people to love what you command
and to desire what you promise,
that, amid the uncertainties of this world,
our hearts may be fixed on that place
where true gladness is found.
Through our Lord Jesus Christ, your Son,
who lives and reigns with you in the unity of the Holy Spirit,
one God, for ever and ever.
Amen.

FIRST READING
A reading from the prophet Isaiah 22:19-23

Thus says the Lord of hosts to Shebna, the master of the palace:

> I dismiss you from your office,
> I remove you from your post,
> and the same day I call on my servant
> Eliakim son of Hilkiah.

I invest him with your robe,
gird him with your sash,
entrust him with your authority;
and he shall be a father
to the inhabitants of Jerusalem
and to the House of Judah.
I place the key of the House of David
on his shoulder;
should he open, no one shall close,
should he close, no one shall open.
I drive him like a peg
into a firm place;
he will become a throne of glory
for his father's house.

The word of the Lord.

Responsorial Psalm   Ps 137:1-3. 6. 8. ℟ v.8

℟   **Your love, O Lord, is eternal,
discard not the work of your hands.**

1   I thank you, Lord, with all my heart,
you have heard the words of my mouth.
Before the angels I will bless you.
I will adore before your holy temple.   ℟

2   I thank you for your faithfulness and love
which excel all we ever knew of you.
On the day I called, you answered;
you increased the strength of my soul.   ℟.

3   The Lord is high yet he looks on the lowly
and the haughty he knows from afar.
Your love, O Lord, is eternal,
discard not the work of your hands.   ℟

SECOND READING

A reading from the letter of St Paul to the Romans   11:33-36

How rich are the depths of God – how deep his wisdom and knowledge – and how impossible to penetrate his motives or understand his methods! Who could ever know the mind of the Lord? Who could ever be his counsellor? Who could ever give him anything or lend him anything? All that exists comes from him; all is by him and for him. To him be glory for ever! Amen.

The word of the Lord.

Gospel Acclamation 2 Cor 5:19
Alleluia, alleluia!
God in Christ was reconciling the world to himself,
and he has entrusted to us the news that they are reconciled.
Alleluia!

or Mt 16:18

Alleluia, alleluia!
You are Peter
and on this rock I will build my Church.
And the gates of the underworld can never hold out against it.
Alleluia!

GOSPEL
A reading from the holy Gospel according to Matthew 16:13-20

When Jesus came to the region of Caesarea Philippi he put this question to his disciples, 'Who do people say the Son of Man is?' And they said, 'Some say he is John the Baptist, some Elijah, and others Jeremiah or one of the prophets.' 'But you,' he said, 'who do you say I am?' Then Simon Peter spoke up, 'You are the Christ,' he said, 'the Son of the living God.' Jesus replied, 'Simon son of Jonah, you are a happy man! Because it was not flesh and blood that revealed this to you but my Father in heaven. So I now say to you: You are Peter and on this rock I will build my Church. And the gates of the underworld can never hold out against it. I will give you the keys of the kingdom of heaven; whatever you bind on earth shall be considered bound in heaven; whatever you loose on earth shall be considered loosed in heaven.' Then he gave the disciples strict orders not to tell anyone that he was the Christ.

The Gospel of the Lord.

The Creed is said.

Prayer over the Offerings
O Lord, who gained for yourself a people by adoption
through the one sacrifice offered once for all,
bestow graciously on us, we pray,
the gifts of unity and peace in your Church.
Through Christ our Lord.
Amen.

Twenty-Second Sunday in Ordinary Time, Year A 553

Communion Antiphon Cf. Ps 103:13-15
The earth is replete with the fruits of your work, O Lord;
you bring forth bread from the earth
and wine to cheer the heart.

or Cf. Jn 6:54
Whoever eats my flesh and drinks my blood
has eternal life, says the Lord,
and I will raise him up on the last day.

Prayer after Communion
Complete within us, O Lord, we pray,
the healing work of your mercy
and graciously perfect and sustain us,
so that in all things we may please you.
Through Christ our Lord.
Amen.

TWENTY-SECOND SUNDAY IN ORDINARY TIME A

Christ Who Overcame the Reluctance of the Flesh

It comes to us as no surprise that the Prophet Jeremiah should have felt reluctance to offer himself as a living sacrifice to God's will, because we all experience the same reluctance to accept the cross. But what consolation it is to know that Christ experienced the same reluctance of the flesh and had to struggle to overcome it.

Entrance Antiphon Cf. Ps 85:3. 5
Have mercy on me, O Lord, for I cry to you all the day long.
O Lord, you are good and forgiving,
full of mercy to all who call to you.

The Gloria in excelsis (Glory to God in the highest) is said.

Collect
God of might, giver of every good gift,
put into our hearts the love of your name,
so that, by deepening our sense of reverence,
you may nurture in us what is good
and, by your watchful care,
keep safe what you have nurtured.
Through our Lord Jesus Christ, your Son,
who lives and reigns with you in the unity of the Holy Spirit,
one God, for ever and ever.
Amen.

Twenty-Second Sunday in Ordinary Time, Year A

FIRST READING
A reading from the prophet Jeremiah   20:7-9

You have seduced me, Lord, and I have let myself be seduced;
you have overpowered me: you were the stronger.
I am a daily laughing-stock,
everybody's butt.
Each time I speak the word, I have to howl
and proclaim: 'Violence and ruin!'
The word of the Lord has meant for me
insult, derision, all day long.
I used to say, 'I will not think about him,
I will not speak in his name any more.'
Then there seemed to be a fire burning in my heart,
imprisoned in my bones.
The effort to restrain it wearied me,
I could not bear it.

The word of the Lord.

Responsorial Psalm   Ps 62:2-6. 8-9. R/ v.2
  R/ **For you my soul is thirsting, O Lord my God.**

1   O God, you are my God, for you I long;
    for you my soul is thirsting.
    My body pines for you
    like a dry, weary land without water. R/

2   So I gaze on you in the sanctuary
    to see your strength and your glory.
    For your love is better than life,
    my lips will speak your praise. R/

3   So I will bless you all my life,
    in your name I will lift up my hands.
    My soul shall be filled as with a banquet,
    my mouth shall praise you with joy. R/

4   For you have been my help;
    in the shadow of your wings I rejoice.
    My soul clings to you;
    your right hand holds me fast. R/

Twenty-Second Sunday in Ordinary Time, Year A

SECOND READING
A reading from the letter of St Paul to the Romans 12:1-2

Think of God's mercy, my brothers, and worship him, I beg you, in a way that is worthy of thinking beings, by offering your living bodies as a holy sacrifice, truly pleasing to God. Do not model yourselves on the behaviour of the world around you, but let your behaviour change, modelled by your new mind. This is the only way to discover the will of God and know what is good, what it is that God wants, what is the perfect thing to do.

The word of the Lord.

Gospel Acclamation Cf. Eph 1:17-18
Alleluia, alleluia!
May the Father of our Lord Jesus Christ
enlighten the eyes of our mind,
so that we can see
what hope his call holds for us.
Alleluia!

GOSPEL
A reading from the holy Gospel according to Matthew 16:21-27

Jesus began to make it clear to his disciples that he was destined to go to Jerusalem and suffer grievously at the hands of the elders and chief priests and scribes, to be put to death and to be raised up on the third day. Then, taking him aside, Peter started to remonstrate with him. 'Heaven preserve you, Lord,' he said. 'This must not happen to you.' But he turned and said to Peter, 'Get behind me, Satan! You are an obstacle in my path, because the way you think is not God's way but man's.'

Then Jesus said to his disciples, 'If anyone wants to be a follower of mine, let him renounce himself and take up his cross and follow me. For anyone who wants to save his life will lose it; but anyone who loses his life for my sake will find it. What, then, will a man gain if he wins the whole world and ruins his life? Or what has a man to offer in exchange for his life?

'For the Son of Man is going to come in the glory of his Father with his angels, and, when he does, he will reward each one according to his behaviour.'

The Gospel of the Lord.

The Creed is said.

Prayer over the Offerings
May this sacred offering, O Lord,
confer on us always the blessing of salvation,
that what it celebrates in mystery
it may accomplish in power.
Through Christ our Lord.
Amen.

Communion Antiphon   Ps 30:20
How great is the goodness, Lord,
that you keep for those who fear you.

or   Mt 5:9-10

Blessed are the peacemakers,
for they shall be called children of God.
Blessed are they who are persecuted for the sake of righteousness,
for theirs is the Kingdom of Heaven.

Prayer after Communion
Renewed by this bread from the heavenly table,
we beseech you, Lord,
that, being the food of charity,
it may confirm our hearts
and stir us to serve you in our neighbour.
Through Christ our Lord.
Amen.

TWENTY-THIRD SUNDAY IN ORDINARY TIME   A

Christ Who Paid the Debt of Love

Christ became our brother and made himself responsible for us, his brothers and sisters. He contracted the debt of mutual love. All he asks of us is that we should do the same.

Entrance Antiphon   Ps 118:137. 124
You are just, O Lord, and your judgement is right;
treat your servant in accord with your merciful love.

The Gloria in excelsis (Glory to God in the highest) is said.

Twenty-Third Sunday in Ordinary Time, Year A

Collect
O God, by whom we are redeemed and receive adoption,
look graciously upon your beloved sons and daughters,
that those who believe in Christ
may receive true freedom
and an everlasting inheritance.
Through our Lord Jesus Christ, your Son,
who lives and reigns with you in the unity of the Holy Spirit,
one God, for ever and ever.
Amen.

FIRST READING
A reading from the prophet Ezekiel   33:7-9

The word of the Lord was addressed to me as follows, 'Son of man, I have appointed you as sentry to the House of Israel. When you hear a word from my mouth, warn them in my name. If I say to a wicked man: Wicked wretch, you are to die, and you do not speak to warn the wicked man to renounce his ways, then he shall die for his sin, but I will hold you responsible for his death. If, however, you do warn a wicked man to renounce his ways and repent, and he does not repent, then he shall die for his sin, but you yourself will have saved your life.'

The word of the Lord.

Responsorial Psalm   Ps 94:1-2. 6-9. R̸ v.8
**R̸ O that today you would listen to his voice!
Harden not your hearts.**

1   Come, ring out our joy to the Lord;
    hail the rock who saves us.
    Let us come before him, giving thanks,
    with songs let us hail the Lord.   R̸

2   Come in; let us bow and bend low;
    let us kneel before the God who made us
    for he is our God and we
    the people who belong to his pasture,
    the flock that is led by his hand.   R̸

3   O that today you would listen to his voice!
    'Harden not your hearts as at Meribah,
    as on that day at Massah in the desert
    when your fathers put me to the test;
    when they tried me, though they saw my work.   R̸

Twenty-Third Sunday in Ordinary Time, Year A

SECOND READING
A reading from the letter of St Paul to the Romans   13:8-10

Avoid getting into debt, except the debt of mutual love. If you love your fellow men you have carried out your obligations. All the commandments: You shall not commit adultery, you shall not kill, you shall not steal, you shall not covet, and so on, are summed up in this single command: You must love your neighbour as yourself. Love is the one thing that cannot hurt your neighbour; that is why it is the answer to every one of the commandments.

The word of the Lord.

Gospel Acclamation   Jn 17:17
Alleluia, alleluia!
Your word is truth, O Lord,
consecrate us in the truth.
Alleluia!

or   2 Cor 5:19
Alleluia, alleluia!
God in Christ was reconciling the world to himself,
and he has entrusted to us the news that they are reconciled.
Alleluia!

GOSPEL
A reading from the holy Gospel according to Matthew   18:15-20

Jesus said to his disciples: 'If your brother does something wrong, go and have it out with him alone, between your two selves. If he listens to you, you have won back your brother. If he does not listen, take one or two others along with you: the evidence of two or three witnesses is required to sustain any charge. But if he refuses to listen to these, report it to the community; and if he refuses to listen to the community, treat him like a pagan or a tax collector.

'I tell you solemnly, whatever you bind on earth shall be considered bound in heaven; whatever you loose on earth shall be considered loosed in heaven.

'I tell you solemnly once again, if two of you on earth agree to ask anything at all, it will be granted to you by my Father in heaven. For where two or three meet in my name, I shall be there with them.'

The Gospel of the Lord.

The Creed is said.

Prayer over the Offerings
O God, who give us the gift of true prayer and of peace,
graciously grant that through this offering,
we may do fitting homage to your divine majesty
and, by partaking of the sacred mystery,
we may be faithfully united in mind and heart.
Through Christ our Lord.
Amen.

Communion Antiphon   Cf. Ps 41:2-3
Like the deer that yearns for running streams,
so my soul is yearning for you, my God;
my soul is thirsting for God, the living God.

or   Jn 8:12
I am the light of the world, says the Lord;
whoever follows me will not walk in darkness,
but will have the light of life.

Prayer after Communion
Grant that your faithful, O Lord,
whom you nourish and endow with life
through the food of your Word and heavenly Sacrament,
may so benefit from your beloved Son's great gifts
that we may merit an eternal share in his life.
Who lives and reigns for ever and ever.
Amen.

TWENTY-FOURTH SUNDAY IN ORDINARY TIME   A

Our Forgiving Lord

We cannot celebrate today the Lord of compassion and love, the Lord who died for us and who lives to intercede for us, unless each of us has forgiven our brother and sister from our hearts.

Entrance Antiphon   Cf. Sir 36:18
Give peace, O Lord, to those who wait for you,
that your prophets be found true.
Hear the prayers of your servant,
and of your people Israel.

The Gloria in excelsis (Glory to God in the highest) is said.

Collect
Look upon us, O God,
Creator and ruler of all things,
and, that we may feel the working of your mercy,
grant that we may serve you with all our heart.
Through our Lord Jesus Christ, your Son,
who lives and reigns with you in the unity of the Holy Spirit,
one God, for ever and ever.
Amen.

FIRST READING
A reading from the book of Ecclesiasticus 27:30 – 28:7

Resentment and anger, these are foul things,
and both are found with the sinner.
He who exacts vengeance will experience the vengeance of the Lord,
who keeps strict account of sin.
Forgive your neighbour the hurt he does you,
and when you pray, your sins will be forgiven.
If a man nurses anger against another,
can he then demand compassion from the Lord?
Showing no pity for a man like himself,
can he then plead for his own sins?
Mere creature of flesh, he cherishes resentment;
who will forgive him his sins?
Remember the last things, and stop hating,
remember dissolution and death, and live by the commandments.
Remember the commandments, and do not bear your neighbour ill-will;
remember the covenant of the Most High, and overlook the offence.

The word of the Lord.

Responsorial Psalm
Ps 102:1-4. 9-12. ℟ v.8

℟ **The Lord is compassion and love,
slow to anger and rich in mercy.**

1   My soul, give thanks to the Lord,
    all my being, bless his holy name.
    My soul, give thanks to the Lord
    and never forget all his blessings.   ℟

Twenty-Fourth Sunday in Ordinary Time, Year A

2 It is he who forgives all your guilt,
who heals every one of your ills,
who redeems your life from the grave,
who crowns you with love and compassion. ℟

3 His wrath will come to an end;
he will not be angry for ever.
He does not treat us according to our sins
nor repay us according to our faults. ℟

4 For as the heavens are high above the earth
so strong is his love for those who fear him.
As far as the east is from the west
so far does he remove our sins. ℟

SECOND READING
A reading from the letter of St Paul to the Romans   14:7-9

The life and death of each of us has its influence on others; if we live, we live for the Lord; and if we die, we die for the Lord, so that alive or dead we belong to the Lord. This explains why Christ both died and came to life, it was so that he might be Lord both of the dead and of the living.

The word of the Lord.

Gospel Acclamation   1 Sam 3:9; Jn 6:68

Alleluia, alleluia!
Speak, Lord, your servant is listening:
you have the message of eternal life.
Alleluia!

or   Jn 13:34

Alleluia, alleluia!
I give you a new commandmant:
love one another, just as I have loved you,
says the Lord.
Alleluia!

GOSPEL
A reading from the holy Gospel according to Matthew   18:21-35

Peter went up to Jesus and said, 'Lord, how often must I forgive my brother if he wrongs me? As often as seven times?' Jesus answered, 'Not seven, I tell you, but seventy-seven times.

'And so the kingdom of heaven may be compared to a king who decided to settle his accounts with his servants. When the reckoning began, they brought him a man who owed ten thousand talents; but he had no means of paying, so his master gave orders that he should be sold, together with his wife and children and all his possessions, to meet the debt. At this, the servant threw himself down at his master's feet. "Give me time," he said, "and I will pay the whole sum." And the servant's master felt so sorry for him that he let him go and cancelled the debt. Now as this servant went out, he happened to meet a fellow servant who owed him one hundred denarii; and he seized him by the throat and began to throttle him. "Pay what you owe me," he said. His fellow servant fell at his feet and implored him, saying, "Give me time and I will pay you." But the other would not agree; on the contrary, he had him thrown into prison till he should pay the debt. His fellow servants were deeply distressed when they saw what had happened, and they went to their master and reported the whole affair to him. Then the master sent for him. "You wicked servant," he said, "I cancelled all that debt of yours when you appealed to me. Were you not bound, then, to have pity on your fellow servant just as I had pity on you?" And in his anger the master handed him over to the torturers till he should pay all his debt. And that is how my heavenly Father will deal with you unless you each forgive your brother from your heart.'

The Gospel of the Lord.

The Creed is said.

Prayer over the Offerings
Look with favour on our supplications, O Lord,
and in your kindness accept these, your servants' offerings,
that what each has offered to the honour of your name
may serve the salvation of all.
Through Christ our Lord.
Amen.

Communion Antiphon Cf. Ps 35:8
How precious is your mercy, O God!
The *children of men seek shelter in the shadow of your wings.*

or Cf. 1 Cor 10:16
The chalice of blessing that we bless
is a communion in the Blood of Christ;
and the bread that we break
is a sharing in the Body of the Lord.

Prayer after Communion
May the working of this heavenly gift, O Lord, we pray,
take possession of our minds and bodies,
so that its effects, and not our own desires,
may always prevail in us.
Through Christ our Lord.
Amen.

TWENTY-FIFTH SUNDAY IN ORDINARY TIME   A

The Generous Love of God

The love of God cannot be measured by any human standard. It is incalculable. By human reckoning it must even appear foolish. What sensible employer would behave like the man in the Gospel parable? We see a reflection of that love in St Paul's dilemma. He loved so much that he could not decide whether it was better to live or to die.

Entrance Antiphon
I am the salvation of the people, says the Lord.
Should they cry to me in any distress,
I will hear them, and I will be their Lord for ever.

The Gloria in excelsis (Glory to God in the highest) is said.

Collect
O God, who founded all the commands of your sacred Law
upon love of you and of our neighbour,
grant that, by keeping your precepts,
we may merit to attain eternal life.
Through our Lord Jesus Christ, your Son,
who lives and reigns with you in the unity of the Holy Spirit,
one God, for ever and ever.
Amen.

FIRST READING
A reading from the prophet Isaiah   55:6-9

Seek the Lord while he is still to be found,
call to him while he is still near.
Let the wicked man abandon his way,
the evil man his thoughts.
Let him turn back to the Lord who will take pity on him,
to our God who is rich in forgiving;
for my thoughts are not your thoughts,

my ways not your ways – it is the Lord who speaks.
Yes, the heavens are as high above earth
as my ways are above your ways,
my thoughts above your thoughts.

 The word of the Lord.

Responsorial Psalm   Ps 144:2-3. 8-9. 17-18. R℣ v.18
 R℣ **The Lord is close to all who call him.**

1   I will bless you day after day
   and praise your name for ever.
   The Lord is great, highly to be praised,
   his greatness cannot be measured.   R℣

2   The Lord is kind and full of compassion,
   slow to anger, abounding in love.
   How good is the Lord to all,
   compassionate to all his creatures.   R℣

3   The Lord is just in all his ways
   and loving in all his deeds.
   He is close to all who call him,
   who call on him from their hearts.   R℣

SECOND READING
A reading from the letter of St Paul to the Philippians   1:20-24. 27

Christ will be glorified in my body, whether by my life or by my death. Life to me, of course, is Christ, but then death would bring me something more; but then again, if living in this body means doing work which is having good results – I do not know what I should choose. I am caught in this dilemma: I want to be gone and be with Christ, which would be very much the better, but for me to stay alive in this body is a more urgent need for your sake. Avoid anything in your everyday lives that would be unworthy of the gospel of Christ.

 The word of the Lord.

Gospel Acclamation   Lk 19:38
 Alleluia, alleluia!
 Blessings on the King who comes,
 in the name of the Lord!
 Peace in heaven
 and glory in the highest heavens!

Alleluia!

or Cf. Acts 16:14

Alleluia, alleluia!
Open our heart, O Lord,
to accept the words of your Son.
Alleluia!

GOSPEL

A reading from the holy Gospel according to Matthew 20:1-16

Jesus said to his disciples: 'The kingdom of heaven is like a landowner going out at daybreak to hire workers for his vineyard. He made an agreement with the workers for one denarius a day, and sent them to his vineyard. Going out at about the third hour he saw others standing idle in the market place and said to them, "You go to my vineyard too and I will give you a fair wage." So they went. At about the sixth hour and again at about the ninth hour, he went out and did the same. Then at about the eleventh hour he went out and found more men standing round, and he said to them, "Why have you been standing here idle all day?" "Because no one has hired us" they answered. He said to them, "You go into my vineyard too". In the evening, the owner of the vineyard said to his bailiff, "Call the workers and pay them their wages, starting with the last arrivals and ending with the first." So those who were hired at about the eleventh hour came forward and received one denarius each. When the first came, they expected to get more, but they too received one denarius each. They took it, but grumbled at the landowner. "The men who came last" they said "have done only one hour, and you have treated them the same as us, though we have done a heavy day's work in all the heat." He answered one of them and said, "My friend, I am not being unjust to you; did we not agree on one denarius? Take your earnings and go. I choose to pay the last-comer as much as I pay you. Have I no right to do what I like with my own? Why be envious because I am generous?" Thus the last will be first, and the first, last.'

The Gospel of the Lord.

The Creed is said.

Prayer over the Offerings

Receive with favour, O Lord, we pray,
the offerings of your people,

that what they profess with devotion and faith
may be theirs through these heavenly mysteries.
Through Christ our Lord.
Amen.

Communion Antiphon   Ps 118:4-5
You have laid down your precepts to be carefully kept;
may my ways be firm in keeping your statutes.

or   Jn 10:14
I am the Good Shepherd, says the Lord;
I know my sheep, and mine know me.

Prayer after Communion
Graciously raise up, O Lord,
those you renew with this Sacrament,
that we may come to possess your redemption
both in mystery and in the manner of our life.
Through Christ our Lord.
Amen.

TWENTY-SIXTH SUNDAY IN ORDINARY TIME   A

Christ Obedient Unto Death

We celebrate Christ who obeyed his Father's will not only in word but also in deed. And Christ assures us that it is never too late to turn to God and to do his will.

Entrance Antiphon   Dn 3:31. 29. 30. 43. 42
All that you have done to us, O Lord,
you have done with true judgement,
for we have sinned against you
and not obeyed your commandments.
But give glory to your name
and deal with us according to the bounty of your mercy.

The Gloria in excelsis (Glory to God in the highest) is said.

Collect
O God, who manifest your almighty power
above all by pardoning and showing mercy,
bestow, we pray, your grace abundantly upon us
and make those hastening to attain your promises

heirs to the treasures of heaven.
Through our Lord Jesus Christ, your Son,
who lives and reigns with you in the unity of the Holy Spirit,
one God, for ever and ever.
Amen.

FIRST READING
A reading from the prophet Ezekiel   18:25-28

The word of the Lord was addressed to me as follows: 'You object, "What the Lord does is unjust." Listen, you House of Israel: is what I do unjust? Is it not what you do that is unjust? When the upright man renounces his integrity to commit sin and dies because of this, he dies because of the evil that he himself has committed. When the sinner renounces sin to become law-abiding and honest, he deserves to live. He has chosen to renounce all his previous sins; he shall certainly live; he shall not die.'

The word of the Lord.

Responsorial Psalm   Ps 24:4-9. R̷ v.6
  R̷ **Remember your mercy, Lord.**

1   Lord, make me know your ways.
    Lord, teach me your paths.
    Make me walk in your truth, and teach me:
    for you are God my saviour.   R̷

2   Remember your mercy, Lord,
    and the love you have shown from of old.
    Do not remember the sins of my youth.
    In your love remember me,
    because of your goodness, O Lord.   R̷

3   The Lord is good and upright.
    He shows the path to those who stray,
    he guides the humble in the right path;
    he teaches his way to the poor.   R̷

SECOND READING
A reading from the letter of St Paul to the Philippians   2:1-11

If our life in Christ means anything to you, if love can persuade at all, or the Spirit that we have in common, or any tenderness and sympathy, then be united in your convictions and united in your love, with a common purpose and a common mind. That is the one thing which would make me completely happy. There must be no competition among you, no conceit; but everybody is to be self-effacing. Always consider the other person to be better than yourself, so that nobody thinks of his own interests first but everybody thinks of other people's interests instead. In your minds you must be the same as Christ Jesus:

> His state was divine,
> yet he did not cling
> to his equality with God
> but emptied himself
> to assume the condition of a slave,
> and became as men are;
> and being as all men are,
> he was humbler yet,
> even to accepting death,
> death on a cross.
> But God raised him high
> and gave him the name
> which is above all other names
> so that all beings
> in the heavens, on earth and in the underworld,
> should bend the knee at the name of Jesus
> and that every tongue should acclaim
> Jesus Christ as Lord,
> to the glory of God the Father.

The word of the Lord

Shorter Form, verses 1-5. Read between

Gospel Acclamation   Jn 14:23
> Alleluia, alleluia!
> If anyone loves me he will keep my word.
> and my Father will love him,
> and we shall come to him.
> Alleluia!

or   Jn 10:27
> Alleluia, alleluia!
> The sheep that belong to me listen to my voice,
> says the Lord,
> I know them and they follow me.
> Alleluia!

GOSPEL

A reading from the holy Gospel according to Matthew 21:28-32

Jesus said to the chief priests and the elders of the people, 'What is your opinion? A man had two sons. He went and said to the first, "My boy, you go and work in the vineyard today." He answered, "I will not go", but afterwards thought better of it and went. The man then went and said the same thing to the second who answered, "Certainly, sir", but did not go. Which of the two did the father's will?' 'The first' they said. Jesus said to them, 'I tell you solemnly, tax collectors and prostitutes are making their way into the kingdom of God before you. For John came to you, a pattern of true righteousness, but you did not believe him, and yet the tax collectors and prostitutes did. Even after seeing that, you refused to think better of it and believe in him.'

The Gospel of the Lord.

The Creed is said.

Prayer over the Offerings
Grant us, O merciful God,
that this our offering may find acceptance with you
and that through it the wellspring of all blessing
may be laid open before us.
Through Christ our Lord.
Amen.

Communion Antiphon Cf. Ps 118:49-50
Remember your word to your servant, O Lord,
by which you have given me hope.
This is my comfort when I am brought low.

or 1 Jn 3:16

By this we came to know the love of God:
that Christ laid down his life for us;
so we ought to lay down our lives for one another.

Prayer after Communion
May this heavenly mystery, O Lord,
restore us in mind and body,
that we may be coheirs in glory with Christ,
to whose suffering we are united
whenever we proclaim his Death.
Who lives and reigns for ever and ever.
Amen.

TWENTY-SEVENTH SUNDAY IN ORDINARY TIME A

The Vineyard of the Lord

The Church rejoices in being the vineyard of the Lord. At the same time we have cause here for much heart-searching and prayer.

Entrance Antiphon
Cf. Est 4:17

Within your will, O Lord, all things are established,
and there is none that can resist your will.
For you have made all things, the heaven and the earth,
and all that is held within the circle of heaven;
you are the Lord of all.

The Gloria in excelsis (Glory to God in the highest) is said.

Collect

Almighty ever-living God,
who in the abundance of your kindness
surpass the merits and the desires of those who entreat you,
pour out your mercy upon us
to pardon what conscience dreads
and to give what prayer does not dare to ask.
Through our Lord Jesus Christ, your Son,
who lives and reigns with you in the unity of the Holy Spirit,
one God, for ever and ever.
Amen.

FIRST READING

A reading from the prophet Isaiah
5:1-7

Let me sing to my friend
the song of his love for his vineyard.
My friend had a vineyard
on a fertile hillside.
He dug the soil, cleared it of stones,
and planted choice vines in it.
In the middle he built a tower,
he dug a press there too.
He expected it to yield grapes,
but sour grapes were all that it gave.

And now, inhabitants of Jerusalem
and men of Judah,
I ask you to judge
between my vineyard and me.

What could I have done for my vineyard
that I have not done?
I expected it to yield grapes.
Why did it yield sour grapes instead?

Very well, I will tell you
what I am going to do to my vineyard:
I will take away its hedge for it to be grazed on,
and knock down its wall for it to be trampled on.
I will lay it waste, unpruned, undug;
overgrown by the briar and the thorn.
I will command the clouds
to rain no rain on it.
Yes, the vineyard of the Lord of hosts
is the House of Israel,
and the men of Judah
that chosen plant.
He expected justice, but found bloodshed,
integrity, but only a cry of distress.

The word of the Lord.

Responsorial Psalm   Ps 79:9. 12-16. 19-20. ℟ Is 5:7
   ℟ **The vineyard of the Lord is the House of Israel.**

1. You brought a vine out of Egypt;
   to plant it you drove out the nations.
   It stretched out its branches to the sea,
   to the Great River it stretched out its shoots. ℟

2. Then why have you broken down its walls?
   It is plucked by all who pass by.
   It is ravaged by the boar of the forest,
   devoured by the beasts of the field. ℟

3. God of hosts, turn again, we implore,
   look down from heaven and see.
   Visit this vine and protect it,
   the vine your right hand has planted. ℟

4. And we shall never forsake you again:
   give us life that we may call upon your name.
   God of hosts, bring us back;
   let your face shine on us and we shall be saved. ℟

SECOND READING

A reading from the letter of St Paul to the Philippians   4:6-9

There is no need to worry; but if there is anything you need, pray for it, asking God for it with prayer and thanksgiving, and that peace of God, which is so much greater than we can understand, will guard your hearts and your thoughts, in Christ Jesus. Finally, brothers, fill your minds with everything that is true, everything that is noble, everything that is good and pure, everything that we love and honour, and everything that can be thought virtuous or worthy of praise. Keep doing all the things that you learnt from me and have been taught by me and have heard or seen that I do. Then the God of peace will be with you.

The word of the Lord.

Gospel Acclamation   Jn 15:15
Alleluia, alleluia!
I call you friends, says the Lord,
because I have made known to you
everything I have learnt from my Father.
Alleluia!

or   Cf. Jn 15:16

Alleluia, alleluia!
I chose you from the world
to go out and bear fruit,
fruit that will last,
says the Lord.
Alleluia!

GOSPEL

A reading from the holy Gospel according to Matthew   21:33-43

Jesus said to the chief priests and the elders of the people, 'Listen to another parable. There was a man, a landowner, who planted a vineyard; he fenced it round, dug a winepress in it and built a tower; then he leased it to tenants and went abroad. When vintage time drew near he sent his servants to the tenants to collect his produce. But the tenants seized his servants, thrashed one, killed another and stoned a third. Next he sent some more servants, this time a larger number, and they dealt with them in the same way. Finally he sent his son to them. "They will respect my son" he said. But when the tenants saw the son, they said to each other, "This is the heir. Come on, let us kill him and take over his inheritance." So they seized him and threw him out of the vineyard and killed him. Now when the owner of the vineyard comes, what will he do to those tenants?' They answered, 'He will bring those wretches to a wretched end and lease the vineyard to other tenants who will deliver the produce to him when the season arrives.' Jesus said to them, 'Have you never read in the scriptures:

> It was the stone rejected by the builders
> that became the keystone.
> This was the Lord's doing
> and it is wonderful to see?

'I tell you, then, that the kingdom of God will be taken from you and given to a people who will produce its fruit.'

The Gospel of the Lord.

The Creed is said.

Prayer over the Offerings
Accept, O Lord, we pray,
the sacrifices instituted by your commands
and, through the sacred mysteries,
which we celebrate with dutiful service,
graciously complete the sanctifying work
by which you are pleased to redeem us.
Through Christ our Lord.
Amen.

Communion Antiphon Lam 3:25
The Lord is good to those who hope in him,
to the soul that seeks him.
or Cf. 1 Cor 10:17
Though many, we are one bread, one body,
for we all partake of the one Bread and one Chalice.

Prayer after Communion
Grant us, almighty God,
that we may be refreshed and nourished
by the Sacrament which we have received,
so as to be transformed into what we consume.
Through Christ our Lord.
Amen.

TWENTY-EIGHTH SUNDAY IN ORDINARY TIME   A

The Lord's Wedding Feast

In Christ Jesus, God fulfils all our needs, as lavishly as only God can. All of us, no matter how unworthy we may be, are invited to the wedding feast of his Son. We have only to respond to his invitation to come, and enter.

Entrance Antiphon   Ps 129:3-4
If you, O Lord, should mark iniquities,
Lord, who could stand?
But with you is found forgiveness,
O God of Israel.

The Gloria in excelsis (Glory to God in the highest) is said.

Collect
May your grace, O Lord, we pray,
at all times go before us and follow after
and make us always determined
to carry out good works.
Through our Lord Jesus Christ, your Son,
who lives and reigns with you in the unity of the Holy Spirit,
one God, for ever and ever.
Amen.

FIRST READING
A reading from the prophet Isaiah   25:6-10

On this mountain,
the Lord of hosts will prepare for all people
a banquet of rich food, a banquet of fine wines,
of food rich and juicy, of fine strained wines.
On this mountain he will remove
the mourning veil covering all peoples,
and the shroud enwrapping all nations,
he will destroy Death for ever.
The Lord will wipe away
the tears from every cheek;
he will take away his people's shame
everywhere on earth,
for the Lord has said so.
That day, it will be said: See, this is our God
in whom we hoped for salvation;
the Lord is the one in whom we hoped.
We exult and we rejoice

that he has saved us;
for the hand of the Lord
rests on this mountain.

    The word of the Lord.

Responsorial Psalm   Ps 22. ℟ v.6
   ℟ **In the Lord's own house shall I dwell
for ever and ever.**

1. The Lord is my shepherd;
   there is nothing I shall want.
   Fresh and green are the pastures
   where he gives me repose.
   Near restful waters he leads me,
   to revive my drooping spirit. ℟

2. He guides me along the right path;
   he is true to his name.
   If I should walk in the valley of darkness
   no evil would I fear.
   You are there with your crook and your staff;
   with these you give me comfort. ℟

3. You have prepared a banquet for me
   in the sight of my foes.
   My head you have anointed with oil;
   my cup is overflowing. ℟

4. Surely goodness and kindness shall follow me
   all the days of my life
   In the Lord's own house shall I dwell
   for ever and ever. ℟

SECOND READING

A reading from the letter of St Paul   4:12-14. 19-20
to the Philippians

I know how to be poor and I know how to be rich too. I have been through my initiation and now I am ready for anything anywhere: full stomach or empty stomach, poverty or plenty. There is nothing I cannot master with the help of the One who gives me strength. All the same, it was good of you to share with me in my hardships. In return my God will fulfil all your needs, in Christ Jesus, as lavishly as only God can. Glory to God, our Father, for ever and ever. Amen.

    The word of the Lord.

Gospel Acclamation   Jn 1:12. 14

Alleluia, alleluia!
The Word was made flesh and lived among us;
to all who did accept him
he gave power to become children of God.
Alleluia!

or   Cf. Eph 1:17-18

Alleluia, alleluia!
May the Father of our Lord Jesus Christ
enlighten the eyes of our mind,
so that we can see what hope his call holds for us.
Alleluia!

GOSPEL

A reading from the holy Gospel according to Matthew   22:1-14

Jesus said to the chief priests and elders of the people: 'The kingdom of heaven may be compared to a king who gave a feast for his son's wedding. He sent his servants to call those who had been invited, but they would not come. Next he sent some more servants. "Tell those who have been invited" he said "that I have my banquet all prepared, my oxen and fattened cattle have been slaughtered, everything is ready. Come to the wedding." But they were not interested: one went off to his farm, another to his business, and the rest seized his servants, maltreated them and killed them. The king was furious. He despatched his troops, destroyed those murderers and burnt their town. Then he said to his servants, "The wedding is ready; but as those who were invited proved to be unworthy, go to the crossroads in the town and invite everyone you can find to the wedding." So these servants went out on to the roads and collected together everyone they could find, bad and good alike; and the wedding hall was filled with guests. When the king came in to look at the guests he noticed one man who was not wearing a wedding garment, and said to him, "How did you get in here, my friend, without a wedding garment?" And the man was silent. Then the king said to the attendants, "Bind him hand and foot and throw him out into the dark, where there will be weeping and grinding of teeth." For many are called, but few are chosen.'

The Gospel of the Lord.

Shorter Form, verses 1-10. Read between

Twenty-Ninth Sunday in Ordinary Time, Year A

The Creed is said.

Prayer over the Offerings
Accept, O Lord, the prayers of your faithful
with the sacrificial offerings,
that, through these acts of devotedness,
we may pass over to the glory of heaven.
Through Christ our Lord.
Amen.

Communion Antiphon
Cf. Ps 33:11
The rich suffer want and go hungry,
but those who seek the Lord lack no blessing.

or
1 Jn 3:2
When the Lord appears, we shall be like him,
for we shall see him as he is.

Prayer after Communion
We entreat your majesty most humbly, O Lord,
that, as you feed us with the nourishment
which comes from the most holy Body and Blood of your Son,
so you may make us sharers of his divine nature.
Who lives and reigns for ever and ever.
Amen.

TWENTY-NINTH SUNDAY IN ORDINARY TIME   A

The Lord of History

God is king. Earthly rulers, political regimes, Cyrus or Caesar, are called by God to reveal something of his power and majesty and his plan for the human race. But they only hold their power for a short time. Our concern is not with them, but with God whom we worship in this celebration.

Entrance Antiphon
Cf. Ps 16:6. 8
To you I call; for you will surely heed me, O God;
turn your ear to me; hear my words.
Guard me as the apple of your eye;
in the shadow of your wings protect me.

The Gloria in excelsis (Glory to God in the highest) is said.

Collect
Almighty ever-living God,
grant that we may always conform our will to yours
and serve your majesty in sincerity of heart.

Through our Lord Jesus Christ, your Son,
who lives and reigns with you in the unity of the Holy Spirit,
one God, for ever and ever.
Amen.

FIRST READING

A reading from the prophet Isaiah 45:1. 4-6

Thus says the Lord to his anointed, to Cyrus,
whom he has taken by his right hand
to subdue nations before him
and strip the loins of kings,
to force gateways before him
that their gates be closed no more:

> It is for the sake of my servant Jacob,
> of Israel my chosen one,
> that I have called you by your name,
> conferring a title though you do not know me.
> I am the Lord, unrivalled;
> there is no other God besides me.
> Though you do not know me, I arm you
> that men may know from the rising to the setting of the sun
> that, apart from me, all is nothing.

The word of the Lord.

Responsorial Psalm Ps 95:1. 3-5. 7-10. ℟ v.7

℟ **Give the Lord glory and power.**

1 O sing a new song to the Lord,
   sing to the Lord all the earth.
   Tell among the nations his glory
   and his wonders among all the peoples. ℟

2 The Lord is great and worthy of praise,
   to be feared above all gods;
   the gods of the heathens are naught.
   It was the Lord who made the heavens. ℟

3 Give the Lord, you families of peoples,
   give the Lord glory and power,
   give the Lord the glory of his name.
   Bring an offering and enter his courts. ℟

4 Worship the Lord in his temple.
O earth, tremble before him.
Proclaim to the nations: 'God is king.'
He will judge the peoples in fairness. ℟

SECOND READING
A reading from the first letter of St Paul to the Thessalonians 1:1-5

From Paul, Silvanus and Timothy, to the Church in Thessalonika which is in God the Father and the Lord Jesus Christ; wishing you grace and peace from God the Father and the Lord Jesus Christ.
We always mention you in our prayers and thank God for you all, and constantly remember before God our Father how you have shown your faith in action, worked for love and persevered through hope, in our Lord Jesus Christ.

We know, brothers, that God loves you and that you have been chosen, because when we brought the Good News to you, it came to you not only as words, but as power and as the Holy Spirit and as utter conviction.

The word of the Lord.

Gospel Acclamation   Jn 17:17
Alleluia, alleluia!
Your word is truth, O Lord,
consecrate us in the truth.
Alleluia!

or   Phil 2:15-16
Alleluia, alleluia!
You will shine in the world like bright stars
because you are offering it the word of life.
Alleluia!

GOSPEL
A reading from the holy Gospel according to Matthew 22:15-21

The Pharisees went away to work out between them how to trap Jesus in what he said. And they sent their disciples to him, together with the Herodians, to say, 'Master, we know that you are an honest man and teach the way of God in an honest way, and that you are not afraid of anyone, because a man's rank means nothing to you. Tell us your opinion, then. Is it permissible to pay taxes to Caesar or not?' But Jesus was aware of their malice and replied, 'You hypocrites! Why do you set this trap for me? Let me see the money you pay the tax with.' They handed him a denarius and he said, 'Whose head is this? Whose name?' 'Caesar's' they replied. He then said to them, 'Very well, give back to Caesar what belongs to Caesar – and to God what belongs to God.'

The Gospel of the Lord.

The Creed is said.

Prayer over the Offerings
Grant us, Lord, we pray,
a sincere respect for your gifts,
that, through the purifying action of your grace,
we may be cleansed by the very mysteries we serve.
Through Christ our Lord.
Amen.

Communion Antiphon Cf. Ps 32:18-19
Behold, the eyes of the Lord
are on those who fear him,
who hope in his merciful love,
to rescue their souls from death,
to keep them alive in famine.

or Mk 10:45
The Son of Man has come
to give his life as a ransom for many.

Prayer after Communion
Grant, O Lord, we pray,
that, benefiting from participation in heavenly things,
we may be helped by what you give in this present age
and prepared for the gifts that are eternal.
Through Christ our Lord.
Amen.

THIRTIETH SUNDAY IN ORDINARY TIME   A

The Commandment of Love
Today, through the strength that Christ gives us, we can celebrate with the joy of the Holy Spirit that great commandment of love which once had to be imposed on people under threat of God's avenging anger.

Entrance Antiphon Cf. Ps 104:3-4
Let the hearts that seek the Lord rejoice;
turn to the Lord and his strength;
constantly seek his face.

Thirtieth Sunday in Ordinary Time, Year A

The Gloria in excelsis (Glory to God in the highest) is said.

Collect
Almighty ever-living God,
increase our faith, hope and charity,
and make us love what you command,
so that we may merit what you promise.
Through our Lord Jesus Christ, your Son,
who lives and reigns with you in the unity of the Holy Spirit,
one God, for ever and ever.
Amen.

FIRST READING
A reading from the book of Exodus 22:20-26

The Lord said to Moses, 'Tell the sons of Israel this, "You must not molest the stranger or oppress him, for you lived as strangers in the land of Egypt. You must not be harsh with the widow, or with the orphan; if you are harsh with them, they will surely cry out to me, and be sure I shall hear their cry; my anger will flare and I shall kill you with the sword, your own wives will be widows, your own children orphans.

"If you lend money to any of my people, to any poor man among you, you must not play the usurer with him: you must not demand interest from him.

"If you take another's cloak as a pledge, you must give it back to him before sunset. It is all the covering he has; it is the cloak he wraps his body in; what else would he sleep in? If he cries to me, I will listen, for I am full of pity."'

The word of the Lord.

Responsorial Psalm   Ps 17:2-4. 47. 51. R̷ v.2
R̷ **I love you, Lord, my strength.**

1   I love you, Lord, my strength,
    my rock, my fortress, my saviour.
    My God is the rock where I take refuge;
    my shield, my mighty help, my stronghold.
    The Lord is worthy of all praise:
    when I call I am saved from my foes.   R̷

2   Long life to the Lord, my rock!
    Praised be the God who saves me.
    He has given great victories to his king
    and shown his love for his anointed.   R̷

SECOND READING

A reading from the first letter of St Paul
to the Thessalonians   1:5-10

You observed the sort of life we lived when we were with you, which was for your instruction, and you were led to become imitators of us, and of the Lord; and it was with the joy of the Holy Spirit that you took to the gospel, in spite of the great opposition all round you. This has made you the great example to all believers in Macedonia and Achaia since it was from you that the word of the Lord started to spread – and not only throughout Macedonia and Achaia, for the news of your faith in God has spread everywhere. We do not need to tell other people about it: other people tell us how we started the work among you, how you broke with idolatry when you were converted to God and became servants of the real, living God; and how you are now waiting for Jesus, his Son, whom he raised from the dead, to come from heaven to save us from the retribution which is coming.

The word of the Lord.

Gospel Acclamation   Cf. Acts 16:14
Alleluia, alleluia!
Open our heart, O Lord,
to accept the words of your Son.
Alleluia!

or   Jn 14:23

Alleluia, alleluia!
If anyone loves me he will keep my word,
and my Father will love him,
and we shall come to him.
Alleluia!

GOSPEL

A reading from the holy Gospel according to Matthew   22:34-40

When the Pharisees heard that Jesus had silenced the Sadducees they got together and, to disconcert him, one of them put a question, 'Master, which is the greatest commandment of the Law?' Jesus said, 'You must love the Lord your God with all your heart, with all your soul, and with all your mind. This is the greatest and the first commandment. The second resembles it: you must love your neighbour as yourself. On these two commandments hang the whole Law, and the Prophets also.'

The Gospel of the Lord.

The Creed is said.

Prayer over the Offerings
Look, we pray, O Lord,
on the offerings we make to your majesty,
that whatever is done by us in your service
may be directed above all to your glory.
Through Christ our Lord.
Amen.

Communion Antiphon Cf. Ps 19:6
We will ring out our joy at your saving help
and exult in the name of our God.

or Eph 5:2

Christ loved us and gave himself up for us,
as a fragrant offering to God.

Prayer after Communion
May your Sacraments, O Lord, we pray,
perfect in us what lies within them,
that what we now celebrate in signs
we may one day possess in truth.
Through Christ our Lord.
Amen.

THIRTY-FIRST SUNDAY IN ORDINARY TIME A

God's Message of Eternal Life

How easy it is for human pride to falsify God's message, to make capital out of it. Today let us honour God in humility, sincerity and truth.

Entrance Antiphon Cf. Ps 37:22-23
Forsake me not, O Lord, my God;
be not far from me!
Make haste and come to my help,
O Lord, my strong salvation!

The Gloria in excelsis (Glory to God in the highest) is said.

Collect
Almighty and merciful God,
by whose gift your faithful offer you
right and praiseworthy service,
grant, we pray,
that we may hasten without stumbling

to receive the things you have promised.
Through our Lord Jesus Christ, your Son,
who lives and reigns with you in the unity of the Holy Spirit,
one God, for ever and ever.
Amen.

FIRST READING
A reading from the prophet Malachi 1:14 – 2:2. 8-10

I am a great king, says the Lord of hosts, and my name is feared throughout the nations. And now, priests, this warning is for you. If you do not listen, if you do not find it in your heart to glorify my name, says the Lord of hosts, I will send the curse on you and curse your very blessing. You have strayed from the way; you have caused many to stumble by your teaching. You have destroyed the covenant of Levi, says the Lord of hosts. And so I in my turn have made you contemptible and vile in the eyes of the whole people in repayment for the way you have not kept to my paths but have shown partiality in your administration.

Have we not all one Father? Did not one God create us? Why, then, do we break faith with one another, profaning the covenant of our ancestors?

The word of the Lord.

Responsorial Psalm
Ps 130

℟ **Keep my soul in peace before you, O Lord.**

1 O Lord, my heart is not proud
    nor haughty my eyes.
    I have not gone after things too great
    nor marvels beyond me. ℟

2 Truly I have set my soul
    in silence and peace.
    A weaned child on its mother's breast,
    even so is my soul. ℟

3 O Israel, hope in the Lord
    both now and for ever. ℟

SECOND READING

A reading from the first letter of St Paul to the Thessalonians 2:7-9. 13

Like a mother feeding and looking after her own children, we felt so devoted and protective towards you, and had come to love you so much, that we were eager to hand over to you not only the Good News but our whole lives as well. Let me remind you, brothers, how hard we used to work, slaving night and day so as not to be a burden on any one of you while we were proclaiming God's Good News to you.

Another reason why we constantly thank God for you is that as soon as you heard the message that we brought you as God's message, you accepted it for what it really is, God's message and not some human thinking; and it is still a living power among you who believe it.

The word of the Lord.

Gospel Acclamation 1 Sam 3:9; Jn 6:68

Alleluia, alleluia!
Speak, Lord, your servant is listening:
you have the message of eternal life.
Alleluia!

or Mt 23:9-10

Alleluia, alleluia!
You have only one Father, and he is in heaven;
you have only one Teacher, the Christ!
Alleluia!

GOSPEL

A reading from the holy Gospel according to Matthew 23:1-12

Addressing the people and his disciples Jesus said, 'The scribes and the Pharisees occupy the chair of Moses. You must therefore do what they tell you and listen to what they say; but do not be guided by what they do: since they do not practise what they preach. They tie up heavy burdens and lay them on men's shoulders, but will they lift a finger to move them? Not they! Everything they do is done to attract attention, like wearing broader phylacteries and longer tassels, like wanting to take the place of honour at banquets and the front seats in the synagogues, being greeted obsequiously in the market squares and having people call them Rabbi.

'You, however, must not allow yourselves to be called Rabbi, since you have only one Master, and you are all brothers. You must call no one on earth your father, since you have only one Father, and he is in heaven. Nor must you allow yourselves to be called teachers, for you have only one Teacher, the Christ. The greatest among you must be your servant. Anyone who exalts himself will be humbled, and anyone who humbles himself will be exalted.'

The Gospel of the Lord.

The Creed is said.

Prayer over the Offerings
May these sacrificial offerings, O Lord,
become for you a pure oblation,
and for us a holy outpouring of your mercy.
Through Christ our Lord.
Amen.

Communion Antiphon Cf. Ps 15:11
You will show me the path of life,
the fullness of joy in your presence, O Lord.

or Jn 6:58

Just as the living Father sent me
and I have life because of the Father,
so whoever feeds on me
shall have life because of me, says the Lord.

Prayer after Communion
May the working of your power, O Lord,
increase in us, we pray,
so that, renewed by these heavenly Sacraments,
we may be prepared by your gift
for receiving what they promise.
Through Christ our Lord.
Amen.

THIRTY-SECOND SUNDAY IN ORDINARY TIME A

The Bridegroom Is Here!

The whole of the Christian life, our response to the love of Christ, our waiting with joyful hope for his coming, is summed up in today's celebration in a single word: Wisdom.

Thirty-Second Sunday in Ordinary Time, Year A

Entrance Antiphon   Cf. Ps 87:3
Let my prayer come into your presence.
Incline your ear to my cry for help, O Lord.

The Gloria in excelsis (Glory to God in the highest) is said.

Collect
Almighty and merciful God,
graciously keep from us all adversity,
so that, unhindered in mind and body alike,
we may pursue in freedom of heart
the things that are yours.
Through our Lord Jesus Christ, your Son,
who lives and reigns with you in the unity of the Holy Spirit,
one God, for ever and ever.
Amen.

FIRST READING

A reading from the book of Wisdom   6:12-16

Wisdom is bright, and does not grow dim.
By those who love her she is readily seen,
and found by those who look for her.
Quick to anticipate those who desire her, she makes herself
    known to them.
Watch for her early and you will have no trouble;
you will find her sitting at your gates.
Even to think about her is understanding fully grown;
be on the alert for her and anxiety will quickly leave you.
She herself walks about looking for those who are worthy of her
and graciously shows herself to them as they go,
in every thought of theirs coming to meet them.

    The word of the Lord.

Responsorial Psalm   Ps 62:2-8. ℟ v.2
    ℟ **For you my soul is thirsting, O God, my God.**

1   O God, you are my God, for you I long;
     for you my soul is thirsting.
     My body pines for you
     like a dry, weary land without water.   ℟

2   So I gaze on you in the sanctuary
     to see your strength and your glory.
     For your love is better than life,
     my lips will speak your praise.   ℟

3   So I will bless you all my life,
    in your name I will lift up my hands.
    My soul shall be filled as with a banquet,
    my mouth shall praise you with joy. ℟

4   On my bed I remember you.
    On you I muse through the night
    for you have been my help;
    in the shadow of your wings I rejoice. ℟

SECOND READING

A reading from the first letter of St Paul to the Thessalonians   4:13-18

We want you to be quite certain, brothers, about those who have died, to make sure that you do not grieve about them, like the other people who have no hope. We believe that Jesus died and rose again, and that it will be the same for those who have died in Jesus: God will bring them with him. We can tell you this from the Lord's own teaching, that any of us who are left alive until the Lord's coming will not have any advantage over those who have died. At the trumpet of God, the voice of the archangel will call out the command and the Lord himself will come down from heaven; those who have died in Christ will be the first to rise, and then those of us who are still alive will be taken up in the clouds, together with them, to meet the Lord in the air. So we shall stay with the Lord for ever. With such thoughts as these you should comfort one another.

The word of the Lord.

Shorter Form, verses 13-14. Read between

Gospel Acclamation   Mt 24:42, 44
Alleluia, alleluia!
Stay awake and stand ready,
because you do not know the hour
when the Son of Man is coming.
Alleluia!

GOSPEL

A reading from the holy Gospel according to Matthew   25:1-13

Jesus told this parable to his disciples: 'The kingdom of heaven will be like this: Ten bridesmaids took their lamps and went to meet the bridegroom. Five of them were foolish and five were sensible: the foolish ones did take their lamps, but they brought no oil, whereas the sensible ones took flasks of oil as well as their lamps. The bridegroom was late, and they all grew drowsy and fell asleep. But at midnight there was a cry, "The bridegroom is here! Go out and meet him." At this, all those bridesmaids woke up and trimmed their lamps, and the foolish ones said to the sensible ones, "Give us some of your oil: our lamps are going out." But they replied, "There may not be enough for us and for you; you had better go to those who sell it and buy some for yourselves." They had gone off to buy it when the bridegroom arrived. Those who were ready went in with him to the wedding hall and the door was closed. The other bridesmaids arrived later. "Lord, Lord," they said "open the door for us." But he replied, "I tell you solemnly, I do not know you." So stay awake, because you do not know either the day or the hour.'

The Gospel of the Lord.

The Creed is said.

Prayer over the Offerings
Look with favour, we pray, O Lord,
upon the sacrificial gifts offered here,
that, celebrating in mystery the Passion of your Son,
we may honour it with loving devotion.
Through Christ our Lord.
Amen.

Communion Antiphon Cf. Ps 22:1-2
The Lord is my shepherd; there is nothing I shall want.
Fresh and green are the pastures where he gives me repose,
near restful waters he leads me.

or Cf. Lk 24:35

The disciples recognized the Lord Jesus in the breaking of bread.

Prayer after Communion
Nourished by this sacred gift, O Lord,
we give you thanks and beseech your mercy,
that, by the pouring forth of your Spirit,
the grace of integrity may endure
in those your heavenly power has entered.
Through Christ our Lord.
Amen.

THIRTY-THIRD SUNDAY IN ORDINARY TIME   A

Christ, the Head of His Household

Christ's family, the Church, today holds festival in honour of its Head, and brings to him the talents of a good wife, devoted children, and faithful servants.

Entrance Antiphon   Jer 29:11-12. 14
The Lord said: I think thoughts of peace and not of affliction.
You will call upon me, and I will answer you,
and I will lead back your captives from every place.

The Gloria in excelsis (Glory to God in the highest) is said.

Collect
Grant us, we pray, O Lord our God,
the constant gladness of being devoted to you,
for it is full and lasting happiness
to serve with constancy
the author of all that is good.
Through our Lord Jesus Christ, your Son,
who lives and reigns with you in the unity of the Holy Spirit,
one God, for ever and ever.
Amen.

FIRST READING

A reading from the book of Proverbs   31:10-13. 19-20. 30-31

A perfect wife – who can find her?
She is far beyond the price of pearls.
Her husband's heart has confidence in her,
from her he will derive no little profit.
Advantage and not hurt she brings him
all the days of her life.
She is always busy with wool and with flax,
she does her work with eager hands.
She sets her hands to the distaff,
her fingers grasp the spindle.
She holds out her hand to the poor,
she opens her arms to the needy.
Charm is deceitful, and beauty empty;
the woman who is wise is the one to praise.
Give her a share in what her hands have worked for,
and let her works tell her praises at the city gates.

     The word of the Lord.

Thirty-Third Sunday in Ordinary Time, Year A

Responsorial Psalm Ps 127:1-5. ℟ v.1
℟ **O blessed are those who fear the Lord.**

1 O blessed are those who fear the Lord
   and walk in his ways!
   By the labour of your hands you shall eat.
   You will be happy and prosper. ℟

2 Your wife like a fruitful vine
   in the heart of your house;
   your children like shoots of the olive,
   around your table. ℟

3 Indeed thus shall be blessed
   the man who fears the Lord.
   May the Lord bless you from Zion
   in a happy Jerusalem
   all the days of your life. ℟

SECOND READING
A reading from the first letter of St Paul to the Thessalonians 5:1-6

You will not be expecting us to write anything to you, brothers, about 'times and seasons', since you know very well that the Day of the Lord is going to come like a thief in the night. It is when people are saying, 'How quiet and peaceful it is' that the worst suddenly happens, as suddenly as labour pains come on a pregnant woman; and there will be no way for anybody to evade it.

But it is not as if you live in the dark, my brothers, for that Day to overtake you like a thief. No, you are all sons of light and sons of the day: we do not belong to the night or to darkness, so we should not go on sleeping, as everyone else does, but stay wide awake and sober.

The word of the Lord.

Gospel Acclamation Apoc 2:10
   Alleluia, alleluia!
   Even if you have to die, says the Lord,
   keep faithful, and I will give you
   the crown of life.
   Alleluia!

or Jn 15:4.5

> Alleluia, alleluia!
> Make your home in me, as I make mine in you,
> says the Lord.
> Whoever remains in me bears fruit in plenty.
> Alleluia!

GOSPEL
A reading from the holy Gospel according to Matthew 25:14-30

Jesus spoke this parable to his disciples: 'The kingdom of heaven is like a man on his way abroad who summoned his servants and entrusted his property to them. To one he gave five talents, to another two, to a third one; each in proportion to his ability. Then he set out.

The man who had received the five talents promptly went and traded with them and made five more. The man who had received two made two more in the same way. But the man who had received one went off and dug a hole in the ground and hid his master's money.

Now a long time after, the master of those servants came back and went through his accounts with them. The man who had received the five talents came forward bringing five more. "Sir," he said " you entrusted me with five talents; here are five more than I have made."

His master said to him, "Well done, good and faithful servant; you have shown you can be faithful in small things, I will trust you with greater; come and join in your master's happiness." Next the man with the two talents came forward. "Sir," he said "you entrusted me with two talents; here are two more that I have made." His master said to him, "Well done, good and faithful servant; you have shown you can be faithful in small things, I will trust you with greater; come and join in your master's happiness." Last came forward the man who had the one talent. "Sir," said he "I had heard you were a hard man, reaping where you have not sown and gathering where you have not scattered; so I was afraid, and I went off and hid your talent in the ground. Here it is; it was yours, you have it back. " But his master answered him, "You wicked and lazy servant! So you knew that I reap where I have not sown and gather where I have not scattered? Well then, you should have deposited my money with the bankers, and on my return I would have recovered my capital with interest. So now, take the talent from him and give it to the man who has the five talents. For to everyone who has will be given more, and he will have more than enough; but from the man who has not, even what he has will be taken away. As for this good-for-nothing servant, throw him out into the dark, where there will be weeping and grinding of teeth." '

The Gospel of the Lord.

Shorter Form, verses 14-15, 19-20. Read between

The Creed is said.

Prayer over the Offerings
Grant, O Lord, we pray,
that what we offer in the sight of your majesty
may obtain for us the grace of being devoted to you
and gain us the prize of everlasting happiness.
Through Christ our Lord.
Amen.

Communion Antiphon   Ps 72:28
To be near God is my happiness,
to place my hope in God the Lord.

or   Mk 11:23-24

Amen, I say to you, whatever you ask in prayer,
believe that you will receive,
and it shall be given to you, says the Lord.

Prayer after Communion
We have partaken of the gifts of this sacred mystery,
humbly imploring, O Lord,
that what your Son commanded us to do
in memory of him
may bring us growth in charity.
Through Christ our Lord.
Amen.

Last Sunday in Ordinary Time
OUR LORD JESUS CHRIST, KING OF THE UNIVERSE A
Solemnity

Christ, the King

Christ is a King on the model of the homeric kings who called themselves 'shepherds of the people'. As a royal shepherd he is leading us to the Kingdom of his Father.

Entrance Antiphon ℟ v.5:12; 1:6
How worthy is the Lamb who was slain,
to receive power and divinity,
and wisdom and strength and honour.
To him belong glory and power for ever and ever.

The Gloria in excelsis (Glory to God in the highest) is said.

Collect
Almighty ever-living God,
whose will is to restore all things
in your beloved Son, the King of the universe,
grant, we pray,
that the whole creation, set free from slavery,
may render your majesty service
and ceaselessly proclaim your praise.
Through our Lord Jesus Christ, your Son,
who lives and reigns with you in the unity of the Holy Spirit,
one God, for ever and ever.
Amen.

FIRST READING
A reading from the prophet Ezekiel 34:11-12. 15-17

The Lord says this: I am going to look after my flock myself and keep all of it in view. As a shepherd keeps all his flock in view when he stands up in the middle of his scattered sheep, so shall I keep my sheep in view. I shall rescue them from wherever they have been scattered during the mist and darkness. I myself will pasture my sheep, I myself will show them where to rest – it is the Lord who speaks. I shall look for the lost one, bring back the stray, bandage the wounded and make the weak strong. I shall watch over the fat and healthy. I shall be a true shepherd to them.

As for you, my sheep, the Lord says this: I will judge between sheep and sheep, between rams and he-goats.

The word of the Lord.

Responsorial Psalm
Ps 22:1-3. 5-6. ℟ v.1

℟ **The Lord is my shepherd;
there is nothing I shall want.**

1 The Lord is my shepherd;
   there is nothing I shall want.
   Fresh and green are the pastures
   where he gives me repose.   ℟

2 Near restful waters he leads me,
   to revive my drooping spirit.
   He guides me along the right path;
   he is true to his name.   ℟

3 You have prepared a banquet for me
   in the sight of my foes.
   My head you have anointed with oil;
   my cup is overflowing.   ℟

4 Surely goodness and kindness shall follow me
   all the days of my life.
   In the Lord's own house shall I dwell
   for ever and ever.   ℟

SECOND READING
A reading from the first letter of St Paul 15:20-26. 28
to the Corinthians

Christ has been raised from the dead, the first-fruits of all who have fallen asleep. Death came through one man and in the same way the resurrection of the dead has come through one man. Just as all men die in Adam, so all men will be brought to life in Christ; but all of them in their proper order: Christ as the first-fruits and then, after the coming of Christ, those who belong to him. After that will come the end, when he hands over the kingdom to God the Father, having done away with every sovereignty, authority and power. For he must be king until he has put all his enemies under his feet and the last of the enemies to be destroyed is death. And when everything is subjected to him, then the Son himself will be subject in his turn to the One who subjected all things to him, so that God may be all in all.

The word of the Lord.

Gospel Acclamation   Mk 11:10
Alleluia, alleluia!
Blessings on him who comes in the name of the Lord!
Blessings on the coming kingdom of our father David!
Alleluia!

GOSPEL
A reading from the holy Gospel according to Matthew   25:31-46

Jesus said to his disciples: 'When the Son of Man comes in his glory, escorted by all the angels, then he will take his seat on his throne of glory. All the nations will be assembled before him and he will separate men one from another as the shepherd separates sheep from goats. He will place the sheep on his right hand and the goats on his left. Then the King will say to those on his right hand, "Come, you whom my Father has blessed, take for your heritage the kingdom prepared for you since the foundation of the world. For I was hungry and you gave me food; I was thirsty and you gave me drink; I was a stranger and you made me welcome; naked and you clothed me, sick and you visited me, in prison and you came to see me." Then the virtuous will say to him in reply, "Lord, when did we see you hungry and feed you; or thirsty and give you drink? When did we see you a stranger and make you welcome; naked and clothe you; sick or in prison and go to see you?" And the King will answer, "I tell you solemnly, in so far as you did this to one of the least of these brothers of mine, you did it to me." Next he will say to those on his left hand, "Go away from me, with your curse upon you, to the eternal fire prepared for the devil and his angels. For I was hungry and you never gave me food; I was thirsty and you never gave me anything to drink; I was a stranger and you never made me welcome, naked and you never clothed me, sick and in prison and you never visited me." Then it will be their turn to ask, "Lord, when did we see you hungry or thirsty, a stranger or naked, sick or in prison, and did not come to your help?" Then he will answer, "I tell you solemnly, in so far as you neglected to do this to one of the least of these, you neglected to do it to me." And they will go away to eternal punishment, and the virtuous to eternal life.'

The Gospel of the Lord.

Our Lord Jesus Christ, King of the Universe, Year A

The Creed is said.

Prayer over the Offerings
As we offer you, O Lord, the sacrifice
by which the human race is reconciled to you,
we humbly pray,
that your Son himself may bestow on all nations
the gifts of unity and peace.
Through Christ our Lord.
Amen.

Preface of Christ, King of the Universe, pp.40-41.

Communion Antiphon Ps 28:10-11
The Lord sits as King for ever.
The Lord will bless his people with peace.

Prayer after Communion
Having received the food of immortality,
we ask, O Lord,
that, glorying in obedience
to the commands of Christ, the King of the universe,
we may live with him eternally in his heavenly Kingdom.
Who lives and reigns for ever and ever.
Amen.

APPENDIX TO YEAR A

MUSICAL SETTINGS
PALM SUNDAY

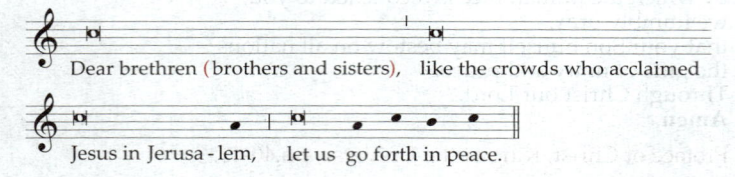

Dear brethren (brothers and sisters), like the crowds who acclaimed Jesus in Jerusalem, let us go forth in peace.

THE SHOWING OF THE HOLY CROSS

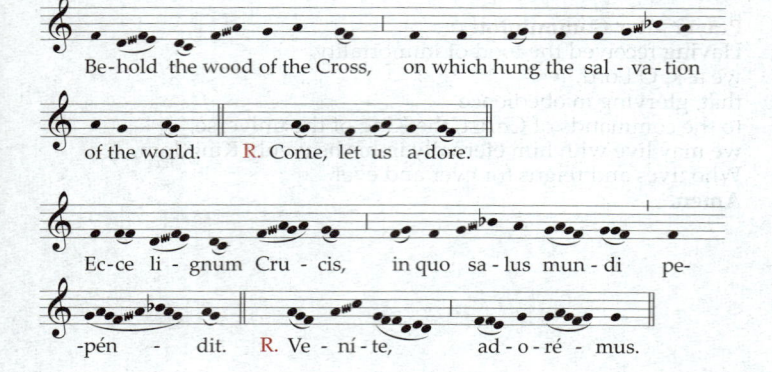

Behold the wood of the Cross, on which hung the salvation of the world. ℟. Come, let us adore.

Ecce lignum Crucis, in quo salus mundi pependit. ℟. Veníte, adorémus.

VIGIL PROCESSION

The Light of Christ.

Lumen Christi.

EXSULTET (LONG FORM)

Ex-ult, let them ex-ult, the hosts of heav-en, ex-ult, let Angel minis-ters of God ex-ult, let the trum-pet of sal-va-tion sound a-loud our might-y King's tri-umph! Be glad, let earth be glad, as glo-ry floods her, a-blaze with light from her e-ter-nal King, let all cor-ners of the earth be glad, know-ing an end to gloom and dark-ness. Re-joice, let Mother Church al-so re-joice, arrayed with the lightning of his glo-ry, let this ho-ly build-ing shake with joy, filled with the might-y voic-es of the peo-ples. (There-fore, dearest friends, standing in the awe-some glo-ry of this ho-ly light, in-voke with me, I ask you, the mer-cy of God al-might-y, that he, who has been pleased to number me, though un-wor-thy, a-mong the Le-vites, may pour into me his light un-shad-owed,

that I may sing this can-dle's per-fect prais-es.)

(V. The Lord be with you. R. And with your spir-it.)

V. Lift up your hearts. R. We lift them up to the Lord.

V. Let us give thanks to the Lord our God. R. It is right and just.

It is truly right and just, with ardent love of mind and heart and

with devoted service of our voice, to acclaim our God in-vis-i-ble,

the al-might-y Fa-ther, and Jesus Christ, our Lord, his Son, his

On-ly Be-got-ten. Who for our sake paid Adam's debt to the e-

-ter-nal Fa-ther, and, pouring out his own dear Blood, wiped clean

the re-cord of our an-cient sin-ful-ness. These then are the feasts

Musical Settings   601

of Pass-o-ver, in which is slain the Lamb, the one true Lamb, whose Blood anoints the door-posts of be-liev-ers. This is the night, when once you led our fore-bears, Is-ra-el's chil-dren, from slaver-y in E-gypt and made them pass dry-shod through the Red Sea. This is the night that with a pil-lar of fire banished the dark-ness of sin. This is the night that even now, throughout the world, sets Christian believers apart from world-ly vic-es and from the gloom of sin, lead-ing them to grace and join-ing them to his ho-ly ones. This is the night, when Christ broke the prison-bars of death and rose vic-to-ri-ous from the un-der-world. Our birth would have been no gain, had we not been redeemed. O wonder of your humble care for us! O love, O charity beyond all telling, to ransom a slave you gave away your Son! O truly necessary sin of Adam, destroyed completely by the Death of Christ! O happy fault that earned so great, so glorious a Redeemer!

O truly blessed night, worthy alone to know the time and hour when Christ rose from the underworld! This is the night of which it is written: The night shall be as bright as day, dazzling is the night for me, and full of gladness. The sanctifying power of this night dispels wickedness, washes faults away, restores innocence to the fallen, and joy to mourners, drives out ha-tred, fos-ters con-cord, and brings down the might-y.

On this, your night of grace, O ho-ly Fa-ther, accept this candle, a

sol-emn of-fer-ing, the work of bees and of your serv-ants' hands,

an evening sacri-fice of praise, this gift from your most ho-ly

Church. But now we know the praises of this pil-lar, which glow-

-ing fire ig-nites for God's hon-our, a fire into many flames

di-vid-ed, yet nev-er dimmed by shar-ing of its light, for it is

fed by melt-ing wax, drawn out by moth-er bees to build a torch

so pre-cious. O truly bless-ed night, when things of heaven

are wed to those of earth, and di-vine to the hu-man.

There-fore, O Lord, we pray you that this candle, hallowed to the honor of your name, may persevere undimmed, to overcome the darkness of this night. Receive it as a pleasing fragrance, and let it mingle with the lights of heaven. May this flame be found still burning by the Morning Star: the one Morning Star who never sets, Christ your Son, who, coming back from death's domain, has shed his peaceful light on humanity, and lives and reigns for ever and ever. R. Amen.

EXSULTET (SHORT FORM)

Exult, let them exult, the hosts of heaven, exult, let Angel ministers of God exult, let the trumpet of salvation sound aloud our mighty King's triumph! Be glad, let earth be glad, as glory floods her, ablaze with light from her eternal King, let all cor-ners of the earth be glad, know-ing an end to gloom and dark-ness. Re-joice, let Mother Church al-so re-joice, arrayed with the lightning of his glo-ry, let this ho-ly build-ing shake with joy, filled with the might-y voic-es of the peo-ples.

(V. The Lord be with you. R. And with your spir-it.)

V. Lift up your hearts. R. We lift them up to the Lord.

V. Let us give thanks to the Lord our God. R. It is right and just.

It is truly right and just, with ardent love of mind and heart and with devoted service of our voice, to acclaim our God in-vis-i-ble, the al-might-y Fa-ther, and Jesus Christ, our Lord, his Son, his On-ly Be-got-ten. Who for our sake paid Adam's debt to the e--ter-nal Fa-ther, and, pouring out his own dear Blood, wiped clean the re-cord of our an-cient sin-ful-ness. These then are the feasts of Pass-o-ver, in which is slain the Lamb, the one true Lamb, whose Blood anoints the door-posts of be-liev-ers. This is the night, when once you led our fore-bears, Is-ra-el's chil-dren, from slaver-y in E-gypt and made them pass dry-shod through the Red Sea. This is the night that with a pil-lar of fire banished the dark-ness of sin. This is the night that even now, throughout the world, sets Christian believers apart from world-ly vic-es and from the gloom of sin, lead-ing them to grace and join-ing them to his ho-ly ones. This is the night, when Christ broke the prison-bars of death and rose vic-to-ri-ous from the un-der-world. O wonder of your hum-ble care for us!

O love, O char-i-ty be-yond all tell-ing, to ran-som a slave you gave a-way your Son! O tru-ly nec-es-sar-y sin of Ad-am, de-stroyed com-plete-ly by the Death of Christ! O hap-py fault that earned so great, so glo-ri-ous a Re-deem-er! The sanctifying power of this night dis-pels wick-ed-ness, washes faults a-way, re-stores innocence to the fall-en, and joy to mourn-ers, O truly bless-ed night, when things of heaven are wed to those of earth, and di-vine to the hu-man.

On this, your night of grace, O ho-ly Fa-ther, accept this candle, a sol-emn of-fer-ing, the work of bees and of your serv-ants' hands, an evening sacri-fice of praise, this gift from your most ho-ly Church.

There-fore, O Lord, we pray you that this candle, hallowed to the honour of your name, may perse-vere un-dimmed, to overcome the dark-ness of this night. Re-ceive it as a pleas-ing fra-grance, and let it min-gle with the lights of heav-en. May this flame be found still burn-ing by the Morn-ing Star: the one Morning Star who nev-er sets, Christ your Son, who, coming back from death's do-main, has shed his peaceful light on hu-man-i-ty, and lives and reigns for ev-er and ev-er. R. A-men.

GLORIA

Gló-ri-a in ex-cél-sis De-o.

BAPTISMAL LITURGY

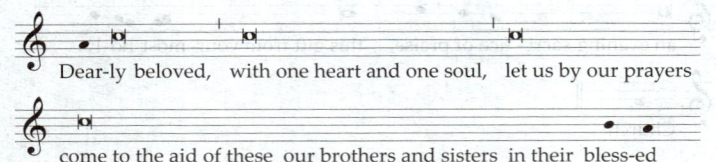

Dear-ly beloved, with one heart and one soul, let us by our prayers come to the aid of these our brothers and sisters in their bless-ed hope, so that, as they approach the font of re-birth, the almighty Father may bestow on them all his merciful help.

Dearly beloved, let us humbly invoke upon this font the grace of God the almighty Father, that those who from it are born anew may be numbered among the children of adoption in Christ.

BLESSING OF BAPTISMAL WATER

O God, who by invisible power accomplish a wondrous effect through sacramental signs and who in many ways have prepared water, your creation, to show forth the grace of Baptism;

O God, whose Spirit in the first moments of the world's creation hovered over the waters, so that the very substance of water would even then take to itself the power to sanctify;

O God, who by the outpouring of the flood forshadowed regeneration, so that from the mystery of one and the same ele-ment of wa-ter would come an end to vice and a be-gin-ning of vir-tue; O God, who caused the children of Abraham to pass dry-shod through through the Red Sea, so that the chosen people, set free from slav--ery to Phar-aoh, would prefigure the people of the bap-tized; O God, whose Son, baptized by John in the waters of the Jordan, was a--nointed with the Ho-ly Spir-it, and, as he hung upon the Cross, gave forth water from his side a-long with blood, and after his Res--urrection, commanded his dis-ci-ples: 'Go forth, teach all na-tions, baptizing them in the name of the Father and of the Son and of the

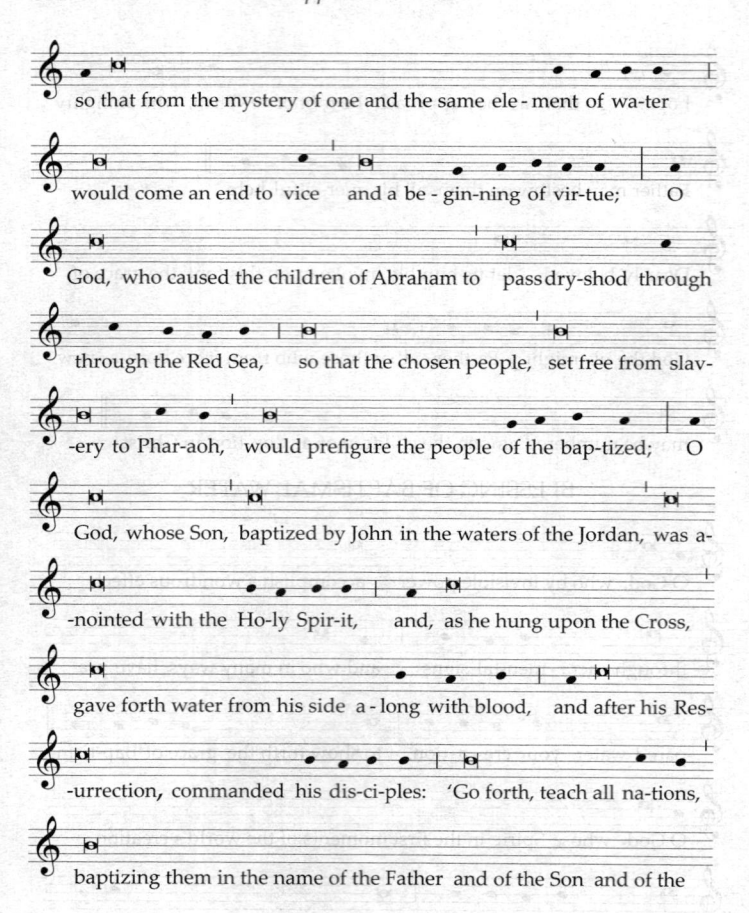

Ho-ly Spir-it,' look now, we pray, upon the face of your Church and graciously un-seal for her the foun-tain of Bap-tism. May this water receive by the Holy Spirit the grace of your Only Be-got-ten Son, so that human nature, created in your im-age and washed clean through the Sacrament of Baptism from all the squalor of the life of old, may be found worthy to rise to the life of new-born chil-dren through water and the Ho-ly Spir-it.

May the power of the Holy Spirit, O Lord, we pray, come down through your Son into the fullness of this font, so that all who have been buried with Christ by Baptism in-to death may rise again to life with him. Who lives and reigns with you in the unity of the Ho-ly Spir-it, one God, for ev-er and ev-er.

R. A-men.

Springs of wa-ter, bless the Lord; praise and exalt him above all for e-ver.

Dear brothers and sisters, let us humbly beseech the Lord our God to bless this water he has cre-at-ed, which will be sprinkled upon us as a memorial of our Bap-tism. May he graciously renew us, that we may remain faithful to the Spirit whom we have re-ceived.

Lord our God, in your mercy be present to your people who keep vigil on this most sacred night, and, for us who recall the wondrous work of our creation and the still greater work of our redemption, graciously bless this wa-ter. For you created water to make the fields fruit-ful and to refresh and cleanse our bod-ies. You also made water the instrument of your mer-cy: for through water you freed your people from slavery and quenched their thirst in the de-sert; through water the Prophets proclaimed the new covenant you were to enter upon with the human race; and last of all, through water, which Christ made holy in the Jor-dan, you have renewed our cor--rupted nature in the bath of re-gen-er-a-tion. There-fore, may this water be for us a memorial of the Baptism we have re-ceived, and grant that we may share in the gladness of our brothers and sisters, who at Easter have re-ceived their Baptism Through Christ our Lord. R. A-men.

I saw water flowing from the Temple, from its right-hand side, alleluia; and all to whom this water came were saved and shall say: Alleluia, alleluia.

Vidi aquam egrediéntem de templo, a látere dextro, allelúia; et omnes, ad quos pervénit aqua ista, salvi facti sunt et dicent: Allelúia, allelúia.

SUNDAY MASSES

Year B

SUNDAY MASSES

Year B

THE SEASON OF ADVENT

FIRST SUNDAY OF ADVENT   B

Waiting for the Lord

Our life is a long vigil, waiting for the Lord to be revealed in all his glory. We wait with longing and with 'joyful hope', for his Spirit is with us, and we know that God is faithful to his promises.

Entrance Antiphon   Cf. Ps 24:1-3
To you, I lift up my soul, O my God.
In you, I have trusted; let me not be put to shame.
Nor let my enemies exult over me;
and let none who hope in you be put to shame.

The Gloria in excelsis (Glory to God in the highest) is not said.

Collect
Grant your faithful, we pray, almighty God,
the resolve to run forth to meet your Christ
with righteous deeds at his coming,
so that, gathered at his right hand,
they may be worthy to possess the heavenly Kingdom.
Through our Lord Jesus Christ, your Son,
who lives and reigns with you in the unity of the Holy Spirit,
one God, for ever and ever.
Amen.

FIRST READING
A reading from the prophet Isaiah   63:16-17; 64:1. 3-8

You, Lord, yourself are our Father,
Our Redeemer is your ancient name.
Why, Lord, leave us to stray from your ways

and harden our hearts against fearing you?
Return, for the sake of your servants,
the tribes of your inheritance.
Oh, that you would tear the heavens open and come down
– at your Presence the mountains would melt.
No ear has heard,
no eye has seen
any god but you act like this
for those who trust him.
You guide those who act with integrity
and keep your ways in mind.
You were angry when we were sinners;
we had long been rebels against you.
We were all like men unclean,
all that integrity of ours like filthy clothing.
We have all withered like leaves
and our sins blew us away like the wind.
No one invoked your name
or roused himself to catch hold of you.
For you hid your face from us
and gave us up to the power of our sins.
And yet, Lord, you are our Father;
we the clay, you the potter,
we are all the work of your hand.

The word of the Lord.

Responsional Psalm   Ps 79:2-3. 15-16. 18-19. R̸ v.4
    R̸ **God of hosts, bring us back;**
       let your face shine on us and we shall be saved.

1   O shepherd of Israel, hear us,
     shine forth from your cherubim throne.
     O Lord, rouse up your might,
     O Lord, come to our help.   R̸

2   God of hosts, turn again, we implore,
     look down from heaven and see.
     Visit this vine and protect it,
     the vine your right hand has planted.   R̸

3   May your hand be on the man you have chosen,
     the man you have given your strength.
     And we shall never forsake you again:
     give us life that we may call upon your name.   R̸

First Sunday of Advent, Year B

SECOND READING
A reading from the first letter of St Paul to the Corinthians   1:3-9

May God our Father and the Lord Jesus Christ send you grace and peace.

I never stop thanking God for all the graces you have received through Jesus Christ. I thank him that you have been enriched in so many ways, especially in your teachers and preachers; the witness to Christ has indeed been strong among you so that you will not be without any of the gifts of the Spirit while you are waiting for our Lord Jesus Christ to be revealed; and he will keep you steady and without blame until the last day, the day of our Lord Jesus Christ, because God by calling you has joined you to his Son, Jesus Christ; and God is faithful.

The word of the Lord.

Gospel Acclamation   Ps 84:8
Alleluia, alleluia!
Let us see, O Lord, your mercy
and give us your saving help.
Alleluia!

GOSPEL
A reading from the holy Gospel according to Mark   13:33-37

Jesus said to his disciples: 'Be on your guard, stay awake, because you never know when the time will come. It is like a man travelling abroad: he has gone from home, and left his servants in charge, each with his own task; and he has told the doorkeeper to stay awake. So stay awake, because you do not know when the master of the house is coming, evening, midnight, cockcrow, dawn; if he comes unexpectedly, he must not find you asleep. And what I say to you I say to all: Stay awake!'

The Gospel of the Lord.

The Creed is said.

Prayer over the Offerings
Accept, we pray, O Lord, these offerings we make,
gathered from among your gifts to us,
and may what you grant us to celebrate devoutly here below
gain for us the prize of eternal redemption.
Through Christ our Lord.
Amen.

Preface I of Advent, p.19.

Communion Antiphon
Ps 84:13
The Lord will bestow his bounty, and our earth shall yield its increase.

Prayer after Communion
May these mysteries, O Lord,
in which we have participated,
profit us, we pray,
for even now, as we walk amid passing things,
you teach us by them to love the things of heaven
and hold fast to what endures.
Through Christ our Lord.
Amen.

A formula of Solemn Blessing, pp.94-5, may be used.

SECOND SUNDAY OF ADVENT   B

The Good News

Today we celebrate the Good News of God's incredible love for all his people. Every messenger of this Good News says the same thing: he is coming to save you; he will make all things new; prepare a way for him; take him to your heart.

Entrance Antiphon
Cf. Is 30:19. 30
O people of Sion, behold,
the Lord will come to save the nations,
and the Lord will make the glory of his voice heard
in the joy of your heart.

The Gloria in excelsis (Glory to God in the highest) is not said.

Collect
Almighty and merciful God,
may no earthly undertaking hinder those
who set out in haste to meet your Son,
but may our learning of heavenly wisdom
gain us admittance to his company.
Who lives and reigns with you in the unity of the Holy Spirit,
one God, for ever and ever.
Amen.

Second Sunday of Advent, Year B

FIRST READING
A reading from the prophet Isaiah   40:1-5. 9-11

'Console my people, console them'
says your God.
'Speak to the heart of Jerusalem
and call to her
that her time of service is ended,
that her sin is atoned for,
that she has received from the hand of the Lord
double punishment for all her crimes.'

A voice cries, 'Prepare in the wilderness
a way for the Lord.
Make a straight highway for our God
across the desert.
Let every valley be filled in,
every mountain and hill be laid low,
let every cliff become a plain,
and the ridges a valley;
then the glory of the Lord shall be revealed
and all mankind shall see it;
for the mouth of the Lord has spoken.'

Go up on a high mountain,
joyful messenger to Zion.
Shout with a loud voice,
joyful messenger to Jerusalem.
Shout without fear,
say to the towns of Judah,
'Here is your God.'
Here is the Lord coming with power,
his arm subduing all things to him.
The prize of his victory is with him,
his trophies all go before him.
He is like a shepherd feeding his flock,
gathering lambs in his arms,
holding them against his breast
and leading to their rest the mother ewes.

The word of the Lord.

Responsional Psalm Ps 84:9-14. ℟ v.8

℟ **Let us see, O Lord, your mercy
and give us your saving help.**

1 I will hear what the Lord God has to say,
   a voice that speaks of peace,
   peace for his people.
   His help is near for those who fear him
   and his glory will dwell in our land. ℟

2 Mercy and faithfulness have met;
   justice and peace have embraced.
   Faithfulness shall spring from the earth
   and justice look down from heaven. ℟

3 The Lord will make us prosper
   and our earth shall yield its fruit.
   Justice shall march before him
   and peace shall follow his steps. ℟

SECOND READING
A reading from the second letter of St Peter 3:8-14

There is one thing, my friends, that you must never forget: that with the Lord, 'a day' can mean a thousand years, and a thousand years is like a day. The Lord is not being slow to carry out his promises, as anybody else might be called slow; but he is being patient with you all, wanting nobody to be lost and everybody to be brought to change his ways. The Day of the Lord will come like a thief, and then with a roar the sky will vanish, the elements will catch fire and fall apart, the earth and all that it contains will be burnt up.

Since everything is coming to an end like this, you should be living holy and saintly lives while you wait and long for the Day of God to come, when the sky will dissolve in flames and the elements melt in the heat. What we are waiting for is what he promised; the new heavens and new earth, the place where righteousness will be at home. So then, my friends, while you are waiting, do your best to live lives without spot or stain so that he will find you at peace.

The word of the Lord.

Gospel Acclamation Lk 3:4. 6
  Alleluia, alleluia!
  Prepare a way for the Lord.
  make his paths straight,

Second Sunday of Advent, Year B

and all mankind shall see the salvation of God.
Alleluia!

GOSPEL
A reading from the holy Gospel according to Mark　　　1:1-8

The beginning of the Good News about Jesus Christ, the Son of God. It is written in the book of the prophet Isaiah:

> Look, I am going to send my messenger before you;
> he will prepare your way.
> A voice cries in the wilderness:
> Prepare a way for the Lord,
> make his paths straight,

and so it was that John the Baptist appeared in the wilderness, proclaiming a baptism of repentance for the forgiveness of sins. All Judaea and all the people of Jerusalem made their way to him, and as they were baptised by him in the river Jordan they confessed their sins. John wore a garment of camel-skin, and he lived on locusts and wild honey. In the course of his preaching he said, 'Someone is following me, someone who is more powerful than I am, and I am not fit to kneel down and undo the strap of his sandals. I have baptised you with water, but he will baptise you with the Holy Spirit.'

The Gospel of the Lord.

The Creed is said.

Prayer over the Offerings
Be pleased, O Lord, with our humble prayers and offerings,
and, since we have no merits to plead our cause,
come, we pray, to our rescue
with the protection of your mercy.
Through Christ our Lord.
Amen.

Preface I of Advent, p.19.

Communion Antiphon　　　Bar 5:5; 4:36
Jerusalem, arise and stand upon the heights,
and behold the joy which comes to you from God.

Prayer after Communion
Replenished by the food of spiritual nourishment,
we humbly beseech you, O Lord,
that, through our partaking in this mystery,
you may teach us to judge wisely the things of earth
and hold firm to the things of heaven.
Through Christ our Lord.
Amen.

A formula of Solemn Blessing, pp.94-5, may be used.

THIRD SUNDAY OF ADVENT   B

Our Joy In Christ

We celebrate our joy in Christ's redeeming work among us, realising that he who is to come is indeed already with us, 'unknown to us.'

In this Mass the colour violet or rose is used.

Entrance Antiphon   Phil 4:4-5
Rejoice in the Lord always; again I say, rejoice.
Indeed, the Lord is near.

The Gloria in excelsis (Glory to God in the highest) is not said.

Collect

O God, who see how your people
faithfully await the feast of the Lord's Nativity,
enable us, we pray,
to attain the joys of so great a salvation
and to celebrate them always
with solemn worship and glad rejoicing.
Through our Lord Jesus Christ, your Son,
who lives and reigns with you in the unity of the Holy Spirit,
one God, for ever and ever.
Amen.

FIRST READING

A reading from the prophet Isaiah   61:1-2. 10-11

The spirit of the Lord has been given to me,
for the Lord has anointed me.
He has sent me to bring good news to the poor,
to bind up hearts that are broken;

Third Sunday of Advent, Year B

to proclaim liberty to captives,
freedom to those in prison;
to proclaim a year of favour from the Lord.

'I exult for joy in the Lord,
my soul rejoices in my God,
for he has clothed me in the garments of salvation,
he has wrapped me in the cloak of integrity,
like a bridegroom wearing his wreath,
like a bride adorned in her jewels.

'For as the earth makes fresh things grow,
as a garden makes seeds spring up,
so will the Lord make both integrity and praise
spring up in the sight of the nations.'

The word of the Lord.

Responsorial Psalm   Lk 1:46-50. 53-54. ℟ Is 61:10

℟ **My soul rejoices in my God.**

1   My soul glorifies the Lord,
    my spirit rejoices in God, my Saviour.
    He looks on his servant in her nothingness;
    henceforth all ages will call me blessed. ℟

2   The Almighty works marvels for me.
    Holy his name!
    His mercy is from age to age,
    on those who fear him. ℟

3   He fills the starving with good things,
    sends the rich away empty.
    He protects Israel, his servant,
    remembering his mercy. ℟

SECOND READING

A reading from the first letter of St Paul   5:16-24
to the Thessalonians

Be happy at all times; pray constantly; and for all things give thanks to God, because this is what God expects you to do in Christ Jesus.

Never try to suppress the Spirit or treat the gift of prophecy with contempt; think before you do anything – hold on to what is good and avoid every form of evil.

May the God of peace make you perfect and holy; and may you all be kept safe and blameless, spirit, soul and body, for the coming of our Lord Jesus Christ. God has called you and he will not fail you.

The word of the Lord.

Gospel Acclamation Is 61:1 (Lk 4:18)
Alleluia, alleluia!
The spirit of the Lord has been given to me.
He has sent me to bring good news to the poor.
Alleluia!

GOSPEL

A reading from the holy Gospel according to John 1:6-8. 19-28

A man came, sent by God.
His name was John.
He came as a witness,
as a witness to speak for the light,
so that everyone might believe through him.
He was not the light,
only a witness to speak for the light.

This is how John appeared as a witness. When the Jews sent priests and Levites from Jerusalem to ask him, 'Who are you?' he not only declared, but he declared quite openly, 'I am not the Christ.' 'Well then,' they asked 'are you Elijah?' 'I am not' he said. 'Are you the Prophet?' He answered, 'No.' So they said to him, 'Who are you? We must take back an answer to those who sent us. What have you to say about yourself?' So John said, 'I am, as Isaiah prophesied:

a voice that cries in the wilderness:
Make a straight way for the Lord.'

Now these men had been sent by the Pharisees, and they put this further question to him, 'Why are you baptising if you are not the Christ, and not Elijah, and not the prophet?' John replied, 'I baptise with water; but there stands among you – unknown to you – the one who is coming after me; and I am not fit to undo his sandal-strap.' This happened at Bethany, on the far side of the Jordan, where John was baptising.

The Gospel of the Lord.

The Creed is said.

Prayer over the Offerings
May the sacrifice of our worship, Lord, we pray,
be offered to you unceasingly,
to complete what was begun in sacred mystery
and powerfully accomplish for us your saving work.
Through Christ our Lord.

Amen.

Preface I or II of Advent, pp.19-20.

Communion Antiphon Cf. Is 35:4
Say to the faint of heart: Be strong and do not fear.
Behold, our God will come, and he will save us.

Prayer after Communion
We implore your mercy, Lord,
that this divine sustenance may cleanse us of our faults
and prepare us for the coming feasts.
Through Christ our Lord.
Amen.

A formula of Solemn Blessing, pp.94-5, may be used.

When during the week a Mass of the weekday is to be said, the texts given below are used, unless the day is one of the Advent weekdays that occur from 17 to 24 December.

FOURTH SUNDAY OF ADVENT B

Mary, the Ark of God's Covenant

Today's Mass is a great song to the everlasting love of God revealed in his covenant (love-pact) with his people. We praise the mystery of his love kept secret for endless ages, but now revealed through a new ark of the covenant, Mary of Nazareth.

Entrance Antiphon Cf. Is 45:8
Drop down dew from above, you heavens,
and let the clouds rain down the Just One;
let the earth be opened and bring forth a Saviour.

The Gloria in excelsis (Glory to God in the highest) is not said.

Collect
Pour forth, we beseech you, O Lord,
your grace into our hearts,
that we, to whom the Incarnation of Christ your Son

was made known by the message of an Angel,
may by his Passion and Cross
be brought to the glory of his Resurrection.
Who lives and reigns with you in the unity of the Holy Spirit,
one God, for ever and ever.
Amen.

FIRST READING

A reading from the second book of Samuel 7:1-5. 8-12. 14. 16

Once David had settled into his house and the Lord had given him rest from all the enemies surrounding him, the king said to the prophet Nathan, 'Look, I am living in a house of cedar while the ark of God dwells in a tent.' Nathan said to the king, 'Go and do all that is in your mind, for the Lord is with you.'

But that very night the word of the Lord came to Nathan:

'Go and tell my servant David, "Thus the Lord speaks: Are you the man to build me a house to dwell in? I took you from the pasture, from following the sheep, to be leader of my people Israel; I have been with you on all your expeditions; I have cut off all your enemies before you. I will give you fame as great as the fame of the greatest on earth. I will provide a place for my people Israel; I will plant them there and they shall dwell in that place and never be disturbed again; nor shall the wicked continue to oppress them as they did, in the days when I appointed judges over my people Israel; I will give them rest from all their enemies. The Lord will make you great; the Lord will make you a House. And when your days are ended and you are laid to rest with your ancestors, I will preserve the offspring of your body after you and make his sovereignty secure. I will be a father to him and he a son to me. Your House and your sovereignty will always stand secure before me and your throne be established for ever."'

The word of the Lord.

Responsorial Psalm Ps 88:2-5. 27. 29. ℟ cf. v.2

  ℟ **I will sing for ever of your love, O Lord.**

1 I will sing for ever of your love, O Lord;
   through all ages my mouth will proclaim your truth.
   Of this I am sure, that your love lasts for ever,
   that your truth is firmly established as the heavens. ℟

2 'I have made a covenant with my chosen one;
   I have sworn to David my servant:

Fourth Sunday of Advent, Year B

> I will establish your dynasty for ever
> and set up your throne through all ages.' ℟

> 3 He will say to me: 'You are my father,
> my God, the rock who saves me.'
> I will keep my love for him always;
> for him my covenant shall endure. ℟

SECOND READING
A reading from the letter of St Paul to the Romans   16:25-27

Glory to him who is able to give you the strength to live according to the Good News I preach, and in which I proclaim Jesus Christ, the revelation of a mystery kept secret for endless ages, but now so clear that it must be broadcast to pagans everywhere to bring them to the obedience of faith. This is only what scripture has predicted, and it is all part of the way the eternal God wants things to be. He alone is wisdom; give glory therefore to him through Jesus Christ for ever and ever. Amen.

The word of the Lord.

Gospel Acclamation   Lk 1:38
> Alleluia, alleluia!
> I am the handmaid of the Lord:
> let what you have said be done to me.
> Alleluia!

GOSPEL
A reading from the holy Gospel according to Luke   1:26-38

The angel Gabriel was sent by God to a town in Galilee called Nazareth, to a virgin betrothed to a man named Joseph, of the House of David; and the virgin's name was Mary. He went in and said to her, 'Rejoice, so highly favoured! The Lord is with you.' She was deeply disturbed by these words and asked herself what this greeting could mean, but the angel said to her, 'Mary, do not be afraid; you have won God's favour. Listen! You are to conceive and bear a son, and you must name him Jesus. He will be great and will be called Son of the Most High. The Lord God will give him the throne of his ancestor David; he will rule over the House of Jacob for ever and his reign will have no end.' Mary said to the angel, 'But how can this come about, since I am a virgin?' 'The Holy Spirit will come upon you' the angel answered 'and the power of the Most High will cover you with its shadow. And so the child will be holy and will be called Son of God. Know this too: your kinswoman Elizabeth has, in her old age, herself conceived a son, and she whom people called barren is now in her sixth month, for nothing is impossible to God.' 'I am the handmaid of the Lord,' said Mary 'let what you have said be done to me.' And the angel left her.

The Gospel of the Lord.

The Creed is said.

Prayer over the Offerings
May the Holy Spirit, O Lord,
sanctify these gifts laid upon your altar,
just as he filled with his power the womb of the Blessed Virgin Mary.
Through Christ our Lord.
Amen.

Preface II of Advent, pp.19-20.

Communion Antiphon Is 7:14
Behold, a Virgin shall conceive and bear a son;
and his name will be called Emmanuel.

Prayer after Communion
Having received this pledge of eternal redemption,
we pray, almighty God,
that, as the feast day of our salvation draws ever nearer,
so we may press forward all the more eagerly
to the worthy celebration of the mystery of your Son's Nativity.
Who lives and reigns for ever and ever.
Amen.

A formula of Solemn Blessing, pp.94-5, may be used.

CHRISTMAS TIME
25 December

THE NATIVITY OF THE LORD
Solemnity

CHRISTMAS DAY: VIGIL MASS
See above, pp.208ff.

CHRISTMAS DAY
See above, pp.216ff.

The Sunday within the Octave of the Nativity of the Lord,
or, if there is no Sunday, 30 December

THE HOLY FAMILY OF JESUS, MARY AND JOSEPH   B
Feast

Holy Family

We celebrate the Holy Family of Nazareth which is the model for all who fear the Lord and walk in his ways.

Entrance Antiphon   Lk 2:16
The shepherds went in haste,
and found Mary and Joseph and the Infant lying in a manger.

The Gloria in excelsis (Glory to God in the highest) is said.

The Holy Family of Jesus, Mary and Joseph, Year B

Collect
O God, who were pleased to give us
the shining example of the Holy Family,
graciously grant that we may imitate them
in practising the virtues of family life and in the bonds of charity,
and so, in the joy of your house,
delight one day in eternal rewards.
Through our Lord Jesus Christ, your Son,
who lives and reigns with you in the unity of the Holy Spirit,
one God, for ever and ever.
Amen.

The First Reading, Psalm, Second Reading and Gospel Acclamation given for Year A, pp.224ff., may be used, with the Gospel below. Or the alternative readings given below may be used.

FIRST READING
A reading from the book of Genesis   15:1-6; 21:1-3

The word of the Lord was spoken to Abram in a vision, 'Have no fear, Abram, I am your shield; your reward will be very great'.

'My Lord,' Abram replied 'what do you intend to give me? I go childless...' Then Abram said, 'See, you have given me no descendants; some man of my household will be my heir.' And then this word of the Lord was spoken to him, 'He shall not be your heir; your heir shall be of your own flesh and blood.' Then taking him outside he said, 'Look up to heaven and count the stars if you can. Such will be your descendants' he told him. Abram put his faith in the Lord, who counted this as making him justified.

The Lord dealt kindly with Sarah as he had said, and did what he had promised her. So Sarah conceived and bore a son to Abraham in his old age, at the time God had promised. Abraham named the son born to him Isaac, the son to whom Sarah had given birth.

The word of the Lord.

Responsorial Psalm   Ps 104:1-6. 8-9. R/ vv.7-8

   R/ **He, the Lord, is our God.**
       He remembers his covenant for ever.

1   Give thanks to the Lord, tell his name,
     make known his deeds among the peoples.

The Holy Family of Jesus, Mary and Joseph, Year B 633

O sing to him, sing his praise;
tell all his wonderful works! ℟

2 Be proud of his holy name,
let the hearts that seek the Lord rejoice.
Consider the Lord and his strength;
constantly seek his face. ℟

3 Remember the wonders he has done,
his miracles, the judgements he spoke.
O children of Abraham, his servant,
O sons of the Jacob he chose. ℟

4 He remembers his covenant for ever,
his promise for a thousand generations,
the covenant he made with Abraham,
the oath he swore to Isaac. ℟

SECOND READING
A reading from the letter to the Hebrews   11:8. 11-12. 17-19

It was by faith that Abraham obeyed the call to set out for a country that was the inheritance given to him and his descendants, and that he set out without knowing where he was going.

It was equally by faith that Sarah, in spite of being past the age, was made able to conceive, because she believed that he who had made the promise would be faithful to it. Because of this, there came from one man, and one who was already as good as dead himself, more descendants than could be counted, as many as the stars of heaven or the grains of sand on the seashore.

It was by faith that Abraham, when put to the test, offered up Isaac. He offered to sacrifice his only son even though the promises had been made to him and he had been told: It is through Isaac that your name will be carried on. He was confident that God had the power even to raise the dead; and so, figuratively speaking, he was given back Isaac from the dead.

The word of the Lord.

Gospel Acclamation   Heb 1:1-2
Alleluia, alleluia!
At various times in the past
and in various different ways,
God spoke to our ancestors through the prophets;
but in our own time, the last days,

he has spoken to us through his Son.
Alleluia!

GOSPEL
A reading from the holy Gospel according to Luke 2:22-40

When the day came for them to be purified as laid down by the Law of Moses, the parents of Jesus took him up to Jerusalem to present him to the Lord – observing what stands written in the law of the Lord: Every first-born male must be consecrated to the Lord – and also to offer in sacrifice, in accordance with what is said in the Law of the Lord, a pair of turtledoves or two young pigeons. Now in Jerusalem there was a man named Simeon. He was an upright and devout man; he looked forward to Israel's comforting and the Holy Spirit rested on him. It had been revealed to him by the Holy Spirit that he would not see death until he had set eyes on the Christ of the Lord. Prompted by the Spirit he came to the Temple; and when the parents brought in the child Jesus to do for him what the Law required, he took him into his arms and blessed God; and he said:

'Now, Master, you can let your servant go in peace,
just as you promised;
because my eyes have seen the salvation
which you have prepared for all the nations to see,
a light to enlighten the pagans
and the glory of your people Israel.'

As the child's father and mother stood there wondering at the things that were being said about him, Simeon blessed them and said to Mary his mother, 'You see this child: he is destined for the fall and for the rising of many in Israel, destined to be a sign that is rejected – and a sword will pierce your own soul too – so that the secret thoughts of many may be laid bare.'

There was a prophetess also, Anna, the daughter of Phanuel, of the tribe of Asher. She was well on in years. Her days of girlhood over, she had been married for seven years before becoming a widow. She was now eighty-four years old and never left the Temple, serving God night and day with fasting and prayer. She came by just at that moment and began to praise God; and she spoke of the child to all who looked forward to the deliverance of Jerusalem.

*When they had done everything the Law of the Lord required, they went back to Galilee, to their own town of Nazareth. Meanwhile the child grew to maturity, and he was filled with wisdom; and God's favour was with him.

The Gospel of the Lord.*

Shorter Form, verses 22. 39-40. Read between

When this Feast is celebrated on Sunday, the Creed is said.

Prayer over the Offerings
We offer you, Lord, the sacrifice of conciliation,
humbly asking that,
through the intercession of the Virgin Mother of God and Saint Joseph,
you may establish our families firmly in your grace and your peace.
Through Christ our Lord.
Amen.

Preface I, II or III of the Nativity of the Lord, pp.20-21.

When the Roman Canon is used, the proper form of the Communicantes (In communion with those) is said.

Communion Antiphon Bar 3:38
Our God has appeared on the earth, and lived among us.

Prayer after Communion
Bring those you refresh with this heavenly Sacrament,
most merciful Father,
to imitate constantly the example of the Holy Family,
so that, after the trials of this world,
we may share their company for ever.
Through Christ our Lord.
Amen.

1 January: Octave of Christmas
SOLEMNITY OF MARY, MOTHER OF GOD
See above, pp.227ff.

SECOND SUNDAY AFTER CHRISTMAS
See above, pp.230ff.

The Baptism of the Lord, Year B

6 January (or Sunday between 2 January and 8 January)
THE EPIPHANY OF THE LORD
See above, pp.234ff.

Sunday after 6 January
THE BAPTISM OF THE LORD   B
Feast

Where the Solemnity of the Epiphany is transferred to Sunday, if this Sunday occurs on 7 or 8 January, the Feast of the Baptism of the Lord is celebrated on the following Monday.

The Baptism of the Lord

At Jesus' baptism by John in the Jordan, the Father anointed his beloved Son, with the Holy Spirit and with power, to bring healing and peace to all the nations.

Entrance Antiphon   Cf. Mt 3:16-17
After the Lord was baptized, the heavens were opened,
and the Spirit descended upon him like a dove,
and the voice of the Father thundered:
This is my beloved Son, with whom I am well pleased.

The Gloria in excelsis (Glory to God in the highest) is said.

Collect
Almighty ever-living God,
who, when Christ had been baptized in the River Jordan
and as the Holy Spirit descended upon him,
solemnly declared him your beloved Son,
grant that your children by adoption,
reborn of water and the Holy Spirit,
may always be well pleasing to you.
Through our Lord Jesus Christ, your Son,
who lives and reigns with you in the unity of the Holy Spirit,
one God, for ever and ever.

or

O God, whose Only Begotten Son
has appeared in our very flesh,
grant, we pray, that we may be inwardly transformed

The Baptism of the Lord, Year B

through him whom we recognize as outwardly like ourselves.
Who lives and reigns with you in the unity of the Holy Spirit,
one God, for ever and ever.
Amen.

The First Reading, Psalm, Second Reading and Gospel Acclamation given for Year A, pp.240ff., may be used, with the Gospel given below. Or the alternative readings given below may be used.

FIRST READING
A reading from the prophet Isaiah 55:1-11

Oh, come to the water all you who are thirsty;
though you have no money, come!
Buy corn without money, and eat,
and, at no cost, wine and milk.
Why spend money on what is not bread,
your wages on what fails to satisfy?
Listen, listen to me, and you will have good things to eat
and rich food to enjoy.
Pay attention, come to me;
listen, and your soul will live.

With you I will make an everlasting covenant
out of the favours promised to David.
See, I have made of you a witness to the peoples,
a leader and a master of the nations.
See, you will summon a nation you never knew,
those unknown will come hurrying to you,
for the sake of the Lord your God,
of the Holy One of Israel who will glorify you.

Seek the Lord while he is still to be found,
call to him while he is still near.
Let the wicked man abandon his way,
the evil man his thoughts.
Let him turn back to the Lord who will take pity on him,
to our God who is rich in forgiving;
for my thoughts are not your thoughts,
my ways not your ways – it is the Lord who speaks.
Yes, the heavens are as high above earth
as my ways are above your ways,
my thoughts above your thoughts.

Yes, as the rain and the snow come down from the heavens and do not return without watering the earth, making it yield and giving growth to provide seed for the sower and bread for the eating, so the word that goes from my mouth does not return to me empty, without carrying out my will and succeeding in what it was sent to do.

The word of the Lord.

Responsorial Psalm   Is 12:2-6. ℟ v.3

℟ **With joy you will draw water
from the wells of salvation.**

1. Truly, God is my salvation,
I trust, I shall not fear.
For the Lord is my strength, my song,
he became my saviour.
With joy you will draw water
from the wells of salvation. ℟

2. Give thanks to the Lord, give praise to his name!
Make his mighty deeds known to the peoples!
Declare the greatness of his name. ℟

3. Sing a psalm to the Lord
for he has done glorious deeds,
make them known to all the earth!
People of Zion, sing and shout for joy
for great in your midst is the Holy One of Israel. ℟

SECOND READING

A reading from the first letter of St John   5:1-9

Whoever believes that Jesus is the Christ
has been begotten by God;
and whoever loves the Father that begot him
loves the child whom he begets.
We can be sure that we love God's children
if we love God himself and do what he has commanded us;
this is what loving God is –
keeping his commandments;
and his commandments are not difficult,
because anyone who has been begotten by God
has already overcome the world;
this is the victory over the world –

our faith.
Who can overcome the world?
Only the man who believes that Jesus is the Son of God:
Jesus Christ who came by water and blood,
not with water only,
but with water and blood;
with the Spirit as another witness –
since the Spirit is the truth –
so that there are three witnesses,
the Spirit, the water and the blood,
and all three of them agree.
We accept the testimony of human witnesses,
but God's testimony is much greater,
and this is God's testimony,
given as evidence for his Son.

The word of the Lord.

Gospel Acclamation cf. Jn 1:29
Alleluia, alleluia!
John saw Jesus coming towards him, and said:
This is the Lamb of God who takes away the sin of the world.
Alleluia!

GOSPEL

A reading from the holy Gospel according to Mark 1:7-11

In the course of his preaching John the Baptist said, 'Someone is following me, someone who is more powerful than I am, and I am not fit to kneel down and undo the strap of his sandals. I have baptised you with water, but he will baptise you with the Holy Spirit.'

It was at this time that Jesus came from Nazareth in Galilee and was baptised in the Jordan by John. No sooner had he come up out of the water than he saw the heavens torn apart and the Spirit, like a dove, descending on him. And a voice came from heaven, 'You are my Son, the Beloved; my favour rests on you.'

The Gospel of the Lord.

The Creed is said.

Prayer over the Offerings
Accept, O Lord, the offerings
we have brought to honour the revealing of your beloved Son,
so that the oblation of your faithful
may be transformed into the sacrifice of him
who willed in his compassion
to wash away the sins of the world.
Who lives and reigns for ever and ever.
Amen.

Preface of the Baptism of the Lord, p.22.

Communion Antiphon   Jn 1: 32. 34
Behold the One of whom John said:
I have seen and testified that this is the Son of God.

Prayer after Communion
Nourished with these sacred gifts,
we humbly entreat your mercy, O Lord,
that, faithfully listening to your Only Begotten Son,
we may be your children in name and in truth.
Through Christ our Lord.
Amen.

Ordinary Time lasts from the Monday after this Sunday to the Tuesday before Lent. For Sunday Masses the texts given below on pp.707ff. are used.

THE SEASON OF LENT

For a Note on Preparation for Baptism, see above, pp.243-4.

ASH WEDNESDAY
See above, pp.244ff.

FIRST SUNDAY OF LENT   B

On this Sunday is celebrated the rite of 'election' or 'enrolment of names' for the catechumens who are to be admitted to the Sacraments of Christian Initiation at the Easter Vigil, using the proper prayers and intercessions.

The Good News of the Covenant

At the beginning of Lent we renew our response to the Covenant, the pact of love that God made with each of us at our baptism. Imagine what good news it must have been to Noah, alone in a drowned world, when he learned that God's love had not abandoned, nor ever would abandon, the earth and its creatures.

Entrance Antiphon   Cf. Ps 90:15-16
When he calls on me, I will answer him;
I will deliver him and give him glory,
I will grant him length of days.

The Gloria in excelsis (Glory to God in the highest) is not said.

Collect
Grant, almighty God,
through the yearly observances of holy Lent,
that we may grow in understanding
of the riches hidden in Christ

and by worthy conduct pursue their effects.
Through our Lord Jesus Christ, your Son,
who lives and reigns with you in the unity of the Holy Spirit,
one God, for ever and ever.
Amen.

FIRST READING
A reading from the book of Genesis 9:8-15

God spoke to Noah and his sons, 'See, I establish my Covenant with you, and with your descendants after you; also with every living creature to be found with you, birds, cattle and every wild beast with you: everything that came out of the ark, everything that lives on the earth. I establish my Covenant with you: no thing of flesh shall be swept away again by the waters of the flood. There shall be no flood to destroy the earth again.'

God said, 'Here is the sign of the Covenant I make between myself and you and every living creature with you for all generations: I set my bow in the clouds and it shall be a sign of the Covenant between me and the earth. When I gather the clouds over the earth and the bow appears in the clouds, I will recall the Covenant between myself and you and every living creature of every kind. And so the waters shall never again become a flood to destroy all things of flesh.'

The word of the Lord.

Responsional Psalm Ps 24:4-9. ℟ cf. v.10

℟ **Your ways, Lord, are faithfulness and love
for those who keep your covenant.**

1 Lord, make me know your ways.
  Lord, teach me your paths.
  Make me walk in your truth, and teach me:
  for you are God my saviour. ℟

2 Remember your mercy, Lord,
  and the love you have shown from of old.
  In your love remember me,
  because of your goodness, O Lord. ℟

3 The Lord is good and upright.
  He shows the path to those who stray,
  he guides the humble in the right path;
  he teaches his way to the poor. ℟

SECOND READING
A reading from the first letter of St Peter   3:18-22

Christ himself, innocent though he was, died once for sins, died for the guilty, to lead us to God. In the body he was put to death, in the spirit he was raised to life, and, in the spirit, he went to preach to the spirits in prison. Now it was long ago, when Noah was still building that ark which saved only a small group of eight people 'by water', and when God was still waiting patiently, that these spirits refused to believe. That water is a type of the baptism which saves you now, and which is not the washing off of physical dirt but a pledge made to God from a good conscience, through the resurrection of Jesus Christ, who has entered heaven and is at God's right hand, now that he has made the angels of the Dominations and Powers his subjects.

The word of the Lord.

Gospel Acclamation   Mt 4:4
Praise to you, O Christ, king of eternal glory!
Man does not live on bread alone,
but on every word that comes from the mouth of God.
Praise to you, O Christ, king of eternal glory!

GOSPEL
A reading from the holy Gospel according to Mark   1:12-15

The Spirit drove Jesus out into the wilderness and he remained there for forty days, and was tempted by Satan. He was with the wild beasts, and the angels looked after him.

After John had been arrested, Jesus went into Galilee. There he proclaimed the Good News from God. 'The time has come' he said 'and the kingdom of God is close at hand. Repent, and believe the Good News.'

The Gospel of the Lord.

After the Homily, the Election or Enrolment of Candidates for Baptism may take place.

The Creed is said.

Prayer over the Offerings
Give us the right dispositions, O Lord, we pray,
to make these offerings,
for with them we celebrate the beginning
of this venerable and sacred time.

Through Christ our Lord.
Amen.

Preface of the Temptation of the Lord, p.24.

Communion Antiphon Mt 4:4
One does not live by bread alone,
but by every word that comes forth from the mouth of God.

or Cf. Ps 90:4

The Lord will conceal you with his pinions,
and under his wings you will trust.

Prayer after Communion
Renewed now with heavenly bread,
by which faith is nourished, hope increased,
and charity strengthened,
we pray, O Lord,
that we may learn to hunger for Christ,
the true and living Bread,
and strive to live by every word
which proceeds from your mouth.
Through Christ our Lord.
Amen.

Prayer over the People
May bountiful blessing, O Lord, we pray,
come down upon your people,
that hope may grow in tribulation,
virtue be strengthened in temptation,
and eternal redemption be assured.
Through Christ our Lord.
Amen.

SECOND SUNDAY OF LENT B

God's Gift to Us: His Son

Abraham was prepared to give God his only son, Isaac, in sacrifice. God would do no less. 'This is my Son, the Beloved,' he says to us. 'Listen to him.'

Entrance Antiphon Cf. Ps 26:8-9
Of you my heart has spoken: Seek his face.
It is your face, O Lord, that I seek;
hide not your face from me.

or   Cf. Ps 24:6. 2. 22

Remember your compassion, O Lord,
and your merciful love, for they are from of old.
Let not our enemies exult over us.
Redeem us, O God of Israel, from all our distress.

The Gloria in excelsis (Glory to God in the highest) is not said.

Collect

O God, who have commanded us
to listen to your beloved Son,
be pleased, we pray,
to nourish us inwardly by your word,
that, with spiritual sight made pure,
we may rejoice to behold your glory.
Through our Lord Jesus Christ, your Son,
who lives and reigns with you in the unity of the Holy Spirit,
one God, for ever and ever.
Amen.

FIRST READING

A reading from the book of Genesis   22:1-2. 9-13. 15-18

God put Abraham to the test. 'Abraham, Abraham' he called. 'Here I am' he replied. 'Take your son,' God said, 'your only child Isaac, whom you love, and go to the land of Moriah. There you shall offer him as a burnt-offering, on a mountain I will point out to you.'

When they arrived at the place God had pointed out to him, Abraham built an altar there and arranged the wood. Then he stretched out his hand and seized the knife to kill his son.

But the angel of the Lord called to him from heaven. 'Abraham, Abraham' he said. 'I am here' he replied. 'Do not raise your hand against the boy' the angel said. 'Do not harm him, for now I know you fear God. You have not refused me your son, your only son.' Then looking up, Abraham saw a ram caught by its horns in a bush. Abraham took the ram and offered it as a burnt-offering in place of his son.

The angel of the Lord called Abraham a second time from heaven. 'I swear by my own self – it is the Lord who speaks – because you have done this, because you have not refused me your son, your only son, I will shower blessings on you, I will make your descendants as many as the stars of heaven and the grains of sand on the seashore. Your descendants shall gain possession of the gates of their enemies. All the nations of the earth shall bless themselves by your descendants, as a reward for your obedience.'

The word of the Lord.

Responsorial Psalm Ps 115:10. 15-19. ℟ Ps 114:9
℟ **I will walk in the presence of the Lord
in the land of the living.**

1 I trusted, even when I said:
 'I am sorely afflicted.'
 O precious in the eyes of the Lord
 is the death of his faithful. ℟

2 Your servant, Lord, your servant am I;
 you have loosened my bonds.
 A thanksgiving sacrifice I make:
 I will call on the Lord's name. ℟

3 My vows to the Lord I will fulfil
 before all his people,
 in the courts of the house of the Lord,
 in your midst, O Jerusalem. ℟

SECOND READING
A reading from the letter of St Paul to the Romans 8:31-34

With God on our side who can be against us? Since God did not spare his own Son, but gave him up to benefit us all, we may be certain, after such a gift, that he will not refuse anything he can give. Could anyone accuse those that God has chosen? When God acquits, could anyone condemn? Could Christ Jesus? No! He not only died for us – he rose from the dead, and there at God's right hand he stands and pleads for us.

The word of the Lord.

Gospel Acclamation Mt 17:5
Glory and praise to you, O Christ!
From the bright cloud the Father's voice was heard:
'This is my Son, the Beloved. Listen to him!'
Glory and praise to you, O Christ!

GOSPEL
A reading from the holy Gospel according to Mark 9:2-10

Jesus took with him Peter and James and John and led them up a high mountain where they could be alone by themselves. There in their presence he was transfigured: his clothes became dazzlingly white, whiter than any earthly bleacher could make them. Elijah appeared to them with Moses; and they were talking with Jesus. Then Peter spoke to Jesus. 'Rabbi', he said 'it is wonderful for us to be here; so let us make three tents, one for you, one for Moses and one for Elijah.' He did not know what to say; they were so frightened. And a cloud came, covering them in shadow; and there came a voice from the cloud, 'This is my Son, the Beloved. Listen to him.' Then suddenly, when they looked round, they saw no one with them any more but only Jesus.

As they came down the mountain he warned them to tell no one what they had seen, until after the Son of Man had risen from the dead. They observed the warning faithfully, though among themselves they discussed what 'rising from the dead' could mean.

The Gospel of the Lord.

The Creed is said.

Prayer over the Offerings
May this sacrifice, O Lord, we pray,
cleanse us of our faults
and sanctify your faithful in body and mind
for the celebration of the paschal festivities.
Through Christ our Lord.
Amen.

Preface of the Transfiguration of the Lord, p.24.

Communion Antiphon Mt 17:5
This is my beloved Son, with whom I am well pleased;
listen to him.

Prayer after Communion
As we receive these glorious mysteries,
we make thanksgiving to you, O Lord,
for allowing us while still on earth
to be partakers even now of the things of heaven.
Through Christ our Lord.
Amen.

Prayer over the People
Bless your faithful, we pray, O Lord,
with a blessing that endures for ever,
and keep them faithful
to the Gospel of your Only Begotten Son,
so that they may always desire and at last attain

that glory whose beauty he showed in his own Body,
to the amazement of his Apostles.
Through Christ our Lord.
Amen.

THIRD SUNDAY OF LENT   B

On this Sunday is celebrated the First Scrutiny in preparation for the Baptism of the catechumens who are to be admitted to the Sacraments of Christian Initiation at the Easter Vigil, using the proper prayers and intercessions as given above, pp.263-8.

Christ the Wisdom of God

Today, we celebrate the foolishness of God that is wiser than any human wisdom: the utter folly of his love that allowed the destruction of the temple of the body of his Son Jesus. And we dedicate ourselves anew to the Law of the Lord which gives wisdom to the simple.

Entrance Antiphon   Cf. Ps 24:15-16
My eyes are always on the Lord,
for he rescues my feet from the snare.
Turn to me and have mercy on me,
for I am alone and poor.

    or   Cf. Ez 36:23-26

When I prove my holiness among you,
I will gather you from all the foreign lands;
and I will pour clean water upon you
and cleanse you from all your impurities,
and I will give you a new spirit, says the Lord.

The Gloria in excelsis (Glory to God in the highest) is not said.

Collect
O God, author of every mercy and of all goodness,
who in fasting, prayer and almsgiving
have shown us a remedy for sin,
look graciously on this confession of our lowliness,
that we, who are bowed down by our conscience,
may always be lifted up by your mercy.
Through our Lord Jesus Christ, your Son,
who lives and reigns with you in the unity of the Holy Spirit,
one God, for ever and ever.
Amen.

The readings for Year A may be used as alternative readings, see above, pp.259ff. If this is done, the Preface and Communion Antiphon as at Year A are used. If a pre-baptismal scrutiny is held today, the readings for Year A are mandatory.

FIRST READING
A reading from the book of Exodus 20:1-17

*God spoke all these words. He said, 'I am the Lord your God who brought you out of the land of Egypt, out of the house of slavery.

'You shall have no gods except me.*

'You shall not make yourself a carved image or any likeness of anything in heaven or on earth beneath or in the waters under the earth; you shall not bow down to them or serve them. For I, the Lord your God, am a jealous God and I punish the father's fault in the sons, the grandsons, and the great-grandsons of those who hate me; but I show kindness to thousands of those who love me and keep my commandments.

*'You shall not utter the name of the Lord your God to misuse it, for the Lord will not leave unpunished the man who utters his name to misuse it.

'Remember the sabbath day and keep it holy.* For six days you shall labour and do all your work, but the seventh day is a sabbath for the Lord your God. You shall do no work that day, neither you nor your son nor your daughter nor your servants, men or women, nor your animals nor the stranger who lives with you. For in six days the Lord made the heavens and the earth and the sea and all that these hold, but on the seventh day he rested; that is why the Lord has blessed the sabbath day and made it sacred.

*'Honour your father and your mother so that you may have a long life in the land that the Lord your God has given to you.

'You shall not kill.

'You shall not commit adultery.

'You shall not steal.

'You shall not bear false witness against your neighbour.

'You shall not covet your neighbour's house. You shall not covet your neighbour's wife, or his servant, man or woman, or his ox, or his donkey, or anything that is his.'

The word of the Lord.*

Shorter Form, verses 1-3. 7-8. 12-17. Read between

Responsorial Psalm　　　　　　　　　　　　Ps 18:8-11. ℟ Jn 6:68

℟　**You, Lord, have the message of eternal life.**

1　The law of the Lord is perfect,
　　it revives the soul.
　　The rule of the Lord is to be trusted,
　　it gives wisdom to the simple.　℟

2　The precepts of the Lord are right,
　　they gladden the heart.
　　The command of the Lord is clear,
　　it gives light to the eyes.　℟

3　The fear of the Lord is holy,
　　abiding for ever.
　　The decrees of the Lord are truth
　　and all of them just.　℟

4　They are more to be desired than gold,
　　than the purest of gold
　　and sweeter are they than honey,
　　than honey from the comb.　℟

SECOND READING

A reading from the first letter of St Paul to the Corinthians　1:22-25

While the Jews demand miracles and the Greeks look for wisdom, here are we preaching a crucified Christ; to the Jews an obstacle that they cannot get over, to the pagans madness, but to those who have been called, whether they are Jews or Greeks, a Christ who is the power and the wisdom of God. For God's foolishness is wiser than human wisdom, and God's weakness is stronger than human strength.

　　The word of the Lord.

Gospel Acclamation　　　　　　　　　　　　　　　　Jn 11:25-26
　　Praise to you, O Christ, king of eternal glory!
　　I am the resurrection and the life, says the Lord,
　　whoever believes in me will never die.
　　Praise to you, O Christ, king of eternal glory!

or　　　　　　　　　　　　　　　　　　　　　　　　　　Jn 3:16

　　Praise to you, O Christ, king of eternal glory!
　　God loved the world so much that he gave his only Son;

Third Sunday of Lent, Year B 651

everyone who believes in him has eternal life.
Praise to you, O Christ, king of eternal glory!

GOSPEL
A reading from the holy Gospel according to John 2:13-25

Just before the Jewish Passover Jesus went up to Jerusalem, and in the Temple he found people selling cattle and sheep and pigeons, and the money changers sitting at their counters there. Making a whip out of some cord, he drove them all out of the Temple, cattle and sheep as well, scattered the money changers' coins, knocked their tables over and said to the pigeon-sellers, 'Take all this out of here and stop turning my Father's house into a market.' Then his disciples remembered the words of scripture: Zeal for your house will devour me. The Jews intervened and said, 'What sign can you show us to justify what you have done?' Jesus answered, 'Destroy this sanctuary, and in three days I will raise it up.' The Jews replied, 'It has taken forty-six years to build this sanctuary: are you going to raise it up in three days?' But he was speaking of the sanctuary that was his body, and when Jesus rose from the dead, his disciples remembered that he had said this, and they believed the scripture and the words he had said.

During his stay in Jerusalem for the Passover many believed in his name when they saw the signs that he gave, but Jesus knew them all and did not trust himself to them; he never needed evidence about any man; he could tell what a man had in him.

The Gospel of the Lord.

After the Homily, the First Scrutiny of Candidates for Baptism may take place. See above, pp.263-8.

If there is no Scrutiny, the Creed is said.

Prayer over the Offerings
Be pleased, O Lord, with these sacrificial offerings,
and grant that we who beseech pardon for our own sins,
may take care to forgive our neighbour.
Through Christ our Lord.
Amen.

Preface of the Samaritan Woman, p.25. When the Gospel of the Samaritan Woman is not read, Preface I or II of Lent, pp.22-3, is used.

Communion Antiphon

When the Gospel of the Samaritan Woman is read: Jn 4:13-14
For anyone who drinks it, says the Lord,
the water I shall give will become in him
a spring welling up to eternal life.

When another Gospel is read: Cf. Ps 83:4-5
The sparrow finds a home,
and the swallow a nest for her young:
by your altars, O Lord of hosts, my King and my God.
Blessed are they who dwell in your house,
for ever singing your praise.

Prayer after Communion

As we receive the pledge
of things yet hidden in heaven
and are nourished while still on earth
with the Bread that comes from on high,
we humbly entreat you, O Lord,
that what is being brought about in us in mystery
may come to true completion.
Through Christ our Lord.
Amen.

Prayer over the People

Direct, O Lord, we pray, the hearts of your faithful,
and in your kindness grant your servants this grace:
that, abiding in the love of you and their neighbour,
they may fulfil the whole of your commands.
Through Christ our Lord.
Amen.

FOURTH SUNDAY OF LENT   B

In this Mass, the colour violet or rose is used. Instrumental music is permitted, and the altar may be decorated with flowers.

On this Sunday is celebrated the Second Scrutiny in preparation for the Baptism of the catechumens who are to be admitted to the Sacraments of Christian Initiation at the Easter Vigil, using the proper prayers and intercessions as given above, pp.274-9.

Christ the Redeemer

Our sins had made us exiles from God's kingdom. But just as God sent Cyrus, the King of Persia, to bring his people back from Babylon, so in his great love he sent his Son, Jesus Christ, to bring us back to the new

Jerusalem 'to live the good life as from the beginning he had meant us to live it'.

Entrance Antiphon
Cf. Is 66:10-11

Rejoice, Jerusalem, and all who love her.
Be joyful, all who were in mourning;
exult and be satisfied at her consoling breast.

The Gloria in excelsis (Glory to God in the highest) is not said.

Collect
O God, who through your Word
reconcile the human race to yourself in a wonderful way,
grant, we pray,
that with prompt devotion and eager faith
the Christian people may hasten
toward the solemn celebrations to come.
Through our Lord Jesus Christ, your Son,
who lives and reigns with you in the unity of the Holy Spirit,
one God, for ever and ever.
Amen.

The readings for Year A may be used as alternative readings, see above, pp.269-70. If this is done, the Preface and Communion Antiphon as at Year A are used. If a pre-baptismal scrutiny is held today, the readings for Year A are mandatory.

FIRST READING
A reading from the second book of Chronicles 36:14-16. 19-23

All the heads of the priesthood, and the people too, added infidelity to infidelity, copying all the shameful practices of the nations and defiling the Temple that the Lord had consecrated for himself in Jerusalem. The Lord, the God of their ancestors, tirelessly sent them messenger after messenger, since he wished to spare his people and his house. But they ridiculed the messengers of God, they despised his words, they laughed at his prophets, until at last the wrath of the Lord rose so high against his people that there was no further remedy.

Their enemies burned down the Temple of God, demolished the walls of Jerusalem, set fire to all its palaces, and destroyed everything of value in it. The survivors were deported by Nebuchadnezzar to Babylon; they were to serve him and his sons until the kingdom of Persia came to power. This is how the word of the Lord was fulfilled that he spoke through Jeremiah, 'Until this land has enjoyed its sabbath rest, until seventy years have gone by, it will keep sabbath throughout the days of its desolation.'

And in the first year of Cyrus king of Persia, to fulfil the word of the Lord that was spoken through Jeremiah, the Lord roused the spirit of Cyrus king of Persia to issue a proclamation and to have it publicly displayed throughout his kingdom: 'Thus speaks Cyrus king of Persia, "The Lord, the God of heaven, has given me all the kingdoms of the earth; he has ordered me to build him a Temple in Jerusalem, in Judah. Whoever there is among you of all his people, may his God be with him! Let him go up."'

The word of the Lord.

Responsional Psalm Ps 136:1-6. ℟ v.6

℟ **O let my tongue
    cleave to my mouth
    if I remember you not!**

1 By the rivers of Babylon
   there we sat and wept,
   remembering Zion;
   on the poplars that grew there
   we hung up our harps. ℟

2 For it was there that they asked us,
   our captors, for songs,
   our oppressors, for joy.
   'Sing to us,' they said,
   'one of Zion's songs.' ℟

3 O how could we sing
   the song of the Lord
   on alien soil?
   If I forget you, Jerusalem,
   let my right hand wither! ℟

4 O let my tongue
   cleave to my mouth
   if I remember you not,
   if I prize not Jerusalem
   above all my joys! ℟

SECOND READING

A reading from the letter of St Paul to the Ephesians 2:4-10

God loved us with so much love that he was generous with his mercy: when we were dead through our sins, he brought us to life with Christ – it is through grace that you have been saved – and raised us up with him and gave us a place with him in heaven, in Christ Jesus.

This was to show for all ages to come, through his goodness towards us in Christ Jesus, how infinitely rich he is in grace. Because it is by grace that you have been saved, through faith; not by anything of your own, but by a gift from God; not by anything that you have done, so that nobody can claim the credit. We are God's work of art, created in Christ Jesus to live the good life as from the beginning he had meant us to live it.

The word of the Lord.

Gospel Acclamation
Jn 3:16

Glory and praise to you, O Christ!
God loved the world so much that he gave his only Son;
everyone who believes in him has eternal life.
Glory and praise to you, O Christ!

GOSPEL

A reading from the holy Gospel according to John 3:14-21

Jesus said to Nicodemus:

'The Son of Man must be lifted up
as Moses lifted up the serpent in the desert,
so that everyone who believes may have eternal life in him.
Yes, God loved the world so much
that he gave his only Son,
so that everyone who believes in him may not be lost
but may have eternal life.
For God sent his Son into the world
not to condemn the world,
but so that through him the world might be saved.
No one who believes in him will be condemned;
but whoever refuses to believe is condemned already,
because he has refused to believe
in the name of God's only Son.
On these grounds is sentence pronounced:
that though the light has come into the world
men have shown they prefer
darkness to the light
because their deeds were evil.
And indeed, everybody who does wrong
hates the light and avoids it,

for fear his actions should be exposed;
but the man who lives by the truth
comes out into the light,
so that it may be plainly seen that what he does is done in God.'

The Gospel of the Lord.

After the Homily, the Second Scrutiny of Candidates for Baptism may take place. See above, pp.274-9ff.

If there is no Scrutiny, the Creed is said.

Prayer over the Offerings
We place before you with joy these offerings,
which bring eternal remedy, O Lord,
praying that we may both faithfully revere them
and present them to you, as is fitting,
for the salvation of all the world.
Through Christ our Lord.
Amen.

Preface of the Man Born Blind, p.25. When the Gospel of the Man Born Blind is not read, Preface I or II of Lent, pp.22-3, is used.

Communion Antiphon
When the Gospel of the Man Born Blind is read: Cf. Jn 9:11. 38
The Lord anointed my eyes: I went, I washed,
I saw and I believed in God.

When another Gospel is read: Cf. Ps 121:3-4
Jerusalem is built as a city bonded as one together.
It is there that the tribes go up, the tribes of the Lord,
to praise the name of the Lord.

Prayer after Communion
O God, who enlighten everyone who comes into this world,
illuminate our hearts, we pray,
with the splendour of your grace,
that we may always ponder
what is worthy and pleasing to your majesty
and love you in all sincerity.
Through Christ our Lord.
Amen.

Prayer over the People
Look upon those who call to you, O Lord,
and sustain the weak;
give life by your unfailing light
to those who walk in the shadow of death,
and bring those rescued by your mercy from every evil
to reach the highest good.
Through Christ our Lord.
Amen.

FIFTH SUNDAY OF LENT   B

The practice of covering crosses and images throughout the church from this Sunday may be observed, if the Conference of Bishops so decides. Crosses remain covered until the end of the celebration of the Lord's Passion on Good Friday, but images remain covered until the beginning of the Easter Vigil.

On this Sunday is celebrated the Third Scrutiny in preparation for the Baptism of the catechumens who are to be admitted to the Sacraments of Christian Initiation at the Easter Vigil, using the proper prayers and intercessions as given below, pp.285-9.

Entrance Antiphon   Cf. Ps 42:1-2
Give me justice, O God,
and plead my cause against a nation that is faithless.
From the deceitful and cunning rescue me,
for you, O God, are my strength.

The Gloria in excelsis (Glory to God in the highest) is not said.

Collect
By your help, we beseech you, Lord our God,
may we walk eagerly in that same charity
with which, out of love for the world,
your Son handed himself over to death.
Through our Lord Jesus Christ, your Son,
who lives and reigns with you in the unity of the Holy Spirit,
one God, for ever and ever.
Amen.

The readings for Cycle A may be used as alternative readings, see above, pp.280-81ff. If this is done, the Preface and Communion Antiphon as at Cycle A are used. If a pre-baptismal scrutiny is held today, the readings for Year A are mandatory.

FIRST READING

A reading from the prophet Jeremiah   31:31-34

See, the days are coming – it is the Lord who speaks – when I will make a new covenant with the House of Israel and the House of Judah, but not a covenant like the one I made with their ancestors on the day I took them by the hand to bring them out of the land of Egypt. They broke that covenant of mine, so I had to show them who was master. It is the Lord who speaks. No, this is the covenant I will make with the House of Israel when those days arrive – it is the Lord who speaks. Deep within them I will plant my Law, writing it on their hearts. Then I will be their God and they shall be my people. There will be no further need for neighbour to try to teach neighbour, or brother to say to brother, 'Learn to know the Lord!' No, they will all know me, the least no less than the greatest – it is the Lord who speaks – since I will forgive their iniquity and never call their sin to mind.

The word of the Lord.

Responsorial Psalm   Ps 50:3-4. 12-15. ℟ v.12

    ℟ **A pure heart create for me, O God.**

1   Have mercy on me, God, in your kindness.
     In your compassion blot out my offence.
     O wash me more and more from my guilt
     and cleanse me from my sin. ℟

2   A pure heart create for me, O God,
     put a steadfast spirit within me.
     Do not cast me away from your presence,
     nor deprive me of your holy spirit. ℟

3   Give me again the joy of your help;
     with a spirit of fervour sustain me,
     that I may teach transgressors your ways
     and sinners may return to you. ℟

SECOND READING

A reading from the letter to the Hebrews   5:7-9

During his life on earth, Christ offered up prayer and entreaty, aloud and in silent tears, to the one who had the power to save him out of death, and he submitted so humbly that his prayer was heard. Although he was Son, he learnt to obey through suffering;

but having been made perfect, he became for all who obey him the source of eternal salvation.

The word of the Lord.

Gospel Acclamation
Jn 12:26
Glory to you, O Christ, you are the Word of God!
If a man serves me, says the Lord, he must follow me;
wherever I am, my servant will be there too.
Glory to you, O Christ, you are the Word of God!

GOSPEL
A reading from the holy Gospel according to John 12:20-30

Among those who went up to worship at the festival were some Greeks. These approached Philip, who came from Bethsaida in Galilee, and put this request to him, 'Sir, we should like to see Jesus.' Philip went to tell Andrew, and Andrew and Philip together went to tell Jesus. Jesus replied to them:

'Now the hour has come
for the Son of Man to be glorified.
I tell you, most solemnly,
unless a wheat grain falls on the ground and dies,
it remains only a single grain;
but if it dies,
it yields a rich harvest.
Anyone who loves his life loses it;
anyone who hates his life in this world
will keep it for the eternal life.
If a man serves me, he must follow me,
wherever I am, my servant will be there too.
If anyone serves me, my Father will honour him.
Now my soul is troubled.
What shall I say:
Father, save me from this hour?
But it was for this very reason that I have come to this hour.
Father, glorify your name!'

A voice came from heaven, 'I have glorified it, and I will glorify it again.'

People standing by, who heard this, said it was a clap of thunder; others said, 'It was an angel speaking to him.' Jesus answered, 'It was not for my sake that this voice came, but for yours.

'Now sentence is being passed on this world;
now the prince of this world is to be overthrown.
And when I am lifted up from the earth,
I shall draw all men to myself.'

By these words he indicated the kind of death he would die.

The Gospel of the Lord.

After the Homily, the Third Scrutiny of Candidates for Baptism may take place. See above, pp.285-9ff.

If there is no Scrutiny, the Creed is said.

Prayer over the Offerings
Hear us, almighty God,
and, having instilled in your servants
the teachings of the Christian faith,
graciously purify them
by the working of this sacrifice.
Through Christ our Lord.
Amen.

Preface of Lazarus, p.26. When the Gospel of Lazarus is not read, Preface I or II of Lent, pp.22-3, is used.

Communion Antiphon
When the Gospel of Lazarus is read: Cf. Jn 11:26
Everyone who lives and believes in me
will not die for ever, says the Lord.

When another Gospel is read:
Amen, Amen I say to you: Unless a grain of wheat
falls to the ground and dies, it remains a single grain.
But if it dies, it bears much fruit.

Prayer after Communion
We pray, almighty God,
that we may always be counted among the members of Christ,
in whose Body and Blood we have communion.
Who lives and reigns for ever and ever.
Amen.

Fifth Sunday of Lent, Year B

Prayer over the People
Bless, O Lord, your people,
who long for the gift of your mercy,
and grant that what, at your prompting, they desire
they may receive by your generous gift.
Through Christ our Lord.
Amen.

HOLY WEEK

PASSION SUNDAY (PALM SUNDAY)

See above, pp.290ff.

HOLY THURSDAY: CHRISM MASS

See above, pp.329ff.

THE EASTER TRIDUUM

HOLY THURSDAY
(Mass of the Lord's Supper)

See above, pp.342ff.

GOOD FRIDAY
(Celebration of the Lord's Passion)

See above, pp.355ff.

THE EASTER VIGIL

See above, pp.383ff.

EASTER DAY

See above, pp.423ff.

THE SEASON OF EASTER

SECOND SUNDAY OF EASTER   B
(or of Divine Mercy)

Faith: Our Victory over the World

We come together today like that first group of believers, united heart and soul, and celebrating our victory over the world through our faith in Christ, the Son of God.

Entrance Antiphon   1 Pt 2:2
Like newborn infants, you must long for the pure, spiritual milk,
that in him you may grow to salvation, alleluia.

or   4 Esdr 2:36-37

Receive the joy of your glory, giving thanks to God,
who has called you into the heavenly kingdom, alleluia.

The Gloria in excelsis (Glory to God in the highest) is said.

Collect
God of everlasting mercy,
who, in the very recurrence of the paschal feast
kindle the faith of the people you have made your own,
increase, we pray, the grace you have bestowed,
that all may grasp and rightly understand
in what font they have been washed,
by whose Spirit they have been reborn,
by whose Blood they have been redeemed.
Through our Lord Jesus Christ, your Son,
who lives and reigns with you in the unity of the Holy Spirit,
one God, for ever and ever.
Amen.

Second Sunday of Easter, Year B

FIRST READING
A reading from the Acts of the Apostles 4:32-35

The whole group of believers was united, heart and soul; no one claimed for his own use anything that he had, as everything they owned was held in common.

The apostles continued to testify to the resurrection of the Lord Jesus with great power, and they were all given great respect.

None of their members was ever in want, as all those who owned land or houses would sell them, and bring the money from them, to present it to the apostles; it was then distributed to any members who might be in need.

The word of the Lord.

Responsorial Psalm Ps 117:2-4. 15-18. 22-24. R̸ v.1

   R̸ **Give thanks to the Lord for he is good,**
      for his love has no end.

or
   R̸ **Alleluia, alleluia, alleluia!**

1. Let the sons of Israel say:
   'His love has no end.'
   Let the sons of Aaron say:
   'His love has no end.'
   Let those who fear the Lord say:
   'His love has no end.' R̸

2. The Lord's right hand has triumphed;
   his right hand raised me up.
   I shall not die, I shall live
   and recount his deeds.
   I was punished, I was punished by the Lord,
   but not doomed to die. R̸

3. The stone which the builders rejected
   has become the corner stone.
   This is the work of the Lord,
   a marvel in our eyes.
   This day was made by the Lord;
   we rejoice and are glad. R̸

SECOND READING

A reading from the first letter of St John   5:1-6

Whoever believes that Jesus is the Christ
has been begotten by God;
and whoever loves the Father that begot him
loves the child whom he begets.
We can be sure that we love God's children
if we love God himself and do what he has commanded us;
this is what loving God is –
keeping his commandments;
and his commandments are not difficult,
because anyone who has been begotten by God
has already overcome the world;
this is the victory over the world –
our faith.
Who can overcome the world?
only the man who believes that Jesus is the Son of God;
Jesus Christ who came by water and blood,
not with water only,
but with water and blood;
with the Spirit as another witness –
since the Spirit is the truth.

The word of the Lord.

Gospel Acclamation   Jn 20:29

Alleluia, alleluia!
Jesus said: 'You believe because you can see me.
Happy are those who have not seen and yet believe.'
Alleluia!

GOSPEL

A reading from the holy Gospel according to John   20:19-31

In the evening of that same day, the first day of the week, the doors were closed in the room where the disciples were, for fear of the Jews. Jesus came and stood among them. He said to them, 'Peace be with you,' and showed them his hands and his side. The disciples were filled with joy when they saw the Lord, and he said to them again, 'Peace be with you.

'As the Father sent me,
so am I sending you.'

After saying this he breathed on them and said:

'Receive the Holy Spirit.
For those whose sins you forgive,
they are forgiven;
for those whose sins you retain,
they are retained.'

Thomas, called the Twin, who was one of the Twelve, was not with them when Jesus came. When the disciples said, 'We have seen the Lord,' he answered, 'Unless I see the holes that the nails made in his hands and can put my finger into the holes they made, and unless I can put my hand into his side, I refuse to believe.' Eight days later the disciples were in the house again and Thomas was with them. The doors were closed, but Jesus came in and stood among them. 'Peace be with you,' he said. Then he spoke to Thomas, 'Put your finger here; look, here are my hands. Give me your hand; put it into my side. Doubt no longer but believe.' Thomas replied, 'My Lord and my God!' Jesus said to him:

'You believe because you can see me.
Happy are those who have not seen and yet believe.'

There were many other signs that Jesus worked and the disciples saw, but they are not recorded in this book. These are recorded so that you may believe that Jesus is the Christ, the Son of God, and that believing this you may have life through his name.

The Gospel of the Lord.

The Creed is said.

Prayer over the Offerings
Accept, O Lord, we pray,
the oblations of your people
(and of those you have brought to new birth),
that, renewed by confession of your name and by Baptism,
they may attain unending happiness.
Through Christ our Lord.
Amen.

Preface I of Easter (... on this day above all ...), p.28.

When the Roman Canon is used, the proper forms of the Communicantes (In communion with those) and Hanc igitur (Therefore, Lord, we pray) are said.

Communion Antiphon
Cf. Jn 20:27
Bring your hand and feel the place of the nails,
and do not be unbelieving but believing, alleluia.

Prayer after Communion
Grant, we pray, almighty God,
that our reception of this paschal Sacrament
may have a continuing effect
in our minds and hearts.
Through Christ our Lord.
Amen.

A formula of Solemn Blessing, p.97, may be used.

For the dismissal of the people, there is sung (as below, p.695) or said: Go forth, the Mass is ended, alleluia, alleluia. Or Go in peace, alleluia, alleluia. The people respond: **Thanks be to God, alleluia, alleluia.**

THIRD SUNDAY OF EASTER   B

Our Advocate with the Father

We celebrate with the living Christ, our advocate with the Father, in whose name repentance for the forgiveness of sins is preached to all the world.

Entrance Antiphon
Cf. Ps 65:1-2
Cry out with joy to God, all the earth;
O sing to the glory of his name.
O render him glorious praise, alleluia.

The Gloria in excelsis (Glory to God in the highest) is said.

Collect
May your people exult for ever, O God,
in renewed youthfulness of spirit,
so that, rejoicing now in the restored glory of our adoption,
we may look forward in confident hope
to the rejoicing of the day of resurrection.
Through our Lord Jesus Christ, your Son,
who lives and reigns with you in the unity of the Holy Spirit,
one God, for ever and ever.
Amen.

Third Sunday of Easter, Year B

FIRST READING
A reading from the Acts of the Apostles 3:13-15. 17-19

Peter said to the people: 'You are Israelites, and it is the God of Abraham, Isaac and Jacob, the God of our ancestors, who has glorified his servant Jesus, the same Jesus you handed over and then disowned in the presence of Pilate, after Pilate had decided to release him. It was you who accused the Holy One, the Just One, you who demanded the reprieve of a murderer while you killed the prince of life. God, however, raised him from the dead, and to that fact we are the witnesses.

'Now I know, brothers, that neither you nor your leaders had any idea what you were really doing; this was the way God carried out what he had foretold, when he said through all his prophets that his Christ would suffer. Now you must repent and turn to God, so that your sins may be wiped out.'

The word of the Lord.

Responsorial Psalm
Ps 4:2. 4. 7. 9. R/ v.7

R/ **Lift up the light of your face on us, O Lord.**

or

R/ **Alleluia!**

1 When I call, answer me, O God of justice;
   from anguish you released me, have mercy and hear me! R/

2 It is the Lord who grants favours to those whom he loves;
   the Lord hears me whenever I call him. R/

3 'What can bring us happiness?' many say.
   Lift up the light of your face on us, O Lord. R/

4 I will lie down in peace and sleep comes at once,
   for you alone, Lord, make me dwell in safety. R/

SECOND READING
A reading from the first letter of St John 2:1-5

I am writing this, my children,
to stop you sinning;
but if anyone should sin,
we have our advocate with the Father,
Jesus Christ, who is just;
he is the sacrifice that takes our sins away,
and not only ours,

but the whole world's.
We can be sure that we know God
only by keeping his commandments.
Anyone who says, 'I know him',
and does not keep his commandments,
is a liar,
refusing to admit the truth.
But when anyone does obey what he has said,
God's love comes to perfection in him.

The word of the Lord.

Gospel Acclamation   cf. Lk 24:32
Alleluia, alleluia!
Lord Jesus, explain the scriptures to us.
Make our hearts burn within us as you talk to us.
Alleluia!

GOSPEL
A reading from the holy Gospel according to Luke   24:35-48

The disciples told their story of what had happened on the road and how they had recognised Jesus at the breaking of bread.

They were still talking about this when Jesus himself stood among them and said to them, 'Peace be with you!' In a state of alarm and fright, they thought they were seeing a ghost. But he said, 'Why are you so agitated, and why are these doubts rising in your hearts? Look at my hands and feet; yes, it is I indeed. Touch me and see for yourselves; a ghost has no flesh and bones as you can see I have.' And as he said this he showed them his hands and feet. Their joy was so great that they could not believe it, and they stood dumbfounded; so he said to them, 'Have you anything here to eat?' And they offered him a piece of grilled fish, which he took and ate before their eyes.

Then he told them, 'This is what I meant when I said, while I was still with you, that everything written about me in the Law of Moses, in the Prophets and in the Psalms, has to be fulfilled.' He then opened their minds to understand the scriptures, and he said to them, 'So you see how it is written that the Christ would suffer and on the third day rise from the dead, and that, in his name, repentance for the forgiveness of sins would be preached to all the nations, beginning from Jerusalem. You are witnesses to this.'

The Gospel of the Lord.

The Creed is said.

Prayer over the Offerings
Receive, O Lord, we pray,
these offerings of your exultant Church,
and, as you have given her cause for such great gladness,
grant also that the gifts we bring
may bear fruit in perpetual happiness.
Through Christ our Lord.
Amen.

An appropriate Preface of Easter, pp.28-30.

Communion Antiphon   Lk 24:35
The disciples recognized the Lord Jesus
in the breaking of the bread, alleluia.

Optional for Year B: Lk 24:46-47
The Christ had to suffer and on the third day rise from the dead;
in his name repentance and remission of sins
must be preached to all the nations, alleluia.

Prayer after Communion
Look with kindness upon your people, O Lord,
and grant, we pray,
that those you were pleased to renew by eternal mysteries
may attain in their flesh
the incorruptible glory of the resurrection.
Through Christ our Lord.
Amen.

A formula of Solemn Blessing, p.97, may be used.

FOURTH SUNDAY OF EASTER   B

Entrance Antiphon   Cf. Ps 32:5-6
The merciful love of the Lord fills the earth;
by the word of the Lord the heavens were made, alleluia.

The Gloria in excelsis (Glory to God in the highest) is said.

Collect
Almighty ever-living God,
lead us to a share in the joys of heaven,
so that the humble flock may reach
where the brave Shepherd has gone before.

Fourth Sunday of Easter, Year B

Who lives and reigns with you in the unity of the Holy Spirit,
one God, for ever and ever.
Amen.

FIRST READING
A reading from the Acts of the Apostles 4:8-12

Filled with the Holy Spirit, Peter said: 'Rulers of the people, and elders! If you are questioning us today about an act of kindness to a cripple, and asking us how he was healed, then I am glad to tell you all, and would indeed be glad to tell the whole people of Israel, that it was by the name of Jesus Christ the Nazarene, the one you crucified, whom God raised from the dead, by this name and by no other that this man is able to stand up perfectly healthy, here in your presence today. This is the stone rejected by you the builders, but which has proved to be the keystone. For of all the names in the world given to men, this is the only one by which we can be saved.'

The word of the Lord.

Responsorial Psalm   Ps 117:1. 8-9. 21-23. 26. 28-29. R̥ v.22
  R̥ **The stone which the builders rejected
     has become the corner stone.**

or
  R̥ **Alleluia!**

1   Give thanks to the Lord for he is good,
    for his love has no end.
    It is better to take refuge in the Lord
    than to trust in men:
    it is better to take refuge in the Lord
    than to trust in princes.   R̥

2   I will thank you for you have given answer
    and you are my saviour.
    The stone which the builders rejected
    has become the corner stone.
    This is the work of the Lord,
    a marvel in our eyes.   R̥

3   Blessed in the name of the Lord
    is he who comes.
    We bless you from the house of the Lord;

I will thank you for you have given answer
and you are my saviour.
Give thanks to the Lord for he is good;
for his love has no end. ℟

SECOND READING
A reading from the first letter of St John   3:1-2

Think of the love that the Father has lavished on us,
by letting us be called God's children;
and that is what we are.
Because the world refused to acknowledge him,
therefore it does not acknowledge us.
My dear people, we are already the children of God
but what we are to be in the future has not yet been revealed;
all we know is, that when it is revealed
we shall be like him
because we shall see him as he really is.

The word of the Lord.

Gospel Acclamation   Jn 10:14
Alleluia, alleluia!
I am the good shepherd, says the Lord;
I know my own sheep and my own know me.
Alleluia!

GOSPEL
A reading from the holy Gospel according to John   10:11-18

Jesus said:

'I am the good shepherd:
the good shepherd is one who lays down his life for his sheep.
The hired man, since he is not the shepherd
and the sheep do not belong to him,
abandons the sheep and runs away
as soon as he sees a wolf coming,
and then the wolf attacks and scatters the sheep;
this is because he is only a hired man
and has no concern for the sheep.
I am the good shepherd;
I know my own
and my own know me,
just as the Father knows me

Fourth Sunday of Easter, Year B

and I know the Father;
and I lay down my life for my sheep.
And there are other sheep I have
that are not of this fold,
and these I have to lead as well.
They too will listen to my voice,
and there will be only one flock
and one shepherd.
The Father loves me,
because I lay down my life
in order to take it up again.
No one takes it from me;
I lay it down of my own free will,
and as it is in my power to lay it down,
so it is in my power to take it up again;
and this is the command I have been given by my Father.'

The Gospel of the Lord.

The Creed is said.

Prayer over the Offerings
Grant, we pray, O Lord,
that we may always find delight in these paschal mysteries,
so that the renewal constantly at work within us
may be the cause of our unending joy.
Through Christ our Lord.
Amen.

An appropriate Preface of Easter, pp.28-30.

Communion Antiphon
The Good Shepherd has risen,
who laid down his life for his sheep
and willingly died for his flock, alleluia.

Prayer after Communion
Look upon your flock, kind Shepherd,
and be pleased to settle in eternal pastures
the sheep you have redeemed
by the Precious Blood of your Son.
Who lives and reigns for ever and ever.
Amen.

A formula of Solemn Blessing, p.97, may be used.

FIFTH SUNDAY OF EASTER B

Christ the True Vine

When, like St Paul, we 'believe in the name of Jesus Christ', God lives in us and we in him. We become branches of the true vine, Jesus Christ.

Entrance Antiphon Cf. Ps 97:1-2
O sing a new song to the Lord,
for he has worked wonders;
in the sight of the nations
he has shown his deliverance, alleluia.

The Gloria in excelsis (Glory to God in the highest) is said.

Collect
Almighty ever-living God,
constantly accomplish the Paschal Mystery within us,
that those you were pleased to make new in Holy Baptism
may, under your protective care, bear much fruit
and come to the joys of life eternal.
Through our Lord Jesus Christ, your Son,
who lives and reigns with you in the unity of the Holy Spirit,
one God, for ever and ever.
Amen.

FIRST READING
A reading from the Acts of the Apostles 9:26-31

When Saul got to Jerusalem he tried to join the disciples, but they were all afraid of him: they could not believe he was really a disciple. Barnabas, however, took charge of him, introduced him to the apostles, and explained how the Lord had appeared to Saul and spoken to him on his journey, and how he had preached boldly at Damascus in the name of Jesus. Saul now started to go round with them in Jerusalem, preaching fearlessly in the name of the Lord. But after he had spoken to the Hellenists, and argued with them, they became determined to kill him. When the brothers knew, they took him to Caesarea, and sent him off from there to Tarsus.

The churches throughout Judaea, Galilee and Samaria were now left in peace, building themselves up, living in the fear of the Lord, and filled with the consolation of the Holy Spirit.

The word of the Lord.

Responsorial Psalm   Ps 21:26-28. 30-32. ℟ v.26

    ℟   **You, Lord, are my praise in the great assembly.**

or

    ℟   **Alleluia!**

1   My vows I will pay before those who fear him.
     The poor shall eat and shall have their fill.
     They shall praise the Lord, those who seek him.
     May their hearts live for ever and ever!   ℟

2   All the earth shall remember and return to the Lord,
     all families of the nations worship before him.
     They shall worship him, all the mighty of the earth;
     before him shall bow all who go down to the dust.   ℟

3   And my soul shall live for him, my children serve him.
     They shall tell of the Lord to generations yet to come,
     declare his faithfulness to peoples yet unborn:
     'These things the Lord has done.'   ℟

SECOND READING

A reading from the first letter of St John   3:18-24

My children,
our love is not to be just words or mere talk,
but something real and active;
only by this can we be certain
that we are the children of the truth
and be able to quieten our conscience in his presence,
whatever accusations it may raise against us,
because God is greater than our conscience and he knows
    everything.
My dear people,
if we cannot be condemned by our own conscience,
we need not be afraid in God's presence,
and whatever we ask him,
we shall receive,
because we keep his commandments
and live the kind of life that he wants.
His commandments are these:
that we believe in the name of his Son Jesus Christ
and that we love one another
as he told us to.

Whoever keeps his commandments
lives in God and God lives in him.
We know that he lives in us
by the Spirit that he has given us.

The word of the Lord.

Gospel Acclamation   Jn 15:4-5
Alleluia, alleluia!
Make your home in me, as I make mine in you.
Whoever remains in me bears fruit in plenty.
Alleluia!

GOSPEL

A reading from the holy Gospel according to John   15:1-8

Jesus said to his disciples:
'I am the true vine,
and my Father is the vinedresser.
Every branch in me that bears no fruit
he cuts away,
and every branch that does bear fruit he prunes
to make it bear even more.
You are pruned already,
by means of the word that I have spoken to you.
Make your home in me, as I make mine in you.
As a branch cannot bear fruit all by itself,
but must remain part of the vine,
neither can you unless you remain in me.
I am the vine,
you are the branches.
Whoever remains in me, with me in him,
bears fruit in plenty;
for cut off from me you can do nothing.
Anyone who does not remain in me
is like a branch that has been thrown away
– he withers;
these branches are collected and thrown on the fire,
and they are burnt.
If you remain in me
and my words remain in you,
you may ask what you will
and you shall get it.

It is to the glory of my Father that you should bear much fruit,
and then you will be my disciples.'

The Gospel of the Lord.

The Creed is said.

Prayer over the Offerings
O God, who by the wonderful exchange effected in this sacrifice
has made us partakers of the one supreme Godhead,
grant, we pray,
that, as we have come to know your truth,
we may make it ours by a worthy way of life.
Through Christ our Lord.
Amen.

An appropriate Preface of Easter, pp.28-30.

Communion Antiphon Cf. Jn 15:1. 5
I am the true vine and you are the branches, says the Lord.
Whoever remains in me, and I in him, bears fruit in plenty,
alleluia.

Prayer after Communion
Graciously be present to your people, we pray, O Lord,
and lead those you have imbued with heavenly mysteries
to pass from former ways to newness of life.
Through Christ our Lord.
Amen.

A formula of Solemn Blessing, p.97, may be used.

SIXTH SUNDAY OF EASTER   B

The Spirit of God's Love

We celebrate the coming of the Spirit of God's love on the Church. And because God does not have favourites, the Spirit is communicated through the Church to the whole world.

Entrance Antiphon Cf. Is 48:20
Proclaim a joyful sound and let it be heard;
proclaim to the ends of the earth:
The Lord has freed his people, alleluia.

The Gloria in excelsis (Glory to God in the highest) is said.

Collect

Grant, almighty God,
that we may celebrate with heartfelt devotion these days of joy,
which we keep in honour of the risen Lord,
and that what we relive in remembrance
we may always hold to in what we do.
Through our Lord Jesus Christ, your Son,
who lives and reigns with you in the unity of the Holy Spirit,
one God, for ever and ever.
Amen.

FIRST READING

A reading from the Acts of the Apostles   10:25-26. 34-35. 44-48

As Peter reached the house Cornelius went out to meet him, knelt at his feet and prostrated himself. But Peter helped him up. 'Stand up,' he said 'I am only a man after all!'

Then Peter addressed them: 'The truth I have now come to realise' he said 'is that God does not have favourites, but that anybody of any nationality who fears God and does what is right is acceptable to him.'

While Peter was still speaking the Holy Spirit came down on all the listeners. Jewish believers who had accompanied Peter were all astonished that the gift of the Holy Spirit should be poured out on the pagans too, since they could hear them speaking strange languages and proclaiming the greatness of God. Peter himself then said, 'Could anyone refuse the water of baptism to these people, now they have received the Holy Spirit just as much as we have?' He then gave orders for them to be baptised in the name of Jesus Christ. Afterwards they begged him to stay on for some days.

The word of the Lord.

Responsorial Psalm   Ps 97:1-4. ℟ cf. v.2

℟   **The Lord has shown his salvation to the nations.**

or

℟   **Alleluia!**

1   Sing a new song to the Lord
     for he has worked wonders.
     His right hand and his holy arm
     have brought salvation. ℟

2. The Lord has made known his salvation;
has shown his justice to the nations.
He has remembered his truth and love
for the house of Israel. ℟

3. All the ends of the earth have seen
the salvation of our God.
Shout to the Lord all the earth,
ring out your joy. ℟

When the Ascension of the Lord is celebrated on the Seventh Sunday of Easter, the second reading and Gospel assigned to the Seventh Sunday (see below, pp.688-90ff.) may be read on the Sixth Sunday.

SECOND READING

A reading from the first letter of St John 4:7-10

My dear people,
let us love one another
since love comes from God
and everyone who loves is begotten by God and knows God.
Anyone who fails to love can never have known God,
because God is love.
God's love for us was revealed
when God sent into the world his only Son
so that we could have life through him;
this is the love I mean:
not our love for God,
but God's love for us when he sent his Son
to be the sacrifice that takes our sins away.

The word of the Lord.

Gospel Acclamation

Jn 14:23

Alleluia, alleluia!
Jesus said: 'If anyone loves me he will keep my word,
and my Father will love him, and we shall come to him.
Alleluia!'

GOSPEL

A reading from the holy Gospel according to John 15:9-17

Jesus said to his disciples:
'As the Father has loved me,
so I have loved you.

Remain in my love.
If you keep my commandments
you will remain in my love,
just as I have kept my Father's commandments
and remain in his love.
I have told you this
so that my own joy may be in you
and your joy be complete.
This is my commandment:
love one another,
as I have loved you.
A man can have no greater love
than to lay down his life for his friends.
You are my friends,
if you do what I command you.
I shall not call you servants any more,
because a servant does not know
his master's business;
I call you friends,
because I have made known to you
everything I have learnt from my Father.
You did not choose me,
no, I chose you;
and I commissioned you
to go out and to bear fruit,
fruit that will last;
and then the Father will give you
anything you ask him in my name.
What I command you
is to love one another.'

    The Gospel of the Lord.

The Creed is said.

Prayer over the Offerings
May our prayers rise up to you, O Lord,
together with the sacrificial offerings,
so that, purified by your graciousness,
we may be conformed to the mysteries of your mighty love.
Through Christ our Lord.
Amen.

An appropriate Preface of Easter, pp.28-30.

The Ascension of the Lord, Year B 681

Communion Antiphon Jn 14:15-16
If you love me, keep my commandments, says the Lord,
and I will ask the Father and he will send you another Paraclete,
to abide with you for ever, alleluia.

Prayer after Communion
Almighty ever-living God,
who restore us to eternal life in the Resurrection of Christ,
increase in us, we pray, the fruits of this paschal Sacrament
and pour into our hearts the strength of this saving food.
Through Christ our Lord.
Amen.

A formula of Solemn Blessing, p.97, may be used.

THE ASCENSION OF THE LORD B
Solemnity

Christ's Eternal Glory

We celebrate today Christ's ascension to his eternal glory in heaven and express our Christian hope that where he, our Head, has gone before us, his Body, we will one day follow, to live for ever in the Kingdom of our Father.

Where the Solemnity of the Ascension is not to be observed as a Holyday of Obligation, it is assigned to the Seventh Sunday of Easter as its proper day.

At the Vigil Mass

This Mass is used on the evening of the day before the Solemnity, either before or after First Vespers (Evening Prayer I) of the Ascension.

Entrance Antiphon Ps 67:33. 35
You kingdoms of the earth, sing to God;
praise the Lord, who ascends above the highest heavens;
his majesty and might are in the skies, alleluia.

The Gloria in excelsis (Glory to God in the highest) is said.

Collect
O God, whose Son today ascended to the heavens
as the Apostles looked on,
grant, we pray, that, in accordance with his promise,

The Ascension of the Lord, Year B

we may be worthy for him to live with us always on earth,
and we with him in heaven.
Who lives and reigns with you in the unity of the Holy Spirit,
one God, for ever and ever.
Amen.

For the Readings, Gospel Acclamation and Gospel, see the Mass during the Day (pp.683-5).

The Creed is said.

Prayer over the Offerings
O God, whose Only Begotten Son, our High Priest,
is seated ever-living at your right hand to intercede for us,
grant that we may approach with confidence the throne of grace
and there obtain your mercy.
Through Christ our Lord.
Amen.

Preface I or II of the Ascension, p.31.

When the Roman Canon is used, the proper form of the Communicantes (In communion with those) is said.

Communion Antiphon   Cf. Heb 10:12
Christ, offering a single sacrifice for sins,
is seated for ever at God's right hand, alleluia.

Prayer after Communion
May the gifts we have received from your altar, Lord,
kindle in our hearts a longing for the heavenly homeland
and cause us to press forward, following in the Saviour's
　　footsteps,
to the place where for our sake he entered before us.
Who lives and reigns for ever and ever.
Amen.

A formula of Solemn Blessing, pp.97-8, may be used.

At the Mass during the Day

Entrance Antiphon   Acts 1:11
Men of Galilee, why gaze in wonder at the heavens?
This Jesus whom you saw ascending into heaven
will return as you saw him go, alleluia.

The Gloria in excelsis (Glory to God in the highest) is said.

The Ascension of the Lord, Year B

Collect

Gladden us with holy joys, almighty God,
and make us rejoice with devout thanksgiving,
for the Ascension of Christ your Son
is our exaltation,
and, where the Head has gone before in glory,
the Body is called to follow in hope.
Through our Lord Jesus Christ, your Son,
who lives and reigns with you in the unity of the Holy Spirit,
one God, for ever and ever.

or

Grant, we pray, almighty God,
that we, who believe that your Only Begotten Son, our Redeemer,
ascended this day to the heavens,
may in spirit dwell already in heavenly realms.
Who lives and reigns with you in the unity of the Holy Spirit,
one God, for ever and ever.
Amen.

FIRST READING

A reading from the Acts of the Apostles   1:1-11

In my earlier work, Theophilus, I dealt with everything Jesus had done and taught from the beginning until the day he gave his instructions to the apostles he had chosen through the Holy Spirit, and was taken up to heaven. He had shown himself alive to them after his Passion by many demonstrations: for forty days he had continued to appear to them and tell them about the kingdom of God. When he had been at table with them, he had told them not to leave Jerusalem, but to wait there for what the Father had promised. 'It is,' he had said, 'what you have heard me speak about: John baptised with water but you, not many days from now, will be baptised with the Holy Spirit.'

Now having met together, they asked him, 'Lord, has the time come? Are you going to restore the kingdom to Israel?' He replied, 'It is not for you to know times or dates that the Father has decided by his own authority, but you will receive power when the Holy Spirit comes on you, and then you will be my witnesses not only in Jerusalem but throughout Judaea and Samaria, and indeed to the ends of the earth.'

As he said this he was lifted up while they looked on, and a cloud took him from their sight. They were still staring into the sky when suddenly two men in white were standing near them and they said, 'Why are you men from Galilee standing here looking into the sky? Jesus who has been taken up from you into heaven, this same Jesus will come back in the same way as you have seen him go there.'

The word of the Lord.

Responsorial Psalm Ps 46:2-3. 6-9. ℟ v.6

℟ **God goes up with shouts of joy;**
the Lord goes up with trumpet blast.

or

℟ **Alleluia!**

1 All peoples, clap your hands,
   cry to God with shouts of joy!
   For the Lord, the Most High, we must fear,
   great king over all the earth. ℟

2 God goes up with shouts of joy;
   the Lord goes up with trumpet blast.
   Sing praise for God, sing praise,
   sing praise to our king, sing praise. ℟

3 God is king of all the earth.
   Sing praise with all your skill.
   God is king over the nations;
   God reigns on his holy throne. ℟

SECOND READING

The reading of Year A, Eph 1:17-23, p.450-51 (above), may be used in place of the following.

A reading from the letter of St Paul to the Ephesians 4:1-13

I, the prisoner in the Lord, implore you to lead a life worthy of your vocation. Bear with one another charitably, in complete selflessness, gentleness and patience. Do all you can to preserve the unity of the Spirit by the peace that binds you together. There is one Body, one Spirit, just as you were all called into one and the same hope when you were called. There is one Lord, one faith, one baptism, and one God who is Father of all, over all, through all and within all. Each one of us, however, has been given his own share of grace, given as Christ allotted it. It was said that he would:

When he ascended to the height, he captured prisoners,
he gave gifts to men.

When it says, 'he ascended', what can it mean if not that he descended right down to the lower regions of the earth? The one who rose higher than all the heavens to fill all things is none other than the one who descended. And* to some, his gift was that they should be apostles; to some, prophets; to some, evangelists; to some, pastors and teachers; so that the saints together make a unity in the work of service, building up the body of Christ. In this way we are all to come to unity in our faith and in our knowledge of the Son of God, until we become the perfect Man, fully mature with the fullness of Christ himself.

The word of the Lord.*

Shorter Form, verses 1-7. 11-13. Read between

Gospel Acclamation Mt 28:19-20
Alleluia, alleluia!
Go, make disciples of all the nations;
I am with you always; yes, to the end of time.
Alleluia!

GOSPEL
A reading from the holy Gospel according to Mark 16:15-20

Jesus showed himself to the Eleven, and said to them, 'Go out to the whole world; proclaim the Good News to all creation. He who believes and is baptised will be saved; he who does not believe will be condemned. These are the signs that will be associated with believers: in my name they will cast out devils; they will have the gift of tongues; they will pick up snakes in their hands, and be unharmed should they drink deadly poison; they will lay their hands on the sick, who will recover.'

And so the Lord Jesus, after he had spoken to them, was taken up into heaven: there at the right hand of God he took his place, while they, going out, preached everywhere, the Lord working with them and confirming the word by the signs that accompanied it.

The Gospel of the Lord.

The Creed is said.

Prayer over the Offerings
We offer sacrifice now in supplication, O Lord,
to honour the wondrous Ascension of your Son:

grant, we pray,
that through this most holy exchange
we, too, may rise up to the heavenly realms.
Through Christ our Lord.
Amen.

Preface I or II of the Ascension of the Lord, p.31.

When the Roman Canon is used, the proper form of the Communicantes (In communion with those) is said.

Communion Antiphon   Mt 28:20
Behold, I am with you always,
even to the end of the age, alleluia.

Prayer after Communion
Almighty ever-living God,
who allow those on earth to celebrate divine mysteries,
grant, we pray,
that Christian hope may draw us onward
to where our nature is united with you.
Through Christ our Lord.
Amen.

A formula of Solemn Blessing, pp.97-8, may be used.

SEVENTH SUNDAY OF EASTER   B

Where the Ascension is not a holiday of obligation, it is celebrated on this Sunday.

The Spirit of God's Life

The Holy Spirit is the soul of the Church, the principle of its life and unity. God is living in us because he lets us share his Spirit.

Entrance Antiphon   Cf. Ps 26:7-9
O Lord, hear my voice, for I have called to you;
of you my heart has spoken: Seek his face;
hide not your face from me, alleluia.

The Gloria in excelsis (Glory to God in the highest) is said.

Collect
Graciously hear our supplications, O Lord,
so that we, who believe that the Saviour of the human race
is with you in your glory,

may experience, as he promised,
until the end of the world,
his abiding presence among us.
Who lives and reigns with you in the unity of the Holy Spirit,
one God, for ever and ever.
Amen.

FIRST READING
A reading from the Acts of the Apostles   1:15-17. 20-26

One day Peter stood up to speak to the brothers – there were about a hundred and twenty persons in the congregation: 'Brothers, the passage of scripture had to be fulfilled in which the Holy Spirit, speaking through David, foretells the fate of Judas, who offered himself as a guide to the men who arrested Jesus – after having been one of our number and actually sharing this ministry of ours.

'In the Book of Psalms it says:

Let someone else take his office.

'We must therefore choose someone who has been with us the whole time that the Lord Jesus was travelling around with us, someone who was with us right from the time when John was baptising until the day when he was taken up from us – and he can act with us as a witness to his resurrection.'

Having nominated two candidates, Joseph known as Barsabbas, whose surname was Justus, and Matthias, they prayed, 'Lord, you can read everyone's heart; show us therefore which of these two you have chosen to take over this ministry and apostolate, which Judas abandoned to go to his proper place.' They then drew lots for them, and as the lot fell to Matthias, he was listed as one of the twelve apostles.

The word of the Lord.

Responsorial Psalm   Ps 102:1-2. 11-12. 19-20. ℟ v.19
  ℟   **The Lord has set his sway in heaven.**

or
  ℟   **Alleluia!**

1   My soul, give thanks to the Lord;
     all my being, bless his holy name.
     My soul, give thanks to the Lord
     and never forget all his blessings.   ℟

2 For as the heavens are high above the earth
so strong is his love for those who fear him.
As far as the east is from the west
so far does he remove our sins. ℟

3 The Lord has set his sway in heaven
and his kingdom is ruling over all.
Give thanks to the Lord, all his angels,
mighty in power, fulfilling his word. ℟

SECOND READING
A reading from the first letter of St John   4:11-16

My dear people,
since God has loved us so much,
we too should love one another.
No one has ever seen God;
but as long as we love one another
God will live in us
and his love will be complete in us.
We can know that we are living in him
and he is living in us
because he lets us share his Spirit.
We ourselves saw and we testify
that the Father sent his Son
as saviour of the world.
If anyone acknowledges that Jesus is the Son of God,
God lives in him, and he in God.
We ourselves have known and put our faith in
God's love towards ourselves.
God is love
and anyone who lives in love lives in God,
and God lives in him.

  The word of the Lord.

Gospel Acclamation   Cf. Jn 14:18
Alleluia, alleluia!
I will not leave your orphans, says the Lord;
I will come back to you, and your hearts will be full of joy.
Alleluia!

GOSPEL

A reading from the holy Gospel according to John 17:11-19

Jesus raised his eyes to heaven and said:
'Holy Father,
keep those you have given me true to your name,
so that they may be one like us.
While I was with them,
I kept those you had given me true to your name.
I have watched over them and not one is lost
except the one who chose to be lost,
and this was to fulfil the scriptures.
But now I am coming to you
and while still in the world I say these things
to share my joy with them to the full.
I passed your word on to them,
and the world hated them,
because they belong to the world
no more than I belong to the world.
I am not asking you to remove them from the world,
but to protect them from the evil one.
They do not belong to the world
any more than I belong to the world.
Consecrate them in the truth;
your word is truth.
As you sent me into the world,
I have sent them into the world,
and for their sake I consecrate myself
so that they too may be consecrated in truth.'

   The Gospel of the Lord.

The Creed is said.

Prayer over the Offerings
Accept, O Lord, the prayers of your faithful
with the sacrificial offerings,
that through these acts of devotedness
we may pass over to the glory of heaven.
Through Christ our Lord.
Amen.

An appropriate Preface of Easter, or of the Ascension, pp.28-31.

Communion Antiphon Jn 17:22
Father, I pray that they may be one
as we also are one, alleluia.

Prayer after Communion
Hear us, O God our Saviour,
and grant us confidence,
that through these sacred mysteries
there will be accomplished in the body of the whole Church
what has already come to pass in Christ her Head.
Who lives and reigns for ever and ever.
Amen.

A formula of Solemn Blessing, pp.97-8, may be used.

PENTECOST SUNDAY B
Solemnity

Simple and extended forms of the Vigil Mass, which is celebrated on Saturday evening, will be found under Year A, pp.456ff.

At the Mass During the Day

The Day of Pentecost

Today we celebrate the great day of Pentecost when Christ filled the Church with the power of his spirit and sent it out into the world to bring his peace, joy and forgiveness to all peoples.

Entrance Antiphon Wis 1:7
The Spirit of the Lord has filled the whole world
and that which contains all things
understands what is said, alleluia.

or Rm 5:5; cf. 8:11
The love of God has been poured into our hearts
through the Spirit of God dwelling within us, alleluia.

The Gloria is excelsis (Glory or God is in the highest) is said.

Collect
O God, who by the mystery of today's great feast
sanctify your whole Church in every people and nation,
pour out, we pray, the gifts of the Holy Spirit
across the face of the earth

and, with the divine grace that was at work
when the Gospel was first proclaimed,
fill now once more the hearts of believers.
Through our Lord Jesus Christ, your Son,
who lives and reigns with you in the unity of the Holy Spirit,
one God, for ever and ever.
Amen.

FIRST READING
A reading from the Acts of the Apostles 2:1-11

When Pentecost day came round, the apostles had all met in one room, when suddenly they heard what sounded like a powerful wind from heaven, the noise of which filled the entire house in which they were sitting; and something appeared to them that seemed like tongues of fire; these separated and came to rest on the head of each of them. They were all filled with the Holy Spirit, and began to speak foreign languages as the Spirit gave them the gift of speech.

Now there were devout men living in Jerusalem from every nation under heaven, and at this sound they all assembled, each one bewildered to hear these men speaking his own language. They were amazed and astonished. 'Surely' they said 'all these men speaking are Galileans? How does it happen that each of us hears them in his own native language? Parthians, Medes and Elamites; people from Mesopotamia, Judaea and Cappadocia, Pontus and Asia, Phrygia and Pamphylia, Egypt and the parts of Libya round Cyrene; as well as visitors from Rome – Jews and proselytes alike – Cretans and Arabs; we hear them preaching in our own language about the marvels of God.'

The word of the Lord.

Responsorial Psalm Ps 103:1. 24. 29-31. 34. ℞ cf. v.30

℞ **Send forth your Spirit, O Lord,
and renew the face of the earth.**

or

℞ **Alleluia.**

1 Bless the Lord, my soul!
 Lord God, how great you are,
 How many are your works, O Lord!
 The earth is full of your riches. ℞

2   You take back your spirit, they die,
    returning to the dust from which they came.
    You send forth your spirit, they are created;
    and you renew the face of the earth. ℟

3   May the glory of the Lord last for ever!
    May the Lord rejoice in his works!
    May my thoughts be pleasing to him.
    I find my joy in the Lord. ℟

The Second Reading and the Gospel may be taken from Year A, see above, pp.468ff. Alternatively, the Second Reading and the Gospel given below may be used.

SECOND READING

A reading from the letter of St Paul to the Galatians   5:16-25

If you are guided by the Spirit you will be in no danger of yielding to self-indulgence, since self-indulgence is the opposite of the Spirit, the Spirit is totally against such a thing, and it is precisely because the two are so opposed that you do not always carry out your good intentions. If you are led by the Spirit, no law can touch you. When self-indulgence is at work the results are obvious: fornication, gross indecency and sexual irresponsibility; idolatry and sorcery; feuds and wrangling, jealousy, bad temper and quarrels; disagreements, factions, envy; drunkenness, orgies and similar things. I warn you now, as I warned you before: those who behave like this will not inherit the kingdom of God. What the Spirit brings is very different: love, joy, peace, patience, kindness, goodness, trustfulness, gentleness and self-control. There can be no law against things like that, of course. You cannot belong to Christ Jesus unless you crucify all self-indulgent passions and desire.

Since the Spirit is our life, let us be directed by the Spirit.

The word of the Lord.

SEQUENCE

The sequence may be said or sung.

Holy Spirit, Lord of light,
   From the clear celestial height
Thy pure beaming radiance give.

Come, thou Father of the poor,
   Come with treasures which endure;
Come, thou light of all that live!

Thou, of all consolers best,
  Thou, the soul's delightful guest,
Dost refreshing peace bestow;

Thou in toil art comfort sweet;
  Pleasant coolness in the heat;
Solace in the midst of woe.

Light immortal, light divine,
  Visit thou these hearts of thine,
And our inmost being fill:

If thou take thy grace away,
  Nothing pure in man will stay;
All his good is turned to ill.

Heal our wounds, our strength renew;
  On our dryness pour thy dew;
Wash the stains of guilt away:

Bend the stubborn heart and will;
  Melt the frozen, warm the chill;
Guide the steps that go astray.

Thou, on us who evermore
  Thee confess and thee adore,
With thy sevenfold gifts descend:

Give us comfort when we die;
  Give us life with thee on high;
Give us joys that never end.

Gospel Acclamation
Alleluia, alleluia!
Come, Holy Spirit, fill the hearts of your faithful
and kindle in them the fire of your love.
Alleluia!

GOSPEL

A reading from the holy Gospel 15:26-27; 16:12-15
according to John

Jesus said to his disciples:
'When the Advocate comes,
whom I shall send to you from the Father,
the Spirit of truth who issues from the Father,
he will be my witness.
And you too will be witnesses,

because you have been with me from the outset.
I still have many things to say to you
but they would be too much for you now.
But when the Spirit of truth comes
he will lead you to the complete truth,
since he will not be speaking as from himself
but will say only what he has learnt;
and he will tell you of the things to come.
He will glorify me,
since all he tells you
will be taken from what is mine.
Everything the Father has is mine;
that is why I said:
All he tells you
will be taken from what is mine.'

The Gospel of the Lord.

The Creed is said.

Prayer over the Offerings
Grant, we pray, O Lord,
that, as promised by your Son,
the Holy Spirit may reveal to us more abundantly
the hidden mystery of this sacrifice
and graciously lead us into all truth.
Through Christ our Lord.
Amen.

Preface of the Mystery of Pentecost, p.32.

When the Roman Canon is used, the proper form of the Communicantes (In communion with those) is said.

Communion Antiphon   Acts 2:4. 11
They were all filled with the Holy Spirit
and spoke of the marvels of God, alleluia.

Prayer after Communion
O God, who bestow heavenly gifts upon your Church,
safeguard, we pray, the grace you have given,
that the gift of the Holy Spirit poured out upon her
may retain all its force
and that this spiritual food
may gain her abundance of eternal redemption.
Through Christ our Lord.
Amen.

Pentecost Sunday, Year B

A formula of Solemn Blessing, p.98, may be used.

To dismiss the people the Deacon or, if there is no Deacon, the Priest himself sings or says:

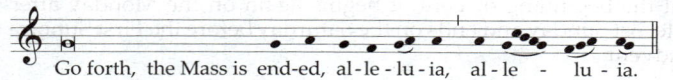

Go forth, the Mass is end-ed, al-le-lu-ia, al-le-lu-ia.

or

Go in peace, al-le-lu-ia, al-le-lu-ia.

Thanks be to God, al-le-lu-ia, al-le-lu-ia.

With Easter Time now concluded, the paschal candle is extinguished. It is desirable to keep the paschal candle in the baptistery with due honour so that it is lit at the celebration of Baptism and the candles of those baptized are lit from it.

ORDINARY TIME

Ordinary Time contains thirty-three or thirty-four weeks. It begins on the Monday following the Sunday after 6 January and continues until the beginning of Lent; it begins again on the Monday after Pentecost Sunday and ends on the Saturday before the First Sunday of Advent.

THE SOLEMNITIES OF THE LORD DURING ORDINARY TIME

First Sunday after Pentecost
THE MOST HOLY TRINITY B
Solemnity

Abba, Father!

We celebrate our baptism in the name of the Trinity as a result of which we have received the spirit of sons and daughters, privileged to call the great God of glory and majesty our Father.

Entrance Antiphon
Blest be God the Father,
and the Only Begotten Son of God,
and also the Holy Spirit,
for he has shown us his merciful love.

The Gloria in excelsis (Glory to God in the highest) is said.

Collect
God our Father, who by sending into the world
the Word of truth and the Spirit of sanctification
made known to the human race your wondrous mystery,
grant us, we pray, that in professing the true faith,
we may acknowledge the Trinity of eternal glory
and adore your Unity, powerful in majesty.
Through our Lord Jesus Christ, your Son,
who lives and reigns with you in the unity of the Holy Spirit,
one God, for ever and ever.
Amen.

FIRST READING
A reading from the book of Deuteronomy 4:32-34. 39-40

Moses said to the people: 'Put this question to the ages that are past, that went before you, from the time God created man on earth: Was there ever a word so majestic, from one end of heaven to the other? Was anything ever heard? Did ever a people hear the voice of the living God speaking from the heart of the fire, as you heard it, and remain alive? Has any god ventured to take to himself one nation from the midst of another by ordeals, signs, wonders, war with mighty hand and outstretched arm, by fearsome terrors – all this that the Lord your God did for you before your eyes in Egypt?

'Understand this today, therefore, and take it to heart: The Lord is God indeed, in heaven above as on earth beneath, he and no other. Keep his laws and commandments as I give them to you today so that you and your children may prosper and live long in the land that the Lord your God gives you for ever.'

The word of the Lord.

Responsorial Psalm Ps 32:4-6. 9. 18-20. 22. ℟ v.12

℟ **Happy the people the Lord has chosen as his own.**

1. The word of the Lord is faithful
and all his works to be trusted.
The Lord loves justice and right
and fills the earth with his love. ℟

2. By his word the heavens were made,
by the breath of his mouth all the stars.
He spoke; and they came to be.
He commanded; they sprang into being. ℟

3. The Lord looks on those who revere him,
on those who hope in his love,
to rescue their souls from death,
to keep them alive in famine. ℟

4. Our soul is waiting for the Lord.
The Lord is our help and our shield.
May your love be upon us, O Lord,
as we place all our hope in you. ℟

SECOND READING
A reading from the letter of St Paul to the Romans   8:14-17

Everyone moved by the Spirit is a son of God. The spirit you received is not the spirit of slaves bringing fear into your lives again; it is the spirit of sons, and it makes us cry out, 'Abba, Father!' The Spirit himself and our spirit bear united witness that we are children of God. And if we are children we are heirs as well: heirs of God and co-heirs with Christ, sharing his sufferings so as to share his glory.

The word of the Lord.

Gospel Acclamation   Cf. Apoc 1:8
Alleluia, alleluia!
Glory be to the Father, and to the Son, and to the Holy Spirit,
the God who is, who was, and who is to come.
Alleluia!

GOSPEL
A reading from the holy Gospel according to Matthew   28:16-20

The eleven disciples set out for Galilee, to the mountain where Jesus had arranged to meet them. When they saw him they fell down before him, though some hesitated. Jesus came up and spoke to them. He said, 'All authority in heaven and on earth has been given to me. Go, therefore, make disciples of all the nations; baptise them in the name of the Father and of the Son and of the Holy Spirit, and teach them to observe all the commands I gave you. And know that I am with you always; yes, to the end of time.'

The Gospel of the Lord.

The Creed is said.

Prayer over the Offerings
Sanctify by the invocation of your name,
we pray, O Lord our God,
this oblation of our service,
and by it make of us an eternal offering to you.
Through Christ our Lord.
Amen.

Preface of the Mystery of the Most Holy Trinity, p.36.

Communion Antiphon   Gal 4:6
Since you are children of God,
God has sent into your hearts the Spirit of his Son,
the Spirit who cries out: Abba, Father.

Prayer after Communion
May receiving this Sacrament, O Lord our God,
bring us health of body and soul,
as we confess your eternal holy Trinity and undivided Unity.
Through Christ our Lord.
Amen.

Thursday after the Most Holy Trinity

THE MOST HOLY BODY AND BLOOD OF CHRIST

(CORPUS CHRISTI)
Solemnity

Where the Solemnity of the Most Holy Body and Blood of Christ is not a Holyday of Obligation, it is assigned to the Sunday after the Most Holy Trinity as its proper day.

The Blood of the Covenant

The old covenant was sealed with the blood of the sacrifice which Moses sprinkled on the people. The new covenant was sealed with the blood of Christ who offered himself as a perfect sacrifice to God.

Entrance Antiphon   Cf. Ps 80:17
He fed them with the finest wheat
and satisfied them with honey from the rock.

The Gloria in excelsis (Glory to God in the highest) is said.

Collect
O God, who in this wonderful Sacrament
have left us a memorial of your Passion,
grant us, we pray,
so to revere the sacred mysteries of your Body and Blood
that we may always experience in ourselves
the fruits of your redemption.

Who live and reign with God the Father
in the unity of the Holy Spirit,
one God, for ever and ever.
Amen.

FIRST READING

A reading from the book of Exodus 24:3-8

Moses went and told the people all the commands of the Lord and all the ordinances. In answer, all the people said with one voice, 'We will observe all the commands that the Lord has decreed.' Moses put all the commands of the Lord into writing, and early next morning he built an altar at the foot of the mountain, with twelve standing-stones for the twelve tribes of Israel. Then he directed certain young Israelites to offer holocausts and to immolate bullocks to the Lord as communion sacrifices. Half of the blood Moses took up and put into basins, the other half he cast on the altar. And taking the Book of the Covenant he read it to the listening people, and they said, 'We will observe all that the Lord has decreed; we will obey.' Then Moses took the blood and cast it towards the people. 'This' he said 'is the blood of the Covenant that the Lord has made with you, containing all these rules.'

The word of the Lord.

Responsorial Psalm Ps 115:12-13. 15-18 ℟ v.13

℟ **The cup of salvation I will raise;
I will call on the Lord's name.**

or

℟ **Alleluia!**

1 How can I repay the Lord
 for his goodness to me?
 The cup of salvation I will raise;
 I will call on the Lord's name. ℟

2 O precious in the eyes of the Lord
 is the death of his faithful.
 Your servant, Lord, your servant am I;
 you have loosened my bonds. ℟

3 A thanksgiving sacrifice I make:
 I will call on the Lord's name.
 My vows to the Lord I will fulfil
 before all his people. ℟

SECOND READING
A reading from the letter to the Hebrews 9:11-15

Now Christ has come, as the high priest of all the blessings which were to come. He has passed through the greater, the more perfect tent, which is better than one made by men's hands because it is not of this created order; and he has entered the sanctuary once and for all, taking with him not the blood of goats and bull calves, but his own blood, having won an eternal redemption for us. The blood of goats and bulls and the ashes of a heifer are sprinkled on those who have incurred defilement and they restore the holiness of their outward lives; how much more effectively the blood of Christ, who offered himself as the perfect sacrifice to God through the eternal Spirit, can purify our inner self from dead actions so that we do our service to the living God.

He brings a new covenant, as the mediator, only so that the people who were called to an eternal inheritance may actually receive what was promised: his death took place to cancel the sins that infringed the earlier covenant.

The word of the Lord.

The Sequence Sing forth, O Zion may be said or sung in its longer or shorter form. See above, pp.479ff.

Gospel Acclamation
Jn 6:51-52

Alleluia, alleluia!
I am the living bread which has come down from heaven,
says the Lord.
Anyone who eats this bread will live for ever.
Alleluia!

GOSPEL
A reading from the holy Gospel according to Mark 14:12-16. 22-26

On the first day of Unleavened Bread, when the Passover lamb was sacrificed, his disciples said to Jesus, 'Where do you want us to go and make the preparations for you to eat the passover?' So he sent two of his disciples, saying to them, 'Go into the city and you will meet a man carrying a pitcher of water. Follow him, and say to the owner of the house which he enters, "The Master says: Where is my dining room in which I can eat the passover with my disciples?" He will show you a large upper room furnished with couches, all prepared. Make the preparations for us there.' The disciples set out and went to the city and found everything as he had told them, and prepared the Passover.

And as they were eating he took some bread, and when he had said the blessing he broke it and gave it to them. 'Take it,' he said 'this is my body.' Then he took a cup, and when he had returned thanks he gave it to them, and all drank from it, and he said to them, 'This is my blood, the blood of the covenant, which is to be poured out for many. I tell you solemnly, I shall not drink any more wine until the day I drink the new wine in the kingdom of God.'

After psalms had been sung they left for the Mount of Olives.

The Gospel of the Lord.

The Creed is said.

Prayer over the Offerings
Grant your Church, O Lord, we pray,
the gifts of unity and peace,
whose signs are to be seen in mystery
in the offerings we here present.
Through Christ our Lord.
Amen.

Preface I or II of the Most Holy Eucharist, pp.38-9.

Communion Antiphon Jn 6:57
Whoever eats my flesh and drinks my blood
remains in me and I in him, says the Lord.

Prayer after Communion
Grant, O Lord, we pray,
that we may delight for all eternity
in that share in your divine life,
which is foreshadowed in the present age
by our reception of your precious Body and Blood.
Who live and reign for ever and ever.
Amen.

It is desirable that a procession take place after the Mass in which the Host to be carried in the procession is consecrated. However, nothing prohibits a procession from taking place even after a public and lengthy period of adoration following the Mass. If a procession takes place after Mass, when the Communion of the faithful is over, the monstrance in which the consecrated host has been placed is set on the altar. When the Prayer after Communion has been said, the Concluding Rites are omitted and the procession forms.

Friday after the Second Sunday after Pentecost
THE MOST SACRED HEART OF JESUS   B
Solemnity

The Heart That Was Pierced

Our rejection of God's love is tragically symbolised by the piercing of the heart of Christ on the cross.

Entrance Antiphon   Ps 32:11. 19
The designs of his Heart are from age to age,
to rescue their souls from death,
and to keep them alive in famine.

The Gloria in excelsis (Glory to God in the highest) is said.

Collect
Grant, we pray, almighty God,
that we, who glory in the Heart of your beloved Son
and recall the wonders of his love for us,
may be made worthy to receive
an overflowing measure of grace
from that fount of heavenly gifts.
Through our Lord Jesus Christ, your Son,
who lives and reigns with you in the unity of the Holy Spirit,
one God, for ever and ever.

or

O God, who in the Heart of your Son,
wounded by our sins,
bestow on us in mercy
the boundless treasures of your love,
grant, we pray,
that, in paying him the homage of our devotion,
we may also offer worthy reparation.
Through our Lord Jesus Christ, your Son,
who lives and reigns with you in the unity of the Holy Spirit,
one God, for ever and ever.
Amen.

FIRST READING

A reading from the prophet Hosea 11:1. 3-4. 8-9

Listen to the word of the Lord:

> When Israel was a child I loved him,
> and I called my son out of Egypt.
> I myself taught Ephraim to walk,
> I took them in my arms;
> yet they have not understood that I was the one looking after them.
> I led them with reins of kindness,
> with leading-strings of love.
> I was like someone who lifts an infant close against his cheek;
> stooping down to him I gave him his food.
> How could I treat you like Admah,
> or deal with you like Zeboiim?
> My heart recoils from it,
> my whole being trembles at the thought.
> I will not give rein to my fierce anger,
> I will not destroy Ephraim again,
> for I am God, not man:
> I am the Holy One in your midst
> and have no wish to destroy.

The word of the Lord.

Responsorial Psalm Is 12:2-6. ℟ v.3

℟ **With joy you will draw water
from the wells of the Saviour.**

1. Truly God is my salvation,
I trust, I shall not fear.
For the Lord is my strength, my song,
he became my saviour.
With joy you will draw water
from the wells of salvation. ℟

2. Give thanks to the Lord, give praise to his name!
Make his mighty deeds known to the peoples!
Declare the greatness of his name. ℟

3. Sing a psalm to the Lord
for he has done glorious deeds;
make them known to all the earth!
People of Zion, sing and shout for joy
for great in your midst is the Holy One of Israel. ℟

SECOND READING
A reading from the letter of St Paul to the Ephesians 3:8-12. 14-19

I, Paul, who am less than the least of all the saints, have been entrusted with this special grace, not only of proclaiming to the pagans the infinite treasure of Christ but also of explaining how the mystery is to be dispensed. Through all the ages, this has been kept hidden in God, the creator of everything. Why? So that the Sovereignties and Powers should learn only now, through the Church, how comprehensive God's wisdom really is, exactly according to the plan which he had had from all eternity in Christ Jesus our Lord. This is why we are bold enough to approach God in complete confidence, through our faith in him. This, then, is what I pray, kneeling before the Father, from whom every family, whether spiritual or natural, takes its name: Out of his infinite glory, may he give you the power through his Spirit for your hidden self to grow strong, so that Christ may live in your hearts through faith, and then, planted in love and built on love, you will with all the saints have strength to grasp the breadth and the length, the height and the depth; until, knowing the love of Christ, which is beyond all knowledge, you are filled with the utter fullness of God.

The word of the Lord.

Gospel Acclamation
Mt 11:29
Alleluia, alleluia!
Shoulder my yoke and learn from me,
for I am gentle and humble in heart.
Alleluia!

Alternative Gospel Acclamation
1 Jn 4:10
Alleluia, alleluia!
This is the love I mean:
God's love for us when he sent his Son
to be the sacrifice that takes our sins away.
Alleluia!

GOSPEL
A reading from the holy Gospel according to John 19:31-37

It was Preparation Day, and to prevent the bodies remaining on the cross during the sabbath since that sabbath was a day of special solemnity – the Jews asked Pilate to have the legs broken and the bodies taken away. Consequently the soldiers came and broke the legs of the first man who had been crucified with him and then of the other. When they came to Jesus, they found he was already dead, and so instead of breaking his legs one of the soldiers pierced his side with a lance; and immediately there came out blood and water. This is the evidence of one who saw it – trustworthy evidence, and he knows he speaks the truth – and he gives it so that you may believe as well. Because all this happened to fulfil the words of scripture:

> Not one bone of his will be broken.

And again, in another place scripture says:

> They will look on the one they have pierced.

The Gospel of the Lord.

Prayer over the Offerings
Look, O Lord, we pray, on the surpassing charity
in the Heart of your beloved Son,
that what we offer may be a gift acceptable to you
and an expiation of our offences.
Through Christ our Lord.
Amen.

Preface of the Sacred Heart, p.37.

Communion Antiphon Cf. Jn 7:37-38
Thus says the Lord:
Let whoever is thirsty come to me and drink.
Streams of living water will flow
from within the one who believes in me.

or Jn 19:34

One of the soldiers opened his side with a lance,
and at once there came forth blood and water.

Prayer after Communion
May this sacrament of charity, O Lord,
make us fervent with the fire of holy love,
so that, drawn always to your Son,
we may learn to see him in our neighbour.
Through Christ our Lord.
Amen.

SUNDAYS IN ORDINARY TIME

Year B

The cycle of Sundays in Ordinary Time runs from the end of the Christmas season to the beginning of Lent; it recommences after Trinity Sunday, and runs until the beginning of Advent. The number of Sundays in Ordinary Time before Lent, and between Trinity Sunday and Advent, varies: see the Table of Principal Celebrations.

The first week of Ordinary Time begins on the Monday following the Feast of the Baptism of the Lord. In Cycle B, the Gospel Readings are taken mainly from the Gospel According to St Mark.

THE BAPTISM OF THE LORD

See above, p.239.

SECOND SUNDAY IN ORDINARY TIME   B

Answering God's Call

Christ calls each of us by name. In this celebration we listen to what he has to say to us, prepared to use in his service the body that he has given us for the glory of God. We say with him, 'This is my body which is given up for you.'

Entrance Antiphon   Ps 65:4
All the earth shall bow down before you, O God,
and shall sing to you,
shall sing to your name, O Most High!

Second Sunday in Ordinary Time, Year B

Collect

Almighty ever-living God,
who govern all things,
both in heaven and on earth,
mercifully hear the pleading of your people
and bestow your peace on our times.
Through our Lord Jesus Christ, your Son,
who lives and reigns with you in the unity of the Holy Spirit,
one God, for ever and ever.
Amen.

FIRST READING

A reading from the first book of Samuel   3:3-10. 19

Samuel was lying in the sanctuary of the Lord where the ark of God was, when the Lord called, 'Samuel! Samuel!' He answered, 'Here I am.' Then he ran to Eli and said, 'Here I am, since you called me.' Eli said, 'I did not call. Go back and lie down.' So he went and lay down. Once again the Lord called, 'Samuel! Samuel!' Samuel got up and went to Eli and said, 'Here I am, since you called me.' He replied, 'I did not call you, my son; go back and lie down.' Samuel had as yet no knowledge of the Lord and the word of the Lord had not yet been revealed to him. Once again the Lord called, the third time. He got up and went to Eli and said, 'Here I am, since you called me.' Eli then understood that it was the Lord who was calling the boy, and he said to Samuel, 'Go and lie down, and if someone calls say, "Speak, Lord, your servant is listening."' So Samuel went and lay down in his place.

The Lord then came and stood by, calling as he had done before, 'Samuel! Samuel!' Samuel answered, 'Speak, Lord, your servant is listening.'

Samuel grew up and the Lord was with him and let no word of his fall to the ground.

The word of the Lord.

Responsorial Psalm   Ps 39:2. 4. 7-10. ℟ vv.8-9

℟ **Here I am, Lord!**
   I come to do your will.

1   I waited, I waited for the Lord
    and he stooped down to me;
    he heard my cry.
    He put a new song into my mouth,
    praise of our God.   ℟

Second Sunday in Ordinary Time, Year B

2   You do not ask for sacrifice and offerings,
    but an open ear.
    You do not ask for holocaust and victim.
    Instead, here am I.   ℟

3   In the scroll of the book it stands written
    that I should do your will.
    My God, I delight in your law
    in the depth of my heart.   ℟

4   Your justice I have proclaimed
    in the great assembly.
    My lips I have not sealed;
    you know it, O Lord.   ℟

SECOND READING

A reading from the first letter of St Paul to the Corinthians   6:13-15. 17-20

The body is not meant for fornication; it is for the Lord, and the Lord for the body. God who raised the Lord from the dead, will by his power raise us up too.

You know, surely, that your bodies are members making up the body of Christ; anyone who is joined to the Lord is one spirit with him.

Keep away from fornication. All the other sins are committed outside the body; but to fornicate is to sin against your own body. Your body, you know, is the temple of the Holy Spirit, who is in you since you received him from God. You are not your own property; you have been bought and paid for. That is why you should use your body for the glory of God.

The word of the Lord.

Gospel Acclamation   1 Sam 3:9; Jn 6:68
Alleluia, alleluia!
Speak, Lord, your servant is listening:
you have the message of eternal life.
Alleluia!

or   Jn 1:41. 17

Alleluia, alleluia!
We have found the Messiah – which means the Christ –
grace and truth have come through him.
Alleluia!

GOSPEL

A reading from the holy Gospel according to John   1:35-42

As John stood with two of his disciples, Jesus passed, and John stared hard at him and said, 'Look, there is the lamb of God.' Hearing this, the two disciples followed Jesus. Jesus turned round, saw them following and said, 'What do you want?' They answered, 'Rabbi,' – which means Teacher – 'where do you live?' 'Come and see' he replied; so they went and saw where he lived, and stayed with him the rest of that day. It was about the tenth hour.

One of these two who became followers of Jesus after hearing what John had said was Andrew, the brother of Simon Peter. Early next morning, Andrew met his brother and said to him, 'We have found the Messiah' – which means the Christ – and he took Simon to Jesus. Jesus looked hard at him and said, 'You are Simon son of John; you are to be called Cephas' – meaning Rock.

The Gospel of the Lord.

The Creed is said.

Prayer over the Offerings
Grant us, O Lord, we pray,
that we may participate worthily in these mysteries,
for whenever the memorial of this sacrifice is celebrated
the work of our redemption is accomplished.
Through Christ our Lord.
Amen.

Communion Antiphon   Cf. Ps 22:5
You have prepared a table before me,
and how precious is the chalice that quenches my thirst.

or   1 Jn 4:16

We have come to know and to believe
in the love that God has for us.

Prayer after Communion
Pour on us, O Lord, the Spirit of your love,
and in your kindness
make those you have nourished
by this one heavenly Bread
one in mind and heart.
Through Christ our Lord.
Amen.

THIRD SUNDAY IN ORDINARY TIME   B

The Lord Who Teaches Us His Ways

Like Jonah, Christ was sent to preach repentance. He calls us to change our ways. We are not to become engrossed in the world, but to believe the good news and live for the kingdom of God.

Entrance Antiphon
Cf. Ps 95:1. 6

O sing a new song to the Lord;
sing to the Lord, all the earth.
In his presence are majesty and splendour,
strength and honour in his holy place.

Collect

Almighty ever-living God,
direct our actions according to your good pleasure,
that in the name of your beloved Son
we may abound in good works.
Through our Lord Jesus Christ, your Son,
who lives and reigns with you in the unity of the Holy Spirit,
one God, for ever and ever.
Amen.

FIRST READING

A reading from the prophet Jonah   3:1-5. 10

The word of the Lord was addressed to Jonah: 'Up!' he said 'Go to Nineveh, the great city, and preach to them as I told you to.' Jonah set out and went to Nineveh in obedience to the word of the Lord. Now Nineveh was a city great beyond compare: it took three days to cross it. Jonah went on into the city, making a day's journey. He preached in these words, 'Only forty days more and Nineveh is going to be destroyed.' And the people of Nineveh believed in God; they proclaimed a fast and put on sackcloth, from the greatest to the least.

God saw their efforts to renounce their evil behaviour. And God relented: he did not inflict on them the disaster which he had threatened.

The word of the Lord.

Responsorial Psalm Ps 24:4-9. ℟ v.4
  ℟ **Lord, make me know your ways.**

1 Lord, make me know your ways.
   Lord, teach me your paths.
   Make me walk in your truth, and teach me:
   for you are God my saviour. ℟

2 Remember your mercy, Lord,
   and the love you have shown from of old.
   In your love remember me,
   because of your goodness, O Lord. ℟

3 The Lord is good and upright.
   He shows the path to those who stray,
   he guides the humble in the right path;
   he teaches his way to the poor. ℟

SECOND READING
A reading from the first letter of St Paul to the Corinthians 7:29-31

Brothers: our time is growing short. Those who have wives should live as though they had none, and those who mourn should live as though they had nothing to mourn for; those who are enjoying life should live as though there were nothing to laugh about; those whose life is buying things should live as though they had nothing of their own; and those who have to deal with the world should not become engrossed in it. I say this because the world as we know it is passing away.

   The word of the Lord.

Gospel Acclamation Mk 1:15
   Alleluia, alleluia!
   The kingdom of God is close at hand;
   believe the Good News.
   Alleluia!

GOSPEL
A reading from the holy Gospel according to Mark 1:14-20

After John had been arrested, Jesus went into Galilee. There he proclaimed the Good News from God. 'The time has come' he said

Third Sunday in Ordinary Time, Year B

'and the kingdom of God is close at hand. Repent, and believe the Good News.'

As he was walking along by the Sea of Galilee he saw Simon and his brother Andrew casting a net in the lake – for they were fishermen. And Jesus said to them, 'Follow me and I will make you into fishers of men.' And at once they left their nets and followed him.

Going on a little further, he saw James son of Zebedee and his brother John; they too were in their boat, mending their nets. He called them at once and, leaving their father Zebedee in the boat with the men he employed, they went after him.

The Gospel of the Lord.

The Creed is said.

Prayer over the Offerings
Accept our offerings, O Lord, we pray,
and in sanctifying them
grant that they may profit us for salvation.
Through Christ our Lord.
Amen.

Communion Antiphon   Cf. Ps 33:6
Look toward the Lord and be radiant;
let your faces not be abashed.

or   Jn 8:12

I am the light of the world, says the Lord;
whoever follows me will not walk in darkness,
but will have the light of life.

Prayer after Communion
Grant, we pray, almighty God,
that, receiving the grace
by which you bring us to new life,
we may always glory in your gift.
Through Christ our Lord.
Amen.

FOURTH SUNDAY IN ORDINARY TIME B

The Lord, Our Teacher

Today we celebrate the Lord Jesus Christ, who speaks with authority and to whom we must give our undivided attention.

Entrance Antiphon Ps 105:47
Save us, O Lord our God!
And gather us from the nations,
to give thanks to your holy name,
and make it our glory to praise you.

Collect
Grant us, Lord our God,
that we may honour you with all our mind,
and love everyone in truth of heart.
Through our Lord Jesus Christ, your Son,
who lives and reigns with you in the unity of the Holy Spirit,
one God, for ever and ever.
Amen.

FIRST READING
A reading from the book of Deuteronomy 18:15-20

Moses said to the people: 'Your God will raise up for you a prophet like myself, from among yourselves, from your own brothers; to him you must listen. This is what you yourselves asked of the Lord your God at Horeb on the day of the Assembly. "Do not let me hear again" you said "the voice of the Lord my God, nor look any longer on this great fire, or I shall die"; and the Lord said to me, "All they have spoken is well said. I will raise up a prophet like yourself for them from their own brothers; I will put my words into his mouth and he shall tell them all I command him. The man who does not listen to my words that he speaks in my name, shall be held answerable to me for it. But the prophet who presumes to say in my name a thing I have not commanded him to say, or who speaks in the name of other gods, that prophet shall die."'

The word of the Lord.

Responsorial Psalm Ps 94:1-2. 6-9. ℟ v.9

℟ **O that today you would listen to his voice!**
Harden not your hearts.

1   Come, ring out our joy to the Lord;
    hail the rock who saves us.
    Let us come before him, giving thanks,
    with songs let us hail the Lord. ℟

2   Come in; let us kneel and bend low;
    let us kneel before the God who made us
    for he is our God and we
    the people who belong to his pasture,
    the flock that is led by his hand. ℟

3   O that today you would listen to his voice!
    'Harden not your hearts as at Meribah,
    as on that day at Massah in the desert
    when your fathers put me to the test;
    when they tried me, though they saw my work.' ℟

SECOND READING

A reading from the first letter of St Paul to the Corinthians 7:32-35

I would like to see you free from all worry. An unmarried man can devote himself to the Lord's affairs, all he need worry about is pleasing the Lord; but a married man has to bother about the world's affairs and devote himself to pleasing his wife: he is torn two ways. In the same way an unmarried woman, like a young girl, can devote herself to the Lord's affairs; all she need worry about is being holy in body and spirit. The married woman, on the other hand, has to worry about the world's affairs and devote herself to pleasing her husband. I say this only to help you, not to put a halter round your necks, but simply to make sure that everything is as it should be, and that you give your undivided attention to the Lord.

The word of the Lord.

Gospel Acclamation Cf. Mt 11:25
Alleluia, alleluia!
Blessed are you, Father,
Lord of heaven and earth,
for revealing the mysteries of the kingdom
to mere children.
Alleluia!

or   Mt 4:16
> Alleluia, alleluia!
> The people that lived in darkness
> has seen a great light;
> on those who dwell in the land and shadow of death
> a light has dawned.
> Alleluia!

GOSPEL

A reading from the holy Gospel according to Mark   1:21-28

Jesus and his followers went as far as Capernaum, and as soon as the sabbath came Jesus went to the synagogue and began to teach. And his teaching made a deep impression on them because, unlike the scribes, he taught them with authority.

In their synagogue just then there was a man possessed by an unclean spirit, and it shouted, 'What do you want with us, Jesus of Nazareth? Have you come to destroy us? I know who you are: the Holy One of God.' But Jesus said sharply, 'Be quiet! Come out of him!' And the unclean spirit threw the man into convulsions and with a loud cry went out of him. The people were so astonished that they started asking each other what it all meant. 'Here is a teaching that is new' they said 'and with authority behind it: he gives orders even to unclean spirits and they obey him.' And his reputation rapidly spread everywhere, through all the surrounding Galilean countryside.

The Gospel of the Lord.

The Creed is said.

Prayer over the Offerings

O Lord, we bring to your altar
these offerings of our service:
be pleased to receive them, we pray,
and transform them
into the Sacrament of our redemption.
Through Christ our Lord.
Amen.

Communion Antiphon   Cf. Ps 30:17-18

Let your face shine on your servant.
Save me in your merciful love.
O Lord, let me never be put to shame, for I call on you.

or Mt 5:3-4

Blessed are the poor in spirit,
for theirs is the Kingdom of Heaven.
Blessed are the meek, for they shall possess the land.

Prayer after Communion
Nourished by these redeeming gifts,
we pray, O Lord,
that through this help to eternal salvation
true faith may ever increase.
Through Christ our Lord.
Amen.

FIFTH SUNDAY IN ORDINARY TIME   B

Christ Who Makes Us Free to Serve

Without Christ our lives would be pure drudgery. We would be like slaves, or like workmen with nothing to look forward to but our wages. But the healing power of Christ has transformed our lives: now we are free to make ourselves like him, the slaves of everyone, offering all the good news without asking for anything in return.

Entrance Antiphon Ps 94:6-7
O come, let us worship God
and bow low before the God who made us,
for he is the Lord our God.

Collect
Keep your family safe, O Lord, with unfailing care,
that, relying solely on the hope of heavenly grace,
they may be defended always by your protection.
Through our Lord Jesus Christ, your Son,
who lives and reigns with you in the unity of the Holy Spirit,
one God, for ever and ever.
Amen.

FIRST READING
A reading from the book of Job 7:1-4. 6-7

Job began to speak:

  Is not man's life on earth nothing more than pressed service,
  his time no better than hired drudgery?
  Like the slave, sighing for the shade,
  or the workman with no thought but his wages,
  months of delusion I have assigned to me,

nothing for my own but nights of grief.
Lying in bed I wonder, 'When will it be day?'
Risen I think, 'How slowly evening comes!'
Restlessly I fret till twilight falls.
Swifter than a weaver's shuttle my days have passed,
and vanished, leaving no hope behind.
Remember that my life is but a breath,
and that my eyes will never again see joy.

The word of the Lord.

Responsorial Psalm   Ps 146:1-6. R℣ v.3

    R℣ **Praise the Lord who heals the broken-hearted.**

or

    R℣ **Alleluia!**

1   Praise the Lord for he is good;
     sing to our God for he is loving:
     to him our praise is due. R℣

2   The Lord builds up Jerusalem
     and brings back Israel's exiles,
     he heals the broken-hearted,
     he binds up all their wounds.
     He fixes the number of the stars;
     he calls each one by its name. R℣

3   Our Lord is great and almighty;
     his wisdom can never be measured.
     The Lord raises the lowly;
     he humbles the wicked to the dust. R℣

SECOND READING

A reading from the first letter of St Paul   9:16-19. 22-23
to the Corinthians

I do not boast of preaching the gospel, since it is a duty which has been laid on me; I should be punished if I did not preach it! If I had chosen this work myself, I might have been paid for it, but as I have not, it is a responsibility which has been put into my hands. Do you know what my reward is? It is this: in my preaching, to be able to offer the Good News free, and not insist on the rights which the gospel gives me.

Fifth Sunday in Ordinary Time, Year B

So though I am not a slave of any man I have made myself the slave of everyone so as to win as many as I could. For the weak I made myself weak. I made myself all things to all men in order to save some at any cost; and I still do this, for the sake of the gospel, to have a share in its blessing.

The word of the Lord.

Gospel Acclamation Jn 8:12
Alleluia, alleluia!
I am the light of the world, says the Lord,
anyone who follows me
will have the light of life.
Alleluia!

or Mt 8:17

Alleluia, alleluia!
He took our sicknesses away,
and carried our diseases for us.
Alleluia!

GOSPEL
A reading from the holy Gospel according to Mark 1:29-39

On leaving the synagogue, Jesus went with James and John straight to the house of Simon and Andrew. Now Simon's mother-in-law had gone to bed with fever, and they told him about her straightaway. He went to her, took her by the hand and helped her up. And the fever left her and she began to wait on them. That evening, after sunset, they brought to him all who were sick and those who were possessed by devils. The whole town came crowding round the door, and he cured many who were suffering from diseases of one kind or another; he also cast out many devils, but he would not allow them to speak, because they knew who he was.

In the morning, long before dawn, he got up and left the house, and went off to a lonely place and prayed there. Simon and his companions set out in search of him, and when they found him they said, 'Everybody is looking for you.' He answered, 'Let us go elsewhere, to the neighbouring country towns, so that I can preach there too, because that is why I came.' And he went all through Galilee, preaching in their synagogues and casting out devils.

The Gospel of the Lord.

The Creed is said.

Prayer over the Offerings
O Lord, our God,
who once established these created things
to sustain us in our frailty,
grant, we pray,
that they may become for us now
the Sacrament of eternal life.
Through Christ our Lord.
Amen.

Communion Antiphon Cf. Ps 106:8-9
Let them thank the Lord for his mercy,
his wonders for the children of men,
for he satisfies the thirsty soul,
and the hungry he fills with good things.

or Mt 5:5-6

Blessed are those who mourn, for they shall be consoled.
Blessed are those who hunger and thirst for righteousness,
for they shall have their fill.

Prayer after Communion
O God, who have willed that we be partakers
in the one Bread and the one Chalice,
grant us, we pray, so to live
that, made one in Christ,
we may joyfully bear fruit
for the salvation of the world.
Through Christ our Lord.
Amen.

SIXTH SUNDAY IN ORDINARY TIME B

Jesus, Friend of Outcasts

To bring help to outcasts, Jesus himself had to become an outcast and 'stay outside in places where nobody lived'.

Entrance Antiphon Cf. Ps 30:3-4
Be my protector, O God,
a mighty stronghold to save me.
For you are my rock, my stronghold!
Lead me, guide me, for the sake of your name.

Sixth Sunday in Ordinary Time, Year B

Collect
O God, who teach us that you abide
in hearts that are just and true,
grant that we may be so fashioned by your grace
as to become a dwelling pleasing to you.
Through our Lord Jesus Christ, your Son,
who lives and reigns with you in the unity of the Holy Spirit,
one God, for ever and ever.
Amen.

FIRST READING
A reading from the book of Leviticus   13:1-2. 44-46

The Lord said to Moses and Aaron, 'If a swelling or scab or shiny spot appears on a man's skin, a case of leprosy of the skin is to be suspected. The man must be taken to Aaron, the priest, or to one of the priests who are his sons.

'The man is leprous: he is unclean. The priest must declare him unclean; he is suffering from leprosy of the head. A man infected with leprosy must wear his clothing torn and his hair disordered; he must shield his upper lip and cry, "Unclean, unclean." As long as the disease lasts he must be unclean; and therefore he must live apart; he must live outside the camp.'

The word of the Lord.

Responsional Psalm   Ps 31:1-2. 5. 11. ℟ v.7
℟ **You are my refuge, O Lord;
you fill me with the joy of salvation.**

1   Happy the man whose offence is forgiven,
    whose sin is remitted.
    O happy the man to whom the Lord
    imputes no guilt,
    in whose spirit is no guile. ℟

2   But now I have acknowledged my sins;
    my guilt I did not hide.
    I said: 'I will confess
    my offence to the Lord.'
    And you, Lord, have forgiven
    the guilt of my sin. ℟

3   Rejoice, rejoice in the Lord,
    exult, you just!
    O come, ring out your joy,
    all you upright of heart. ℟

SECOND READING

A reading from the first letter of St Paul 10:31 – 11:1
to the Corinthians

Whatever you eat, whatever you drink, whatever you do at all, do it for the glory of God. Never do anything offensive to anyone – to Jews or Greeks or to the Church of God; just as I try to be helpful to everyone at all times, not anxious for my own advantage but for the advantage of everybody else, so that they may be saved.

Take me for your model, as I take Christ.

The word of the Lord.

Gospel Acclamation   Cf. Eph 1:17-18
    Alleluia, alleluia!
    May the Father of our Lord Jesus Christ
    enlighten the eyes of our mind,
    so that we can see what hope his call holds for us.
    Alleluia!

or   Lk 7:16

    Alleluia, alleluia!
    A great prophet has appeared among us;
    God has visited his people.
    Alleluia!

GOSPEL

A reading from the holy Gospel according to Mark 1:40-45

A leper came to Jesus and pleaded on his knees: 'If you want to' he said 'you can cure me.' Feeling sorry for him, Jesus stretched out his hand and touched him. 'Of course I want to!' he said. 'Be cured!' And the leprosy left him at once and he was cured. Jesus immediately sent him away and sternly ordered him, 'Mind you say nothing to anyone, but go and show yourself to the priest, and make the offering for your healing prescribed by Moses as evidence of your recovery.' The man went away, but then started talking about it freely and telling the story everywhere, so that Jesus could no longer go openly into any town, but had to stay outside in places where nobody lived. Even so, people from all around would come to him.

The Gospel of the Lord.

The Creed is said.

Prayer over the Offerings
May this oblation, O Lord, we pray,
cleanse and renew us
and may it become for those who do your will
the source of eternal reward.
Through Christ our Lord.
Amen.

Communion Antiphon Cf. Ps 77:29-30
They ate and had their fill,
and what they craved the Lord gave them;
they were not disappointed in what they craved.

or Jn 3:16

God so loved the world
that he gave his Only Begotten Son,
so that all who believe in him may not perish,
but may have eternal life.

Prayer after Communion
Having fed upon these heavenly delights,
we pray, O Lord,
that we may always long
for that food by which we truly live.
Through Christ our Lord.
Amen.

SEVENTH SUNDAY IN ORDINARY TIME B

Christ Forgives Our Sins

Today we say Yes to the Lord who comes to forgive us our sins, and we praise him who shows such mercy to the poor and the weak.

Entrance Antiphon Ps 12:6
O Lord, I trust in your merciful love.
My heart will rejoice in your salvation.
I will sing to the Lord who has been bountiful with me.

Collect

Grant, we pray, almighty God,
that, always pondering spiritual things,
we may carry out in both word and deed
that which is pleasing to you.
Through our Lord Jesus Christ, your Son,
who lives and reigns with you in the unity of the Holy Spirit,
one God, for ever and ever.
Amen.

FIRST READING

A reading from the prophet Isaiah   43:18-19. 21-22. 24-25

Thus says the Lord:
   No need to recall the past,
   no need to think about what was done before.
   See, I am doing a new deed,
   even now it comes to light; can you not see it?
   Yes, I am making a road in the wilderness,
   paths in the wilds.
   The people I have formed for myself
   will sing my praises.
   Jacob, you have not invoked me,
   you have not troubled yourself, Israel, on my behalf.
   Instead you have burdened me with your sins,
   troubled me with your iniquities.
   I it is, I it is, who must blot out everything
   and not remember your sins.

The word of the Lord.

Responsorial Psalm   Ps 40:2-5. 13-14. ℟ v.5

   ℟   **Heal my soul for I have sinned against you.**

1 Happy the man who considers the poor and the weak.
   The Lord will save him in the day of evil,
   will guard him, give him life, make him happy in the land
   and will not give him up to the will of his foes.   ℟

2 The Lord will help him on his bed of pain,
   he will bring him back from sickness to health.
   As for me, I said: 'Lord, have mercy on me,
   heal my soul for I have sinned against you.'   ℟

3   If you uphold me I shall be unharmed
    and set in your presence for evermore.
    Blessed be the Lord, the God of Israel
    from age to age. Amen. Amen. ℟

SECOND READING

A reading from the second letter of St Paul   1:18-22
to the Corinthians

I swear by God's truth, there is no Yes and No about what we say to you. The Son of God, the Christ Jesus that We proclaimed among you – I mean Silvanus and Timothy and I – was never Yes and No: with him it was always Yes, and however many the promises God made, the Yes to them all is in him. That is why it is 'through him' that we answer Amen to the praise of God. Remember it is God himself who assures us all, and you, of our standing in Christ, and has anointed us, marking us with his seal and giving us the pledge, the Spirit, that we carry in our hearts.

The word of the Lord.

Gospel Acclamation   Jn 1:14. 12
    Alleluia, alleluia!
    The Word was made flesh and lived among us;
    to all who did accept him
    he gave power to become children of God.
    Alleluia!

or   Cf.Lk 4:18

    Alleluia, alleluia!
    The Lord has sent me to bring the good news to the poor,
    to proclaim liberty to captives.
    Alleluia!

GOSPEL

A reading from the holy Gospel according to Mark   2:1-12

When Jesus returned to Capernaum, word went round that he was back; and so many people collected that there was no room left, even in front of the door. He was preaching the word to them when some people came bringing him a paralytic carried by four men, but as the crowds made it impossible to get the man to him, they stripped the roof over the place where Jesus was; and when they had made an opening, they lowered the stretcher on which the paralytic lay. Seeing their faith, Jesus said to the paralytic, 'My child, your sins are forgiven.' Now some scribes were sitting there, and they thought to themselves, 'How can this man talk like that? He is blaspheming. Who can forgive sins but God?' Jesus, inwardly aware that this was what they were thinking, said to them, 'Why do you have these thoughts in your hearts? Which of these is easier: to say to the paralytic, "Your sins are forgiven" or to say, "Get up, pick up your stretcher and walk?" But to prove to you that the Son of Man has authority on earth to forgive sins,' – he said to the paralytic – 'I order you: get up, pick up your stretcher, and go off home.' And the man got up, picked up his stretcher at once and walked out in front of everyone, so that they were all astounded and praised God saying, 'We have never seen anything like this.'

The Gospel of the Lord.

The Creed is said.

Prayer over the Offerings
As we celebrate your mysteries, O Lord,
with the observance that is your due,
we humbly ask you,
that what we offer to the honour of your majesty
may profit us for salvation.
Through Christ our Lord.
Amen.

Communion Antiphon   Ps 9:2-3
I will recount all your wonders,
I will rejoice in you and be glad,
and sing psalms to your name, O Most High.

or   Jn 11:27

Lord, I have come to believe that you are the Christ,
the Son of the living God, who is coming into this world.

Prayer after Communion
Grant, we pray, almighty God,
that we may experience the effects of the salvation
which is pledged to us by these mysteries.
Through Christ our Lord.
Amen.

EIGHTH SUNDAY IN ORDINARY TIME   B

Christ the Bridegroom

Today the love of Christ for his Church is shown to be no less than the love of a bridegroom for his bride. His love-letter is written on every Christian heart.

Entrance Antiphon
Cf. Ps 17:19-20

The Lord became my protector.
He brought me out to a place of freedom;
he saved me because he delighted in me.

Collect
Grant us, O Lord, we pray,
that the course of our world
may be directed by your peaceful rule
and that your Church may rejoice,
untroubled in her devotion.
Through our Lord Jesus Christ, your Son,
who lives and reigns with you in the unity of the Holy Spirit,
one God, for ever and ever.
Amen.

FIRST READING
A reading from the prophet Hosea   2:16-17. 21-22

Thus says the Lord:
 I am going to lure her
 and lead her out into the wilderness
 and speak to her heart.
 There she will respond to me as she did when she was young,
 as she did when she came out of the land of Egypt.
 I will betroth you to myself for ever,
 betroth you with integrity and justice,
 with tenderness and love;
 I will betroth you to myself with faithfulness,
 and you will come to know the Lord.

The word of the Lord.

Responsorial Psalm   Ps 102:1-4. 8. 10. 12-13. ℟ v.8

℟   **The Lord is compassion and love.**

1. My soul, give thanks to the Lord,
   all my being, bless his holy name.
   My soul, give thanks to the Lord
   and never forget all his blessings. ℟

2. It is he who forgives all your guilt,
   who heals every one of your ills,
   who redeems your life from the grave,
   who crowns you with love and compassion. ℟

3. The Lord is compassion and love,
   slow to anger and rich in mercy.
   He does not treat us according to our sins
   nor repay us according to our faults. ℟

4. So far as the east is from the west
   so far does he remove our sins.
   As a father has compassion on his sons,
   the Lord has pity on those who fear him. ℟

SECOND READING

A reading from the second letter of St Paul   3:1-6
to the Corinthians

Unlike other people, we need no letters of recommendation either to you or from you, because you are yourselves our letter, written in our hearts, that anybody can see and read, and it is plain that you are a letter from Christ, drawn up by us, and written not with ink but with the Spirit of the living God, not on stone tablets but on the tablets of your living hearts.

    Before God, we are confident of this through Christ: not that we are qualified in ourselves to claim anything as our own work: all our qualifications come from God. He is the one who has given us the qualifications to be the administrators of this new covenant, which is not a covenant of written letters but of the Spirit: the written letters bring death, but the Spirit gives life.

    The word of the Lord.

Gospel Acclamation   Jn 10:27
    Alleluia, alleluia!
    The sheep that belong to me listen to my voice,

says the Lord,
I know them and they follow me.
Alleluia!

or   James 1:18

Alleluia, alleluia!
By his own choice the Father made us his children
by the message of the truth,
so that we should be a sort of first-fruits
of all that he created.
Alleluia!

GOSPEL
A reading from the holy Gospel according to Mark   2:18-22

One day when John's disciples and the Pharisees were fasting, some people came and said to Jesus, 'Why is it that John's disciples and the disciples of the Pharisees fast, but your disciples do not?' Jesus replied, 'Surely the bridegroom's attendants would never think of fasting while the bridegroom is still with them? As long as they have the bridegroom with them, they could not think of fasting. But the time will come for the bridegroom to be taken away from them, and then, on that day, they will fast. No one sews a piece of unshrunken cloth on an old cloak; if he does, the patch pulls away from it, the new from the old, and the tear gets worse. And nobody puts new wine into old wineskins; if he does, the wine will burst the skins, and the wine is lost and the skins too. No! New wine, fresh skins!'

The Gospel of the Lord.

The Creed is said.

Prayer over the Offerings
O God, who provide gifts to be offered to your name
and count our oblations as signs
of our desire to serve you with devotion,
we ask of your mercy
that what you grant as the source of merit
may also help us to attain merit's reward.
Through Christ our Lord.
Amen.

Communion Antiphon   Cf. Ps 12:6
I will sing to the Lord who has been bountiful with me,
sing psalms to the name of the Lord Most High.

or   Mt 28:20

Behold, I am with you always,
even to the end of the age, says the Lord.

Prayer after Communion
Nourished by your saving gifts,
we beseech your mercy, Lord,
that by this same Sacrament
with which you feed us in the present age,
you may make us partakers of life eternal.
Through Christ our Lord.
Amen.

NINTH SUNDAY IN ORDINARY TIME   B

The Lord of the Sabbath

The Christian Sabbath is the Lord's day: the day of his triumph over sin and death. It is our day of respite from the drabness of the daily routine, the day on which in our mortal flesh the life of Jesus is openly shown.

Entrance Antiphon   Cf. Ps 24:16. 18
Turn to me and have mercy on me, O Lord,
for I am alone and poor.
See my lowliness and suffering
and take away all my sins, my God.

Collect
O God, whose providence never fails in its design,
keep from us, we humbly beseech you,
all that might harm us
and grant all that works for our good.
Through our Lord Jesus Christ, your Son,
who lives and reigns with you in the unity of the Holy Spirit,
one God, for ever and ever.
Amen.

Ninth Sunday in Ordinary Time, Year B 731

FIRST READING
A reading from the book of Deuteronomy 5:12-15

The Lord says this: 'Observe the sabbath day and keep it holy, as the Lord your God has commanded you. For six days you shall labour and do all your work, but the seventh day is a sabbath for the Lord your God. You shall do no work that day, neither you nor your son nor your daughter nor your servants, men or women, nor your ox nor your donkey nor any of your animals, nor the stranger who lives with you. Thus your servant, man or woman, shall rest as you do. Remember that you were a servant in the land of Egypt, and that the Lord your God brought you out from there with mighty hand and outstretched arm; because of this, the Lord your God has commanded you to keep the sabbath day.'

The word of the Lord.

Responsorial Psalm Ps 80:3-8. 10-11. ℟ v.2

℟ **Ring out your joy to God our strength.**

1 Raise a song and sound the timbrel,
 the sweet-sounding harp and the lute,
 blow the trumpet at the new moon,
 when the moon is full, on our feast. ℟

2 For this is Israel's law,
 a command of the God of Jacob.
 He imposed it as a rule on Joseph,
 when he went out against the land of Egypt. ℟

3 A voice I did not know said to me:
 'I freed your shoulder from the burden;
 your hands were freed from the load.
 You called in distress and I saved you. ℟

4 'Let there be no foreign god among you,
 no worship of an alien god.
 I am the Lord your God,
 who brought you from the land of Egypt.' ℟

SECOND READING

A reading from the second letter of St Paul to the Corinthians   4:6-11

It is the same God that said, 'Let there be light shining out of darkness,' who has shone in our minds to radiate the light of the knowledge of God's glory, the glory on the face of Christ.

We are only the earthenware jars that hold this treasure, to make it clear that such an overwhelming power comes from God and not from us. We are in difficulties on all sides, but never cornered; we see no answer to our problems, but never despair; we have been persecuted, but never deserted; knocked down, but never killed; always, wherever we may be, we carry with us in our body the death of Jesus, so that the life of Jesus, too, may always be seen in our body. Indeed, while we are still alive, we are consigned to our death every day, for the sake of Jesus, so that in our mortal flesh the life of Jesus, too, may be openly shown.

The word of the Lord.

Gospel Acclamation   Cf. Jn 6:63. 68
Alleluia, alleluia!
Your words are spirit, Lord, and they are life:
you have the message of eternal life.
Alleluia!

or   Cf. Jn 17:17

Alleluia, alleluia!
Your word is truth, O Lord,
consecrate us in the truth.
Alleluia!

GOSPEL

A reading from the holy Gospel according to Mark   2:23 – 3:6

*One sabbath day Jesus happened to be taking a walk through the cornfields, and his disciples began to pick ears of corn as they went along. And the Pharisees said to him, 'Look, why are they doing something on the sabbath day that is forbidden?' And he replied, 'Did you ever read what David did in his time of need when he and his followers were hungry – how he went into the house of God when Abiathar was high priest, and ate the loaves of offering which only the priests are allowed to eat, and how he also gave some to the men with him?'

Ninth Sunday in Ordinary Time, Year B

And he said to them, 'The sabbath was made for man, not man for the sabbath; so the Son of Man is master even of the sabbath.'*

He went again into a synagogue, and there was a man there who had a withered hand. And they were watching him to see if he would cure him on the sabbath day, hoping for something to use against him. He said to the man with the withered hand, 'Stand up out in the middle!' Then he said to them, 'Is it against the law on the sabbath day to do good, or to do evil; to save life, or to kill?' But they said nothing. Then, grieved to find them so obstinate, he looked angrily round at them, and said to the man, 'Stretch out your hand.' He stretched it out and his hand was better. The Pharisees went out and at once began to plot with the Herodians against him, discussing how to destroy him.

The Gospel of the Lord.

Shorter Form, verses 23-28, read between

The Creed is said.

Prayer over the Offerings
Trusting in your compassion, O Lord,
we come eagerly with our offerings to your sacred altar,
that, through the purifying action of your grace,
we may be cleansed by the very mysteries we serve.
Through Christ our Lord.
Amen.

Communion Antiphon   Cf. Ps 16:6
To you I call, for you will surely heed me, O God;
turn your ear to me; hear my words.

or   Mk 11:23-24

Amen, I say to you: Whatever you ask for in prayer,
believe you will receive it,
and it will be yours, says the Lord.

Prayer after Communion
Govern by your Spirit, we pray, O Lord,
those you feed with the Body and Blood of your Son,
that, professing you not just in word or in speech,
but also in works and in truth,
we may merit to enter the Kingdom of Heaven.
Through Christ our Lord.
Amen.

TENTH SUNDAY IN ORDINARY TIME — B

Mary, the Type of the Church

In Mary, we see the fullness of redemption. Today we celebrate with her, who did the will of God throughout her life and who was the first whom God raised with Jesus and put by his side.

Entrance Antiphon — Cf. Ps 26:1-2

The Lord is my light and my salvation; whom shall I fear?
The Lord is the stronghold of my life; whom should I dread?
When those who do evil draw near, they stumble and fall.

Collect

O God, from whom all good things come,
grant that we, who call on you in our need,
may at your prompting discern what is right,
and by your guidance do it.
Through our Lord Jesus Christ, your Son,
who lives and reigns with you in the unity of the Holy Spirit,
one God, for ever and ever.
Amen.

FIRST READING

A reading from the book of Genesis — 3:9-15

The Lord God called to the man after he had eaten of the tree. 'Where are you?' he asked. 'I heard the sound of you in the garden;' he replied 'I was afraid because I was naked, so I hid.' 'Who told you that you were naked?' he asked. 'Have you been eating of the tree I forbade you to eat?' The man replied, 'It was the woman you put with me; she gave me the fruit, and I ate it.'

Then the Lord God asked the woman, 'What is this you have done?' The woman replied, 'The serpent tempted me and I ate.'

Then the Lord God said to the serpent, 'Because you have done this,

'Be accursed beyond all cattle,
all wild beasts.
You shall crawl on your belly and eat dust
every day of your life.
I will make you enemies of each other:
you and the woman,
your offspring and her offspring.

It will crush your head
and you will strike its heel.'

The word of the Lord.

Responsional Psalm   Ps 129. ℟ v.7
℟ **With the Lord there is mercy
and fullness of redemption.**

1. Out of the depths I cry to you, O Lord,
Lord, hear my voice!
O let your ears be attentive
to the voice of my pleading. ℟

2. If you, O Lord, should mark our guilt,
Lord, who would survive?
But with you is found forgiveness:
for this we revere you. ℟

3. My soul is waiting for the Lord,
I count on his word.
My soul is longing for the Lord
more than watchman for daybreak. ℟

4. Because with the Lord there is mercy
and fullness of redemption,
Israel indeed he will redeem
from all its iniquity. ℟

SECOND READING

A reading from the second letter of St Paul   4:13 – 5:1
to the Corinthians

As we have the same spirit of faith that is mentioned in scripture – I believed, and therefore I spoke – we too believe and therefore we too speak, knowing that he who raised the Lord Jesus to life will raise us with Jesus in our turn, and put us by his side and you with us. You see, all this is for your benefit, so that the more grace is multiplied among people, the more thanksgiving there will be, to the glory of God.

That is why there is no weakening on our part, and instead, though this outer man of ours may be falling into decay, the inner man is renewed day by day. Yes, the troubles which are soon over, though they weigh little, train us for the carrying of a weight of eternal glory which is out of all proportion to them. And so we have no eyes for things that are visible, but only for things that are invisible; for visible things last only for a time, and the invisible things are eternal.

For we know that when the tent that we live in on earth is folded up, there is a house built by God for us, an everlasting home not made by human hands, in the heavens.

The word of the Lord.

Gospel Acclamation Jn 14:23

Alleluia, alleluia!
If anyone loves me he will keep my word,
and my Father will love him,
and we shall come to him.
Alleluia!

or Jn 12:31-32

Alleluia, alleluia!
Now the prince of this world is to be overthrown,
says the Lord.
And when I am lifted up from the earth,
I shall draw all men to myself.
Alleluia!

GOSPEL

A reading from the holy Gospel according to Mark 3:20-35

Jesus went home with his disciples, and such a crowd collected that they could not even have a meal. When his relatives heard of this, they set out to take charge of him, convinced he was out of his mind.

The scribes who had come down from Jerusalem were saying, 'Beelzebul is in him,' and, 'It is through the prince of devils that he casts devils out.' So he called them to him and spoke to them in parables, 'How can Satan cast out Satan? If a kingdom is divided against itself, that kingdom cannot last. And if a household is divided against itself, that household can never stand. Now if Satan has rebelled against himself and is divided, he cannot stand either – it is the end of him. But no one can make his way into a strong man's house and burgle his property unless he has tied up the strong man first. Only then can he burgle his house.

'I tell you solemnly, all men's sins will be forgiven, and all their blasphemies; but let anyone blaspheme against the Holy Spirit and he will never have forgiveness: he is guilty of an eternal sin.' This was because they were saying, 'An unclean spirit is in him.'

His mother and brothers now arrived and, standing outside, sent in a message asking for him. A crowd was sitting round him at the time the message was passed to him, 'Your mother and brothers and sisters are outside asking for you.' He replied, 'Who are my mother and my brothers?' And looking round at those sitting in a circle about him, he said, 'Here are my mother and my brothers. Anyone who does the will of God, that person is my brother and sister and mother.'

The Gospel of the Lord.

The Creed is said.

Prayer over the Offerings
Look kindly upon our service, O Lord, we pray,
that what we offer
may be an acceptable oblation to you
and lead us to grow in charity.
Through Christ our Lord.
Amen.

Communion Antiphon   Ps 17:3
The Lord is my rock, my fortress, and my deliverer;
my God is my saving strength.

or   1 Jn 4: 16

God is love, and whoever abides in love
abides in God, and God in him.

Prayer after Communion
May your healing work, O Lord,
free us, we pray, from doing evil
and lead us to what is right.
Through Christ our Lord.
Amen.

ELEVENTH SUNDAY IN ORDINARY TIME   B

The Cedar of Lebanon

The Church of Christ is like a tree that God planted in the world. From the smallest of seeds it became the noblest of trees and filled the earth. We are like the birds of the air who make their home in him.

Eleventh Sunday in Ordinary Time, Year B

Entrance Antiphon Cf. Ps 26:7. 9
O Lord, hear my voice, for I have called to you; be my help.
Do not abandon or forsake me, O God, my Saviour!

Collect
O God, strength of those who hope in you,
graciously hear our pleas,
and, since without you mortal frailty can do nothing,
grant us always the help of your grace,
that in following your commands
we may please you by our resolve and our deeds.
Through our Lord Jesus Christ, your Son,
who lives and reigns with you in the unity of the Holy Spirit,
one God, for ever and ever.
Amen.

FIRST READING
A reading from the prophet Ezekiel 17:22-24

The Lord says this:

'From the top of the cedar,
from the highest branch I will take a shoot
and plant it myself on a very high mountain.
I will plant it on the high mountain of Israel.
It will sprout branches and bear fruit,
and become a noble cedar.
Every kind of bird will live beneath it,
every winged creature rest in the shade of its branches.
And every tree of the field will learn that I, the Lord, am the one
who stunts tall trees and makes the low ones grow,
who withers green trees and makes the withered green.
I, the Lord, have spoken, and I will do it.'

The word of the Lord.

Responsorial Psalm Ps 91:2-3. 13-16. ℟ cf. v.2
  ℟ **It is good to give you thanks, O Lord.**

1   It is good to give thanks to the Lord
    to make music to your name, O Most High,
    to proclaim your love in the morning
    and your truth in the watches of the night. ℟

Eleventh Sunday in Ordinary Time, Year B

2 The just will flourish like the palm-tree
   and grow like a Lebanon cedar. ℟

3 Planted in the house of the Lord
   they will flourish in the courts of our God,
   still bearing fruit when they are old,
   still full of sap, still green,
   to proclaim that the Lord is just.
   In him, my rock, there is no wrong. ℟

SECOND READING

A reading from the second letter of St Paul
to the Corinthians   5:6-10

We are always full of confidence when we remember that to live in the body means to be exiled from the Lord, going as we do by faith and not by sight – we are full of confidence, I say, and actually want to be exiled from the body and make our home with the Lord. Whether we are living in the body or exiled from it, we are intent on pleasing him. For all the truth about us will be brought out in the law court of Christ, and each of us will get what he deserves for the things he did in the body, good or bad.

The word of the Lord.

Gospel Acclamation   Jn 15:15
   Alleluia, alleluia!
   I call you friends, says the Lord,
   because I have made known to you
   everything I have learnt from my Father.
   Alleluia!

or

   Alleluia, alleluia!
   The seed is the word of God, Christ the sower;
   whoever finds the seed will remain for ever.
   Alleluia!

GOSPEL

A reading from the holy Gospel according to Mark   4:26-34

Jesus said to the crowds: 'This is what the kingdom of God is like. A man throws seed on the land. Night and day, while he sleeps, when he is awake, the seed is sprouting and growing; how, he does not know. Of its own accord the land produces first the shoot, then the ear, then the full grain in the ear. And when the crop is ready, he loses no time: he starts to reap because the harvest has come.'

He also said, 'What can we say the kingdom of God is like? What parable can we find for it? It is like a mustard seed which at the time of its sowing in the soil is the smallest of all the seeds on earth; yet once it is sown it grows into the biggest shrub of them all and puts out big branches so that the birds of the air can shelter in its shade.'

Using many parables like these, he spoke the word to them, so far as they were capable of understanding it. He would not speak to them except in parables, but he explained everything to his disciples when they were alone.

The Gospel of the Lord.

The Creed is said.

Prayer over the Offerings
O God, who in the offerings presented here
provide for the twofold needs of human nature,
nourishing us with food
and renewing us with your Sacrament,
grant, we pray,
that the sustenance they provide
may not fail us in body or in spirit.
Through Christ our Lord.
Amen.

Communion Antiphon   Ps 26:4
There is one thing I ask of the Lord, only this do I seek:
to live in the house of the Lord all the days of my life.

or   Jn 17:11

Holy Father, keep in your name those you have given me,
that they may be one as we are one, says the Lord.

Prayer after Communion
As this reception of your Holy Communion, O Lord,
foreshadows the union of the faithful in you,
so may it bring about unity in your Church.
Through Christ our Lord.
Amen.

Twelfth Sunday in Ordinary Time, Year B

TWELFTH SUNDAY IN ORDINARY TIME   B

The Lord of the Storm

Just to know that Christ is with us amid all the turbulence of life is a great cause for celebration and thanksgiving. With Christ the turbulence can become the birth pangs of a new creation.

Entrance Antiphon   Cf. Ps 27:8-9
The Lord is the strength of his people,
a saving refuge for the one he has anointed.
Save your people, Lord, and bless your heritage,
and govern them for ever.

Collect
Grant, O Lord,
that we may always revere and love your holy name,
for you never deprive of your guidance
those you set firm on the foundation of your love.
Through our Lord Jesus Christ, your Son,
who lives and reigns with you in the unity of the Holy Spirit,
one God, for ever and ever.
Amen.

FIRST READING
A reading from the book of Job   3:1. 8-11

From the heart of tempest the Lord gave Job his answer. He said:

> Who pent up the sea behind closed doors
> when it leapt tumultuous out of the womb,
> when I wrapped it in a robe of mist
> and made black clouds its swaddling bands;
> when I marked the bounds it was not to cross
> and made it fast with a bolted gate?
> Come thus far, I said, and no farther:
> here your proud waves shall break.

The word of the Lord.

Responsorial Psalm   Ps 106:23-26. 28-31. ℟ v.1
℟ **O give thanks to the Lord,
for his love endures for ever.**

or

℟ **Alleluia!**

1. Some sailed to the sea in ships
   to trade on the mighty waters.
   These men have seen the Lord's deeds,
   the wonders he does in the deep. ℟

2. For he spoke; he summoned the gale.
   tossing the waves of the sea
   up to heaven and back into the deep;
   their soul melted away in their distress. ℟

3. Then they cried to the Lord in their need
   and he rescued them from their distress
   He stilled the storm to a whisper:
   all the waves of the sea were hushed. ℟

4. They rejoiced because of the calm
   and he led them to the haven they desired.
   Let them thank the Lord for his love,
   the wonders he does for men. ℟

SECOND READING

A reading from the second letter of St Paul 5:14-17
to the Corinthians

The love of Christ overwhelms us when we reflect that if one man has died for all, then all men should be dead; and the reason he died for all was so that living men should live no longer for themselves, but for him who died and was raised to life for them.

From now onwards, therefore, we do not judge anyone by the standards of the flesh. Even if we did once know Christ in the flesh, that is not how we know him now. And for anyone who is in Christ, there is a new creation; the old creation has gone, and now the new one is here.

The word of the Lord.

Gospel Acclamation   Cf. Eph 1:17-18

Alleluia, alleluia!
May the Father of our Lord Jesus Christ
enlighten the eyes of our mind,
so that we can see what hope his call holds for us.
Alleluia!

or Lk 7:16

Alleluia, alleluia!
A great prophet has appeared among us;
God has visited his people.
Alleluia!

GOSPEL

A reading from the holy Gospel according to Mark 4:35-41

With the coming of evening, Jesus said to his disciples, 'Let us cross over to the other side.' And leaving the crowd behind they took him, just as he was, in the boat; and there were other boats with him. Then it began to blow a gale and the waves were breaking into the boat so that it was almost swamped. But he was in the stern, his head on the cushion, asleep. They woke him and said to him, 'Master, do you not care? We are going down!' And he woke up and rebuked the wind and said to the sea, 'Quiet now! Be calm!' And the wind dropped, and all was calm again. Then he said to them, 'Why are you so frightened? How is it that you have no faith?' They were filled with awe and said to one another, 'Who can this be? Even the wind and the sea obey him.'

The Gospel of the Lord.

The Creed is said.

Prayer over the Offerings
Receive, O Lord, the sacrifice of conciliation and praise
and grant that, cleansed by its action,
we may make offering of a heart pleasing to you.
Through Christ our Lord.
Amen.

Communion Antiphon Ps 144:15
The eyes of all look to you, Lord,
and you give them their food in due season.

or Jn 10:11. 15

I am the Good Shepherd,
and I lay down my life for my sheep, says the Lord.

Prayer after Communion
Renewed and nourished
by the Sacred Body and Precious Blood of your Son,
we ask of your mercy, O Lord,
that what we celebrate with constant devotion

may be our sure pledge of redemption.
Through Christ our Lord.
Amen.

THIRTEENTH SUNDAY IN ORDINARY TIME   B

The Lord Who Gives Life

The Lord made us to live. Death is totally opposed to God, who is life itself. And yet Christ accepted death in order that we might live. He took our poverty to make us rich.

Entrance Antiphon   Ps 46:2
All peoples, clap your hands.
Cry to God with shouts of joy!

Collect
O God, who through the grace of adoption
chose us to be children of light,
grant, we pray,
that we may not be wrapped in the darkness of error
but always be seen to stand in the bright light of truth.
Through our Lord Jesus Christ, your Son,
who lives and regins with you in the unity of the Holy Spirit,
one God, for ever and ever.
Amen.

FIRST READING
A reading from the book of Wisdom   1:13-15; 2:23-24

Death was not God's doing,
he takes no pleasure in the extinction of the living.
To be – for this he created all;
the world's created things have health in them,
in them no fatal poison can be found,
and Hades holds no power on earth;
for virtue is undying.
Yet God did make man imperishable,
he made him in the image of his own nature;
it was the devil's envy that brought death into the world,
as those who are his partners will discover.

    The word of the Lord.

Responsorial Psalm   Ps 29:2. 4-6. 11-13. ℟ v.2
  ℟ **I will praise you, Lord, you have rescued me.**

Thirteenth Sunday in Ordinary Time, Year B

1 I will praise you, Lord, you have rescued me
  and have not let my enemies rejoice over me.
  O Lord, you have raised my soul from the dead,
  restored me to life from those who sink into the grave. ℟

2 Sing psalms to the Lord, you who love him,
  give thanks to his holy name.
  His anger lasts but a moment; his favour through life.
  At night there are tears, but joy comes with dawn. ℟

3 The Lord listened and had pity.
  The Lord came to my help.
  For me you have changed my mourning into dancing,
  O Lord my God, I will thank you for ever. ℟

SECOND READING

A reading from the second letter of St Paul 8:7. 9. 13-15
to the Corinthians

You always have the most of everything – of faith, of eloquence, of understanding, of keenness for any cause, and the biggest share of our affection – so we expect you to put the most into this work of mercy too. Remember how generous the Lord Jesus was: he was rich, but he became poor for your sake, to make you rich out of his poverty. This does not mean that to give relief to others you ought to make things difficult for yourselves: it is a question of balancing what happens to be your surplus now against their present need, and one day they may have something to spare that will supply your own need. That is how we strike a balance: as scripture says: The man who gathered much had none too much, the man who gathered little did not go short.

The word of the Lord.

Gospel Acclamation Cf. Jn 6:63. 68
  Alleluia, alleluia!
  Your words are spirit, Lord,
  and they are life:
  you have the message of eternal life.
  Alleluia!

or Cf. 2 Tim 1:10

  Alleluia, alleluia!
  Our Saviour Christ Jesus abolished death,
  and he has proclaimed life through the Good News.
  Alleluia!

Thirteenth Sunday in Ordinary Time, Year B

GOSPEL

A reading from the holy Gospel according to Mark   5:21-43

When Jesus had crossed in the boat to the other side, a large crowd gathered round him and he stayed by the lakeside. Then one of the synagogue officials came up, Jairus by name, and seeing him, fell at his feet and pleaded with him earnestly, saying, 'My little daughter is desperately sick. Do come and lay your hands on her to make her better and save her life.' Jesus went with him and a large crowd followed him; they were pressing all round him.

Now there was a woman who had suffered from a haemorrhage for twelve years; after long and painful treatment under various doctors, she had spent all she had without being any the better for it, in fact, she was getting worse. She had heard about Jesus, and she came up behind him through the crowd and touched his cloak. 'If I can touch even his clothes,' she had told herself 'I shall be well again.' And the source of the bleeding dried up instantly, and she felt in herself that she was cured of her complaint. Immediately aware that power had gone out from him Jesus turned round in the crowd and said, 'Who touched my clothes?' His disciples said to him, 'You see how the crowd is pressing round you and yet you say, "Who touched me?" ' But he continued to look all round to see who had done it. Then the woman came forward, frightened and trembling because she knew what had happened to her, and she fell at his feet and told him the whole truth. 'My daughter,' he said 'your faith has restored you to health; go in peace and be free from your complaint.'

While he was still speaking* some people arrived from the house of the synagogue offical to say, 'Your daughter is dead: why put the Master to any further trouble?' But Jesus had overheard this remark of theirs and he said to the official, 'Do not be afraid; only have faith.' And he allowed no one to go with him except Peter and James and John the brother of James. So they came to the official's house and Jesus noticed all the commotion, with people weeping and wailing unrestrainedly. He went in and said to them, 'Why all this commotion and crying? The child is not dead, but asleep.' But they laughed at him. So he turned them all out and, taking with him the child's father and mother and his own companions, he went into the place where the child lay. And taking the child by the hand he said to her, 'Talitha, kum!' which means, 'Little girl, I tell you to get up.' The little girl got up at once and began to walk about, for she was twelve years old. At this they were overcome with astonishment, and he ordered them strictly not to let anyone know about it, and told them to give her something to eat.

The Gospel of the Lord.*

Shorter Form, verses 21-24. 35-43. Read between

The Creed is said.

Prayer over the Offerings
O God, who graciously accomplish
the effects of your mysteries,
grant, we pray,
that the deeds by which we serve you
may be worthy of these sacred gifts.
Through Christ our Lord.
Amen.

Communion Antiphon   Cf. Ps 102:1
Bless the Lord, O my soul,
and all within me, his holy name.

or   Jn 17:20-21

O Father, I pray for them, that they may be one in us,
that the world may believe that you have sent me, says the Lord.

Prayer after Communion
May this divine sacrifice we have offered and received
fill us with life, O Lord, we pray,
so that, bound to you in lasting charity,
we may bear fruit that lasts for ever.
Through Christ our Lord.
Amen.

FOURTEENTH SUNDAY IN ORDINARY TIME   B

The Church as Prophet of God

The Church rejoices in the spirit of prophecy, even though the exercise of that charism does not bring her any honour from the world. It is exercised in weakness.

Entrance Antiphon   Cf. Ps 47:10-11
Your merciful love, O God,
we have received in the midst of your temple.
Your praise, O God, like your name,
reaches the ends of the earth;
your right hand is filled with saving justice.

Collect
O God, who in the abasement of your Son
have raised up a fallen world,
fill your faithful with holy joy,

for on those you have rescued from slavery to sin
you bestow eternal gladness.
Through our Lord Jesus Christ, your Son,
who lives and reigns with you in the unity of the Holy Spirit,
one God, for ever and ever.
Amen.

FIRST READING
A reading from the prophet Ezekiel 2:2-5

The spirit came into me and made me stand up, and I heard the Lord speaking to me. He said, 'Son of man, I am sending you to the Israelites, to the rebels who have turned against me. Till now they and their ancestors have been in revolt against me. The sons are defiant and obstinate; I am sending you to them, to say, "The Lord says this." Whether they listen or not, this set of rebels shall know there is a prophet among them.'

The word of the Lord.

Responsorial Psalm Ps 122. ℟ v.2

℟ **Our eyes are on the Lord
till he show us his mercy.**

1   To you have I lifted up my eyes,
    you who dwell in the heavens:
    my eyes, like the eyes of slaves
    on the hand of their lords.   ℟

2   Like the eyes of a servant
    on the hand of her mistress,
    so our eyes are on the Lord our God
    till he show us his mercy.   ℟

3   Have mercy on us, Lord, have mercy.
    We are filled with contempt.
    Indeed all too full is our soul
    with the scorn of the rich,
    with the proud man's disdain.   ℟

SECOND READING
A reading from the second letter of St Paul 12:7-10
to the Corinthians

In view of the extraordinary nature of these revelations, to stop me from getting too proud I was given a thorn in the flesh, an angel of Satan to beat me and stop me from getting too proud! About this thing, I have pleaded with the Lord three times for it to leave me, but he has said, 'My grace is enough for you: my power is at its best in weakness.' So I shall be very happy to make my weaknesses my special boast so that the power of Christ may stay over me, and that is why I am quite content with my weaknesses, and with insults, hardships, persecutions, and the agonies I go through for Christ's sake. For it is when I am weak that I am strong.

The word of the Lord.

Gospel Acclamation Jn 1:14. 12
Alleluia, alleluia!
The Word was made flesh and lived among us;
to all who did accept him
he gave power to become children of God.
Alleluia!

or Lk 4:18

Alleluia, alleluia!
The Lord has sent me to bring the good news to the poor,
to proclaim liberty to captives.
Alleluia!

GOSPEL
A reading from the holy Gospel according to Mark 6:1-6

Jesus went to his home town and his disciples accompanied him. With the coming of the sabbath he began teaching in the synagogue and most of them were astonished when they heard him. They said, 'Where did the man get all this? What is this wisdom that has been granted him, and these miracles that are worked through him? This is the carpenter, surely, the son of Mary, the brother of James and Joset and Jude and Simon? His sisters, too, are they not here with us?' And they would not accept him. And Jesus said to them, 'A prophet is only despised in his own country among his own relations and in his own house'; and he could work no miracle there, though he cured a few sick people by laying his hands on them. He was amazed at their lack of faith.

The Gospel of the Lord.

The Creed is said.

Prayer over the Offerings
May this oblation dedicated to your name
purify us, O Lord,

and day by day bring our conduct
closer to the life of heaven.
Through Christ our Lord.
Amen.

Communion Antiphon Ps 33:9
Taste and see that the Lord is good;
blessed the man who seeks refuge in him.

or Mt 11:28

Come to me, all who labour and are burdened,
and I will refresh you, says the Lord.

Prayer after Communion
Grant, we pray, O Lord,
that, having been replenished by such great gifts,
we may gain the prize of salvation
and never cease to praise you.
Through Christ our Lord.
Amen.

FIFTEENTH SUNDAY IN ORDINARY TIME   B

The Missionary Church

'Go, tell my people,' is the command we have been given by God. And the message is the most stupendous one imaginable: that God has blessed us with all the spiritual blessings from heaven in Christ.

Entrance Antiphon Cf. Ps 16:15
As for me, in justice I shall behold your face;
I shall be filled with the vision of your glory.

Collect
O God, who show the light of your truth
to those who go astray,
so that they may return to the right path,
give all who for the faith they profess
are accounted Christians
the grace to reject whatever is contrary to the name of Christ
and to strive after all that does it honour.
Through our Lord Jesus Christ, your Son,
who lives and reigns with you in the unity of the Holy Spirit,
one God, for ever and ever.
Amen.

Fifteenth Sunday in Ordinary Time, Year B

FIRST READING

A reading from the prophet Amos   7:12-15

Amaziah, the priest of Bethel, said to Amos, 'Go away, seer; get back to the land of Judah; earn your bread there, do your prophesying there. We want no more prophesying in Bethel; this is the royal sanctuary, the national temple.' 'I was no prophet, neither did I belong to any of the brotherhoods of prophets,' Amos replied to Amaziah. 'I was a shepherd, and looked after sycamores: but it was the Lord who took me from herding the flock, and the Lord who said, "Go, prophesy to my people Israel."'

The word of the Lord.

Responsorial Psalm   Ps 84:9-14. ℟ v.8

℟ **Let us see, O Lord, your mercy**
and give us your saving help.

1   I will hear what the Lord God has to say,
    a voice that speaks of peace,
    peace for his people.
    His help is near for those who fear him
    and his glory will dwell in our land.   ℟

2   Mercy and faithfulness have met;
    justice and peace have embraced.
    Faithfulness shall spring from the earth
    and justice look down from heaven.   ℟

3   The Lord will make us prosper
    and our earth shall yield its fruit.
    Justice shall march before him
    and peace shall follow his steps.   ℟

SECOND READING

A reading from the letter of St Paul to the Ephesians   1:3-14

*Blessed be God the Father of our Lord Jesus Christ,
who has blessed us with all the spiritual blessings of heaven in Christ.
Before the world was made, he chose us, chose us in Christ,
to be holy and spotless, and to live through love in his presence,
determining that we should become his adopted sons, through
    Jesus Christ
for his own kind purposes,
to make us praise the glory of his grace,
his free gift to us in the Beloved

in whom, through his blood, we gain our freedom, the
    forgiveness of our sins.
Such is the richness of the grace
which he has showered on us
in all wisdom and insight.
He has let us know the mystery of his purpose,
the hidden plan he so kindly made in Christ from the beginning
to act upon when the times had run their course to the end:
that he would bring everything together under Christ, as head,
everything in the heavens and everything on earth.*

And it is in him that we were claimed as God's own,
chosen from the beginning,
under the predetermined plan of the one who guides all things
as he decides by his own will;
chosen to be,
for his greater glory,
the people who would put their hopes in Christ before he came.
Now you too, in him,
have heard the message of the truth and the good news of your
    salvation,
and have believed it:
and you too have been stamped with the seal of the Holy Spirit of
  the Promise,
the pledge of our inheritance
which brings freedom for those whom God has taken for his
  own,
to make his glory praised.

The word of the Lord.

Shorter Form, verses 3-10. Read between

Gospel Acclamation Cf. Jn 6:63. 68
  Alleluia, alleluia!
  Your words are spirit, Lord,
  and they are life:
  you have the message of eternal life.
  Alleluia!

or Cf. Eph 1:17-18

  Alleluia, alleluia!
  May the Father of our Lord Jesus Christ
  enlighten the eyes of our mind,
  so that we can see what hope his call holds for us.
  Alleluia!

GOSPEL

A reading from the holy Gospel according to Mark   6:7-13

Jesus summoned the Twelve and began to send them out in pairs giving them authority over the unclean spirits. And he instructed them to take nothing for the journey except a staff – no bread, no haversack, no coppers for their purses. They were to wear sandals but, he added, 'Do not take a spare tunic.' And he said to them, 'If you enter a house anywhere, stay there until you leave the district. And if any place does not welcome you and people refuse to listen to you, as you walk away shake off the dust from under your feet as a sign to them.' So they set off to preach repentance; and they cast out many devils, and anointed many sick people with oil and cured them.

The Gospel of the Lord.

The Creed is said.

Prayer over the Offerings
Look upon the offerings of the Church, O Lord,
as she makes her prayer to you,
and grant that, when consumed by those who believe,
they may bring ever greater holiness.
Through Christ our Lord.
Amen.

Communion Antiphon   Cf. Ps 83:4-5
The sparrow finds a home,
and the swallow a nest for her young:
by your altars, O Lord of hosts, my King and my God.
Blessed are they who dwell in your house,
for ever singing your praise.

or   Jn 6:57

Whoever eats my flesh and drinks my blood
remains in me and I in him, says the Lord.

Prayer after Communion
Having consumed these gifts, we pray, O Lord,
that, by our participation in this mystery,
its saving effects upon us may grow.
Through Christ our Lord.
Amen.

SIXTEENTH SUNDAY IN ORDINARY TIME B

Christ the Good Shepherd

Today we celebrate the Shepherd who leads all people to the Father, however far apart they may be in race or culture.

Entrance Antiphon
Ps 53:6. 8

See, I have God for my help.
The Lord sustains my soul.
I will sacrifice to you with willing heart,
and praise your name, O Lord, for it is good.

Collect
Show favour, O Lord, to your servants
and mercifully increase the gifts of your grace,
that, made fervent in hope, faith and charity,
they may be ever watchful in keeping your commands.
Through our Lord Jesus Christ, your Son,
who lives and reigns with you in the unity of the Holy Spirit,
one God, for ever and ever.
Amen.

FIRST READING
A reading from the prophet Jeremiah
23:1-6

'Doom for the shepherds who allow the flock of my pasture to be destroyed and scattered – it is the Lord who speaks! This, therefore, is what the Lord, the God of Israel, says about the shepherds in charge of my people: You have let my flock be scattered and go wandering and have not taken care of them. Right, I will take care of you for your misdeeds – it is the Lord who speaks! But the remnant of my flock I myself will gather from all the countries where I have dispersed them, and will bring them back to their pastures: they shall be fruitful and increase in numbers. I will raise up shepherds to look after them and pasture them; no fear, no terror for them any more; not one shall be lost – it is the Lord who speaks!

'See, the days are coming – it is the Lord who speaks –
when I will raise a virtuous Branch for David,
who will reign as true king and be wise,
practising honesty and integrity in the land.
In his days Judah will be saved
and Israel dwell in confidence.

And this is the name he will be called:
The Lord-our-integrity.'

The word of the Lord.

Responsorial Psalm Ps 22. ℟ v.1

℟ **The Lord is my shepherd;
there is nothing I shall want.**

1. The Lord is my shepherd;
   there is nothing I shall want.
   Fresh and green are the pastures
   where he gives me repose.
   Near restful waters he leads me,
   to revive my drooping spirit. ℟

2. He guides me along the right path;
   he is true to his name.
   If I should walk in the valley of darkness
   no evil would I fear.
   You are there with your crook and your staff;
   with these you give me comfort. ℟

3. You have prepared a banquet for me
   in the sight of my foes.
   My head you have anointed with oil;
   my cup is overflowing. ℟

4. Surely goodness and kindness shall follow me
   all the days of my life.
   In the Lord's own house shall I dwell
   for ever and ever. ℟

SECOND READING
A reading from the letter of St Paul to the Ephesians 2:13-18

In Christ Jesus, you that used to be so far apart from us have been brought very close, by the blood of Christ. For he is the peace between us, and has made the two into one and broken down the barrier which used to keep them apart, actually destroying in his own person the hostility caused by the rules and decrees of the Law. This was to create one single New Man in himself out of the two of them and by restoring peace through the cross, to unite them both in a single Body and reconcile them with God. In his own person he killed the hostility. Later he came to bring the good news of peace,

peace to you who were far away and peace to those who were near at hand. Through him, both of us have in the one Spirit our way to come to the Father.

The word of the Lord.

Gospel Acclamation   Jn 10:27
Alleluia, alleluia!
The sheep that belong to me listen to my voice,
says the Lord,
I know them and they follow me.
Alleluia!

GOSPEL
A reading from the holy Gospel according to Mark   6:30-34

The apostles rejoined Jesus and told him all they had done and taught. Then he said to them, 'You must come away to some lonely place all by yourselves and rest for a while'; for there were so many coming and going that the apostles had no time even to eat. So they went off in a boat to a lonely place where they could be by themselves. But people saw them going, and many could guess where; and from every town they all hurried to the place on foot and reached it before them. So as he stepped ashore he saw a large crowd; and he took pity on them because they were like sheep without a shepherd, and he set himself to teach them at some length.

The Gospel of the Lord.

The Creed is said.

Prayer over the Offerings
O God, who in the one perfect sacrifice
brought to completion varied offerings of the law,
accept, we pray, this sacrifice from your faithful servants
and make it holy, as you blessed the gifts of Abel,
so that what each has offered to the honour of your majesty
may benefit the salvation of all.
Through Christ our Lord.
Amen.

Communion Antiphon   Ps 110:4-5
The Lord, the gracious, the merciful,
has made a memorial of his wonders;
he gives food to those who fear him.

or Rv 3:20
Behold, I stand at the door and knock, says the Lord.
If anyone hears my voice and opens the door to me,
I will enter his house and dine with him, and he with me.

Prayer after Communion
Graciously be present to your people, we pray, O Lord,
and lead those you have imbued with heavenly mysteries
to pass from former ways to newness of life.
Through Christ our Lord.
Amen.

SEVENTEENTH SUNDAY IN ORDINARY TIME   B

Christ Who Feeds Us

We celebrate today the new Elisha who feeds his people and makes us one body, one spirit, in himself.

Entrance Antiphon Cf. Ps 67:6-7. 36
God is in his holy place,
God who unites those who dwell in his house;
he himself gives might and strength to his people.

Collect
O God, protector of those who hope in you,
without whom nothing has firm foundation, nothing is holy,
bestow in abundance your mercy upon us
and grant that, with you as our ruler and guide,
we may use the good things that pass
in such a way as to hold fast even now
to those that ever endure.
Through our Lord Jesus Christ, your Son,
who lives and reigns with you in the unity of the Holy Spirit,
one God, for ever and ever.
Amen.

FIRST READING
A reading from the second book of the Kings 4:42-44

A man came from Baal-shalishah, bringing Elisha, the man of God, bread from the first-fruits, twenty barley loaves and fresh grain in the ear. 'Give it to the people to eat,' Elisha said. But his servant replied, 'How can I serve this to a hundred men?' 'Give it to the people to eat' he insisted 'for the Lord says this, "They will eat and have some left over."' He served them; they ate and had some over, as the Lord had said.

The word of the Lord.

Responsorial Psalm   Ps 144:10-11. 15-18. ℟ v.16
  ℟ **You open wide your hand, O Lord,
     and grant our desires.**

1. All your creatures shall thank you, O Lord,
   and your friends shall repeat their blessing.
   They shall speak of the glory of your reign
   and declare your might, O God. ℟

2. The eyes of all creatures look to you
   and you give them their food in due time.
   You open wide your hand,
   grant the desires of all who live. ℟

3. The Lord is just in all his ways
   and loving in all his deeds.
   He is close to all who call him,
   who call on him from their hearts. ℟

SECOND READING
A reading from the letter of St Paul to the Ephesians   4:1-6

I, the prisoner in the Lord, implore you to lead a life worthy of your vocation. Bear with one another charitably, in complete selflessness, gentleness and patience. Do all you can to preserve the unity of the Spirit by the peace that binds you together. There is one Body, one Spirit, just as you were all called into one and the same hope when you were called. There is one Lord, one faith, one baptism, and one God who is Father of all, through all and within all.

The word of the Lord.

Gospel Acclamation   Cf. Jn 6:63. 68
  Alleluia, alleluia!
  Your words are spirit, Lord,
  and they are life:
  you have the message of eternal life.
  Alleluia!

Seventeenth Sunday in Ordinary Time, Year B

or   Lk 7:16

Alleluia, alleluia!
A great prophet has appeared among us;
God has visited his people.
Alleluia!

GOSPEL
A reading from the holy Gospel according to John   6:1-15

Jesus went off to the other side of the Sea of Galilee – or of Tiberias – and a large crowd followed him, impressed by the signs he gave by curing the sick. Jesus climbed the hillside, and sat down there with his disciples. It was shortly before the Jewish feast of Passover.

Looking up, Jesus saw the crowds approaching and said to Philip, 'Where can we buy some bread for these people to eat?' He only said this to test Philip; he himself knew exactly what he was going to do. Philip answered, 'Two hundred denarii would only buy enough to give them a small piece each.' One of his disciples, Andrew, Simon Peter's brother, said, 'There is a small boy here with five barley loaves and two fish; but what is that between so many?' Jesus said to them, 'Make the people sit down.' There was plenty of grass there, and as many as five thousand men sat down. Then Jesus took the loaves, gave thanks, and gave them out to all who were sitting ready; he then did the same with the fish, giving out as much as was wanted. When they had eaten enough he said to the disciples, 'Pick up the pieces left over, so that nothing gets wasted.' So they picked them up, and filled twelve hampers with scraps left over from the meal of five barley loaves. The people, seeing this sign that he had given, said, 'This really is the prophet who is to come into the world.' Jesus, who could see they were about to come and take him by force and make him king, escaped back to the hills by himself.

The Gospel of the Lord.

The Creed is said.

Prayer over the Offerings
Accept, O Lord, we pray, the offerings
which we bring from the abundance of your gifts,
that through the powerful working of your grace
these most sacred mysteries may sanctify our present way of life
and lead us to eternal gladness.
Through Christ our Lord.
Amen.

Communion Antiphon   Ps 102:2
Bless the Lord, O my soul,
and never forget all his benefits.

or   Mt 5:7-8

Blessed are the merciful, for they shall receive mercy.
Blessed are the clean of heart, for they shall see God.

Prayer after Communion
We have consumed, O Lord, this divine Sacrament,
the perpetual memorial of the Passion of your Son;
grant, we pray, that this gift,
which he himself gave us with love beyond all telling,
may profit us for salvation.
Through Christ our Lord.
Amen.

EIGHTEENTH SUNDAY IN ORDINARY TIME   B

Bread from Heaven

Through Christ we have undergone what St Paul calls a spiritual revolution and we can no longer be satisfied with material things. We need the food that comes from heaven, the bread of life which we receive at this Mass.

Entrance Antiphon   Ps 69:2. 6
O God, come to my assistance;
O Lord, make haste to help me!
You are my rescuer, my help;
O Lord, do not delay.

Collect
Draw near to your servants, O Lord,
and answer their prayers with unceasing kindness,
that, for those who glory in you as their Creator and guide,
you may restore what you have created
and keep safe what you have restored.
Through our Lord Jesus Christ, your Son,
who lives and reigns with you in the unity of the Holy Spirit,
one God, for ever and ever.
Amen.

Eighteenth Sunday in Ordinary Time, Year B

FIRST READING
A reading from the first book of Exodus   16:2-4. 12-15

The whole community of the sons of Israel began to complain against Moses and Aaron in the wilderness and said to them, 'Why did we not die at the Lord's hand in the land of Egypt, when we were able to sit down to pans of meat and could eat bread to our heart's content! As it is, you have brought us to this wilderness to starve this whole company to death!'

Then the Lord said to Moses, 'Now I will rain down bread for you from the heavens. Each day the people are to go out and gather the day's portion; I propose to test them in this way to see whether they will follow my law or not.'

'I have heard the complaints of the sons of Israel. Say this to them, "Between the two evenings you shall eat meat, and in the morning you shall have bread to your heart's content. Then you will learn that I, the Lord, am your God."' And so it came about: quails flew up in the evening, and they covered the camp; in the morning there was a coating of dew all round the camp. When the coating of dew lifted, there on the surface of the desert was a thing delicate, powdery, as fine as hoarfrost on the ground. When they saw this, the sons of Israel said to one another, 'What is that?' not knowing what it was. 'That' said Moses to them 'is the bread the Lord gives you to eat.'

The word of the Lord.

Responsorial Psalm   Ps 77:3-4. 23-25. 54. ℟ v.24
℟ **The Lord gave them bread from heaven.**

1   The things we have heard and understood,
     the things our fathers have told us,
     we will tell to the next generation:
     the glories of the Lord and his might. ℟

2   He commanded the clouds above
     and opened the gates of heaven.
     He rained down manna for their food,
     and gave them bread from heaven. ℟

3   Mere men ate the bread of angels.
     He sent them abundance of food.
     He brought them to his holy land,
     to the mountain which his right hand had won. ℟

SECOND READING
A reading from the letter of St Paul to the Ephesians 4:17. 20-24

I want to urge you in the name of the Lord, not to go on living the aimless kind of life that pagans live. Now that is hardly the way you have learnt from Christ, unless you failed to hear him properly when you were taught what the truth is in Jesus. You must give up your old way of life; you must put aside your old self, which gets corrupted by following illusory desires. Your mind must be renewed by a spiritual revolution so that you can put on the new self that has been created in God's way, in the goodness and holiness of the truth.

The word of the Lord.

Gospel Acclamation Jn 14:5
Alleluia, alleluia!
I am the Way, the Truth and the Life, says the Lord;
no one can come to the Father except through me.
Alleluia!

or Mt 4:4

Alleluia, alleluia!
Man does not live on bread alone,
but on every word that comes from the mouth of God.
Alleluia!

GOSPEL
A reading from the holy Gospel according to John 6:24-35

When the people saw that neither Jesus nor his disciples were there, they got into boats and crossed to Capernaum to look for Jesus. When they found him on the other side, they said to him, 'Rabbi, when did you come here?' Jesus answered:

'I tell you most solemnly,
you are not looking for me
because you have seen the signs
but because you had all the bread you wanted to eat.
Do not work for food that cannot last,
but work for food that endures to eternal life,
the kind of food the Son of Man is offering you,
for on him the Father, God himself, has set his seal.'

Then they said to him, 'What must we do if we are to do the works that God wants?' Jesus gave them this answer, 'This is working for

Eighteenth Sunday in Ordinary Time, Year B

God: you must believe in the one he has sent.' So they said, 'What sign will you give to show us that we should believe in you? What work will you do? Our fathers had manna to eat in the desert; as scripture says: He gave them bread from heaven to eat.'

Jesus answered:

'I tell you most solemnly,
it was not Moses who gave you bread from heaven,
it is my Father who gives you the bread from heaven,
the true bread;
for the bread of God
is that which comes down from heaven
and gives life to the world.'

'Sir,' they said 'give us that bread always.' Jesus answered:

'I am the bread of life.
He who comes to me will never be hungry;
he who believes in me will never thirst.'

The Gospel of the Lord.

The Creed is said.

Prayer over the Offerings
Graciously sanctify these gifts, O Lord, we pray,
and, accepting the oblation of this spiritual sacrifice,
make of us an eternal offering to you.
Through Christ our Lord.
Amen.

Communion Antiphon   Wis 16:20
You have given us, O Lord, bread from heaven,
endowed with all delights and sweetness in every taste.

or   Jn 6:35

I am the bread of life, says the Lord;
whoever comes to me will not hunger
and whoever believes in me will not thirst.

Prayer after Communion
Accompany with constant protection, O Lord,
those you renew with these heavenly gifts
and, in your never-failing care for them,
make them worthy of eternal redemption.
Through Christ our Lord.
Amen.

NINETEENTH SUNDAY IN ORDINARY TIME   B

The Father Who Draws Us to Himself

Elijah was drawn to the mountain of God by the Lord who gave him food and drink. The Father is drawing us to himself by offering us the bread of life at this Eucharist.

Entrance Antiphon   Cf. Ps 73:20. 19. 22. 23
Look to your covenant, O Lord,
and forget not the life of your poor ones for ever.
Arise, O God, and defend your cause,
and forget not the cries of those who seek you.

Collect
Almighty ever-living God,
whom, taught by the Holy Spirit,
we dare to call our Father,
bring, we pray, to perfection in our hearts
the spirit of adoption as your sons and daughters,
that we may merit to enter into the inheritance
which you have promised.
Through our Lord Jesus Christ, your Son,
who lives and reigns with you in the unity of the Holy Spirit,
one God, for ever and ever.
Amen.

FIRST READING
A reading from the first book of Kings   19:4-8

Elijah went into the wilderness, a day's journey, and sitting under a furze bush wished he were dead. 'Lord,' he said 'I have had enough. Take my life; I am no better than my ancestors.' Then he lay down and went to sleep. But an angel touched him and said, 'Get up and eat.' He looked round, and there at his head was a scone baked on hot stones, and a jar of water. He ate and drank and then lay down again. But the angel of the Lord came back a second time and touched him and said, 'Get up and eat, or the journey will be too long for you.' So he got up and ate and drank, and strengthened by that food he walked for forty days and forty nights until he reached Horeb, the mountain of God.

The word of the Lord.

Nineteenth Sunday in Ordinary Time, Year B

Responsorial Psalm   Ps 33:2-9. ℟ v.9
   ℟ **Taste and see that the Lord is good.**

1. I will bless the Lord at all times,
   his praise always on my lips;
   in the Lord my soul shall make its boast.
   The humble shall hear and be glad. ℟

2. Glorify the Lord with me.
   Together let us praise his name.
   I sought the Lord and he answered me;
   from all my terrors he set me free. ℟

3. Look towards him and be radiant;
   let your faces not be abashed.
   This poor man called; the Lord heard him
   and rescued him from all his distress. ℟

4. The angel of the Lord is encamped
   around those who revere him, to rescue them.
   Taste and see that the Lord is good.
   He is happy who seeks refuge in him. ℟

SECOND READING
A reading from the letter of St Paul to the Ephesians   4:30 – 5:2

Do not grieve the Holy Spirit of God who has marked you with his seal for you to be set free when the day comes. Never have grudges against others, or lose your temper, or raise your voice to anybody, or call each other names, or allow any sort of spitefulness. Be friends with one another, and kind, forgiving each other as readily as God forgave you in Christ.

   Try, then, to imitate God, as children of his that he loves, and follow Christ by loving as he loved you, giving himself up in our place as a fragrant offering and a sacrifice to God.

   The word of the Lord.

Gospel Acclamation   Jn 14:23
   Alleluia, alleluia!
   If anyone loves me he will keep my word,
   and my Father will love him,
   and we shall come to him.
   Alleluia!

or Jn 6:51

Alleluia, alleluia!
I am the living bread which has come down from heaven,
says the Lord.
Anyone who eats this bread will live for ever.
Alleluia!

GOSPEL

A reading from the holy Gospel according to John 6:41-51

The Jews were complaining to each other about Jesus, because he had said, 'I am the bread that came down from heaven.' 'Surely this is Jesus son of Joseph' they said. 'We know his father and mother. How can he now say, "I have come down from heaven"?' Jesus said in reply, 'Stop complaining to each other.

> 'No one can come to me
> unless he is drawn by the Father who sent me,
> and I will raise him up at the last day.
> It is written in the prophets:
> They will all be taught by God,
> and to hear the teaching of the Father,
> and learn from it,
> is to come to me.
> Not that anybody has seen the Father,
> except the one who comes from God:
> he has seen the Father.
> I tell you most solemnly,
> everybody who believes has eternal life.
> I am the bread of life.
> Your fathers ate the manna in the desert
> and they are dead;
> but this is the bread that comes down from heaven,
> so that a man may eat it and not die.
> I am the living bread which has come down from heaven.
> Anyone who eats this bread will live for ever;
> and the bread that I shall give
> is my flesh, for the life of the world.'

The Gospel of the Lord.

The Creed is said.

Prayer over the Offerings
Be pleased, O Lord, to accept the offerings of your Church,
for in your mercy you have given them to be offered

Twentieth Sunday in Ordinary Time, Year B

and by your power you transform them
into the mystery of our salvation.
Through Christ our Lord.
Amen.

Communion Antiphon — Ps 147:12. 14
O Jerusalem, glorify the Lord,
who gives you your fill of finest wheat.

or — Cf. Jn 6:51

The bread that I will give, says the Lord,
is my flesh for the life of the world.

Prayer after Communion
May the communion in your Sacrament
that we have consumed, save us, O Lord,
and confirm us in the light of your truth.
Through Christ our Lord.
Amen.

TWENTIETH SUNDAY IN ORDINARY TIME   B

Our Eucharist: Thanksgiving

Eucharist means thanksgiving. Today, filled with the Spirit, we make thanksgiving to God for the bread of life.

Entrance Antiphon — Ps 83:10-11
Turn your eyes, O God, our shield;
and look on the face of your anointed one;
one day within your courts
is better than a thousand elsewhere.

Collect
O God, who have prepared for those who love you
good things which no eye can see,
fill our hearts, we pray, with the warmth of your love,
so that, loving you in all things and above all things,
we may attain your promises,
which surpass every human desire.
Through our Lord Jesus Christ, your Son,
who lives and reigns with you in the unity of the Holy Spirit,
one God, for ever and ever.
Amen.

FIRST READING

A reading from the book of Proverbs 9:1-6

Wisdom has built herself a house,
she has erected her seven pillars,
she has slaughtered her beasts, prepared her wine,
she has laid her table.
She has despatched her maidservants
and proclaimed from the city's heights:
'Who is ignorant? Let him step this way.'
To the fool she says,
'Come and eat my bread,
drink the wine I have prepared!
Leave your folly and you will live,
walk in the ways of perception.'

The word of the Lord.

Responsorial Psalm Ps 33:2-3. 10-15. ℟ v.9

℟ **Taste and see that the Lord is good.**

1. I will bless the Lord at all times,
   his praise always on my lips;
   in the Lord my soul shall make its boast.
   The humble shall hear and be glad. ℟

2. Revere the Lord, you his saints.
   They lack nothing, those who revere him.
   Strong lions suffer want and go hungry
   but those who seek the Lord lack no blessing. ℟

3. Come, children, and hear me
   that I may teach you the fear of the Lord.
   Who is he who longs for life
   and many days, to enjoy his prosperity? ℟

4. Then keep your tongue from evil
   and your lips from speaking deceit.
   Turn aside from evil and do good;
   seek and strive after peace. ℟

SECOND READING

A reading from the letter of St Paul to the Ephesians 5:15-20

Be very careful about the sort of lives you lead, like intelligent and not like senseless people. This may be a wicked age, but your lives

Twentieth Sunday in Ordinary Time, Year B

should redeem it. And do not be thoughtless but recognise what is the will of the Lord. Do not drug yourselves with wine, this is simply dissipation; be filled with the Spirit. Sing the words and tunes of the psalms and hymns when you are together, and go on singing and chanting to the Lord in your hearts, so that always and everywhere you are giving thanks to God who is our Father in the name of our Lord Jesus Christ.

The word of the Lord.

Gospel Acclamation Jn 1:14. 12
Alleluia, alleluia!
The Word was made flesh and lived among us;
to all who did accept him
he gave power to become children of God.
Alleluia!

or Jn 6:56

Alleluia, alleluia!
He who eats my flesh and drinks my blood
lives in me, and I live in him,
says the Lord.
Alleluia!

GOSPEL
A reading from the holy Gospel according to John 6:51-58

Jesus said to the crowd:

'I am the living bread which has come down from heaven.
Anyone who eats this bread will live for ever;
and the bread that I shall give
is my flesh, for the life of the world.'

Then the Jews started arguing with one another: 'How can this man give us his flesh to eat?' they said. Jesus replied:

'I tell you most solemnly,
if you do not eat the flesh of the Son of Man
and drink his blood,
you will not have life in you.
Anyone who does eat my flesh and drink my blood
has eternal life,
and I shall raise him up on the last day.
For my flesh is real food
and my blood is real drink.

He who eats my flesh and drinks my blood
lives in me
and I live in him.
As I, who am sent by the living Father,
myself draw life from the Father,
so whoever eats me will draw life from me.
This is the bread come down from heaven;
not like the bread our ancestors ate:
they are dead,
but anyone who eats this bread will live for ever.'

The Gospel of the Lord.

The Creed is said.

Prayer over the Offerings
Receive our oblation, O Lord,
by which is brought about a glorious exchange,
that, by offering what you have given,
we may merit to receive your very self.
Through Christ our Lord.
Amen.

Communion Antiphon   Ps 129:7
With the Lord there is mercy;
in him is plentiful redemption.

or   Jn 6:51-52

I am the living bread that came down from heaven, says the Lord.
Whoever eats of this bread will live for ever.

Prayer after Communion
Made partakers of Christ through these Sacraments,
we humbly implore your mercy, Lord,
that, conformed to his image on earth,
we may merit also to be his coheirs in heaven.
Who lives and reigns for ever and ever.
Amen.

TWENTY-FIRST SUNDAY IN ORDINARY TIME   B

The Holy One of God

Today, as we celebrate the marriage feast of Christ with his Church, we consciously choose him who is the Holy One of God.

Twenty-First Sunday in Ordinary Time, Year B

Entrance Antiphon Cf. Ps 85:1-3
Turn your ear, O Lord, and answer me;
save the servant who trusts in you, my God.
Have mercy on me, O Lord, for I cry to you all the day long.

Collect
O God, who cause the minds of the faithful
to unite in a single purpose,
grant your people to love what you command
and to desire what you promise,
that, amid the uncertainties of this world,
our hearts may be fixed on that place
where true gladness is found.
Through our Lord Jesus Christ, your Son,
who lives and reigns with you in the unity of the Holy Spirit,
one God, for ever and ever.
Amen.

FIRST READING
A reading from the book of Joshua 24:1-2. 15-18

Joshua gathered all the tribes of Israel together at Shechem; then he called the elders, leaders, judges and scribes of Israel, and they presented themselves before God. Then Joshua said to all the people: 'If you will not serve the Lord, choose today whom you wish to serve, whether the gods that your ancestors served beyond the River, or the gods of the Amorites in whose land you are now living. As for me and my House, we will serve the Lord.'

The people answered, 'We have no intention of deserting the Lord our God and serving other gods. Was it not the Lord our God who brought us and our ancestors out of the land of Egypt, the house of slavery, who worked those great wonders before our eyes and preserved us all along the way we travelled and among all the peoples through whom we journeyed. We too will serve the Lord, for he is our God.'

The word of the Lord.

Responsorial Psalm Ps 33:2-3. 16-23. ℟ v.9
℟ **Taste and see that the Lord is good.**

1 I will bless the Lord at all times,
 his praise always on my lips;
 in the Lord my soul shall make its boast.
 The humble shall hear and be glad. ℟

2   The Lord turns his face against the wicked
    to destroy their remembrance from the earth.
    The Lord turns his eyes to the just
    and his ears to their appeal. ℟

3   They call and the Lord hears
    and rescues them in all their distress.
    The Lord is close to the broken-hearted;
    those whose spirit is crushed he will save. ℟

4   Many are the trials of the just man
    but from them all the Lord will rescue him.
    He will keep guard over all his bones,
    not one of his bones shall be broken. ℟

5   Evil brings death to the wicked;
    those who hate the good are doomed.
    The Lord ransoms the souls of his servants.
    Those who hide in him shall not be condemned. ℟

SECOND READING

A reading from the letter of St Paul to the Ephesians   5:21-32

Give way to one another in obedience to Christ. Wives should regard their husbands as they regard the Lord, since as Christ is head of the Church and saves the whole body, so is a husband the head of his wife; and as the Church submits to Christ, so should wives to their husbands, in everything. Husbands should love their wives just as Christ loved the Church and sacrificed himself for her to make her holy. He made her clean by washing her in water with a form of words, so that when he took her to himself she would be glorious, with no speck or wrinkle or anything like that, but holy and faultless. In the same way, husbands must love their wives as they love their own bodies; for a man to love his wife is for him to love himself. A man never hates his own body, but he feeds it and looks after it; and that is the way Christ treats the Church, because it is his body – and we are its living parts. For this reason, a man must leave his father and mother and be joined to his wife, and the two will become one body. This mystery has many implications; but I am saying it applies to Christ and the Church.

The word of the Lord.

Gospel Acclamation   Cf. Jn 6:63. 68
    Alleluia, alleluia!
    Your words are spirit, Lord,

Twenty-First Sunday in Ordinary Time, Year B

and they are life:
you have the message of eternal life.
Alleluia!

GOSPEL

A reading from the holy Gospel according to John 6:60-69

After hearing his doctrine many of the followers of Jesus said, 'This is intolerable language. How could anyone accept it?' Jesus was aware that his followers were complaining about it and said, 'Does this upset you? What if you should see the Son of Man ascend to where he was before?

'It is the spirit that gives life,
the flesh has nothing to offer.
The words I have spoken to you are spirit
and they are life.

'But there are some of you who do not believe.' For Jesus knew from the outset those who did not believe, and who it was that would betray him. He went on, 'This is why I told you that no one could come to me unless the Father allows him.' After this, many of his disciples left him and stopped going with him. Then Jesus said to the Twelve, 'What about you, do you want to go away too?' Simon Peter answered, 'Lord, who shall we go to? You have the message of eternal life, and we believe; we know that you are the Holy One of God.'

The Gospel of the Lord.

The Creed is said.

Prayer over the Offerings
O Lord, who gained for yourself a people by adoption
through the one sacrifice offered once for all,
bestow graciously on us, we pray,
the gifts of unity and peace in your Church.
Through Christ our Lord.
Amen.

Communion Antiphon Cf. Ps 103:13-15
The earth is replete with the fruits of your work, O Lord;
you bring forth bread from the earth
and wine to cheer the heart.

or   Cf. Jn 6:54

Whoever eats my flesh and drinks my blood
has eternal life, says the Lord,
and I will raise him up on the last day.

Prayer after Communion
Complete within us, O Lord, we pray,
the healing work of your mercy
and graciously perfect and sustain us,
so that in all things we may please you.
Through Christ our Lord.
Amen.

TWENTY-SECOND SUNDAY IN ORDINARY TIME   B

The Commandments of Life

We rejoice in the Law of God which is pure religion, totally different from any human law or tradition. It is fulfilled in this sacrament of love.

Entrance Antiphon   Cf. Ps 85:3. 5
Have mercy on me, O Lord, for I cry to you all the day long.
O Lord, you are good and forgiving,
full of mercy to all who call to you.

Collect
God of might, giver of every good gift,
put into our hearts the love of your name,
so that, by deepening our sense of reverence,
you may nurture in us what is good
and, by your watchful care,
keep safe what you have nurtured.
Through our Lord Jesus Christ, your Son,
who lives and reigns with you in the unity of the Holy Spirit,
one God, for ever and ever.
Amen.

FIRST READING
A reading from the book of Deuteronomy   4:1-2. 6-8

Moses said to the people: 'Now, Israel, take notice of the laws and customs that I teach you today, and observe them, that you may

Twenty-Second Sunday in Ordinary Time, Year B

have life and may enter and take possession of the land that the Lord the God of your fathers is giving you. You must add nothing to what I command you, and take nothing from it, but keep the commandments of the Lord your God just as I lay them down for you. Keep them, observe them, and they will demonstrate to the peoples your wisdom and understanding. When they come to know of all these laws they will exclaim, "No other people is as wise and prudent as this great nation." And indeed, what great nation is there that has its gods so near as the Lord our God is to us whenever we call to him? And what great nation is there that has laws and customs to match this whole Law that I put before you today?'

The word of the Lord.

Responsorial Psalm   Ps 14:2-5. ℟ v.1

   ℟   **The just will live in the presence of the Lord.**

1   Lord, who shall dwell on your holy mountain?
     He who walks without fault;
     he who acts with justice
     and speaks the truth from his heart.   ℟

2   He who does no wrong to his brother,
     who casts no slur on his neighbour,
     who holds the godless in disdain,
     but honours those who fear the Lord.   ℟

3   He who keeps his pledge, come what may;
     who takes no interest on a loan
     and accepts no bribes against the innocent.
     Such a man will stand firm for ever.   ℟

SECOND READING

A reading from the letter of St James   1:17-18. 21-22. 27

It is all that is good, everything that is perfect, which is given us from above; it comes down from the Father of all light; with him there is no such thing as alteration, no shadow of a change. By his own choice he made us his children by the message of the truth so that we should be a sort of first-fruits of all that he had created.

    Accept and submit to the word which has been planted in you and can save your souls. But you must do what the word tells you, and not just listen to it and deceive yourselves.

Pure unspoilt religion, in the eyes of God our Father is this: coming to the help of orphans and widows when they need it, and keeping oneself uncontaminated by the world.

The word of the Lord.

Gospel Acclamation   Cf. Jn 6:63. 68
Alleluia, alleluia!
Your words are spirit, Lord,
and they are life:
you have the message of eternal life.
Alleluia!

or   James 1:18

Alleluia, alleluia!
By his own choice the Father made us his children
by the message of the truth,
so that we should be a sort of first-fruits
of all that he created.
Alleluia!

GOSPEL

A reading from the holy Gospel   7:1-8. 14-15. 21-23
according to Mark

The Pharisees and some of the scribes who had come from Jerusalem gathered round Jesus, and they noticed that some of his disciples were eating with unclean hands, that is, without washing them. For the Pharisees, and the Jews in general, follow the tradition of the elders and never eat without washing their arms as far as the elbow; and on returning from the market place they never eat without first sprinkling themselves. There are also many other observances which have been handed down to them concerning the washing of cups and pots and bronze dishes. So these Pharisees and scribes asked him, 'Why do your disciples not respect the tradition of the elders but eat their food with unclean hands?' He answered, 'It was of you hypocrites that Isaiah so rightly prophesied in this passage of scripture:

This people honours me only with lip-service,
while their hearts are far from me.
The worship they offer me is worthless,
the doctrines they teach are only human regulations.

You put aside the commandment of God to cling to human traditions.'

Twenty-Third Sunday in Ordinary Time, Year B

He called the people to him again and said, 'Listen to me, all of you, and understand. Nothing that goes into a man from outside can make him unclean; it is the things that come out of a man that make him unclean. For it is from within, from men's hearts, that evil intentions emerge: fornication, theft, murder, adultery, avarice, malice, deceit, indecency, envy, slander, pride, folly. All these evil things come from within and make a man unclean.'

The Gospel of the Lord.

The Creed is said.

Prayer over the Offerings
May this sacred offering, O Lord,
confer on us always the blessing of salvation,
that what it celebrates in mystery
it may accomplish in power.
Through Christ our Lord.
Amen.

Communion Antiphon   Ps 30:20
How great is the goodness, Lord,
that you keep for those who fear you.

or   Mt 5:9-10

Blessed are the peacemakers,
for they shall be called children of God.
Blessed are they who are persecuted for the sake of righteousness,
for theirs is the Kingdom of Heaven.

Prayer after Communion
Renewed by this bread from the heavenly table,
we beseech you, Lord,
that, being the food of charity,
it may confirm our hearts
and stir us to serve you in our neighbour.
Through Christ our Lord.
Amen.

TWENTY-THIRD SUNDAY IN ORDINARY TIME   B

The Lord Who Does All Things Well

Today we celebrate our 'unbounded admiration' for the Lord who makes no distinctions between classes of people, but makes the poor rich in faith, the deaf hear and the dumb speak.

Twenty-Third Sunday in Ordinary Time, Year B

Entrance Antiphon   Ps 118:137. 124
You are just, O Lord, and your judgement is right;
treat your servant in accord with your merciful love.

Collect
O God, by whom we are redeemed and receive adoption,
look graciously upon your beloved sons and daughters,
that those who believe in Christ
may receive true freedom
and an everlasting inheritance.
Through our Lord Jesus Christ, your Son,
who lives and reigns with you in the unity of the Holy Spirit,
one God, for ever and ever.
Amen.

FIRST READING
A reading from the prophet Isaiah   35:4-7

Say to all faint hearts,
'Courage! Do not be afraid.

'Look, your God is coming,
vengeance is coming,
the retribution of God;
he is coming to save you.'

Then the eyes of the blind shall be opened,
the ears of the deaf unsealed,
then the lame shall leap like a deer
and the tongues of the dumb sing for joy;

for water gushes in the desert,
streams in the wasteland,
the scorched earth becomes a lake,
the parched land springs of water.

    The word of the Lord.

Responsorial Psalm   Ps 145:7-10. ℟ v.1
   ℟   **My soul, give praise to the Lord.**

or
   ℟   **Alleluia!**

1   It is the Lord who keeps faith for ever,
     who is just to those who are oppressed.

Twenty-Third Sunday in Ordinary Time, Year B

It is he who gives bread to the hungry,
the Lord, who sets prisoners free. ℟

2 It is the Lord who gives sight to the blind,
who raises up those who are bowed down,
the Lord who loves the just,
the Lord, who protects the stranger. ℟

3 The Lord upholds the widow and orphan,
but thwarts the path of the wicked.
The Lord will reign for ever,
Zion's God, from age to age. ℟

SECOND READING

A reading from the letter of St James   2:1-5

My brothers, do not try to combine faith in Jesus Christ, our glorified Lord, with the making of distinctions between classes of people. Now suppose a man comes into your synagogue, beautifully dressed and with a gold ring on, and at the same time a poor man comes in, in shabby clothes, and you take notice of the well-dressed man, and say, 'Come this way to the best seats'; then you tell the poor man, 'Stand over there' or 'You can sit on the floor by my foot-rest.' Can't you see that you have used two different standards in your mind, and turned yourselves into judges, and corrupt judges at that?

Listen, my dear brothers: it was those who are poor according to the world that God chose, to be rich in faith and to be the heirs to the kingdom which he promised to those who love him.

The word of the Lord.

Gospel Acclamation   1 Sam 3:9; Jn 6:68
Alleluia, alleluia!
Speak, Lord, your servant is listening:
you have the message of eternal life.
Alleluia!

or   Cf. Mt 4:23

Alleluia, alleluia!
Jesus proclaimed the Good News of the kingdom,
and cured all kinds of sickness among the people.
Alleluia!

GOSPEL

A reading from the holy Gospel according to Mark 7:31-37

Returning from the district of Tyre, Jesus went by way of Sidon towards the Sea of Galilee, right through the Decapolis region. And they brought him a deaf man who had an impediment in his speech; and they asked him to lay his hand on him. He took him aside in private, away from the crowd, put his fingers into the man's ears and touched his tongue with spittle. Then looking up to heaven he sighed; and he said to him, 'Ephphatha,' that is, 'Be opened.' And his ears were opened, and the ligament of his tongue was loosened and he spoke clearly. And Jesus ordered them to tell no one about it, but the more he insisted, the more widely they published it. Their admiration was unbounded. 'He has done all things well,' they said 'he makes the deaf hear and the dumb speak.'

The Gospel of the Lord.

The Creed is said.

Prayer over the Offerings
O God, who give us the gift of true prayer and of peace,
graciously grant that through this offering,
we may do fitting homage to your divine majesty
and, by partaking of the sacred mystery,
we may be faithfully united in mind and heart.
Through Christ our Lord.
Amen.

Communion Antiphon   Cf. Ps 41:2-3
Like the deer that yearns for running streams,
so my soul is yearning for you, my God;
my soul is thirsting for God, the living God.

or   Jn 8:12

I am the light of the world, says the Lord;
whoever follows me will not walk in darkness,
but will have the light of life.

Prayer after Communion
Grant that your faithful, O Lord,
whom you nourish and endow with life
through the food of your Word and heavenly Sacrament,
may so benefit from your beloved Son's great gifts
that we may merit an eternal share in his life.
Who lives and reigns for ever and ever.
Amen.

TWENTY-FOURTH SUNDAY IN ORDINARY TIME B

Christ, the Son of Man

We worship the man Christ, who accepted every weakness of our human condition, renouncing himself and taking up the cross.

Entrance Antiphon
Cf. Sir 36:18

Give peace, O Lord, to those who wait for you,
that your prophets be found true.
Hear the prayers of your servant,
and of your people Israel.

Collect

Look upon us, O God,
Creator and ruler of all things,
and, that we may feel the working of your mercy,
grant that we may serve you with all our heart.
Through our Lord Jesus Christ, your Son,
who lives and reigns with you in the unity of the Holy Spirit,
one God, for ever and ever.
Amen.

FIRST READING

A reading from the prophet Isaiah 50:5-9

The Lord has opened my ear.

For my part, I made no resistance,
neither did I turn away.
I offered my back to those who struck me,
my cheeks to those who tore at my beard;
I did not cover my face
against insult and spittle.

The Lord comes to my help,
so that I am untouched by the insults.
So, too, I set my face like flint;
I know I shall not be shamed.

My vindicator is here at hand. Does anyone start proceedings
  against me?
Then let us go to court together.
Who thinks he has a case against me?
Let him approach me.

The Lord is coming to my help,
who dare condemn me?

    The word of the Lord.

Responsorial Psalm   Ps 114:1-6. 8-9. ℟ v.9

    ℟   **I will walk in the presence of the Lord,
in the land of the living.**

or

    ℟   **Alleluia!**

1   I love the Lord for he has heard
the cry of my appeal;
for he turned his ear to me
in the day when I called him.   ℟

2   They surrounded me, the snares of death,
with the anguish of the tomb;
they caught me, sorrow and distress.
I called on the Lord's name.
O Lord my God, deliver me!   ℟

3   How gracious is the Lord, and just;
our God has compassion.
The Lord protects the simple hearts;
I was helpless so he saved me.   ℟

4   He has kept my soul from death,
my eyes from tears
and my feet from stumbling.
I will walk in the presence of the Lord
in the land of the living.   ℟

SECOND READING

A reading from the letter of St James   2:14-18

Take the case, my brothers, of someone who has never done a single good act but claims that he has faith. Will that faith save him? If one of the brothers or one of the sisters is in need of clothes and has not enough food to live on, and one of you says to them, 'I wish you well; keep yourself warm and eat plenty,' without giving them these bare necessities of life, then what good is that? Faith is like that: if good works do not go with it, it is quite dead.

    This is the way to talk to people of that kind: 'You say you have faith and I have good deeds; I will prove to you that I have faith by

Twenty-Fourth Sunday in Ordinary Time, Year B

showing you my good deeds – now you prove to me that you have faith without any good deeds to show.'

The word of the Lord.

Gospel Acclamation Jn 14:5
Alleluia, alleluia!
I am the Way, the Truth and the Life, says the Lord;
no one can come to the Father except through me.
Alleluia!

or Gal 6:14

Alleluia, alleluia!
The only thing I can boast about is the cross of our Lord,
through whom the world is crucified to me, and I to the world.
Alleluia!

GOSPEL
A reading from the holy Gospel according to Mark 8:27-35

Jesus and his disciples left for the villages round Caesarea Philippi. On the way he put this question to his disciples, 'Who do people say I am?' And they told him. 'John the Baptist,' they said 'others Elijah; others again, one of the prophets.' 'But you,' he asked 'who do you say I am?' Peter spoke up and said to him, 'You are the Christ.' And he gave them strict orders not to tell anyone about him.

And he began to teach them that the Son of Man was destined to suffer grievously, to be rejected by the elders and the chief priests and the scribes, and to be put to death, and after three days to rise again; and he said all this quite openly. Then, taking him aside, Peter started to remonstrate with him. But, turning and seeing his disciples, he rebuked Peter and said to him, 'Get behind me, Satan! Because the way you think is not God's way but man's.'

He called the people and his disciples to him and said, 'If anyone wants to be a follower of mine, let him renounce himself and take up his cross and follow me. For anyone who wants to save his life will lose it; but anyone who loses his life for my sake, and for the sake of the gospel, will save it.'

The Gospel of the Lord.

The Creed is said.

Prayer over the Offerings
Look with favour on our supplications, O Lord,
and in your kindness accept these, your servants' offerings,
that what each has offered to the honour of your name
may serve the salvation of all.
Through Christ our Lord.
Amen.

Communion Antiphon   Cf. Ps 35:8
How precious is your mercy, O God!
The children of men seek shelter in the shadow of your wings.

or   Cf. 1 Cor 10:16

The chalice of blessing that we bless
is a communion in the Blood of Christ;
and the bread that we break
is a sharing in the Body of the Lord.

Prayer after Communion
May the working of this heavenly gift, O Lord, we pray,
take possession of our minds and bodies,
so that its effects, and not our own desires,
may always prevail in us.
Through Christ our Lord.
Amen.

TWENTY-FIFTH SUNDAY IN ORDINARY TIME   B

Christ, the Son of God

We worship the Son of God, the wisdom that came down from above and became the servant of all.

Entrance Antiphon
I am the salvation of the people, says the Lord.
Should they cry to me in any distress,
I will hear them, and I will be their Lord for ever.

Collect
O God, who founded all the commands of your sacred Law
upon love of you and of our neighbour,
grant that, by keeping your precepts,
we may merit to attain eternal life.
Through our Lord Jesus Christ, your Son,

Twenty-Fifth Sunday in Ordinary Time, Year B

who lives and reigns with you in the unity of the Holy Spirit,
one God, for ever and ever.
Amen.

FIRST READING
A reading from the book of Wisdom   2:12. 17-20

The godless say to themselves,
'Let us lie in wait for the virtuous man, since he annoys us
and opposes our way of life,
reproaches us for our breaches of the law
and accuses us of playing false to our upbringing.
Let us see if what he says is true,
let us observe what kind of end he himself will have.
If the virtuous man is God's son, God will take his part
and rescue him from the clutches of his enemies.
Let us test him with cruelty and with torture,
and thus explore this gentleness of his
and put his endurance to the proof.
Let us condemn him to a shameful death
since he will be looked after – we have his word for it.'

The word of the Lord.

Responsorial Psalm   Ps 53:3-6. 8. ℟ v.6
   ℟   **The Lord upholds my life.**

1   O God, save me by your name;
    by your power, uphold my cause.
    O God, hear my prayer;
    listen to the words of my mouth.   ℟

2   For proud men have risen against me,
    ruthless men seek my life.
    They have no regard for God.   ℟

3   But I have God for my help.
    The Lord upholds my life.
    I will sacrifice to you with willing heart
    and praise your name for it is good.   ℟

SECOND READING
A reading from the letter of St James   3:16 – 4:3

Wherever you find jealousy and ambition, you find disharmony, and wicked things of every kind being done; whereas the wisdom that comes down from above is essentially something pure; it also makes for peace, and is kindly and considerate; it is full of compassion and shows itself by doing good; nor is there any trace of partiality or hypocrisy in it. Peacemakers, when they work for peace, sow the seeds which will bear fruit in holiness.

Where do these wars and battles between yourselves first start? Isn't it precisely in the desires fighting inside your own selves? You want something and you haven't got it; so you are prepared to kill. You have an ambition that you cannot satisfy; so you fight to get your way by force. Why you don't have what you want is because you don't pray for it; when you do pray and don't get it, it is because you have not prayed properly, you have prayed for something to indulge your own desires.

The word of the Lord.

Gospel Acclamation   Jn 8:12

Alleluia, alleluia!
I am the light of the world, says the Lord,
anyone who follows me
will have the light of life.
Alleluia!

or   Cf. 2 Thess 2:14

Alleluia, alleluia!
Through the Good News God called us
to share the glory of our Lord Jesus Christ.
Alleluia!

GOSPEL

A reading from the holy Gospel according to Mark   9:30-37

After leaving the mountain Jesus and his disciples made their way through Galilee; and he did not want anyone to know, because he was instructing his disciples; he was telling them, 'The Son of Man will be delivered into the hands of men; they will put him to death; and three days after he has been put to death he will rise again.' But they did not understand what he said and were afraid to ask him.

They came to Capernaum, and when he was in the house he asked them, 'What were you arguing about on the road?' They said nothing because they had been arguing which of them was the greatest. So he sat down, called the Twelve to him and said, 'If anyone wants to be first, he must make himself last of all and servant of all.' He then took a little child, set him in front of them, put his arms round him, and said to them, 'Anyone who welcomes one of these little children in my name, welcomes me; and anyone who welcomes me welcomes not me but the one who sent me.'

The Gospel of the Lord.

The Creed is said.

Prayer over the Offerings
Receive with favour, O Lord, we pray,
the offerings of your people,
that what they profess with devotion and faith
may be theirs through these heavenly mysteries.
Through Christ our Lord.
Amen.

Communion Antiphon Ps 118:4-5
You have laid down your precepts to be carefully kept;
may my ways be firm in keeping your statutes.

or Jn 10:14

I am the Good Shepherd, says the Lord;
I know my sheep, and mine know me.

Prayer after Communion
Graciously raise up, O Lord,
those you renew with this Sacrament,
that we may come to possess your redemption
both in mystery and in the manner of our life.
Through Christ our Lord.
Amen.

TWENTY-SIXTH SUNDAY IN ORDINARY TIME B

God's Spirit in the World

We praise God for all his prophets: men and women of every nation and creed who have resisted evil and manifested the Spirit in their lives.

Entrance Antiphon Dn 3:31. 29. 30. 43. 42
All that you have done to us, O Lord,
you have done with true judgement,
for we have sinned against you
and not obeyed your commandments.
But give glory to your name
and deal with us according to the bounty of your mercy.

Twenty-Sixth Sunday in Ordinary Time, Year B

Collect
O God, who manifest your almighty power
above all by pardoning and showing mercy,
bestow, we pray, your grace abundantly upon us
and make those hastening to attain your promises
heirs to the treasures of heaven.
Through our Lord Jesus Christ, your Son,
who lives and reigns with you in the unity of the Holy Spirit,
one God, for ever and ever.
Amen.

FIRST READING

A reading from the book of Numbers   11:25-29

The Lord came down in the Cloud. He spoke with Moses, but took some of the spirit that was on him and put it on the seventy elders. When the spirit came on them they prophesied, but not again.

Two men had stayed back in the camp; one was called Eldad and the other Medad. The spirit came down on them; though they had not gone to the Tent, their names were enrolled among the rest. These began to prophesy in the camp. The young man ran to tell this to Moses, 'Look,' he said 'Eldad and Medad are prophesying in the camp.' Then said Joshua the son of Nun, who had served Moses from his youth, 'My Lord Moses, stop them!' Moses answered him, 'Are you jealous on my account? If only the whole people of the Lord were prophets, and the Lord gave his Spirit to them all!'

The word of the Lord.

Responsorial Psalm   Ps 18:8. 10. 12-14. ℟ v.9
   ℟   **The precepts of the Lord gladden the heart.**

1   The law of the Lord is perfect,
     it revives the soul.
     The rule of the Lord is to be trusted,
     it gives wisdom to the simple. ℟

2   The fear of the Lord is holy,
     abiding for ever.
     The decrees of the Lord are truth
     and all of them just. ℟

3   So in them your servant finds instruction;
     great reward is in their keeping.
     But who can detect all his errors?
     From hidden faults acquit me. ℟

Twenty-Sixth Sunday in Ordinary Time, Year B

4   From presumption restrain your servant
    and let it not rule me.
    Then shall I be blameless,
    clean from grave sin. ℟

SECOND READING
A reading from the letter of St James   5:1-6

An answer for the rich. Start crying, weep for the miseries that are coming to you. Your wealth is all rotting, your clothes are all eaten up by moths. All your gold and your silver are corroding away, and the same corrosion will be your own sentence, and eat into your body. It was a burning fire that you stored up as your treasure for the last days. Labourers mowed your fields, and you cheated them – listen to the wages that you kept back, calling out; realise that the cries of the reapers have reached the ears of the Lord of hosts. On earth you have had a life of comfort and luxury; in the time of slaughter you went on eating to your heart's content. It was you who condemned the innocent and killed them; they offered you no resistance.

   The word of the Lord.

Gospel Acclamation   Cf. Jn 17:17
   Alleluia, alleluia!
   Your word is truth, O Lord,
   consecrate us in the truth.
   Alleluia!

GOSPEL
A reading from the holy Gospel   9:38-43. 45. 47-48
according to Mark

John said to Jesus, 'Master, we saw a man who is not one of us casting out devils in your name; and because he was not one of us we tried to stop him.' But Jesus said, 'You must not stop him: no one who works a miracle in my name is likely to speak evil of me. Anyone who is not against us is for us.

   'If anyone gives you a cup of water to drink just because you belong to Christ, then I tell you solemnly, he will most certainly not lose his reward.

   'But anyone who is an obstacle to bring down one of these little ones who have faith, would be better thrown into the sea with a great millstone round his neck. And if your hand should cause you to sin, cut it off; it is better for you to enter into life crippled, than to have two hands and go to hell, into the fire that cannot be put out. And if your foot should cause you to sin, cut it off; it is better for you to enter into life lame, than to have two feet and be thrown into hell. And if your eye should cause you to sin, tear it out; it is better for you to enter into the kingdom of God with one eye, than to have two eyes and be thrown into hell where their worm does not die nor their fire go out.'

The Gospel of the Lord.

The Creed is said.

Prayer over the Offerings
Grant us, O merciful God,
that this our offering may find acceptance with you
and that through it the wellspring of all blessing
may be laid open before us.
Through Christ our Lord.
Amen.

Communion Antiphon Cf. Ps 118:49-50
Remember your word to your servant, O Lord,
by which you have given me hope.
This is my comfort when I am brought low.

or 1 Jn 3:16

By this we came to know the love of God:
that Christ laid down his life for us;
so we ought to lay down our lives for one another.

Prayer after Communion
May this heavenly mystery, O Lord,
restore us in mind and body,
that we may be coheirs in glory with Christ,
to whose suffering we are united
whenever we proclaim his Death.
Who lives and reigns for ever and ever.
Amen.

TWENTY-SEVENTH SUNDAY IN ORDINARY TIME B

The Family of God

We celebrate today our belonging together as the family of God. Christ has made us his brothers and sisters, and children of our heavenly Father. The

Twenty-Seventh Sunday in Ordinary Time, Year B

love and respect we show for each other in this celebration will be largely dependent on the love and respect that exists in our own human families.

Entrance Antiphon
Cf. Est 4:17

Within your will, O Lord, all things are established,
and there is none that can resist your will.
For you have made all things, the heaven and the earth,
and all that is held within the circle of heaven;
you are the Lord of all.

Collect
Almighty ever-living God,
who in the abundance of your kindness
surpass the merits and the desires of those who entreat you,
pour out your mercy upon us
to pardon what conscience dreads
and to give what prayer does not dare to ask.
Through our Lord Jesus Christ, your Son,
who lives and reigns with you in the unity of the Holy Spirit,
one God, for ever and ever.
Amen.

FIRST READING

A reading from the book of Genesis 2:18-24

The Lord God said, 'It is not good that the man should be alone. I will make him a helpmate.' So from the soil the Lord God fashioned all the wild beasts and all the birds of heaven. These he brought to the man to see what he would call them; each one was to bear the name the man would give it. The man gave names to all the cattle, all the birds of heaven and all the wild beasts. But no helpmate suitable for man was found for him. So the Lord God made the man fall into a deep sleep. And while he slept, he took one of his ribs and enclosed it in flesh. The Lord God built the rib he had taken from the man into a woman, and brought her to the man. The man exclaimed:

> 'This at last is bone from my bones
> and flesh from my flesh!
> This is to be called woman,
> for this was taken from man.'

This is why a man leaves his father and mother and joins himself to his wife, and they become one body.

The word of the Lord.

Responsorial Psalm Ps 127. ℟ v.5
℟ **May the Lord bless us
all the days of our life.**

1   O blessed are those who fear the Lord
    and walk in his ways!
    by the labour of your hands you shall eat.
    You will be happy and prosper. ℟

2   Your wife will be like a fruitful vine
    in the heart of your house;
    your children like shoots of the olive,
    around your table. ℟

3   Indeed thus shall be blessed
    the man who fears the Lord.
    May the Lord bless you from Zion
    in a happy Jerusalem
    all the days of your life!
    May you see your children's children.
    On Israel, peace! ℟

SECOND READING
A reading from the letter to the Hebrews   2:9-11

We see in Jesus one who was for a short while made lower than the angels and is now crowned with glory and splendour because he submitted to death; by God's grace he had to experience death for all mankind.

As it was his purpose to bring a great many of his sons into glory, it was appropriate that God, for whom everything exists and through whom everything exists, should make perfect, through suffering, the leader who would take them to their salvation. For the one who sanctifies, and the ones who are sanctified, are of the same stock; that is why he openly calls them brothers.

The word of the Lord.

Gospel Acclamation   Cf. Jn 17:17
    Alleluia, alleluia!
    Your word is truth, O Lord,
    consecrate us in the truth.
    Alleluia!

or 1 Jn 4:12

Alleluia, alleluia!
As long as we love one another
God will live in us
and his love will be complete in us.
Alleluia!

GOSPEL

A reading from the holy Gospel according to Mark 10:2-16

Some Pharisees approached Jesus and asked, 'Is it against the law for a man to divorce his wife?' They were testing him. He answered them, 'What did Moses command you?' 'Moses allowed us' they said 'to draw up a writ of dismissal and so to divorce.' Then Jesus said to them, 'It was because you were so unteachable that he wrote this commandment for you. But from the beginning of creation God made them male and female. This is why a man must leave father and mother, and the two become one body. They are no longer two, therefore, but one body. So then, what God has united, man must not divide.' Back in the house the disciples questioned him again about this, and he said to them, 'The man who divorces his wife and marries another is guilty of adultery against her. And if a woman divorces her husband and marries another she is guilty of adultery too.'

People were bringing little children to him, for him to touch them. The disciples turned them away, but when Jesus saw this he was indignant and said to them, 'Let the little children come to me; do not stop them; for it is to such as these that the kingdom of God belongs. I tell you solemnly, anyone who does not welcome the kingdom of God like a little child will never enter it.' Then he put his arms round them, laid his hands on them and gave them his blessing.

The Gospel of the Lord.

Shorter Form, verses 2-12. Read between

The Creed is said.

Prayer over the Offerings
Accept, O Lord, we pray,
the sacrifices instituted by your commands
and, through the sacred mysteries,
which we celebrate with dutiful service,
graciously complete the sanctifying work
by which you are pleased to redeem us.

Through Christ our Lord.
Amen.

Communion Antiphon Lam 3:25
The Lord is good to those who hope in him,
to the soul that seeks him.

or Cf. 1 Cor 10:17

Though many, we are one bread, one body,
for we all partake of the one Bread and one Chalice.

Prayer after Communion
Grant us, almighty God,
that we may be refreshed and nourished
by the Sacrament which we have received,
so as to be transformed into what we consume.
Through Christ our Lord.
Amen.

TWENTY-EIGHTH SUNDAY IN ORDINARY TIME   B

Christ, Our Wealth

Even though we had nothing in this world that we could call our own, in having Christ, the wisdom of God, we possess all things; we are rich in him. He is the word of God that is alive and active in our hearts.

Entrance Antiphon Ps 129:3-4
If you, O Lord, should mark iniquities,
Lord, who could stand?
But with you is found forgiveness,
O God of Israel.

Collect
May your grace, O Lord, we pray,
at all times go before us and follow after
and make us always determined
to carry out good works.
Through our Lord Jesus Christ, your Son,
who lives and reigns with you in the unity of the Holy Spirit,
one God, for ever and ever.
Amen.

Twenty-Eighth Sunday in Ordinary Time, Year B 795

FIRST READING

A reading from the book of Wisdom 7:7-11

I prayed, and understanding was given me;
I entreated, and the spirit of Wisdom came to me.
I esteemed her more than sceptres and thrones;
compared with her, I held riches as nothing.
I reckoned no priceless stone to be her peer,
for compared with her, all gold is a pinch of sand,
and beside her silver ranks as mud.
I loved her more than health or beauty,
preferred her to the light,
since her radiance never sleeps.
In her company all good things came to me,
at her hands riches not to be numbered.

The word of the Lord.

Responsorial Psalm Ps 89:12-17. ℟ v.14

℟ **Fill us with your love that we may rejoice.**

1. Make us know the shortness of our life
   that we may gain wisdom of heart.
   Lord, relent! Is your anger for ever?
   Show pity to your servants. ℟

2. In the morning, fill us with your love;
   we shall exult and rejoice all our days.
   Give us joy to balance our affliction
   for the years when we knew misfortune. ℟

3. Show forth your work to your servants;
   let your glory shine on their children.
   Let the favour of the Lord be upon us:
   give success to the work of our hands. ℟

SECOND READING

A reading from the letter to the Hebrews 4:12-13

The word of God is something alive and active: it cuts like any double-edged sword but more finely: it can slip through the place where the soul is divided from the spirit, or joints from the marrow; it can judge the secret emotions and thoughts. No created thing can hide from him; everything is uncovered and open to the eyes of the one to whom we must give account of ourselves.

The word of the Lord.

Gospel Acclamation   Cf. Mt 11:25
Alleluia, alleluia!
Blessed are you, Father,
Lord of heaven and earth,
for revealing the mysteries of the kingdom
to mere children.
Alleluia!

or   Mt 5:3

Alleluia, alleluia!
How happy are the poor in spirit;
theirs is the kingdom of heaven.
Alleluia!

GOSPEL

A reading from the holy Gospel according to Mark   10:17-30

*Jesus was setting out on a journey when a man ran up, knelt before him and put this question to him, 'Good master, what must I do to inherit eternal life?' Jesus said to him, 'Why do you call me good? No one is good but God alone. You know the commandments: You must not kill; You must not commit adultery; You must not steal; You must not bring false witness; You must not defraud; Honour your father and mother.' And he said to him, 'Master, I have kept all these from my earliest days.' Jesus looked steadily at him and loved him, and he said, 'There is one thing you lack. Go and sell everything you own and give the money to the poor, and you will have treasure in heaven; then come, follow me.' But his face fell at these words and he went away sad, for he was a man of great wealth.

Jesus looked round and said to his disciples, 'How hard it is for those who have riches to enter the kingdom of God!' The disciples were astounded by these words, but Jesus insisted, 'My children,' he said to them, 'how hard it is to enter the kingdom of God! It is easier for a camel to pass through the eye of a needle than for a rich man to enter the kingdom of God.' They were more astonished than ever. 'In that case' they said to one another 'who can be saved?' Jesus gazed at them. 'For men' he said 'it is impossible, but not for God: because everything is possible for God.'*

Peter took this up. 'What about us?' he asked him. 'We have left everything and followed you.' Jesus said, 'I tell you solemnly, there is no one who has left house, brothers, sisters, father, children or land for my sake and for the sake of the gospel who will not be repaid a hundred times over, houses, brothers, sisters, mothers, children and land – not without persecutions – now in this present time and, in the world to come, eternal life.'

The Gospel of the Lord.

Shorter Form, verses 17-27. Read between

The Creed is said.

Prayer over the Offerings
Accept, O Lord, the prayers of your faithful
with the sacrificial offerings,
that, through these acts of devotedness,
we may pass over to the glory of heaven.
Through Christ our Lord.
Amen.

Communion Antiphon　　　　　　　　　　　　　　　　　Cf. Ps 33:11
The rich suffer want and go hungry,
but those who seek the Lord lack no blessing.

or　　　　　　　　　　　　　　　　　　　　　　　　　　　　1 Jn 3:2

When the Lord appears, we shall be like him,
for we shall see him as he is.

Prayer after Communion
We entreat your majesty most humbly, O Lord,
that, as you feed us with the nourishment
which comes from the most holy Body and Blood of your Son,
so you may make us sharers of his divine nature.
Who lives and reigns for ever and ever.
Amen.

TWENTY-NINTH SUNDAY IN ORDINARY TIME　　B

Christ the Suffering Servant of God

Today we celebrate the Christ who gives meaning to all human suffering. By taking on himself the role of a servant and redeeming us by his sufferings, he has turned all our human values upside down. It is the weak who have become strong.

Twenty-Ninth Sunday in Ordinary Time, Year B

Entrance Antiphon   Cf. Ps 16:6. 8
To you I call; for you will surely heed me, O God;
turn your ear to me; hear my words.
Guard me as the apple of your eye;
in the shadow of your wings protect me.

Collect
Almighty ever-living God,
grant that we may always conform our will to yours
and serve your majesty in sincerity of heart.
Through our Lord Jesus Christ, your Son,
who lives and reigns with you in the unity of the Holy Spirit,
one God, for ever and ever.
Amen.

FIRST READING

A reading from the prophet Isaiah   53:10-11

The Lord has been pleased to crush his servant with suffering.
If he offers his life in atonement,
he shall see his heirs, he shall have a long life
and through him what the Lord wishes will be done.
His soul's anguish over
he shall see the light and be content.
By his sufferings shall my servant justify many,
taking their faults on himself.

    The word of the Lord.

Responsorial Psalm   Ps 32:4-5. 18-20. 22. ℟ v.22
   ℟ **May your love be upon us, O Lord,**
      as we place all our hope in you.

1   The word of the Lord is faithful
      and all his works to be trusted.
      The Lord loves justice and right
      and fills the earth with his love.   ℟

2   The Lord looks on those who revere him,
      on those who hope in his love,
      to rescue their souls from death,
      to keep them alive in famine.   ℟

3   Our soul is waiting for the Lord.
      The Lord is our help and our shield.

Twenty-Ninth Sunday in Ordinary Time, Year B

May your love be upon us, O Lord,
as we place all our hope in you. ℟

SECOND READING
A reading from the letter to the Hebrews   4:14-16

Since in Jesus, the Son of God, we have the supreme high priest who has gone through to the highest heaven, we must never let go of the faith that we have professed. For it is not as if we had a high priest who was incapable of feeling our weaknesses with us; but we have one who has been tempted in every way that we are, though he is without sin. Let us be confident, then, in approaching the throne of grace, that we shall have mercy from him and find grace when we are in need of help.

The word of the Lord.

Gospel Acclamation   Jn 14:6
Alleluia, alleluia!
I am the Way, the Truth and the Life, says the Lord;
no one can come to the Father except through me.
Alleluia!

or   Mk 10:45

Alleluia, alleluia!
The Son of Man came to serve,
and to give his life as a ransom for many.
Alleluia!

GOSPEL
A reading from the holy Gospel according to Mark   10:35-45

James and John, the sons of Zebedee, approached Jesus. 'Master,' they said to him 'we want you to do us a favour.' He said to them, 'What is it you want me to do for you?' They said to him, 'Allow us to sit one at your right hand and the other at your left in your glory.' 'You do not know what you are asking' Jesus said to them. 'Can you drink the cup that I must drink, or be baptised with the baptism with which I must be baptised?' They replied, 'We can.' Jesus said to them, 'The cup that I must drink you shall drink, and with the baptism with which I must be baptised you shall be baptised, but as for seats at my right hand or my left, these are not mine to grant; they belong to those to whom they have been allotted.'

When the other ten heard this they began to feel indignant with James and John, so *Jesus called them to him and said to them, 'You know that among the pagans their so-called rulers lord it over them, and their great men make their authority felt. This is not to happen among you. No; anyone who wants to become great among you must be your servant, and anyone who wants to be first among you must be slave to all. For the Son of Man himself did not come to be served but to serve, and to give his life as a ransom for many.'

The Gospel of the Lord.*

Shorter Form, verses 42-45. Read between

The Creed is said.

Prayer over the Offerings
Grant us, Lord, we pray,
a sincere respect for your gifts,
that, through the purifying action of your grace,
we may be cleansed by the very mysteries we serve.
Through Christ our Lord.
Amen.

Communion Antiphon   Cf. Ps 32:18-19
Behold, the eyes of the Lord
are on those who fear him,
who hope in his merciful love,
to rescue their souls from death,
to keep them alive in famine.

or   Mk 10:45

The Son of Man has come
to give his life as a ransom for many.

Prayer after Communion
Grant, O Lord, we pray,
that, benefiting from participation in heavenly things,
we may be helped by what you give in this present age
and prepared for the gifts that are eternal.
Through Christ our Lord.
Amen.

THIRTIETH SUNDAY IN ORDINARY TIME   B

The Lord Who Works Marvels

We worship Christ who opens our eyes to see the marvels that he has done for us as our high priest and mediator with the Father.

Entrance Antiphon   Cf. Ps 104:3-4
Let the hearts that seek the Lord rejoice;
turn to the Lord and his strength;
constantly seek his face.

Collect
Almighty ever-living God,
increase our faith, hope and charity,
and make us love what you command,
so that we may merit what you promise.
Through our Lord Jesus Christ, your Son,
who lives and reigns with you in the unity of the Holy Spirit,
one God, for ever and ever.
Amen.

FIRST READING
A reading from the prophet Jeremiah   31:7-9

The Lord says this:

> Shout with joy for Jacob!
> Hail the chief of nations!
> Proclaim! Praise! Shout!
> 'The Lord has saved his people,
> the remnant of Israel!'
> See, I will bring them back
> from the land of the North
> and gather them from the far ends of earth;
> all of them: the blind and the lame,
> women with child, women in labour:
> a great company returning here.
> They had left in tears,
> I will comfort them as I lead them back;
> I will guide them to streams of water,
> by a smooth path where they will not stumble.
> For I am a father to Israel,
> and Ephraim is my first-born son.

The word of the Lord.

Responsorial Psalm Ps 125. ℟ v.3

℟ **What marvels the Lord worked for us!
Indeed we were glad.**

1 When the Lord delivered Zion from bondage,
it seemed like a dream.
Then was our mouth filled with laughter,
on our lips there were songs. ℟

2 The heathens themselves said: 'What marvels
the Lord worked for them!'
What marvels the Lord worked for us!
Indeed we were glad. ℟

3 Deliver us, O Lord, from our bondage
as streams in dry land.
Those who are sowing in tears
will sing when they reap. ℟

4 They go out, they go out, full of tears,
carrying seed for the sowing:
they come back, they come back, full of song,
carrying their sheaves. ℟

SECOND READING

A reading from the letter to the Hebrews 5:1-6

Every high priest has been taken out of mankind and is appointed to act for men in their relations with God, to offer gifts and sacrifices for sins; and so he can sympathise with those who are ignorant or uncertain because he too lives in the limitations of weakness. That is why he has to make sin offerings for himself as well as for the people. No one takes this honour on himself, but each one is called by God, as Aaron was. Nor did Christ give himself the glory of becoming high priest, but he had it from the one who said to him: You are my son, today I have become your father, and in another text: You are a priest of the order of Melchizedek, and for ever.

The word of the Lord.

Gospel Acclamation Jn 8:12
Alleluia, alleluia!
I am the light of the world, says the Lord,
anyone who follows me

will have the light of life.
Alleluia!

or Cf. 2 Tim 1:10

Alleluia, alleluia!
Our Saviour Christ Jesus abolished death,
and he has proclaimed life through the Good News.
Alleluia!

GOSPEL
A reading from the holy Gospel according to Mark 10:46-52

As Jesus left Jericho with his disciples and a large crowd, Bartimaeus (that is, the son of Timaeus), a blind beggar, was sitting at the side of the road. When he heard that it was Jesus of Nazareth, he began to shout and to say, 'Son of David, Jesus, have pity on me.' And many of them scolded him and told him to keep quiet, but he only shouted all the louder, 'Son of David, have pity on me.' Jesus stopped and said, 'Call him here.' So they called the blind man. 'Courage,' they said 'get up; he is calling you.' So throwing off his cloak, he jumped up and went to Jesus. Then Jesus spoke, 'What do you want me to do for you?' 'Rabbuni,' the blind man said to him 'Master, let me see again.' Jesus said to him, 'Go; your faith has saved you.' And immediately his sight returned and he followed him along the road.

The Gospel of the Lord.

The Creed is said.

Prayer over the Offerings
Look, we pray, O Lord,
on the offerings we make to your majesty,
that whatever is done by us in your service
may be directed above all to your glory.
Through Christ our Lord.
Amen.

Communion Antiphon Cf. Ps 19:6
We will ring out our joy at your saving help
and exult in the name of our God.

or Eph 5:2

Christ loved us and gave himself up for us,
as a fragrant offering to God.

Prayer after Communion
May your Sacraments, O Lord, we pray,
perfect in us what lies within them,
that what we now celebrate in signs
we may one day possess in truth.
Through Christ our Lord.
Amen.

THIRTY-FIRST SUNDAY IN ORDINARY TIME B

Christ the Priest of the New Covenant

Through, with, and in Christ we offer the sacrifice of the new covenant which gives perfect glory to the Father and enables us to give him a fitting return of love.

Entrance Antiphon   Cf. Ps 37:22-23
Forsake me not, O Lord, my God;
be not far from me!
Make haste and come to my help,
O Lord, my strong salvation!

Collect
Almighty and merciful God,
by whose gift your faithful offer you
right and praiseworthy service,
grant, we pray,
that we may hasten without stumbling
to receive the things you have promised.
Through our Lord Jesus Christ, your Son,
who lives and reigns with you in the unity of the Holy Spirit,
one God, for ever and ever.
Amen.

FIRST READING
A reading from the book of Deuteronomy   6:2-6

Moses said to the people: 'If you fear the Lord your God all the days of your life and if you keep all his laws and commandments which I lay on you, you will have a long life, you and your son and your grandson. Listen then, Israel, keep and observe what will make you prosper and give you great increase, as the Lord God of your fathers has promised you, giving you a land where milk and honey flow.

'Listen, Israel: The Lord our God is the one Lord. You shall love the Lord your God with all your heart, with all your soul, with all your strength. Let these words I urge on you today be written on your heart.'

The word of the Lord.

Responsorial Psalm Ps 17:2-4. 47. 51. ℟ v.2

℟ **I love you, Lord, my strength.**

1 I love you, Lord, my strength,
   my rock, my fortress, my saviour.
   My God is the rock where I take refuge;
   my shield, my mighty help, my stronghold.
   The Lord is worthy of all praise:
   when I call I am saved from my foes. ℟

2 Long life to the Lord, my rock!
   Praised be the God who saves me.
   He has given great victories to his king
   and shown his love for his anointed. ℟

SECOND READING

A reading from the letter to the Hebrews 7:23-28

There used to be a great number of priests under the former covenant, because death put an end to each one of them; but this one, Christ, because he remains for ever, can never lose his priesthood. It follows then, that his power to save is utterly certain, since he is living for ever to intercede for all who come to God through him.

To suit us, the ideal high priest would have to be holy, innocent and uncontaminated, beyond the influence of sinners, and raised up above the heavens; one who would not need to offer sacrifices every day, as the other high priests do for their own sins and then for those of the people, because he has done this once and for all by offering himself. The Law appoints high priests who are men subject to weakness; but the promise on oath, which came after the Law, appointed the Son who is made perfect for ever.

The word of the Lord.

Gospel Acclamation Cf. Jn 6:63. 68

Alleluia, alleluia!
Your words are spirit, Lord,
and they are life:

you have the message of eternal life.
Alleluia!

or   Jn 14:23

Alleluia, alleluia!
If anyone loves me he will keep my word,
and my Father will love him,
and we shall come to him.
Alleluia!

GOSPEL
A reading from the holy Gospel according to Mark   12:28-34

One of the scribes came up to Jesus and put a question to him, 'Which is the first of all the commandments?' Jesus replied, 'This is the first: Listen, Israel, the Lord our God is the one Lord, and you must love the Lord your God with all your heart, with all your soul, with all your mind and with all your strength. The second is this: You must love your neighbour as yourself. There is no commandment greater than these.' The scribe said to him, 'Well spoken, Master; what you have said is true: that he is one and there is no other. To love with all your heart, with all your understanding and strength and to love your neighbour as yourself, this is far more important than any holocaust or sacrifice.' Jesus, seeing how wisely he had spoken said, 'You are not far from the kingdom of God.' And after that no one dared to question him any more.

The Gospel of the Lord.

The Creed is said.

Prayer over the Offerings
May these sacrificial offerings, O Lord,
become for you a pure oblation,
and for us a holy outpouring of your mercy.
Through Christ our Lord.
Amen.

Communion Antiphon   Cf. Ps 15:11
You will show me the path of life,
the fullness of joy in your presence, O Lord.

or   Jn 6:58

Just as the living Father sent me
and I have life because of the Father,

so whoever feeds on me
shall have life because of me, says the Lord.

Prayer after Communion
May the working of your power, O Lord,
increase in us, we pray,
so that, renewed by these heavenly Sacraments,
we may be prepared by your gift
for receiving what they promise.
Through Christ our Lord.
Amen.

THIRTY-SECOND SUNDAY IN ORDINARY TIME B

God in Whom We Trust

We must not be afraid to give, for Christ gave himself completely and will reward with salvation all those who are waiting for him.

Entrance Antiphon Cf. Ps 87:3
Let my prayer come into your presence.
Incline your ear to my cry for help, O Lord.

Collect
Almighty and merciful God,
graciously keep from us all adversity,
so that, unhindered in mind and body alike,
we may pursue in freedom of heart
the things that are yours.
Through our Lord Jesus Christ, your Son,
who lives and reigns with you in the unity of the Holy Spirit,
one God, for ever and ever.
Amen.

FIRST READING
A reading from the first book of the Kings 17:10-16

Elijah the Prophet went off to Sidon. And when he reached the city gate, there was a widow gathering sticks; addressing her he said, 'Please bring a little water in a vessel for me to drink.' She was setting off to bring it when he called after her. 'Please' he said 'bring me a scrap of bread in your hand.' 'As the Lord your God lives,' she replied 'I have no baked bread, but only a handful of meal in a jar and a little oil in a jug; I am just gathering a stick or two to go and prepare this for myself and my son to eat, and then we shall die.' But Elijah said to her, 'Do not be afraid, go and do as you have said; but first make a little scone of it for me and bring it to me, and then make some for yourself and for your son. For thus the Lord speaks, the God of Israel:

"Jar of meal shall not be spent,
jug of oil shall not be emptied,
before the day when the Lord sends
rain on the face of the earth."'

The woman went and did as Elijah told her and they ate the food, she, himself and her son. The jar of meal was not spent nor the jug of oil emptied, just as the Lord had foretold through Elijah.

The word of the Lord.

Responsorial Psalm   Ps 145:7-10. R℣ v.2
    R℣ **My soul, give praise to the Lord.**

or
    R℣ **Alleluia!**

1   It is the Lord who keeps faith for ever,
    who is just to those who are oppressed.
    It is he who gives bread to the hungry,
    the Lord, who sets prisoners free.   R℣

2   It is the Lord who gives sight to the blind,
    who raises up those who are bowed down.
    It is the Lord who loves the just,
    the Lord, who protects the stranger.   R℣

3   The Lord upholds the widow and orphan
    but thwarts the path of the wicked.
    The Lord will reign for ever,
    Zion's God, from age to age.   R℣

SECOND READING
A reading from the letter to the Hebrews   9:24-28

It is not as though Christ had entered a man-made sanctuary which was only modelled on the real one; but it was heaven itself, so that he could appear in the actual presence of God on our behalf. And he does not have to offer himself again and again, like the high priest going into the sanctuary year after year with the blood that is not his own, or else he would have had to suffer over and over again since the world began. Instead of that, he has made his appearance once and for all, now at the end of the last age, to do away with sin by sacrificing himself. Since men only die once, and after that comes judgement, so Christ, too, offers himself only once to take the faults of many on himself, and when he appears a second time, it will not be to deal with sin but to reward with salvation those who are waiting for him.

The word of the Lord.

Gospel Acclamation Apoc 2:10
Alleluia, alleluia!
Even if you have to die, says the Lord,
keep faithful, and I will give you
the crown of life.
Alleluia!

or Mt 5:3

Alleluia, alleluia!
How happy are the poor in spirit;
theirs is the kingdom of heaven.
Alleluia!

GOSPEL
A reading from the holy Gospel according to Mark 12:38-44

In his teaching Jesus said, 'Beware of the scribes who like to walk about in long robes, to be greeted obsequiously in the market squares, to take the front seats in the synagogues and the places of honour at banquets; these are the men who swallow the property of widows, while making a show of lengthy prayers. The more severe will be the sentence they receive.'

*He sat down opposite the treasury and watched the people putting money into the treasury, and many of the rich put in a great deal. A poor widow came and put in two small coins, the equivalent of a penny. Then he called his disciples and said to them, 'I tell you solemnly, this poor widow has put more in than all who have contributed to the treasury; for they have all put in money they had over, but she from the little she had has put in everything she possessed, all she had to live on.'

The Gospel of the Lord.*

Shorter Form, verses 41-44. Read between
The Creed is said.

Prayer over the Offerings
Look with favour, we pray, O Lord,
upon the sacrificial gifts offered here,
that, celebrating in mystery the Passion of your Son,
we may honour it with loving devotion.
Through Christ our Lord.
Amen.

Communion Antiphon Cf. Ps 22:1-2
The Lord is my shepherd; there is nothing I shall want.
Fresh and green are the pastures where he gives me repose,
near restful waters he leads me.

or Cf. Lk 24:35

The disciples recognized the Lord Jesus in the breaking of bread.

Prayer after Communion
Nourished by this sacred gift, O Lord,
we give you thanks and beseech your mercy,
that, by the pouring forth of your Spirit,
the grace of integrity may endure
in those your heavenly power has entered.
Through Christ our Lord.
Amen.

THIRTY-THIRD SUNDAY IN ORDINARY TIME B

The Eternal Perfection of All Whom Christ Is Sanctifying

We celebrate today the final consummation at the end of time. Each Mass continues Christ's redemptive work in the world and brings us nearer to the final Eucharist when that work of sanctification will be complete.

Entrance Antiphon Jer 29:11-12. 14
The Lord said: I think thoughts of peace and not of affliction.
You will call upon me, and I will answer you,
and I will lead back your captives from every place.

Collect
Grant us, we pray, O Lord our God,
the constant gladness of being devoted to you,
for it is full and lasting happiness
to serve with constancy
the author of all that is good.
Through our Lord Jesus Christ, your Son,

Thirty-Third Sunday in Ordinary Time, Year B

who lives and reigns with you in the unity of the Holy Spirit, one God, for ever and ever.
Amen.

FIRST READING
A reading from the prophet Daniel   12:1-13

'At that time Michael will stand up, the great prince who mounts guard over your people. There is going to be a time of great distress, unparalleled since nations first came into existence. When that time comes, your own people will be spared, all those whose names are found written in the Book. Of those who lie sleeping in the dust of the earth many will awake, some to everlasting life, some to shame and everlasting disgrace. The learned will shine as brightly as the vault of heaven, and those who have instructed many in virtue, as bright as stars for all eternity.'

The word of the Lord.

Responsorial Psalm   Ps 15:5. 8-11. ℟ v.1

℟ **Preserve me, God, I take refuge in you.**

1   O Lord, it is you who are my portion and cup;
    it is you yourself who are my prize.
    I keep the Lord ever in my sight:
    since he is at my right hand, I shall stand firm.   ℟

2   And so my heart rejoices, my soul is glad;
    even my body shall rest in safety.
    For you will not leave my soul among the dead,
    nor let your beloved know decay.   ℟

3   You will show me the path of life,
    the fullness of joy in your presence,
    at your right hand happiness for ever.   ℟

SECOND READING
A reading from the letter to the Hebrews   10:11-14. 18

All the priests stand at their duties every day, offering over and over again the same sacrifices which are quite incapable of taking sins away. Christ, on the other hand, has offered one single sacrifice for sins, and then taken his place for ever, at the right hand of God, where he is now waiting until his enemies are made into a footstool for him. By virtue of that one single offering, he has achieved the eternal perfection of all whom he is sanctifying. When all sins have been forgiven, there can be no more sin offerings.

The word of the Lord.

Gospel Acclamation   Mt 24:42. 44
Alleluia, alleluia!
Stay awake and stand ready,
because you do not know the hour
when the Son of Man is coming.
Alleluia!

or   Lk 21:36

Alleluia, alleluia!
Stay awake, praying at all times
for the strength to stand with confidence
before the Son of Man.
Alleluia!

GOSPEL
A reading from the holy Gospel according to Mark   13:24-32

Jesus said to his disciples: 'In those days, after the time of distress, the sun will be darkened, the moon will lose its brightness, the stars will come falling from heaven and the powers in the heavens will be shaken. And then they will see the Son of Man coming in the clouds with great power and glory; then too he will send the angels to gather his chosen from the four winds, from the ends of the world to the ends of heaven.

'Take the fig tree as a parable: as soon as its twigs grow supple and its leaves come out, you know that summer is near. So with you, when you see these things happening: know that he is near, at the very gates. I tell you solemnly, before this generation has passed away all these things will have taken place. Heaven and earth will pass away, but my words will not pass away.

'But as for that day or hour, nobody knows it, neither the angels of heaven, nor the Son; no one but the Father.'

The Gospel of the Lord.

The Creed is said.

Prayer over the Offerings
Grant, O Lord, we pray,
that what we offer in the sight of your majesty

may obtain for us the grace of being devoted to you
and gain us the prize of everlasting happiness.
Through Christ our Lord.
Amen.

Communion Antiphon Ps 72:28
To be near God is my happiness,
to place my hope in God the Lord.

or Mk 11:23-24

Amen, I say to you: Whatever you ask in prayer,
believe that you will receive,
and it shall be given to you, says the Lord.

Prayer after Communion
We have partaken of the gifts of this sacred mystery,
humbly imploring, O Lord,
that what your Son commanded us to do
in memory of him
may bring us growth in charity.
Through Christ our Lord.
Amen.

Last Sunday in Ordinary Time

OUR LORD JESUS CHRIST, B
KING OF THE UNIVERSE
Solemnity

Christ the King

Today we celebrate Christ the universal King. He did not claim to be only the king of the Jews. His kingdom was not to be an exclusive one. He is king of all who are on the side of truth and listen to his voice.

Entrance Antiphon Rv 5:12; 1:6
How worthy is the Lamb who was slain,
to receive power and divinity,
and wisdom and strength and honour.
To him belong glory and power for ever and ever.

The Gloria in excelsis (Glory to God in the highest) is said.

Our Lord Jesus Christ, King of the Universe, Year B

Collect
Almighty ever-living God,
whose will is to restore all things
in your beloved Son, the King of the universe,
grant, we pray,
that the whole creation, set free from slavery,
may render your majesty service
and ceaselessly proclaim your praise.
Through our Lord Jesus Christ, your Son,
who lives and reigns with you in the unity of the Holy Spirit,
one God, for ever and ever.
Amen.

FIRST READING
A reading from the prophet Daniel   7:13-14

I gazed into the visions of the night.
And I saw, coming on the clouds of heaven,
one like a son of man.
He came to the one of great age
and was led into his presence.
On him was conferred sovereignty,
glory and kingship,
and men of all peoples, nations and languages became his
   servants.
His sovereignty is an eternal sovereignty
which shall never pass away,
nor will his empire be destroyed.

This is the word of the the Lord.

Responsorial Psalm   Ps 92:1-2. 5. R℣ v.1
   R℣   **The Lord is king, with majesty enrobed.**

1   The Lord is king, with majesty enrobed;
    the Lord has robed himself with might,
    he has girded himself with power.   R℣

2   The world you made firm, not to be moved;
    your throne has stood firm from of old.
    From all eternity, O Lord, you are.   R℣

3   Truly your decrees are to be trusted.
    Holiness is fitting to your house,
    O Lord, until the end of time.   R℣

SECOND READING
A reading from the book of the Apocalypse   1:5-8

Jesus Christ is the faithful witness, the First-born from the dead, the Ruler of the kings of the earth. He loves us and has washed away our sins with his blood, and made us a line of kings, priests to serve his God and Father; to him, then, be glory and power for ever and ever. Amen. It is he who is coming on the clouds; everyone will see him, even those who pierced him, and all the races of the earth will mourn over him. This is the truth. Amen. 'I am the Alpha and the Omega' says the Lord God, who is, who was, and who is to come, the Almighty.

The word of the Lord.

Gospel Acclamation   Mk 11:9-10
Alleluia, alleluia!
Blessings on him who comes in the name of the Lord!
Blessings on the coming kingdom of our father David!
Alleluia!

GOSPEL
A reading from the holy Gospel according to John   18:33-37

'Are you the king of the Jews?' Pilate asked. Jesus replied, 'Do you ask this of your own accord, or have others spoken to you about me?' Pilate answered, 'Am I a Jew? It is your own people and the chief priests who have handed you over to me: what have you done?' Jesus replied, 'Mine is not a kingdom of this world; if my kingdom were of this world, my men would have fought to prevent my being surrendered to the Jews. But my kingdom is not of this kind.' 'So you are a king then?' said Pilate. 'It is you who say it' answered Jesus. 'Yes, I am a king. I was born for this, I came into the world for this: to bear witness to the truth; and all who are on the side of truth listen to my voice.'

The Gospel of the Lord.

The Creed is said.

Prayer over the Offerings
As we offer you, O Lord, the sacrifice
by which the human race is reconciled to you,
we humbly pray,
that your Son himself may bestow on all nations

the gifts of unity and peace.
Through Christ our Lord.
Amen.

Preface of Christ, King of the Universe, pp.40-41.

Communion Antiphon Ps 28:10-11
The Lord sits as King for ever.
The Lord will bless his people with peace.

Prayer after Communion
Having received the food of immortality,
we ask, O Lord,
that, glorying in obedience
to the commands of Christ, the King of the universe,
we may live with him eternally in his heavenly Kingdom.
Who lives and reigns for ever and ever.
Amen.

SUNDAY MASSES

Year C

THE SEASON OF ADVENT

FIRST SUNDAY OF ADVENT C

Our Hope and Trust in Christ Is Our Liberation from Fear

Fear is one of the most crippling of all the emotions and there are many things in life and in the world to make us afraid. But today we lift up our souls to Christ who comes to deliver us from fear; in him we trust and hope. We can stand erect, hold our heads high, and dwell in confidence.

Entrance Antiphon Cf. Ps 24:1-3
To you, I lift up my soul, O my God.
In you, I have trusted; let me not be put to shame.
Nor let my enemies exult over me;
and let none who hope in you be put to shame.

The Gloria in excelsis (Glory to God in the highest) is not said.

Collect
Grant your faithful, we pray, almighty God,
the resolve to run forth to meet your Christ
with righteous deeds at his coming,
so that, gathered at his right hand,
they may be worthy to possess the heavenly Kingdom.
Through our Lord Jesus Christ, your Son,
who lives and reigns with you in the unity of the Holy Spirit,
one God, for ever and ever.
Amen.

FIRST READING
A reading from the prophet Jeremiah 33:14-16

See, the days are coming – it is the Lord who speaks – when I am going to fulfil the promise I made to the House of Israel and the House of Judah:

'In those days and at that time,
I will make a virtuous Branch grow for David,
who shall practise honesty and integrity in the land.
In those days Judah shall be saved
and Israel shall dwell in confidence.
And this is the name the city will be called:
The Lord-our-integrity.'

The word of the Lord.

Responsorial Psalm   Ps 24:4-5. 8-9. 10. 14. ℟ v.1

℟   **To you, O Lord, I lift up my soul.**

1   Lord, make me know your ways.
    Lord, teach me your paths.
    Make me walk in your truth, and teach me:
    for you are God my saviour.   ℟

2   The Lord is good and upright.
    He shows the path to those who stray,
    he guides the humble in the right path;
    he teaches his way to the poor.   ℟

3   His ways are faithfulness and love
    for those who keep his covenant and will.
    The Lord's friendship is for those who revere him;
    to them he reveals his covenant.   ℟

SECOND READING

A reading from the first letter of St Paul   3:12 – 4:2
to the Thessalonians

May the Lord be generous in increasing your love and make you love one another and the whole human race as much as we love you. And may he so confirm your hearts in holiness that you may be blameless in the sight of our God and Father when our Lord Jesus Christ comes with all his saints.

Finally, brothers, we urge you and appeal to you in the Lord Jesus to make more and more progress in the kind of life that you are meant to live: the life that God wants, as you learnt from us, and as you are already living it. You have not forgotten the instructions we gave you on the authority of the Lord Jesus.

The word of the Lord.

Gospel Acclamation Ps 84:8
Alleluia, alleluia!
Let us see, O Lord, your mercy
and give us your saving help.
Alleluia!

GOSPEL

A reading from the holy Gospel according to Luke 21:25-28. 34-36

Jesus said to his disciples: 'There will be signs in the sun and moon and stars; on earth nations in agony, bewildered by the clamour of the ocean and its waves; men dying of fear as they await what menaces the world, for the powers of heaven will be shaken. And then they will see the Son of Man coming in a cloud with power and great glory. When these things begin to take place, stand erect, hold your heads high, because your liberation is near at hand.'

'Watch yourselves, or your hearts will be coarsened with debauchery and drunkenness and the cares of life, and that day will be sprung on you suddenly, like a trap. For it will come down on every living man on the face of the earth. Stay awake, praying at all times for the strength to survive all that is going to happen, and to stand with confidence before the Son of Man.'

The Gospel of the Lord.

The Creed is said.

Prayer over the Offerings
Accept, we pray, O Lord, these offerings we make,
gathered from among your gifts to us,
and may what you grant us to celebrate devoutly here below
gain for us the prize of eternal redemption.
Through Christ our Lord.
Amen.

Preface I of Advent, p.19.

Communion Antiphon Ps 84:13
The Lord will bestow his bounty, and our earth shall yield its increase.

Prayer after Communion
May these mysteries, O Lord,
in which we have participated,
profit us, we pray,
for even now, as we walk amid passing things,

you teach us by them to love the things of heaven
and hold fast to what endures.
Through Christ our Lord.
Amen.

A formula of Solemn Blessing, pp.94-5, may be used.

SECOND SUNDAY OF ADVENT   C

The Joy of Salvation

As we await and celebrate with joyful hope that 'Day of the Lord' when his work in us will be complete, we rejoice in the marvels God has worked for us in sending us his mercy and forgiveness, and calling us to share his glory.

Entrance Antiphon   Cf. Is 30:19. 30
O people of Sion, behold,
the Lord will come to save the nations,
and the Lord will make the glory of his voice heard
in the joy of your heart.

The Gloria in excelsis (Glory to God in the highest) is not said.

Collect
Almighty and merciful God,
may no earthly undertaking hinder those
who set out in haste to meet your Son,
but may our learning of heavenly wisdom
gain us admittance to his company.
Who lives and reigns with you in the unity of the Holy Spirit,
one God, for ever and ever.
Amen.

FIRST READING
A reading from the prophet Baruch   5:1-9

Jerusalem, take off your dress of sorrow and distress,
put on the beauty of the glory of God for ever,
wrap the cloak of the integrity of God around you,
put the diadem of the glory of the Eternal on your head:
since God means to show your splendour to every nation under
   heaven,
since the name God gives you for ever will be,
'Peace through integrity, and honour through devotedness'.

Arise, Jerusalem, stand on the heights
and turn your eyes to the east:
see your sons reassembled from west and east
at the command of the Holy One, jubilant that God has
    remembered them.
Though they left you on foot,
with enemies for an escort,
now God brings them back to you
like royal princes carried back in glory.
For God has decreed the flattening
of each high mountain, of the everlasting hills,
the filling of the valleys to make the ground level
so that Israel can walk in safety under the glory of God.
And the forests and every fragrant tree will provide shade
for Israel at the command of God;
for God will guide Israel in joy by the light of his glory
with his mercy and integrity for escort.

The word of the Lord.

Responsorial Psalm   Ps 125. ℟ v.3℟

℟ **What marvels the Lord worked for us!**
   Indeed we were glad.

1 When the Lord delivered Zion from bondage,
it seemed like a dream.
Then was our mouth filled with laughter,
on our lips there were songs. ℟

2 The heathens themselves said: 'What marvels
the Lord worked for them!'
What marvels the Lord worked for us!
Indeed we were glad. ℟

3 Deliver us, O Lord, from our bondage
as streams in dry land.
Those who are sowing in tears
will sing when they reap. ℟

4 They go out, they go out, full of tears
carrying seed for the sowing:
they come back, they come back, full of song,
carrying their sheaves. ℟

SECOND READING
A reading from the letter of St Paul to the Philippians   1:3-6. 8-11

Every time I pray for all of you, I pray with joy, remembering how you have helped to spread the Good News from the day you first heard it right up to the present. I am quite certain that the One who began this good work in you will see that it is finished when the Day of Christ Jesus comes. God knows how much I miss you all, loving you as Christ Jesus loves you. My prayer is that your love for each other may increase more and more and never stop improving your knowledge and deepening your perception so that you can always recognise what is best. This will help you to become pure and blameless, and prepare you for the Day of Christ, when you will reach the perfect goodness which Jesus Christ produces in us for the glory and praise of God.

The word of the Lord.

Gospel Acclamation Lk 3:4. 6
Alleluia, alleluia!
Prepare a way for the Lord,
make his paths straight,
and all mankind shall see the salvation of God.
Alleluia!

GOSPEL
A reading from the holy Gospel according to Luke 3:1-6

In the fifteenth year of Tiberius Caesar's reign, when Pontius Pilate was governor of Judaea, Herod tetrarch of Galilee, his brother Philip tetrarch of the lands of Ituraea and Trachonitis, Lysanias tetrarch of Abilene, during the pontificate of Annas and Caiaphas, the word of God came to John son of Zechariah, in the wilderness. He went through the whole Jordan district proclaiming a baptism of repentance for the forgiveness of sins, as it is written in the book of the sayings of the prophet Isaiah:

A voice cries in the wilderness;
Prepare a way for the Lord,
make his paths straight.
Every valley will be filled in,
every mountain and hill be laid low,
winding ways will be straightened
and rough roads made smooth.
And all mankind shall see the salvation of God.

Third Sunday of Advent, Year C

The Gospel of the Lord.

The Creed is said.

Prayer over the Offerings
Be pleased, O Lord, with our humble prayers and offerings,
and, since we have no merits to plead our cause,
come, we pray, to our rescue
with the protection of your mercy.
Through Christ our Lord.
Amen.

Preface I of Advent, p.19.

Communion Antiphon Bar 5:5; 4:36
Jerusalem, arise and stand upon the heights,
and behold the joy which comes to you from God.

Prayer after Communion
Replenished by the food of spiritual nourishment,
we humbly beseech you, O Lord,
that, through our partaking in this mystery,
you may teach us to judge wisely the things of earth
and hold firm to the things of heaven.
Through Christ our Lord.
Amen.

A formula of Solemn Blessing, p.94-5, may be used.

THIRD SUNDAY OF ADVENT C

In this Mass the colour violet or rose is used.

A Day of Festival

Today is a day when we rejoice and exult with all our heart. Let us sing and shout for joy with Christ, the Lord of the Dance, who brings us the Good News of our redemption, and renews us by his love.

Entrance Antiphon Phil 4:4-5
Rejoice in the Lord always; again I say, rejoice.
Indeed, the Lord is near.

The Gloria in excelsis (Glory to God in the highest) is not said.

Collect
O God, who see how your people

faithfully await the feast of the Lord's Nativity,
enable us, we pray,
to attain the joys of so great a salvation
and to celebrate them always
with solemn worship and glad rejoicing.
Through our Lord Jesus Christ, your Son,
who lives and reigns with you in the unity of the Holy Spirit,
one God, for ever and ever.
Amen.

FIRST READING
A reading from the prophet Zephaniah　　　　　　　　3:14-18

Shout for joy, daughter of Zion,
Israel, shout aloud!
Rejoice, exult with all your heart,
daughter of Jerusalem!
The Lord has repealed your sentence;
he has driven your enemies away.
The Lord, the king of Israel, is in your midst;
you have no more evil to fear.
When that day comes, word will come to Jerusalem:
Zion, have no fear,
do not let your hands fall limp.
The Lord your God is in your midst,
a victorious warrior.
He will exult with joy over you,
he will renew you by his love;
he will dance with shouts of joy for you
as on a day of festival.

　　The word of the Lord.

Responsorial Psalm　　　　　　　　　　　　　　Is 12:2-6. ℟ v.6
　℟　**Sing and shout for joy**
　　　for great in your midst is the Holy One of Israel.

1　Truly, God is my salvation,
　I trust, I shall not fear.
　For the Lord is my strength, my song,
　he became my saviour.
　With joy you will draw water

Third Sunday of Advent, Year C

from the wells of salvation. ℟

2   Give thanks to the Lord, give praise to his name!
    Make his mighty deeds known to the peoples!
    Declare the greatness of his name.   ℟

3   Sing a psalm to the Lord
    for he has done glorious deeds,
    make them known to all the earth!
    People of Zion, sing and shout for joy
    for great in your midst is the Holy One of Israel.   ℟

SECOND READING
A reading from the letter of St Paul to the Philippians   4:4-7

I want you to be happy, always happy in the Lord; I repeat, what I want is your happiness. Let your tolerance be evident to everyone: the Lord is very near. There is no need to worry; but if there is anything you need, pray for it, asking God for it with prayer and thanksgiving, and that peace of God, which is so much greater than we can understand, will guard your hearts and your thoughts, in Christ Jesus.

The word of the Lord.

Gospel Acclamation   Is 61:1 (Lk 4:18)
    Alleluia, alleluia!
    The spirit of the Lord has been given to me.
    He has sent me to bring good news to the poor.
    Alleluia!

GOSPEL
A reading from the holy Gospel according to Luke   3:10-18

When all the people asked John, 'What must we do?' he answered, 'If anyone has two tunics he must share with the man who has none, and the one with something to eat must do the same.' There were tax collectors too who came for baptism, and these said to him, 'Master what must we do?' He said to them, 'Exact no more than your rate.' Some soldiers asked him in their turn, 'What about us? What must we do?' He said to them, 'No intimidation! No extortion! Be content with your pay!'

A feeling of expectancy had grown among the people, who were beginning to think that John might be the Christ, so John declared before them all, 'I baptise you with water, but someone is coming, someone who is more powerful than I am, and I am not fit to undo the strap of his sandals; he will baptise you with the Holy Spirit and fire. His winnowing-fan is in his hand to clear his threshing-floor and to gather the wheat into his barn; but the chaff he will burn in a fire that will never go out.' As well as this, there were many other things he said to exhort the people and to announce the Good News to them.

The Gospel of the Lord.

The Creed is said.

Prayer over the Offerings
May the sacrifice of our worship, Lord, we pray,
be offered to you unceasingly,
to complete what was begun in sacred mystery
and powerfully accomplish for us your saving work.
Through Christ our Lord.
Amen.

Preface I or II of Advent, pp.19-20.

Communion Antiphon Cf. Is 35:4
Say to the faint of heart: Be strong and do not fear.
Behold, our God will come, and he will save us.

Prayer after Communion
We implore your mercy, Lord,
that this divine sustenance may cleanse us of our faults
and prepare us for the coming feasts.
Through Christ our Lord.
Amen.

A formula of Solemn Blessing, p.94-5, may be used.

FOURTH SUNDAY OF ADVENT   C

Mary's Child: The Prince of Peace

From the least of the clans of Judah, from Mary his lowly handmaid, God prepared a human body for his Christ, who through his incarnation comes to fill the world with his spirit of peace.

Entrance Antiphon Cf. Is 45:8
Drop down dew from above, you heavens,

Fourth Sunday of Advent, Year C

and let the clouds rain down the Just One;
let the earth be opened and bring forth a Saviour.

The Gloria in excelsis (Glory to God in the highest) is not said.

Collect
Pour forth, we beseech you, O Lord,
your grace into our hearts,
that we, to whom the Incarnation of Christ your Son
was made known by the message of an Angel,
may by his Passion and Cross
be brought to the glory of his Resurrection.
Who lives and reigns with you in the unity of the Holy Spirit,
one God, for ever and ever.
Amen.

FIRST READING
A reading from the prophet Micah 5:1-4

The Lord says this:
You, Bethlehem Ephrathah,
the least of the clans of Judah,
out of you will be born for me
the one who is to rule over Israel;
his origin goes back to the distant past,
to the days of old.
The Lord is therefore going to abandon them
till the time when she who is to give birth gives birth.
Then the remnant of his brothers will come back
to the sons of Israel.
He will stand and feed his flock
with the power of the Lord,
with the majesty of the name of his God.
They will live secure, for from then on he will extend his power
to the ends of the land.
He himself will be peace.

    The word of the Lord.

Responsorial Psalm
Ps 79:2-3. 15-16. 18-19. R̷ v.4

R̷ **God of hosts, bring us back;
let your face shine on us and we shall be saved.**

1   O shepherd of Israel, hear us,
    shine forth from your cherubim throne.

O Lord, rouse up your might,
O Lord, come to our help.

2 God of hosts, turn again, we implore,
look down from heaven and see.
Visit this vine and protect it,
the vine your right hand has planted.

3 May your hand be on the man you have chosen,
the man you have given your strength.
And we shall never forsake you again:
give us life that we may call upon your name.

SECOND READING

A reading from the letter to the Hebrews 10:5-10

This is what Christ said, on coming into the world:

> You who wanted no sacrifice or oblation,
> prepared a body for me.
> You took no pleasure in holocausts or sacrifices for sin;
> then I said,
> just as I was commanded in the scroll of the book,
> 'God, here I am! I am coming to obey your will.'

Notice that he says first: You did not want what the Law lays down as the things to be offered, that is: the sacrifices, the oblations, the holocausts and the sacrifices for sin, and you took no pleasure in them; and then he says: Here I am! I am coming to obey your will. He is abolishing the first sort to replace it with the second. And this will was for us to be made holy by the offering of his body made once and for all by Jesus Christ.

The word of the Lord.

Gospel Acclamation Lk 1:38
Alleluia, alleluia!
I am the handmaid of the Lord:
let what you have said be done to me.
Alleluia!

GOSPEL

A reading from the holy Gospel according to Luke   1:39-44

Mary set out and went as quickly as she could to a town in the hill country of Judah. She went into Zechariah's house and greeted Elizabeth. Now as soon as Elizabeth heard Mary's greeting, the child leapt in her womb and Elizabeth was filled with the Holy Spirit. She gave a loud cry and said, 'Of all women you are the most blessed, and blessed is the fruit of your womb. Why should I be honoured with a visit from the mother of my Lord? For the moment your greeting reached my ears, the child in my womb leapt for joy. Yes, blessed is she who believed that the promise made her by the Lord would be fulfilled.'

The Gospel of the Lord.

The Creed is said.

Prayer over the Offerings
May the Holy Spirit, O Lord,
sanctify these gifts laid upon your altar,
just as he filled with his power the womb of the Blessed Virgin Mary.
Through Christ our Lord.
Amen.

Preface II of Advent, pp.19-20.

Communion Antiphon   Is 7:14
Behold, a Virgin shall conceive and bear a son;
and his name will be called Emmanuel.

Prayer after Communion
Having received this pledge of eternal redemption,
we pray, almighty God,
that, as the feast day of our salvation draws ever nearer,
so we may press forward all the more eagerly
to the worthy celebration of the mystery of your Son's Nativity.
Who lives and reigns for ever and ever.
Amen.

A formula of Solemn Blessing, p.94-5, may be used.

CHRISTMAS TIME
25 December

THE NATIVITY OF THE LORD
Solemnity

CHRISTMAS DAY: VIGIL MASS

See above, pp.208ff.

CHRISTMAS DAY

See above, pp.216ff.

The Sunday within the Octave of the Nativity of the Lord,
or, if there is no Sunday, 30 December

THE HOLY FAMILY OF JESUS, MARY AND JOSEPH C
Feast

Where there is no Sunday occurring between 25 December and 1 January, this feast is celebrated on 30 December, with one reading only before the Gospel.

The Holy Family

We celebrate the Holy Family of Nazareth, a model for us to imitate by practising the virtues of family life and the bonds of love, so that we may all truly fear the Lord and walk in his ways.

The Holy Family of Jesus, Mary and Joseph, Year C

Entrance Antiphon   Lk 2:16
The shepherds went in haste,
and found Mary and Joseph and the Infant lying in a manger.

The Gloria in excelsis (Glory to God in the highest) is said.

Collect
O God, who were pleased to give us
the shining example of the Holy Family,
graciously grant that we may imitate them
in practising the virtues of family life and in the bonds of charity,
and so, in the joy of your house,
delight one day in eternal rewards.
Through our Lord Jesus Christ, your Son,
who lives and reigns with you in the unity of the Holy Spirit,
one God, for ever and ever.
Amen.

The First Reading, Psalm, Second Reading and Gospel Acclamation given for Year A, pp.224ff., may be used, with the Gospel below. Or the alternative readings given below may be used.

FIRST READING
A reading from the first book of Samuel   1:20-22. 24-28

Hannah conceived and gave birth to a son, and called him Samuel 'since' she said 'I asked the Lord for him.'

When a year had gone by, the husband Elkanah went up again with all his family to offer the annual sacrifice to the Lord and to fulfil his vow. Hannah, however, did not go up, having said to her husband, 'Not before the child is weaned. Then I will bring him and present him before the Lord and he shall stay there for ever.'

When she had weaned him, she took him up with her together with a three-year old bull, an ephah of flour and a skin of wine, and she brought him to the temple of the Lord at Shiloh; and the child was with them. They slaughtered the bull and the child's mother came to Eli. She said, 'If you please, my lord. As you live, my lord, I am the woman who stood here beside you, praying to the Lord. This is the child I prayed for, and the Lord granted me what I asked him. Now I make him over to the Lord for the whole of his life. He is made over to the Lord.' There she left him, for the Lord.

The word of the Lord.

Responsorial Psalm   Ps 83:2-3. 5-6. 9-10. ℟ v.5

  ℟ **They are happy who dwell in your house, O Lord.**

1   How lovely is your dwelling place,
    Lord, God of hosts.
    My soul is longing and yearning,
    is yearning for the courts of the Lord.
    My heart and my soul ring out their joy
    to God, the living God. ℟

2   They are happy, who dwell in your house,
    for ever singing your praise.
    They are happy, whose strength is in you;
    they walk with ever growing strength. ℟

3   O Lord, God of hosts, hear my prayer,
    give ear, O God of Jacob.
    Turn your eyes, O God, our shield,
    look on the face of your anointed. ℟

SECOND READING

A reading from the first letter of St John   3:1-2. 21-24

Think of the love that the Father has lavished on us,
by letting us be called God's children;
and that is what we are.
Because the world refused to acknowledge him,
therefore it does not acknowledge us.
My dear people, we are already the children of God
but what we are to be in the future has not yet been revealed,
all we know is, that when it is revealed
we shall be like him
because we shall see him as he really is.

My dear people,
if we cannot be condemned by our own conscience,
we need not be afraid in God's presence,
and whatever we ask him,
we shall receive,
because we keep his commandments
and live the kind of life that he wants.
His commandments are these:
that we believe in the name of his Son Jesus Christ
and that we love one another
as he told us to.
Whoever keeps his commandments
lives in God and God lives in him.

The Holy Family of Jesus, Mary and Joseph, Year C

We know that he lives in us
by the Spirit that he has given us.

The word of the Lord.

Gospel Acclamation
Cf. Acts 16:14
Alleluia, alleluia!
Open our heart, O Lord,
to accept the words of your Son.
Alleluia!

GOSPEL
A reading from the holy Gospel according to Luke 2:41-52

Every year the parents of Jesus used to go to Jerusalem for the feast of the Passover. When he was twelve years old, they went up for the feast as usual. When they were on their way home after the feast, the boy Jesus stayed behind in Jerusalem without his parents knowing it. They assumed he was with the caravan, and it was only after a day's journey that they went to look for him among their relations and acquaintances. When they failed to find him they went back to Jerusalem looking for him everywhere.

Three days later, they found him in the Temple, sitting among the doctors, listening to them, and asking them questions; and all those who heard him were astounded at his intelligence and his replies. They were overcome when they saw him, and his mother said to him, 'My child, why have you done this to us? See how worried your father and I have been, looking for you.' 'Why were you looking for me?' he replied. 'Did you not know that I must be busy with my Father's affairs?' But they did not understand what he meant.

He then went down with them and came to Nazareth and lived under their authority. His mother stored up all these things in her heart. And Jesus increased in wisdom, in stature, and in favour with God and men.

The Gospel of the Lord.

When this Feast is celebrated on Sunday, the Creed is said.

Prayer over the Offerings
We offer you, Lord, the sacrifice of conciliation,
humbly asking that,
through the intercession of the Virgin Mother of God and Saint
    Joseph,
you may establish our families firmly in your grace and your
    peace.
Through Christ our Lord.
Amen.

Preface I, II or III of the Nativity of the Lord, pp.20-21.

When the Roman Canon is used, the proper form of the Communicantes (In communion with those) is said.

Communion Antiphon Bar 3:38
Our God has appeared on the earth, and lived among us.

Prayer after Communion
Bring those you refresh with this heavenly Sacrament,
most merciful Father,
to imitate constantly the example of the Holy Family,
so that, after the trials of this world,
we may share their company for ever.
Through Christ our Lord.
Amen.

1 January: Octave of Christmas
SOLEMNITY OF MARY, MOTHER OF GOD

See above, pp.227ff.

SECOND SUNDAY AFTER CHRISTMAS

See above, pp.230ff.

6 January (or the Sunday between 2 January and 8 January)
THE EPIPHANY OF THE LORD

See above, pp.234ff.

Sunday after 6 January
THE BAPTISM OF THE LORD   C
Feast

Where the Solemnity of the Epiphany is transferred to Sunday, if this Sunday occurs on 7 or 8 January, the Feast of the Baptism of the Lord is celebrated on the following Monday. This feast is omitted when the Epiphany is celebrated on this Sunday.

The Baptism of the Lord

At his baptism by John in the Jordan, the Father anointed Jesus his beloved son to bring healing and peace to all the nations.

The Baptism of the Lord, Year C

Entrance Antiphon   Cf. Mt 3:16-17
After the Lord was baptized, the heavens were opened,
and the Spirit descended upon him like a dove,
and the voice of the Father thundered:
This is my beloved Son, with whom I am well pleased.

The Gloria in excelsis (Glory to God in the highest) is said.

Collect
Almighty ever-living God,
who, when Christ had been baptized in the River Jordan
and as the Holy Spirit descended upon him,
solemnly declared him your beloved Son,
grant that your children by adoption,
reborn of water and the Holy Spirit,
may always be well pleasing to you.
Through our Lord Jesus Christ, your Son,
who lives and reigns with you in the unity of the Holy Spirit,
one God, for ever and ever.
Amen.

or

O God, whose Only Begotten Son
has appeared in our very flesh,
grant, we pray, that we may be inwardly transformed
through him whom we recognize as outwardly like ourselves.
Who lives and reigns with you in the unity of the Holy Spirit,
one God, for ever and ever.
Amen.

The First Reading, Psalm, Second Reading and Gospel Acclamation given for Year A, pp.240ff., may be used, with the Gospel below. Or the alternative readings given below may be used.

FIRST READING

A reading from the prophet Isaiah   40:1-5. 9-11

'Console my people, console them'
says your God.
'Speak to the heart of Jerusalem
and call to her
that her time of service is ended,
that her sin is atoned for,

that she has received from the hand of the Lord
double punishment for all her crimes.'

A voice cries, 'Prepare in the wilderness
a way for the Lord.
Make a straight highway for our God
across the desert.
Let every valley be filled in,
every mountain and hill be laid low,
let every cliff become a plain,
and the ridges a valley;
then the glory of the Lord shall be revealed
and all mankind shall see it;
for the mouth of the Lord has spoken.'

Go up on a high mountain,
joyful messenger to Zion.
Shout with a loud voice,
joyful messenger to Jerusalem.
Shout without fear,
say to the towns of Judah,
'Here is your God.'
Here is the Lord coming with power,
his arm subduing all things to him.
The prize of his victory is with him,
his trophies all go before him.
He is like a shepherd feeding his flock,
gathering lambs in his arms,
holding them against his breast
and leading to their rest the mother ewes.

    The word of the Lord.

Responsorial Psalm   Ps 103:1-2. 3-4. 24-25. 27-30. ℟ v.1
  ℟   **Bless the Lord, my soul!**
      Lord God, how great you are.

1   Lord God, how great you are,
    clothed in majesty and glory,
    wrapped in light as in a robe!
    You stretch out the heavens like a tent. ℟

2   Above the rains you build your dwelling.
    You make the clouds your chariot,
    you walk on the wings of the wind,
    you make the winds your messengers
    and flashing fire your servants. ℟

3   How many are your works, O Lord!
    In wisdom you have made them all.
    The earth is full of your riches.
    There is the sea, vast and wide,
    with its moving swarms past counting,
    living things great and small.   ℟

4   All of these look to you
    to give them their food in due season.
    You give it, they gather it up:
    you open your hand, they have their fill.   ℟

5   You take back your spirit, they die,
    returning to the dust from which they came.
    You send forth your spirit, they are created;
    and you renew the face of the earth.   ℟

SECOND READING
A reading from the letter of St Paul to Titus   2:11-14; 3:4-7

God's grace has been revealed, and it has made salvation possible for the whole human race and taught us that what we have to do is to give up everything that does not lead to God, and all our worldly ambitions; we must be self-restrained and live good and religious lives here in this present world, while we are waiting in hope for the blessing which will come with the Appearing of the glory of our great God and saviour Christ Jesus. He sacrificed himself for us in order to set us free from all wickedness and to purify a people so that it could be his very own and would have no ambition except to do good.

When the kindness and love of God our saviour for mankind were revealed, it was not because he was concerned with any righteous actions we might have done ourselves; it was for no reason except his own compassion that he saved us, by means of the cleansing water of rebirth and by renewing us with the Holy Spirit which he has so generously poured over us through Jesus Christ our saviour. He did this so that we should be justified by his grace, to become heirs looking forward to inheriting eternal life.

The word of the Lord.

Gospel Acclamation   Cf. Lk 3:16
    Alleluia, alleluia!
    Someone is coming, said John, someone greater than I.
    He will baptize you with the Holy Spirit and with fire.
    Alleluia!

GOSPEL

A reading from the holy Gospel according to Luke   3:15-16. 21-22

A feeling of expectancy had grown among the people, who were beginning to think that John might be the Christ, so John declared before them all, 'I baptise you with water, but someone is coming, someone who is more powerful than I am and I am not fit to undo the strap of his sandals; he will baptise you with the Holy Spirit and fire.'

Now when all the people had been baptised and while Jesus after his own baptism was at prayer, heaven opened and the Holy Spirit descended on him in bodily shape, like a dove. And a voice came from heaven, 'You are my Son, the Beloved; my favour rests on you.'

The Gospel of the Lord.

The Creed is said.

Prayer over the Offerings
Accept, O Lord, the offerings
we have brought to honour the revealing of your beloved Son,
so that the oblation of your faithful
may be transformed into the sacrifice of him
who willed in his compassion
to wash away the sins of the world.
Who lives and reigns for ever and ever.
Amen.

Preface of the Baptism of the Lord, p.22.

Communion Antiphon   Jn 1:32. 34
Behold the One of whom John said:
I have seen and testified that this is the Son of God.

Prayer after Communion
Nourished with these sacred gifts,
we humbly entreat your mercy, O Lord,
that, faithfully listening to your Only Begotten Son,
we may be your children in name and in truth.
Through Christ our Lord.
Amen.

Ordinary Time lasts from the Monday after this Sunday to the Tuesday before Lent. For Sunday Masses the texts given below on pp.908ff. are used.

THE SEASON OF LENT

For a Note on Preparation for Baptism, see above, pp.243-4.

ASH WEDNESDAY
See above, pp.244ff.

FIRST SUNDAY OF LENT   C

On this Sunday is celebrated the rite of 'election' or 'enrolment of names' for the catechumens who are to be admitted to the Sacraments of Christian Initiation at the Easter Vigil, using the proper prayers and intercessions.

Jesus Is Lord

Today we praise God for the marvellous things he did for our ancestors, when he heard their cry of distress and with his mighty hand and outstretched arm led them to freedom. What he did for them he still does for us, in Jesus the Lord who conquered sin and death.

Entrance Antiphon   Cf. Ps 90:15-16
When he calls on me, I will answer him;
I will deliver him and give him glory,
I will grant him length of days.

The Gloria in excelsis (Glory to God in the highest) is not said.

Collect
Grant, almighty God,
through the yearly observances of holy Lent,
that we may grow in understanding
of the riches hidden in Christ
and by worthy conduct pursue their effects.
Through our Lord Jesus Christ, your Son,

First Sunday of Lent, Year C

who lives and reigns with you in the unity of the Holy Spirit,
one God, for ever and ever.
Amen.

FIRST READING
A reading from the book of Deuteronomy   26:4-10

Moses said to the people: 'The priest shall take the pannier from your hand and lay it before the altar of the Lord your God. Then, in the sight of the Lord your God, you must make this pronouncement:

'"My father was a wandering Aramaean. He went down into Egypt to find refuge there, few in numbers; but there he became a nation, great, mighty, and strong. The Egyptians ill-treated us, they gave us no peace and inflicted harsh slavery on us. But we called on the Lord, the God of our fathers. The Lord heard our voice and saw our misery, our toil and our oppression; and the Lord brought us out of Egypt with mighty hand and outstretched arm, with great terror, and with signs and wonders. He brought us here and gave us this land, a land where milk and honey flow. Here then I bring the first-fruits of the produce of the soil that you, Lord, have given me." You must then lay them before the Lord your God, and bow down in the sight of the Lord your God.'

The word of the Lord.

Responsorial Psalm   Ps 90:1-2. 10-15. ℟ v.15

℟ **Be with me, O Lord, in my distress.**

1   He who dwells in the shelter of the Most High
    and abides in the shade of the Almighty
    says to the Lord: 'My refuge,
    my stronghold, my God in whom I trust!'   ℟

2   Upon you no evil shall fall,
    no plague approach where you dwell.
    For you has he commanded his angels,
    to keep you in all your ways.   ℟

3   They shall bear you upon their hands
    lest you strike your foot against a stone.
    On the lion and the viper you will tread
    and trample the young lion and the dragon.   ℟

4   His love he set on me, so I will rescue him;
    protect him for he knows my name.

When he calls I shall answer: 'I am with you.'
I will save him in distress and give him glory. ℟

SECOND READING

A reading from the letter of St Paul to the Romans   10:8-13

Scripture says: The word, that is the faith we proclaim, is very near to you, it is on your lips and in your heart. If your lips confess that Jesus is Lord and if you believe in your heart that God raised him from the dead, then you will be saved. By believing from the heart you are made righteous; by confessing with your lips you are saved. When scripture says: those who believe in him will have no cause for shame, it makes no distinction between Jew and Greek: all belong to the same Lord who is rich enough, however many ask for his help, for everyone who calls on the name of the Lord will be saved.

The word of the Lord.

Gospel Acclamation   Mt 4:4

Praise to you, O Christ, king of eternal glory!
Man does not live on bread alone
but on every word that comes from the mouth of God.
Praise to you, O Christ, king of eternal glory!

GOSPEL

A reading from the holy Gospel according to Luke   4:1-13

Filled with the Holy Spirit, Jesus left the Jordan and was led by the Spirit through the wilderness, being tempted there by the devil for forty days. During that time he ate nothing and at the end he was hungry. Then the devil said to him, 'If you are the Son of God, tell this stone to turn into a loaf.' But Jesus replied, 'Scripture says: Man does not live on bread alone.'

Then leading him to a height, the devil showed him in a moment of time all the kingdoms of the world and said to him, 'I will give you all this power and the glory of these kingdoms, for it has been committed to me and I give it to anyone I choose. Worship me, then, and it shall all be yours.' But Jesus answered him. 'Scripture says:

You must worship the Lord your God,
and serve him alone.'

Then he led him to Jerusalem and made him stand on the parapet of the Temple. 'If you are the Son of God,' he said to him 'throw yourself down from here, for scripture says:

> He will put his angels in charge of you
> to guard you,

and again:

> They will hold you up on their hands
> in case you hurt your foot against a stone.'

But Jesus answered him, 'It has been said:

> You must not put the Lord your God to the test.'

Having exhausted all these ways of tempting him, the devil left him, to return at the appointed time.

> The Gospel of the Lord.

After the Homily, the Election or Enrolment of Candidates for Baptism may follow.

The Creed is said.

Prayer over the Offerings
Give us the right dispositions, O Lord, we pray,
to make these offerings,
for with them we celebrate the beginning
of this venerable and sacred time.
Through Christ our Lord.
Amen.

Preface of the Temptation of the Lord, p.24.

Communion Antiphon Mt 4:4
One does not live by bread alone,
but by every word that comes forth from the mouth of God.

or Cf. Ps 90:4

The Lord will conceal you with his pinions,
and under his wings you will trust.

Prayer after Communion
Renewed now with heavenly bread,
by which faith is nourished, hope increased,
and charity strengthened,
we pray, O Lord,

that we may learn to hunger for Christ,
the true and living Bread,
and strive to live by every word
which proceeds from your mouth.
Through Christ our Lord.
Amen.

Prayer over the People
May bountiful blessing, O Lord, we pray,
come down upon your people,
that hope may grow in tribulation,
virtue be strengthened in temptation,
and eternal redemption be assured.
Through Christ our Lord.
Amen.

SECOND SUNDAY OF LENT   C

The Lord in Whom We Put Our Faith

Like Abraham, our father in faith, we are called by God to a new homeland. We are not to rest in the material comforts of this world, but to move onwards towards the land of promise, where the Lord in whom we put our faith will transfigure our mortal bodies into the likeness of his glorified body.

Entrance Antiphon   Cf. Ps 26:8-9
Of you my heart has spoken: Seek his face.
It is your face, O Lord, that I seek;
hide not your face from me.

or   Cf. Ps 24:6. 2. 22

Remember your compassion, O Lord,
and your merciful love, for they are from of old.
Let not our enemies exult over us.
Redeem us, O God of Israel, from all our distress.

The Gloria in excelsis (Glory to God in the highest) is not said.

Collect
O God, who have commanded us
to listen to your beloved Son,
be pleased, we pray,
to nourish us inwardly by your word,
that, with spiritual sight made pure,
we may rejoice to behold your glory.

Through our Lord Jesus Christ, your Son,
who lives and reigns with you in the unity of the Holy Spirit,
one God, for ever and ever.
Amen.

FIRST READING
A reading from the book of Genesis 15:5-12. 17-18

Taking Abram outside the Lord said, 'Look up to heaven and count the stars if you can. Such will be your descendants' he told him. Abram put his faith in the Lord, who counted this as making him justified.

'I am the Lord' he said to him 'who brought you out of Ur of the Chaldaeans to make you heir to this land.' 'My Lord, the Lord' Abram replied 'how am I to know that I shall inherit it?' He said to him, 'Get me a three-year-old heifer, a three-year-old goat, a three-year-old ram, a turtledove and a young pigeon.' He brought him all these, cut them in half and put half on one side and half facing it on the other; but the birds he did not cut in half. Birds of prey came down on the carcasses but Abram drove them off.

Now as the sun was setting Abram fell into a deep sleep, and terror seized him. When the sun had set and darkness had fallen, there appeared a smoking furnace and a firebrand that went between the halves. That day the Lord made a Covenant with Abram in these terms:

'To your descendants I give this land,
from the wadi of Egypt to the Great River.'

The word of the Lord.

Responsorial Psalm Ps 26:1. 7-9. 13-14. ℟ v.1

℟ **The Lord is my light and my help.**

1 The Lord is my light and my help;
 whom shall I fear?
 The Lord is the stronghold of my life;
 before whom shall I shrink?

2 O Lord, hear my voice when I call;
 have mercy and answer.
 Of you my heart has spoken:
 'Seek his face.'

3   It is your face, O Lord, that I seek;
    hide not your face.
    Dismiss not your servant in anger;
    you have been my help.

4   I am sure I shall see the Lord's goodness
    in the land of the living.
    Hope in him, hold firm and take heart.
    Hope in the Lord!

SECOND READING
A reading from the letter of St Paul to the Philippians   3:17–4:1

My brothers, be united in following my rule of life. Take as your models everybody who is already doing this and study them as you used to study us. I have told you often, and I repeat it today with tears, there are many who are behaving as the enemies of the cross of Christ. They are destined to be lost. They make foods into their god and they are proudest of something they ought to think shameful; the things they think important are earthly things. *For us, our homeland is in heaven, and from heaven comes the saviour we are waiting for, the Lord Jesus Christ, and he will transfigure these wretched bodies of ours into copies of his glorious body. He will do that by the same power with which he can subdue the whole universe.

So then, my brothers and dear friends, do not give way but remain faithful in the Lord. I miss you very much, dear friends; you are my joy and my crown.

The word of the Lord.*

Shorter Form, 3:20–4:1. Read between

Gospel Acclamation   Mt 17:5
Glory and praise to you, O Christ!
From the bright cloud, the Father's voice was heard:
'This is my Son, the Beloved. Listen to him!'
Glory and praise to you, O Christ!

GOSPEL
A reading from the holy Gospel according to Luke   9:28-36

Jesus took with him Peter and John and James and went up the mountain to pray. As he prayed, the aspect of his face was changed and his clothing became brilliant as lightning. Suddenly there were two men there talking to him; they were Moses and Elijah appearing in glory, and they were speaking of his passing which he was to accomplish in Jerusalem. Peter and his companions were heavy with sleep, but they kept awake and saw his glory and the two men standing with him. As these were leaving him, Peter said to Jesus, 'Master, it is wonderful for us to be here; so let us make three tents, one for you, one for Moses and one for Elijah.' – He did not know what he was saying. As he spoke, a cloud came and covered them with shadow; and when they went into the cloud the disciples were afraid. And a voice came from the cloud saying, 'This is my Son, the Chosen One. Listen to him'. And after the voice had spoken, Jesus was found alone. The disciples kept silence and, at that time, told no one what they had seen.

The Gospel of the Lord.

The Creed is said.

Prayer over the Offerings
May this sacrifice, O Lord, we pray,
cleanse us of our faults
and sanctify your faithful in body and mind
for the celebration of the paschal festivities.
Through Christ our Lord.
Amen.

Preface of the Transfiguration of the Lord, p.40.

Communion Antiphon   Mt 17:5
This is my beloved Son, with whom I am well pleased;
listen to him.

Prayer after Communion
As we receive these glorious mysteries,
we make thanksgiving to you, O Lord,
for allowing us while still on earth
to be partakers even now of the things of heaven.
Through Christ our Lord.
Amen.

Prayer over the People
Bless your faithful, we pray, O Lord,
with a blessing that endures for ever,
and keep them faithful
to the Gospel of your Only Begotten Son,
so that they may always desire and at last attain

that glory whose beauty he showed in his own Body,
to the amazement of his Apostles.
Through Christ our Lord.
Amen.

THIRD SUNDAY OF LENT   C

On this Sunday is celebrated the First Scrutiny in preparation for the Baptism of the catechumens who are to be admitted to the Sacraments of Christian Initiation at the Easter Vigil, using the proper prayers and intercessions as given above, pp.263-8.

The Lord of Compassion and Love

We celebrate today the Lord of compassion, who resolves to rescue and free us from our slavery to sin, if only we will listen to his serious warnings to us to repent.

Entrance Antiphon   Cf. Ps 24:15-16
My eyes are always on the Lord,
for he rescues my feet from the snare.
Turn to me and have mercy on me,
for I am alone and poor.

or   Cf. Ez 36:23-26

When I prove my holiness among you,
I will gather you from all the foreign lands;
and I will pour clean water upon you
and cleanse you from all your impurities,
and I will give you a new spirit, says the Lord.

The Gloria in excelsis (Glory to God in the highest) is not said.

Collect
O God, author of every mercy and of all goodness,
who in fasting, prayer and almsgiving
have shown us a remedy for sin,
look graciously on this confession of our lowliness,
that we, who are bowed down by our conscience,
may always be lifted up by your mercy.
Through our Lord Jesus Christ, your Son,
who lives and reigns with you in the unity of the Holy Spirit,
one God, for ever and ever.
Amen.

850   *Third Sunday of Lent, Year C*

The readings for Cycle A may be used as alternative readings, see above, pp.259ff. If this is done, the Preface and Communion Antiphon as at Cycle A are used. If a pre-baptismal scrutiny is held today, the readings for Year A are mandatory.

FIRST READING

A reading from the book of Exodus   3:1-8. 13-15

Moses was looking after the flock of Jethro, his father-in-law, priest of Midian. He led his flock to the far side of the wilderness and came to Horeb, the mountain of God. There the angel of the Lord appeared to him in the shape of a flame of fire, coming from the middle of a bush. Moses looked; there was the bush blazing but it was not being burnt up. 'I must go and look at this strange sight,' Moses said 'and see why the bush is not burnt.' Now the Lord saw him go forward to look, and God called to him from the middle of the bush. 'Moses, Moses!' he said. 'Here I am' he answered. 'Come no nearer' he said. 'Take off your shoes, for the place on which you stand is holy ground. I am the God of your father,' he said 'the God of Abraham, the God of Isaac and the God of Jacob.' At this Moses covered his face, afraid to look at God.

And the Lord said, 'I have seen the miserable state of my people in Egypt. I have heard their appeal to be free of their slave-drivers. Yes, I am well aware of their sufferings. I mean to deliver them out of the hands of the Egyptians and bring them up out of that land to a land rich and broad, a land where milk and honey flow.'

Then Moses said to God, 'I am to go, then, to the sons of Israel and say to them, "The God of your fathers has sent me to you." But if they ask me what his name is, what am I to tell them?' And God said to Moses, 'I Am who I Am. This' he added 'is what you must say to the sons of Israel: "The Lord, the God of your fathers, the God of Abraham, the God of Isaac, and the God of Jacob, has sent me to you." This is my name for all time; by this name I shall be invoked for all generations to come.'

The word of the Lord.

Responsorial Psalm   Ps 102:1-4. 6-8. 11. ℟ v.8

   ℟   **The Lord is compassion and love.**

1   My soul, give thanks to the Lord,
      all my being, bless his holy name.

Third Sunday of Lent, Year C

    My soul give thanks to the Lord
and never forget all his blessings. ℟

2   It is he who forgives all your guilt,
who heals every one of your ills,
who redeems your life from the grave,
who crowns you with love and compassion. ℟

3   The Lord does deeds of justice,
gives judgement for all who are oppressed.
He made known his ways to Moses
and his deeds to Israel's sons. ℟

4   The Lord is compassion and love,
slow to anger and rich in mercy.
For as the heavens are high above the earth
so strong is his love for those who fear him. ℟

SECOND READING

A reading from the first letter of St Paul   10:1-6. 10-12
to the Corinthians

I want to remind you, brothers, how our fathers were all guided by a cloud above them and how they all passed through the sea. They were all baptised into Moses in this cloud and in this sea; all ate the same spiritual food and all drank the same spiritual drink, since they all drank from the spiritual rock that followed them as they went, and that rock was Christ. In spite of this, most of them failed to please God and their corpses littered the desert.

These things all happened as warnings for us, not to have the wicked lusts for forbidden things that they had. You must never complain: some of them did, and they were killed by the Destroyer.

All this happened to them as a warning and it was written down to be a lesson for us who are living at the end of the age. The man who thinks he is safe must be careful that he does not fall.

The word of the Lord.

Gospel Acclamation   Mt 4:17
    Glory to you, O Christ, you are the Word of God!
Repent, says the Lord,
for the kingdom of heaven is close at hand.
Glory to you, O Christ, you are the Word of God!

GOSPEL
A reading from the holy Gospel according to Luke 13:1-9

Some people arrived and told Jesus about the Galileans whose blood Pilate had mingled with that of their sacrifices. At this he said to them, 'Do you suppose these Galileans who suffered like that were greater sinners than any other Galileans? They were not, I tell you. No; but unless you repent you will all perish as they did. Or those eighteen on whom the tower at Siloam fell and killed them? Do you suppose that they were more guilty than all the other people living in Jerusalem? They were not, I tell you. No; but unless you repent you will all perish as they did.'

He told this parable: 'A man had a fig tree planted in his vineyard and he came looking for fruit on it but found none. He said to the man who looked after the vineyard, "Look here, for three years now I have been coming to look for fruit on this fig tree and finding none. Cut it down: why should it be taking up the ground?" "Sir," the man replied "leave it one more year and give me time to dig round it and manure it: it may bear fruit next year; if not, then you can cut it down."'

The Gospel of the Lord.

After the Homily, the First Scrutiny of Candidates for Baptism may follow. See above, pp.263-8.

If there is no Scrutiny, the Creed is said.

Prayer over the Offerings
Be pleased, O Lord, with these sacrificial offerings,
and grant that we who beseech pardon for our own sins,
may take care to forgive our neighbour.
Through Christ our Lord.
Amen.

Preface of the Samaritan Woman, p.25.

When the Gospel of the Samaritan Woman is not read, Preface I or II of Lent, pp.22-3, is used.

Communion Antiphon

When the Gospel of the Samaritan Woman is read: Jn 4:13-14
For anyone who drinks it, says the Lord,
the water I shall give will become in him
a spring welling up to eternal life.

Fourth Sunday of Lent, Year C 853

When another Gospel is read: Cf. Ps 83:4-5
The sparrow finds a home,
and the swallow a nest for her young:
by your altars, O Lord of hosts, my King and my God.
Blessed are they who dwell in your house,
for ever singing your praise.

Prayer after Communion
As we receive the pledge
of things yet hidden in heaven
and are nourished while still on earth
with the Bread that comes from on high,
we humbly entreat you, O Lord,
that what is being brought about in us in mystery
may come to true completion.
Through Christ our Lord.
Amen.

Prayer over the People
Direct, O Lord, we pray, the hearts of your faithful,
and in your kindness grant your servants this grace:
that, abiding in the love of you and their neighbour,
they may fulfil the whole of your commands.
Through Christ our Lord.
Amen.

FOURTH SUNDAY OF LENT C

In this Mass, the colour violet or rose is used. Instrumental music is permitted, and the altar may be decorated with flowers.

On this Sunday is celebrated the Second Scrutiny in preparation for the Baptism of the catechumens who are to be admitted to the Sacraments of Christian Initiation at the Easter Vigil, using the proper prayers and intercessions as given above, pp.274-9.

The Lord Who Welcomes Sinners

We too taste and see that the Lord is good and celebrate this Mass in the joy of forgiveness. We gratefully eat the manna, the food that our Father gives us for our journey to the kingdom where his banquet is prepared for us.

Entrance Antiphon Cf. Is 66:10-11
Rejoice, Jerusalem, and all who love her.
Be joyful, all who were in mourning;
exult and be satisfied at her consoling breast.

Fourth Sunday of Lent, Year C

The Gloria in excelsis (Glory to God in the highest) is not said.

Collect
O God, who through your Word
reconcile the human race to yourself in a wonderful way,
grant, we pray,
that with prompt devotion and eager faith
the Christian people may hasten
toward the solemn celebrations to come.
Through our Lord Jesus Christ, your Son,
who lives and reigns with you in the unity of the Holy Spirit,
one God, for ever and ever.
Amen.

The readings for Year A may be used as alternative readings, see above, pp.269-71ff. If this is done, the Preface and Communion Antiphon as at Year A are used. If a pre-baptismal scrutiny is held today, the readings for Year A are mandatory.

FIRST READING
A reading from the book of Joshua   5:9-12

The Lord said to Joshua, 'Today I have taken the shame of Egypt away from you.'

    The Israelites pitched their camp at Gilgal and kept the Passover there on the fourteenth day of the month, at evening in the plain of Jericho. On the morrow of the Passover they tasted the produce of that country, unleavened bread and roasted ears of corn, that same day. From that time, from their first eating of the produce of that country, the manna stopped falling. And having manna no longer, the Israelites fed from that year onwards on what the land of Canaan yielded.

    The word of the Lord.

Responsorial Psalm   Ps 33:2-7. ℟ v.9
   ℟   **Taste and see that the Lord is good.**

1   I will bless the Lord at all times,
     his praise always on my lips;
     in the Lord my soul shall make its boast.
     The humble shall hear and be glad.

2   Glorify the Lord with me.
     Together let us praise his name.
     I sought the Lord and he answered me;
     from all my terrors he set me free.

3   Look towards him and be radiant;
    let your faces not be abashed.
    This poor man called; the Lord heard him
    and rescued him from all his distress.

SECOND READING

A reading from the second letter of St Paul to the Corinthians   5:17-21

For anyone who is in Christ, there is a new creation; the old creation has gone, and now the new one is here. It is all God's work. It was God who reconciled us to himself through Christ and gave us the work of handing on his reconciliation. In other words, God in Christ was reconciling the world to himself, not holding men's faults against them, and he has entrusted to us the news that they are reconciled. So we are ambassadors for Christ; it is as though God were appearing through us, and the appeal that we make in Christ's name is: be reconciled to God. For our sake God made the sinless one into sin, so that in him we might become the goodness of God.

The word of the Lord.

Gospel Acclamation   Lk 15:18

Praise and honour to you, Lord Jesus!
I will leave this place and go to my father and say:
'Father, I have sinned against heaven and against you.'
Praise and honour to you, Lord Jesus!

GOSPEL

A reading from the holy Gospel according to Luke   15:1-3. 11-32

The tax collectors and the sinners were all seeking the company of Jesus to hear what he had to say, and the Pharisees and the scribes complained. 'This man,' they said, 'welcomes sinners and eats with them.' So he spoke this parable to them:

'A man had two sons. The younger said to his father, "Father, let me have the share of the estate that would come to me." So the father divided the property between them. A few days later, the younger son got together everything he had and left for a distant country where he squandered his money on a life of debauchery.

'When he had spent it all, that country experienced a severe famine, and now he began to feel the pinch, so he hired himself out to one of the local inhabitants who put him on his farm to feed the pigs. And he would willingly have filled his belly with the husks the pigs were eating but no one offered him anything. Then he came to his senses and said, "How many of my father's paid servants have more food than they want, and here am I dying of hunger! I will leave this place and go to my father and say: Father, I have sinned against heaven and against you; I no longer deserve to be called your son; treat me as one of your paid servants." So he left the place and went back to his father.

'While he was still a long way off, his father saw him and was moved with pity. He ran to the boy, clasped him in his arms and kissed him tenderly. Then his son said, "Father, I have sinned against heaven and against you. I no longer deserve to be called your son." But the father said to his servants, "Quick! Bring out the best robe and put it on him; put a ring on his finger and sandals on his feet. Bring the calf we have been fattening, and kill it; we are going to have a feast, a celebration, because this son of mine was dead and has come back to life; he was lost and is found." And they began to celebrate.

'Now the elder son was out in the fields, and on his way back, as he drew near the house, he could hear music and dancing. Calling one of the servants he asked what it was all about. "Your brother has come" replied the servant "and your father has killed the calf we had fattened because he has got him back safe and sound." He was angry then and refused to go in, and his father came out to plead with him; but he answered his father, "Look, all these years I have slaved for you and never once disobeyed your orders, yet you never offered me so much as a kid for me to celebrate with my friends. But for this son of yours, when he comes back after swallowing up your property – he and his women – you kill the calf we had been fattening."

'The father said, "My son, you are with me always and all I have is yours. But it is only right we should celebrate and rejoice, because your brother here was dead and has come to life; he was lost and is found."'

The Gospel of the Lord.

After the Homily, the Second Scrutiny of Candidates for Baptism may follow. See above, pp.274-9ff.

If there is no Scrutiny, the Creed is said.

Prayer over the Offerings
We place before you with joy these offerings,
which bring eternal remedy, O Lord,

praying that we may both faithfully revere them
and present them to you, as is fitting,
for the salvation of all the world.
Through Christ our Lord.
Amen.

Preface of The Man Born Blind, p.25.

When the Gospel of the Man Born Blind is not read, Preface I or II of Lent, pp.22-3, is used.

Communion Antiphon
When the Gospel of the Man Born Blind is read: Cf. Jn 9:11. 38
The Lord anointed my eyes: I went, I washed,
I saw and I believed in God.

When the Gospel of the Prodigal Son is read: Lk 15:32
You must rejoice, my son,
for your brother was dead and has come to life;
he was lost and is found.

Prayer after Communion
O God, who enlighten everyone who comes into this world,
illuminate our hearts, we pray,
with the splendour of your grace,
that we may always ponder
what is worthy and pleasing to your majesty
and love you in all sincerity.
Through Christ our Lord.
Amen.

Prayer over the People
Look upon those who call to you, O Lord,
and sustain the weak;
give life by your unfailing light
to those who walk in the shadow of death,
and bring those rescued by your mercy from every evil
to reach the highest good.
Through Christ our Lord.
Amen.

FIFTH SUNDAY OF LENT C

The practice of covering crosses and images throughout the church from this Sunday may be observed, if the Conference of Bishops so decides. Crosses remain covered until the end of the celebration of the Lord's Passion on Good Friday, but images remain covered until the beginning of the Easter Vigil.

On this Sunday is celebrated the Third Scrutiny in preparation for the Baptism of the catechumens who are to be admitted to the Sacraments of Christian Initiation at the Easter Vigil, using the proper prayers and intercessions as given above, pp.285-9.

The Lord Who Has Wiped Out Our Past Sinfulness

The utter completeness of Christ's forgiveness is almost incredible. When he says to us 'Neither do I condemn you', the past is dead, snuffed out like a wick, forgotten. Laughter and song fill our hearts. It seems like a dream.

Entrance Antiphon
Cf. Ps 42:1-2

Give me justice, O God,
and plead my cause against a nation that is faithless.
From the deceitful and cunning rescue me,
for you, O God, are my strength.

The Gloria in excelsis (Glory to God in the highest) is not said.

Collect

By your help, we beseech you, Lord our God,
may we walk eagerly in that same charity
with which, out of love for the world,
your Son handed himself over to death.
Through our Lord Jesus Christ, your Son,
who lives and reigns with you in the unity of the Holy Spirit,
one God, for ever and ever.
Amen.

The readings for Cycle A may be used as alternative readings, see above, pp.280-82ff. If this is done, the Preface and Communion Antiphon as at Year A are used. If a pre-baptismal scrutiny is held today, the readings for Year A are mandatory.

FIRST READING

A reading from the prophet Isaiah 43:16-21

Thus says the Lord,
who made a way through the sea,

a path in the great waters;
who put chariots and horse in the field
and a powerful army,
which lay there never to rise again,
snuffed out, put out like a wick:

> No need to recall the past,
> no need to think about what was done before.
> See, I am doing a new deed,
> even now it comes to light; can you not see it?
> Yes, I am making a road in the wilderness,
> paths in the wilds.
>
> The wild beasts will honour me,
> jackals and ostriches,
> because I am putting water in the wilderness
> (rivers in the wild)
> to give my chosen people drink.
> The people I have formed for myself
> will sing my praises.

The word of the Lord.

Responsorial Psalm   Ps 125. ℟ v.3

> ℟ **What marvels the Lord worked for us!**
> **Indeed we were glad.**

1. When the Lord delivered Zion from bondage,
   it seemed like a dream.
   Then was our mouth filled with laughter,
   on our lips there were songs.

2. The heathens themselves said: 'What marvels
   the Lord worked for them!'
   What marvels the Lord worked for us!
   Indeed we were glad.

3. Deliver us, O Lord, from our bondage
   as streams in dry land.
   Those who are sowing in tears
   will sing when they reap.

4. They go out, they go out, full of tears,
   carrying seed for the sowing:
   they come back, they come back, full of song,
   carrying their sheaves.

SECOND READING
A reading from the letter of St Paul to the Philippians   3:8-14

I believe nothing can happen that will outweigh the supreme advantage of knowing Christ Jesus my Lord. For him I have accepted the loss of everything, and I look on everything as so much rubbish if only I can have Christ and be given a place in him. I am no longer trying for perfection by my own efforts, the perfection that comes from the Law, but I want only the perfection that comes through faith in Christ, and is from God and based on faith. All I want is to know Christ and the power of his resurrection and to share his sufferings by reproducing the pattern of his death. That is the way I can hope to take my place in the resurrection of the dead. Not that I have become perfect yet: I have not yet won, but I am still running, trying to capture the prize for which Christ Jesus captured me. I can assure you my brothers, I am far from thinking that I have already won. All I can say is that I forget the past and I strain ahead for what is still to come; I am racing for the finish, for the prize to which God calls us upwards to receive in Christ Jesus.

The word of the Lord.

Gospel Acclamation   Cf. Amos 5:14
Praise to you, O Christ, king of eternal glory!
Seek good and not evil so that you may live,
and that the Lord God of hosts may really be with you.
Praise to you, O Christ, king of eternal glory!

or   Joel 2:12-13

Praise to you, O Christ, king of eternal glory!
Now, now – it is the Lord who speaks –
come back to me with all your heart,
for I am all tenderness and compassion.
Praise to you, O Christ, king of eternal glory!

GOSPEL
A reading from the holy Gospel according to John   8:1-11

Jesus went to the Mount of Olives. At daybreak he appeared in the Temple again; and as all the people came to him, he sat down and began to teach them.

The scribes and Pharisees brought a woman along who had been caught committing adultery; and making her stand there in full view of everybody, they said to Jesus, 'Master, this woman was caught in the very act of committing adultery, and Moses

Fifth Sunday of Lent, Year C

has ordered us in the Law to condemn women like this to death by stoning. What have you to say?' They asked him this as a test, looking for something to use against him. But Jesus bent down and started writing on the ground with his finger. As they persisted with their question, he looked up and said, 'If there is one of you who has not sinned, let him be the first to throw a stone at her.' Then he bent down and wrote on the ground again. When they heard this they went away one by one, beginning with the eldest, until Jesus was left alone with the woman, who remained standing there. He looked up and said, 'Woman, where are they? Has no one condemned you?' 'No one, sir,' she replied. 'Neither do I condemn you,' said Jesush, 'go away, and don't sin any more.'

The Gospel of the Lord.

After the Homily, the Third Scrutiny of Candidates for Baptism may follow. See above, pp.285-9ff.

If there is no Scrutiny, the Creed is said.

Prayer over the Offerings
Hear us, almighty God,
and, having instilled in your servants
the teachings of the Christian faith,
graciously purify them
by the working of this sacrifice.
Through Christ our Lord.
Amen.

Preface of Lazarus, see p.26.

When the Gospel of Lazarus is not read, Preface I or II of Lent, pp.22-3, is used.

Communion Antiphon
When the Gospel of Lazarus is read: Cf. Jn 11:26
Everyone who lives and believes in me
will not die for ever, says the Lord.

When the Gospel of the Adulterous Woman is read: Jn 8:10-11
Has no one condemned you, woman? No one, Lord.
Neither shall I condemn you. From now on, sin no more.

Prayer after Communion
We pray, almighty God,
that we may always be counted among the members of Christ,
in whose Body and Blood we have communion.
Who lives and reigns for ever and ever.
Amen.

Prayer over the People
Bless, O Lord, your people,
who long for the gift of your mercy,
and grant that what, at your prompting, they desire
they may receive by your generous gift.
Through Christ our Lord.
Amen.

HOLY WEEK

PASSION SUNDAY (PALM SUNDAY)

See above, pp.290ff.

HOLY THURSDAY: CHRISM MASS

See above, pp.329ff.

THE EASTER TRIDUUM

HOLY THURSDAY
(Mass of the Lord's Supper)

See above, pp.342ff.

GOOD FRIDAY
(Celebration of the Lord's Passion)

See above, pp.355ff.

EASTER VIGIL

See above, pp.383ff.

EASTER SUNDAY

See above, pp.423ff.

THE SEASON OF EASTER

SECOND SUNDAY OF EASTER   C
(or of Divine Mercy)

The Living One

We worship Christ who was dead and is now alive for ever and ever. He is always present in our midst, bringing healing and peace.

Entrance Antiphon   1 Pt 2:2
Like newborn infants, you must long for the pure, spiritual milk,
that in him you may grow to salvation, alleluia.

or   4 Esdr 2:36-37

Receive the joy of your glory, giving thanks to God,
who has called you into the heavenly kingdom, alleluia.

The Gloria in excelsis (Glory to God in the highest) is said.

Collect
God of everlasting mercy,
who, in the very recurrence of the paschal feast
kindle the faith of the people you have made your own,
increase, we pray, the grace you have bestowed,
that all may grasp and rightly understand
in what font they have been washed,
by whose Spirit they have been reborn,
by whose Blood they have been redeemed.
Through our Lord Jesus Christ, your Son,
who lives and reigns with you in the unity of the Holy Spirit,
one God, for ever and ever.
Amen.

FIRST READING
A reading from the Acts of the Apostles 5:12-16

The faithful all used to meet by common consent in the Portico of Solomon. No one else ever dared to join them, but the people were loud in their praise and the numbers of men and women who came to believe in the Lord increased steadily. So many signs and wonders were worked among the people at the hands of the apostles that the sick were even taken out into the streets and laid on beds and sleeping-mats in the hope that at least the shadow of Peter might fall across some of them as he went past. People even came crowding in from the towns round about Jerusalem, bringing with them their sick and those tormented by unclean spirits, and all of them were cured.

The word of the Lord.

Responsorial Psalm Ps 117:2-4. 22-27. R̸ v.1

R̸ **Give thanks to the Lord for he is good,
for his love has no end.**

or

R̸ **Alleluia, alleluia, alleluia!**

1 Let the sons of Israel say:
 'His love has no end.'
 Let the sons of Aaron say:
 'His love has no end.'
 Let those who fear the Lord say:
 'His love has no end.' R̸

2 The stone which the builders rejected
 has become the corner stone.
 This is the work of the Lord,
 a marvel in our eyes.
 This day was made by the Lord;
 we rejoice and are glad. R̸

3 O Lord, grant us salvation;
 O Lord grant success.
 Blessed in the name of the Lord
 is he who comes.
 We bless you from the house of the Lord;
 the Lord God is our light. R̸

SECOND READING

A reading from the book of the Apocalypse   1:9-13. 17-19

My name is John, and through our union in Jesus I am your brother and share your sufferings, your kingdom, and all you endure. I was on the island of Patmos for having preached God's word and witnessed for Jesus; it was the Lord's day and the Spirit possessed me, and I heard a voice behind me, shouting like a trumpet, 'Write down all that you see in a book.' I turned round to see who had spoken to me, and when I turned I saw seven golden lamp-stands and, surrounded by them, a figure like a Son of man, dressed in a long robe tied at the waist with a golden girdle.

When I saw him, I fell in a dead faint at his feet, but he touched me with his right hand and said, 'Do not be afraid; it is I, the First and the Last; I am the Living One. I was dead and now I am to live for ever and ever, and I hold the keys of death and of the underworld. Now write down all that you see of present happenings and things that are still to come.'

The word of the Lord.

Gospel Acclamation   Jn 20:29

Alleluia, alleluia!
Jesus said: 'You believe because you can see me.
Happy are those who have not seen and yet believe.'
Alleluia!

GOSPEL

A reading from the holy Gospel according to John   20:19-31

In the evening of that same day, the first day of the week, the doors were closed in the room where the disciples were, for fear of the Jews. Jesus came and stood among them. He said to them, 'Peace be with you,' and showed them his hands and his side. The disciples were filled with joy when they saw the Lord, and he said to them again, 'Peace be with you.

'As the Father sent me,
so am I sending you.'

After saying this he breathed on them and said:

'Receive the Holy Spirit.
For those whose sins you forgive,
they are forgiven;

Second Sunday of Easter, Year C

for those whose sins you retain,
they are retained.'

Thomas, called the Twin, who was one of the Twelve, was not with them when Jesus came. When the disciples said, 'We have seen the Lord', he answered, 'Unless I see the holes that the nails made in his hands and can put my finger into the holes they made, and unless I can put my hand into his side, I refuse to believe.' Eight days later the disciples were in the house again and Thomas was with them. The doors were closed, but Jesus came in and stood among them. 'Peace be with you,' he said. Then he spoke to Thomas, 'Put your finger here; look, here are my hands. Give me your hand; put it into my side. Doubt no longer but believe.' Thomas replied, 'My Lord and my God!' Jesus said to him:

'You believe because you can see me.
Happy are those who have not seen and yet believe.'

There were many other signs that Jesus worked and the disciples saw, but they are not recorded in this book. These are recorded so that you may believe that Jesus is the Christ, the Son of God, and that believing this you may have life through his name.

The Gospel of the Lord.

The Creed is said.

Prayer over the Offerings
Accept, O Lord, we pray,
the oblations of your people
(and of those you have brought to new birth),
that, renewed by confession of your name and by Baptism,
they may attain unending happiness.
Through Christ our Lord.
Amen.

Preface I of Easter (... on this day above all ...), p.28.

When the Roman Canon is used, the proper forms of the Communicantes (In communion with those) and Hanc igitur (Therefore, Lord, we pray) are said.

Communion Antiphon　　　　　　　　　　　　　　　　Cf. Jn 20:27
Bring your hand and feel the place of the nails,
and do not be unbelieving but believing, alleluia.

Prayer after Communion
Grant, we pray, almighty God,
that our reception of this paschal Sacrament
may have a continuing effect
in our minds and hearts.
Through Christ our Lord.
Amen.

A formula of Solemn Blessing, p.97, may be used.

For the dismissal of the people, there is sung (as below, p.896) or said: Go forth, the Mass is ended, alleluia, alleluia. Or: Go in peace, alleluia, alleluia. The people respond: **Thanks be to God, alleluia, alleluia.**

THIRD SUNDAY OF EASTER C

'It Is The Lord'

In this eucharist we proclaim that Christ is the Lord, the Lamb that was sacrificed and who is worthy to be given power, riches, wisdom, strength, honour, glory and blessing. Obedient to God, the apostles accepted every kind of humiliation rather than give up proclaiming the name of Jesus.

Entrance Antiphon Cf. Ps 65:1-2
Cry out with joy to God, all the earth;
O sing to the glory of his name.
O render him glorious praise, alleluia.

The Gloria in excelsis (Glory to God in the highest) is said.

Collect
May your people exult for ever, O God,
in renewed youthfulness of spirit,
so that, rejoicing now in the restored glory of our adoption,
we may look forward in confident hope
to the rejoicing of the day of resurrection.
Through our Lord Jesus Christ, your Son,
who lives and reigns with you in the unity of the Holy Spirit,
one God, for ever and ever.
Amen.

FIRST READING

A reading from the Acts of the Apostles   5:27-32. 40-41

The high priest demanded an explanation of the apostles. 'We gave you a formal warning,' he said 'not to preach in this name, and what have you done? You have filled Jerusalem with your teaching, and seem determined to fix the guilt of this man's death on us.' In reply Peter and the apostles said, 'Obedience to God comes before obedience to men; it was the God of our ancestors who raised up Jesus, but it was you who had him executed by hanging on a tree. By his own right hand God has now raised him up to be leader and saviour, to give repentance and forgiveness of sins through him to Israel. We are witnesses to all this, we and the Holy Spirit whom God has given to those who obey him.'

They warned the apostles not to speak in the name of Jesus and released them. And so they left the presence of the Sanhedrin glad to have had the honour of suffering humiliation for the sake of the name.

The word of the Lord.

Responsorial Psalm   Ps 29:2. 4-6. 11-13. ℟ v.2

℟ **I will praise you, Lord,**
    you have rescued me.

or

℟ **Alleluia!**

1 I will praise you, Lord, you have rescued me
    and have not let my enemies rejoice over me.
    O Lord, you have raised my soul from the dead,
    restored me to life from those who sink into the grave.   ℟

2 Sing psalms to the Lord, you who love him,
    give thanks to his holy name.
    His anger lasts but a moment; his favour through life.
    At night there are tears, but joy comes with dawn.   ℟

3 The Lord listened and had pity.
    The Lord came to my help.
    For me you have changed my mourning into dancing;
    O Lord my God, I will thank you for ever.   ℟

SECOND READING
A reading from the book of the Apocalypse   5:11-14

In my vision, I, John, heard the sound of an immense number of angels gathered round the throne and the animals and the elders; there were ten thousand times ten thousand of them and thousands upon thousands, shouting, 'The Lamb that was sacrificed is worthy to be given power, riches, wisdom, strength, honour, glory and blessing.' Then I heard all the living things in creation – everything that lives in the air, and on the ground, and under the ground, and in the sea, crying, 'To the One who is sitting on the throne and to the Lamb, be all praise, honour, glory and power, for ever and ever. Amen.' And the four animals said, 'Amen'; and the elders prostrated themselves to worship.

The word of the Lord.

Gospel Acclamation   Cf. Lk 24:32
Alleluia, alleluia!
Lord Jesus, explain the scriptures to us.
Make our hearts burn within us as you talk to us.
Alleluia!

or

Alleluia, alleluia!
Christ has risen: he who created all things,
and has granted his mercy to men.
Alleluia!

GOSPEL
A reading from the holy Gospel according to John   21:1-19

*Jesus showed himself again to the disciples. It was by the Sea of Tiberias, and it happened like this: Simon Peter, Thomas called the Twin, Nathanael from Cana in Galilee, the sons of Zebedee and two more of his disciples were together. Simon Peter said, 'I'm going fishing.' They replied, 'We'll come with you.' They went out and got into the boat but caught nothing that night.

It was light by now and there stood Jesus on the shore, though the disciples did not realise that it was Jesus. Jesus called out, 'Have you caught anything, friends?' And when they answered, 'No', he said, 'Throw the net out to starboard and you'll find something.' So they dropped the net, and there were so many fish that they could not haul it in. The disciple Jesus loved said to Peter, 'It is the Lord.' At these words 'It is the Lord', Simon Peter, who had practically nothing on, wrapped his cloak round him and jumped into the water. The other disciples came on in the boat, towing the net and the fish; they were only about a hundred yards from land.

As soon as they came ashore they saw that there was some bread there, and a charcoal fire with fish cooking on it. Jesus said, 'Bring some of the fish you have just caught.' Simon Peter went aboard and dragged the net to the shore, full of big fish, one hundred and fifty-three of them; and in spite of there being so many the net was not broken. Jesus said to them, 'Come and have breakfast.' None of the disciples was bold enough to ask, 'Who are you?'; they knew quite well it was the Lord. Jesus then stepped forward, took the bread and gave it to them, and the same with the fish. This was the third time that Jesus showed himself to the disciples after rising from the dead.*

After the meal Jesus said to Simon Peter, 'Simon son of John, do you love me more than these others do?' He answered, 'Yes Lord, you know I love you.' Jesus said to him, 'Feed my lambs.' A second time he said to him, 'Simon son of John, do you love me?' He replied 'Yes, Lord, you know I love you.' Jesus said to him, 'Look after my sheep.' Then he said to him a third time, 'Simon son of John, do you love me?' Peter was upset that he asked him the third time, 'Do you love me?' and said, 'Lord, you know everything; you know I love you.' Jesus said to him, 'Feed my sheep.

'I tell you most solemnly,
when you were young
you put on your own belt
and walked where you liked;
but when you grow old
you will stretch out your hands,
and somebody else will put a belt round you
and take you where you would rather not go.'

In these words he indicated the kind of death by which Peter would give glory to God. After this he said, 'Follow me.'

The Gospel of the Lord.

Shorter Form, verses 1-14. Read between

The Creed is said.

Prayer over the Offerings
Receive, O Lord, we pray,
these offerings of your exultant Church,
and, as you have given her cause for such great gladness,

grant also that the gifts we bring
may bear fruit in perpetual happiness.
Through Christ our Lord.
Amen.

An appropriate Preface of Easter, pp.28-30.

Communion Antiphon Lk 24:35
The disciples recognized the Lord Jesus
in the breaking of the bread, alleluia.

Optional for Year C: Cf. Jn 21:12-13
Jesus said to his disciples: Come and eat.
And he took bread and gave it to them, alleluia.

Prayer after Communion
Look with kindness upon your people, O Lord,
and grant, we pray,
that those you were pleased to renew by eternal mysteries
may attain in their flesh
the incorruptible glory of the resurrection.
Through Christ our Lord.
Amen.

A formula of Solemn Blessing, p.97, may be used.

FOURTH SUNDAY OF EASTER C

The Lamb Will Be Our Shepherd

We offer in sacrifice the Lamb that takes away the sins of the world. He who was slain is now our Shepherd. He will lead to springs of living water all who do not reject him.

Entrance Antiphon Cf. Ps 32:5-6
The merciful love of the Lord fills the earth;
by the word of the Lord the heavens were made, alleluia.

The Gloria in excelsis (Glory to God in the highest) is said.

Collect
Almighty ever-living God,
lead us to a share in the joys of heaven,
so that the humble flock may reach
where the brave Shepherd has gone before.

Fourth Sunday of Easter, Year C

Who lives and reigns with you in the unity of the Holy Spirit,
one God, for ever and ever.
Amen.

FIRST READING

A reading from the Acts of the Apostles   13:14. 43-52

Paul and Barnabas carried on from Perga till they reached Antioch in Pisidia. Here they went to synagogue on the sabbath and took their seats.

When the meeting broke up, many Jews and devout converts joined Paul and Barnabas, and in their talks with them Paul and Barnabas urged them to remain faithful to the grace God had given them.

The next sabbath almost the whole town assembled to hear the word of God. When they saw the crowds, the Jews, prompted by jealousy, used blasphemies and contradicted everything Paul said. Then Paul and Barnabas spoke out boldly, 'We had to proclaim the word of God to you first, but since you have rejected it, since you do not think yourselves worthy of eternal life, we must turn to the pagans. For this is what the Lord commanded us to do when he said:

> I have made you a light for the nations,
> so that my salvation may reach the ends of the earth.'

It made the pagans very happy to hear this and they thanked the Lord for his message; all who were destined for eternal life became believers. Thus the word of the Lord spread through the whole countryside.

But the Jews worked upon some of the devout women of the upper classes and the leading men of the city and persuaded them to turn against Paul and Barnabas and expel them from their territory. So they shook the dust from their feet in defiance and went off to Iconium; but the disciples were filled with joy and the Holy Spirit.

The word of the Lord.

Responsorial Psalm   Ps 99:1-3. 5. ℟ v.3

   ℟   **We are his people, the sheep of his flock.**

or

        Alleluia!

1. Cry out with joy to the Lord, all the earth.
   Serve the Lord with gladness.
   Come before him, singing for joy. ℟

2. Know that he, the Lord, is God.
   He made us, we belong to him,
   we are his people, the sheep of his flock. ℟

3. Indeed, how good is the Lord,
   eternal his merciful love.
   He is faithful from age to age. ℟

SECOND READING

A reading from the book of the Apocalypse   7:9. 14-17

I, John, saw a huge number, impossible to count, of people from every nation, race, tribe and language; they were standing in front of the throne and in front of the Lamb, dressed in white robes and holding palms in their hands. One of the elders said to me, 'These are the people who have been through the great persecution, and because they have washed their robes white again in the blood of the Lamb, they now stand in front of God's throne and serve him day and night in his sanctuary; and the One who sits on the throne will spread his tent over them. They will never hunger or thirst again; neither the sun nor scorching wind will ever plague them, because the Lamb who is at the throne will be their shepherd and will lead them to springs of living water; and God will wipe away all tears from their eyes.'

The word of the Lord.

Gospel Acclamation   Jn 10:14
Alleluia, alleluia!
I am the good shepherd, says the Lord;
I know my own sheep and my own know me.
Alleluia!

GOSPEL

A reading from the holy Gospel according to John   10:27-30

Jesus said:

'The sheep that belong to me listen to my voice;
I know them and they follow me.

I give them eternal life;
they will never be lost
and no one will ever steal them from me.
The Father who gave them to me is greater than anyone,
and no one can steal them from the Father.
The Father and I are one.'

The Gospel of the Lord.

The Creed is said.

Prayer over the Offerings
Grant, we pray, O Lord,
that we may always find delight in these paschal mysteries,
so that the renewal constantly at work within us
may be the cause of our unending joy.
Through Christ our Lord.
Amen.

An appropriate Preface of Easter, pp.28-30.

Communion Antiphon
The Good Shepherd has risen,
who laid down his life for his sheep
and willingly died for his flock, alleluia.

Prayer after Communion
Look upon your flock, kind Shepherd,
and be pleased to settle in eternal pastures
the sheep you have redeemed
by the Precious Blood of your Son.
Who lives and reigns for ever and ever.
Amen.

A formula of Solemn Blessing, p.97, may be used.

FIFTH SUNDAY OF EASTER C

The New Creation

At this season, Christ puts fresh heart in us, so that we may spread his kingdom. He gives us his new commandment of love and encourages us with the promise of the new Jerusalem.

Fifth Sunday of Easter, Year C

Entrance Antiphon   Cf. Ps 97:1-2
O sing a new song to the Lord,
for he has worked wonders;
in the sight of the nations
he has shown his deliverance, alleluia.

The Gloria in excelsis (Glory to God in the highest) is said.

Collect
Almighty ever-living God,
constantly accomplish the Paschal Mystery within us,
that those you were pleased to make new in Holy Baptism
may, under your protective care, bear much fruit
and come to the joys of life eternal.
Through our Lord Jesus Christ, your Son,
who lives and reigns with you in the unity of the Holy Spirit,
one God, for ever and ever.
Amen.

FIRST READING

A reading from the Acts of the Apostles   14:21-27

Paul and Barnabas went back through Lystra and Iconium to Antioch. They put fresh heart into the disciples, encouraging them to persevere in the faith. 'We all have to experience many hardships' they said 'before we enter the kingdom of God.' In each of these churches they appointed elders, and with prayer and fasting they commended them to the Lord in whom they had come to believe.

They passed through Pisidia and reached Pamphylia. Then after proclaiming the word at Perga they went down to Attalia and from there sailed for Antioch, where they had originally been commended to the grace of God for the work they had now completed.

On their arrival they assembled the church and gave an account of all that God had done with them, and how he had opened the door of faith to the pagans.

The word of the Lord.

Responsorial Psalm   Ps 144:8-13. ℟ cf. v.1
   ℟ **I will bless your name for ever, O God my King.**

or
   ℟ **Alleluia!**

1. The Lord is kind and full of compassion,
   slow to anger, abounding in love.
   How good is the Lord to all,
   compassionate to all his creatures. ℟

2. All your creatures shall thank you, O Lord,
   and your friends shall repeat their blessing.
   They shall speak of the glory of your reign
   and declare your might, O God,
   to make known to men your mighty deeds
   and the glorious splendour of your reign. ℟

3. Yours is an everlasting kingdom;
   your rule lasts from age to age. ℟

SECOND READING

A reading from the book of the Apocalypse   21:1-5

I, John, saw a new heaven and a new earth; the first heaven and the first earth had disappeared now, and there was no longer any sea. I saw the holy city, and the new Jerusalem, coming down from God out of heaven, as beautiful as a bride all dressed for her husband. Then I heard a loud voice call from the throne, 'You see this city? Here God lives among men. He will make his home among them; they shall be his people, and he will be their God; his name is God-with-them. He will wipe away all tears from their eyes; there will be no more death, and no more mourning or sadness. The world of the past has gone.'

Then the One sitting on the throne spoke: 'Now I am making the whole of creation new'.

The word of the Lord.

Gospel Acclamation   Jn 13:34
    Alleluia, alleluia!
    Jesus said: 'I give you a new commandment:
    love one another, just as I have loved you.'
    Alleluia!

GOSPEL

A reading from the holy Gospel according to John   13:31-35

When Judas had gone Jesus said:
'Now has the Son of Man been glorified,
and in him God has been glorified.

If God has been glorified in him,
God will in turn glorify him in himself,
and will glorify him very soon.
My little children,
I shall not be with you much longer.
I give you a new commandment:
love one another;
just as I have loved you,
you also must love one another.
By this love you have for one another,
everyone will know that you are my disciples.'

The Gospel of the Lord.

The Creed is said.

Prayer over the Offerings
O God, who by the wonderful exchange effected in this sacrifice
have made us partakers of the one supreme Godhead,
grant, we pray,
that, as we have come to know your truth,
we may make it ours by a worthy way of life.
Through Christ our Lord.
Amen.

An appropriate Preface of Easter, pp.28-30.

Communion Antiphon
Cf. Jn 15:1. 5
I am the true vine and you are the branches, says the Lord.
Whoever remains in me, and I in him, bears fruit in plenty,
    alleluia.

Prayer after Communion
Graciously be present to your people, we pray, O Lord,
and lead those you have imbued with heavenly mysteries
to pass from former ways to newness of life.
Through Christ our Lord.
Amen.

A formula of Solemn Blessing, p.97, may be used.

SIXTH SUNDAY OF EASTER   C

The Radiant Glory of God

The Holy Spirit is the radiant glory of God that enlightens the Church and guides it on its way through the world in all its decision.

Entrance Antiphon   Cf. Is 48:20
Proclaim a joyful sound and let it be heard;
proclaim to the ends of the earth:
The Lord has freed his people, alleluia.

The Gloria in excelsis (Glory to God in the highest) is said.

Collect
Grant, almighty God,
that we may celebrate with heartfelt devotion these days of joy,
which we keep in honour of the risen Lord,
and that what we relive in remembrance
we may always hold to in what we do.
Through our Lord Jesus Christ, your Son,
who lives and reigns with you in the unity of the Holy Spirit,
one God, for ever and ever.
Amen.

FIRST READING
A reading from the Acts of the Apostles   15:1-2. 22-29

Some men came down from Judaea and taught the brothers, 'Unless you have yourselves circumcised in the tradition of Moses you cannot be saved.' This led to disagreement, and after Paul and Barnabas had had a long argument with these men it was arranged that Paul and Barnabas and others of the church should go up to Jerusalem and discuss the problem with the apostles and elders.

Then the apostles and elders decided to choose delegates to send to Antioch with Paul and Barnabas; the whole church concurred with this. They chose Judas known as Barsabbas and Silas, both leading men in the brotherhood, and gave them this letter to take with them:

'The apostles and elders, your brothers, send greetings to the brothers of pagan birth in Antioch, Syria and Cilicia. We hear that some of our members have disturbed you with their demands and have unsettled your minds. They acted without any authority from us, and so we have decided unanimously to elect delegates and to send them to you with Barnabas and Paul, men we highly respect who have dedicated their lives to the name of our Lord Jesus Christ. Accordingly we are sending you Judas and Silas, who will confirm by word of mouth what we have written in this letter. It has been decided by the Holy Spirit and by ourselves not to saddle you with any burden beyond these essentials: you are to abstain from food sacrificed to idols, from blood, from the meat of strangled animals and from fornication. Avoid these, and you will do what is right. Farewell.'

The word of the Lord.

Responsional Psalm Ps 66:2-3. 5-6. 8. ℟ v.4

℟ **Let the peoples praise you, O God;**
  let all the peoples praise you.

or

℟ **Alleluia!**

1 O God, be gracious and bless us
  and let your face shed its light upon us.
  So will your ways be known upon earth.
  and all nations learn your saving help. ℟

2 Let the nations be glad and exult
  for you rule the world with justice.
  With fairness you rule the peoples,
  you guide the nations on earth. ℟

3 Let the peoples praise you, O God;
  let all the peoples praise you.
  May God still give us his blessing
  till the ends of the earth revere him. ℟

When the Ascension of the Lord is celebrated on the Seventh Sunday of Easter, the Second Reading and Gospel assigned to the Seventh Sunday (see below, pp.889-91ff.) may be read on the Sixth Sunday.

SECOND READING

A reading from the book of the Apocalypse 21:10-14. 22-23

In the spirit, the angel took me to the top of an enormous high mountain and showed me Jerusalem, the holy city, coming down from God out of heaven. It had all the radiant glory of God and glittered like some precious jewel of crystal-clear diamond. The walls of it were of a great height, and had twelve gates; at each of the twelve gates there was an angel, and over the gates were written the names of the twelve tribes of Israel; on the east there were three gates, on the north three gates, on the south three gates, and on the west three gates. The city walls stood on twelve foundation stones, each one of which bore the name of one of the twelve apostles of the Lamb.

I saw that there was no temple in the city since the Lord God Almighty and the Lamb were themselves the temple, and the city did not need the sun or the moon for light, since it was lit by the radiant glory of God and the Lamb was a lighted torch for it.

The word of the Lord.

Gospel Acclamation Jn 14:23
Alleluia, alleluia!
Jesus said: 'If anyone loves me he will keep my word,
and my Father will love him, and we shall come to him.
Alleluia!

GOSPEL
A reading from the holy Gospel according to John 14:23-29

Jesus said to his disciples:

'If anyone loves me he will keep my word,
and my Father will love him,
and we shall come to him
and make our home with him.
Those who do not love me do not keep my words.
And my word is not my own:
it is the word of the one who sent me.
I have said these things to you
while still with you;
but the Advocate, the Holy Spirit,
whom the Father will send in my name,
will teach you everything
and remind you of all I have said to you.
Peace I bequeath to you,
my own peace I give you,
a peace the world cannot give, this is my gift to you.
Do not let your hearts be troubled or afraid.
You heard me say:
I am going away, and shall return.
If you loved me you would have been glad to know that I am

going to the Father,
for the Father is greater than I.
I have told you this now before it happens,
so that when it does happen you may believe.'

The Gospel of the Lord.

The Creed is said.

Prayer over the Offerings
May our prayers rise up to you, O Lord,
together with the sacrificial offerings,
so that, purified by your graciousness,
we may be conformed to the mysteries of your mighty love.
Through Christ our Lord.
Amen.

An appropriate Preface of Easter, pp.28-30.

Communion Antiphon Jn 14:15-16
If you love me, keep my commandments, says the Lord,
and I will ask the Father and he will send you another Paraclete,
to abide with you for ever, alleluia.

Prayer after Communion
Almighty ever-living God,
who restore us to eternal life in the Resurrection of Christ,
increase in us, we pray, the fruits of this paschal Sacrament
and pour into our hearts the strength of this saving food.
Through Christ our Lord.
Amen.

A formula of Solemn Blessing, p.97, may be used.

THE ASCENSION OF THE LORD C
Solemnity

Christ's Eternal Glory

Today we celebrate Christ's ascension to his eternal glory in heaven and express our Christian hope that where he, our Head, has gone before us, we, his Body, will one day follow, to live for ever in the Kingdom of our Father.

Where the Solemnity of the Ascension is not to be observed as a Holyday of Obligation, it is assigned to the Seventh Sunday of Easter as its proper day.

The Ascension of the Lord, Year C

At the Vigil Mass

This Mass is used on the evening of the day before the Solemnity, either before or after First Vespers (Evening Prayer I) of the Ascension.

Entrance Antiphon — Ps 67:33. 35
You kingdoms of the earth, sing to God;
praise the Lord, who ascends above the highest heavens;
his majesty and might are in the skies, alleluia.

The Gloria in excelsis (Glory to God in the highest) is said.

Collect
O God, whose Son today ascended to the heavens
as the Apostles looked on,
grant, we pray, that, in accordance with his promise,
we may be worthy for him to live with us always on earth,
and we with him in heaven.
Who lives and reigns with you in the unity of the Holy Spirit,
one God, for ever and ever.
Amen.

For the Readings, Gospel Acclamation and Gospel, see the Mass during the Day (pp.884ff).

The Creed is said.

Prayer over the Offerings
O God, whose Only Begotten Son, our High Priest,
is seated ever-living at your right hand to intercede for us,
grant that we may approach with confidence the throne of grace
and there obtain your mercy.
Through Christ our Lord.
Amen.

Preface I or II of the Ascension, p.31.

When the Roman Canon is used, the proper form of the Communicantes (In communion with those) is said.

Communion Antiphon — Cf. Heb 10:12
Christ, offering a single sacrifice for sins,
is seated for ever at God's right hand, alleluia.

Prayer after Communion
May the gifts we have received from your altar, Lord,
kindle in our hearts a longing for the heavenly homeland
and cause us to press forward, following in the Saviour's
    footsteps,
to the place where for our sake he entered before us.
Who lives and reigns for ever and ever.
Amen.

A formula of Solemn Blessing, pp.97-8, may be used.

At the Mass during the Day

Entrance Antiphon Acts 1:11
Men of Galilee, why gaze in wonder at the heavens?
This Jesus whom you saw ascending into heaven
will return as you saw him go, alleluia.

The Gloria in excelsis (Glory to God in the highest) is said.

Collect
Gladden us with holy joys, almighty God,
and make us rejoice with devout thanksgiving,
for the Ascension of Christ your Son
is our exaltation,
and, where the Head has gone before in glory,
the Body is called to follow in hope.
Through our Lord Jesus Christ, your Son,
who lives and reigns with you in the unity of the Holy Spirit,
one God, for ever and ever.

or

Grant, we pray, almighty God,
that we, who believe that your Only Begotten Son, our Redeemer,
ascended this day to the heavens,
may in spirit dwell already in heavenly realms.
Who lives and reigns with you in the unity of the Holy Spirit,
one God, for ever and ever.
Amen.

FIRST READING
A reading from the Acts of the Apostles 1:1-11

In my earlier work, Theophilus, I dealt with everything Jesus had done and taught from the beginning until the day he gave his instructions to the apostles he had chosen through the Holy Spirit, and was taken up to heaven. He had shown himself alive to them after his Passion by many demonstrations: for forty days he had continued to appear to them and tell them about the kingdom of God. When he had been at table with them, he had told them not to leave Jerusalem, but to wait there for what the Father had promised. 'It is,' he had said, 'what you have heard me speak about: John baptised with water but you, not many days from now, will be baptised with the Holy Spirit.'

Now having met together, they asked him, 'Lord, has the time come? Are you going to restore the kingdom to Israel?' He replied, 'It is not for you to know times or dates that the Father has decided by his own authority, but you will receive power when the Holy Spirit comes on you, and then you will be my witnesses not only in Jerusalem but throughout Judaea and Samaria, and indeed to the ends of the earth.'

As he said this he was lifted up while they looked on, and a cloud took him from their sight. They were still staring into the sky when suddenly two men in white were standing near them and they said, 'Why are you men from Galilee standing here looking into the sky? Jesus who has been taken up from you into heaven, this same Jesus will come back in the same way as you have seen him go there.'

The word of the Lord.

Responsorial Psalm　　　　　　　　　　Ps 46:2-3. 6-7. 8-9. ℟ v.6

℟　**God goes up with shouts of joy;**
the Lord goes up with trumpet blast.

or

℟　**Alleluia!**

1　All peoples, clap your hands,
　　cry to God with shouts of joy!
　　For the Lord, the Most High, we must fear,
　　great king over all the earth.　℟

2　God goes up with shouts of joy;
　　the Lord goes up with trumpet blast.
　　Sing praise for God, sing praise,
　　sing praise to our king, sing praise.　℟

3　God is king of all the earth.
　　Sing praise with all your skill.

God is king over the nations;
God reigns on his holy throne. ℟

SECOND READING

A reading from the letter of St Paul to the Ephesians   1:17-23

May the God of our Lord Jesus Christ, the Father of glory, give you a spirit of wisdom and perception of what is revealed, to bring you to full knowledge of him. May he enlighten the eyes of your mind so that you can see what hope his call holds for you, what rich glories he has promised the saints will inherit and how infinitely great is the power that he has exercised for us believers. This you can tell from the strength of his power at work in Christ, when he used it to raise him from the dead and to make him sit at his right hand, in heaven, far above every Sovereignty, Authority, Power, or Domination, or any other name that can be named, not only in this age, but also in the age to come. He has put all things under his feet, and made him, as the ruler of everything, the head of the Church; which is his body, the fullness of him who fills the whole creation.

The word of the Lord.

Optional Second Reading for Year C

A reading from the letter to the Hebrews   9:24-28; 10:19-23

It is not as though Christ had entered a man-made sanctuary which was only modelled on the real one; but it was heaven itself, so that he could appear in the actual presence of God on our behalf. And he does not have to offer himself again and again, like the high priest going into the sanctuary year after year with the blood that is not his own, or else he would have had to suffer over and over again since the world began. Instead of that, he has made his appearance once and for all, now at the end of the last age, to do away with sin by sacrificing himself. Since men only die once, and after that comes judgement, so Christ, too, offers himself only once to take the faults of many on himself, and when he appears a second time, it will not be to deal with sin but to reward with salvation those who are waiting for him.

In other words, brothers, through the blood of Jesus we have the right to enter the sanctuary, by a new way which he had opened for us, a living opening through the curtain, that is to say, his body. And we have the supreme high priest over all the house of God. So as we go in, let us be sincere in heart and filled with faith, our minds sprinkled and free from any trace of bad conscience and our bodies washed with pure water. Let us keep firm in the hope we profess, because the one who made the promise is faithful.

The word of the Lord.

Gospel Acclamation Mt 28:19-20
Alleluia, alleluia!
Go, make disciples of all the nations;
I am with you always; yes, to the end of time.
Alleluia!

GOSPEL
A reading from the holy Gospel according to Luke 24:46-53

Jesus said to his disciples: 'You see how it is written that the Christ would suffer and on the third day rise from the dead, and that, in his name, repentance for the forgiveness of sins would be preached to all the nations, beginning from Jerusalem. You are witnesses to this.

'And now I am sending down to you what the Father has promised. Stay in the city then, until you are clothed with the power from on high.' Then he took them out as far as the outskirts of Bethany, and lifting up his hands he blessed them. Now as he blessed them, he withdrew from them and was carried up to heaven. They worshipped him and then went back to Jerusalem full of joy; and they were continually in the Temple praising God.

The Gospel of the Lord.

The Creed is said.

Prayer over the Offerings
We offer sacrifice now in supplication, O Lord,
to honour the wondrous Ascension of your Son:
grant, we pray,
that through this most holy exchange
we, too, may rise up to the heavenly realms.
Through Christ our Lord.
Amen.

Preface I or II of the Ascension of the Lord, p.31.

When the Roman Canon is used, the proper form of the Communicantes (In communion with those) is said.

Communion Antiphon Mt 28:20
Behold, I am with you always,
even to the end of the age, alleluia.

Prayer after Communion
Almighty ever-living God,
who allow those on earth to celebrate divine mysteries,
grant, we pray,
that Christian hope may draw us onward
to where our nature is united with you.
Through Christ our Lord.
Amen.

A formula of Solemn Blessing, pp.97-8, may be used.

SEVENTH SUNDAY OF EASTER C

Where the Ascension is not a holiday of obligation, it is celebrated on this Sunday.

The Spirit and the Bride

The Church is wedded to Christ in the love of the Spirit and looks forward to the final fulfilment of that love in the glory of heaven.

Entrance Antiphon Cf. Ps 26:7-9
O Lord, hear my voice, for I have called to you;
of you my heart has spoken: Seek his face;
hide not your face from me, alleluia.

The Gloria in excelsis (Glory to God in the highest) is said.

Collect
Graciously hear our supplications, O Lord,
so that we, who believe that the Saviour of the human race
is with you in your glory,
may experience, as he promised,
until the end of the world,
his abiding presence among us.
Who lives and reigns with you in the unity of the Holy Spirit,
one God, for ever and ever.
Amen.

FIRST READING
A reading from the Acts of the Apostles 7:55-60

Stephen, filled with the Holy Spirit, gazed into heaven and saw the glory of God, and Jesus standing at God's right hand. 'I can see heaven thrown open' he said 'and the Son of Man standing at the right hand of God.' At this all the members of the council shouted out and stopped their ears with their hands; then they all rushed at him, sent him out of the city and stoned him. The witnesses put down their clothes at the feet of a young man called Saul. As they were stoning him, Stephen said in invocation, 'Lord Jesus, receive my spirit.' Then he knelt down and said aloud, 'Lord, do not hold this sin against them'; and with these words he fell asleep.

The word of the Lord.

Responsorial Psalm Ps 96:1-2. 6-7. 9. R/ vv.1. 9

  R/ **The Lord is king, most high above all the earth.**

or

  R/ **Alleluia!**

1. The Lord is king, let earth rejoice,
the many coastlands be glad.
His throne is justice and right. R/

2. The skies proclaim his justice;
all peoples see his glory.
All you spirits, worship him. R/

3. For you indeed are the Lord
most high above all the earth
exalted far above all spirits. R/

SECOND READING
A reading from the book of the Apocalypse 22:12-14. 16-17. 20

I, John, heard a voice speaking to me: 'Very soon now, I shall be with you again, bringing the reward to be given to every man according to what he deserves. I am the Alpha and the Omega, the First and the Last, the Beginning and the End. Happy are those who will have washed their robes clean, so that they will have the right to feed on the tree of life and can come through the gates into the city.'

I, Jesus, have sent my angel to make these revelations to you for the sake of the churches. I am of David's line, the root of David and the bright star of the morning.

The Spirit and the Bride say, 'Come.' Let everyone who listens answer, 'Come.' Then let all who are thirsty come; all who want it may have the water of life, and have it free. The one who guarantees these revelations repeats his promise: I shall indeed be with you soon. Amen; come, Lord Jesus.

The word of the Lord.

Gospel Acclamation   Cf. Jn 14:18
Alleluia, alleluia!
I will not leave you orphans, says the Lord;
I will come back to you, and your hearts will be full of joy.
Alleluia!

GOSPEL

A reading from the holy Gospel according to John   17:20-26

Jesus raised his eyes to heaven and said:
'Holy Father,
I pray not only for these,
but for those also
who through their words will believe in me.
May they all be one.
Father, may they be one in us,
as you are in me and I am in you,
so that the world may believe it was you who sent me.
I have given them the glory you gave to me,
that they may be one as we are one.
With me in them and you in me,
may they be so completely one
that the world will realise that it was you who sent me
and that I have loved them as much as you love me.
Father,
I want those you have given me
to be with me where I am,
so that they may always see the glory
you have given me
because you loved me
before the foundation of the world.
Father, Righteous One,
the world has not known you,
but I have known you,
and these have known
that you have sent me.
I have made your name known to them

and will continue to make it known,
so that the love with which you loved me may be in them,
and so that I may be in them.'

The Gospel of the Lord.

The Creed is said.

Prayer over the Offerings
Accept, O Lord, the prayers of your faithful
with the sacrificial offerings,
that through these acts of devotedness
we may pass over to the glory of heaven.
Through Christ our Lord.
Amen.

An appropriate Preface of Easter, or of the Ascension, pp.28-31.

Communion Antiphon   Jn 17:22
Father, I pray that they may be one
as we also are one, alleluia.

Prayer after Communion
Hear us, O God our Saviour,
and grant us confidence,
that through these sacred mysteries
there will be accomplished in the body of the whole Church
what has already come to pass in Christ her Head.
Who lives and reigns for ever and ever.
Amen.

A formula of Solemn Blessing, p.97-8, may be used.

PENTECOST SUNDAY   C
Solemnity

Simple and extended forms of the Vigil Mass, which is celebrated on Saturday evening, will be found under Year A, pp.456ff.

At the Mass during the Day

The Day of Pentecost

Today we celebrate the great day of Pentecost when Christ filled the Church with the power of his Spirit and sent it out into the world to bring his peace, joy and forgiveness to all people.

Pentecost Sunday, Year C

Entrance Antiphon   Wis 1:7
The Spirit of the Lord has filled the whole world
and that which contains all things
understands what is said, alleluia.

or   Rm 5:5; cf. 8:11

The love of God has been poured into our hearts
through the Spirit of God dwelling within us, alleluia.

The Gloria is excelsis (Glory or God is in the highest) is said.

Collect
O God, who by the mystery of today's great feast
sanctify your whole Church in every people and nation,
pour out, we pray, the gifts of the Holy Spirit
across the face of the earth
and, with the divine grace that was at work
when the Gospel was first proclaimed,
fill now once more the hearts of believers.
Through our Lord Jesus Christ, your Son,
who lives and reigns with you in the unity of the Holy Spirit,
one God, for ever and ever.
Amen.

FIRST READING
A reading from the Acts of the Apostles   2:1-11

When Pentecost day came round, the apostles had all met in one room, when suddenly they heard what sounded like a powerful wind from heaven, the noise of which filled the entire house in which they were sitting; and something appeared to them that seemed like tongues of fire; these separated and came to rest on the head of each of them. They were all filled with the Holy Spirit, and began to speak foreign languages as the Spirit gave them the gift of speech.

    Now there were devout men living in Jerusalem from every nation under heaven, and at this sound they all assembled, each one bewildered to hear these men speaking his own language. They were amazed and astonished. 'Surely' they said 'all these men speaking are Galileans? How does it happen that each of us hears them in his own native language? Parthians, Medes and Elamites; people from Mesopotamia, Judaea and Cappadocia, Pontus and Asia, Phrygia and Pamphylia, Egypt and the parts of Libya round Cyrene; as well as visitors from Rome – Jews and proselytes alike

– Cretans and Arabs; we hear them preaching in our own language about the marvels of God.'

The word of the Lord.

Responsorial Psalm   Ps 103:1. 24. 29-31. 34. ℟ cf v.30

℟ **Send forth your Spirit, O Lord,**
   and renew the face of the earth.

or

℟ **Alleluia.**

1. Bless the Lord, my soul!
Lord God, how great you are,
How many are your works, O Lord!
The earth is full of your riches. ℟

2. You take back your spirit, they die,
returning to the dust from which they came.
You send forth your spirit, they are created;
and you renew the face of the earth. ℟

3. May the glory of the Lord last for ever!
May the Lord rejoice in his works!
May my thoughts be pleasing to him.
I find my joy in the Lord. ℟

The Second Reading and Gospel may be taken from Year A, see above pp.468ff. Alternatively, the Second Reading and Gospel given below may be used.

SECOND READING

A reading from the letter of St Paul to the Romans   8:8-17

People who are interested only in unspiritual things can never be pleasing to God. Your interests, however, are not in the unspiritual, but in the spiritual, since the Spirit of God has made his home in you. In fact, unless you possessed the Spirit of Christ you would not belong to him. Though your body may be dead it is because of sin, but if Christ is in you then your spirit is life itself because you have been justified; and if the Spirit of him who raised Jesus from the dead is living in you, then he who raised Jesus from the dead will give life to your own mortal bodies through his Spirit living in you.

So then, my brothers, there is no necessity for us to obey our unspiritual selves or to live unspiritual lives. If you do live in that way, you are doomed to die; but if by the Spirit you put an end to the misdeeds of the body you will live.

Everyone moved by the Spirit is a son of God. The spirit you received is not the spirit of slaves bringing fear into your lives again; it is the spirit of sons, and it makes us cry out, 'Abba, Father!' The Spirit himself and our spirit bear united witness that we are children of God. And if we are children we are heirs as well: heirs of God and coheirs with Christ, sharing his sufferings so as to share his glory.

The word of the Lord.

SEQUENCE

The sequence may be said or sung.

Holy Spirit, Lord of light,
From the clear celestial height
Thy pure beaming radiance give.

Come, thou Father of the poor,
Come with treasures which endure;
Come, thou light of all that live!

Thou, of all consolers best,
Thou, the soul's delightful guest,
Dost refreshing peace bestow;

Thou in toil art comfort sweet;
Pleasant coolness in the heat;
Solace in the midst of woe.

Light immortal, light divine,
Visit thou these hearts of thine,
And our inmost being fill:

If thou take thy grace away,
Nothing pure in man will stay;
All his good is turned to ill.

Heal our wounds, our strength renew;
On our dryness pour thy dew;
Wash the stains of guilt away:

Bend the stubborn heart and will;
Melt the frozen, warm the chill;
Guide the steps that go astray.

Thou, on us who evermore
　　Thee confess and thee adore,
With thy sevenfold gifts descend:

Give us comfort when we die;
　　Give us life with thee on high;
Give us joys that never end.

Gospel Acclamation
　　Alleluia, alleluia!
　　Come, Holy Spirit, fill the hearts of your faithful
　　and kindle in them the fire of your love.
　　Alleluia!

GOSPEL

A reading from the holy Gospel according to John   14:15-16. 23-26

Jesus said to his disciples

'If you love me you will keep my commandments.
I shall ask the Father
and he will give you another Advocate
to be with you for ever.
If anyone loves me he will keep my word,
and my Father will love him,
and we shall come to him
and make our home with him.
Those who do not love me do not keep my words.
And my word is not my own;
it is the word of the one who sent me.
I have said these things to you
while still with you;
but the Advocate, the Holy Spirit,
whom the Father will send in my name,
will teach you everything
and remind you of all I have said to you.'

The Gospel of the Lord.

The Creed is said.

Prayer over the Offerings
Grant, we pray, O Lord,
that, as promised by your Son,
the Holy Spirit may reveal to us more abundantly
the hidden mystery of this sacrifice

and graciously lead us into all truth.
Through Christ our Lord.
Amen.

Preface of the Mystery of Pentecost, p.32.

When the Roman Canon is used, the proper form of the Communicantes (In communion with those) is said.

Communion Antiphon
Acts 2:4. 11

They were all filled with the Holy Spirit
and spoke of the marvels of God, alleluia.

Prayer after Communion
O God, who bestow heavenly gifts upon your Church,
safeguard, we pray, the grace you have given,
that the gift of the Holy Spirit poured out upon her
may retain all its force
and that this spiritual food
may gain her abundance of eternal redemption.
Through Christ our Lord.
Amen.

A formula of Solemn Blessing, p.98, may be used. To dismiss the people the Deacon or, if there is no Deacon, the Priest himself sings or says:

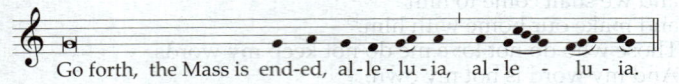

Go forth, the Mass is end-ed, al-le-lu-ia, al-le - lu-ia.

or

Go in peace, al-le-lu-ia, al-le - lu-ia.

Thanks be to God, al-le-lu-ia, al-le - lu-ia.

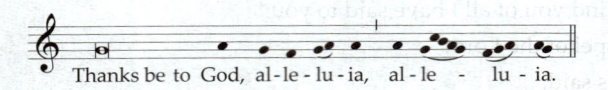

With Easter Time now concluded, the paschal candle is extinguished. It is desirable to keep the paschal candle in the baptistery with due honour so that it is lit at the celebration of Baptism and the candles of those baptized are lit from it.

ORDINARY TIME

Ordinary Time contains thirty-three or thirty-four weeks. It begins on the Monday following the Sunday after 6 January and continues until the beginning of Lent; it begins again on the Monday after Pentecost Sunday and ends on the Saturday before the First Sunday of Advent.

THE SOLEMNITIES OF THE LORD
DURING ORDINARY TIME

First Sunday after Pentecost
THE MOST HOLY TRINITY   C
Solemnity

Glory to the Father, the Son, and the Holy Spirit

The Spirit glorifies the Son of the eternal Father, and today we in the Spirit give glory to God, for the love of God has been poured into our hearts by the Holy Spirit who has been given to us.

Entrance Antiphon
Blest be God the Father,
and the Only Begotten Son of God,
and also the Holy Spirit,
for he has shown us his merciful love.

The Gloria in excelsis (Glory to God in the highest) is said.

Collect
God our Father, who by sending into the world
the Word of truth and the Spirit of sanctification
made known to the human race your wondrous mystery,
grant us, we pray, that in professing the true faith,
we may acknowledge the Trinity of eternal glory
and adore your Unity, powerful in majesty.
Through our Lord Jesus Christ, your Son,
who lives and reigns with you in the unity of the Holy Spirit,
one God, for ever and ever.
Amen.

FIRST READING

A reading from the book of Proverbs   8:22-31

The Wisdom of God cries aloud:

> The Lord created me when his purpose first unfolded,
> before the oldest of his works.
> From everlasting I was firmly set,
> from the beginning, before earth came into being.
> The deep was not, when I was born,
> there were no springs to gush with water.
> Before the mountains were settled,
> before the hills, I came to birth;
> before he made the earth, the countryside,
> or the first grains of the world's dust.
> When he fixed the heavens firm, I was there,
> when he drew a ring on the surface of the deep,
> when he thickened the clouds above,
> when he fixed fast the springs of the deep,
> when he assigned the sea its boundaries
> – and the waters will not invade the shore –
> when he laid down the foundations of the earth,
> I was by his side, a master craftsman,
> delighting him day after day,
> ever at play in his presence,
> at play everywhere in his world,
> delighting to be with the sons of men.

The word of the Lord.

Responsorial Psalm   Ps 8:4-9. ℟ v.2

℟ **How great is your name, O Lord our God,
through all the earth!**

1 When I see the heavens, the work of your hands,
the moon and the stars which you arranged,
what is man that you should keep him in mind,
mortal man that you care for him? ℟

2 Yet you have made him little less than a god;
with glory and honour you crowned him,
gave him power over the works of your hand,
put all things under his feet. ℟

3 All of them, sheep and cattle,
yes, even the savage beasts,

birds of the air, and fish
that make their way through the waters. ℟

SECOND READING
A reading from the letter of St Paul to the Romans 5:1-5

Through our Lord Jesus Christ, by faith we are judged righteous and at peace with God, since it is by faith and through Jesus that we have entered this state of grace in which we can boast about looking forward to God's glory. But that is not all we can boast about; we can boast about our sufferings. These sufferings bring patience, as we know, and patience brings perseverance, and perseverance brings hope, and this hope is not deceptive, because the love of God has been poured into our hearts by the Holy Spirit which has been given us.

The word of the Lord.

Gospel Acclamation Cf. Apoc 1:8
Alleluia, alleluia!
Glory be to the Father, and to the Son, and to the Holy Spirit,
the God who is, who was, and who is to come.
Alleluia!

GOSPEL
A reading from the holy Gospel according to John 16:12-15

Jesus said to his disciples:

'I still have many things to say to you
but they would be too much for you now.
But when the Spirit of truth comes
he will lead you to the complete truth,
since he will not be speaking as from himself
but will say only what he has learnt;
and he will tell you of the things to come.
He will glorify me
since all he tells you
will be taken from what is mine.
Everything the Father has is mine;
that is why I said:
All he tells you
will be taken from what is mine.'

The Gospel of the Lord.

The Creed is said.

Prayer over the Offerings
Sanctify by the invocation of your name,
we pray, O Lord our God,
this oblation of our service,
and by it make of us an eternal offering to you.
Through Christ our Lord.
Amen.

Preface of the Mystery of the Most Holy Trinity, p.36.

Communion Antiphon
Gal 4:6
Since you are children of God,
God has sent into your hearts the Spirit of his Son,
the Spirit who cries out: Abba, Father.

Prayer after Communion
May receiving this Sacrament, O Lord our God,
bring us health of body and soul,
as we confess your eternal holy Trinity and undivided Unity.
Through Christ our Lord.
Amen.

Thursday after the Most Holy Trinity
THE MOST HOLY BODY AND BLOOD OF CHRIST C
(CORPUS CHRISTI)
Solemnity

The Priesthood of Melchizedek

Like Melchizedek of old we bring bread and wine to the altar and Christ, through the action of the Holy Spirit, transforms it into his own body and blood so that we may all experience in ourselves the fruits of redemption

Where the Solemnity of the Most Holy Body and Blood of Christ is not a Holyday of Obligation, it is assigned to the Sunday after the Most Holy Trinity as its proper day.

Entrance Antiphon
Cf. Ps 80:17
He fed them with the finest wheat
and satisfied them with honey from the rock.

The Gloria in excelsis (Glory to God in the highest) is said.

Collect

O God, who in this wonderful Sacrament
have left us a memorial of your Passion,
grant us, we pray,
so to revere the sacred mysteries of your Body and Blood
that we may always experience in ourselves
the fruits of your redemption.
Who live and reign with God the Father
in the unity of the Holy Spirit,
one God, for ever and ever.
Amen.

FIRST READING

A reading from the book of Genesis 14:18-20

Melchizedek king of Salem brought bread and wine; he was a priest of God Most High. He pronounced this blessing:

'Blessed be Abraham by God Most High, creator of heaven
    and earth,
and blessed be God Most High for handing over your enemies
    to you.'

And Abraham gave him a tithe of everything.

The word of the Lord.

Responsorial Psalm   Ps 109:1-4. ℟ v.4

℟ **You are a priest for ever,
a priest like Melchizedek of old.**

1   The Lord's revelation to my Master:
    'Sit on my right:
    I will put your foes beneath your feet.' ℟

2   The Lord will send from Zion
    your sceptre of power:
    rule in the midst of all your foes. ℟

3   A prince from the day of your birth
    on the holy mountains;
    from the womb before the daybreak I begot you. ℟

4   The Lord has sworn an oath he will not change.
    'You are a priest for ever,
    a priest like Melchizedek of old.' ℟

SECOND READING

A reading from the first letter of St Paul 11:23-26
to the Corinthians

This is what I received from the Lord, and in turn passed on to you: that on the same night that he was betrayed, the Lord Jesus took some bread, and thanked God for it and broke it, and he said, 'This is my body, which is for you; do this as a memorial of me.' In the same way he took the cup after supper, and said, 'This cup is the new covenant in my blood. Whenever you drink it, do this as a memorial of me.' Until the Lord comes, therefore, every time you eat this bread and drink this cup, you are proclaiming his death.

The word of the Lord.

The sequence, Sing forth, O Zion, may be said or sung in its longer or shorter form. See above, pp.471ff.

Gospel Acclamation Jn 6:51-52

Alleluia, alleluia!
I am the living bread which has come down from heaven,
says the Lord.
Anyone who eats this bread will live for ever.
Alleluia!

GOSPEL

A reading from the holy Gospel according to Luke 9:11-17

Jesus made the crowds welcome and talked to them about the kingdom of God; and he cured those who were in need of healing.

It was late afternoon when the Twelve came to him and said, 'Send the people away, and they can go to the villages and farms round about to find lodging and food; for we are in a lonely place here.' He replied, 'Give them something to eat yourselves.' But they said, 'We have no more than five loaves and two fish, unless we are to go ourselves and buy food for all these people.' For there were about five thousand men. But he said to his disciples, 'Get them to sit down in parties of about fifty.' They did so and made them all sit down. Then he took the five loaves and the two fish, raised his eyes to heaven, and said the blessing over them; then he broke them and handed them to his disciples to distribute among the crowd. They all ate as much as they wanted, and when the scraps remaining were collected they filled twelve baskets.

The Gospel of the Lord.

The Creed is said.

Prayer over the Offerings
Grant your Church, O Lord, we pray,
the gifts of unity and peace,
whose signs are to be seen in mystery
in the offerings we here present.
Through Christ our Lord.
Amen.

Preface I or II of the Most Holy Eucharist, pp.38-9.

Communion Antiphon — Jn 6:57
Whoever eats my flesh and drinks my blood
remains in me and I in him, says the Lord.

Prayer after Communion
Grant, O Lord, we pray,
that we may delight for all eternity
in that share in your divine life,
which is foreshadowed in the present age
by our reception of your precious Body and Blood.
Who live and reign for ever and ever.
Amen.

It is desirable that a procession take place after the Mass in which the Host to be carried in the procession is consecrated. However, nothing prohibits a procession from taking place even after a public and lengthy period of adoration following the Mass. If a procession takes place after Mass, when the Communion of the faithful is over, the monstrance in which the consecrated host has been placed is set on the altar. When the Prayer after Communion has been said, the Concluding Rites are omitted and the procession forms.

Friday after the Second Sunday after Pentecost
THE MOST SACRED HEART OF JESUS   C
Solemnity

The Heart of the Shepherd

We celebrate the love of Christ the Good Shepherd who gave his life for his sheep and continually guides us along the right path.

Entrance Antiphon   Ps 32:11. 19
The designs of his Heart are from age to age,
to rescue their souls from death,
and to keep them alive in famine.

The Gloria in excelsis (Glory to God in the highest) is said.

Collect
Grant, we pray, almighty God,
that we, who glory in the Heart of your beloved Son
and recall the wonders of his love for us,
may be made worthy to receive
an overflowing measure of grace
from that fount of heavenly gifts.
Through our Lord Jesus Christ, your Son,
who lives and reigns with you in the unity of the Holy Spirit,
one God, for ever and ever.
Amen.

or

O God, who in the Heart of your Son,
wounded by our sins,
bestow on us in mercy
the boundless treasures of your love,
grant, we pray,
that, in paying him the homage of our devotion,
we may also offer worthy reparation.
Through our Lord Jesus Christ, your Son,
who lives and reigns with you in the unity of the Holy Spirit,
one God, for ever and ever.
Amen.

The Most Sacred Heart of Jesus, Year C 905

FIRST READING
A reading from the prophet Ezekiel 34:11-16

The Lord God says this: I am going to look after my flock myself and keep all of it in view. As a shepherd keeps all his flock in view when he stands up in the middle of his scattered sheep, so shall I keep my sheep in view. I shall rescue them from wherever they have been scattered during the mist and darkness. I shall bring them out of the countries where they are; I shall gather them together from foreign countries and bring them back to their own land. I shall pasture them on the mountains of Israel, in the ravines and in every inhabited place in the land. I shall feed them in good pasturage; the high mountains of Israel will be their grazing ground. There they will rest in good grazing ground; they will browse in rich pastures on the mountains of Israel. I myself will pasture my sheep, I myself will show them where to rest – it is the Lord who speaks. I shall look for the lost one, bring back the stray, bandage the wounded and make the weak strong. I shall watch over the fat and healthy. I shall be a true shepherd to them.

The word of the Lord.

Responsorial Psalm Ps 22. ℟ v.1
℟ **The Lord is my shepherd;**
there is nothing I shall want.

1 The Lord is my shepherd;
   there is nothing I shall want.
   Fresh and green are the pastures
   where he gives me repose.
   Near restful waters he leads me,
   to revive my drooping spirit. ℟

2 He guides me along the right path;
   he is true to his name.
   If I should walk in the valley of darkness
   no evil would I fear.
   You are there with your crook and your staff;
   with these you give me comfort. ℟

3 You have prepared a banquet for me
   in the sight of my foes.
   My head you have anointed with oil;
   my cup is overflowing. ℟

4 Surely goodness and kindness shall follow me
   all the days of my life.
   In the Lord's own house shall I dwell
   for ever and ever. ℟

SECOND READING
A reading from the letter of St Paul to the Romans   5:5-11

The love of God has been poured into our hearts by the Holy Spirit which has been given us. We were still helpless when at his appointed moment Christ died for sinful men. It is not easy to die even for a good man – though of course for someone really worthy, a man might be prepared to die – but what proves that God loves us is that Christ died for us while we were still sinners. Having died to make us righteous, is it likely that he would now fail to save us from God's anger? When we were reconciled to God by the death of his Son, we were still enemies; now that we have been reconciled, surely we may count on being saved by the life of his Son? Not merely because we have been reconciled but because we are filled with joyful trust in God, through our Lord Jesus Christ, through whom we have already gained our reconciliation.

   The word of the Lord.

Gospel Acclamation   Mt 11:29
   Alleluia, alleluia!
   Shoulder my yoke and learn from me,
   for I am gentle and humble in heart.
   Alleluia!

Alternative Gospel Acclamation   Jn 10:14
   Alleluia, alleluia!
   I am the good shepherd, says the Lord;
   I know my own sheep and my own know me.
   Alleluia!

GOSPEL
A reading from the holy Gospel according to Luke   15:3-7

Jesus spoke this parable to the scribes and Pharisees:
   'What man among you with a hundred sheep, losing one, would not leave the ninety-nine in the wilderness and go after the missing one till he found it? And when he found it, would he not joyfully take it on his shoulders and then, when he got home, call together his friends and neighbours? "Rejoice with me," he would

say "I have found my sheep that was lost." In the same way, I tell you, there will be more rejoicing in heaven over one repentant sinner than over ninety-nine virtuous men who have no need of repentance.'

The Gospel of the Lord.

The Creed is said.

Prayer over the Offerings
Look, O Lord, we pray, on the surpassing charity
in the Heart of your beloved Son,
that what we offer may be a gift acceptable to you
and an expiation of our offences.
Through Christ our Lord.
Amen.

Preface of the Sacred Heart, p.37.

Communion Antiphon Cf. Jn 7:37-38
Thus says the Lord:
Let whoever is thirsty come to me and drink.
Streams of living water will flow
from within the one who believes in me.

or Jn 19:34

One of the soldiers opened his side with a lance,
and at once there came forth blood and water.

Prayer after Communion
May this sacrament of charity, O Lord,
make us fervent with the fire of holy love,
so that, drawn always to your Son,
we may learn to see him in our neighbour.
Through Christ our Lord.
Amen.

SUNDAYS IN ORDINARY TIME   C

The cycle of Sundays in Ordinary Time runs from the end of the Christmas season to the beginning of Lent; it recommences after Trinity Sunday, and runs until the beginning of Advent. The number of Sundays in Ordinary Time before Lent, and between Trinity Sunday and Advent, varies: see the Table of Principal Celebrations.

The first week of Ordinary Time begins on the Monday following the Feast of the Baptism of the Lord. In Cycle C, the Gospel Readings are taken mainly from the Gospel According to St Luke.

THE BAPTISM OF THE LORD
Feast

See above, pp.239ff.

SECOND SUNDAY IN ORDINARY TIME   C

The Church's Bridegroom

The Church rejoices in her Bridegroom who will cherish her, delight in her, lavish upon her the many gifts of his Spirit, and transform her into a new creation as he transformed water into wine.

Entrance Antiphon   Ps 65:4
All the earth shall bow down before you, O God,
and shall sing to you,
shall sing to your name, O Most High!

Collect

Almighty ever-living God,
who govern all things,
both in heaven and on earth,
mercifully hear the pleading of your people
and bestow your peace on our times.
Through our Lord Jesus Christ, your Son,
who lives and reigns with you in the unity of the Holy Spirit,
one God, for ever and ever.
Amen.

FIRST READING

A reading from the prophet Isaiah 62:1-5

About Zion I will not be silent.
about Jerusalem I will not grow weary,
until her integrity shines out like the dawn
and her salvation flames like a torch.
The nations then will see your integrity,
all the kings your glory,
and you will be called by a new name,
one which the mouth of the Lord will confer.
You are to be a crown of splendour in the hand of the Lord,
a princely diadem in the hand of your God;
no longer are you to be named 'Forsaken',
nor your land 'Abandoned',
but you shall be called 'My Delight'
and your land 'The Wedded';
for the Lord takes delight in you
and your land will have its wedding.
Like a young man marrying a virgin,
so will the one who built you wed you,
and as the bridegroom rejoices in his bride,
so will your God rejoice in you.

The word of the Lord.

Responsorial Psalm

Ps 95:1-3. 7-10. ℟ v.3

℟ **Proclaim the wonders of the
Lord among all the peoples.**

1 O sing a new song to the Lord,
   sing to the Lord all the earth.
   O sing to the Lord, bless his name. ℟

2　Proclaim his help day by day,
　　tell among the nations his glory
　　and his wonders among all the peoples. ℟

3　Give the Lord, you families of peoples,
　　give the Lord glory and power,
　　give the Lord the glory of his name. ℟

4　Worship the Lord in his temple.
　　O earth, tremble before him.
　　Proclaim to the nations: 'God is king.'
　　He will judge the peoples in fairness. ℟

SECOND READING
A reading from the first letter of St Paul to the Corinthians　12:4-11

There is a variety of gifts but always the same Spirit; there are all sorts of service to be done, but always to the same Lord; working in all sorts of different ways in different people, it is the same God who is working in all of them. The particular way in which the Spirit is given to each person is for a good purpose. One may have the gift of preaching with wisdom given him by the Spirit; another may have the gift of preaching instruction given him by the same Spirit; and another the gift of faith given by the same Spirit; another again the gift of healing, through this one Spirit; one, the power of miracles; another, prophecy; another the gift of recognising spirits; another the gift of tongues and another the ability to interpret them. All these are the work of one and the same Spirit, who distributes different gifts to different people just as he chooses.

　　The word of the Lord.

Gospel Acclamation　　　　　　　　　　　　　　　　　Cf. Jn 6:63. 68
　　Alleluia, alleluia!
　　Your words are spirit, Lord,
　　and they are life:
　　you have the message of eternal life.
　　Alleluia!

or　　　　　　　　　　　　　　　　　　　　　　　　　Cf. 2 Thess 2:14

　　Alleluia, alleluia!
　　Through the Good News God called us
　　to share the glory of our Lord Jesus Christ.
　　Alleluia!

Second Sunday in Ordinary Time, Year C

GOSPEL
A reading from the holy Gospel according to John • 2:1-11

There was a wedding at Cana in Galilee. The mother of Jesus was there, and Jesus and his disciples had also been invited. When they ran out of wine, since the wine provided for the wedding was all finished, the mother of Jesus said to him, 'They have no wine.' Jesus said, 'Woman why turn to me? My hour has not come yet.' His mother said to the servants, 'Do whatever he tells you.' There were six stone water jars standing there, meant for the ablutions that are customary among the Jews; each could hold twenty or thirty gallons. Jesus said to the servants, 'Fill the jars with water,' and they filled them to the brim. 'Draw some out now' he told them 'and take it to the steward.' They did this; the steward tasted the water, and it had turned into wine. Having no idea where it came from – only the servants who had drawn the water knew – the steward called the bridegroom and said, 'People generally serve the best wine first, and keep the cheaper sort till the guests have had plenty to drink; but you have kept the best wine till now.'

This was the first of the signs given by Jesus: it was given at Cana in Galilee. He let his glory be seen, and his disciples believed in him.

The Gospel of the Lord.

The Creed is said.

Prayer over the Offerings
Grant us, O Lord, we pray,
that we may participate worthily in these mysteries,
for whenever the memorial of this sacrifice is celebrated
the work of our redemption is accomplished.
Through Christ our Lord.
Amen.

Communion Antiphon
Cf. Ps 22:5

You have prepared a table before me,
and how precious is the chalice that quenches my thirst.

or • 1 Jn 4:16

We have come to know and to believe
in the love that God has for us.

Prayer after Communion
Pour on us, O Lord, the Spirit of your love,
and in your kindness
make those you have nourished
by this one heavenly Bread
one in mind and heart.
Through Christ our Lord.
Amen.

THIRD SUNDAY IN ORDINARY TIME C

The Law of the Lord

Today is a day of rejoicing in the New Law which Christ has given us and which unites us with him, binds us together as his people, and enables us to work together for his Kingdom. We listen to the words of the Law and ponder them in our hearts.

Entrance Antiphon Cf. Ps 95:1. 6
O sing a new song to the Lord;
sing to the Lord, all the earth.
In his presence are majesty and splendour,
strength and honour in his holy place.

Collect
Almighty ever-living God,
direct our actions according to your good pleasure,
that in the name of your beloved Son
we may abound in good works.
Through our Lord Jesus Christ, your Son,
who lives and reigns with you in the unity of the Holy Spirit,
one God, for ever and ever.
Amen.

FIRST READING
A reading from the book of Nehemiah 8:2-6. 8-10

Ezra the priest brought the Law before the assembly, consisting of men, women, and children old enough to understand. This was the first day of the seventh month. On the square before the Water Gate, in the presence of the men and women, and children old enough to understand, he read from the book from early morning till noon; all the people listened attentively to the Book of the Law.

Third Sunday in Ordinary Time, Year C

Ezra the scribe stood on a wooden dais erected for the purpose. In full view of all the people – since he stood higher than all the people – Ezra opened the book; and when he opened it all the people stood up. Then Ezra blessed the Lord, the great God, and all the people raised their hands and answered, 'Amen! Amen!'; then they bowed down and, face to the ground, prostrated themselves before the Lord. And Ezra read from the Law of God, translating and giving the sense, so that the people understood what was read.

Then Nehemiah – His Excellency – and Ezra, priest and scribe (and the Levites who were instructing the people) said to all the people, 'This day is sacred to the Lord your God. Do not be mournful, do not weep.' For the people were all in tears as they listened to the words of the Law.

He then said, 'Go, eat the fat, drink the sweet wine, and send a portion to the man who has nothing prepared ready. For this day is sacred to our Lord. Do not be sad: the joy of the Lord is your stronghold.'

The word of the Lord.

Responsorial Psalm Ps 18:8-10. 15. ℟ Jn 6:63

℟ **Your words are spirit, Lord, and they are life.**

1 The law of the Lord is perfect,
 it revives the soul.
 The rule of the Lord is to be trusted,
 it gives wisdom to the simple. ℟

2 The precepts of the Lord are right,
 they gladden the heart.
 The command of the Lord is clear,
 it gives light to the eyes. ℟

3 The fear of the Lord is holy,
 abiding for ever.
 The decrees of the Lord are truth
 and all of them just. ℟

4 May the spoken words of my mouth,
 the thoughts of my heart,
 win favour in your sight, O Lord,
 my rescuer, my rock! ℟

Third Sunday in Ordinary Time, Year C

SECOND READING

A reading from the first letter of St Paul to the Corinthians   12:12-30

*Just as a human body, though it is made up of many parts is a single unit because all these parts, though many, make one body, so it is with Christ. In the one Spirit we were all baptised, Jews as well as Greeks, slaves as well as citizens, and one Spirit was given to us all to drink.

Nor is the body to be identified with any one of its many parts.* If the foot were to say, 'I am not a hand and so I do not belong to the body', would that mean that it stopped being part of the body? If the ear were to say, 'I am not an eye, and so I do not belong to the body,' would that mean that it is not a part of the body? If your whole body was just one eye, how would you hear anything? If it was just one ear, how would you smell anything?

Instead of that, God put all the separate parts into the body on purpose. If all the parts were the same, how could it be a body? As it is, the parts are many but the body is one. The eye cannot say to the hand, 'I do not need you,' nor can the head say to the feet, 'I do not need you.'

What is more, it is precisely the parts of the body that seem to be the weakest which are the indispensable ones; and it is the least honourable parts of the body that we clothe with the greatest care. So our more improper parts get decorated in a way that our more proper parts do not need. God has arranged the body so that more dignity is given to the parts which are without it, and so that there may not be disagreements inside the body, but that each part may be equally concerned for all the others. If one part is hurt, all parts are hurt with it. If one part is given special honour, all parts enjoy it.

Now you together are Christ's body; but each of you is a different part of it. In the Church, God has given the first place to apostles, the second to prophets, the third to teachers; after them, miracles, and after them the gift of healing; helpers, good leaders, those with many languages. Are all of them apostles, or all of them prophets, or all of them teachers? Do they all have the gift of miracles, or all have the gift of healing? Do all speak strange languages, and all interpret them?

The word of the Lord.

Shorter Form, verses 12-14. 27. Read between

Gospel Acclamation   Lk 4:18
Alleluia, alleluia!
The Lord has sent me to bring the good news to the poor,
to proclaim liberty to captives.
Alleluia!

GOSPEL
A reading from the holy Gospel according to Luke   1:1-4; 4:14-21

Seeing that many others have undertaken to draw up accounts of the events that have taken place among us, exactly as these were handed down to us by those who from the outset were eyewitnesses and ministers of the word, I in my turn, after carefully going over the whole story from the beginning, have decided to write an ordered account for you, Theophilus, so that your Excellency may learn how well founded the teaching is that you have received.

Jesus, with the power of the Spirit in him, returned to Galilee; and his reputation spread throughout the countryside. He taught in their synagogues and everyone praised him.

He came to Nazara, where he had been brought up, and went into the synagogue on the sabbath day as he usually did. He stood up to read, and they handed him the scroll of the prophet Isaiah. Unrolling the scroll he found the place where it is written:

> The spirit of the Lord has been given to me, for he has
>   anointed me.
> He has sent me to bring the good news to the poor,
> to proclaim liberty to captives
> and to the blind new sight,
> to set the downtrodden free,
> to proclaim the Lord's year of favour.

He then rolled up the scroll, gave it back to the assistant and sat down. And all eyes in the synagogue were fixed on him. Then he began to speak to them, 'This text is being fulfilled today even as you listen.'

The Gospel of the Lord.

The Creed is said.

Prayer over the Offerings
Accept our offerings, O Lord, we pray,
and in sanctifying them

grant that they may profit us for salvation.
Through Christ our Lord.
Amen.

Communion Antiphon Cf. Ps 33:6
Look toward the Lord and be radiant;
let your faces not be abashed.

or Jn 8:12

I am the light of the world, says the Lord;
whoever follows me will not walk in darkness,
but will have the light of life.

Prayer after Communion
Grant, we pray, almighty God,
that, receiving the grace
by which you bring us to new life,
we may always glory in your gift.
Through Christ our Lord.
Amen.

FOURTH SUNDAY IN ORDINARY TIME C

The Church as the Prophet of God

We are privileged to be called by God to be his prophets: to take his words on our lips and proclaim them to the world. But the gift of prophecy is of no help to us without the gift of love: a Christ-like love of the world which is proof even against the world's rejection of us.

Entrance Antiphon Ps 105:47
Save us, O Lord our God!
And gather us from the nations,
to give thanks to your holy name,
and make it our glory to praise you.

Collect
Grant us, Lord our God,
that we may honour you with all our mind,
and love everyone in truth of heart.
Through our Lord Jesus Christ, your Son,
who lives and reigns with you in the unity of the Holy Spirit,
one God, for ever and ever.
Amen.

Fourth Sunday in Ordinary Time, Year C

FIRST READING
A reading from the prophet Jeremiah   1:4-5. 17-19

In the days of Josiah, the word of the Lord was addressed to me, saying,

> 'Before I formed you in the womb I knew you;
> before you came to birth I consecrated you;
> I have appointed you as prophet to the nations.
> So now brace yourself for action.
> Stand up and tell them
> all I command you.
> Do not be dismayed at their presence,
> or in their presence I will make you dismayed.
> I, for my part, today will make you
> into a fortified city,
> a pillar of iron,
> and a wall of bronze
> to confront all this land:
> the kings of Judah, its princes,
> its priests and the country people.
> They will fight against you
> but shall not overcome you,
> for I am with you to deliver you –
> it is the Lord who speaks.'

The word of the Lord.

Responsorial Psalm   Ps 70:1-6. 15. 17. ℟ v.15

℟   **My lips will tell of your help.**

1   In you, O Lord, I take refuge;
    let me never be put to shame.
    In your justice rescue me, free me:
    pay heed to me and save me.   ℟

2   Be a rock where I can take refuge,
    a mighty stronghold to save me;
    for you are my rock, my stronghold.
    Free me from the hand of the wicked.   ℟

3   It is you, O Lord, who are my hope,
    my trust, O Lord, since my youth.
    On you I have leaned from my birth,
    from my mother's womb you have been my help.   ℟

4 My lips will tell of your justice
   and day by day of your help.
   O God, you have taught me from my youth
   and I proclaim your wonders still. ℟

SECOND READING

A reading from the first letter of St Paul to the Corinthians   12:31 – 13:13

Be ambitious for the higher gifts. And I am going to show you a way that is better than any of them.

If I have all the eloquence of men or of angels, but speak without love, I am simply a gong booming or a cymbal clashing. If I have the gift of prophecy, understanding all the mysteries there are, and knowing everything, and if I have faith in all its fulness, to move mountains, but without love, then I am nothing at all. If I give away all that I possess, piece by piece, and if I even let them take my body to burn it, but am without love, it will do me no good whatever.

*Love is always patient and kind: it is never jealous; love is never boastful or conceited; it is never rude or selfish; it does not take offence, and is not resentful. Love takes no pleasure in other people's sins but delights in the truth; it is always ready to excuse, to trust, to hope, and to endure whatever comes.

Love does not come to an end. But if there are gifts of prophecy, the time will come when they must fail; or the gift of languages, it will not continue for ever; and knowledge – for this, too, the time will come when it must fail. For our knowledge is imperfect and our prophesying is imperfect; but once perfection comes, all imperfect things will disappear. When I was a child, I used to talk like a child, and think like a child, and argue like a child, but now I am a man, all childish ways are put behind me. Now we are seeing a dim reflection in a mirror; but then we shall be seeing face to face. The knowledge that I have now is imperfect; but then I shall know as fully as I am known.

In short, there are three things that last: faith, hope and love; and the greatest of these is love.

The word of the Lord.*

Shorter Form, verses 4-13. Read between

Gospel Acclamation   Jn 14:5
   Alleluia, alleluia!
   I am the Way, the Truth and the Life, says the Lord;
   no one can come to the Father except through me.
   Alleluia!

Fourth Sunday in Ordinary Time, Year C

or   Lk 4:18

Alleluia, alleluia!
The Lord has sent me to bring the good news to the poor,
to proclaim liberty to captives.
Alleluia!

GOSPEL

A reading from the holy Gospel according to Luke   4:21-30

Jesus began to speak in the synagogue, 'This text is being fulfilled today even as you listen.' And he won the approval of all, and they were astonished by the gracious words that came from his lips.

They said, 'This is Joseph's son, surely?' But he replied, 'No doubt you will quote me the saying, "Physician, heal yourself" and tell me, "We have heard all that happened in Capernaum, do the same here in your own countryside."' And he went on, 'I tell you solemnly, no prophet is ever accepted in his own country.

'There were many widows in Israel, I can assure you, in Elijah's day, when heaven remained shut for three years and six months and a great famine raged throughout the land, but Elijah was not sent to any one of these: he was sent to a widow at Zarephath, Sidonian town. And in the prophet Elisha's time there were many lepers in Israel, but none of these was cured, except the Syrian, Naaman.'

When they heard this everyone in the synagogue was enraged. They sprang to their feet and hustled him out of the town; and they took him up to the brow of the hill their town was built on, intending to throw him down the cliff, but he slipped through the crowd and walked away.

The Gospel of the Lord.

The Creed is said.

Prayer over the Offerings
O Lord, we bring to your altar
these offerings of our service:
be pleased to receive them, we pray,
and transform them
into the Sacrament of our redemption.
Through Christ our Lord.
Amen.

Communion Antiphon
Cf. Ps 30:17-18

Let your face shine on your servant.
Save me in your merciful love.
O Lord, let me never be put to shame, for I call on you.

or
Mt 5:3-4

Blessed are the poor in spirit,
for theirs is the Kingdom of Heaven.
Blessed are the meek, for they shall possess the land.

Prayer after Communion
Nourished by these redeeming gifts,
we pray, O Lord,
that through this help to eternal salvation
true faith may ever increase.
Through Christ our Lord.
Amen.

FIFTH SUNDAY IN ORDINARY TIME   C

Christ Makes Us His Apostles

We are utterly unworthy to be the apostles of Christ and yet he sends us out to be fishers of all. He cleanses us from our sins and gives us the strength to say: 'Here I am, Lord, send me.'

Entrance Antiphon
Ps 94:6-7

O come, let us worship God
and bow low before the God who made us,
for he is the Lord our God.

Collect
Keep your family safe, O Lord, with unfailing care,
that, relying solely on the hope of heavenly grace,
they may be defended always by your protection.
Through our Lord Jesus Christ, your Son,
who lives and reigns with you in the unity of the Holy Spirit,
one God, for ever and ever.
Amen.

FIRST READING
A reading from the prophet Isaiah
6:1-8

In the year of King Uzziah's death I saw the Lord seated on a high throne; his train filled the sanctuary; above him stood seraphs, each one with six wings.

Fifth Sunday in Ordinary Time, Year C

And they cried out one to another in this way,

'Holy, holy, holy is the Lord of hosts.
His glory fills the whole earth.'

The foundations of the threshold shook with the voice of the one who cried out, and the Temple was filled with smoke. I said:

'What a wretched state I am in! I am lost,
for I am a man of unclean lips
and I live among a people of unclean lips,
and my eyes have looked at the King, the Lord of hosts.'

Then one of the seraphs flew to me, holding in his hand a live coal which he had taken from the altar with a pair of tongs. With this he touched my mouth and said:

'See now, this has touched your lips,
your sin is taken away,
your iniquity is purged.'

Then I heard the voice of the Lord saying:

'Whom shall I send? Who will be our messenger?'

I answered, 'Here I am, send me.'

The word of the Lord.

Responsional Psalm   Ps 137:1-5. 7-8. ℟ v.1

℟ **Before the angels I will bless you, O Lord.**

1   I thank you, Lord, with all my heart,
    you have heard the words of my mouth.
    Before the angels I will bless you.
    I will adore before your holy temple.   ℟

2   I thank you for your faithfulness and love
    which excel all we ever knew of you.
    On the day I called, you answered;
    you increased the strength of my soul.   ℟

3   All earth's kings shall thank you
    when they hear the words of your mouth.
    They shall sing of the Lord's ways:
    'How great is the glory of the Lord!'   ℟

4   You stretch out your hand and save me,
    your hand will do all things for me.
    Your love, O Lord, is eternal,
    discard not the work of your hand.   ℟

SECOND READING

A reading from the first letter of St Paul to the Corinthians   15:1-11

Brothers, I want to remind you of the gospel I preached to you, the gospel that you received and in which you are firmly established; because the gospel will save you only if you keep believing exactly what I preached to you – believing anything else will not lead to anything.

Well then,* in the first place, I taught you what I had been taught myself, namely that Christ died for our sins, in accordance with the scriptures; that he was buried; and that he was raised to life on the third day, in accordance with the scriptures; that he appeared first to Cephas and secondly to the Twelve. Next he appeared to more than five hundred of the brothers at the same time, most of whom are still alive, though some have died; then he appeared to James, and then to all the apostles; and last of all he appeared to me too; it was as though I was born when no one expected it.*

I am the least of the apostles; in fact, since I persecuted the Church of God, I hardly deserve the name apostle; but by God's grace that is what I am, and the grace that he gave me has not been fruitless. On the contrary, I, or rather the grace of God that is with me, have worked harder than any of the others; *but what matters is that I preach what they preach, and this is what you all believed.

The word of the Lord.*

Shorter Form, verses 3-8. 11. Read between

Gospel Acclamation   Jn 15:15

Alleluia, alleluia!
I call you friends, says the Lord,
because I have made known to you
everything I have learnt from my Father.
Alleluia!

or   Mt 4:19

Alleluia, alleluia!
Follow me, says the Lord,
and I will make you fishers of men.
Alleluia!

Fifth Sunday in Ordinary Time, Year C

GOSPEL
A reading from the holy Gospel according to Luke 5:1-11

Jesus was standing one day by the lake of Gennesaret, with the crowd pressing round him listening to the word of God, when he caught sight of two boats close to the bank. The fishermen had gone out of them and were washing their nets. He got into one of the boats – it was Simon's – and asked him to put out a little from the shore. Then he sat down and taught the crowds from the boat.

When he had finished speaking he said to Simon, 'Put out into deep water and pay out your nets for a catch.' 'Master,' Simon replied 'we worked hard all night long and caught nothing, but if you say so, I will pay out the nets.' And when they had done this they netted such a huge number of fish that their nets began to tear, so they signalled to their companions in the other boats to come and help them; when these came, they filled the two boats to sinking point.

When Simon Peter saw this he fell at the knees of Jesus saying, 'Leave me, Lord; I am a sinful man.' For he and all his companions were completely overcome by the catch they had made; so also were James and John, sons of Zebedee, who were Simon's partners. But Jesus said to Simon, 'Do not be afraid; from now on it is men you will catch.' Then, bringing their boats back to land, they left everything and followed him.

The Gospel of the Lord.

The Creed is said.

Prayer over the Offerings
O Lord, our God,
who once established these created things
to sustain us in our frailty,
grant, we pray,
that they may become for us now
the Sacrament of eternal life.
Through Christ our Lord.
Amen.

Communion Antiphon   Cf. Ps 106:8-9
Let them thank the Lord for his mercy,
his wonders for the children of men,
for he satisfies the thirsty soul,
and the hungry he fills with good things.

or Mt 5:5-6
Blessed are those who mourn, for they shall be consoled.
Blessed are those who hunger and thirst for righteousness,
for they shall have their fill.

Prayer after Communion
O God, who have willed that we be partakers
in the one Bread and the one Chalice,
grant us, we pray, so to live
that, made one in Christ,
we may joyfully bear fruit
for the salvation of the world.
Through Christ our Lord.
Amen.

SIXTH SUNDAY IN ORDINARY TIME C

Our Trust in the Lord

Nothing in this world can rob us of our peace of mind and interior joy, because our trust is not in people, but in the crucified and risen Christ.

Entrance Antiphon Cf. Ps 30:3-4
Be my protector, O God,
a mighty stronghold to save me.
For you are my rock, my stronghold!
Lead me, guide me, for the sake of your name.

Collect
O God, who teach us that you abide
in hearts that are just and true,
grant that we may be so fashioned by your grace
as to become a dwelling pleasing to you.
Through our Lord Jesus Christ, your Son,
who lives and reigns with you in the unity of the Holy Spirit,
one God, for ever and ever.
Amen.

FIRST READING
A reading from the prophet Jeremiah 17:5-8

The Lord says this:

'A curse on the man who puts his trust in man,
who relies on things of flesh,
whose heart turns from the Lord.

He is like dry scrub in the wastelands:
if good comes, he has no eyes for it,
he settles in the parched places of the wilderness,
a salt land, uninhabited.

'A blessing on the man who puts his trust in the Lord,
with the Lord for his hope.
He is like a tree by the waterside
that thrusts its roots to the stream:
when the heat comes it feels no alarm,
its foliage stays green;
it has no worries in a year of drought,
and never ceases to bear fruit.'

The word of the Lord.

Responsorial Psalm   Ps 1:1-4. 6. ℟ Ps 39:5

℟ **Happy the man who has placed
his trust in the Lord.**

1 Happy indeed is the man
who follows not the counsel of the wicked;
nor lingers in the way of sinners
nor sits in the company of scorners,
but whose delight is the law of the Lord
and who ponders his law day and night. ℟

2 He is like a tree that is planted
beside the flowing waters,
that yields its fruit in due season
and whose leaves shall never fade;
and all that he does shall prosper. ℟

3 Not so are the wicked, not so!
For they like winnowed chaff
shall be driven away by the wind.
For the Lord guards the way of the just
but the way of the wicked leads to doom. ℟

SECOND READING
A reading from the first letter of St Paul   15:12. 16-20
to the Corinthians

If Christ raised from the dead is what has been preached, how can some of you be saying that there is no resurrection of the dead? For if the dead are not raised, Christ has not been raised, and if Christ

has not been raised, you are still in your sins. And what is more serious, all who have died in Christ have perished. If our hope in Christ has been for this life only, we are the most unfortunate of all people.
But Christ has in fact been raised from the dead, the first-fruits of all who have fallen asleep.

The word of the Lord.

Gospel Acclamation Cf. Mt 11:25
Alleluia, alleluia!
Blessed are you, Father,
Lord of heaven and earth,
for revealing the mysteries of the kingdom
to mere children.
Alleluia!

or Lk 6:23

Alleluia, alleluia!
Rejoice and be glad:
your reward will be great in heaven.
Alleluia!

GOSPEL

A reading from the holy Gospel according to Luke 6:17. 20-26

Jesus came down with the Twelve and stopped at a piece of level ground where there was a large gathering of his disciples with a great crowd of people from all parts of Judaea and from Jerusalem and from the coastal region of Tyre and Sidon who had come to hear him and to be cured of their diseases. Then fixing his eyes on his disciples he said:

'How happy are you who are poor; yours is the kingdom of God.
Happy you who are hungry now: you shall be satisfied.
Happy you who weep now: you shall laugh.

'Happy are you when people hate you, drive you out, abuse you, denounce your name as criminal, on account of the Son of Man. Rejoice when that day comes and dance for joy, for then your reward will be great in heaven. This was the way their ancestors treated the prophets.

'But alas for you who are rich: you are having your consolation now.

Alas for you who have your fill now: you shall go hungry.
Alas for you who laugh now: you shall mourn and weep.

'Alas for you when the world speaks well of you! This was the way their ancestors treated the false prophets.'

The Gospel of the Lord.

The Creed is said.

Prayer over the Offerings
May this oblation, O Lord, we pray,
cleanse and renew us
and may it become for those who do your will
the source of eternal reward.
Through Christ our Lord.
Amen.

Communion Antiphon Cf. Ps 77:29-30
They ate and had their fill,
and what they craved the Lord gave them;
they were not disappointed in what they craved.

or Jn 3:16

God so loved the world
that he gave his Only Begotten Son,
so that all who believe in him may not perish,
but may have eternal life.

Prayer after Communion
Having fed upon these heavenly delights,
we pray, O Lord,
that we may always long
for that food by which we truly live.
Through Christ our Lord.
Amen.

SEVENTH SUNDAY IN ORDINARY TIME   C

The Love of Our Father

God's love is so overwhelming, he loves us totally, however hateful, sinful and unworthy we may be. There is no way to express this love in our own lives except by modelling ourselves on Christ, and loving our enemies as he loves them. It is then that we are most like our Father in heaven.

Seventh Sunday in Ordinary Time, Year C

Entrance Antiphon Ps 12:6
O Lord, I trust in your merciful love.
My heart will rejoice in your salvation.
I will sing to the Lord who has been bountiful with me.

Collect
Grant, we pray, almighty God,
that, always pondering spiritual things,
we may carry out in both word and deed
that which is pleasing to you.
Through our Lord Jesus Christ, your Son,
who lives and reigns with you in the unity of the Holy Spirit,
one God, for ever and ever.
Amen.

FIRST READING
A reading from the first book of Samuel 26:2. 7-9. 12-13. 22-23

Saul set off and went down to the wilderness of Ziph, accompanied by three thousand men chosen from Israel to search for David in the wilderness of Ziph.

So in the dark David and Abishai made their way towards the force, where they found Saul asleep inside the camp, his spear stuck in the ground beside his head, with Abner and the troops lying round him.

Then Abishai said to David, 'Today God has put your enemy in your power; so now let me pin him to the ground with his own spear. Just one stroke! I will not need to strike him twice.' David answered Abishai, 'Do not kill him, for who can lift his hand against the Lord's anointed and be without guilt?' David took the spear and the pitcher of water from beside Saul's head, and they made off. No one saw, no one knew, no one woke up; they were all asleep, for a deep sleep from the Lord had fallen on them.

David crossed to the other side and halted on the top of the mountain a long way off; there was a wide space between them. David then called out, 'Here is the king's spear. Let one of the soldiers come across and take it. The Lord repays everyone for his uprightness and loyalty. Today the Lord put you in my power, but I would not raise my hand against the Lord's anointed.'

The word of the Lord.

Responsorial Psalm   Ps 102:1-4. 8. 10. 12-13. ℟ v.8

℟ **The Lord is compassion and love.**

1. My soul, give thanks to the Lord,
   all my being, bless his holy name.
   My soul, give thanks to the Lord
   and never forget all his blessings. ℟

2. It is he who forgives all your guilt,
   who heals every one of your ills,
   who redeems your life from the grave,
   who crowns you with love and compassion. ℟

3. The Lord is compassion and love,
   slow to anger and rich in mercy.
   He does not treat us according to our sins
   nor repay us according to our faults. ℟

4. As far as the east is from the west
   so far does he remove our sins.
   As a father has compassion on his sons,
   the Lord has pity on those who fear him. ℟

SECOND READING

A reading from the first letter of St Paul   15:45-49
to the Corinthians

The first man, Adam, as scripture says, became a living soul; but the last Adam has become a life-giving spirit. That is, first the one with the soul, not the spirit, and after that, the one with the spirit. The first man, being from the earth, is earthly by nature; the second man is from heaven. As this earthly man was, so are we on earth; and as the heavenly man is, so are we in heaven. And we, who have been modelled on the earthly man, will be modelled on the heavenly man.

    The word of the Lord.

Gospel Acclamation   Cf. Acts 16:14

Alleluia, alleluia!
Open our heart, O Lord,
to accept the words of your Son.
Alleluia!

or Jn 13:34

Alleluia, alleluia!
I give you a new commandment:
love one another,
just as I have loved you,
says the Lord.
Alleluia!

GOSPEL

A reading from the holy Gospel according to Luke 6:27-38

Jesus said to his disciples: 'I say this to you who are listening: Love your enemies, do good to those who hate you, bless those who curse you, pray for those who treat you badly. To the man who slaps you on one cheek, present the other cheek too; to the man who takes your cloak from you, do not refuse your tunic. Give to everyone who asks you, and do not ask for your property back from the man who robs you. Treat others as you would like them to treat you. If you love those who love you, what thanks can you expect? Even sinners love those who love them. And if you do good to those who do good to you, what thanks can you expect? For even sinners do that much. And if you lend to those from whom you hope to receive, what thanks can you expect? Even sinners lend to sinners to get back the same amount. Instead, love your enemies and do good, and lend without any hope of return. You will have a great reward, and you will be sons of the Most High, for he himself is kind to the ungrateful and the wicked.

'Be compassionate as your Father is compassionate. Do not judge, and you will not be judged yourselves; do not condemn, and you will not be condemned yourselves; grant pardon, and you will be pardoned. Give, and there will be gifts for you: a full measure, pressed down, shaken together, and running over, will be poured into your lap; because the amount you measure out is the amount you will be given back.'

The Gospel of the Lord.

The Creed is said.

Prayer over the Offerings
As we celebrate your mysteries, O Lord,
with the observance that is your due,
we humbly ask you,
that what we offer to the honour of your majesty

may profit us for salvation.
Through Christ our Lord.
Amen.

Communion Antiphon Ps 9:2-3
I will recount all your wonders,
I will rejoice in you and be glad,
and sing psalms to your name, O Most High.

or Jn 11:27

Lord, I have come to believe that you are the Christ,
the Son of the living God, who is coming into this world.

Prayer after Communion
Grant, we pray, almighty God,
that we may experience the effects of the salvation
which is pledged to us by these mysteries.
Through Christ our Lord.
Amen.

EIGHTH SUNDAY IN ORDINARY TIME C

Praise and Thanksgiving

Today let our hearts be so filled with the joy of the risen Christ that we can proclaim his love, praise and thank him with sincerity and truth.

Entrance Antiphon Cf. Ps 17:19-20
The Lord became my protector.
He brought me out to a place of freedom;
he saved me because he delighted in me.

Collect
Grant us, O Lord, we pray,
that the course of our world
may be directed by your peaceful rule
and that your Church may rejoice,
untroubled in her devotion.
Through our Lord Jesus Christ, your Son,
who lives and reigns with you in the unity of the Holy Spirit,
one God, for ever and ever.
Amen.

Eighth Sunday in Ordinary Time, Year C

FIRST READING
A reading from the book of Ecclesiasticus 27:4-7

In a shaken sieve the rubbish is left behind,
so too the defects of a man appear in his talk.
The kiln tests the work of the potter,
the test of a man is in his conversation.
The orchard where the tree grows is judged on the quality of its fruit,
similarly a man's words betray what he feels.
Do not praise a man before he has spoken,
since this is the test of men.

The word of the Lord.

Responsorial Psalm   Ps 91:2-3. 13-16. ℟ cf. v.2
℟ **It is good to give you thanks, O Lord.**

1   It is good to give thanks to the Lord
    to make music to your name, O Most High,
    to proclaim your love in the morning
    and your truth in the watches of the night. ℟

2   The just will flourish like the palm-tree
    and grow like a Lebanon cedar. ℟

3   Planted in the house of the Lord
    they will flourish in the courts of our God,
    still bearing fruit when they are old,
    still full of sap, still green,
    to proclaim that the Lord is just.
    In him, my rock, there is no wrong. ℟

SECOND READING
A reading from the first letter of St Paul 15:54-58
to the Corinthians

When this perishable nature has put on imperishability, and when this mortal nature has put on immortality, then the words of scripture will come true: Death is swallowed up in victory. Death, where is your victory? Death, where is your sting? Now the sting of death is sin, and sin gets its power from the Law. So let us thank God for giving us the victory through our Lord Jesus Christ.

Eighth Sunday in Ordinary Time, Year C

Never give in then, my dear brothers, never admit defeat; keep on working at the Lord's work always, knowing that, in the Lord, you cannot be labouring in vain.

The word of the Lord.

Gospel Acclamation Cf. Acts 16:14
Alleluia, alleluia!
Open our hearts, O Lord,
to accept the words of your Son.
Alleluia!

or Phil 2:15-16

Alleluia, alleluia!
You will shine in the world like bright stars
because you are offering it the word of life.
Alleluia!

GOSPEL
A reading from the holy Gospel according to Luke 6:39-45

Jesus told a parable to his disciples. 'Can one blind man guide another? Surely both will fall into a pit? The disciple is not superior to his teacher; the fully trained disciple will always be like his teacher. Why do you observe the splinter in your brother's eye and never notice the plank in your own? How can you say to your brother, "Brother, let me take out the splinter that is in your eye," when you cannot see the plank in your own? Hypocrite! Take the plank out of your own eye first, and then you will see clearly enough to take out the splinter that is in your brother's eye.

'There is no sound tree that produces rotten fruit, nor again a rotten tree that produces sound fruit. For every tree can be told by its own fruit; people do not pick figs from thorns, nor gather grapes from brambles. A good man draws what is good from the store of goodness in his heart; a bad man draws what is bad from the store of badness. For a man's words flow out of what fills his heart.'

The Gospel of the Lord.

The Creed is said.

Prayer over the Offerings
O God, who provide gifts to be offered to your name
and count our oblations as signs
of our desire to serve you with devotion,
we ask of your mercy

that what you grant as the source of merit
may also help us to attain merit's reward.
Through Christ our Lord.
Amen.

Communion Antiphon   Cf. Ps 12:6
I will sing to the Lord who has been bountiful with me,
sing psalms to the name of the Lord Most High.

or   Mt 28:20

Behold, I am with you always,
even to the end of the age, says the Lord.

Prayer after Communion
Nourished by your saving gifts,
we beseech your mercy, Lord,
that by this same Sacrament
with which you feed us in the present age,
you may make us partakers of life eternal.
Through Christ our Lord.
Amen.

NINTH SUNDAY IN ORDINARY TIME   C

The Church for All Men

The Good News is that God loves all people. Any version of the Gospel which makes God's love the private possession of a coterie is all wrong. We rejoice today in the healing work of Christ everywhere throughout the world.

Entrance Antiphon   Cf. Ps 24:16. 18
Turn to me and have mercy on me, O Lord,
for I am alone and poor.
See my lowliness and suffering
and take away all my sins, my God.

Collect
O God, whose providence never fails in its design,
keep from us, we humbly beseech you,
all that might harm us
and grant all that works for our good.
Through our Lord Jesus Christ, your Son,

who lives and reigns with you in the unity of the Holy Spirit,
one God, for ever and ever.
Amen.

FIRST READING
A reading from the first book of the Kings 8:41-43

Solomon stood before the altar of the Lord and, stretching out his hands towards heaven, said:

'If a foreigner, not belonging to your people Israel, comes from a distant country for the sake of your name – for men will hear of your name, of your mighty hand and outstretched arm – if he comes and prays in this Temple, hear from heaven where your home is, and grant all the foreigner asks, so that all the peoples of the earth may come to know your name and, like your people Israel, revere you, and know that your name is given to the Temple I have built.'

The word of the Lord.

Responsorial Psalm Ps 116:1-2. ℟ Mk. 16:15

℟ **Go out to the whole world
and proclaim the Good News.**

or

Alleluia!

1 O praise the Lord, all you nations,
acclaim him all you peoples! ℟

2 Strong is his love for us;
he is faithful for ever. ℟

SECOND READING
A reading from the letter of St Paul to the Galatians 1:1-2. 6-10

From Paul to the churches of Galatia, and from all the brothers who are here with me, an apostle who does not owe his authority to men or his appointment to any human being but who has been appointed by Jesus Christ and by God the Father who raised Jesus from the dead.

I am astonished at the promptness with which you have turned away from the one who called you and have decided to follow a different version of the Good News. Not that there can be more than one Good News; it is merely that some troublemakers among you want to change the Good News of Christ; and let me warn you that if anyone preaches a version of the Good News different from the one we have already preached to you, whether it be ourselves or an angel from heaven, he is to be condemned. I am only repeating what we told you before: if anyone preaches a version of the Good News different from the one you have already heard, he is to be condemned. So now whom am I trying to please – man, or God? Would you say it is men's approval I am looking for? If I still wanted that, I should not be what I am – a servant of Christ.

The word of the Lord.

Gospel Acclamation   Jn 1:14. 12
    Alleluia, alleluia!
    The Word was made flesh and lived among us;
    to all who did accept him
    he gave power to become children of God.
    Alleluia!

or   Jn 3:16

    Alleluia, alleluia!
    God loved the world so much
    that he gave his only Son
    so that everyone who believes in him
    may have eternal life.
    Alleluia!

GOSPEL

A reading from the holy Gospel according to Luke   7:1-10

When Jesus had come to the end of all he wanted the people to hear, he went into Capernaum. A centurion there had a servant, a favourite of his, who was sick and near death. Having heard about Jesus he sent some Jewish elders to him to ask him to come and heal his servant. When they came to Jesus they pleaded earnestly with him. 'He deserves this of you,' they said 'because he is friendly towards our people; in fact, he is the one who built the synagogue.' So Jesus went with them, and was not very far from the house when the centurion sent word to him by some friends: 'Sir,' he said 'do not put yourself to trouble; because I am not worthy to have you under my roof; and for this same reason I did not presume to come to you myself; but give the word and let my servant be cured. For I am under authority myself, and have soldiers under me; and I say to one man: Go, and he goes; to another: Come here, and he comes; to my servant: Do this, and he does it.' When Jesus heard these words he was astonished at him and, turning round, said to the crowd following him, 'I tell you, not even in Israel have I found faith like this.' And when the messengers got back to the house they found the servant in perfect health.

The Gospel of the Lord.

The Creed is said.

Prayer over the Offerings
Trusting in your compassion, O Lord,
we come eagerly with our offerings to your sacred altar,
that, through the purifying action of your grace,
we may be cleansed by the very mysteries we serve.
Through Christ our Lord.
Amen.

Communion Antiphon Cf. Ps 16:6
To you I call, for you will surely heed me, O God;
turn your ear to me; hear my words.

or Mk 11:23-24

Amen, I say to you: Whatever you ask for in prayer,
believe you will receive it,
and it will be yours, says the Lord.

Prayer after Communion
Govern by your Spirit, we pray, O Lord,
those you feed with the Body and Blood of your Son,
that, professing you not just in word or in speech,
but also in works and in truth,
we may merit to enter the Kingdom of Heaven.
Through Christ our Lord.
Amen.

TENTH SUNDAY IN ORDINARY TIME C

Christ Who Restores Us to Life

Every conversion, like St Paul's for example, is a raising to new life. It is like Christ saying to our mother, the Church, 'Look, your child is alive again,' and 'her mourning is changed into dancing'.

Entrance Antiphon Cf. Ps 26:1-2
The Lord is my light and my salvation; whom shall I fear?
The Lord is the stronghold of my life; whom should I dread?
When those who do evil draw near, they stumble and fall.

Tenth Sunday in Ordinary Time, Year C

Collect
O God, from whom all good things come,
grant that we, who call on you in our need,
may at your prompting discern what is right,
and by your guidance do it.
Through our Lord Jesus Christ, your Son,
who lives and reigns with you in the unity of the Holy Spirit,
one God, for ever and ever.
Amen.

FIRST READING
A reading from the first book of the Kings   17:17-24

The son of the mistress of the house fell sick; his illness was so severe that in the end he had no breath left in him. And the woman said to Elijah, 'What quarrel have you with me, man of God? Have you come here to bring my sins home to me and to kill my son?' 'Give me your son,' he said, and taking him from her lap, carried him to the upper room where he was staying and laid him on his own bed. He cried out to the Lord, 'Lord my God, do you mean to bring grief to the widow who is looking after me by killing her son?' He stretched himself on the child three times and cried out to the Lord, 'Lord my God, may the soul of this child, I beg you, come into him again!' The Lord heard the prayer of Elijah and the soul of the child returned to him again and he revived. Elijah took the child, brought him down from the upper room into the house, and gave him to his mother. 'Look,' Elijah said 'your son is alive.' And the woman replied, 'Now I know you are a man of God and the word of the Lord in your mouth is truth itself.'

The word of the Lord.

Responsorial Psalm   Ps 29:2. 4-6. 11-13. ℟ v.2
  ℟ **I will praise you, Lord,
      you have rescued me.**

1   I will praise you, Lord, you have rescued me
    and have not let my enemies rejoice over me.
    O Lord, you have raised my soul from the dead,
    restored me to life from those who sink into the grave.   ℟

2   Sing psalms to the Lord, you who love him,
    give thanks to his holy name.
    His anger lasts a moment; his favour through life.
    At night there are tears, but joy comes with dawn.   ℟

3   The Lord listened and had pity.
    The Lord came to my help.
    For me you have changed my mourning into dancing;
    O Lord my God, I will thank you for ever.   ℟

SECOND READING
A reading from the letter of St Paul to the Galatians   1:11-19

The Good News I preached is not a human message that I was given by men, it is something I learnt only through a revelation of Jesus Christ. You must have heard of my career as a practising Jew, how merciless I was in persecuting the Church of God, how much damage I did to it, how I stood out among other Jews of my generation, and how enthusiastic I was for the traditions of my ancestors.

Then God, who had specially chosen me while I was still in my mother's womb, called me through his grace and chose to reveal his Son in me, so that I might preach the Good News about him to the pagans. I did not stop to discuss this with any human being, nor did I go up to Jerusalem to see those who were already apostles before me, but I went off to Arabia at once and later went straight back from there to Damascus. Even when after three years I went up to Jerusalem to visit Cephas and stayed with him for fifteen days, I did not see any of the other apostles; I only saw James, the brother of the Lord.

The word of the Lord.

Gospel Acclamation   Cf. Eph 1:17-18
    Alleluia, alleluia!
    May the Father of our Lord Jesus Christ
    enlighten the eyes of our mind,
    so that we can see what hope his call holds for us.
    Alleluia!

or   Lk 7:16

    Alleluia, alleluia!
    A great prophet has appeared among us;
    God has visited his people.
    Alleluia!

GOSPEL
A reading from the holy Gospel according to Luke   7:11-17

Jesus went to a town called Nain, accompanied by his disciples and a great number of people. When he was near the gate of the town it happened that a dead man was being carried out for burial, the only son of his mother, and she was a widow. And a considerable number of the townspeople were with her. When the Lord saw her he felt sorry for her. 'Do not cry' he said. Then he went up and put his hand on the bier and the bearers stood still, and he said, 'Young man, I tell you to get up.' And the dead man sat up and began to walk, and Jesus gave him to his mother. Everyone was filled with awe and praised God saying, 'A great prophet has appeared among us; God has visited his people.' And this opinion of him spread throughout Judaea and all over the countryside.

The Gospel of the Lord.

The Creed is said.

Prayer over the Offerings
Look kindly upon our service, O Lord, we pray,
that what we offer
may be an acceptable oblation to you
and lead us to grow in charity.
Through Christ our Lord.
Amen.

Communion Antiphon Ps 17:3
The Lord is my rock, my fortress, and my deliverer;
my God is my saving strength.

or 1 Jn 4:16

God is love, and whoever abides in love
abides in God, and God in him.

Prayer after Communion
May your healing work, O Lord,
free us, we pray, from doing evil
and lead us to what is right.
Through Christ our Lord.
Amen.

ELEVENTH SUNDAY IN ORDINARY TIME C

The Forgiving Christ

With David and with Mary of Magdala we celebrate today the forgiveness of Christ and our faith in the Son of God who loved us and who sacrificed himself for our sake.

Eleventh Sunday in Ordinary Time, Year C

Entrance Antiphon Cf. Ps 26:7. 9
O Lord, hear my voice, for I have called to you; be my help.
Do not abandon or forsake me, O God, my Saviour!

Collect
O God, strength of those who hope in you,
graciously hear our pleas,
and, since without you mortal frailty can do nothing,
grant us always the help of your grace,
that in following your commands
we may please you by our resolve and our deeds.
Through our Lord Jesus Christ, your Son,
who lives and reigns with you in the unity of the Holy Spirit,
one God, for ever and ever.
Amen.

FIRST READING
A reading from the second book of Samuel 12:7-10. 13

Nathan said to David, 'The Lord the God of Israel says this, "I anointed you king over Israel; I delivered you from the hands of Saul; I gave your master's house to you, his wives into your arms; I gave you the House of Israel and of Judah; and if this were not enough, I would add as much again for you. Why have you shown contempt for the Lord, doing what displeases him? You have struck down Uriah the Hittite with the sword, taken his wife for your own, and killed him with the sword of the Ammonites. So now the sword will never be far from your House, since you have shown contempt for me and taken the wife of Uriah the Hittite to be your wife."'

David said to Nathan, 'I have sinned against the Lord.' Then Nathan said to David, 'The Lord, for his part, forgives your sin; you are not to die.'

The word of the Lord.

Responsorial Psalm Ps 31:1-2. 5. 7. 11. ℟ cf. v.5
  ℟ **Forgive, Lord, the guilt of my sin.**

1 Happy the man whose offence is forgiven
    whose sin is remitted.
    O happy the man to whom the Lord
    imputes no guilt,
    in whose spirit is no guile. ℟

2   But now I have acknowledged my sins:
    my guilt I did not hide.
    I said: 'I will confess
    my offence to the Lord.'
    And you, Lord, have forgiven
    the guilt of my sin.   ℟

3   You are my hiding place, O Lord;
    you save me from distress.
    You surround me with cries of deliverance.   ℟

4   Rejoice, rejoice in the Lord,
    exult, you just!
    O come, ring out your joy,
    all you upright of heart.   ℟

SECOND READING
A reading from the letter of St Paul to the Galatians   2:16. 19-21

We acknowledge that what makes a man righteous is not obedience to the Law, but faith in Jesus Christ. We had to become believers in Christ Jesus no less than you had, and now we hold that faith in Christ rather than fidelity to the Law is what justifies us, and that no one can be justified by keeping the Law. In other words, through the Law I am dead to the Law, so that now I can live for God. I have been crucified with Christ, and I live now not with my own life but with the life of Christ who lives in me. The life I now live in this body I live in faith: faith in the Son of God who loved me and who sacrificed himself for my sake. I cannot bring myself to give up God's gift: if the Law can justify us, there is no point in the death of Christ.

The word of the Lord.

Gospel Acclamation   Jn 14:6
Alleluia, alleluia!
I am the Way, the Truth and the Life, says the Lord;
no one can come to the Father except through me.
Alleluia!

or   1 Jn 4:10

Alleluia, alleluia!
God so loved us when he sent his Son
to be the sacrifice that takes our sins away.
Alleluia!

Eleventh Sunday in Ordinary Time, Year C 943

GOSPEL

A reading from the holy Gospel according to Luke 7:36 – 8:3

*One of the Pharisees invited Jesus to a meal. When he arrived at the Pharisee's house and took his place at table, a woman came in, who had a bad name in the town. She had heard he was dining with the Pharisee and had brought with her an alabaster jar of ointment. She waited behind him at his feet, weeping, and her tears fell on his feet, and she wiped them away with her hair; then she covered his feet with kisses and anointed them with the ointment.

When the Pharisee who had invited him saw this, he said to himself, 'If this man were a prophet, he would know who this woman is that is touching him and what a bad name she has.' Then Jesus took him up and said, 'Simon, I have something to say to you.' 'Speak Master' was the reply. 'There was once a creditor who had two men in his debt; one owed him five hundred denarii, the other fifty. They were unable to pay, so he pardoned them both. Which of them will love him more?' 'The one who was pardoned more, I suppose' answered Simon. Jesus said, 'You are right.'

Then he turned to the woman. 'Simon', he said 'you see this woman? I came into your house, and you poured no water over my feet, but she has poured out her tears over my feet and wiped them away with her hair. You gave me no kiss, but she has been covering my feet with kisses ever since I came in. You did not anoint my head with oil, but she has anointed my feet with ointment. For this reason I tell you that her sins, her many sins, must have been forgiven her, or she would not have shown such great love. It is the man who is forgiven little who shows little love.' Then he said to her, 'Your sins are forgiven.' Those who were with him at table began to say to themselves, 'Who is this man, that he even forgives sins?' But he said to the woman 'Your faith has saved you; go in peace.'*

Now after this he made his way through towns and villages, preaching, and proclaiming the Good News of the kingdom of God. With him went the Twelve, as well as certain women who had been cured of evil spirits and ailments: Mary surnamed the Magdalene, from whom seven demons had gone out, Joanna the wife of Herod's steward Chuza, Susanna, and several others who provided for them out of their own resources.

The Gospel of the Lord.

Shorter Form, verses 36-50. Read between

The Creed is said.

Prayer over the Offerings
O God, who in the offerings presented here
provide for the twofold needs of human nature,
nourishing us with food
and renewing us with your Sacrament,
grant, we pray,
that the sustenance they provide
may not fail us in body or in spirit.
Through Christ our Lord.
Amen.

Communion Antiphon   Ps 26:4
There is one thing I ask of the Lord, only this do I seek:
to live in the house of the Lord all the days of my life.

or   Jn 17:11

Holy Father, keep in your name those you have given me,
that they may be one as we are one, says the Lord.

Prayer after Communion
As this reception of your Holy Communion, O Lord,
foreshadows the union of the faithful in you,
so may it bring about unity in your Church.
Through Christ our Lord.
Amen.

TWELFTH SUNDAY IN ORDINARY TIME   C

The One Whom We Have Pierced

In today's celebration, with all our differences, we become one as we gaze in prayer on the Christ we have pierced and who gave his life for our sake.

Entrance Antiphon   Cf. Ps 27:8-9
The Lord is the strength of his people,
a saving refuge for the one he has anointed.
Save your people, Lord, and bless your heritage,
and govern them for ever.

Collect
Grant, O Lord,
that we may always revere and love your holy name,
for you never deprive of your guidance

those you set firm on the foundation of your love.
Through our Lord Jesus Christ, your Son,
who lives and reigns with you in the unity of the Holy Spirit,
one God, for ever and ever.
Amen.

FIRST READING
A reading from the prophet Zechariah 12:10-11; 13:1

It is the Lord who speaks: 'Over the House of David and the citizens of Jerusalem I will pour out a spirit of kindness and prayer. They will look on the one whom they have pierced; they will mourn for him as for an only son, and weep for him as people weep for a first-born child. When that day comes, there will be great mourning in Judah, like the mourning of Hadad-rimmon in the plain of Megiddo. When that day comes, a fountain will be opened for the House of David and the citizens of Jerusalem, for sin and impurity.'

The word of the Lord.

Responsorial Psalm Ps 62:2-6. 8-9. ℟ v.2

℟ **For you my soul is thirsting,**
 O God, my God.

1 O God, you are my God, for you I long;
 for you my soul is thirsting.
 My body pines for you
 like a dry, weary land without water. ℟

2 So I gaze on you in the sanctuary
 to see your strength and your glory.
 For your love is better than life,
 my lips will speak your praise. ℟

3 So I will bless you all my life,
 in your name I will lift up my hands.
 My soul shall be filled as with a banquet,
 my mouth shall praise you with joy. ℟

4 For you have been my help;
 in the shadow of your wings I rejoice.
 My soul clings to you;
 your right hand holds me fast. ℟

SECOND READING
A reading from the letter of St Paul to the Galatians 3:26-29

You are, all of you, sons of God through faith in Christ Jesus. All baptised in Christ, you have all clothed yourselves in Christ, and there are no more distinctions between Jew and Greek, slave and free, male and female, but all of you are one in Christ Jesus. Merely by belonging to Christ you are the posterity of Abraham, the heirs he was promised.

The word of the Lord.

Gospel Acclamation
Jn 8:12

Alleluia, alleluia!
I am the light of the world, says the Lord,
anyone who follows me
will have the light of life.
Alleluia!

or
Jn 10:27

Alleluia, alleluia!
The sheep that belong to me listen to my voice,
says the Lord,
I know them and they follow me.
Alleluia!

GOSPEL
A reading from the holy Gospel according to Luke 9:18-24

One day when Jesus was praying alone in the presence of his disciples he put this question to them, 'Who do the crowds say I am?' And they answered, 'John the Baptist; others Elijah; and others say one of the ancient prophets come back to life.' 'But you,' he said 'who do you say I am?' It was Peter who spoke up. 'The Christ of God' he said. But he gave them strict orders not to tell anyone anything about this.

'The Son of Man' he said 'is destined to suffer grievously, to be rejected by the elders and chief priests and scribes and to be put to death, and to be raised up on the third day.'

Then to all he said, 'If anyone wants to be a follower of mine, let him renounce himself and take up his cross every day and follow me. For anyone who wants to save his life will lose it; but anyone who loses his life for my sake, that man will save it.'

The Gospel of the Lord.

The Creed is said.

Prayer over the Offerings
Receive, O Lord, the sacrifice of conciliation and praise
and grant that, cleansed by its action,
we may make offering of a heart pleasing to you.
Through Christ our Lord.
Amen.

Communion Antiphon — Ps 144:15
The eyes of all look to you, Lord,
and you give them their food in due season.

or — Jn 10:11. 15

I am the Good Shepherd,
and I lay down my life for my sheep, says the Lord.

Prayer after Communion
Renewed and nourished
by the Sacred Body and Precious Blood of your Son,
we ask of your mercy, O Lord,
that what we celebrate with constant devotion
may be our sure pledge of redemption.
Through Christ our Lord.
Amen.

THIRTEENTH SUNDAY IN ORDINARY TIME   C

The Lord We Serve

We acclaim Christ who is more to us than all the world and whose Spirit has made us resolve to follow him wherever he leads us.

Entrance Antiphon — Ps 46:2
All peoples, clap your hands.
Cry to God with shouts of joy!

Collect
O God, who through the grace of adoption
chose us to be children of light,
grant, we pray,
that we may not be wrapped in the darkness of error
but always be seen to stand in the bright light of truth.

Through our Lord Jesus Christ, your Son,
who lives and reigns with you in the unity of the Holy Spirit,
one God, for ever and ever.
Amen.

FIRST READING

A reading from the first book of the Kings   19:16. 19-21

The Lord said to Elijah: 'Go, you are to anoint Elisha son of Shaphat, of Abel Meholah, as prophet to succeed you.' Leaving there, Elijah came on Elisha son of Shaphat as he was ploughing behind twelve yoke of oxen, he himself being with the twelfth. Elijah passed near to him and threw his cloak over him. Elisha left his oxen and ran after Elijah. 'Let me kiss my father and mother, then I will follow you' he said. Elijah answered, 'Go, go back; for have I done anything to you?' Elisha turned away, took the pair of oxen and slaughtered them. He used the plough for cooking the oxen, then gave to his men, who ate. He then rose, and followed Elijah and became his servant.

The word of the Lord.

Responsional Psalm   Ps 15:1-2. 5. 7-11. ℟ cf. v.5

℟   **O Lord, it is you who are my portion.**

1   Preserve me, God, I take refuge in you.
    I say to the Lord: 'You are my God.'
    O Lord, it is you who are my portion and cup;
    it is you yourself who are my prize.   ℟

2   I will bless the Lord who gives me counsel,
    who even at night directs my heart.
    I keep the Lord ever in my sight:
    since he is at my right hand, I shall stand firm.   ℟

3   And so my heart rejoices, my soul is glad;
    even my body shall rest in safety.
    For you will not leave my soul among the dead,
    nor let your beloved know decay.   ℟

4   You will show me the path of life,
    the fullness of joy in your presence,
    at your right hand happiness for ever.   ℟

Thirteenth Sunday in Ordinary Time, Year C

SECOND READING
A reading from the letter of St Paul to the Galatians 5:1. 13-18

When Christ freed us, he meant us to remain free. Stand firm, therefore, and do not submit again to the yoke of slavery.

My brothers, you were called, as you know, to liberty; but be careful, or this liberty will provide an opening for self-indulgence. Serve one another, rather, in works of love, since the whole of the Law is summarised in a single command: Love your neighbour as yourself. If you go snapping at each other and tearing each other to pieces, you had better watch or you will destroy the whole community.

Let me put it like this: if you are guided by the Spirit you will be in no danger of yielding to self-indulgence, since self-indulgence is the opposite of the Spirit, the Spirit is totally against such a thing, and it is precisely because the two are so opposed that you do not always carry out your good intentions. If you are led by the Spirit, no law can touch you.

The word of the Lord.

Gospel Acclamation
1 Sam 3:9; Jn 6:68

Alleluia, alleluia!
Speak, Lord, your servant is listening:
you have the message of eternal life.
Alleluia!

GOSPEL
A reading from the holy Gospel according to Luke 9:51-62

As the time drew near for him to be taken up to heaven, Jesus resolutely took the road for Jerusalem and sent messengers ahead of him. These set out, and they went into a Samaritan village to make preparations for him, but the people would not receive him because he was making for Jerusalem. Seeing this, the disciples James and John said, 'Lord, do you want us to call down fire from heaven to burn them up?' But he turned and rebuked them, and they went off to another village.

As they travelled along they met a man on the road who said to him, 'I will follow you wherever you go.' Jesus answered, 'Foxes have holes and the birds of the air have nests, but the Son of Man has nowhere to lay his head.' Another to whom he said, 'Follow me,' replied, 'Let me go and bury my father first.' But he answered, 'Leave the dead to bury their dead; your duty is to go and spread the news of the kingdom of God.'

Another said, 'I will follow you, sir, but first let me go and say good-bye to my people at home.' Jesus said to him, 'Once the hand is laid on the plough, no one who looks back is fit for the kingdom of God.'

The Gospel of the Lord.

The Creed is said.

Prayer over the Offerings
O God, who graciously accomplishes
the effects of your mysteries,
grant, we pray,
that the deeds by which we serve you
may be worthy of these sacred gifts.
Through Christ our Lord.
Amen.

Communion Antiphon   Cf. Ps 102:1
Bless the Lord, O my soul,
and all within me, his holy name.

or   Jn 17:20-21

O Father, I pray for them, that they may be one in us,
that the world may believe that you have sent me, says the Lord.

Prayer after Communion
May this divine sacrifice we have offered and received
fill us with life, O Lord, we pray,
so that, bound to you in lasting charity,
we may bear fruit that lasts for ever.
Through Christ our Lord.
Amen.

FOURTEENTH SUNDAY IN ORDINARY TIME   C

Christ Our Peace

The peace of Christ which we celebrate today should leave its mark on us so that we become messengers of peace of all around us.

Entrance Antiphon   Cf. Ps 47:10-11
Your merciful love, O God,
we have received in the midst of your temple.
Your praise, O God, like your name,

reaches the ends of the earth;
your right hand is filled with saving justice.

Collect
O God, who in the abasement of your Son
have raised up a fallen world,
fill your faithful with holy joy,
for on those you have rescued from slavery to sin
you bestow eternal gladness.
Through our Lord Jesus Christ, your Son,
who lives and reigns with you in the unity of the Holy Spirit,
one God, for ever and ever.
Amen.

FIRST READING
A reading from the prophet Isaiah 66:10-14

Rejoice, Jerusalem,
be glad for her, all you who love her!
Rejoice, rejoice for her,
all you who mourned her!

That you may be suckled, filled,
from her consoling breast,
that you may savour with delight
her glorious breasts.

For thus says the Lord:
Now towards her I send flowing
peace, like a river,
and like a stream in spate
the glory of the nations.

At her breast will her nurslings be carried
and fondled in her lap.
Like a son comforted by his mother
will I comfort you.
And by Jerusalem you will be comforted.

At the sight your heart will rejoice,
and your bones flourish like the grass.
To his servants the Lord will reveal his hand.

The word of the Lord.

Responsorial Psalm   Ps 65:1-7. 16. 20. ℟ v.1
   ℟   **Cry out with joy to God all the earth.**

1   Cry out with joy to God all the earth,
     O sing to the glory of his name.
     O render him glorious praise.
     Say to God: 'How tremendous your deeds!' ℟

2   'Before you all the earth shall bow;
     shall sing to you, sing to your name!'
     Come and see the works of God,
     tremendous his deeds among men. ℟

3   He turned the sea into dry land,
     they passed through the river dry-shod.
     Let our joy then be in him;
     he rules for ever by his might. ℟

4   Come and hear, all who fear God.
     I will tell what he did for my soul.
     Blessed be God who did not reject my prayer
     nor withhold his love from me. ℟

SECOND READING
A reading from the letter of St Paul to the Galatians   6:14-18

The only thing I can boast about is the cross of our Lord Jesus Christ, through whom the world is crucified to me, and I to the world. It does not matter if a person is circumcised or not; what matters is for him to become an altogether new creature. Peace and mercy to all who follow this rule, who form the Israel of God.

    I want no more trouble from anybody after this; the marks on my body are those of Jesus. The grace of our Lord Jesus Christ be with your spirit, my brothers. Amen.

    The word of the Lord.

Gospel Acclamation   Jn 15:15
    Alleluia, alleluia!
    I call you friends, says the Lord,
    because I have made known to you
    everything I have learnt from my Father.
    Alleluia!

Fourteenth Sunday in Ordinary Time, Year C

or   Col 3:15-16

Alleluia, alleluia!
May the peace of Christ
reign in your hearts,
because it is for this that you were called together
as parts of one body.
Alleluia!

GOSPEL

A reading from the holy Gospel according to Luke   10:1-12. 17-20

The Lord appointed seventy-two others and sent them out ahead of him, in pairs, to all the towns and places he himself was to visit. He said to them, 'The harvest is rich but the labourers are few, so ask the Lord of the harvest to send labourers to his harvest. Start off now, but remember, I am sending you out like lambs among wolves. Carry no purse, no haversack, no sandals. Salute no one on the road. Whatever house you go into, let your first words be, "Peace to this house!" And if a man of peace lives there, your peace will go and rest on him; if not, it will come back to you. Stay in the same house, taking what food and drink they have to offer, for the labourer deserves his wages; do not move from house to house. Whenever you go into a town where they make you welcome, eat what is set before you. Cure those in it who are sick, and say, "The kingdom of God is very near to you." But whenever you enter a town and they do not make you welcome, go out into its streets and say, "We wipe off the very dust of your town that clings to our feet, and leave it with you. Yet be sure of this: the kingdom of God is very near." I tell you, that on that day it will not go as hard with Sodom as with that town.'

The seventy-two came back rejoicing. 'Lord,' they said 'even the devils submit to us when we use your name.' He said to them, 'I watched Satan fall like lightning from heaven. Yes, I have given you power to tread underfoot serpents and scorpions and the whole strength of the enemy; nothing shall ever hurt you. Yet do not rejoice that the spirits submit to you; rejoice rather that your names are written in heaven.'

The Gospel of the Lord.

Shorter Form, verses 1-9. Read between

The Creed is said.

Prayer over the Offerings
May this oblation dedicated to your name
purify us, O Lord,
and day by day bring our conduct
closer to the life of heaven.
Through Christ our Lord.
Amen.

Communion Antiphon   Ps 33:9
Taste and see that the Lord is good;
blessed the man who seeks refuge in him.

or   Mt 11:28

Come to me, all who labour and are burdened,
and I will refresh you, says the Lord.

Prayer after Communion
Grant, we pray, O Lord,
that, having been replenished by such great gifts,
we may gain the prize of salvation
and never cease to praise you.
Through Christ our Lord.
Amen.

FIFTEENTH SUNDAY IN ORDINARY TIME   C

His Word Is Near

We celebrate the nearness of the Lord to us his people. He is the Good Samaritan who comes close to us and heals us, raising us to life as his own body.

Entrance Antiphon   Cf. Ps 16:15
As for me, in justice I shall behold your face;
I shall be filled with the vision of your glory.

Collect
O God, who show the light of your truth
to those who go astray,
so that they may return to the right path,
give all who for the faith they profess
are accounted Christians
the grace to reject whatever is contrary to the name of Christ
and to strive after all that does it honour.
Through our Lord Jesus Christ, your Son,

Fifteenth Sunday in Ordinary Time, Year C

who lives and reigns with you in the unity of the Holy Spirit,
one God, for ever and ever.
Amen.

FIRST READING
A reading from the book of Deuteronomy   30:10-14

Moses said to the people: 'Obey the voice of the Lord your God, keeping those commandments and laws of his that are written in the Book of this Law, and you shall return to the Lord your God with all your heart and soul.

'For this Law that I enjoin on you today is not beyond your strength or beyond your reach. It is not in heaven, so that you need to wonder, "Who will go up to heaven for us and bring it down to us, so that we may hear it and keep it?" Nor is it beyond the seas, so that you need to wonder, "Who will cross the seas for us and bring it back to us, so that we may hear it and keep it?" No, the Word is very near to you, it is in your mouth and in your heart for your observance.'

The word of the Lord.

Responsorial Psalm   Ps 68:14. 17. 30-31. 33-34. 36-37. ℟ cf. v.33
  ℟ **Seek the Lord, you who are poor,
      and your hearts will revive.**

1   This is my prayer to you,
    my prayer for your favour.
    In your great love, answer me, O God,
    with your help that never fails:
    Lord, answer, for your love is kind;
    in your compassion, turn towards me.   ℟

2   As for me in my poverty and pain
    let your help, O God, lift me up.
    I will praise God's name with a song;
    I will glorify him with thanksgiving.   ℟

3   The poor when they see it will be glad
    and God-seeking hearts will revive;
    for the Lord listens to the needy
    and does not spurn his servants in their chains.   ℟

4   For God will bring help to Zion
    and rebuild the cities of Judah.

(continued)

The sons of his servants shall inherit it;
those who love his name shall dwell there. ℟

Alternative Responsorial Psalm   Ps 18:8-11. ℟ v.9

   ℟ **The precepts of the Lord**
      gladden the heart.

1. The law of the Lord is perfect,
it revives the soul.
The rule of the Lord is to be trusted,
it gives wisdom to the simple. ℟

2. The precepts of the Lord are right,
they gladden the heart.
The command of the Lord is clear,
it gives light to the eyes. ℟

3. The fear of the Lord is holy,
abiding for ever.
The decrees of the Lord are truth
and all of them just. ℟

4. They are more to be desired than gold,
than the purest of gold
and sweeter are they than honey,
than honey from the comb. ℟

SECOND READING
A reading from the letter of St Paul to the Colossians   1:15-20

Christ Jesus is the image of the unseen God
and the first-born of all creation,
for in him were created
all things in heaven and on earth:
everything visible and everything invisible,
Thrones, Dominations, Sovereignties, Powers –
all things were created through him and for him.
Before anything was created, he existed,
and he holds all things in unity.
Now the Church is his body,
he is its head.
As he is the Beginning,
he was first to be born from the dead,
so that he should be first in every way;
because God wanted all perfection
to be found in him

and all things to be reconciled through him and for him,
everything in heaven and everything on earth,
when he made peace
by his death on the cross.

The word of the Lord.

Gospel Acclamation Jn 10:27

Alleluia, alleluia!
The sheep that belong to me listen to my voice,
says the Lord,
I know them and they follow me.
Alleluia!

or Cf. Jn 6:63. 68

Alleluia, alleluia!
Your words are spirit, Lord,
and they are life:
you have the message of eternal life.
Alleluia!

GOSPEL

A reading from the holy Gospel according to Luke 10:25-37

There was a lawyer who, to disconcert Jesus, stood up and said to him, 'Master, what must I do to inherit eternal life?' He said to him, 'What is written in the law? What do you read there?' He replied, 'You must love the Lord your God with all your heart, with all your soul, with all your strength, and with all your mind, and your neighbour as yourself.' 'You have answered right,' said Jesus, 'do this and life is yours.'

But the man was anxious to justify himself and said to Jesus, 'And who is my neighbour?' Jesus replied, 'A man was once on his way down from Jerusalem to Jericho and fell into the hands of brigands; they took all he had, beat him and then made off, leaving him half dead. Now a priest happened to be travelling down the same road, but when he saw the man, he passed by on the other side. In the same way a Levite who came to the place saw him, and passed by on the other side. But a Samaritan traveller who came upon him was moved with compassion when he saw him. He went up and bandaged his wounds, pouring oil and wine on them. He then lifted him on to his own mount, carried him to the inn and looked after him. Next day, he took out two denarii and handed them to the innkeeper. "Look after him," he said "and on my way back I will make good any extra expense you have." Which of these three, do you think, proved himself a neighbour to the man who fell into the brigands' hands?' 'The one, who took pity on him' he replied. Jesus said to him, 'Go, and do the same yourself.'

The Gospel of the Lord.

The Creed is said.

Prayer over the Offerings
Look upon the offerings of the Church, O Lord,
as she makes her prayer to you,
and grant that, when consumed by those who believe,
they may bring ever greater holiness.
Through Christ our Lord.
Amen.

Communion Antiphon   Cf. Ps 83:4-5
The sparrow finds a home,
and the swallow a nest for her young:
by your altars, O Lord of hosts, my King and my God.
Blessed are they who dwell in your house,
for ever singing your praise.

or   Jn 6:57

Whoever eats my flesh and drinks my blood
remains in me and I in him, says the Lord.

Prayer after Communion
Having consumed these gifts, we pray, O Lord,
that, by our participation in this mystery,
its saving effects upon us may grow.
Through Christ our Lord.
Amen.

SIXTEENTH SUNDAY IN ORDINARY TIME   C

Jesus Our Friend

The mystery of today's celebration is Christ among us as our friend. We welcome him as Abraham and Sarah welcomed the Lord at Mamre, and Martha and Mary welcomed Christ at Bethany.

Entrance Antiphon   Ps 53:6. 8
See, I have God for my help.
The Lord sustains my soul.
I will sacrifice to you with willing heart,
and praise your name, O Lord, for it is good.

Sixteenth Sunday in Ordinary Time, Year C

Collect
Show favour, O Lord, to your servants
and mercifully increase the gifts of your grace,
that, made fervent in hope, faith and charity,
they may be ever watchful in keeping your commands.
Through our Lord Jesus Christ, your Son,
who lives and reigns with you in the unity of the Holy Spirit,
one God, for ever and ever.
Amen.

FIRST READING
A reading from the book of Genesis 18:1-10

The Lord appeared to Abraham at the Oak of Mamre while he was sitting by the entrance of the tent during the hottest part of the day. He looked up, and there he saw three men standing near him. As soon as he saw them he ran from the entrance of the tent to meet them, and bowed to the ground. 'My Lord,' he said 'I beg you, if I find favour with you, kindly do not pass your servant by. A little water shall be brought; you shall wash your feet and lie down under the tree. Let me fetch a little bread and you shall refresh yourselves before going further. That is why you have come in your servant's direction.' They replied, 'Do as you say.'

Abraham hastened to the tent to find Sarah. 'Hurry,' he said 'knead three bushels of flour and make loaves.' Then running to the cattle Abraham took a fine and tender calf and gave it to the servant, who hurried to prepare it. Then taking cream, milk and the calf he had prepared, he laid all before them, and they ate while he remained standing near them under the tree. 'Where is your wife Sarah?' they asked him. 'She is in the tent' he replied. Then his guest said, 'I shall visit you again next year without fail and your wife will then have a son.'

The word of the Lord.

Responsorial Psalm Ps 14:2-5. ℟ v.1
 ℟ **The just will live in the presence of the Lord.**

1 Lord, who shall dwell on your holy mountain?
 He who walks without fault;
 he who acts with justice
 and speaks the truth from his heart;
 he who does not slander with his tongue. ℟

2 He who does no wrong to his brother,
   who casts no slur on his neighbour,
   who holds the godless in disdain,
   but honours those who fear the Lord ℟

3 He who keeps his pledge, come what may;
   who takes no interest on a loan
   and accepts no bribes against the innocent.
   Such a man will stand firm for ever. ℟

SECOND READING
A reading from the letter of St Paul to the Colossians   1:24-28

It makes me happy to suffer for you, as I am suffering now, and in my body to do what I can to make up all that has still to be undergone by Christ for the sake of his body, the Church. I became the servant of the Church when God made me responsible for delivering God's message to you, the message which was a mystery hidden for generations and centuries and has now been revealed to his saints. It was God's purpose to reveal it to them and to show all the rich glory of this mystery to pagans. The mystery is Christ among you, your hope of glory: this is the Christ we proclaim, this is the wisdom in which we thoroughly train everyone and instruct everyone, to make them all perfect in Christ.

The word of the Lord.

Gospel Acclamation   Cf. Acts 16:14
   Alleluia, alleluia!
   Open our heart, O Lord,
   to accept the words of your Son.
   Alleluia!

or   Cf. Lk 8:15

   Alleluia, alleluia!
   Blessed are those who,
   with a noble and generous heart,
   take the word of God to themselves
   and yield a harvest through their perseverance.
   Alleluia!

GOSPEL
A reading from the holy Gospel according to Luke   10:38-42

Jesus came to a village, and a woman named Martha welcomed him into her house. She had a sister called Mary, who sat down at the Lord's feet and listened to him speaking. Now Martha who was distracted with all the serving said, 'Lord, do you not care that my sister is leaving me to do the serving all by myself? Please tell her to help me.' But the Lord answered: 'Martha, Martha,' he said 'you worry and fret about so many things, and yet few are needed, indeed only one. It is Mary who has chosen the better part; it is not to be taken from her.'

The Gospel of the Lord.

The Creed is said.

Prayer over the Offerings
O God, who in the one perfect sacrifice
brought to completion varied offerings of the law,
accept, we pray, this sacrifice from your faithful servants
and make it holy, as you blessed the gifts of Abel,
so that what each has offered to the honour of your majesty
may benefit the salvation of all.
Through Christ our Lord.
Amen.

Communion Antiphon Ps 110:4-5
The Lord, the gracious, the merciful,
has made a memorial of his wonders;
he gives food to those who fear him.

or Rv 3:20
Behold, I stand at the door and knock, says the Lord.
If anyone hears my voice and opens the door,
I will enter his house and dine with him, and he with me.

Prayer after Communion
Graciously be present to your people, we pray, O Lord,
and lead those you have imbued with heavenly mysteries
to pass from former ways to newness of life.
Through Christ our Lord.
Amen.

SEVENTEENTH SUNDAY IN ORDINARY TIME C

Our Father In Heaven

Christ has given us in very truth the power to become the children of God. Compare the timidity and self-abnegation of Abraham's prayer with the confidence with which Christ teaches us to pray to our Father in heaven.

Seventeenth Sunday in Ordinary Time, Year C

Entrance Antiphon Cf. Ps 67:6-7. 36
God is in his holy place,
God who unites those who dwell in his house;
he himself gives might and strength to his people.

Collect
O God, protector of those who hope in you,
without whom nothing has firm foundation, nothing is holy,
bestow in abundance your mercy upon us
and grant that, with you as our ruler and guide,
we may use the good things that pass
in such a way as to hold fast even now
to those that ever endure.
Through our Lord Jesus Christ, your Son,
who lives and reigns with you in the unity of the Holy Spirit,
one God, for ever and ever.
Amen.

FIRST READING
A reading from the book of Genesis 18:20-32

The Lord said, 'How great an outcry there is against Sodom and Gomorrah! How grievous is their sin! I propose to go down and see whether or not they have done all that is alleged in the outcry against them that has come up to me. I am determined to know.'

The men left there and went to Sodom while Abraham remained standing before the Lord. Approaching him he said, 'Are you really going to destroy the just man with the sinner? Perhaps there are fifty just men in the town. Will you really overwhelm them, will you not spare the place for the fifty just men in it? Do not think of doing such a thing: to kill the just man with the sinner, treating just and sinner alike! Do not think of it! Will the judge of the whole earth not administer justice?' The Lord replied, 'If at Sodom I find fifty just men in the town, I will spare the whole place because of them.'

Abraham replied, 'I am bold indeed to speak like this to my Lord, I who am dust and ashes. But perhaps the fifty just men lack five: will you destroy the whole city for five?' 'No,' he replied, 'I *will not destroy it if I find forty-five just men there.*' Again Abraham said to him, 'Perhaps there will only be forty there.' 'I will not do it' he replied 'for the sake of the forty.' Abraham said, 'I trust my Lord will not be angry, but give me leave to speak: perhaps there will only be thirty there.' 'I will not do it' he replied 'if I find thirty there.' He said, 'I am bold indeed to speak like this, but perhaps there will only be twenty there.' 'I will not destroy it' he replied 'for the sake of the twenty.' He said, 'I trust my Lord will not be angry if I speak once more: perhaps there will only be ten.' I will not destroy it' he replied 'for the sake of the ten.'

The word of the Lord.

Responsorial Psalm   Ps 137:1-3. 6-8. ℟ v.3

  ℟ **On the day I called,
you answered me, O Lord.**

1   I thank you, Lord, with all my heart,
you have heard the words of my mouth.
Before the angels I will bless you.
I will adore before your holy temple.   ℟

2   I thank you for your faithfulness and love
which excel all we ever knew of you.
On the day I called, you answered;
you increased the strength of my soul.   ℟

3   The Lord is high yet he looks on the lowly
and the haughty he knows from afar.
Though I walk in the midst of affliction
you give me life and frustrate my foes.   ℟

4   You stretch out your hand and save me,
your hand will do all things for me.
Your love, O Lord, is eternal,
discard not the work of your hands.   ℟

SECOND READING
A reading from the letter of St Paul to the Colossians   2:12-14

You have been buried with Christ, when you were baptised; and by baptism, too, you have been raised up with him through your belief in the power of God who raised him from the dead. You were dead, because you were sinners and had not been circumcised: he has brought you to life with him, he has forgiven us all our sins.

He has overridden the Law, and cancelled every record of the debt that we had to pay; he has done away with it by nailing it to the cross.

The word of the Lord.

Gospel Acclamation   Jn 1:14. 12

    Alleluia, alleluia!
    The Word was made flesh and lived among us;
    to all who did accept him
    he gave power to become children of God.
    Alleluia!

or   Rom 8:15

    Alleluia, alleluia!
    The spirit you received is the spirit of sons,
    and it makes us cry out, 'Abba, Father!'
    Alleluia!

GOSPEL

A reading from the holy Gospel according to Luke   11:1-13

Once Jesus was in a certain place praying, and when he had finished, one of his disciples said, 'Lord, teach us to pray, just as John taught his disciples.' He said to them, 'Say this when you pray:

    "Father, may your name be held holy,
    your kingdom come;
    give us each day our daily bread,
    and forgive us our sins,
    for we ourselves forgive each one who is in debt to us.
    And do not put us to the test."'

He also said to them, 'Suppose one of you has a friend and goes to him in the middle of the night to say, "My friend, lend me three loaves because a friend of mine on his travels has just arrived at my house and I have nothing to offer him"; and the man answers from inside the house, "Do not bother me. The door is bolted now, and my children and I are in bed; I cannot get up to give it to you," I tell you, if the man does not get up and give it him for friendship's sake, persistence will be enough to make him get up and give his friend all he wants.

'So I say to you: Ask, and it will be given to you; search, and you will find; knock, and the door will be opened to you. For the one who asks always receives; the one who searches always finds; the one who knocks will always have the door opened to him. What father among you would hand his son a stone when he asked for bread? Or hand him a snake instead of a fish? Or hand him a scorpion if he asked for an egg? If you then, who are evil, know how to give your children what is good, how much more will the heavenly Father give the Holy Spirit to those who ask him!'

    The Gospel of the Lord.

Eighteenth Sunday in Ordinary Time, Year C

The Creed is said.

Prayer over the Offerings
Accept, O Lord, we pray, the offerings
which we bring from the abundance of your gifts,
that through the powerful working of your grace
these most sacred mysteries may sanctify our present way of life
and lead us to eternal gladness.
Through Christ our Lord.
Amen.

Communion Antiphon Ps 102:2
Bless the Lord, O my soul,
and never forget all his benefits.

or Mt 5:7-8

Blessed are the merciful, for they shall receive mercy.
Blessed are the clean of heart, for they shall see God.

Prayer after Communion
We have consumed, O Lord, this divine Sacrament,
the perpetual memorial of the Passion of your Son;
grant, we pray, that this gift,
which he himself gave us with love beyond all telling,
may profit us for salvation.
Through Christ our Lord.
Amen.

EIGHTEENTH SUNDAY IN ORDINARY TIME   C

Christ Who Is Everything and in Everything

Today our thoughts are on heavenly things, not on the things of earth where without Christ all is vanity and great injustice.

Entrance Antiphon Ps 69:2. 6
O God, come to my assistance;
O Lord, make haste to help me!
You are my rescuer, my help;
O Lord, do not delay.

Collect
Draw near to your servants, O Lord,
and answer their prayers with unceasing kindness,
that, for those who glory in you as their Creator and guide,

you may restore what you have created
and keep safe what you have restored.
Through our Lord Jesus Christ, your Son,
who lives and reigns with you in the unity of the Holy Spirit,
one God, for ever and ever.
Amen.

FIRST READING
A reading from the book of Ecclesiastes   1:2; 2:21-23

Vanity of vanities, the Preacher says. Vanity of vanities. All is vanity!

    For so it is that a man who has laboured wisely, skilfully and successfully must leave what is his own to someone who has not toiled for it at all. This, too, is vanity and great injustice; for what does he gain for all the toil and strain that he has undergone under the sun? What of all his laborious days, his cares of office, his restless nights? This, too, is vanity.

    The word of the Lord.

Responsorial Psalm   Ps 89:3-6. 12-14. 17. ℟ v.1

  ℟ **O Lord, you have been our refuge**
     from one generation to the next.

1   You turn men back into dust
and say: 'Go back, sons of men.'
To your eyes a thousand years
are like yesterday, come and gone,
no more than a watch in the night. ℟

2   You sweep men away like a dream,
like grass which springs up in the morning.
In the morning it springs up and flowers:
by evening it withers and fades. ℟

3   Make us know the shortness of our life
that we may gain wisdom of heart.
Lord, relent! Is your anger for ever?
Show pity to your servants. ℟

4   In the morning, fill us with your love;
we shall exult and rejoice all our days.
Let the favour of the Lord be upon us:
give success to the work of our hands. ℟

Alternative Responsorial Psalm   Ps 94:1-2. 6-9. R̸ vv.7-8

  R̸   **O that today you would listen to his voice!**
        Harden not your hearts.

1   Come, ring out our joy to the Lord;
    hail the rock who saves us.
    Let us come before him, giving thanks,
    with songs let us hail the Lord.   R̸

2   Come in; let us bow and bend low;
    let us kneel before the God who made us
    for he is our God and we
    the people who belong to his pasture,
    the flock that is led by his hand.   R̸

3   O that today you would listen to his voice!
    'Harden not your hearts at Meribah,
    as on that day at Massah in the desert
    when your fathers put me to the test;
    when they tried me, though they saw my work.'   R̸

SECOND READING

A reading from the letter of St Paul to the Colossians   3:1-5. 9-11

Since you have been brought back to true life with Christ, you must look for the things that are in heaven, where Christ is, sitting at God's right hand. Let your thoughts be on heavenly things, not on the things that are on the earth, because you have died, and now the life you have is hidden with Christ in God. But when Christ is revealed – and he is your life – you too will be revealed in all your glory with him.

    That is why you must kill everything in you that belongs only to earthly life: fornication, impurity, guilty passion, evil desires and especially greed, which is the same thing as worshipping a false god; and never tell each other lies. You have stripped off your old behaviour with your old self, and you have put on a new self which will progress towards true knowledge the more it is renewed in the image of its creator; and in that image there is no room for distinction between Greek and Jew, between the circumcised or the uncircumcised, or between barbarian and Scythian, slave and free man. There is only Christ: he is everything and he is in everything.

    The word of the Lord.

Eighteenth Sunday in Ordinary Time, Year C

Gospel Acclamation Cf. Jn 17:17
Alleluia, alleluia!
Your word is truth, O Lord,
consecrate us in the truth.
Alleluia!

or Mt 5:3

Alleluia, alleluia!
How happy are the poor in spirit;
theirs is the kingdom of heaven.
Alleluia!

GOSPEL
A reading from the holy Gospel according to Luke 12:13-21

A man in the crowd said to Jesus, 'Master, tell my brother to give me a share of our inheritance.' 'My friend,' he replied, 'who appointed me your judge, or the arbitrator of your claims?' Then he said to them, 'Watch, and be on your guard against avarice of any kind, for a man's life is not made secure by what he owns, even when he has more than he needs.'

Then he told them a parable: 'There was once a rich man who, having had a good harvest from his land, thought to himself, "What am I to do? I have not enough room to store my crops." Then he said, "This is what I will do: I will pull down my barns and build bigger ones, and store all my grain and my goods in them, and I will say to my soul: My soul, you have plenty of good things laid by for many years to come; take things easy, eat, drink, have a good time." But God said to him, "Fool! This very night the demand will be made for your soul; and this hoard of yours, whose will it be then?" So it is when a man stores up treasure for himself in place of making himself rich in the sight of God.'

The Gospel of the Lord.

The Creed is said.

Prayer over the Offerings
Graciously sanctify these gifts, O Lord, we pray,
and, accepting the oblation of this spiritual sacrifice,
make of us an eternal offering to you.
Through Christ our Lord.
Amen.

Communion Antiphon
Wis 16:20

You have given us, O Lord, bread from heaven,
endowed with all delights and sweetness in every taste.

or
Jn 6:35

I am the bread of life, says the Lord;
whoever comes to me will not hunger
and whoever believes in me will not thirst.

Prayer after Communion
Accompany with constant protection, O Lord,
those you renew with these heavenly gifts
and, in your never-failing care for them,
make them worthy of eternal redemption.
Through Christ our Lord.
Amen.

NINETEENTH SUNDAY IN ORDINARY TIME   C

The Lord Our God

The Lord has chosen us to be his people. Though a little flock, our history goes back into the dim and distant past. The God we worship is the God of Abraham, Isaac and Jacob. We also look forward in hope to a glorious future in the Kingdom of our Father.

Entrance Antiphon
Cf. Ps 73:20. 19. 22-23

Look to your covenant, O Lord,
and forget not the life of your poor ones for ever.
Arise, O God, and defend your cause,
and forget not the cries of those who seek you.

Collect
Almighty ever-living God,
whom, taught by the Holy Spirit,
we dare to call our Father,
bring, we pray, to perfection in our hearts
the spirit of adoption as your sons and daughters,
that we may merit to enter into the inheritance
which you have promised.
Through our Lord Jesus Christ, your Son,
who lives and reigns with you in the unity of the Holy Spirit,
one God, for ever and ever.
Amen.

FIRST READING
A reading from the book of Wisdom   18:6-9

That night had been foretold to our ancestors, so that,
once they saw what kind of oaths they had put their trust in
they would joyfully take courage.
This was the expectation of your people,
the saving of the virtuous and the ruin of their enemies;
for by the same act with which you took vengeance on our foes
you made us glorious by calling us to you.
The devout children of worthy men offered sacrifice in secret
and this divine pact they struck with one accord:
that the saints would share the same blessings and dangers alike;
and forthwith they had begun to chant the hymns of the fathers.

The word of the Lord.

Responsorial Psalm   Ps 32:1. 12. 18-20. 22. ℟ v.12

℟ **Happy are the people the Lord has chosen as his own.**

1 Ring out your joy to the Lord, O you just;
 for praise is fitting for loyal hearts.
 They are happy, whose God is the Lord,
 the people he has chosen as his own. ℟

2 The Lord looks on those who revere him,
 on those who hope in his love,
 to rescue their souls from death,
 to keep them alive in famine. ℟

3 Our soul is waiting for the Lord.
 The Lord is our help and our shield.
 May your love be upon us, O Lord,
 as we place all our hope in you. ℟

SECOND READING
A reading from the letter to the Hebrews   11:1-2. 8-19

*Only faith can guarantee the blessings that we hope for, or prove the existence of the realities that at present remain unseen. It was for faith that our ancestors were commended.

It was by faith that Abraham obeyed the call to set out for a country that was the inheritance given to him and his descendants, and that he set out without knowing where he was going. By faith he arrived, as a foreigner, in the Promised Land, and lived there as if in a strange country, with Isaac and Jacob, who were heirs with him of the same promise. They lived there in tents while he looked forward to a city founded, designed and built by God.

It was equally by faith that Sarah, in spite of being past the age, was made able to conceive, because she believed that he who had made the promise would be faithful to it. Because of this, there came from one man, and one who was already as good as dead himself, more descendants than could be counted, as many as the stars of heaven or the grains of sand on the seashore.*

All these died in faith, before receiving any of the things that had been promised, but they saw them in the far distance and welcomed them, recognising that they were only strangers and nomads on earth. People who use such terms about themselves make it quite plain that they are in search of their real homeland. They can hardly have meant the country they came from, since they had the opportunity to go back to it; but in fact they were longing for a better homeland, their heavenly homeland. That is why God is not ashamed to be called their God, since he has founded the city for them.

It was by faith that Abraham, when put to the test, offered up Isaac. He offered to sacrifice his only son even though the promises had been made to him and he had been told: It is through Isaac that your name will be carried on. He was confident that God had the power even to raise the dead; and so, figuratively speaking, he was given back Isaac from the dead.

The word of the Lord.

Shorter Form, verses 1-2. 8-12. Read between

Gospel Acclamation
Cf. Mt 11:25

Alleluia, alleluia!
Blessed are you, Father,
Lord of heaven and earth,
for revealing the mysteries of the kingdom
to mere children.
Alleluia!

or
Mt 24:42. 44

Alleluia, alleluia!
Stay awake and stand ready,
because you do not know the hour
when the Son of Man is coming.
Alleluia!

GOSPEL

A reading from the holy Gospel according to Luke   12:32-48

Jesus said to his disciples: 'There is no need to be afraid, little flock, for it has pleased your Father to give you the kingdom.

'Sell your possessions and give alms. Get yourselves purses that do not wear out, treasure that will not fail you, in heaven where no thief can reach it and no moth destroy it. For where your treasure is, there will your heart be also.

'See that you are dressed for action and have your lamps lit. Be like men waiting for their master to return from the wedding feast, ready to open the door as soon as he comes and knocks. Happy those servants whom the master finds awake when he comes. I tell you solemnly, he will put on an apron, sit them down at table and wait on them. It may be in the second watch he comes, or in the third, but happy those servants if he finds them ready. You may be quite sure of this, that if the householder had known at what hour the burglar would come, he would not have let anyone break through the wall of his house. You too must stand ready, because the Son of Man is coming at an hour you do not expect.'

Peter said, 'Lord, do you mean this parable for us, or for everyone?' The Lord replied, 'What sort of steward, then, is faithful and wise enough for the master to place him over his household to give them their allowance of food at the proper time? Happy that servant if his master's arrival finds him at this employment. I tell you truly, he will place him over everything he owns. But as for the servant who says to himself, "My master is taking his time coming", and sets about beating the menservants and the maids, and eating and drinking and getting drunk, his master will come on a day he does not expect and at an hour he does not know. The master will cut him off and send him to the same fate as the unfaithful.

'The servant who knows what his master wants, but has not even started to carry out those wishes, will receive very many strokes of the lash. The one who did not know, but deserves to be beaten for what he has done, will receive fewer strokes. When a man has had a great deal given him, a great deal will be demanded of him; when a man has had a great deal given him on trust, even more will be expected of him.'

The Gospel of the Lord.

Shorter Form, verses 35-40. Read between

The Creed is said.

Prayer over the Offerings
Be pleased, O Lord, to accept the offerings of your Church,
for in your mercy you have given them to be offered
and by your power you transform them
into the mystery of our salvation.
Through Christ our Lord.
Amen.

Communion Antiphon Ps 147:12. 14
O Jerusalem, glorify the Lord,
who gives you your fill of finest wheat.

or Cf. Jn 6:51

The bread that I will give, says the Lord,
is my flesh for the life of the world.

Prayer after Communion
May the communion in your Sacrament
that we have consumed, save us, O Lord,
and confirm us in the light of your truth.
Through Christ our Lord.
Amen.

TWENTIETH SUNDAY IN ORDINARY TIME C

Victory with Christ

Today's celebration should raise our morale in the fight against evil. Christ our Leader, who came to bring fire on the earth, communicates to us something of his tremendous zeal.

Entrance Antiphon Ps 83:10-11
Turn your eyes, O God, our shield;
and look on the face of your anointed one;
one day within your courts
is better than a thousand elsewhere.

Collect
O God, who have prepared for those who love you
good things which no eye can see,
fill our hearts, we pray, with the warmth of your love,
so that, loving you in all things and above all things,
we may attain your promises,
which surpass every human desire.
Through our Lord Jesus Christ, your Son,

who lives and reigns with you in the unity of the Holy Spirit,
one God, for ever and ever.
Amen.

FIRST READING

A reading from the prophet Jeremiah   38:4-6. 8-10

The king's leading men spoke to the king. 'Let Jeremiah be put to death: he is unquestionably disheartening the remaining soldiers in the city, and all the people too, by talking like this. The fellow does not have the welfare of this people at heart so much as its ruin.' 'He is in your hands as you know,' King Zedekiah answered 'for the king is powerless against you.' So they took Jeremiah and threw him into the well of Prince Malchiah in the Court of the Guard, letting him down with ropes. There was no water in the well, only mud, and into the mud Jeremiah sank. Ebed-melech came out from the palace and spoke to the king.

'My lord king,' he said 'these men have done a wicked thing by treating the prophet Jeremiah like this: they have thrown him into the well where he will die.' At this the king gave Ebed-melech the Cushite the following order: 'Take three men with you from here and pull the prophet Jeremiah out of the well before he dies.'

The word of the Lord.

Responsorial Psalm   Ps 39:2-4. 18. ℟ v.14

℟   **Lord, come to my aid!**

1   I waited, I waited for the Lord
    and he stooped down to me;
    he heard my cry.   ℟

2   He drew me from the deadly pit,
    from the miry clay.
    He set my feet upon a rock
    and made my footsteps firm.   ℟

3   He put a new song into my mouth,
    praise of our God.
    Many shall see and fear
    and shall trust in the Lord.   ℟

4   As for me, wretched and poor,
    the Lord thinks of me.
    You are my rescuer, my help,
    O God, do not delay.   ℟

SECOND READING
A reading from the letter to the Hebrews 12:1-4

With so many witnesses in a great cloud on every side of us, we too, then, should throw off everything that hinders us, especially the sin that clings so easily, and keep running steadily in the race we have started. Let us not lose sight of Jesus, who leads us in our faith and brings it to perfection: for the sake of the joy which was still in the future, he endured the cross, disregarding the shamefulness of it, and from now on has taken his place at the right of God's throne. Think of the way he stood such opposition from sinners and then you will not give up for want of courage. In the fight against sin, you have not yet had to keep fighting to the point of death.

The word of the Lord.

Gospel Acclamation
Cf. Acts 16:14
    Alleluia, alleluia!
    Open our heart, O Lord,
    to accept the words of your Son.
    Alleluia!

or
Jn 10:27
    Alleluia, alleluia!
    The sheep that belong to me listen to my voice,
    says the Lord,
    I know them and they follow me.
    Alleluia!

GOSPEL
A reading from the holy Gospel according to Luke 12:49-53

Jesus said to his disciples: 'I have come to bring fire to the earth, and how I wish it were blazing already! There is a baptism I must still receive, and how great is my distress till it is over!

'Do you suppose that I am here to bring peace on earth? No, I tell you, but rather division. For from now on a household of five will be divided: three against two and two against three; the father divided against the son, son against father, mother against daughter, daughter against mother, mother-in-law against daughter-in-law, daughter-in-law against mother-in-law.'

The Gospel of the Lord.

The Creed is said.

Prayer over the Offerings
Receive our oblation, O Lord,
by which is brought about a glorious exchange,
that, by offering what you have given,
we may merit to receive your very self.
Through Christ our Lord.
Amen.

Communion Antiphon   Ps 129:7
With the Lord there is mercy;
in him is plentiful redemption.

or   Jn 6:51-52

I am the living bread that came down from heaven, says the Lord.
Whoever eats of this bread will live for ever.

Prayer after Communion
Made partakers of Christ through these Sacraments,
we humbly implore your mercy, Lord,
that, conformed to his image on earth,
we may merit also to be his coheirs in heaven.
Who lives and reigns for ever and ever.
Amen.

TWENTY-FIRST SUNDAY IN ORDINARY TIME   C

The Lord Gathers a People to Himself

Today, as sons and daughters of God, we submit ourselves to his loving discipline, remembering that it was not just the Jews, nor will it be just Christians whom the Lord will gather to himself. Many more worthy than us will come from East and West to share the banquet of his kingdom.

Entrance Antiphon   Cf. Ps 85:1-3
Turn your ear, O Lord, and answer me;
save the servant who trusts in you, my God.
Have mercy on me, O Lord, for I cry to you all the day long.

Collect
O God, who cause the minds of the faithful
to unite in a single purpose,
grant your people to love what you command
and to desire what you promise,
that, amid the uncertainties of this world,

Twenty-First Sunday in Ordinary Time, Year C

our hearts may be fixed on that place
where true gladness is found.
Through our Lord Jesus Christ, your Son,
who lives and reigns with you in the unity of the Holy Spirit,
one God, for ever and ever.
Amen.

FIRST READING
A reading from the prophet Isaiah 66:18-21

The Lord says this: I am coming to gather the nations of every language. They shall come to witness my glory. I will give them a sign and send some of their survivors to the nations: to Tarshish, Put, Lud, Moshech, Rosh, Tubal, and Javan, to the distant islands that have never heard of me or seen my glory. They will proclaim my glory to the nations. As an offering to the Lord they will bring all your brothers, in horses, in chariots, in litters, on mules, on dromedaries, from all the nations to my holy mountain in Jerusalem, says the Lord, like Israelites bringing oblations in clean vessels to the Temple of the Lord. And of some of them I will make priests and Levites, says the Lord.

The word of the Lord.

Responsorial Psalm Ps 116. ℟ Mk 16:15

℟ **Go out to the whole world;
proclaim the Good News.**

or

℟ **Alleluia!**

1 O praise the Lord, all you nations,
acclaim him all you peoples! ℟

2 Strong is his love for us;
he is faithful for ever. ℟

SECOND READING
A reading from the letter to the Hebrews 12:5-7. 11-13

Have you forgotten that encouraging text in which you are addressed as sons? My son, when the Lord corrects you, do not treat it lightly; but do not get discouraged when he reprimands you. For the Lord trains the ones that he loves and he punishes all those that he acknowledges as his sons. Suffering is part of your training; God is treating you as his sons. Has there ever been any son whose father did not train him? Of course, any punishment is most painful at the time, and far from pleasant; but later, in those on whom it has been used, it bears fruit in peace and goodness. So hold up your limp arms and steady your trembling knees and smooth out the path you tread; then the injured limb will not be wrenched, it will grow strong again.

The word of the Lord.

Gospel Acclamation Jn 14:23
Alleluia, alleluia!
If anyone loves me he will keep my word,
and my Father will love him,
and we shall come to him.
Alleluia!

or Jn 14:6

Alleluia, alleluia!
I am the Way, the Truth and the Life, says the Lord;
no one can come to the Father except through me.
Alleluia!

GOSPEL

A reading from the holy Gospel according to Luke 13:22-30

Through towns and villages Jesus went teaching, making his way to Jerusalem. Someone said to him, 'Sir, will there be only a few saved?' He said to them, 'Try your best to enter by the narrow door, because I tell you, many will try to enter and will not succeed.

'Once the master of the house has got up and locked the door, you may find yourself knocking on the door, saying, "Lord, open to us" but he will answer, "I do not know where you come from."

'Then you will find yourself saying, "We once ate and drank in your company; you taught in our streets" but he will reply, "I do not know where you come from. Away from me, all you wicked men!"

'Then there will be weeping and grinding of teeth, when you see Abraham and Isaac and Jacob and all the prophets in the kingdom of God, and yourselves turned outside. And men from east and west, from north and south, will come to take their places at the feast in the kingdom of God.

'Yes, there are those now last who will be first, and those now first who will be last.'

The Gospel of the Lord.

The Creed is said.

Prayer over the Offerings
O Lord, who gained for yourself a people by adoption
through the one sacrifice offered once for all,
bestow graciously on us, we pray,
the gifts of unity and peace in your Church.
Through Christ our Lord.
Amen.

Communion Antiphon Cf. Ps 103:13-15
The earth is replete with the fruits of your work, O Lord;
you bring forth bread from the earth
and wine to cheer the heart.

or Cf. Jn 6:54

Whoever eats my flesh and drinks my blood
has eternal life, says the Lord,
and I will raise him up on the last day.

Prayer after Communion
Complete within us, O Lord, we pray,
the healing work of your mercy
and graciously perfect and sustain us,
so that in all things we may please you.
Through Christ our Lord.
Amen.

TWENTY-SECOND SUNDAY IN ORDINARY TIME   C

Jesus, the Mediator of a New Covenant

God made the new covenant of his love with the poor, the lowly, the downtrodden and the oppressed. It is therefore in a spirit of humility, the spirit of Jesus, that we make our celebration today, asking him to accept the homage of the humble.

Entrance Antiphon Cf. Ps 85:3. 5
Have mercy on me, O Lord, for I cry to you all the day long.
O Lord, you are good and forgiving,
full of mercy to all who call to you.

Collect
God of might, giver of every good gift,
put into our hearts the love of your name,

so that, by deepening our sense of reverence,
you may nurture in us what is good
and, by your watchful care,
keep safe what you have nurtured.
Through our Lord Jesus Christ, your Son,
who lives and reigns with you in the unity of the Holy Spirit,
one God, for ever and ever.
Amen.

FIRST READING
A reading from the book of Ecclesiasticus 3:17-20. 28-29

My son, be gentle in carrying out your business,
and you will be better loved than a lavish giver.
The greater you are, the more you should behave humbly,
and then you will find favour with the Lord;
for great though the power of the Lord is,
he accepts the homage of the humble.
There is no cure for the proud man's malady,
since an evil growth has taken root in him.
The heart of a sensible man will reflect on parables,
an attentive ear is the sage's dream.

The word of the Lord.

Responsorial Psalm Ps 67:4-7. 10-11. ℟ cf. v.11
℟   **In your goodness, O God, you prepared a home for the poor.**

1   The just shall rejoice at the presence of God,
    they shall exult and dance for joy.
    O sing to the Lord, make music to his name;
    rejoice in the Lord, exult at his presence. ℟

2   Father of the orphan, defender of the widow,
    such is God in his holy place.
    God gives the lonely a home to live in;
    he leads the prisoners forth into freedom. ℟

3   You poured down, O God, a generous rain:
    when your people were starved you gave them new life.
    It was there that your people found a home,
    prepared in your goodness, O God, for the poor. ℟

SECOND READING
A reading from the letter to the Hebrews   12:18-19. 22-24

What you have come to is nothing known to the senses: not a blazing fire, or a gloom turning to total darkness, or a storm; or trumpeting thunder or the great voice speaking which made everyone that heard it beg that no more should be said to them. But what you have come to is Mount Zion and the city of the living God, the heavenly Jerusalem where the millions of angels have gathered for the festival, with the whole Church in which everyone is a 'firstborn son' and a citizen of heaven. You have come to God himself, the supreme Judge, and been placed with spirits of the saints who have been made perfect; and to Jesus, the mediator who brings a new covenant.

The word of the Lord.

Gospel Acclamation   Jn 14:23
Alleluia, alleluia!
If anyone loves me he will keep my word,
and my Father will love him,
and we shall come to him.
Alleluia!

or   Mt 11:29

Alleluia, alleluia!
Shoulder my yoke and learn from me,
for I am gentle and humble in heart.
Alleluia!

GOSPEL
A reading from the holy Gospel according to Luke   14:1. 7-14

On a sabbath day Jesus had gone for a meal to the house of one of the leading Pharisees; and they watched him closely. He then told the guests a parable, because he had noticed how they picked the places of honour. He said this, 'When someone invites you to a wedding feast, do not take your seat in the place of honour. A more distinguished person than you may have been invited, and the person who invited you both may come and say, "Give up your place to this man." And then, to your embarrassment, you would have to go and take the lowest place. No; when you are a guest, make your way to the lowest place and sit there, so that, when your host comes, he may say, "My friend, move up higher." In that way, everyone with you at the table will see you honoured. For everyone who exalts himself will be humbled, and the man who humbles himself will be exalted.'

Then he said to his host, 'When you give a lunch or a dinner, do not ask your friends, brothers, relations or rich neighbours, for fear they repay your courtesy by inviting you in return. No; when you have a party, invite the poor, the crippled, the lame, the blind; that they cannot pay you back means that you are fortunate, because repayment will be made to you when the virtuous rise again.'

The Gospel of the Lord.

The Creed is said.

Prayer over the Offerings
May this sacred offering, O Lord,
confer on us always the blessing of salvation,
that what it celebrates in mystery
it may accomplish in power.
Through Christ our Lord.
Amen.

Communion Antiphon Ps 30:20
How great is the goodness, Lord,
that you keep for those who fear you.

or Mt 5:9-10

Blessed are the peacemakers,
for they shall be called children of God.
Blessed are they who are persecuted for the sake of righteousness,
for theirs is the Kingdom of Heaven.

Prayer after Communion
Renewed by this bread from the heavenly table,
we beseech you, Lord,
that, being the food of charity,
it may confirm our hearts
and stir us to serve you in our neighbour.
Through Christ our Lord.
Amen.

TWENTY-THIRD SUNDAY IN ORDINARY TIME C

Christ Who Gave Up Everything for Our Sake

We celebrate the self-sacrificing love of Christ, the unfathomable wisdom of God, who was prepared to give up everything out of love for all. In the same spirit St Paul was prepared to send back to Philemon the dear friend of his captivity, Onesimus, a part of his own self.

Entrance Antiphon
Ps 118:137. 124

You are just, O Lord, and your judgement is right;
treat your servant in accord with your merciful love.

Collect
O God, by whom we are redeemed and receive adoption,
look graciously upon your beloved sons and daughters,
that those who believe in Christ
may receive true freedom
and an everlasting inheritance.
Through our Lord Jesus Christ, your Son,
who lives and reigns with you in the unity of the Holy Spirit,
one God, for ever and ever.
Amen.

FIRST READING
A reading from the book of Wisdom 9:13-18

What man can know the intentions of God?
Who can divine the will of the Lord?
The reasonings of mortals are unsure
and our intentions unstable;
for a perishable body presses down the soul,
and this tent of clay weighs down the teeming mind.
It is hard enough for us to work out what is on earth,
laborious to know what lies within our reach;
who, then, can discover what is in the heavens?
As for your intention, who could have learnt it, had you not
    granted Wisdom
and sent your holy spirit from above?
Thus have the paths of those on earth been straightened
and men been taught what pleases you,
and saved, by Wisdom.

The word of the Lord.

Twenty-Third Sunday in Ordinary Time, Year C

Responsorial Psalm Ps 89:3-6. 12-14. 17. ℟ v.1

℟ **O Lord, you have been our refuge
from one generation to the next.**

1. You turn men back into dust
and say: 'Go back, sons of men.'
To your eyes a thousand years
are like yesterday, come and gone,
no more than a watch in the night. ℟

2. You sweep men away like a dream,
like grass which springs up in the morning.
In the morning it springs up and flowers:
by evening it withers and fades. ℟

3. Make us know the shortness of our life
that we may gain wisdom of heart.
Lord, relent! Is your anger for ever?
Show pity to your servants. ℟

4. In the morning, fill us with your love;
we shall exult and rejoice all our days.
Let the favour of the Lord be upon us:
give success to the work of our hands. ℟

SECOND READING

A reading from the letter of St Paul to Philemon 9-10. 12-17

This is Paul writing, an old man now and, what is more, still a prisoner of Christ Jesus. I am appealing to you for a child of mine, whose father I became while wearing these chains: I mean Onesimus. I am sending him back to you, and with him – I could say – a part of my own self. I should have liked to keep him with me; he could have been a substitute for you, to help me while I am in the chains that the Good News has brought me. However, I did not want to do anything without your consent; it would have been forcing your act of kindness, which should be spontaneous. I know you have been deprived of Onesimus for a time, but it was only so that you could have him back for ever, not as a slave any more, but something much better than a slave, a dear brother; especially dear to me, but how much more to you, as a blood-brother as well as a brother in the Lord. So if all that we have in common means anything to you, welcome him as you would me.

The word of the Lord.

Twenty-Third Sunday in Ordinary Time, Year C

Gospel Acclamation   Jn 15:15
> Alleluia, alleluia!
> I call you friends, says the Lord,
> because I have made known to you
> everything I have learnt from my Father.
> Alleluia!

or   Ps 118:135

> Alleluia, alleluia!
> Let your face shine on your servant,
> and teach me your decrees.
> Alleluia!

GOSPEL

A reading from the holy Gospel according to Luke   14:25-33

Great crowds accompanied Jesus on his way and he turned and spoke to them. 'If any man comes to me without hating his father, mother, wife, children, brothers, sisters, yes and his own life too, he cannot be my disciple. Anyone who does not carry his cross and come after me cannot be my disciple.

'And indeed, which of you here, intending to build a tower, would not first sit down and work out the cost to see if he had enough to complete it? Otherwise, if he laid the foundation and then found himself unable to finish the work, the onlookers would all start making fun of him and saying, "Here is a man who started to build and was unable to finish." Or again, what king marching to war against another king would not first sit down and consider whether with ten thousand men he could stand up to the other who advanced against him with twenty thousand? If not, then while the other king was still a long way off, he would send envoys to sue for peace. So in the same way, none of you can be my disciple unless he gives up all his possessions.'

The Gospel of the Lord.

The Creed is said.

Prayer over the Offerings
O God, who give us the gift of true prayer and of peace,
graciously grant that through this offering,
we may do fitting homage to your divine majesty
and, by partaking of the sacred mystery,

we may be faithfully united in mind and heart.
Through Christ our Lord.
Amen.

Communion Antiphon
Cf. Ps 41:2-3
Like the deer that yearns for running streams,
so my soul is yearning for you, my God;
my soul is thirsting for God, the living God.

or
Jn 8:12

I am the light of the world, says the Lord;
whoever follows me will not walk in darkness,
but will have the light of life.

Prayer after Communion
Grant that your faithful, O Lord,
whom you nourish and endow with life
through the food of your Word and heavenly Sacrament,
may so benefit from your beloved Son's great gifts
that we may merit an eternal share in his life.
Who lives and reigns for ever and ever.
Amen.

TWENTY-FOURTH SUNDAY IN ORDINARY TIME C

Christ Who Welcomes Sinners

The Christ we celebrate in this Eucharist is the second Moses who interceded for sinners, who came into the world to save them, and who loves them and welcomes them.

Entrance Antiphon
Cf. Sir 36:18
Give peace, O Lord, to those who wait for you,
that your prophets be found true.
Hear the prayers of your servant,
and of your people Israel.

Collect
Look upon us, O God,
Creator and ruler of all things,
and, that we may feel the working of your mercy,
grant that we may serve you with all our heart.
Through our Lord Jesus Christ, your Son,

Twenty-Fourth Sunday in Ordinary Time, Year C

who lives and reigns with you in the unity of the Holy Spirit,
one God, for ever and ever.
Amen.

FIRST READING
A reading from the book of Exodus   32:7-11. 13-14

The Lord spoke to Moses, 'Go down now, because your people whom you brought out of Egypt have apostasised. They have been quick to leave the way I marked out for them; they have made themselves a calf of molten metal and have worshipped it and offered it sacrifice. "Here is your God, Israel," they have cried "who brought you up from the land of Egypt!" I can see how headstrong these people are! Leave me, now, my wrath shall blaze out against them and devour them; of you, however, I will make a great nation.'

But Moses pleaded with the Lord his God. 'Lord,' he said, 'why should your wrath blaze out against this people of yours whom you brought out of the land of Egypt with arm outstretched and mighty hand? Remember Abraham, Isaac and Jacob, your servants to whom by your own self you swore and made this promise: I will make your offspring as many as the stars of heaven, and all this land which I promised I will give to your descendants, and it shall be their heritage for ever.' So the Lord relented and did not bring on his people the disaster he had threatened.

The word of the Lord.

Responsorial Psalm   Ps 50:3-4. 12-13. 17. 19. ℟ Lk 15:18

  ℟ **I will leave this place and go to my father.**

1. Have mercy on me, God, in your kindness.
    In your compassion blot out my offence.
    O wash me more and more from my guilt
    and cleanse me from my sin.   ℟

2. A pure heart create for me, O God,
    put a steadfast spirit within me.
    Do not cast me away from your presence,
    nor deprive me of your holy spirit.   ℟

3. O Lord, open my lips
    and my mouth shall declare your praise.
    My sacrifice is a contrite spirit;
    a humbled, contrite heart you will not spurn.   ℟

SECOND READING
A reading from the first letter of St Paul to Timothy   1:12-17

I thank Christ Jesus our Lord, who has given me strength, and who judged me faithful enough to call me into his service even though I used to be a blasphemer and did all I could to injure and discredit the faith. Mercy, however, was shown me, because until I became a believer I had been acting in ignorance; and the grace of our Lord filled me with faith and with the love that is in Christ Jesus. Here is a saying that you can rely on and nobody should doubt: that Christ Jesus came into the world to save sinners. I myself am the greatest of them; and if mercy has been shown to me, it is because Jesus Christ meant to make me the greatest evidence of his inexhaustible patience for all the other people who would later have to trust in him to come to eternal life. To the eternal King, the undying, invisible and only God, be honour and glory for ever and ever. Amen.

The word of the Lord.

Gospel Acclamation   Cf. Eph 1:17-18
Alleluia, alleluia!
May the Father of our Lord Jesus Christ
enlighten the eyes of our mind,
so that we can see what hope his call holds for us.
Alleluia!

or   2 Cor 5:19

Alleluia, alleluia!
God in Christ was reconciling the world to himself,
and he has entrusted to us the news that they are reconciled.
Alleluia.

GOSPEL
A reading from the holy Gospel according to Luke   15:1-32

*The tax collectors and the sinners were all seeking the company of Jesus to hear what he had to say, and the Pharisees and the scribes complained. 'This man' they said 'welcomes sinners and eats with them.' So he spoke this parable to them:

'What man among you with a hundred sheep, losing one, would not leave the ninety-nine in the wilderness and go after the missing one till he found it? And when he found it, would he not joyfully take it on his shoulders and then, when he got home, call together his friends, and neighbours? "Rejoice with me," he would say "I have found my sheep that was lost." In the same way, I tell you, there will be more rejoicing in heaven over one repentant sinner than over ninety-nine virtuous men who have no need of repentance.

'Or again, what woman with ten drachmas would not, if she lost one, light a lamp and sweep out the house and search thoroughly till she found it? And then, when she had found it, call together her friends and neighbours? "Rejoice with me," she would say "I have found the drachma I lost." In the same way, I tell you, there is rejoicing among the angels of God over one repentant sinner.'*

He also said, 'A man had two sons. The younger said to his father, "Father, let me have the share of the estate that would come to me." So the father divided the property between them. A few days later, the younger son got together everything he had and left for a distant country where he squandered his money on a life of debauchery.

'When he had spent it all, that country experienced a severe famine, and now he began to feel the pinch, so he hired himself out to one of the local inhabitants who put him on his farm to feed the pigs. And he would willingly have filled his belly with the husks the pigs were eating but no one offered him anything. Then he came to his senses and said, "How many of my father's paid servants have more food than they want, and here am I dying of hunger! I will leave this place and go to my father and say: Father, I have sinned against heaven and against you; I no longer deserve to be called your son; treat me as one of your paid servants." So he left the place and went back to his father.

'While he was still a long way off, his father saw him and was moved with pity. He ran to the boy, clasped him in his arms and kissed him tenderly. Then his son said, "Father, I have sinned against heaven and against you. I no longer deserve to be called your son." But the father said to his servants, "Quick! Bring out the best robe and put it on him; put a ring on his finger and sandals on his feet. Bring the calf we have been fattening, and kill it; we are going to have a feast, a celebration, because this son of mine was dead and has come back to life; he was lost and is found." And they began to celebrate.

'Now the elder son was out in the fields, and on his way back, as he drew near the house, he could hear music and dancing. Calling one of the servants he asked what it was all about. "Your brother has come" replied the servant "and your father has killed the calf we had fattened because he has got him back safe and sound." He was angry then and refused to go in, and his father came out to plead with him; but he answered his father, "Look, all these years I have slaved for you and never once disobeyed your orders, yet you never offered me so much as a kid for me to celebrate with my friends. But, for this son of yours, when he comes back after swallowing up your property – he and his women – you kill the calf we had been fattening."

'The father said, "My son, you are with me always and all I have is yours. But it was only right we should celebrate and rejoice, because your brother here was dead and has come to life; he was lost and is found."'

The Gospel of the Lord.

Shorter Form, verses 1-10. Read between

The Creed is said.

Prayer over the Offerings
Look with favour on our supplications, O Lord,
and in your kindness accept these, your servants' offerings,
that what each has offered to the honour of your name
may serve the salvation of all.
Through Christ our Lord.
Amen.

Communion Antiphon   Cf. Ps 35:8
How precious is your mercy, O God!
The children of men seek shelter in the shadow of your wings.

or   Cf. 1 Cor 10:16

The chalice of blessing that we bless
is a communion in the Blood of Christ;
and the bread that we break
is a sharing in the Body of the Lord.

Prayer after Communion
May the working of this heavenly gift, O Lord, we pray,
take possession of our minds and bodies,
so that its effects, and not our own desires,
may always prevail in us.
Through Christ our Lord.
Amen.

TWENTY-FIFTH SUNDAY IN ORDINARY TIME C

Lord of the Oppressed

Christ is the defender of all who are sacrificed to the god of money, who are manipulated for economic gain. He sacrificed himself as a ransom for them all.

Entrance Antiphon
I am the salvation of the people, says the Lord.
Should they cry to me in any distress,
I will hear them, and I will be their Lord for ever.

Collect
O God, who founded all the commands of your sacred Law
upon love of you and of our neighbour,
grant that, by keeping your precepts,
we may merit to attain eternal life.
Through our Lord Jesus Christ, your Son,
who lives and reigns with you in the unity of the Holy Spirit,
one God, for ever and ever.
Amen.

FIRST READING
A reading from the prophet Amos   8:4-7

Listen to this, you who trample on the needy
and try to suppress the poor people of the country,
you who say, 'When will New Moon be over
so that we can sell our corn,
and sabbath, so that we can market our wheat?
Then by lowering the bushel, raising the shekel,
by swindling and tampering with the scales,
we can buy up the poor for money,
and the needy for a pair of sandals,
and get a price even for the sweepings of the wheat.'
The Lord swears it by the pride of Jacob,
'Never will I forget a single thing you have done.'

The word of the Lord.

Responsional Psalm Ps 112:1-2. 4-8. ℟ cf. vv.1. 7

℟ **Praise the Lord, who raises the poor.**

or

℟ **Alleluia!**

1   Praise, O servants of the Lord,
    praise the name of the Lord!
    May the name of the Lord be blessed
    both now and for evermore! ℟

2   High above all nations is the Lord,
    above the heavens his glory.
    Who is like the Lord, our God,
    who has risen on high to his throne
    yet stoops from the heights to look down,
    to look down upon heaven and earth? ℟

3   From the dust he lifts up the lowly,
    from the dungheap he raises the poor
    to set him in the company of princes,
    yes, with the princes of his people. ℟

SECOND READING

A reading from the first letter of St Paul to Timothy   2:1-8

My advice is that, first of all, there should be prayers offered for everyone – petitions, intercessions and thanksgiving – and especially for kings and others in authority, so that we may be able to live religious and reverent lives in peace and quiet. To do this is right, and will please God our saviour: he wants everyone to be saved and reach full knowledge of the truth. For there is only one God, and there is only one mediator between God and mankind, himself a man, Christ Jesus, who sacrificed himself as a ransom for them all. He is the evidence of this, sent at the appointed time, and I have been named a herald and apostle of it and – I am telling the truth and no lie – a teacher of the faith and the truth to the pagans.

In every place, then, I want the men to lift their hands up reverently in prayer, with no anger or argument.

The word of the Lord.

Gospel Acclamation   Cf. Acts 16:14

Alleluia, alleluia!
Open our heart, O Lord,
to accept the words of your Son,
Alleluia!

or 2 Cor 8:9

Alleluia, alleluia!
Jesus Christ was rich,
but he became poor for your sake,
to make you rich out of his poverty.
Alleluia!

GOSPEL

A reading from the holy Gospel according to Luke 16:1-13

Jesus said to his disciples, 'There was a rich man and he had a steward who was denounced to him for being wasteful with his property. He called for the man and said, "What is this I hear about you? Draw me up an account of your stewardship because you are not to be my steward any longer." Then the steward said to himself, "Now that my master is taking the stewardship from me, what am I to do? Dig? I am not strong enough. Go begging? I should be too ashamed. Ah, I know what I will do to make sure that when I am dismissed from office there will be some to welcome me into their homes."

'Then he called his master's debtors one by one. To the first he said, "How much do you owe my master?" "One hundred measures of oil" was the reply. The steward said, "Here, take your bond; sit down straight away and write fifty." To another he said, "And you, sir, how much do you owe?" "One hundred measures of wheat" was the reply. The steward said, "Here, take your bond and write eighty."

'The master praised the dishonest steward for his astuteness. For the children of this world are more astute in dealing with their own kind than are the children of light.

'And so I tell you this: use money, tainted as it is, to win you friends, and thus make sure that when it fails you, they will welcome you into the tents of eternity. *The man who can be trusted in little things can be trusted in great; the man who is dishonest in little things will be dishonest in great. If then you cannot be trusted with money, that tainted thing, who will trust you with genuine riches? And if you cannot be trusted with what is not yours, who will give you what is your very own?

'No servant can be the slave of two masters: he will either hate the first and love the second, or treat the first with respect and the second with scorn. You cannot be the slave both of God and of money.'

The Gospel of the Lord.*

Shorter Form, verses 10-13. Read between

The Creed is said.

Prayer over the Offerings
Receive with favour, O Lord, we pray,
the offerings of your people,
that what they profess with devotion and faith
may be theirs through these heavenly mysteries.
Through Christ our Lord.
Amen.

Communion Antiphon   Ps 118:4-5
You have laid down your precepts to be carefully kept;
may my ways be firm in keeping your statutes.

or   Jn 10:14

I am the Good Shepherd, says the Lord;
I know my sheep, and mine know me.

Prayer after Communion
Graciously raise up, O Lord,
those you renew with this Sacrament,
that we may come to possess your redemption
both in mystery and in the manner of our life.
Through Christ our Lord.
Amen.

TWENTY-SIXTH SUNDAY IN ORDINARY TIME   C

Behold the Man!

It is our purple and fine linen, our life of ease and our love of wealth, that is mocked today by the lone figure of Christ, the centre of our celebration, who in the presence of Pilate stood like a Lazarus covered with sores and wounds and spoke up as a witness for the truth.

Entrance Antiphon   Dn 3:31. 29. 30. 43. 42
All that you have done to us, O Lord,
you have done with true judgement,
for we have sinned against you
and not obeyed your commandments.
But give glory to your name
and deal with us according to the bounty of your mercy.

Collect

O God, who manifest your almighty power
above all by pardoning and showing mercy,
bestow, we pray, your grace abundantly upon us
and make those hastening to attain your promises
heirs to the treasures of heaven.
Through our Lord Jesus Christ, your Son,
who lives and reigns with you in the unity of the Holy Spirit,
one God, for ever and ever.
Amen.

FIRST READING

A reading from the prophet Amos   6:1. 4-7

The almighty Lord says this:

> Woe to those ensconced so snugly in Zion
> and to those who feel so safe on the mountain of Samaria.
> Lying on ivory beds
> and sprawling on their divans,
> they dine on lambs from the flock,
> and stall-fattened veal;
> they bawl to the sound of the harp,
> they invent new instruments of music like David,
> they drink wine by the bowlful,
> and use the finest oil for anointing themselves,
> but about the ruin of Joseph they do not care at all.
> That is why they will be the first to be exiled;
> the sprawlers' revelry is over.

The word of the Lord.

Responsorial Psalm   Ps 145:6-10. ℟ v.2

℟ **My soul, give praise to the Lord.**

or

℟ **Alleluia!**

1   It is the Lord who keeps faith for ever,
    who is just to those who are oppressed.
    It is he who gives bread to the hungry,
    the Lord, who sets prisoners free.   ℟

2   It is the Lord who gives sight to the blind,
    who raises up those who are bowed down.

It is the Lord who loves the just,
the Lord, who protects the stranger. ℟

3 He upholds the widow and orphan
but thwarts the path of the wicked.
The Lord will reign for ever,
Zion's God, from age to age. ℟

SECOND READING
A reading from the first letter of St Paul to Timothy 6:11-16

As a man dedicated to God, you must aim to be saintly and religious, filled with faith and love, patient and gentle. Fight the good fight of the faith and win for yourself the eternal life to which you were called when you made your profession and spoke up for the truth in front of many witnesses. Now, before God the source of all life and before Jesus Christ, who spoke up as a witness for the truth in front of Pontius Pilate, I put to you the duty of doing all that you have been told, with no faults or failures, until the Appearing of our Lord Jesus Christ,

>who at the due time will be revealed
>by God, the blessed and only Ruler of all,
>the King of kings and the Lord of lords,
>who alone is immortal,
>whose home is in inaccessible light,
>whom no man has seen and no man is able to see:
>to him be honour and everlasting power. Amen.

The word of the Lord.

Gospel Acclamation Jn 10:27
Alleluia, alleluia!
The sheep that belong to me listen to my voice,
says the Lord,
I know them and they follow me.
Alleluia!

or 2 Cor 8:9

Alleluia, alleluia!
Jesus Christ was rich,
but he became poor for your sake,
to make you rich out of his poverty.
Alleluia!

Twenty-Sixth Sunday in Ordinary Time, Year C

GOSPEL
A reading from the holy Gospel according to Luke 16:19-31

Jesus said to the Pharisees: 'There was a rich man who used to dress in purple and fine linen and feast magnificently every day. And at his gate there lay a poor man called Lazarus, covered with sores, who longed to fill himself with the scraps that fell from the rich man's table. Dogs even came and licked his sores. Now the poor man died and was carried away by the angels to the bosom of Abraham. The rich man also died and was buried.

'In his torment in Hades he looked up and saw Abraham a long way off with Lazarus in his bosom. So he cried out, "Father Abraham, pity me and send Lazarus to dip the tip of his finger in water and cool my tongue, for I am in agony in these flames." "My son," Abraham replied "remember that during your life good things came your way, just as bad things came the way of Lazarus. Now he is being comforted here while you are in agony. But that is not all: between us and you a great gulf has been fixed, to stop anyone, if he wanted to, crossing from our side to yours, and to stop any crossing from your side to ours."

'The rich man replied, "Father, I beg you then to send Lazarus to my father's house, since I have five brothers, to give them warning so that they do not come to this place of torment too." "They have Moses and the prophets," said Abraham "let them listen to them." "Ah no, father Abraham," said the rich man "but if someone comes to them from the dead, they will repent." Then Abraham said to him, "If they will not listen either to Moses or to the prophets, they will not be convinced even if someone should rise from the dead."'

The Gospel of the Lord.

The Creed is said.

Prayer over the Offerings
Grant us, O merciful God,
that this our offering may find acceptance with you
and that through it the wellspring of all blessing
may be laid open before us.
Through Christ our Lord.
Amen.

Communion Antiphon
Cf. Ps 118:49-50
Remember your word to your servant, O Lord,
by which you have given me hope.
This is my comfort when I am brought low.

or   1 Jn 3:16

By this we came to know the love of God:
that Christ laid down his life for us;
so we ought to lay down our lives for one another.

Prayer after Communion
May this heavenly mystery, O Lord,
restore us in mind and body,
that we may be coheirs in glory with Christ,
to whose suffering we are united
whenever we proclaim his Death.
Who lives and reigns for ever and ever.
Amen.

TWENTY-SEVENTH SUNDAY IN ORDINARY TIME C

Our Faith

Faith gives us a new vision of the world. Without it we see only the darker side of life. We are still slaves. It is faith which liberates us and makes us see the Spirit of power and love at work in our lives.

Entrance Antiphon   Cf. Est 4:17
Within your will, O Lord, all things are established,
and there is none that can resist your will.
For you have made all things, the heaven and the earth,
and all that is held within the circle of heaven;
you are the Lord of all.

Collect
Almighty ever-living God,
who in the abundance of your kindness
surpass the merits and the desires of those who entreat you,
pour out your mercy upon us
to pardon what conscience dreads
and to give what prayer does not dare to ask.
Through our Lord Jesus Christ, your Son,
who lives and reigns with you in the unity of the Holy Spirit,
one God, for ever and ever.
Amen.

FIRST READING
A reading from the prophet Habakkuk 1:2-3; 2:2-4

How long, Lord, am I to cry for help
while you will not listen;
to cry 'Oppression!' in your ear
and you will not save?
Why do you set injustice before me,
why do you look on where there is tyranny?
Outrage and violence, this is all I see,
all is contention, and discord flourishes.
Then the Lord answered and said,

> 'Write the vision down,
> inscribe it on tablets
> to be easily read,
> since this vision is for its own time only:
> eager for its own fulfilment, it does not deceive;
> if it comes slowly, wait,
> for come it will, without fail.
> See how he flags, he whose soul is not at rights,
> but the upright man will live by his faithfulness.'

The word of the Lord.

Responsorial Psalm
Ps 94:1-2. 6-9. R/ v.8

℟ **O that today you would listen to his voice!**
Harden not your hearts.

1 Come, ring out our joy to the Lord;
hail the rock who saves us.
Let us come before him, giving thanks,
with songs let us hail the Lord. ℟

2 Come in; let us bow and bend low;
let us kneel before the God who made us
for he is our God and we
the people who belong to his pasture,
the flock that is led by his hand. ℟

3 O that today you would listen to his voice!
'Harden not your hearts as at Meribah,
as on that day at Massah in the desert
when your fathers put me to the test;
when they tried me, though they saw my work.' ℟

SECOND READING

A reading from the second letter of St Paul to Timothy 1:6-8. 13-14

I am reminding you to fan into a flame the gift that God gave you when I laid my hands on you. God's gift was not a spirit of timidity, but the Spirit of power, and love, and self-control. So you are never to be ashamed of witnessing to the Lord, or ashamed of me for being his prisoner; but with me, bear the hardships for the sake of the Good News, relying on the power of God.

Keep as your pattern the sound teaching you have heard from me, in the faith and love that are in Christ Jesus. You have been trusted to look after something precious; guard it with the help of the Holy Spirit who lives in us.

The word of the Lord.

Gospel Acclamation 1 Sam 3:9; Jn 6:68
Alleluia, alleluia!
Speak, Lord, your servant is listening:
you have the message of eternal life.
Alleluia!

or 1 Pet 1:25

Alleluia, alleluia!
The word of the Lord remains for ever:
What is this word?
It is the Good News that has been brought to you.
Alleluia!

GOSPEL

A reading from the holy Gospel according to Luke 17:5-10

The apostles said to the Lord, 'Increase our faith.' The Lord replied, 'Were your faith the size of a mustard seed you could say to this mulberry tree, "Be uprooted and planted in the sea," and it would obey you.

'Which of you, with a servant ploughing or minding sheep, would say to him when he returned from the fields, "Come and have your meal immediately?" Would he not be more likely to say, "Get my supper laid; make yourself tidy and wait on me while I eat and drink. You can eat and drink yourself afterwards?" Must he be grateful to the servant for doing what he was told? So with you: when you have done all you have been told to do, say, "We are merely servants: we have done no more than our duty."'

The Gospel of the Lord.

The Creed is said.

Prayer over the Offerings
Accept, O Lord, we pray,
the sacrifices instituted by your commands
and, through the sacred mysteries,
which we celebrate with dutiful service,
graciously complete the sanctifying work
by which you are pleased to redeem us.
Through Christ our Lord.
Amen.

Communion Antiphon Lam 3:25
The Lord is good to those who hope in him,
to the soul that seeks him.

or Cf. 1 Cor 10:17

Though many, we are one bread, one body,
for we all partake of the one Bread and one Chalice.

Prayer after Communion
Grant us, almighty God,
that we may be refreshed and nourished
by the Sacrament which we have received,
so as to be transformed into what we consume.
Through Christ our Lord.
Amen.

TWENTY-EIGHTH SUNDAY IN ORDINARY TIME   C

Thanksgiving

Today we come to give thanks to God and to offer sacrifice to him for having made known to us his salvation and cleansed us from our sins.

Entrance Antiphon Ps 129:3-4
If you, O Lord, should mark iniquities,
Lord, who could stand?
But with you is found forgiveness,
O God of Israel.

Twenty-Eighth Sunday in Ordinary Time, Year C

Collect
May your grace, O Lord, we pray,
at all times go before us and follow after
and make us always determined
to carry out good works.
Through our Lord Jesus Christ, your Son,
who lives and reigns with you in the unity of the Holy Spirit,
one God, for ever and ever.
Amen.

FIRST READING
A reading from the second book of the Kings 5:14-17

Naaman the leper went down and immersed himself seven times in the Jordan, as Elisha had told him to do. And his flesh became clean once more like the flesh of a little child.

Returning to Elisha with his whole escort, he went in and stood before him. 'Now I know' he said 'that there is no God in all the earth except in Israel. Now, please, accept a present from your servant.' But Elisha replied, 'As the Lord lives, whom I serve, I will accept nothing.' Naaman pressed him to accept, but he refused. Then Naaman said, 'Since your answer is "No," allow your servant to be given as much earth as two mules may carry, because your servant will no longer offer holocaust or sacrifice to any god except the Lord.'

The word of the Lord.

Responsorial Psalm Ps 97:1-4. R/ cf. v.2

R/ **The Lord has shown his salvation to the nations.**

1 Sing a new song to the Lord
   for he has worked wonders.
   His right hand and his holy arm
   have brought salvation. R/

2 The Lord has made known his salvation;
   has shown his justice to the nations.
   He has remembered his truth and love
   for the house of Israel. R/

3 All the ends of the earth have seen
   the salvation of our God.
   Shout to the Lord all the earth,
   ring out your joy. R/

SECOND READING
A reading from the second letter of St Paul to Timothy   2:8-13

Remember the Good News that I carry, 'Jesus Christ risen from the dead, sprung from the race of David'; it is on account of this that I have my own hardships to bear, even to being chained like a criminal – but they cannot chain up God's news. So I bear it all for the sake of those who are chosen, so that in the end they may have the salvation that is in Christ Jesus and the eternal glory that comes with it.

Here is a saying that you can rely on:

If we have died with him, then we shall live with him.
If we hold firm, then we shall reign with him.
If we disown him, then he will disown us.
We may be unfaithful, but he is always faithful,
for he cannot disown his own self.

The word of the Lord.

Gospel Acclamation   Cf. Jn 6:63. 68
Alleluia, alleluia!
Your words are spirit, Lord,
and they are life:
you have the message of eternal life.
Alleluia!

or   1 Thess 5:18

Alleluia, alleluia!
For all things give thanks,
because this is what God expects you to do in Christ Jesus.
Alleluia!

GOSPEL
A reading from the holy Gospel according to Luke   17:11-19

On the way to Jerusalem Jesus travelled along the border between Samaria and Galilee. As he entered one of the villages, ten lepers came to meet him. They stood some way off and called to him, 'Jesus! Master! Take pity on us.' When he saw them he said 'Go and show yourselves to the priests.' Now as they were going away they were cleansed. Finding himself cured, one of them turned back praising God at the top of his voice and threw himself at the feet of Jesus and thanked him. The man was a Samaritan. This made Jesus say, 'Were not all ten made clean? The other nine, where are they? It seems that no one has come back to give praise to God, except this foreigner.' And he said to the man, 'Stand up and go on your way. Your faith has saved you.'

The Gospel of the Lord.

The Creed is said.

Prayer over the Offerings
Accept, O Lord, the prayers of your faithful
with the sacrificial offerings,
that, through these acts of devotedness,
we may pass over to the glory of heaven.
Through Christ our Lord.
Amen.

Communion Antiphon Cf. Ps 33:11
The rich suffer want and go hungry,
but those who seek the Lord lack no blessing.

or 1 Jn 3:2
When the Lord appears, we shall be like him,
for we shall see him as he is.

Prayer after Communion
We entreat your majesty most humbly, O Lord,
that, as you feed us with the nourishment
which comes from the most holy Body and Blood of your Son,
so you may make us sharers of his divine nature.
Who lives and reigns for ever and ever.
Amen.

TWENTY-NINTH SUNDAY IN ORDINARY TIME   C

Christ Always Interceding for Us

Christ who 'opened his arms on the cross' is like Moses whose arms were raised in prayer for his people. Today Christ asks us to join him in continual prayer and never to lose heart.

Entrance Antiphon Cf. Ps 16:6. 8
To you I call, for you shall surely heed me, O God;
turn your ear to me; hear my words.

Twenty-Ninth Sunday in Ordinary Time, Year C

Guard me as the apple of your eye;
in the shadow of your wings protect me.

Collect
Almighty ever-living God,
grant that we may always conform our will to yours
and serve your majesty in sincerity of heart.
Through our Lord Jesus Christ, your Son,
who lives and reigns with you in the unity of the Holy Spirit,
one God, for ever and ever.
Amen.

FIRST READING
A reading from the book of Exodus   17:8-13

The Amalekites came and attacked Israel at Rephidim. Moses said to Joshua, 'Pick out men for yourself, and tomorrow morning march out to engage Amalek. I, meanwhile, will stand on the hilltop, the staff of God in my hand.' Joshua did as Moses told him and marched out to engage Amalek, while Moses and Aaron and Hur went up to the top of the hill. As long as Moses kept his arms raised, Israel had the advantage; when he let his arms fall, the advantage went to Amalek. But Moses' arms grew heavy, so they took a stone and put it under him and on this he sat, Aaron and Hur supporting his arms, one on one side, one on the other; and his arms remained firm till sunset. With the edge of the sword Joshua cut down Amalek and his people.

    The word of the Lord.

Responsional Psalm   Ps 120. ℟ cf. v.2
   ℟ **Our help is in the name of the Lord
who made heaven and earth.**

1   I lift up my eyes to the mountains:
     from where shall come my help?
     My help shall come from the Lord
     who made heaven and earth.   ℟

2   May he never allow you to stumble!
     Let him sleep not, your guard.
     No, he sleeps not nor slumbers,
     Israel's guard.   ℟

3   The Lord is your guard and your shade;
    at your right side he stands.
    By day the sun shall not smite you
    nor the moon in the night.   ℟

4   The Lord will guard you from evil,
    he will guard your soul.
    The Lord will guard your going and coming
    both now and for ever.   ℟

SECOND READING

A reading from the second letter of St Paul to Timothy   3:14 – 4:2

You must keep to what you have been taught and know to be true; remember who your teachers were, and how, ever since you were a child, you have known the holy scriptures – from these you can learn the wisdom that leads to salvation through faith in Christ Jesus. All scripture is inspired by God and can profitably be used for teaching, for refuting error, for guiding people's lives and teaching them to be holy. This is how the man who is dedicated to God becomes fully equipped and ready for any good work.

Before God and before Christ Jesus who is to be judge of the living and the dead, I put this duty to you, in the name of his Appearing and of his kingdom: proclaim the message and, welcome or unwelcome, insist on it. Refute falsehood, correct error, call to obedience – but do all with patience and with the intention of teaching.

The word of the Lord.

Gospel Acclamation   Cf. Eph 1:17-18

Alleluia, alleluia!
May the Father of our Lord Jesus Christ
enlighten the eyes of our mind,
so that we can see what hope his call holds for us.
Alleluia!

or   Heb 4:12

Alleluia, alleluia!
The word of God is something alive and active;
it can judge secret emotions and thoughts.
Alleluia!

Twenty-Ninth Sunday in Ordinary Time, Year C

GOSPEL
A reading from the holy Gospel according to Luke   18:1-8

Jesus told his disciples a parable about the need to pray continually and never lose heart. 'There was a judge in a certain town' he said 'who had neither fear of God nor respect for man. In the same town there was a widow who kept on coming to him and saying, "I want justice from you against my enemy!" For a long time he refused, but at last he said to himself, "Maybe I have neither fear of God nor respect for man, but since she keeps pestering me I must give this widow her just rights, or she will persist in coming and worry me to death."'

And the Lord said, 'You notice what the unjust judge has to say? Now will not God see justice done to his chosen who cry to him day and night even when he delays to help them? I promise you, he will see justice done to them, and done speedily. But when the Son of Man comes, will he find any faith on earth?'

The Gospel of the Lord.

The Creed is said.

Prayer over the Offerings
Grant us, Lord, we pray,
a sincere respect for your gifts,
that, through the purifying action of your grace,
we may be cleansed by the very mysteries we serve.
Through Christ our Lord.
Amen.

Communion Antiphon   Cf. Ps 32:18-19
Behold, the eyes of the Lord
are on those who fear him,
who hope in his merciful love,
to rescue their souls from death,
to keep them alive in famine.

or   Mk 10:45

The Son of Man has come
to give his life as a ransom for many.

Prayer after Communion
Grant, O Lord, we pray,
that, benefiting from participation in heavenly things,
we may be helped by what you give in this present age

and prepared for the gifts that are eternal.
Through Christ our Lord.
Amen.

THIRTIETH SUNDAY IN ORDINARY TIME   C

The Lord, the Righteous Judge

The Lord is our judge. The one thing we know for certain about his judgement is that it favours the humble, and the one who humbles themself will be exalted.

Entrance Antiphon   Cf. Ps 104:3-4
Let the hearts that seek the Lord rejoice;
turn to the Lord and his strength;
constantly seek his face.

Collect
Almighty ever-living God,
increase our faith, hope and charity,
and make us love what you command,
so that we may merit what you promise.
Through our Lord Jesus Christ, your Son,
who lives and reigns with you in the unity of the Holy Spirit,
one God, for ever and ever.
Amen.

FIRST READING
A reading from the book of Ecclesiasticus   35:12-14. 16-19

The Lord is a judge
who is no respecter of personages.
He shows no respect of personages to the detriment of a poor man,
he listens to the plea of the injured party.
He does not ignore the orphan's supplication,
nor the widow's as she pours out her story.
The man who with his whole heart serves God will be accepted,
his petitions will carry to the clouds.
The humble man's prayer pierces the clouds,
until it arrives he is inconsolable,
nor will he desist until the Most High takes notice of him,
acquits the virtuous and delivers judgement.

Thirtieth Sunday in Ordinary Time, Year C

And the Lord will not be slow,
nor will he be dilatory on their behalf.

The word of the Lord.

Responsorial Psalm Ps 32:2-3. 17-19. 23. ℟ v.7
℟ **This poor man called; the Lord heard him.**

1 I will bless the Lord at all times,
his praise always on my lips;
in the Lord my soul shall make its boast.
The humble shall hear and be glad. ℟

2 The Lord turns his face against the wicked
to destroy their remembrance from the earth.
The just call and the Lord hears
and rescues them in all their distress. ℟

3 The Lord is close to the broken-hearted;
those whose spirit is crushed he will save.
The Lord ransoms the souls of his servants.
Those who hide in him shall not be condemned. ℟

SECOND READING
A reading from the second letter of St Paul 4:6-8. 16-18
to Timothy

My life is already being poured away as a libation, and the time has come for me to be gone. I have fought the good fight to the end; I have run the race to the finish; I have kept the faith; all there is to come now is the crown of righteousness reserved for me, which the Lord, the righteous judge, will give to me on that Day; and not only to me but to all those who have longed for his Appearing.

The first time I had to present my defence, there was not a single witness to support me. Every one of them deserted me – may they not be held accountable for it. But the Lord stood by me and gave me power, so that through me the whole message might be proclaimed for all the pagans to hear; and so I was rescued from the lion's mouth. The Lord will rescue me from all evil attempts on me, and bring me safely to his heavenly kingdom. To him be glory for ever and ever. Amen.

The word of the Lord.

Gospel Acclamation Cf. Mt 11:25
Alleluia, alleluia!
Blessed are you, Father,

Lord of heaven and earth,
for revealing the mysteries of the kingdom
to mere children.
Alleluia!

or 2 Cor 5:19

Alleluia, alleluia!
God in Christ was reconciling the world to himself.
and he has entrusted to us the news that they are reconciled.
Alleluia!

GOSPEL

A reading from the holy Gospel according to Luke 18:9-14

Jesus spoke the following parable to some people who prided themselves on being virtuous and despised everyone else. 'Two men went up to the Temple to pray, one a Pharisee, the other a tax collector. The Pharisee stood there and said this prayer to himself, "I thank you, God, that I am not grasping, unjust, adulterous like the rest of mankind, and particularly that I am not like this tax collector here. I fast twice a week; I pay tithes on all I get." The tax collector stood some distance away, not daring even to raise his eyes to heaven; but he beat his breast and said, "God, be merciful to me, a sinner." This man, I tell you, went home again at rights with God; the other did not. For everyone who exalts himself will be humbled, but the man who humbles himself will be exalted.'

The Gospel of the Lord.

The Creed is said.

Prayer over the Offerings
Look, we pray, O Lord,
on the offerings we make to your majesty,
that whatever is done by us in your service
may be directed above all to your glory.
Through Christ our Lord.
Amen.

Communion Antiphon
Cf. Ps 19:6

We will ring out our joy at your saving help
and exult in the name of our God.

Thirty-First Sunday in Ordinary Time, Year C

or Eph 5:2

Christ loved us and gave himself up for us,
as a fragrant offering to God.

Prayer after Communion
May your Sacraments, O Lord, we pray,
perfect in us what lies within them,
that what we now celebrate in signs
we may one day possess in truth.
Through Christ our Lord.
Amen.

THIRTY-FIRST SUNDAY IN ORDINARY TIME C

Jesus in Our Midst

To him the whole world is like a grain of dust that tips the scales or morning dew that falls. Yet he loves all that exists, and comes to dwell with sinners.

Entrance Antiphon Cf. Ps 37:22-23
Forsake me not, O Lord, my God;
be not far from me!
Make haste and come to my help,
O Lord, my strong salvation!

Collect
Almighty and merciful God,
by whose gift your faithful offer you
right and praiseworthy service,
grant, we pray,
that we may hasten without stumbling
to receive the things you have promised.
Through our Lord Jesus Christ, your Son,
who lives and reigns with you in the unity of the Holy Spirit,
one God, for ever and ever.
Amen.

FIRST READING
A reading from the book of Wisdom 11:22-12:2

In your sight, Lord, the whole world is like a grain of dust that
  tips the scales,

like a drop of morning dew falling on the ground.
Yet you are merciful to all, because you can do all things
and overlook men's sins so that they can repent.
Yes, you love all that exists, you hold nothing of what you have
 made in abhorrence,
for had you hated anything, you would not have formed it.
And how, had you not willed it, could a thing persist,
how be conserved if not called forth by you?
You spare all things because all things are yours, Lord, lover of
 life,
you whose imperishable spirit is in all.
Little by little, therefore, you correct those who offend,
you admonish and remind them of how they have sinned,
so that they may abstain from evil and trust in you, Lord.

The word of the Lord.

Responsorial Psalm Ps 144:1-2. 8-11. 13-14. ℟ cf. v.1
℟ **I will bless your name for ever,
 O God my King.**

1 I will give you glory, O God my King,
 I will bless your name for ever.
 I will bless you day after day
 and praise your name for ever. ℟

2 The Lord is kind and full of compassion,
 slow to anger, abounding in love.
 How good is the Lord to all,
 compassionate to all his creatures. ℟

3 All your creatures shall thank you, O Lord,
 and your friends shall repeat their blessing.
 They shall speak of the glory of your reign
 and declare your might, O God. ℟

4 The Lord is faithful in all his words
 and loving in all his deeds.
 The Lord supports all who fall
 and raises all who are bowed down. ℟

SECOND READING

A reading from the second letter of St Paul to the Thessalonians   1:11 – 2:2

We pray continually that our God will make you worthy of his call, and by his power fulfil all your desires for goodness and complete all that you have been doing through faith; because in this way the name of our Lord Jesus Christ will be glorified in you and you in him, by the grace of our God and the Lord Jesus Christ.

To turn now, brothers, to the coming of our Lord Jesus Christ and how we shall all be gathered round him: please do not get excited too soon or alarmed by any prediction or rumour or any letter claiming to come from us, implying that the Day of the Lord has already arrived.

The word of the Lord.

Gospel Acclamation   Lk 19:38; 2:14
Alleluia, alleluia!
Blessings on the King who comes,
in the name of the Lord!
Peace in heaven
and glory in the highest heavens!
Alleluia!

or   Jn 3:16

Alleluia, alleluia!
God loved the world so much
that he gave his only Son,
so that everyone who believes in him
may have eternal life.
Alleluia!

GOSPEL

A reading from the holy Gospel according to Luke   19:1-10

Jesus entered Jericho and was going through the town when a man whose name was Zacchaeus made his appearance; he was one of the senior tax collectors and a wealthy man. He was anxious to see what kind of man Jesus was, but he was too short and could not see him for the crowd; so he ran ahead and climbed a sycamore tree to catch a glimpse of Jesus who was to pass that way. When Jesus reached the spot he looked up and spoke to him: 'Zacchaeus, come down. Hurry, because I must stay at your house today.' And he hurried down and welcomed him joyfully. They all complained when they saw what was happening. 'He has gone to stay at a sinner's house' they said. But Zacchaeus stood his ground and said to the Lord, 'Look, sir, I am going to give half my property to the poor, and if I have cheated anybody I will pay him back four times the amount.' And Jesus said to him, 'Today salvation has come to this house, because this man too is a son of Abraham; for the Son of Man has come to seek out and save what was lost.'

The Gospel of the Lord.

The Creed is said.

Prayer over the Offerings
May these sacrificial offerings, O Lord,
become for you a pure oblation,
and for us a holy outpouring of your mercy.
Through Christ our Lord.
Amen.

Communion Antiphon   Cf. Ps 15:11
You will show me the path of life,
the fullness of joy in your presence, O Lord.

or   Jn 6:58

Just as the living Father sent me
and I have life because of the Father,
so whoever feeds on me
shall have life because of me, says the Lord.

Prayer after Communion
May the working of your power, O Lord,
increase in us, we pray,
so that, renewed by these heavenly Sacraments,
we may be prepared by your gift
for receiving what they promise.
Through Christ our Lord.
Amen.

THIRTY-SECOND SUNDAY IN ORDINARY TIME   C

Such Sure Hope

However cruelly the world may treat us, we can always rejoice in the glorious future promised us by Christ, when we will be filled with the vision of God's glory.

Entrance Antiphon
Cf. Ps 87:3

Let my prayer come into your presence.
Incline your ear to my cry for help, O Lord.

Collect
Almighty and merciful God,
graciously keep from us all adversity,
so that, unhindered in mind and body alike,
we may pursue in freedom of heart
the things that are yours.
Through our Lord Jesus Christ, your Son,
who lives and reigns with you in the unity of the Holy Spirit,
one God, for ever and ever.
Amen.

FIRST READING
A reading from the second book of Maccabees   7:1-2. 9-14

There were seven brothers who were arrested with their mother. The king tried to force them to taste pig's flesh, which the Law forbids, by torturing them with whips and scourges. One of them, acting as spokesman for the others, said, 'What are you trying to find out from us? We are prepared to die rather than break the Law of our ancestors.'

With his last breath the second brother exclaimed, 'Inhuman fiend, you may discharge us from this present life, but the King of the world will raise us up, since it is for his laws that we die, to live again for ever.'

After him, they amused themselves with the third, who on being asked for his tongue promptly thrust it out and boldly held out his hands, with these honourable words, 'It was heaven that gave me these limbs; for the sake of his laws I disdain them; from him I hope to receive them again.' The king and his attendants were astounded at the young man's courage and his utter indifference to suffering.

When this one was dead they subjected the fourth to the same savage torture. When he neared his end he cried, 'Ours is the better choice, to meet death at men's hands, yet relying on God's promise that we shall be raised up by him; whereas for you there can be no resurrection, no new life.'

The word of the Lord.

Responsorial Psalm Ps 16:1. 5-6. 8. 15. ℟ v.15
> ℟ **I shall be filled, when I awake,**
> **with the sight of your glory, O Lord.**

1. Lord, hear a cause that is just,
   pay heed to my cry.
   Turn your ear to my prayer:
   no deceit is on my lips. ℟

2. I kept my feet firmly in your paths;
   there was no faltering in my steps.
   I am here and I call, you will hear me, O God.
   Turn your ear to me; hear my words. ℟

3. Guard me as the apple of your eye.
   Hide me in the shadow of your wings.
   As for me, in my justice I shall see your face
   and be filled, when I awake, with the sight of your glory. ℟

SECOND READING

A reading from the second letter of St Paul 2:16–3:5
to the Thessalonians

May our Lord Jesus Christ himself, and God our Father who has given us his love and, through his grace, such inexhaustible comfort and such sure hope, comfort you and strengthen you in everything good that you do or say.

Finally, brothers, pray for us; pray that the Lord's message may spread quickly, and be received with honour as it was among you; and pray that we may be preserved from the interference of bigoted and evil people, for faith is not given to everyone. But the Lord is faithful, and he will give you strength and guard you from the evil one, and we, in the Lord, have every confidence that you are doing and will go on doing all that we tell you. May the Lord turn your hearts towards the love of God and the fortitude of Christ.

The word of the Lord.

Thirty-Second Sunday in Ordinary Time, Year C

Gospel Acclamation   Lk 21:36
> Alleluia, alleluia!
> Stay awake, praying at all times
> for the strength to stand with confidence before the Son of Man.
> Alleluia!

or   Apoc 1:5-6

> Alleluia, alleluia!
> Jesus Christ is the First-born from the dead;
> to him be glory and power for ever and ever.
> Amen.
> Alleluia!

GOSPEL

A reading from the holy Gospel according to Luke   20:27-38

Some Sadducees – those who say that there is no resurrection – approached Jesus and they put this question to him, 'Master, we have it from Moses in writing, that if a man's married brother dies childless, the man must marry the widow to raise up children for his brother. Well, then, there were seven brothers. The first, having married a wife, died childless. The second and then the third married the widow. And the same with all seven, they died leaving no children. Finally the woman herself died. Now, at the resurrection, to which of them will she be wife since she had been married to all seven?'

*Jesus replied, 'The children of this world take wives and husbands, but those who are judged worthy of a place in the other world and in the resurrection from the dead do not marry because they can no longer die, for they are the same as the angels, and being children of the resurrection they are sons of God. And Moses himself implies that the dead rise again, in the passage about the bush where he calls the Lord the God of Abraham, the God of Isaac and the God of Jacob. Now he is God, not of the dead, but of the living; for to him all men are in fact alive.'

The Gospel of the Lord.*

Shorter Form, verses 27. 34-38. Read between

The Creed is said.

Prayer over the Offerings
Look with favour, we pray, O Lord,
upon the sacrificial gifts offered here,

that, celebrating in mystery the Passion of your Son,
we may honour it with loving devotion.
Through Christ our Lord.
Amen.

Communion Antiphon Cf. Ps 22:1-2
The Lord is my shepherd; there is nothing I shall want.
Fresh and green are the pastures where he gives me repose,
near restful waters he leads me.

or Cf. Lk 24:35

The disciples recognized the Lord Jesus in the breaking of bread.

Prayer after Communion
Nourished by this sacred gift, O Lord,
we give you thanks and beseech your mercy,
that, by the pouring forth of your Spirit,
the grace of integrity may endure
in those your heavenly power has entered.
Through Christ our Lord.
Amen.

THIRTY-THIRD SUNDAY IN ORDINARY TIME   C

The Triumph of God

The day is coming when al that is evil will be brought to nothing. Already Christ has given us the strength to overcome evil: we receive it in the Eucharist.

Entrance Antiphon Jer 29:11-12. 14
The Lord said: I think thoughts of peace and not of affliction.
You will call upon me, and I will answer you,
and I will lead back your captives from every place.

Collect
Grant us, we pray, O Lord our God,
the constant gladness of being devoted to you,
for it is full and lasting happiness
to serve with constancy
the author of all that is good.
Through our Lord Jesus Christ, your Son,
who lives and reigns with you in the unity of the Holy Spirit,
one God, for ever and ever.
Amen.

FIRST READING

A reading from the prophet Malachi   3:19-20

The day is coming now, burning like a furnace; and all the arrogant and the evil-doers will be like stubble. The day that is coming is going to burn them up, says the Lord of hosts, leaving them neither root nor stalk. But for you who fear my name, the sun of righteousness will shine out with healing in its rays.

The word of the Lord.

Responsorial Psalm   Ps 97:5-9. ℟ cf. v.9

℟   **The Lord comes to rule the peoples with fairness.**

1   Sing psalms to the Lord with the harp
     with the sound of music.
     With trumpets and the sound of the horn
     acclaim the King, the Lord.   ℟

2   Let the sea and all within it, thunder;
     the world, and all its peoples.
     Let the rivers clap their hands
     and the hills ring out their joy
     at the presence of the Lord.   ℟

3   For the Lord comes,
     he comes to rule the earth.
     He will rule the world with justice
     and the peoples with fairness.   ℟

SECOND READING

A reading from the second letter of St Paul   3:7-12
to the Thessalonians

You know how you are supposed to imitate us: now we were not idle when we were with you, nor did we ever have our meals at anyone's table without paying for them; no, we worked night and day, slaving and straining, so as not to be a burden on any of you. This was not because we had no right to be, but in order to make ourselves an example for you to follow.

We gave you a rule when we were with you: not to let anyone have any food if he refused to do any work. Now we hear that there are some of you who are living in idleness, doing no work themselves but interfering with everyone else's. In the Lord Jesus

Christ, we order and call on people of this kind to go on quietly working and earning the food that they eat.

The word of the Lord.

Gospel Acclamation   Lk 21:36
Alleluia, alleluia!
Stay awake, praying at all times
for the strength to stand with confidence
before the Son of Man.
Alleluia!

or   Lk 21:28

Alleluia, alleluia!
Stand erect, hold your heads high,
because your liberation is near at hand.
Alleluia!

GOSPEL

A reading from the holy Gospel according to Luke   21:5-19

When some were talking about the Temple, remarking how it was adorned with fine stonework and votive offerings, Jesus said, 'All these things you are staring at now – the time will come when not a single stone will be left on another: everything will be destroyed.' And they put to him this question: 'Master,' they said 'when will this happen, then, and what sign will there be that this is about to take place?'

'Take care not to be deceived,' he said 'because many will come using my name and saying, "I am he" and, "The time is near at hand." Refuse to join them. And when you hear of wars and revolutions, do not be frightened, for this is something that must happen but the end is not so soon.' Then he said to them, 'Nation will fight against nation, and kingdom against kingdom. There will be great earthquakes and plagues and famines here and there; there will be fearful sights and great signs from heaven.

'But before all this happens, men will seize you and persecute you; they will hand you over to the synagogues and to imprisonment, and bring you before kings and governors because of my name – and that will be your opportunity to bear witness. Keep this carefully in mind: you are not to prepare your defence, because I myself shall give you an eloquence and a wisdom that none of your opponents will be able to resist or contradict. You will be betrayed even by parents and brothers, relations and friends;

Our Lord Jesus Christ, King of the Universe, Year C

and some of you will be put to death. You will be hated by all men on account of my name, but not a hair of your head will be lost. Your endurance will win you your lives.'

The Gospel of the Lord.

The Creed is said.

Prayer over the Offerings
Grant, O Lord, we pray,
that what we offer in the sight of your majesty
may obtain for us the grace of being devoted to you
and gain us the prize of everlasting happiness.
Through Christ our Lord.
Amen.

Communion Antiphon   Ps 72:28
To be near God is my happiness,
to place my hope in God the Lord.

or   Mk 11:23-24

Amen, I say to you: Whatever you ask in prayer,
believe that you will receive,
and it shall be given to you, says the Lord.

Prayer after Communion
We have partaken of the gifts of this sacred mystery,
humbly imploring, O Lord,
that what your Son commanded us to do
in memory of him
may bring us growth in charity.
Through Christ our Lord.
Amen.

Last Sunday in Ordinary Time
**OUR LORD JESUS CHRIST,
KING OF THE UNIVERSE**   **C**
Solemnity

Christ the King

We celebrate Christ our anointed King who overcame suffering and death and so brought us out of darkness into his kingdom of light.

Entrance Antiphon   Rv 5:12; 1:6
How worthy is the Lamb who was slain,
to receive power and divinity,
and wisdom and strength and honour.
To him belong glory and power for ever and ever.

The Gloria in excelsis (Glory to God in the highest) is said.

Collect
Almighty ever-living God,
whose will is to restore all things
in your beloved Son, the King of the universe,
grant, we pray,
that the whole creation, set free from slavery,
may render your majesty service
and ceaselessly proclaim your praise.
Through our Lord Jesus Christ, your Son,
who lives and reigns with you in the unity of the Holy Spirit,
one God, for ever and ever.
Amen.

FIRST READING
A reading from the second book of Samuel   5:1-3

All the tribes of Israel came to David at Hebron. 'Look,' they said, 'we are your own flesh and blood. In days past when Saul was our king, it was you who led Israel in all their exploits; and the Lord said to you, "You are the man who shall be shepherd of my people Israel, you shall be the leader of Israel."' So all the elders of Israel came to the king at Hebron, and King David made a pact with them at Hebron in the presence of the Lord, and they anointed David king of Israel.

The word of the Lord.

Responsorial Psalm   Ps 121:1-5. ℟ cf. v.2
    ℟ **I rejoiced when I heard them say:**
       'Let us go to God's house.'

1   I rejoiced when I heard them say:
     'Let us go to God's house.'
     And now our feet are standing
     within your gates, O Jerusalem.   ℟

Our Lord Jesus Christ, King of the Universe, Year C

2 Jerusalem is built as a city
   strongly compact.
   It is there that the tribes go up,
   the tribes of the Lord. ℟

3 For Israel's law it is,
   there to praise the Lord's name.
   There were set the thrones of judgement
   of the house of David. ℟

SECOND READING
A reading from the letter of St Paul to the Colossians 1:12-20

We give thanks to the Father who has made it possible for you to join the saints and with them to inherit the light.

Because that is what he has done: he has taken us out of the power of darkness and created a place for us in the kingdom of the Son that he loves, and in him, we gain our freedom, the forgiveness of our sins.

He is the image of the unseen God
and the first-born of all creation,
for in him were created
all things in heaven and on earth:
everything visible and everything invisible,
Thrones, Dominations, Sovereignties, Powers –
all things were created through him and for him.
Before anything was created, he existed,
and he holds all things in unity.
Now the Church is his body,
he is its head.
As he is the Beginning,
he was first to be born from the dead,
so that he should be first in every way;
because God wanted all perfection
to be found in him
and all things to be reconciled through him and for him,
everything in heaven and everything on earth,
when he made peace
by his death on the cross.

The word of the Lord.

Gospel Acclamation
Mk 11:9-10
Alleluia, alleluia!
Blessings on him who comes in the name of the Lord!
Blessings on the coming kingdom of our father David!
Alleluia!

GOSPEL
A reading from the holy Gospel according to Luke 23:35-43

The people stayed there before the cross watching Jesus. As for the leaders, they jeered at him. 'He saved others,' they said 'let him save himself if he is the Christ of God, the Chosen One.' The soldiers mocked him too, and when they approached to offer him vinegar they said, 'If you are the king of the Jews, save yourself.' Above him there was an inscription: 'This is the King of the Jews.'

One of the criminals hanging there abused him. 'Are you not the Christ?' he said. 'Save yourself and us as well.' But the other spoke up and rebuked him. 'Have you no fear of God at all?' he said: 'You got the same sentence as he did, but in our case we deserved it: we are paying for what we did. But this man has done nothing wrong. Jesus,' he said 'remember me when you come into your kingdom.' 'Indeed, I promise you,' he replied 'today you will be with me in paradise.'

The Gospel of the Lord.

The Creed is said.

Prayer over the Offerings
As we offer you, O Lord, the sacrifice
by which the human race is reconciled to you,
we humbly pray,
that your Son himself may bestow on all nations
the gifts of unity and peace.
Through Christ our Lord.
Amen.

Preface of Christ, King of the Universe, p.40-41

Communion Antiphon
Ps 28:10-11
The Lord sits as King for ever.
The Lord will bless his people with peace.

Prayer after Communion
Having received the food of immortality,
we ask, O Lord,

that, glorying in obedience
to the commands of Christ, the King of the universe,
we may live with him eternally in his heavenly Kingdom.
Who lives and reigns for ever and ever.
Amen.

HOLY DAYS
FEASTS OF THE LORD
AND SOLEMNITIES

HOLY DAYS
FEASTS OF THE LORD
AND SOLEMNITIES

2 February
THE PRESENTATION OF THE LORD
Feast

In the Temple Simeon and Anna encountered Christ and recognised him as Lord. Today we celebrate that event, the feast which closes the Christmas festival of light. Candles are blessed and we carry them in procession to welcome Christ, the light to enlighten the Gentiles and the glory of his people.

THE BLESSING OF CANDLES AND THE PROCESSION
First Form: The Procession

At an appropriate hour, a gathering takes place at a smaller church or other suitable place other than inside the church to which the procession will go. The faithful hold in their hands unlighted candles.

The Priest, wearing white vestments as for Mass, approaches with the ministers. Instead of the chasuble, the Priest may wear a cope, which he leaves aside after the procession is over.

While the candles are being lit, the following antiphon or another appropriate chant is sung.

Be-hold, our Lord will come with power, to en-light-en the eyes of his ser-vants, al-le-lu-ia.

or

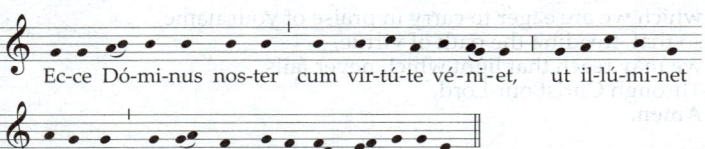

Ec-ce Dó-mi-nus nos-ter cum vir-tú-te vé-ni-et, ut il-lú-mi-net ó-cu-los ser-vó-rum su-ó-rum, al-le-lú-ia.

Holy Days and Feasts of the Lord: General Calendar

When the chant is concluded, the Priest, facing the people, says: In the name of the Father, and of the Son, and of the Holy Spirit. *Then the Priest greets the people in the usual way, and next he gives an introductory address, encouraging the faithful to celebrate the rite of this feast day actively and consciously. He may use these or similar words:*

Dear brethren (brothers and sisters),
forty days have passed since we celebrated the joyful feast
of the Nativity of the Lord.
Today is the blessed day
when Jesus was presented in the Temple by Mary and Joseph.
Outwardly he was fulfilling the Law,
but in reality he was coming to meet his believing people.
Prompted by the Holy Spirit,
Simeon and Anna came to the Temple.
Enlightened by the same Spirit,
they recognized the Lord
and confessed him with exultation.
So let us also, gathered together by the Holy Spirit,
proceed to the house of God to encounter Christ.
There we shall find him
and recognize him in the breaking of the bread,
until he comes again, revealed in glory.

After the address the Priest blesses the candles, saying, with hands extended:

Let us pray.
O God, source and origin of all light,
who on this day showed to the just man Simeon
the Light for revelation to the Gentiles,
we humbly ask that,
in answer to your people's prayers,
you may be pleased to sanctify with your blessing ☩ these candles,
which we are eager to carry in praise of your name,
so that, treading the path of virtue,
we may reach that light which never fails.
Through Christ our Lord.
Amen.

or

O God, true light, who create light eternal,
spreading it far and wide,

pour, we pray, into the hearts of the faithful
the brilliance of perpetual light,
so that all who are brightened in your holy temple
by the splendour of these candles
may happily reach the light of your glory.
Through Christ our Lord.
Amen.

He sprinkles the candles with holy water without saying anything, and puts incense into the thurible for the procession.

Then the Priest receives from the Deacon or a minister the lighted candle prepared for him and the procession begins, with the Deacon announcing (or, if there is no Deacon, the Priest himself):

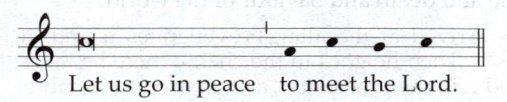

Let us go in peace to meet the Lord.

or

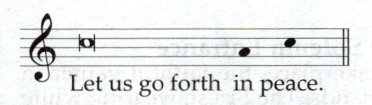

Let us go forth in peace.

In this case, all respond:

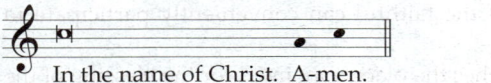

In the name of Christ. A-men.

All carry lighted candles. As the procession moves forward, one or other of the antiphons that follow is sung, namely the antiphon A light for revelation with the canticle (Lk 2:29-32), or the antiphon Sion, adorn your bridal chamber or another appropriate chant.

I

Lk 2:29-32

Ant. A light for revelation to the Gentiles
and the glory of your people Israel.
Lord, now you let your servant go in peace,
in accordance with your word.

Ant. A light for revelation to the Gentiles . . .
For my eyes have seen your salvation.
Ant. A light for revelation to the Gentiles . . .
Which you have prepared in the sight of all peoples.
Ant. A light for revelation to the Gentiles . . .

II

Ant. Sion, adorn your bridal chamber and welcome Christ the King; take Mary in your arms, who is the gate of heaven, for she herself is carrying the King of glory and new light. A Virgin she remains, though bringing in her hands the Son before the morning star begotten, whom Simeon, taking in his arms announced to the peoples as Lord of life and death and Saviour of the world.

When the Priest has arrived at the altar, he venerates it and, if appropriate, incenses it. Then he goes to the chair, where he takes off the cope, if he used it in the procession, and puts on a chasuble. After the singing of the hymn Gloria in excelsis (Glory to God in the highest), he says the Collect as usual. The Mass continues in the usual manner.

Second Form: The Solemn Entrance

Whenever a procession cannot take place, the faithful gather in church, holding candles in their hands. The Priest, wearing white sacred vestments as for Mass, together with the ministers and a representative group of the faithful, goes to a suitable place, either in front of the church door or inside the church itself, where at least a large part of the faithful can conveniently participate in the rite.

When the Priest reaches the place appointed for the blessing of the candles, candles are lit while the antiphon Behold, our Lord (as above) or another appropriate chant is sung.

Then, after the greeting and address, the Priest blesses the candles, as above; and then the procession to the altar takes place, with singing.

At the Mass

Entrance Antiphon Cf. Ps 47:10-11
Your merciful love, O God,
we have received in the midst of your temple.
Your praise, O God, like your name,

reaches the ends of the earth;
your right hand is filled with saving justice.

The Gloria in excelsis (Glory to God in the highest) is said.

Collect
Almighty ever-living God,
we humbly implore your majesty
that, just as your Only Begotten Son
was presented on this day in the Temple
in the substance of our flesh,
so, by your grace,
we may be presented to you with minds made pure.
Through our Lord Jesus Christ, your Son,
who lives and reigns with you in the unity of the Holy Spirit,
one God, for ever and ever.
Amen.

FIRST READING
A reading from the prophet Malachi   3:1-4

The Lord God says this: Look, I am going to send my messenger to prepare a way before me. And the Lord you are seeking will suddenly enter his Temple; and the angel of the covenant whom you are longing for, yes, he is coming, says the Lord of hosts. Who will be able to resist the day of his coming? Who will remain standing when he appears? For he is like the refiner's fire and the fullers' alkali. He will take his seat as refiner and purifier; he will purify the sons of Levi and refine them like gold and silver, and then they will make the offering to the Lord as it should be made. The offering of Judah and Jerusalem will then be welcomed by the Lord as in former days, as in the years of old.

The word of the Lord.

Responsional Psalm   Ps 23:7-10. ℟ v.8
   ℟   **Who is the king of glory?**
         It is the Lord.

1   O gates, lift up your heads;
     grow higher, ancient doors.
     Let him enter, the king of glory! ℟

2   Who is the king of glory?
     The Lord, the mighty, the valiant,
     the Lord, the valiant in war. ℟

3 O gates, lift high your heads;
   grow higher, ancient doors.
   Let him enter, the king of glory! ℟

4 Who is he, the king of glory?
   He, the Lord of armies,
   he is the king of glory. ℟

SECOND READING

A reading from the letter to the Hebrews   2:14-18

Since all the children share the same blood and flesh, Jesus too shared equally in it, so that by his death he could take away all the power of the devil, who had power over death, and set free all those who had been held in slavery all their lives by the fear of death. For it was not the angels that he took to himself; he took to himself descent from Abraham. It was essential that he should in this way become completely like his brothers so that he could be a compassionate and trustworthy high priest of God's religion, able to atone for human sins. That is, because he has himself been through temptation he is able to help others who are tempted.

The word of the Lord.

Gospel Acclamation   Lk 2:32
Alleluia, alleluia!
The light to enlighten the Gentiles
and give glory to Israel, your people.
Alleluia!

GOSPEL

A reading from the holy Gospel according to Luke   2:22-40

*When the day came for them to be purified as laid down by the Law of Moses, the parents of Jesus took him up to Jerusalem to present him to the Lord – observing what stands written in the Law of the Lord: Every first-born male must be consecrated to the Lord – and also to offer in sacrifice, in accordance with what is said in the Law of the Lord, a pair of turtledoves or two young pigeons. Now in Jerusalem there was a man named Simeon. He was an upright and devout man; he looked forward to Israel's comforting and the Holy Spirit rested on him. It had been revealed to him by the Holy Spirit that he would not see death until he had set eyes on the Christ of the Lord. Prompted by the Spirit he came to the Temple; and when the parents brought in the child Jesus to do for him what the law required, he took him into his arms and blessed God; and he said:

'Now, Master, you can let your servant go in peace,
just as you promised;
because my eyes have seen the salvation
which you have prepared for all the nations to see,
a light to enlighten the pagans
and the glory of your people Israel.'*

As the child's father and mother stood there wondering at the things that were being said about him, Simeon blessed them and said to Mary his mother, 'You see this child: he is destined for the fall and for the rising of many in Israel, destined to be a sign that is rejected – and a sword will pierce your own soul too – so that the secret thoughts of many may be laid bare.'

There was a prophetess also, Anna the daughter of Phanuel, of the tribe of Asher. She was well on in years. Her days of girlhood over, she had been married for seven years before becoming a widow. She was now eighty-four years old and never left the Temple, serving God night and day with fasting and prayer. She came by just at that moment and began to praise God; and she spoke of the child to all who looked forward to the deliverance of Jerusalem.

When they had done everything the Law of the Lord required, they went back to Galilee, to their own town of Nazareth. Meanwhile the child grew to maturity, and he was filled with wisdom; and God's favour was with him.

The Gospel of the Lord.

*Shorter Form, Luke 2:22-32. Read between *

When this Feast falls on a Sunday, the Creed is said.

Prayer over the Offerings
May the offering made with exultation by your Church
be pleasing to you, O Lord, we pray,
for you willed that your Only Begotten Son
be offered to you for the life of the world
as the Lamb without blemish.
Who lives and reigns for ever and ever.
Amen.

Preface of the Mystery of the Presentation of the Lord, p.39.

Communion Antiphon
Lk 2:30-31

My eyes have seen your salvation,
which you prepared in the sight of all the peoples.

Prayer after Communion
By these holy gifts which we have received, O Lord,
bring your grace to perfection within us,
and, as you fulfilled Simeon's expectation
that he would not see death
until he had been privileged to welcome the Christ,
so may we, going forth to meet the Lord,
obtain the gift of eternal life.
Through Christ our Lord.
Amen.

19 March
ST JOSEPH
SPOUSE OF THE BLESSED VIRGIN MARY
Solemnity

Joseph, the husband of Mary and guardian of the child Jesus, was of the house and line of David. The humble carpenter from Nazareth is called a 'man of honour' in the gospel and has become for us the guardian and patron of Christ's universal Church.

Entrance Antiphon
Cf. Lk 12:42

Behold, a faithful and prudent steward,
whom the Lord set over his household.

The Gloria in excelsis (Glory to God in the highest) is said.

Collect
Grant, we pray, almighty God,
that by Saint Joseph's intercession
your Church may constantly watch over
the unfolding of the mysteries of human salvation,
whose beginnings you entrusted to his faithful care.
Through our Lord Jesus Christ, your Son,
who lives and reigns with you in the unity of the Holy Spirit,
one God, for ever and ever.
Amen.

19 March: St Joseph, Spouse of the Blessed Virgin Mary

FIRST READING
A reading from the second book of Samuel 7:4-5. 12-14. 16

The word of the Lord came to Nathan:

'Go and tell my servant David, "Thus the Lord speaks: When your days are ended and you are laid to rest with your ancestors, I will preserve the offspring of your body after you and make his sovereignty secure. (It is he who shall build a house for my name, and I will make his royal throne secure for ever.) I will be a father to him and he a son to me. Your House and your sovereignty will always stand secure before me and your throne be established for ever." '

The word of the Lord.

Responsorial Psalm Ps 88:2-5. 27. 29. ℟ v.37

 ℟ **His dynasty shall last for ever.**

1   I will sing for ever of your love, O Lord;
    through all ages my mouth will proclaim your truth.
    Of this I am sure, that your love lasts for ever,
    that your truth is firmly established as the heavens. ℟

2   'I have made a covenant with my chosen one;
    I have sworn to David my servant:
    I will establish your dynasty for ever
    and set up your throne through all ages.' ℟

3   He will say to me: 'You are my father,
    my God, the rock who saves me.'
    I will keep my love for him always;
    for him my covenant shall endure. ℟

SECOND READING
A reading from the letter of St Paul 4:13. 16-18. 22
to the Romans

The promise of inheriting the world was not made to Abraham and his descendants on account of any law but on account of the righteousness which consists in faith. That is why what fulfils the promise depends on faith, so that it may be a free gift and be available to all of Abraham's descendants, not only those who belong to the Law but also those who belong to the faith of Abraham who is the Father of all of us. As scripture says: I have made you the ancestor of many nations – Abraham is our father in the eyes of God, in whom he put his faith, and who brings the dead to life and calls into being what does not exist.

Though it seemed Abraham's hope could not be fullfilled, he hoped and he believed, and through doing so he did become the father of many nations exactly as he had been promised: Your descendants will be as many as the stars. This is the faith that was 'considered as justifying him'.

The word of the Lord.

Gospel Acclamation Ps 83:5
Glory and praise to you, O Christ.
They are happy who dwell in your house, O Lord,
for ever singing your praise.
Glory and praise to you, O Christ.

GOSPEL
A reading from the holy Gospel according to Matthew
1:16. 18-21. 24

Jacob was the father of Joseph the husband of Mary; of her was born Jesus who is called Christ.

This is how Jesus Christ came to be born. His mother Mary was betrothed to Joseph; but before they came to live together she was found to be with child through the Holy Spirit. Her husband Joseph, being a man of honour and wanting to spare her publicity, decided to divorce her informally. He had made up his mind to do this when the angel of the Lord appeared to him in a dream and said, 'Joseph son of David, do not be afraid to take Mary home as your wife, because she has conceived what is in her by the Holy Spirit. She will give birth to a son and you must name him Jesus, because he is the one who is to save his people from their sins.' When Joseph woke up he did what the angel of the Lord had told him to do.

The Gospel of the Lord.

Alternative Gospel
A reading from the holy Gospel according to Luke 2:41-51

Every year the parents of Jesus used to go to Jerusalem to the feast of the Passover. When he was twelve years old, they went up for the feast as usual. When they were on their way home after the feast, the boy Jesus stayed behind in Jerusalem without his parents knowing it. They assumed he was with the caravan, and it was only after a day's journey that they went to look for him among

19 March: St Joseph, Spouse of the Blessed Virgin Mary

their relations and acquaintances. When they failed to find him they went back to Jerusalem looking for him everywhere.

Three days later, they found him in the Temple, sitting among the doctors, listening to them, and asking them questions; and all those who heard him were astounded at his intelligence and his replies. They were overcome when they saw him, and his mother said to him, 'My child, why have you done this to us? See how worried your father and I have been, looking for you.' 'Why were you looking for me?' he replied 'Did you not know that I must be busy with my Father's affairs?' But they did not understand what he meant.

He then went down with them and came to Nazareth and lived under their authority.

The Gospel of the Lord.

The Creed is said.

Prayer over the Offerings
We pray, O Lord,
that, just as Saint Joseph served with loving care
your Only Begotten Son, born of the Virgin Mary,
so we may be worthy to minister
with a pure heart at your altar.
Through Christ our Lord.
Amen.

Preface of the Mission of Saint Joseph, p.45.

Communion Antiphon Mt 25:21
Well done, good and faithful servant.
Come, share your master's joy.

Prayer after Communion
Defend with unfailing protection,
O Lord, we pray,
the family you have nourished
with food from this altar,
as they rejoice at the Solemnity of Saint Joseph,
and graciously keep safe your gifts among them.
Through Christ our Lord.
Amen.

25 March
THE ANNUNCIATION OF THE LORD
Solemnity

This ancient feast of East and West celebrates that great day of decision. Its Greek title means' the spreading of the good news', Mary's acceptance of the role that God had chosen for her in his plan of redemption.

Whenever this Solemnity occurs during Holy Week, it is transferred to the Monday after the Second Sunday of Easter.

Entrance Antiphon
Heb 10:5. 7

The Lord said, as he entered the world:
Behold, I come to do your will, O God.

The Gloria in excelsis Deo (Glory to God in the highest) is said.

Collect
O God, who willed that your Word
should take on the reality of human flesh
in the womb of the Virgin Mary,
grant, we pray,
that we, who confess our Redeemer to be God and man,
may merit to become partakers even in his divine nature.
Who lives and reigns with you in the unity of the Holy Spirit,
one God, for ever and ever.
Amen.

FIRST READING
A reading from the prophet Isaiah   7:10-14. 8:10

The Lord spoke to Ahaz and said, 'Ask the Lord your God for a sign for yourself coming either from the depths of Sheol or from the heights above.' 'No,' Ahaz answered, 'I will not put the Lord to the test.'

Then Isaiah said:

Listen now, House of David:
are you not satisfied with trying the patience of men
without trying the patience of my God, too?
The Lord himself, therefore,
will give you a sign.
It is this: the maiden is with child
and will soon give birth to a son
whom she will call Emmanuel,
a name which means, 'God-is-with-us'.

The word of the Lord.

25 March: The Annunciation of the Lord

Responsorial Psalm   Ps 39:7-11. ℟ vv.8. 9.

   ℟   **Here I am, Lord!**
          I come to do your will.

1. You do not ask for sacrifice and offerings,
   but an open ear.
   You do not ask for holocaust and victim.
   Instead, here am I. ℟

2. In the scroll of the book it stands written
   that I should do your will.
   My God, I delight in your law
   in the depth of my heart. ℟

3. Your justice I have proclaimed
   in the great assembly.
   My lips I have not sealed;
   you know it, O Lord. ℟

4. I have not hidden your justice in my heart
   but declared your faithful help.
   I have not hidden your love and your truth
   from the great assembly. ℟

SECOND READING

A reading from the letter to the Hebrews   10:4-10

Bulls' blood and goats' blood are useless for taking away sins, and this is what Christ said, on coming into the world:

   You who wanted no sacrifice or oblation,
   prepared a body for me.
   You took no pleasure in holocausts or sacrifices for sin;
   then I said,
   just as I was commanded in the scroll of the book,
   'God, here I am! I am coming to obey your will.'

Notice that he says first: You did not want what the Law lays down as the things to be offered, that is: the sacrifices, the oblations, the holocausts and the sacrifices for sin, and you took no pleasure in them; and then he says: Here I am! I am coming to obey your will. He is abolishing the first sort to replace it with the second. And this will was for us to be made holy by the offering of his body made once and for all by Jesus Christ.

   The word of the Lord.

Gospel Acclamation Jn 1:14. 12
> Praise to you, O Christ, king of eternal glory!
> The Word was made flesh,
> he lived among us,
> and we saw his glory.
> Praise to you, O Christ, king of eternal glory!

GOSPEL

A reading from the holy Gospel according to Luke 1:26-38

The angel Gabriel was sent by God to a town in Galilee called Nazareth, to a virgin betrothed to a man named Joseph, of the House of David; and the virgin's name was Mary. He went in and said to her, 'Rejoice, so highly favoured! The Lord is with you.' She was deeply disturbed by these words and asked herself what this greeting could mean, but the angel said to her, 'Mary, do not be afraid; you have won God's favour. Listen! You are to conceive and bear a son, and you must name him Jesus. He will be great and will be called Son of the Most High. The Lord God will give him the throne of his ancestor David; he will rule over the House of Jacob for ever and his reign will have no end.' Mary said to the angel, 'But how can this come about, since I am a virgin?' 'The Holy Spirit will come upon you,' the angel answered, 'and the power of the Most High will cover you with its shadow. And so the child will be holy and will be called Son of God. Know this too: your kinswoman Elizabeth has, in her old age, herself conceived a son, and she whom people called barren is now in her sixth month, for nothing is impossible to God.' 'I am the handmaid of the Lord,' said Mary, 'let what you have said be done to me.' And the angel left her.

The Gospel of the Lord.

The Creed is said. At the words and by the Holy Spirit was incarnate of the Virgin Mary and became man all kneel.

Prayer over the Offerings
Be pleased, almighty God,
to accept your Church's offering,
so that she, who is aware that her beginnings
lie in the Incarnation of your Only Begotten Son,
may rejoice to celebrate his mysteries on this Solemnity.
Who lives and reigns for ever and ever.
Amen.

Preface of the Mystery of the Incarnation, p.37.

Communion Antiphon
Is 7:14

Behold, a Virgin shall conceive and bear a son;
and his name will be called Emmanuel.

Prayer after Communion
Confirm in our minds the mysteries of the true faith,
we pray, O Lord,
so that, confessing that he who was conceived of the Virgin Mary
is true God and true man,
we may, through the saving power of his Resurrection,
merit to attain eternal joy.
Through Christ our Lord.
Amen.

24 June

THE NATIVITY OF SAINT JOHN THE BAPTIST
Solemnity

The birthday of John the Baptist is one of the oldest Christian feasts. Today we celebrate the cousin of Jesus, Elizabeth's son, the prophet who baptised Jesus in the Jordan, the forerunner, specially chosen by God to be the herald of the Saviour and to prepare the people for his coming.

At the Vigil Mass

This Mass is used on the evening of 23 June, either before or after First Vespers (Evening Prayer I) of the Solemnity.

Entrance Antiphon
Lk 1:15. 14

He will be great in the sight of the Lord
and will be filled with the Holy Spirit,
even from his mother's womb;
and many will rejoice at his birth.

The Gloria in excelsis (Glory to God in the highest) is said.

Collect
Grant, we pray, almighty God,
that your family may walk in the way of salvation
and, attentive to what Saint John the Precursor urged,
may come safely to the One he foretold,
our Lord Jesus Christ.
Who lives and reigns with you in the unity of the Holy Spirit,
one God, for ever and ever.
Amen.

FIRST READING

A reading from the prophet Jeremiah   1:4-10

The word of the Lord was addressed to me, saying,
> 'Before I formed you in the womb I knew you;
> before you came to birth I consecrated you;
> I have appointed you as prophet to the nations.'

I said, 'Ah, Lord; look, I do not know how to speak: I am a child!'

But the Lord replied:

> 'Do not say, "I am a child."
> Go now to those to whom I send you
> and say whatever I command you.
> Do not be afraid of them,
> for I am with you to protect you –
> it is the Lord who speaks!'

Then the Lord put out his hand and touched my mouth and said to me:

> 'There! I am putting my words into your mouth.
> Look, today I am setting you
> over nations and over kingdoms,
> to tear up and to knock down,
> to destroy and to overthrow,
> to build and to plant.'

The word of the Lord.

Responsorial Psalm   Ps 70:1-6. 15. 17. ℟ v.6

  ℟ **From my mother's womb you have been my help.**

1   In you, O Lord, I take refuge;
     let me never be put to shame.
     In your justice rescue me, free me:
     pay heed to me and save me.   ℟

2   Be a rock where I can take refuge,
     a mighty stronghold to save me;
     for you are my rock, my stronghold.
     Free me from the hand of the wicked.   ℟

3   It is you, O Lord, who are my hope,
     my trust, O Lord, since my youth.
     On you I have leaned from my birth,
     from my mother's womb you have been my help.   ℟

4   My lips will tell of your justice
    and day by day of your help.
    O God, you have taught me from my youth
    and I proclaim your wonders still.   ℟

SECOND READING
A reading from the first letter of St Peter   1:8-12

You did not see Jesus Christ, yet you love him; and still without seeing him, you are already filled with a joy so glorious that it cannot be described, because you believe; and you are sure of the end to which your faith looks forward, that is, the salvation of your souls.

It was this salvation that the prophets were looking and searching so hard for; their prophecies were about the grace which was to come to you. The Spirit of Christ which was in them foretold the sufferings of Christ and the glories that would come after them, and they tried to find out at what time and in what circumstances all this was to be expected. It was revealed to them that the news they brought of all the things which have now been announced to you, by those who preached to you the Good News through the Holy Spirit sent from heaven, was for you and not for themselves. Even the angels long to catch a glimpse of these things.

The word of the Lord.

Gospel Acclamation   Jn 1:7; Lk 1:17
Alleluia, alleluia!
He came as a witness,
as a witness to speak for the light,
preparing for the Lord a people fit for him.
Alleluia!

GOSPEL
A reading from the holy Gospel according to Luke   1:5-17

In the days of King Herod of Judaea there lived a priest called Zechariah who belonged to the Abijah section of the priesthood, and he had a wife, Elizabeth by name, who was a descendant of Aaron. Both were worthy in the sight of God, and scrupulously observed all the commandments and observances of the Lord. But they were childless: Elizabeth was barren and they were both getting on in years.

Now it was the turn of Zechariah's section to serve, and he was exercising his priestly office before God when it fell to him by lot, as the ritual custom was, to enter the Lord's sanctuary and burn incense there. And at the hour of incense the whole congregation was outside, praying.

Then there appeared to him the angel of the Lord, standing on the right of the altar of incense. The sight disturbed Zechariah and he was overcome with fear. But the angel said to him, 'Zechariah, do not be afraid, your prayer has been heard. Your wife Elizabeth is to bear you a son and you must name him John. He will be your joy and delight and many will rejoice at his birth, for he will be great in the sight of the Lord; he must drink no wine, no strong drink. Even from his mother's womb he will be filled with the Holy Spirit, and he will bring back many of the sons of Israel to the Lord their God. With the spirit and power of Elijah, he will go before him to turn the hearts of fathers towards their children and the disobedient back to the wisdom that the virtuous have, preparing for the Lord a people fit for him.'

The Gospel of the Lord.

The Creed is said.

Prayer over the Offerings
Look with favour, O Lord,
upon the offerings made by your people
on the Solemnity of Saint John the Baptist,
and grant that what we celebrate in mystery
we may follow with deeds of devoted service.
Through Christ our Lord.
Amen.

Preface of the Mission of the Precursor, pp.44-5.

Communion Antiphon Lk 1:68
Blessed be the Lord, the God of Israel!
He has visited his people and redeemed them.

Prayer after Communion
May the marvellous prayer of Saint John the Baptist
accompany us who have eaten our fill
at this sacrificial feast, O Lord,
and, since Saint John proclaimed your Son
to be the Lamb who would take away our sins,
may he implore now for us your favour.
Through Christ our Lord.
Amen.

24 June: The Nativity of Saint John the Baptist

At the Mass during the Day

Entrance Antiphon   Jn 1. 6-7; Lk 1. 17
A man was sent from God, whose name was John.
He came to testify to the light,
to prepare a people fit for the Lord.

The Gloria in excelsis (Glory to God in the highest) is said.

Collect
O God, who raised up Saint John the Baptist
to make ready a nation fit for Christ the Lord,
give your people, we pray,
the grace of spiritual joys
and direct the hearts of all the faithful
into the way of salvation and peace.
Through our Lord Jesus Christ, your Son,
who lives and reigns with you in the unity of the Holy Spirit,
one God, for ever and ever.
Amen.

FIRST READING
A reading from the prophet Isaiah   49:1-6

Islands, listen to me,
pay attention, remotest peoples.
The Lord called me before I was born,
from my mother's womb he pronounced my name.
He made my mouth a sharp sword,
and hid me in the shadow of his hand.
He made me into a sharpened arrow,
and concealed me in his quiver.
He said to me, 'You are my servant (Israel)
in whom I shall be glorified';
while I was thinking 'I have toiled in vain,
I have exhausted myself for nothing';
and all the while my cause was with the Lord,
my reward with my God.
I was honoured in the eyes of the Lord,
my God was my strength.
And now the Lord has spoken,
he who formed me in the womb to be his servant,
to bring Jacob back to him,
to gather Israel to him:
'It is not enough for you to be my servant,

to restore the tribes of Jacob and bring back the survivors of
   Israel;
I will make you the light of the nations
so that my salvation may reach to the ends of the earth.'

The word of the Lord.

Responsorial Psalm   Ps 138:1-3. 13-15. R/ v.14

R/ **I thank you for the wonder of my being.**

1   O Lord, you search me and you know me,
    you know my resting and my rising,
    you discern my purpose from afar.
    You mark when I walk or lie down,
    all my ways lie open to you.   R/

2   For it was you who created my being,
    knit me together in my mother's womb.
    I thank you for the wonder of my being,
    for the wonders of all your creation.   R/

3   Already you knew my soul,
    my body held no secret from you
    when I was being fashioned in secret
    and moulded in the depths of the earth.   R/

SECOND READING

A reading from the Acts of the Apostles   13:22-26

Paul said: 'God made David the king of our ancestors, of whom he approved in these words, "I have selected David son of Jesse, a man after my own heart, who will carry out my whole purpose." To keep his promise, God has raised up for Israel one of David's descendants, Jesus, as Saviour, whose coming was heralded by John when he proclaimed a baptism of repentance for the whole people of Israel. Before John ended his career he said, "I am not the one you imagine me to be; that one is coming after me and I am not fit to undo his sandal."

'My brothers, sons of Abraham's race, and all you who fear God, this message of salvation is meant for you.'

The word of the Lord.

Gospel Acclamation   Cf. Lk 1:76
    Alleluia, alleluia!
    As for you, little child, you shall be called
    a prophet of God, the Most High.

24 June: The Nativity of Saint John the Baptist

You shall go ahead of the Lord
to prepare his ways before him.
Alleluia!

GOSPEL

A reading from the holy Gospel according to Luke 1:57-66. 80

The time came for Elizabeth to have her child, and she gave birth to a son; and when her neighbours and relations heard that the Lord had shown her so great a kindness, they shared her joy.

Now on the eighth day they came to circumcise the child; they were going to call him Zechariah after his father, but his mother spoke up. 'No,' she said 'he is to be called John.' They said to her, 'But no one in your family has that name', and made signs to his father to find out what he wanted him called. The father asked for a writing tablet and wrote, 'His name is John.' And they were all astonished. At that instant his power of speech returned and he spoke and praised God. All their neighbours were filled with awe and the whole affair was talked about throughout the hill country of Judaea. All those who heard of it treasured it in their hearts. 'What will this child turn out to be?' they wondered. And indeed the hand of the Lord was with him. The child grew up and his spirit matured. And he lived out in the wilderness until the day he appeared openly to Israel.

The Gospel of the Lord.

The Creed is said.

Prayer over the Offerings
We place these offerings on your altar, O Lord,
to celebrate with fitting honour the nativity of him
who both foretold the coming of the world's Saviour
and pointed him out when he came.
Who lives and reigns for ever and ever.
Amen.

Preface of the Mission of the Precursor, pp.44-5.

Communion Antiphon Cf. Lk 1:78
Through the tender mercy of our God,
the Dawn from on high will visit us.

Prayer after Communion
Having feasted at the banquet of the heavenly Lamb,
we pray, O Lord,

that, finding joy in the nativity of Saint John the Baptist,
your Church may know as the author of her rebirth
the Christ whose coming John foretold.
Who lives and reigns for ever and ever.
Amen.

29 June
SAINTS PETER AND PAUL, APOSTLES
Solemnity

We celebrate the ancient feast of the martyrdom of Saints Peter and Paul in Rome. They are often referred to as 'princes' of the apostles, from whom we derive our Christian faith. The Lord stood by them and gave them power, so that through them the message of the gospel might be proclaimed for all the world to hear. They kept the faith and received the crown of righteousness.

At the Vigil Mass

This Mass is used on the evening of 28 June, either before or after First Vespers (Evening Prayer I) of the Solemnity.

Entrance Antiphon
Peter the Apostle, and Paul the teacher of the Gentiles,
these have taught us your law, O Lord.

The Gloria in excelsis (Glory to God in the highest) is said.

Collect
Grant, we pray, O Lord our God,
that we may be sustained
by the intercession of the blessed Apostles Peter and Paul,
that, as through them you gave your Church
the foundations of her heavenly office,
so through them you may help her to eternal salvation.
Through our Lord Jesus Christ, your Son,
who lives and reigns with you in the unity of the Holy Spirit,
one God, for ever and ever.
Amen.

FIRST READING
A reading from the Acts of the Apostles 3:1-10

Once, when Peter and John were going up to the Temple for the prayers at the ninth hour, it happened that there was a man being

29 June: Saints Peter and Paul, Apostles

carried past. He was a cripple from birth; and they used to put him down every day near the Temple entrance called the Beautiful Gate so that he could beg from the people going in. When this man saw Peter and John on their way into the Temple he begged from them. Both Peter and John looked straight at him and said, 'Look at us.' He turned to them expectantly, hoping to get something from them, but Peter said, 'I have neither silver nor gold, but I will give you what I have: in the name of Jesus Christ the Nazarene, walk!' Peter then took him by the hand and helped him to stand up. Instantly his feet and ankles became firm, he jumped up, stood, and began to walk, and he went with them into the Temple, walking and jumping and praising God. Everyone could see him walking and praising God, and they recognised him as the man who used to sit begging at the Beautiful Gate of the Temple. They were all astonished and unable to explain what had happened to him.

The word of the Lord.

Responsorial Psalm   Ps 18:2-5. R℣ v.5

   R℣ **Their word goes forth through all the earth.**

1   The heavens proclaim the glory of God
      and the firmament shows forth the work of his hands.
      Day unto day takes up the story
      and night unto night makes known the message.   R℣

2   No speech, no word, no voice is heard
      yet their span extends through all the earth,
      their words to the utmost bounds of the world.   R℣

SECOND READING
A reading from the letter of St Paul to the Galatians   1:11-20

The Good News I preached is not a human message that I was given by men, it is something I learnt only through a revelation of Jesus Christ. You must have heard of my career as a practising Jew, how merciless I was in persecuting the Church of God, how much damage I did to it, how I stood out among other Jews of my generation, and how enthusiastic I was for the traditions of my ancestors.

Then God, who had specially chosen me while I was still in my mother's womb, called me through his grace and chose to reveal his Son to me, so that I might preach the Good News about him to the pagans. I did not stop to discuss this with any human being, nor did I go up to Jerusalem to see those who were already apostles before me, but I went off to Arabia at once and later went straight back from there to Damascus. Even when after three years I went up to Jerusalem to visit Cephas and stayed with him for fifteen days, I did not see any of the other apostles; I only saw James, the brother of the Lord, and I swear before God that what I have just written is the literal truth.

The word of the Lord.

Gospel Acclamation Jn 21:17
Alleluia, alleluia!
Lord, you know everything;
you know I love you.
Alleluia!

GOSPEL

A reading from the holy Gospel according to John 21:15-19

After Jesus had shown himself to his disciples and eaten with them, he said to Simon Peter, 'Simon son of John, do you love me more than these others do?' He answered, 'Yes, Lord, you know I love you.' Jesus said to him, 'Feed my lambs.' A second time he said to him, 'Simon son of John, do you love me?' He replied, 'Yes, Lord, you know I love you.' Jesus said to him, 'Look after my sheep.' Then he said to him a third time, 'Simon son of John, do you love me?' Peter was upset that he asked him the third time, 'Do you love me?' and said, 'Lord, you know everything; you know I love you.' Jesus said to him, 'Feed my sheep.

'I tell you most solemnly,
when you were young
you put on your own belt
and walked where you liked;
but when you grow old
you will stretch out your hands,
and somebody else will put a belt round you
and take you where you would rather not go.'

In these words he indicated the kind of death by which Peter would give glory to God. After this he said, 'Follow me.'

The Gospel of the Lord.

The Creed is said.

Prayer over the Offerings
We bring offerings to your altar, O Lord,
as we glory in the solemn feast

29 June: Saints Peter and Paul, Apostles

of the blessed Apostles Peter and Paul,
so that the more we doubt our own merits,
the more we may rejoice that we are to be saved
by your loving kindness.
Through Christ our Lord.
Amen.

Preface of the Twofold Mission of Peter and Paul in the Church, p.46.

Communion Antiphon
Cf. Jn 21:15. 17
Simon, Son of John, do you love me more than these?
Lord, you know everything; you know that I love you.

Prayer after Communion
By this heavenly Sacrament, O Lord, we pray,
strengthen your faithful,
whom you have enlightened with the teaching of the Apostles.
Through Christ our Lord.
Amen.

The Solemn Blessing formula on pp.101-2 may be used.

At the Mass during the Day

Entrance Antiphon
These are the ones who, living in the flesh,
planted the Church with their blood;
they drank the chalice of the Lord
and became the friends of God.

The Gloria in excelsis (Glory to God in the highest) is said.

Collect
O God, who on the Solemnity of the Apostles Peter and Paul
give us the noble and holy joy of this day,
grant, we pray, that your Church
may in all things follow the teaching
of those through whom she received
the beginnings of right religion.
Through our Lord Jesus Christ, your Son,
who lives and reigns with you in the unity of the Holy Spirit,
one God, for ever and ever.
Amen.

FIRST READING

A reading from the Acts of the Apostles   12:1-11

King Herod started persecuting certain members of the Church. He beheaded James the brother of John, and when he saw that this pleased the Jews he decided to arrest Peter as well. This was during the days of Unleavened Bread, and he put Peter in prison, assigning four squads of four soldiers each to guard him in turns. Herod meant to try Peter in public after the end of Passover week. All the time Peter was under guard the Church prayed to God for him unremittingly.

On the night before Herod was to try him, Peter was sleeping between two soldiers, fastened with double chains, while guards kept watch at the main entrance to the prison. Then suddenly the angel of the Lord stood there, and the cell was filled with light. He tapped Peter on the side and woke him. 'Get up!' he said 'Hurry!' – and the chains fell from his hands. The angel then said, 'Put on your belt and sandals.' After he had done this, the angel next said, 'Wrap your cloak round you and follow me.' Peter followed him, but had no idea that what the angel did was all happening in reality; he thought he was seeing a vision. They passed through two guard posts one after the other, and reached the iron gate leading to the city. This opened of its own accord; they went through it and had walked the whole length of one street when suddenly the angel left him. It was only then that Peter came to himself. 'Now I know it is all true,' he said. 'The Lord really did send his angel and has saved me from Herod and from all that the Jewish people were so certain would happen to me.'

The word of the Lord.

Responsorial Psalm   Ps 33:2-9. ℟ v.5. Alt. ℟ v.8

   ℟   **From all my terrors the Lord set me free.**

or

   ℟   **The angel of the Lord rescues those who revere him.**

1   I will bless the Lord at all times,
    his praise always on my lips;
    in the Lord my soul shall make its boast.
    The humble shall hear and be glad.   ℟

2   Glorify the Lord with me.
    Together let us praise his name.
    I sought the Lord and he answered me;
    from all my terrors he set me free.   ℟

3   Look towards him and be radiant;
    let your faces not be abashed.
    This poor man called; the Lord heard him
    and rescued him from all his distress.   ℟

4   The angel of the Lord is encamped
    around those who revere him, to rescue them.
    Taste and see that the Lord is good.
    He is happy who seeks refuge in him.   ℟

SECOND READING

A reading from the second letter of St Paul to Timothy   4:6-8. 17-18

My life is already being poured away as a libation, and the time has come for me to be gone. I have fought the good fight to the end; I have run the race to the finish; I have kept the faith; all there is to come now is the crown of righteousness reserved for me, which the Lord, the righteous judge, will give to me on that Day; and not only to me but to all those who have longed for his Appearing. The Lord stood by me and gave me power, so that through me the whole message might be proclaimed for all the pagans to hear; and so I was rescued from the lion's mouth. The Lord will rescue me from all evil attempts on me, and bring me safely to his heavenly kingdom. To him be glory for ever and ever. Amen.

The word of the Lord.

Gospel Acclamation   Mt 16:18
Alleluia, alleluia!
You are Peter and on this rock I will build my Church.
And the gates of the underworld can never hold out against it.
Alleluia!

GOSPEL

A reading from the holy Gospel according to Matthew   16:13-19

When Jesus came to the region of Caesarea Philippi he put this question to his disciples, 'Who do people say the Son of Man is?' And they said, 'Some say he is John the Baptist, some Elijah, and others Jeremiah or one of the prophets.' 'But you,' he said 'who do you say I am?' Then Simon Peter spoke up, 'You are the Christ,' he said 'the Son of the living God.' Jesus replied, 'Simon son of Jonah, you are a happy man! Because it was not flesh and blood that revealed this to you but my Father in heaven. So I now say to you: You are Peter and on this rock I will build my Church. And the gates of the underworld can never hold out against it. I will give you the keys of the kingdom of heaven: whatever you bind on earth shall be considered bound in heaven; whatever you loose on earth shall be considered loosed in heaven.'

The Gospel of the Lord.

The Creed is said.

Prayer over the Offerings
May the prayer of the Apostles, O Lord,
accompany the sacrificial gift
that we present to your name for consecration,
and may their intercession make us devoted to you
in celebration of the sacrifice.
Through Christ our Lord.
Amen.

Preface of the Twofold Mission of Peter and Paul in the Church, p.46.

Communion Antiphon   Cf. Mt 16:16. 18
Peter said to Jesus: You are the Christ, the Son of the living God.
And Jesus replied: You are Peter,
and upon this rock I will build my Church.

Prayer after Communion
Grant us, O Lord,
who have been renewed by this Sacrament,
so to live in the Church,
that, persevering in the breaking of the Bread
and in the teaching of the Apostles,
we may be one heart and one soul,
made steadfast in your love.
Through Christ our Lord.
Amen.

The Solemn Blessing formula on pp.101-2 may be used.

6 August
THE TRANSFIGURATION OF THE LORD
Feast

It is wonderful for us to be here today as we celebrate the transfigured Christ, the Christ of prophecy, in whom we have believed. This feast reminds us that Christ is indeed the bridge between heaven and earth.

Entrance Antiphon
Cf. Mt 17:5

In a resplendent cloud the Holy Spirit appeared.
The Father's voice was heard: This is my beloved Son,
with whom I am well pleased. Listen to him.

The Gloria in excelsis (Glory to God in the highest) is said.

Collect
O God, who in the glorious Transfiguration
of your Only Begotten Son
confirmed the mysteries of faith by the witness of the Fathers
and wonderfully prefigured our full adoption to sonship,
grant, we pray, to your servants,
that, listening to the voice of your beloved Son,
we may merit to become coheirs with him.
Who lives and reigns with you in the unity of the Holy Spirit,
one God, for ever and ever.
Amen.

FIRST READING
A reading from the book of Daniel
7:9-10. 13-14

As I watched:
Thrones were set in place
and one of great age took his seat.
His robe was white as snow,
the hair of his head as pure as wool.
His throne was a blaze of flames,
its wheels were a burning fire.
A stream of fire poured out,
issuing from his presence.
A thousand thousand waited on him,
ten thousand times ten thousand stood before him.
A court was held and the books were opened.
I gazed into the visions of the night.
And I saw, coming on the clouds of heaven,
one like a son of man.
He came to the one of great age

and was led into his presence.
On him was conferred sovereignty,
glory and kingship,
and men of all peoples, nations and languages became his
servants.
His sovereignty is an eternal sovereignty
which shall never pass away,
nor will his empire ever be destroyed.

The word of the Lord.

Responsorial Psalm   Ps 96:1-2. 5-6. 9. ℟ vv.1.9

   ℟ **The Lord is king,
      most high above all the earth.**

1. The Lord is king, let earth rejoice,
let all the coastlands be glad.
Cloud and darkness are his raiment;
his throne, justice and right. ℟

2. The mountains melt like wax
before the Lord of all the earth.
The skies proclaim his justice;
all peoples see his glory. ℟

3. For you indeed are the Lord
most high above all the earth
exalted far above all spirits. ℟

SECOND READING
A reading from the second letter of St Peter   1:16-19

It was not any cleverly invented myths that we were repeating when we brought you the knowledge of the power and the coming of our Lord Jesus Christ; we had seen his majesty for ourselves. He was honoured and glorified by God the Father, when the Sublime Glory itself spoke to him and said, 'This is my Son, the Beloved; he enjoys my favour.' We heard this ourselves, spoken from heaven, when we were with him on the holy mountain. So we have confirmation of what was said in prophecies; and you will be right to depend on prophecy and take it as a lamp for lighting a way through the dark until the dawn comes and the morning star rises in your minds.

The word of the Lord.

Gospel Acclamation   Mt 17:5
   Alleluia, alleluia!

> This is my Son, the Beloved,
> he enjoys my favour;
> listen to him.
> Alleluia!

GOSPEL

Year A
A reading from the holy Gospel according to Matthew   17:1-9

Jesus took with him Peter and James and his brother John and led them up a high mountain where they could be alone. There in their presence he was transfigured: his face shone like the sun and his clothes became as white as the light. Suddenly Moses and Elijah appeared to them; they were talking with him. Then Peter spoke to Jesus. 'Lord,' he said 'it is wonderful for us to be here; if you wish, I will make three tents here, one for you, one for Moses and one for Elijah.' He was still speaking when suddenly a bright cloud covered them with shadow, and from the cloud there came a voice which said, 'This is my Son; the Beloved; he enjoys my favour. Listen to him.' When they heard this, the disciples fell on their faces, overcome with fear. But Jesus came up and touched them. 'Stand up,' he said 'do not be afraid.' And when they raised their eyes they saw no one but only Jesus.

As they came down from the mountain Jesus gave them this order, 'Tell no one about the vision until the Son of Man has risen from the dead.'

The Gospel of the Lord.

Year B
A reading from the holy Gospel according to Mark   9:2-10

Jesus took with him Peter and James and John and led them up a high mountain where they could be alone by themselves. There in their presence he was transfigured: his clothes became dazzlingly white, whiter than any earthly bleacher could make them. Elijah appeared to them with Moses; and they were talking with Jesus. Then Peter spoke to Jesus: 'Rabbi,' he said 'it is wonderful for us to be here; so let us make three tents, one for you, one for Moses and one for Elijah.' He did not know what to say; they were so frightened. And a cloud came, covering them in shadow; and there came a voice from the cloud, 'This is my Son, the Beloved. Listen to him.' Then suddenly, when they looked round, they saw no one with them any more but only Jesus.

As they came down from the mountain he warned them to tell no one what they had seen, until after the Son of Man had risen from the dead. They observed the warning faithfully, though among themselves they discussed what 'rising from the dead' could mean.

The Gospel of the Lord.

Year C
A reading from the holy Gospel according to Luke 9:28-36

Jesus took with him Peter and John and James and went up the mountain to pray. As he prayed, the aspect of his face was changed and his clothing became brilliant as lightning. Suddenly there were two men there talking to him; they were Moses and Elijah appearing in glory, and they were speaking of his passing which he was to accomplish in Jerusalem. Peter and his companions were heavy with sleep, but they kept awake and saw his glory and the two men standing with him. As these were leaving him, Peter said to Jesus, 'Master, it is wonderful for us to be here; so let us make three tents, one for you, one for Moses and one for Elijah.' – He did not know what he was saying. As he spoke, a cloud came and covered them with shadow; and when they went into the cloud the disciples were afraid. And a voice came from the cloud, saying, 'This is my Son, the Chosen One. Listen to him.' And after the voice had spoken, Jesus was found alone. The disciples kept silence and, at that time, told no one what they had seen.

The Gospel of the Lord.

When this Feast falls on a Sunday, the Creed is said.

Prayer over the Offerings
Sanctify, O Lord, we pray,
these offerings here made to celebrate
the glorious Transfiguration of your Only Begotten Son,
and by his radiant splendour
cleanse us from the stains of sin.
Through Christ our Lord.
Amen.

Preface of the Mystery of the Transfiguration, p.40.

Communion Antiphon   Cf. 1 Jn 3:2
When Christ appears, we shall be like him,
for we shall see him as he is.

Prayer after Communion
May the heavenly nourishment we have received,
O Lord, we pray,
transform us into the likeness of your Son,
whose radiant splendour you willed to make manifest
in his glorious Transfiguration.
Who lives and reigns for ever and ever.
Amen.

15 August
THE ASSUMPTION
OF THE BLESSED VIRGIN MARY
Solemnity

In Mary's glorious assumption we celebrate the fulfilment of our Christian destiny, and with her we proclaim the greatness of the Lord. Mary is the pledge of the fulfilment of Christ's promise to go and prepare a place for us, that when he comes again he may receive us to himself, so that where he is, we may be also.

At the Vigil Mass

This Mass is used on the evening of 14 August, either before or after First Vespers (Evening Prayer I) of the Solemnity.

Entrance Antiphon
Glorious things are spoken of you, O Mary,
who today were exalted above the choirs of Angels
into eternal triumph with Christ.

The Gloria in excelsis (Glory to God in the highest) is said.

Collect
O God, who, looking on the lowliness of the Blessed Virgin Mary,
raised her to this grace,
that your Only Begotten Son was born of her according
　to the flesh
and that she was crowned this day with surpassing glory,
grant through her prayers,
that, saved by the mystery of your redemption,
we may merit to be exalted by you on high.
Through our Lord Jesus Christ, your Son,
who lives and reigns with you in the unity of the Holy Spirit,
one God, for ever and ever.
Amen.

FIRST READING
A reading from the first book of Chronicles   15:3-4. 15-16; 16:1-2

David gathered all Israel together in Jerusalem to bring the ark of God up to the place he had prepared for it. David called together the sons of Aaron and the sons of Levi. And the Levites carried the ark of God with the shafts on their shoulders, as Moses had ordered in accordance with the word of the Lord.

David then told the heads of the Levites to assign duties for their kinsmen as cantors, with their various instruments of music, harps and lyres and cymbals, to play joyful tunes. They brought the ark of God in and put it inside the tent that David had pitched for it; and they offered holocausts before God, and communion sacrifices. And when David had finished offering holocausts and communion sacrifices, he blessed the people in the name of the Lord.

The word of the Lord.

Responsorial Psalm   Ps 131:6-7. 9-10. 13-14. ℟ v.8

℟   **Go up, Lord, to the place of your rest,
    you and the ark of your strength.**

1   At Ephrata we heard of the ark;
    we found it in the plains of Yearim.
    'Let us go to the place of his dwelling;
    let us go to kneel at his footstool.'   ℟

2   Your priests shall be clothed with holiness:
    your faithful shall ring out their joy.
    For the sake of David your servant
    do not reject your anointed.   ℟

3   For the Lord has chosen Zion;
    he has desired it for his dwelling:
    'This is my resting-place for ever,
    here have I chosen to live.'   ℟

SECOND READING
A reading from the first letter of St Paul
to the Corinthians   15:54-57

When this perishable nature has put on imperishability, and when this mortal nature has put on immortality, then the words of scripture will come true: Death is swallowed up in victory. Death, where is your victory? Death, where is your sting? Now the sting

15 August: The Assumption of the Blessed Virgin Mary

of death is sin, and sin gets its power from the Law. So let us thank God for giving us the victory through our Lord Jesus Christ.

The word of the Lord.

Gospel Acclamation Lk 11:28
Alleluia, alleluia!
Happy are those
who hear the word of God,
and keep it.
Alleluia!

GOSPEL
A reading from the holy Gospel according to Luke 11:27-28

As Jesus was speaking, a woman in the crowd raised her voice and said, 'Happy the womb that bore you and the breasts you sucked!' But he replied, 'Still happier those who hear the word of God and keep it!'

The Gospel of the Lord.

The Creed is said.

Prayer over the Offerings
Receive, we pray, O Lord,
the sacrifice of conciliation and praise,
which we celebrate on the Assumption of the holy Mother of God,
that it may lead us to your pardon
and confirm us in perpetual thanksgiving.
Through Christ our Lord.
Amen.

Preface of the Glory of Mary Assumed into Heaven, pp.43-4.

Communion Antiphon Cf. Lk 11:27
Blessed is the womb of the Virgin Mary,
which bore the Son of the eternal Father.

Prayer after Communion
Having partaken of this heavenly table,
we beseech your mercy, Lord our God,
that we, who honour the Assumption of the Mother of God,
may be freed from every threat of harm.
Through Christ our Lord.
Amen.

The Solemn Blessing formula, p.101, may be used.

At the Mass during the Day

Entrance Antiphon   Cf. Rev 12:1
A great sign appeared in heaven:
a woman clothed with the sun, and the moon beneath her feet,
and on her head a crown of twelve stars.

or

Let us all rejoice in the Lord,
as we celebrate the feast day in honour of the Virgin Mary,
at whose Assumption the Angels rejoice
and praise the Son of God.

The Gloria in excelsis (Glory to God in the highest) is said.

Collect
Almighty ever-living God,
who assumed the Immaculate Virgin Mary, the Mother of your Son,
body and soul into heavenly glory,
grant, we pray,
that, always attentive to the things that are above,
we may merit to be sharers of her glory.
Through our Lord Jesus Christ, your Son,
who lives and reigns with you in the unity of the Holy Spirit,
one God, for ever and ever.
Amen.

FIRST READING
A reading from the book of the Apocalypse   11:19; 12:1-6. 10

The sanctuary of God in heaven opened, and the ark of the covenant could be seen inside it.

    Now a great sign appeared in heaven: a woman, adorned with the sun, standing on the moon, and with the twelve stars on her head for a crown. She was pregnant, and in labour, crying aloud in the pangs of childbirth. Then a second sign appeared in the sky, a huge red dragon which had seven heads and ten horns, and each of the seven heads crowned with a coronet. Its tail dragged a third of the stars from the sky and dropped them to the earth, and the dragon stopped in front of the woman as she was having the child, so that he could eat it as soon as it was born from its mother. The woman brought a male child into the world, the son who was to rule all the nations with an iron sceptre, and the child was taken straight

15 August: The Assumption of the Blessed Virgin Mary

up to God and to his throne, while the woman escaped into the desert, where God had made a place of safety ready. Then I heard a voice shout from heaven, 'Victory and power and empire for ever have been won by our God, and all authority for his Christ.'

The word of the Lord.

Responsional Psalm
Ps 44:10-12. 16. ℟ v.10

℟ **On your right stands the queen, in garments of gold.**

1. The daughters of kings are among your loved ones.
   On your right stands the queen in gold of Ophir.
   Listen, O daughter, give ear to my words:
   forget your own people and your father's house. ℟

2. So will the king desire your beauty:
   He is your lord, pay homage to him.
   They are escorted amid gladness and joy;
   they pass within the palace of the king. ℟

SECOND READING
A reading from the first letter of St Paul to the Corinthians
15:20-26

Christ has been raised from the dead, the first-fruits of all who have fallen asleep. Death came through one man and in the same way the resurrection of the dead has come through one man. Just as all men die in Adam, so all men will be brought to life in Christ; but all of them in their proper order: Christ as the first-fruits and then, after the coming of Christ, those who belong to him. After that will come the end, when he hands over the kingdom to God the Father, having done away with every sovereignty, authority and power. For he must be king until he has put all his enemies under his feet and the last of the enemies to be destroyed is death, for everything is to be put under his feet.

The word of the Lord.

Gospel Acclamation
Alleluia, alleluia!
Mary has been taken up into heaven;
all the choirs of angels are rejoicing.
Alleluia!

GOSPEL

A reading from the holy Gospel according to Luke   1:39-56

Mary set out and went as quickly as she could to a town in the hill country of Judah. She went into Zechariah's house and greeted Elizabeth. Now as soon as Elizabeth heard Mary's greeting, the child leapt in her womb and Elizabeth was filled with the Holy Spirit. She gave a loud cry and said, 'Of all women you are the most blessed, and blessed is the fruit of your womb. Why should I be honoured with a visit from the mother of my Lord? From the moment your greeting reached my ears, the child in my womb leapt for joy. Yes, blessed is she who believed that the promise made her by the Lord would be fulfilled.' And Mary said:

> 'My soul proclaims the greatness of the Lord
> and my spirit exults in God my saviour;
> because he has looked upon his lowly handmaid.
> Yes, from this day forward all generations will call me
>   blessed,
> for the Almighty has done great things for me.
> Holy is his name,
> and his mercy reaches from age to age for those who fear him.
> He has shown the power of his arm,
> he has routed the proud of heart.
> He has pulled down princes from their thrones and exalted
>   the lowly.
> The hungry he has filled with good things, the rich sent
>   empty away.
> He has come to the help of Israel his servant, mindful of his
>   mercy
> – according to the promise he made to our ancestors –
> of his mercy to Abraham and to his descendants for ever.'

Mary stayed with Elizabeth about three months and then went back home.

> The Gospel of the Lord.

The Creed is said.

Prayer over the Offerings

May this oblation, our tribute of homage,
rise up to you, O Lord,
and, through the intercession of the Most Blessed Virgin Mary,
whom you assumed into heaven,

may our hearts, aflame with the fire of love,
constantly long for you.
Through Christ our Lord.
Amen.

Preface of the Glory of Mary Assumed into Heaven, pp.43-4.

Communion Antiphon
Lk 1:48-49
All generations will call me blessed,
for he who is mighty has done great things for me.

Prayer after Communion
Having received the Sacrament of salvation,
we ask you to grant, O Lord,
that, through the intercession of the Blessed Virgin Mary,
whom you assumed into heaven,
we may be brought to the glory of the resurrection.
Through Christ our Lord.
Amen.

The Solemn Blessing formula, p.101, may be used.

14 September
THE EXALTATION OF THE HOLY CROSS
Feast

The cross on which Jesus, the Son of Man, was lifted up has become the universal symbol of his victory over the power of evil. He made the instrument of humiliation, torture and death the instrument of our redemption. Christians 'exalt', raise on high the cross as the symbol of our salvation and resurrection.

Entrance Antiphon
Cf. Gal 6:14
We should glory in the Cross of our Lord Jesus Christ,
in whom is our salvation, life and resurrection,
through whom we are saved and delivered.

The Gloria in excelsis (Glory to God in the highest) is said.

Collect
O God, who willed that your Only Begotten Son
should undergo the Cross to save the human race,
grant, we pray,
that we, who have known his mystery on earth,
may merit the grace of his redemption in heaven.
Through our Lord Jesus Christ, your Son,

who lives and reigns with you in the unity of the Holy Spirit,
one God, for ever and ever.
Amen.

FIRST READING

A reading from the book of Numbers   21:4-9

On the way through the wilderness, the Israelites lost patience. They spoke against God and against Moses, 'Why did you bring us out of Egypt to die in this wilderness? For there is neither bread nor water here; we are sick of this unsatisfying food.'

At this God sent fiery serpents among the people; their bite brought death to many in Israel. The people came and said to Moses, 'We have sinned by speaking against the Lord and against you. Intercede for us with the Lord to save us from these serpents.' Moses interceded for the people, and the Lord answered him, 'Make a fiery serpent and put it on a standard. If anyone is bitten and looks at it, he shall live.' So Moses fashioned a bronze serpent which he put on a standard, and if anyone was bitten by a serpent, he looked at the bronze serpent and lived.

The word of the Lord.

Responsorial Psalm   Ps 77:1-2. 34-38. ℟ v.7

℟ **Never forget the deeds of the Lord.**

1 Give heed, my people, to my teaching;
 turn your ear to the words of my mouth.
 I will open my mouth in a parable
 and reveal hidden lessons of the past. ℟

2 When he slew them then they would seek him,
 return and seek him in earnest.
 They would remember that God was their rock,
 God the Most High their redeemer. ℟

3 But the words they spoke were mere flattery;
 they lied to him with their lips.
 For their hearts were not truly with him;
 they were not faithful to his covenant. ℟

4 Yet he who is full of compassion
 forgave their sin and spared them.
 So often he held back his anger
 when he might have stirred up his rage. ℟

14 September: The Exaltation of the Holy Cross

SECOND READING
A reading from the letter of St Paul to the Philippians   2:6-11

The state of Jesus Christ was divine,
yet he did not cling
to his equality with God
but emptied himself
to assume the condition of a slave,
and became as men are;
and being as all men are,
he was humbler yet,
even to accepting death,
death on a cross.
But God raised him high
and gave him the name
which is above all other names
so that all beings
in the heavens, on earth and in the underworld,
should bend the knee at the name of Jesus
and that every tongue should acclaim
Jesus Christ as Lord,
to the glory of God the Father.

The word of the Lord.

Gospel Acclamation
    Alleluia, alleluia!
    We adore you, O Christ,
    and we bless you;
    because by your cross
    you have redeemed the world.
    Alleluia!

GOSPEL
A reading from the holy Gospel according to John   3:13-17

Jesus said to Nicodemus:

    'No one has gone up to heaven
    except the one who came down from heaven,
    the Son of Man who is in heaven;
    and the Son of Man must be lifted up
    as Moses lifted up the serpent in the desert,
    so that everyone who believes may have eternal life in him.
    Yes, God loved the world so much

that he gave his only Son,
so that everyone who believes in him may not be lost
but may have eternal life.
For God sent his Son into the world
not to condemn the world,
but so that through him the world might be saved.'

The Gospel of the Lord.

When this Feast falls on a Sunday, the Creed is said.

Prayer over the Offerings
May this oblation, O Lord,
which on the altar of the Cross
cancelled the offence of the whole world,
cleanse us, we pray, of all our sins.
Through Christ our Lord.
Amen.

Preface of the Victory of the Glorious Cross, p.38 or Preface I of the Passion of the Lord, p.26, may also be used.

Communion Antiphon   Jn 12:32
When I am lifted up from the earth,
I will draw everyone to myself, says the Lord.

Prayer after Communion
Having been nourished by your holy banquet,
we beseech you, Lord Jesus Christ,
to bring those you have redeemed
by the wood of your life-giving Cross
to the glory of the resurrection.
Who live and reign for ever and ever.
Amen.

1 November
ALL SAINTS
Solemnity

Today we offer the Lamb and celebrate the victory of our God in the company of all the redeemed in the heavenly kingdom. This feast reminds us of the fundamental connection in prayer and love between ourselves and the multitude without number, of every race, tribe, nation and language: the blessed in the kingdom of heaven.

Entrance Antiphon
Let us all rejoice in the Lord,
as we celebrate the feast day in honour of all the Saints,
at whose festival the Angels rejoice
and praise the Son of God.

The Gloria in excelsis (Glory to God in the highest) is said.

Collect
Almighty ever-living God,
by whose gift we venerate in one celebration
the merits of all the Saints,
bestow on us, we pray,
through the prayers of so many intercessors,
an abundance of the reconciliation with you
for which we earnestly long.
Through our Lord Jesus Christ, your Son,
who lives and reigns with you in the unity of the Holy Spirit,
one God, for ever and ever.
Amen.

The Creed is said.

FIRST READING
A reading from the book of the Apocalypse   7:2-4. 9-14

I, John, saw another angel rising where the sun rises, carrying the seal of the living God; he called in a powerful voice to the four angels whose duty was to devastate land and sea, 'Wait before you do any damage on land or at sea or to the trees, until we have put the seal on the foreheads of the servants of our God.' Then I heard how many were sealed: a hundred and forty-four thousand, out of all the tribes of Israel.

After that I saw a huge number, impossible to count, of people from every nation, race, tribe and language; they were standing in front of the throne and in front of the Lamb, dressed in white robes and holding palms in their hands. They shouted aloud, 'Victory to our God, who sits on the throne, and to the Lamb!' And all the angels who were standing in a circle round the throne, surrounding the elders and the four animals, prostrated themselves before the throne, and touched the ground with their foreheads, worshipping God with these words: 'Amen. Praise and glory and wisdom and thanksgiving and honour and power and strength to our God for ever and ever. Amen.'

One of the elders then spoke, and asked me, 'Do you know who these people are, dressed in white robes, and where they have come from?' I answered him, 'You can tell me, my Lord.' Then he said, 'These are the people who have been through the great persecution, and they have washed their robes white again in the blood of the Lamb.'

The word of the Lord.

Responsorial Psalm   Ps 23:1-6. ℟ cf. v.6
   ℟ **Such are the men who seek your face, O Lord.**

1   The Lord's is the earth and its fullness,
    the world and all its peoples.
    It is he who set it on the seas;
    on the waters he made it firm.   ℟

2   Who shall climb the mountain of the Lord?
    Who shall stand in his holy place?
    The man with clean hands and pure heart,
    who desires not worthless things.   ℟

3   He shall receive blessings from the Lord
    and reward from the God who saves him.
    Such are the men who seek him,
    seek the face of the God of Jacob.   ℟

SECOND READING
A reading from the first letter of St John   3:1-3

Think of the love that the Father has lavished on us,
by letting us be called God's children;
and that is what we are.
Because the world refused to acknowledge him,
therefore it does not acknowledge us.
My dear people, we are already the children of God
but what we are to be in the future has not yet been revealed;
all we know is, that when it is revealed
we shall be like him

1 November: All Saints

because we shall see him as he really is.
Surely everyone who entertains this hope
must purify himself, must try to be as pure as Christ.

The word of the Lord.

Gospel Acclamation — Mt 11:28
Alleluia, alleluia!
Come to me, all you who labour and are overburdened,
and I will give you rest, says the Lord.
Alleluia!

GOSPEL

A reading from the holy Gospel according to Matthew — 5:1-12

Seeing the crowds, Jesus went up the hill. There he sat down and was joined by his disciples. Then he began to speak. This is what he taught them:

'How happy are the poor in spirit;
theirs is the kingdom of heaven.
Happy the gentle:
they shall have the earth for their heritage.
Happy those who mourn:
they shall be comforted.
Happy those who hunger and thirst for what is right:
they shall be satisfied.
Happy the merciful:
they shall have mercy shown them.
Happy the pure in heart:
they shall see God.
Happy the peacemakers:
they shall be called sons of God
Happy those who are persecuted in the cause of right:
theirs is the kingdom of heaven.

'Happy are you when people abuse you and persecute you and speak all kinds of calumny against you on my account. Rejoice and be glad, for your reward will be great in heaven.'

The Gospel of the Lord.

The Creed is said.

Prayer over the Offerings
May these offerings we bring in honour of all the Saints
be pleasing to you, O Lord,
and grant that, just as we believe the Saints
to be already assured of immortality,

so we may experience their concern for our salvation.
Through Christ our Lord.
Amen.

Preface of the Glory of Jerusalem, Our Mother, p.48.

Communion Antiphon Mt 5:8-10
Blessed are the clean of heart, for they shall see God.
Blessed are the peacemakers,
for they shall be called children of God.
Blessed are they who are persecuted for the sake of righteousness,
for theirs is the Kingdom of Heaven.

Prayer after Communion
As we adore you, O God, who alone are holy
and wonderful in all your Saints,
we implore your grace,
so that, coming to perfect holiness in the fullness of your love,
we may pass from this pilgrim table
to the banquet of our heavenly homeland.
Through Christ our Lord.
Amen.

The Solemn Blessing formula, pp.102-3, may be used.

2 November
THE COMMEMORATION OF ALL THE FAITHFUL DEPARTED
(All Souls' Day)

Today we remember with love and in prayer all the faithful departed; that having died with Christ, in him they may rise and enter into eternal life.

The Masses that follow may be used at the discretion of the celebrant.[1]

Even when 2 November falls on a Sunday, the Mass celebrated is that of the Commemoration of All the Faithful Departed.

1

FIRST MASS
Entrance Antiphon Cf. 1 Th 4:14; 1 Cor 15:22
Just as Jesus died and has risen again,

---

[1] On this day, any Priest may celebrate three Masses, observing, nevertheless, what was established by Benedict XV in the Apostolic Constitution, *Incruentum Altaris Sacrificium*, 10 August 1915: *Acta Apostolicae Sedis* 7 (1915) pp.401–404.

2 November: The Commemoration of all the Faithful Departed

so through Jesus God will bring with him
those who have fallen asleep;
and as in Adam all die,
so also in Christ will all be brought to life.

Collect
Listen kindly to our prayers, O Lord,
and, as our faith in your Son,
raised from the dead, is deepened,
so may our hope of resurrection for your departed servants
also find new strength.
Through our Lord Jesus Christ, your Son,
who lives and reigns with you in the unity of the Holy Spirit,
one God, for ever and ever.
Amen.

Prayer over the Offerings
Look favourably on our offerings, O Lord,
so that your departed servants
may be taken up into glory with your Son,
in whose great mystery of love we are all united.
Who lives and reigns for ever and ever.
Amen.

An appropriate Preface for the Dead, pp.55-7.

Communion Antiphon   Cf. Jn 11:25-26
I am the Resurrection and the Life, says the Lord.
Whoever believes in me, even though he dies, will live,
and everyone who lives and believes in me will not die for ever.

Prayer after Communion
Grant we pray, O Lord, that your departed servants,
for whom we have celebrated this paschal Sacrament,
may pass over to a dwelling place of light and peace.
Through Christ our Lord.
Amen.

The Solemn Blessing formula, p.104, may be used.

2
SECOND MASS
Entrance Antiphon   Cf. 4 Esdr 2:34-35
Eternal rest grant unto them, O Lord,
and let perpetual light shine upon them.

Collect
O God, glory of the faithful and life of the just,
by the Death and Resurrection of whose Son
we have been redeemed,
look mercifully on your departed servants,
that, just as they professed the mystery of our resurrection,
so they may merit to receive the joys of eternal happiness.
Through our Lord Jesus Christ, your Son,
who lives and reigns with you in the unity of the Holy Spirit,
one God, for ever and ever.
Amen.

Prayer over the Offerings
Almighty and merciful God,
by means of these sacrificial offerings
wash away, we pray, in the Blood of Christ,
the sins of your departed servants,
for you purify unceasingly by your merciful forgiveness
those you once cleansed in the waters of Baptism.
Through Christ our Lord.
Amen.

An appropriate Preface for the Dead, pp.55-7.

Communion Antiphon   Cf. 4 Esdr 2:35. 34
Let perpetual light shine upon them, O Lord,
with your Saints for ever, for you are merciful.

Prayer after Communion
Having received the Sacrament of your Only Begotten Son,
who was sacrificed for us and rose in glory,
we humbly implore you, O Lord,
for your departed servants,
that, cleansed by the paschal mysteries,
they may glory in the gift of the resurrection to come.
Through Christ our Lord.
Amen.

The Solemn Blessing formula, p.104, may be used.

3

THIRD MASS
Entrance Antiphon   Cf. Rom 8:11
God, who raised Jesus from the dead,
will give life also to your mortal bodies,
through his Spirit that dwells in you.

2 November: The Commemoration of all the Faithful Departed 1077

Collect
O God, who willed that your Only Begotten Son,
having conquered death,
should pass over into the realm of heaven,
grant, we pray, to your departed servants
that, with the mortality of this life overcome,
they may gaze eternally on you,
their Creator and Redeemer.
Through our Lord Jesus Christ, your Son,
who lives and reigns with you in the unity of the Holy Spirit,
one God, for ever and ever.
Amen.

Prayer over the Offerings
Receive, Lord, in your kindness,
the sacrificial offering we make
for all your servants who sleep in Christ,
that, set free from the bonds of death
by this singular sacrifice,
they may merit eternal life.
Through Christ our Lord.
Amen.

An appropriate Preface for the Dead, pp.55-7.

Communion Antiphon
Cf. Phil 3:20-21
We await a saviour, the Lord Jesus Christ,
who will change our mortal bodies,
to conform with his glorified body.

Prayer after Communion
Through these sacrificial gifts
which we have received, O Lord,
bestow on your departed servants your great mercy
and, to those you have endowed with the grace of Baptism,
grant also the fullness of eternal joy.
Through Christ our Lord.
Amen.

The Solemn Blessing formula, p.104, may be used.

FIRST READING
A reading from the prophet Isaiah   25:6-9

On this mountain,
the Lord of hosts will prepare for all peoples
a banquet of rich food.

On this mountain he will remove
the mourning veil covering all peoples,
and the shroud enwrapping all nations,
he will destroy Death for ever.
The Lord will wipe away
the tears from every cheek;
he will take away his people's shame
everywhere on earth,
for the Lord has said so.
That day, it will be said: See, this is our God
in whom we hoped for salvation;
the Lord is the one in whom we hoped.
We exult and we rejoice
that he has saved us.

    The word of the Lord.

Responsorial Psalm   Ps 26:1. 4. 7-9. 13-14. ℟ v.1. Alt. ℟ v.13

    ℟ **The Lord is my light and my help.**

or

    ℟ **I am sure I shall see the Lord's goodness
in the land of the living.**

1   The Lord is my light and my help;
whom shall I fear?
The Lord is the stronghold of my life;
before whom shall I shrink? ℟

2   There is one thing I ask of the Lord,
for this I long,
to live in the house of the Lord,
all the days of my life,
to savour the sweetness of the Lord,
to behold his temple. ℟

3   Lord, hear my voice when I call;
have mercy and answer.
It is your face, O Lord, that I seek;
hide not your face. ℟

4   I am sure I shall see the Lord's goodness
in the land of the living.
Hope in him, hold firm and take heart.
Hope in the Lord! ℟

SECOND READING
A reading from the letter of St Paul to the Romans 5:5-11

Hope is not deceptive, because the love of God has been poured into our hearts by the Holy Spirit which has been given us. We were still helpless when at his appointed moment Christ died for sinful men. It is not easy to die even for a good man – though of course for someone really worthy, a man might be prepared to die – but what proves that God loves us is that Christ died for us while we were still sinners. Having died to make us righteous, is it likely that he would now fail to save us from God's anger? When we were reconciled to God by the death of his Son, we were still enemies; now that we have been reconciled, surely we may count on being saved by the life of his Son? Not merely because we have been reconciled but because we are filled with joyful trust in God, through our Lord Jesus Christ, through whom we have already gained our reconciliation.

The word of the Lord.

Gospel Acclamation   Jn 6:39
Alleluia, alleluia!
It is my Father's will, says the Lord,
that I should lose nothing of all that he has given to me,
and that I should raise it up on the last day.
Alleluia!

GOSPEL
Year A
Matthew 11:25-30, see Fourteenth Sunday in Ordinary Time, Year A, p.517 above.

Year B
A reading from the holy Gospel according to Mark 15:33-39; 16:1-6

When the sixth hour came there was darkness over the whole land until the ninth hour. And at the ninth hour Jesus cried out in a loud voice, 'Eloi, Eloi, lama sabachthani?' which means, 'My God, my God, why have you deserted me?' When some of those who stood by heard this, they said, 'Listen, he is calling on Elijah.' Someone ran and soaked a sponge in vinegar and, putting it on a reed, gave it him to drink saying, 'Wait and see if Elijah will come to take him down.' But Jesus gave a loud cry and breathed his last. And the veil of the Temple was torn in two from top to bottom. The centurion, who was standing in front of him, had seen how he had died and he said, 'In truth this man was a son of God.'

When the sabbath was over, Mary of Magdala, Mary the mother of James, and Salome, bought spices with which to go and anoint him. And very early in the morning on the first day of the week they went to the tomb, just as the sun was rising.

They had been saying to one another, 'Who will roll away the stone for us from the entrance to the tomb?' But when they looked they could see that the stone – which was very big – had already been rolled back. On entering the tomb they saw a young man in a white robe seated on the right-hand side, and they were struck with amazement. But he said to them, 'There is no need for alarm. You are looking for Jesus of Nazareth, who was crucified: he has risen, he is not here. See, here is the place where they laid him.'

The Gospel of the Lord.

*Shorter Form, verses 33-39. Read between *

Year C: In Ordinary Time, Luke 7:11-17, see Tenth Sunday, Year C, pp.939-40 above.

9 November
THE DEDICATION OF THE LATERAN BASILICA
Feast

The basilica of St John Lateran is the cathedral of the bishop of Rome. This feast is a celebration in honour of the basilica called the 'mother of all churches in Rome and the world' and is a sign of love and union with the See of Peter.

Entrance Antiphon   Cf. Rev 21: 2
I saw the holy city, a new Jerusalem,
coming down out of heaven from God,
prepared like a bride adorned for her husband.

or   Cf. Rev 21: 3

Behold God's dwelling with the human race.
He will dwell with them and they will be his people,
and God himself with them will be their God.

The Gloria in excelsis (Glory to God in the highest) is said.

Collect
O God, who from living and chosen stones
prepare an eternal dwelling for your majesty,
increase in your Church the spirit of grace you have bestowed,
so that by new growth your faithful people
may build up the heavenly Jerusalem.
Through our Lord Jesus Christ, your Son,

9 November: The Dedication of the Lateran Basilica

who lives and reigns with you in the unity of the Holy Spirit,
one God, for ever and ever.
Amen.
or
O God, who were pleased to call your Church the Bride,
grant that the people that serves your name
may revere you, love you and follow you,
and may be led by you
to attain your promises in heaven.
Through our Lord Jesus Christ, your Son,
who lives and reigns with you in the unity of the Holy Spirit,
one God, for ever and ever.
Amen.

FIRST READING
A reading from the prophet Ezekiel 47:1-2. 8-9. 12

The angel brought me to the entrance of the Temple, where a stream came out from under the Temple threshold and flowed eastwards, since the Temple faced east. The water flowed from under the right side of the Temple, south of the altar. He took me out by the north gate and led me right round outside as far as the outer east gate where the water flowed out on the right-hand side. The man went to the east holding his measuring line and measured off a thousand cubits; he then made me wade across the stream; the water reached my ankles. He measured off another thousand and made me wade across the stream again; the water reached my knees. He measured off another thousand and made me wade across again; the water reached my waist. He measured off another thousand; it was now a river which I could not cross; the stream had swollen and was now deep water, a river impossible to cross. He then said, 'Do you see, son of man?' He took me further, then brought me back to the bank of the river. When I got back, there were many trees on each bank of the river. He said, 'This water flows east down to the Arabah and to the sea; and flowing into the sea it makes its waters wholesome. Wherever the river flows, all living creatures teeming in it will live. Fish will be very plentiful, for wherever the water goes it brings health, and life teems wherever the river flows. Along the river, on either bank, will grow every kind of fruit tree with leaves that never wither and fruit that never fails; they will bear new fruit every month, because this water comes from the sanctuary. And their fruit will be good to eat and the leaves medicinal.'

The word of the Lord.

Responsorial Psalm   Ps 45:2-3. 5-6. 8-9. ℟ v.5

℟ **The waters of a river give joy to God's city,**
the holy place where the Most High dwells.

1. God is for us a refuge and strength,
a helper close at hand, in time of distress:
so we shall not fear though the earth should rock,
though the mountains fall into the depths of the sea. ℟

2. The waters of a river give joy to God's city,
the holy place where the Most High dwells.
God is within, it cannot be shaken;
God will help it at the dawning of the day. ℟

3. The Lord of hosts is with us:
the God of Jacob is our stronghold.
Come, consider the works of the Lord
the redoubtable deeds he has done on the earth. ℟

SECOND READING

A reading from the first letter of St Paul   3:9-11. 16-17
to the Corinthians

You are God's building. By the grace God gave me, I succeeded as an architect and laid the foundations, on which someone else is doing the building. Everyone doing the building must work carefully. For the foundation, nobody can lay any other than the one which has already been laid, that is Jesus Christ. Didn't you realise that you were God's temple and that the Spirit of God was living among you? If anybody should destroy the temple of God, God will destroy him, because the temple of God is sacred; and you are that temple.

The word of the Lord.

Gospel Acclamation   2 Chron 7:16
Alleluia, alleluia!
I have chosen and consecrated this house, says the Lord,
for my name to be there for ever.
Alleluia!

GOSPEL

A reading from the holy Gospel according to John   2:13-22

Just before the Jewish Passover Jesus went up to Jerusalem, and in the Temple he found people selling cattle and sheep and pigeons,

9 November: The Dedication of the Lateran Basilica

and the money changers sitting at their counters there. Making a whip out of some cord, he drove them all out of the Temple, cattle and sheep as well, scattered the money changers' coins, knocked their tables over and said to the pigeon-sellers, 'Take all this out of here and stop turning my Father's house into a market.' Then his disciples remembered the words of scripture: Zeal for your house will devour me. The Jews intervened and said, 'What sign can you show us to justify what you have done?' Jesus answered, 'Destroy this sanctuary, and in three days I will raise it up.' The Jews replied, 'It has taken forty-six years to build this sanctuary: are you going to raise it up in three days?' But he was speaking of the sanctuary that was his body, and when Jesus rose from the dead, his disciples remembered that he had said this, and they believed the scripture and the words he had said.

The Gospel of the Lord.

When this Feast falls on a Sunday, the Creed is said.

Prayer over the Offerings
Accept, we pray, O Lord, the offering made here
and grant that by it those who seek your favour
may receive in this place
the power of the Sacraments
and the answer to their prayers.
Through Christ our Lord.
Amen.

Preface of the Mystery of the Church, the Bride of Christ and the Temple of the Spirit, p.41.

Communion Antiphon   Cf. 1 Pet 2:5
Be built up like living stones,
into a spiritual house, a holy priesthood.

Prayer after Communion
O God, who chose to foreshadow for us
the heavenly Jerusalem
through the sign of your Church on earth,
grant, we pray,
that, by our partaking of this Sacrament,
we may be made the temple of your grace
and may enter the dwelling place of your glory.
Through Christ our Lord.
Amen.

The Solemn Blessing formula, p.103, may be used.

8 December
THE IMMACULATE CONCEPTION OF THE BLESSED VIRGIN MARY
Solemnity

We celebrate the conception of her whom God chose to be the mother of Christ and the new Eve, the mother of all the living. God chose her to be the first of all the redeemed, holy and spotless, to live through love in his presence.

Entrance Antiphon
Is 61:10

I rejoice heartily in the Lord,
in my God is the joy of my soul;
for he has clothed me with a robe of salvation,
and wrapped me in a mantle of justice,
like a bride adorned with her jewels.

The Gloria in excelsis (Glory to God in the highest) is said.

Collect

O God, who by the Immaculate Conception of the Blessed Virgin
prepared a worthy dwelling for your Son,
grant, we pray,
that, as you preserved her from every stain
by virtue of the Death of your Son, which you foresaw,
so, through her intercession,
we, too, may be cleansed and admitted to your presence.
Through our Lord Jesus Christ, your Son,
who lives and reigns with you in the unity of the Holy Spirit,
one God, for ever and ever.
Amen.

FIRST READING
A reading from the book of Genesis   3:9-15. 20

After Adam had eaten of the tree, the Lord God called to him. 'Where are you?' he asked. 'I heard the sound of you in the garden,' he replied. 'I was afraid because I was naked, so I hid.' 'Who told you that you were naked?' he asked. 'Have you been eating of the tree I forbade you to eat?' The man replied, 'It was the woman you put with me; she gave me the fruit, and I ate it.' Then the Lord God asked the woman, 'What is this you have done?' The woman replied, 'The serpent tempted me and I ate.' Then the Lord God said to the serpent, 'Because you have done this,

8 December: The Immaculate Conception 1085

'Be accursed beyond all cattle,
all wild beasts.
You shall crawl on your belly and eat dust
every day of your life.
I will make you enemies of each other:
you and the woman,
your offspring and her offspring.
It will crush your head
and you will strike its heel.'

The man named his wife 'Eve' because she was the mother of all those who live.

The word of the Lord.

Responsorial Psalm Ps 97:1-4. R̸ v.1

R̸ **Sing a new song to the Lord
for he has worked wonders.**

1 Sing a new song to the Lord
 for he has worked wonders.
 His right hand and his holy arm
 have brought salvation. R̸

2 The Lord has made known his salvation;
 has shown his justice to the nations.
 He has remembered his truth and love
 for the house of Israel. R̸

3 All the ends of the earth have seen
 the salvation of our God.
 Shout to the Lord all the earth,
 ring out your joy. R̸

SECOND READING

A reading from the letter of St Paul to the Ephesians 1:3-6. 11-12

Blessed be God the Father of our Lord Jesus Christ,
who has blessed us with all the spiritual blessings of heaven in
 Christ.
Before the world was made, he chose us, chose us in Christ,
to be holy and spotless, and to live through love in his presence,
determining that we should become his adopted sons, through
 Jesus Christ
for his own kind purposes,
to make us praise the glory of his grace,

his free gift to us in the Beloved.
And it is in him that we were claimed as God's own,
chosen from the beginning,
under the predetermined plan of the one who guides all things
as he decides by his own will;
chosen to be,
for his greater glory,
the people who would put their hopes in Christ before he came.

The word of the Lord.

Gospel Acclamation Cf. Lk 1:28
Alleluia, alleluia!
Hail, Mary, full of grace; the Lord is with thee!
Blessed art thou among women.
Alleluia!

GOSPEL

A reading from the holy Gospel according to Luke 1:26-38

The angel Gabriel was sent by God to a town in Galilee called Nazareth, to a virgin betrothed to a man named Joseph, of the House of David; and the virgin's name was Mary. He went in and said to her, 'Rejoice, so highly favoured! The Lord is with you.' She was deeply disturbed by these words and asked herself what this greeting could mean, but the angel said to her, 'Mary, do not be afraid; you have won God's favour. Listen! You are to conceive and bear a son, and you must name him Jesus. He will be great and will be called Son of the Most High. The Lord God will give him the throne of his ancestor David; he will rule over the House of Jacob for ever and his reign will have no end.' Mary said to the angel, 'But how can this come about, since I am a virgin?' 'The Holy Spirit will come upon you,' the angel answered, 'and the power of the Most High will cover you with its shadow. And so the child will be holy and will be called Son of God. Know this too: your kinswoman Elizabeth has, in her old age, herself conceived a son, and she whom people called barren is now in her sixth month, for nothing is impossible to God.' 'I am the handmaid of the Lord,' said Mary, 'let what you have said be done to me.' And the angel left her.

The Gospel of the Lord.

The Creed is said.

8 December: The Immaculate Conception

Prayer over the Offerings
Graciously accept the saving sacrifice
which we offer you, O Lord,
on the Solemnity of the Immaculate Conception
of the Blessed Virgin Mary,
and grant that, as we profess her,
on account of your prevenient grace,
to be untouched by any stain of sin,
so, through her intercession,
we may be delivered from all our faults.
Through Christ our Lord.
Amen.

Preface of the Mystery of Mary and the Church, p.43.

Communion Antiphon
Glorious things are spoken of you, O Mary,
for from you arose the sun of justice,
Christ our God.

Prayer after Communion
May the Sacrament we have received,
O Lord our God,
heal in us the wounds of that fault
from which in a singular way
you preserved Blessed Mary in her Immaculate Conception.
Through Christ our Lord.
Amen.

The Solemn Blessing formula, p.101, may be used.

APPENDIX TO HOLY DAYS, FEASTS OF THE LORD AND SOLEMNITIES

MUSICAL SETTINGS

THE PRESENTATION OF THE LORD

Lu-men ad re-ve-la-ti-ó-nem gén-ti-um, et gló-ri-am ple-bis tu-æ Is-ra-el.

A light for re-ve-la-tion to the Gen-tiles and the glo-ry of your peo-ple Is-ra-el.

Lord, now you let your servant go in peace, in accord-ance with your word:

For my eyes have seen your sal-va-tion, which you have prepared in the sight of all the peo-ples.

FROM THE NATIONAL CALENDARS OF SAINTS FOR ENGLAND, SCOTLAND AND WALES

1 March
SAINT DAVID, BISHOP
Patron of Wales
Feast (Solemnity in Wales)

David was born in the sixth century, the son of the king of Ceredigion; he became well known for teaching and preaching and founded many monasteries and churches in Wales. He was buried at Saint David's Cathedral in Wales, where his relics still remain. He was a popular and much loved saint. His last words were: 'Be joyful, and keep your faith and your creed. Do the little things that you have seen me do and heard about'.

Entrance Antiphon
Is.52:7

How beautiful upon the mountains are the feet of him
who brings glad tidings of peace,
bearing good news, announcing salvation!

The Gloria in excelsis (Glory to God in the highest) is said.

Collect
O God, who graciously bestowed on your Bishop Saint David of Wales
the virtue of wisdom and the gift of eloquence,
and made him an example of prayer and pastoral zeal;
grant that, through his intercession,
your Church may ever prosper and render you joyful praise.
Through our Lord Jesus Christ, your Son,
who lives and reigns with you in the unity of the Holy Spirit,
one God, for ever and ever.
Amen.

FIRST READING
A reading from the letter of St Paul to the Philippians   3:8-14

I believe nothing can happen that will outweigh the supreme advantage of knowing Christ Jesus my Lord. For him I have accepted the loss of everything, and I look on everything as so much rubbish if only I can have Christ and be given a place in him. I am no longer trying for perfection by my own efforts, the perfection that comes from the Law, but I want only the perfection that comes through faith in Christ, and is from God and based on faith. All I want is to know Christ and the power of his resurrection and to share his sufferings by reproducing the pattern of his death. That is the way I can hope to take my place in the resurrection of the dead. Not that I have become perfect yet: I have not yet won, but I am still running, trying to capture the prize for which Christ Jesus captured me. I can assure you my brothers, I am far from thinking that I have already won. All I can say is that I forget the past and I strain ahead for what is still to come; I am racing for the finish, for the prize to which God calls us upwards to receive in Christ Jesus.

The word of the Lord.

Responsorial Psalm   Ps 1:4. 6 ℟ Ps 39:5
    ℟   **Happy the man who has placed his trust in the Lord.**

1   Happy indeed is the man
who follows not the counsel of the wicked;
nor lingers in the way of sinners
nor sits in the company of scorners,
but whose delight is the law of the Lord
and who ponders his law day and night.   ℟

2   He is like a tree that is planted
beside the flowing waters,
that yields its fruit in due season
and whose leaves shall never fade;
and all that he does shall prosper.   ℟

3   Not so are the wicked, not so!
For they like winnowed chaff
shall be driven away by the wind;
for the Lord guards the way of the just
but the way of the wicked leads to doom.   ℟

Gospel Acclamation   Jn 8:31-32

Outside Lent

Alleluia, alleluia!
If you make my word your home
you will indeed be my disciples,
and you will learn the truth, says the Lord.
Alleluia!

In Lent

Glory to you, O Christ, you are the Word of God.
If you make my word your home

you will indeed be my disciples,
and you will learn the truth, says the Lord.
Glory to you, O Christ, you are the Word of God.

GOSPEL

A reading from the holy Gospel according to Matthew 5:13-16

Jesus said to his disciples: 'You are the salt of the earth. But if salt becomes tasteless, what can make it salty again? It is good for nothing, and can only be thrown out to be trampled underfoot by men.

'You are the light of the world. A city built on a hill-top cannot be hidden. No one lights a lamp to put it under a tub; they put it on the lamp-stand where it shines for everyone in the house. In the same way your light must shine in the sight of men, so that, seeing your good works, they may give the praise to your Father in heaven.'

The Gospel of the Lord.

Where this feast is kept as a Solemnity, the Creed is said.

Prayer over the Offerings

Look with favour, O Lord we pray,
on the offerings we set upon this sacred altar
on the feast day of the Bishop Saint David,
that, bestowing on us your pardon,
our oblations may give honour to your name.
Through Christ our Lord.
Amen.

Communion Antiphon   Cf. 1 Cor 1:23-24

We proclaim Christ crucified;
Christ, the power of God and the wisdom of God.

Prayer after Communion

We pray, almighty God,
that we, who are fortified by the power of this Sacrament,
may learn through the example of your Bishop Saint David
to seek you always above all things
and to bear in this world the likeness of New Man.
Through Christ our Lord.
Amen.

17 March
SAINT PATRICK, BISHOP
Patron of Ireland
Feast (In Ireland Solemnity)

Patrick lived in the first half of the fifth century; many later stories were written about him, but from his own words we know he was born into a Christian family somewhere in the north west of England or South West Scotland, called Bana Venta Berniae. He was taken to Ireland as a slave when he was sixteen and lived there for six years until he escaped. Later he was educated by St Germanus of Auxerre and formed part of a mission to Ireland. He was renowned a teacher and pastor, converting many people and ordaining many priests as well as creating religious communities. His tomb is said to be at Downpatrick, Co Down.

Entrance Antiphon
cf. Ps.95:2–3

Proclaim the salvation of God day by day;
tell among the nations his glory.

The Gloria in excelsis (Glory to God in the highest) is said.

Collect
O God, who chose the Bishop Saint Patrick
to preach your glory to the peoples of Ireland,
grant through his merits and intercession,
that those who glory in the name of Christian
may never cease to proclaim your wondrous deeds to all.
Through our Lord Jesus Christ, your Son,
who lives and reigns with you in the unity of the Holy Spirit,
one God, for ever and ever.
Amen.

FIRST READING
A reading from the prophet Jeremiah
1:4-9

The word of the Lord was addressed to me, saying,

'Before I formed you in the womb I knew you;
before you came to birth I consecrated you;
I have appointed you as prophet to the nations.'

I said, 'Ah, Lord God; look, I do not know how to speak: I am a child!'

But the Lord replied,
'Do not say, "I am a child".
Go now to those to whom I send you

17 March: Saint Patrick

and say whatever I command you.
Do not be afraid of them,
for I am with you to protect you –
it is the Lord who speaks!'

Then the Lord put out his hand and touched my mouth and said to me:

'There! I am putting my words into your mouth.'

The word of the Lord.

Responsional Psalm   Ps 116. ℟ Mk 16:15

   ℟ **Go out to all the world,**
      and tell the Good News.

or (outside Lent only)
   ℟ **Alleluia!**

1   O praise the Lord, all you nations,
    acclaim him all you peoples!   ℟

2   Strong is his love for us;
    he is faithful for ever.   ℟

SECOND READING
A reading from the Acts of the Apostles   13:46-49

Paul and Barnabas spoke out boldly to the Jews, 'We had to proclaim the word of God to you first, but since you have rejected it, since you do not think yourselves worthy of eternal life, we must turn to the pagans. For this is what the Lord commanded us to do when he said:

'I have made you a light for the nations,
so that my salvation may reach the ends of the earth.'

It made the pagans very happy to hear this and they thanked the Lord for his message; all who were destined for eternal life became believers. Thus the word of the Lord spread through the whole countryside.

The word of the Lord.

Gospel Acclamation   Lk 4:18

                    Outside Lent
Alleluia, alleluia!
The Lord sent me to bring Good News to the poor,
and freedom to prisoners.
Alleluia!

In Lent
Praise and honour to you, Lord Jesus!
The Lord sent me to bring Good News to the poor,
and freedom to prisoners.
Praise and honour to you, Lord Jesus!

GOSPEL
A reading from the holy Gospel according to Luke   10:1-12. 17-20

The Lord appointed seventy-two others and sent them out ahead of him, in pairs, to all the towns and places he himself was to visit. He said to them, 'The harvest is rich but the labourers are few, so ask the Lord of the harvest to send labourers to his harvest. Start off now, but remember, I am sending you out like lambs among wolves. Carry no purse, no haversack, no sandals. Salute no one on the road. Whatever house you go into, let your first words be, "Peace to this house!" And if a man of peace lives there, your peace will go and rest on him; if not, it will come back to you. Stay in the same house, taking what food and drink they have to offer, for the labourer deserves his wages; do not move from house to house. Whenever you go into a town where they make you welcome, eat what is set before you. Cure those in it who are sick, and say, "The kingdom of God is very near to you." But whenever you enter a town and they do not make you welcome, go out into its streets and say, "We wipe off the very dust of your town that clings to our feet, and leave it with you. Yet be sure of this: the kingdom of God is very near." I tell you, on that day it will not go as hard with Sodom as with that town.'

The seventy-two came back rejoicing. 'Lord,' they said 'even the devils submit to us when we use your name.' He said to them, 'I watched Satan fall like lightning from heaven. Yes, I have given you power to tread underfoot serpents and scorpions and the whole strength of the enemy; nothing shall ever hurt you. Yet do not rejoice that the spirits submit to you; rejoice rather that your names are written in heaven.'

The Gospel of the Lord.

Where this feast is kept as a Solemnity, the Creed is said.

Prayer over the Offerings
Lord, accept this pure sacrifice
which, through the labours of Saint Patrick,

your grateful people make
to the glory of your name.
Through Christ our Lord.
Amen.

Communion Antiphon   Lk.22:29-30
I confer a kingdom on you
just as my Father has conferred one on me,
that you may eat and drink at my table in my kingdom,
   says the Lord.

Prayer after Communion
Strengthen us, O Lord, by this sacrament,
so that we may profess the faith taught by Saint Patrick
and proclaim it by our way of living.
Through Christ our Lord.
Amen.

23 April
SAINT GEORGE, MARTYR
Patron of England
Feast (In England Solemnity)

George was a third/fourth century martyr who lived in Syria Palestina. According to ancient tradition he was a soldier and was martyred for his Christian faith in Nicomedia. His tomb is in Lydda (Lod) in Israel. He was a popular saint, widely venerated in the East; his cult spread to England in the twelfth century through Crusader influence as they adopted him as a patron and used his emblem, the George Cross. In time he became the patron saint of England. The legend of George and the dragon is a much later gloss on his story and has very ancient roots. He is also regarded as a holy person in Islam.

Entrance Antiphon   Cf. Mt 25:34
Rejoice, you Saints, in the presence of the Lamb;
a kingdom has been prepared for you
from the foundation of the world, alleluia.

or   Ps 90:13

On the asp and the viper you will tread,
and trample the young lion and the dragon, alleluia.

The Gloria in excelsis (Glory to God in the highest) is said.

Collect

God of hosts,
who so kindled the fire of charity
in the heart of Saint George your martyr,
that he bore witness to the risen Lord
both by his life and by his death;
grant us through his intercession, we pray,
the same faith and power of love,
that we who rejoice in his triumph
may be led to share with him
in the fullness of the resurrection.
Through our Lord Jesus Christ, your Son,
who lives and reigns with you in the unity of the Holy Spirit,
one God, for ever and ever.
Amen.

FIRST READING

A reading from the book of the Apocalypse   12:10-12

I, John, heard a voice shout from heaven, 'Victory and power and empire for ever have been won by our God, and all authority for his Christ, now that the persecutor, who accused our brothers day and night before our God, has been brought down. They have triumphed over him by the blood of the Lamb and by the witness of their martyrdom, because even in the face of death they would not cling to life. Let the heavens rejoice and all who live there.'

The word of the Lord.

Responsorial Psalm   Ps 125. ℟ v.5

℟ **Those who are sowing in tears
will sing when they reap.**

1   When the Lord delivered Zion from bondage,
    it seemed like a dream.
    Then was our mouth filled with laughter,
    on our lips there were songs. ℟

2   The heathens themselves said: 'What marvels
    the Lord worked for them!'
    What marvels the Lord worked for us!
    Indeed we were glad. ℟

3   Deliver us, O Lord, from our bondage
    as streams in dry land.
    Those who are sowing in tears
    will sing when they reap. ℟

4   They go out, they go out, full of tears,
    carrying seed for the sowing;
    they come back, they come back, full of song,
    carrying their sheaves. ℟

Gospel Acclamation   James 1:12
    Alleluia, alleluia!
    Happy the man who stands firm,
    for he has proved himself,
    and will win the crown of life.
    Alleluia!

GOSPEL

A reading from the holy Gospel according to John   15:18-21

Jesus said to his disciples:

'If the world hates you,
remember that it hated me before you.
If you belonged to the world,
the world would love you as its own;
but because you do not belong to the world,
because my choice withdrew you from the world,
therefore the world hates you.
Remember the words I said to you:
A servant is not greater than his master.
If they persecuted me,
they will persecute you too;
if they kept my word,
they will keep yours as well.
But it will be on my account that they will do this,
because they do not know the one who sent me.'

The Gospel of the Lord.

Alternative Gospel
A reading from the holy Gospel according to John   15:1-8

Jesus said to his disciples:

'I am the true vine,
and my Father is the vinedresser.
Every branch in me that bears no fruit
he cuts away,
and every branch that does bear fruit he prunes
to make it bear even more.

You are pruned already,
by means of the word that I have spoken to you.
Make your home in me, as I make mine in you.
As a branch cannot bear fruit all by itself,
but must remain part of the vine,
neither can you unless you remain in me.
I am the vine,
you are the branches.
Whoever remains in me, with me in him,
bears fruit in plenty;
for cut off from me you can do nothing.
Anyone who does not remain in me
is like a branch that has been thrown away
– he withers;
these branches are collected and thrown on the fire,
and they are burnt.
If you remain in me
and my words remain in you,
you may ask what you will
and you shall get it.
It is to the glory of my Father that you should bear much fruit,
and then you will be my disciples.'

The Gospel of the Lord.

Where this feast is kept as a Solemnity, the Creed is said.

Prayer over the Offerings
Receive, we pray, O Lord,
the sacrifice of conciliation and praise,
which we offer to your majesty
in commemoration of the blessed Martyr Saint George,
that it may lead us to forgiveness
and confirm us in constant thanksgiving.
Through Christ our Lord.
Amen.

Communion Antiphon
Cf. 2 Tim 2:11-12
If we have died with Christ, we shall also live with him;
if we persevere, we shall also reign with him, alleluia.

Prayer after Communion
Rejoicing on this festival day, O Lord,
we have received your heavenly gifts;
grant, we pray,

that we who in this divine banquet
proclaim the death of your Son
may merit with Saint George to be partakers
in his resurrection and glory.
Through Christ our Lord.
Amen.

30 November
SAINT ANDREW, APOSTLE AND MARTYR
Patron of Scotland
Feast (In Scotland: Solemnity)

Andrew is mentioned in the New Testament as the son of John and the brother of Simon Peter, like him a fisherman. He is also known as the 'first called' by the Orthodox in recognition of being the first of the apostles called by Christ to 'follow him'. Church tradition says he preached the gospel in Asia Minor and is associated with the City of Byzantium, which is why the Patriarchate of Constantinople is called the See of Andrew. He was martyred at Patras in present day Greece.

Entrance Antiphon Cf. Mt 4:18-19
Beside the Sea of Galilee,
the Lord saw two brothers, Peter and Andrew,
and he said to them:
Come after me and I will make you fishers of men.

The Gloria in excelsis (Glory to God in the highest) is said.

Collect
We humbly implore your majesty, O Lord,
that, just as the blessed Apostle Andrew
was for your Church a preacher and pastor,
so he may be for us a constant intercessor before you.
Through our Lord Jesus Christ, your Son,
who lives and reigns with you in the unity of the Holy Spirit,
one God, for ever and ever.
Amen.

FIRST READING
A reading from the book of Wisdom 3:1-9

The souls of the virtuous are in the hands of God,
no torment shall ever touch them.

In the eyes of the unwise, they did appear to die,
their going looked like a disaster,
their leaving us, like annihilation;
but they are in peace.
If they experienced punishment as men see it,
their hope was rich with immortality;
slight was their affliction, great will their blessings be.
God has put them to the test
and proved them worthy to be with him;
he has tested them like gold in a furnace,
and accepted them as a holocaust.
When the time comes for his visitation they will shine out;
as sparks run through the stubble, so will they.
They shall judge nations, rule over peoples,
and the Lord will be their king for ever.
They who trust in him will understand the truth,
those who are faithful will live with him in love;
for grace and mercy await those he has chosen.

   The word of the Lord.

Responsorial Psalm Ps 30:3-4. 6. 8. 17. 21. ℟ v.6
   ℟   **Into your hands, O Lord,
       I commend my spirit.**

1   Be a rock of refuge for me,
    a mighty stronghold to save me,
    for you are my rock, my stronghold.
    For your name's sake, lead me and guide me. ℟

2   Into your hands I commend my spirit.
    It is you who will redeem me, Lord.
    As for me, I trust in the Lord:
    let me be glad and rejoice in your love. ℟

3   Let your face shine on your servant.
    Save me in your love.
    You hide them in the shelter of your presence
    from the plotting of men. ℟

SECOND READING
A reading from the letter of St Paul to the Romans 10:9-18

If your lips confess that Jesus is Lord and if you believe in your
heart that God raised him from the dead, then you will be saved.

By believing from the heart you are made righteous; by confessing with your lips you are saved. When scripture says: those who believe in him will have no cause for shame, it makes no distinction between Jew and Greek: all belong to the same Lord who is rich enough, however many ask his help, for everyone who calls on the name of the Lord will be saved.

But they will not ask his help unless they believe in him, and they will not believe in him unless they have heard of him, and they will not hear of him unless they get a preacher, and they will never have a preacher unless one is sent, but as scripture says: The footsteps of those who bring good news are a welcome sound. Not everyone, of course, listens to the Good News. As Isaiah says: Lord, how many believed what we proclaimed? So faith comes from what is preached, and what is preached comes from the word of Christ.

Let me put the question: is it possible that they did not hear? Indeed they did; in the words of the psalm, their voice has gone out through all the earth, and their message to the ends of the world.

The word of the Lord.

Gospel Acclamation Mt 4:19
Alleluia, alleluia!
Follow me, says the Lord,
and I will make you into fishers of men.
Alleluia!

GOSPEL
A reading from the holy Gospel according to Matthew 4:18-22

As Jesus was walking by the Sea of Galilee he saw two brothers, Simon, who was called Peter, and his brother Andrew; they were making a cast in the lake with their net, for they were fishermen. And he said to them, 'Follow me and I will make you fishers of men.' And they left their nets at once and followed him. Going on from there he saw another pair of brothers, James son of Zebedee and his brother John; they were in their boat with their father Zebedee, mending their nets, and he called them. At once, leaving the boat and their father, they followed him.

The Gospel of the Lord.

Where this feast is kept as a Solemnity, the Creed is said.

Prayer over the Offerings
Grant us, almighty God, that through these offerings,
which we bring on the feast day of Saint Andrew,

we may please you by what we have brought
and be given life by what you have accepted.
Through Christ our Lord.
Amen.

An appropriate Preface of the Apostles, pp.46-7.

Communion Antiphon Cf. Jn 1:41-42
Andrew told his brother Simon:
We have found the Messiah, the Christ,
and he brought him to Jesus.

Prayer after Communion
May communion in your Sacrament strengthen us, O Lord,
so that by the example of the blessed Apostle Andrew
we, who carry in our body the Death of Christ,
may merit to live with him in glory.
Who lives and reigns for ever and ever.
Amen.

The Solemn Blessing formula, p.102, may be used.

FROM THE NATIONAL CALENDARS OF SAINTS FOR IRELAND

17 March
SAINT PATRICK, BISHOP, PRINCIPAL PATRON OF IRELAND
Solemnity

Patrick lived in the first half of the fifth century; many later stories were written about him, but from his own words we know he was born into a Christian family somewhere in the north west of England or South West Scotland, called Bana Venta Berniae. He was taken to Ireland as a slave when he was sixteen and lived there for six years until he escaped. Later he was educated by St Germanus of Auxerre and formed part of a mission to Ireland. He was renowned a teacher and pastor, converting many people and ordaining many priests as well as creating religious communities. His tomb is said to be at Downpatrick, Co Down.

Entrance Antiphon
Gen 12:1-2

Go from your country and your kindred and your father's house to the land that I will show you.
I will make of you a great nation, and I will bless you,
and make your name great, so that you will be a blessing.

The Gloria in excelsis (Glory to God in the highest) is said.

Collect
Lord, through the work of Saint Patrick in Ireland
we have come to acknowledge the mystery of the one true God
and give thanks for our salvation in Christ;
grant by his prayers
that we who celebrate this festival
may keep alive the fire of faith he kindled.
Through our Lord Jesus Christ, your Son,
who lives and reigns with you in the unity of the Holy Spirit,
one God, for ever and ever.
Amen.

For readings, see pp.92-5.

Where this feast is kept as a Solemnity, the Creed is said.

Prayer over the Offerings
Lord, accept this pure sacrifice
which, through the labours of Saint Patrick,

your grateful people make
to the glory of your name.
Through Christ our Lord.
Amen.

Preface
℣ The Lord be with you.
℟ **And with your spirit.**
℣ Lift up your hearts.
℟ **We lift them up to the Lord.**
℣ Let us give thanks to the Lord our God.
℟ **It is right and just.**

It is truly right and just, our duty and our salvation,
always and everywhere to give you thanks,
Lord, holy Father, almighty and eternal God,
and to proclaim your greatness with due praise
as we honour Saint Patrick.
For you drew him through daily prayer
in captivity and hardship
to know you as a loving Father.

You chose him out of all the world
to return to the land of his captors,
that they might acknowledge Jesus Christ, their Redeemer.

In the power of your Spirit you directed his paths
to win the sons and daughters of the Irish
to the service of the Triune God.

And so, with the Angels and Archangels,
and with the great multitude of the Saints,
we sing the hymn of your praise,
as without end we acclaim:
Holy, Holy, Holy Lord God of hosts …

Communion Antiphon   Cf. Mt 8:11
Many will come from east and west
and sit down with Abraham, Isaac and Jacob
at the feast in the Kingdom of Heaven, says the Lord.

Prayer after Communion
Strengthen us, O Lord, by this sacrament
so that we may profess the faith taught by Saint Patrick

and to proclaim it in our way of living.
Through Christ our Lord.
Amen.

Solemn Blessing

May God the Father, who called us together
to celebrate this feast of Saint Patrick,
bless you, protect you and keep you faithful.
℟ **Amen.**

May Christ the Lord, the High King of Heaven,
be near you at all times and shield you from evil.
℟ **Amen.**

May the Holy Spirit, who is the source of all holiness,
make you rich in the love of God's people.
℟ **Amen.**

And may the blessing of almighty God,
the Father, and the Son, ✜ and the Holy Spirit,
come down on you and remain with you for ever.
℟ **Amen.**

COMMON OF THE DEDICATION OF A CHURCH

This building in which we assemble to celebrate the divine mysteries is not only the house of God, but the house of the living Temple, the People of God and is a symbol of the universal Church, a people dedicated to God.

ON THE ANNIVERSARY OF THE DEDICATION
I. In the Church that was Dedicated

Entrance Antiphon   Ps 67:36
Wonderful are you, O God in your holy place.
The God of Israel himself gives his people strength and courage.
Blessed be God! (E.T. alleluia).

The Gloria in excelsis (Glory to God in the highest) is said.

Collect
O God, who year by year renew for us the day
when this your holy temple was consecrated,
hear the prayers of your people
and grant that in this place
for you there may always be pure worship
and for us, fullness of redemption.
Through our Lord Jesus Christ, your Son,
who lives and reigns with you in the unity of the Holy Spirit,
one God, for ever and ever.
Amen.

FIRST READING
A reading from the second book of Chronicles   5:6-11. 13-6:2

King Solomon, and all the community of Israel gathering with him in front of the ark, sacrificed sheep and oxen, countless, innumerable. The priests brought the ark of the covenant of the Lord to its place, in the Debir of the Temple, that is, in the Holy of Holies, under the cherubs' wings. For there where the ark was placed the cherubs spread out their wings and sheltered the ark and its shafts. These were long enough for their ends to be seen from the Holy Place in front of the Debir, but not from outside. There was nothing in the ark except the two tablets that Moses had placed in it at Horeb, where the Lord had made a covenant with the Israelites when they came out of Egypt.

Now when the priests came out of the sanctuary, a cloud filled the sanctuary, the Temple of the Lord.

All those who played the trumpet, or who sang, united in giving praise and glory to the Lord. Lifting their voices to the sound of the

Common of the Dedication of a Church

trumpet and cymbal and instruments of music, they gave praise to the Lord, 'for he is good, for his love is everlasting'.

Because of the cloud the priests could no longer perform their duties; the glory of the Lord filled the Temple of God.

Then Solomon said:

'The Lord has chosen to dwell in the thick cloud.
Yes, I have built you a dwelling,
a place for you to live in for ever.'

The word of the Lord.

In the Easter Season

A reading from the Acts of the Apostles 7:44-50

Stephen said to the people, the elders and scribes, 'While they were in the desert our ancestors possessed the Tent of Testimony that had been constructed according to the instructions God gave Moses, telling him to make an exact copy of the pattern he had been shown. It was handed down from one ancestor of ours to another until Joshua brought it into the country we had conquered from the nations which were driven out by God as we advanced. Here it stayed until the time of David. He won God's favour and asked permission to have a temple built for the House of Jacob, though it was Solomon who actually built God's house for him. Even so the Most High does not live in a house that human hands have built: for as the prophet says:

"With heaven my throne
and earth my footstool,
what house could you build me,
what place could you make for my rest?
Was not all this made by my hand?" '

The word of the Lord.

Responsional Psalm Ps 83:3-5. 10-11. ℟ v.2. Alt. ℟ Apoc 21:3

℟ **How lovely is your dwelling place,
Lord, God of hosts.**

or

℟ **Here God lives among men.**

1 My soul is longing and yearning,
is yearning for the courts of the Lord.
My heart and my soul ring out their joy
to God, the living God. ℟

2　The sparrow herself finds a home
　　and the swallow a nest for her brood;
　　she lays her young by your altars,
　　Lord of hosts, my king and my God. ℟

3　They are happy, who dwell in your house
　　for ever singing your praise.
　　Turn your eyes, O God, our shield,
　　look on the face of your anointed. ℟

4　One day within your courts
　　is better than a thousand elsewhere.
　　The threshold of the house of God
　　I prefer to the dwelling of the wicked. ℟

SECOND READING

A reading from the first letter of St Paul to the Corinthians　　　3:9-11. 16-17

You are God's building. By the grace God gave me, I succeeded as an architect and laid the foundations, on which someone else is doing the building. Everyone doing the building must work carefully. For the foundation, nobody can lay any other than the one which has already been laid, that is Jesus Christ.

Didn't you realise that you were God's temple and that the Spirit of God was living among you? If anybody should destroy the temple of God, God will destroy him, because the temple of God is sacred; and you are the temple.

The word of the Lord.

Gospel Acclamation　　　Ez 37:27
　　Alleluia, alleluia!
　　I shall make my home among them, says the Lord;
　　I will be their God,
　　they shall be my people.
　　Alleluia.

GOSPEL

A reading from the holy Gospel according to John　　　4:19-24

The Samaritan woman said to Jesus, 'I see you are a prophet, sir. Our fathers worshipped on this mountain, while you say that Jerusalem is the place where one ought to worship.' Jesus said:

　　'Believe me, woman, the hour is coming
　　when you will worship the Father
　　neither on this mountain nor in Jerusalem.

Common of the Dedication of a Church

You worship what you do not know;
we worship what we do know;
for salvation comes from the Jews.
But the hour will come – in fact it is here already –
when true worshippers will worship the Father in spirit and
    truth:
that is the kind of worshipper
the Father wants.
God is spirit,
and those who worship
must worship in spirit and truth.'

The Gospel of the Lord.

The Creed is said.

Prayer over the Offerings
Recalling the day when you were pleased
to fill your house with glory and holiness, O Lord,
we pray that you may make of us
a sacrificial offering always acceptable to you.
Through Christ our Lord.
Amen.

Preface of the Mystery of the Temple of God, which is the Church, p.41.

Communion Antiphon Cf. 1 Cor 3:16-17
You are the temple of God, and the Spirit of God dwells in you.
The temple of God, which you are, is holy (E.T. alleluia).

Prayer after Communion
May the people consecrated to you, O Lord, we pray,
receive the fruits and joy of your blessing,
that the festive homage
they have offered you today in the body
may redound upon them as a spiritual gift.
Through Christ our Lord.
Amen.

Blessing at the End of Mass
May God, the Lord of heaven and earth,
who has gathered you today
in memory of the dedication of this church,
make you abound in heavenly blessings.
Amen.

And may he, who has willed that all his scattered children
be gathered together in his Son,
grant that you may become his temple
and the dwelling place of the Holy Spirit.
Amen.

Thus, may you be made thoroughly clean,
so that God may dwell within you
and you may possess with all the Saints
the inheritance of eternal happiness.
Amen.

And may the blessing of almighty God,
the Father, and the Son, ✛ and the Holy Spirit,
come down on you and remain with you for ever.
Amen.

II. Outside the Church that was Dedicated

Entrance Antiphon Cf. Rv 21:2
I saw the holy city, a new Jerusalem,
coming down out of heaven from God
prepared like a bride adorned for her husband (E.T. alleluia).

or Cf. Rv 21:3

Behold God's dwelling with the human race.
He will dwell with them
and they will be his people,
and God himself with them will be their God (E.T. alleluia).

The Gloria in excelsis (Glory to God in the highest) is said.

Collect
O God, who from living and chosen stones
prepare an eternal dwelling for your majesty,
increase in your Church the grace you have bestowed,
so that by unceasing growth
your faithful people may build up the heavenly Jerusalem.
Through our Lord Jesus Christ, your Son,
who lives and reigns with you in the unity of the Holy Spirit,
one God, for ever and ever.
Amen.
or

Common of the Dedication of a Church

O God, who were pleased to call your Church the Bride,
grant that the people that serves your name
may revere you, love you and follow you,
and may be led by you
to attain your promises in heaven.
Through our Lord Jesus Christ, your Son,
who lives and reigns with you in the unity of the Holy Spirit,
one God, for ever and ever.
Amen.

For readings, see pp.106-9.

Prayer over the Offerings
Accept, we pray, O Lord, the offering made here
and grant that by it those who seek your favour
may receive in this place
the grace of the Sacraments
and an answer to their prayers.
Through Christ our Lord.
Amen.

Preface of the Mystery of the Church, the Bride of Christ and Temple of the Spirit, pp.41-2.

Communion Antiphon Cf. 1 Pet 2:5
Be built up like living stones,
into a spiritual house, a holy priesthood (E.T. alleluia).

or Cf. Mt 21:13; Lk 11:10

My house shall be a house of prayer, says the Lord:
in that house, everyone who asks receives, and the one who seeks finds,
and to the one who knocks, the door will be opened (E.T. alleluia).

Prayer after Communion
O God, who chose to foreshadow for us
the heavenly Jerusalem
through the sign of your Church on earth,
grant, we pray,
that, by our partaking of this Sacrament,
we may be made the temple of your grace
and may enter the dwelling place of your glory.
Through Christ our Lord.
Amen.

THE SACRAMENTS

Stages in the **Christian Initiation of Adults** are given during the Sundays of Lent Year A as follows:

- First Scrutiny (p.263ff.)
- Second Scrutiny (p.271ff.)
- Third Scrutiny (p.279ff.)

The **Rite of Baptism** below and the **Rite of Confirmation** (p.1117) are given during the Easter Vigil celebration

Extracts from the **Rite of Pardon and Reconciliation** (p.1111), and the **Rites of the Sick and Dying** (p.1118) are given in the pages that follow. A selection of the texts provided for the celebration of the Rite is given in each case. Alternative texts are to be found in the full edition of each Rite. This section is reprinted from the *Glenstal Bible Missal*.

THE RITE OF BAPTISM

Candidates to be baptised renounce the devil individually. Then they are questioned about their faith and are baptised.

Priest: Do you renounce Satan?
Candidates: **I do.**
Priest: And all his works?
Candidates: **I do.**
Priest: And all his empty show?
Candidates: **I do.**

or

Priest: Do you renounce sin,
so as to live in the freedom of the children of God?
Candidates: **I do.**
Priest: Do you renounce the lure of evil,
so that sin may have no mastery over you?
Candidates: **I do.**
Priest: Do you renounce Satan,
the author and prince of sin?
Candidates: **I do.**

If the situation warrants, this second formula may be adapted by Conferences of Bishops according to local needs.

Then the Priest continues:

Priest: Do you believe in God,
the Father almighty,
Creator of heaven and earth?
Candidates: **I do.**
Priest: Do you believe in Jesus Christ, his only Son, our Lord,
who was born of the Virgin Mary,
suffered death and was buried,
rose again from the dead
and is seated at the right hand of the Father?
Candidates: **I do.**
Priest: Do you believe in the Holy Spirit,
the holy Catholic Church,
the communion of saints,
the forgiveness of sins,
the resurrection of the body,
and life everlasting?
Candidates: **I do.**

The candidates are then baptised by the priest who says:

Priest: N., I baptise you in the name of the Father, and of the Son, and of the Holy Spirit.

An acclamation may be sung, for example one of the following:

Rejoice, you newly baptised,
chosen members of the Kingdom.
Buried with Christ in death,
you are reborn in him by faith.

or

Blessed be God who chose you in Christ.

THE RITE OF CONFIRMATION

Adults are confirmed immediately after baptism if a bishop or a priest with the faculty to confirm is present. The neophyte stands in front of the celebrant, who speaks to him in these or similar words:

N., born again in Christ by baptism, you have become a member of Christ and of his priestly people. Now you are to share in the outpouring of the Holy Spirit among us, the Spirit sent by the Lord upon his apostles at Pentecost and given by them and their successors to be baptised.

The promised strength of the Holy Spirit which you are to receive, will make you more like Christ and help you to be a witness to his suffering, death, and resurrection. It will strengthen you to be an active member of the Church and to build up the Body of Christ in faith and love.

Then the celebrant stands and faces the people and says:

My dear friends, let us pray to God our Father,
that he will pour out the Spirit on these newly baptised
to strengthen them with his gifts
and anoint them to be more like Christ, the Son of God.

All pray in silence for a short time.

Then the celebrant lays hands upon the candidate and says:

All-powerful God, Father of our Lord Jesus Christ,
by water and the Holy Spirit
you freed your sons and daughters from sin
and gave them new life.
Send your Holy Spirit upon them
to be their helper and guide.
Give them the spirit of wisdom and understanding,
the spirit of right judgment and courage,
the spirit of knowledge and reverence.
Fill them with the spirit of wonder and awe in your presence.
We ask this through Christ our Lord.
Amen.

The candidate, with the godparents, goes to the celebrant. The godparent places his right hand on the candidate's shoulder and gives the candidate's name to the celebrant, or the candidate may give his own name. The celebrant dips his right thumb in the chrism and makes the sign of the cross on the forehead of the one to be confirmed, saying:

Celebrant: N., be sealed with the gift of the Holy Spirit.
Newly confirmed: **Amen.**
Celebrant: Peace be with you.
Newly confirmed: **And also with you.**

When the rite of baptism (and confirmation) has been completed, all present stand with lighted candles and renew their baptismal promises (see p.419ff.)

THE RITE OF PARDON AND RECONCILIATION
INDIVIDUAL PENITENTS

Greeting, Sign of the Cross and Invitation to Trust in God
The priest welcomes and greets the penitent with kindness.

The penitent makes the sign of the cross which the priest may also make. The priest invites the penitent to trust in God. The following or similar words may be used:

May God, who has enlightened every heart,
help you to know your sins
and trust in his mercy.
Penitent: **Amen.**

LITURGY OF THE WORD (OPTIONAL)

Then the priest may read or say from memory a text of scripture which proclaims God's mercy and calls man to conversion. This text may be read or said by the penitent. If this part of the rite is omitted, it is fitting that the penitent read one of these texts as part of the preparation for reception of the sacrament.

The following texts are suitable:

After John had been arrested, Jesus went into Galilee. There he proclaimed the Good News from God. 'The time has come' he said 'and the kingdom of God is close at hand. Repent, and believe the Good News.' **Mark 1:14-75**

Give thanks to the Father who has made it possible for you to join the saints and with them to inherit the light.
 Because that is what he has done: he has taken us out of the power of darkness and created a place for us in the kingdom of the Son that he loves, and in him, we gain our freedom, the forgiveness of our sins. **Col 1:12-14**

LITURGY OF RECONCILIATION

Confession of Sins and Acceptance of Satisfaction
Where it is the custom, the penitent says a general formula for confession (such as the 'I confess') before the confession of sins.
 The penitent then confesses his or her sins. If necessary the priest helps the penitent to make a full confession and gives suitable counsel. Urging the penitent to be sorry for his or her faults, the

priest recalls that through the sacrament of reconciliation, the Christian dies and rises with Christ and is renewed in the Easter mystery.

The priest proposes an act of penance which the penitent accepts to make satisfaction for sin and to amend his or her life.

Penitent's Prayer of Sorrow
The priest then asks the penitent to express sorrow for sins committed. This may be done by using an Act of Contrition familiar to the penitent or a prayer taken from or based on the scriptures, such as the following:

Lord Jesus,
you opened the eyes of the blind,
healed the sick,
forgave the sinful woman,
and after Peter's denial confirmed him in your love.
Listen to my prayer:
forgive all my sins,
renew your love in my heart,
help me to live in perfect unity with my fellow Christians
that I may proclaim your saving power to all the world.

Absolution
Then the priest extends his hands over the penitent's head (or at least extends his right hand) and says:

God, the Father of mercies,
through the death and resurrection of his Son
has reconciled the world to himself
and sent the Holy Spirit among us
for the forgiveness of sins;
through the ministry of the Church
may God give you pardon and peace,
and I absolve you from your sins
in the name of the Father, and of the Son, ✚
and of the Holy Spirit.
Penitent: **Amen.**

Praise of God and Dismissal
After the absolution the priest continues:

Give thanks to the Lord, for he is good.
Penitent: **His mercy endures for ever.**

Then the priest dismisses the penitent, saying:

The Lord has freed you from your sins. Go in peace.

In place of the proclamation of God's praise and the dismissal, the priest may say the following, or similar, words:

The Lord has freed you from sin.
May he bring you safely to his kingdom in heaven.
Glory to him for ever.
Penitent: **Amen.**

SEVERAL PENITENTS WITH INDIVIDUAL CONFESSION AND ABSOLUTION

INTRODUCTORY RITES

When the faithful have assembled, they may sing a psalm, antiphon, or other appropriate song while the priest is entering the church. After the song, all make the sign of the cross together:

In the name of the Father, and of the Son, and of the Holy Spirit.
Amen.

The priest greets the congregation in these or similar words:

May God open your hearts to his law
and give you peace:
may he answer your prayers
and restore you to friendship.
All: **Amen.**

The greetings from the introductory rites of Mass may also be used. Then the priest or another minister speaks briefly about the importance and purpose of the celebration and the order of the service.

Opening Prayer

The priest invites all to pray. All pray in silence for a brief period.

Then the priest sings or says the opening prayer, for example:

Father of mercies
and God of all consolation,
you do not wish the sinner to die
but to be converted and live.

Come to the aid of your people,
that they may turn from their sins
and live for you alone.
May we be attentive to your word,
confess our sins, receive your forgiveness,
and be always grateful for your loving kindness.
Help us to live the truth in love
and grow into the fullness of Christ, your Son,
who lives and reigns for ever and ever.
All: **Amen.**

LITURGY OF THE WORD

The celebration of the Word follows. A psalm, an appropriate song or a period of silence should punctuate the readings. If there is only one reading, it is preferable that it be from the Gospel. The readings are chosen from those given in the Lectionary.

Homily

Examination of Conscience

A period of time may be spent in making an examination of conscience and in arousing true sorrow for sins. The priest, deacon, or another minister may help the faithful by brief statements or a kind of litany, taking into consideration their circumstances, age, etc.

LITURGY OF RECONCILIATION

General Confession of Sins

The deacon or another minister invites all to kneel or bow, and to join in saying a general formula of confession (e.g. I confess).

Deacon or minister: Brothers and sisters, let us call to mind the goodness of God our Father, and acknowledge our sins, so that we may receive his merciful forgiveness.

All: **I confess to almighty God,
and to you, my brothers and sisters,
that I have sinned through my own fault**

They strike their breast:
**in my thoughts and in my words,
in what I have done,
and in what I have failed to do;
and I ask blessed Mary, ever virgin,
all the angels and saints,**

and you, my brothers and sisters,
to pray for me to the Lord our God.

All stand and say or sing a litany or an appropriate song, for example:

Deacon or minister: Christ our Saviour is our advocate with the Father:
with humble hearts let us ask him to forgive us our sins
and cleanse us from every stain.

You were sent with good news for the poor and healing for the contrite.
All: **Lord, be merciful to me, a sinner.**
or
    Lord, have mercy.

You came to call sinners, not the just.
All: **Lord, be merciful to me, a sinner.**
or
    Lord, have mercy.

You forgave the many sins of the woman who showed you great love.
All: **Lord, be merciful to me, a sinner.**
or
    Lord, have mercy.

You did not shun the company of outcasts and sinners.
All: **Lord, be merciful to me, a sinner.**
or
    Lord, have mercy.

You carried back to the fold the sheep that had strayed.
All: **Lord, be merciful to me, a sinner.**
or
    Lord, have mercy.

You did not condemn the woman taken in adultery, but sent her away in peace.
All: **Lord, be merciful to me, a sinner.**
or
    Lord, have mercy.

You called Zacchaeus to repentance and a new life.
All: **Lord, be merciful to me, a sinner.**
or
    Lord, have mercy.

You promised Paradise to the repentant thief.
All: **Lord, be merciful to me, a sinner.**
or
> Lord, have mercy.

You are always interceding for us at the right hand of the Father.
All: **Lord, be merciful to me, a sinner.**
or
> Lord, have mercy.

Deacon or minister: Now, in obedience to Christ himself, let us join in prayer to the Father, asking him to forgive us as we forgive others.

All: **Our Father . . .**

The priest concludes:

Father, our source of life,
you know our weakness.
May we reach out with joy to grasp your hand
and walk more readily in your ways.
We ask this through Christ our Lord.
All: **Amen.**

Individual Confession and Absolution
Then the penitents go to the priest or priests designated for individual confession, and confess their sins. Each one receives and accepts an appropriate act of satisfaction. The priest may offer suitable counsel. The penitent is then absolved with the formula used for the reconciliation of individual penitents. Everything else which is customary in individual confession is omitted.

Proclamation of God's Mercy
When the individual confessions have been completed, the priest or priests return to the sanctuary. The presiding priest invites all to offer thanks and encourage them to do good works which will proclaim the grace of repentance in the life of the community and in each of its members. It is fitting for all to sing a psalm or hymn or to say a litany in acknowledgement of God's power and mercy.

Concluding Prayer of Thanksgiving
After the song of praise or the litany, the priest concludes with the following or a similar prayer:

Father,
in your love you have brought us
from evil to good and from misery to happiness.

Rite of Reconciliation: Several Penitents

Through your blessings
give the courage of perseverance
to those you have called and justified in faith.
Grant this through Christ our Lord.
All: **Amen.**

Blessing and Dismissal
Then the priest blesses all present in these or similar words:

May the Lord guide your hearts in the way of his love
and fill you with Christ-like patience.
All: **Amen.**

May he give you strength
to walk in newness of life
and to please him in all things.
All: **Amen.**

May almighty God bless you,
the Father, and the Son, ✝ and the Holy Spirit.
All: **Amen.**

The deacon or other minister or the priest himself dismisses the assembly:

The Lord has freed you from your sins. Go in peace.

All: **Amen.**

Any other appropriate form may be used.

THE RITE OF
COMMUNION OF THE SICK

Greeting
The minister greets the sick person and the others present in these or similar words:

The grace of our Lord Jesus Christ
and the love of God
and the fellowship of the Holy Spirit
be with you all.

All: **And also with you.**

[Sprinkling with Holy Water
A priest or deacon may sprinkle the sick person and those present with holy water with these or similar words:

Let this water call to mind our baptism into Christ, who by his death and resurrection has redeemed us.]

If the sacrament of penance is now celebrated, the penitential rite is omitted.

Penitential Rite
The minister invites the sick person and those present to recall their sins and to repent of them in these or similar words:

My brothers and sisters,
to prepare ourselves for this celebration,
let us call to mind our sins.

The minister may continue with one of the penitential rites from the Missal, or all may say: I confess . . .

The minister concludes:

May almighty God have mercy on us,
forgive us our sins,
and bring us to everlasting life.
All: **Amen.**

Liturgy of the Word
Several readings may follow, as at Mass. There should be at least one reading, read by one of those present or by the minister.

Communion of the Sick

A brief period of silence may follow the reading. The minister may give a brief explanation of the reading.

[Prayer of the Faithful
The prayer of the faithful may follow. The minister introduces the prayer and says the concluding prayer. It is desirable that someone other than the minister announce the intentions.]

LITURGY OF HOLY COMMUNION

The Lord's Prayer
The minister introduces the Lord's Prayer in these or similar words:

Now let us pray together to the Father
in the words given us by our Lord Jesus Christ.

All say together:

Our Father . . .

Communion
Then the minister shows the eucharist, saying:

This is the Lamb of God
who takes away the sins of the world.
Happy are those who are called to his supper.

The sick person and other communicants reply:

**Lord, I am not worthy to receive you,
but only say the word and I shall be healed.**

The minister goes to the sick person and, showing the sacrament says:

The body of Christ (or: The blood of Christ)

The sick person replies:

Amen.

Others present then receive communion in the usual manner.

Silent Prayer
A period of silence may be observed.

Prayer after Communion
The minister says the concluding prayer, for example:
Let us pray

God our Father,
you have called us to share the one bread and one cup
and so become one in Christ.

Help us to live in him
that we may bear fruit,
rejoicing that he has redeemed the world.
We ask this through Christ our Lord.
All: **Amen.**

Blessing
A priest or deacon gives the blessing in these or similar words:

May God the Father bless you.
All: **Amen.**
Priest/Deacon: May God the Son heal you.
All: **Amen.**
Priest/Deacon: May God the Holy Spirit enlighten you.
All: **Amen.**
Priest/Deacon: May almighty God bless you
the Father, and the Son, and the Holy Spirit.
All: **Amen.**

A minister who is not a priest or deacon, invokes God's blessing and makes the sign of the cross on himself or herself, saying:

May the Lord bless us,
protect us from all evil,
and bring us to everlasting life.
All: **Amen.**

or

May the almighty and merciful God bless and protect us,
the Father, and the Son, ✠ and the Holy Spirit.
All: **Amen.**

FROM THE MASSES FOR VARIOUS NEEDS AND OCCASIONS

FOR THE EVANGELIZATION OF PEOPLES

This Mass may be used even on Sundays of Ordinary Time, whenever there are special celebrations for the work of the missions, provided it does not occur on a Sunday of Advent, Lent or Easter, or on any Solemnity.

A

Entrance Antiphon Cf. Ps 66:2-3
O God, be gracious and bless us,
and let your face shed its light upon us, and have mercy.
So will your ways be known upon earth
and all nations learn your salvation.

Collect
O God, whose will it is that all should be saved
and come to the knowledge of the truth,
look upon your abundant harvest
and be pleased to send workers to gather it,
that the Gospel may be preached to all creation
and that your people, gathered by the word of life
and sustained by the power of the Sacraments,
may advance in the path of salvation and love.
Through our Lord Jesus Christ, your Son,
who lives and reigns with you in the unity of the Holy Spirit,
one God, for ever and ever.
Amen.

or

O God, who sent your Son into the world as the true light,
pour out, we pray, the Spirit he promised
to sow seeds of truth constantly in people's hearts
and to awaken in them obedience to the faith,
so that, being born to new life through Baptism,
all may become part of your one people.
Through our Lord Jesus Christ, your Son,
who lives and reigns with you in the unity of the Holy Spirit,
one God, for ever and ever.
Amen.

FIRST READING

A reading from the prophet Isaiah   2:1-5

The vision of Isaiah son of Amoz, concerning Judah and
Jerusalem.
In the days to come
the mountain of the Temple of the Lord
shall tower above the mountains
and be lifted higher than the hills.
All the nations will stream to it,
peoples without number will come to it; and they will say:
'Come, let us go up to the mountain of the Lord,
to the Temple of the God of Jacob
that he may teach us his ways
so that we may walk in his paths;
since the Law will go out from Zion,
and the oracle of the Lord from Jerusalem.'
He will wield authority over the nations
and adjudicate between many peoples;
these will hammer their swords into ploughshares,
their spears into sickles.
Nation will not lift sword against nation,
there will be no more training for war.
O House of Jacob, come,
let us walk in the light of the Lord.

The word of the Lord.

Responsorial Psalm   Ps 97:1-6. ℟ v.2. Alt. ℟ v.3

℟ **The Lord has shown his salvation to the nations.**

or

℟ **All the ends of the earth have seen
the salvation of our God.**

1   Sing a new song to the Lord
    for he has worked wonders.
    His right hand and his holy arm
    have brought salvation. ℟

2   The Lord has made known his salvation;
    has shown his justice to the nations.
    He has remembered his truth and love
    for the house of Israel. ℟

3   All the ends of the earth have seen
    the salvation of our God.

Shout to the Lord all the earth,
ring out your joy. R/

4. Sing psalms to the Lord with the harp
with the sound of music.
With trumpets and the sound of the horn
acclaim the King, the Lord. R/

SECOND READING
A reading from the letter of St Paul to the Ephesians 3:2-12

You have probably heard how I have been entrusted by God with the grace he meant for you, and that it was by a revelation that I was given the knowledge of the mystery, as I have just described it very shortly. If you read my words, you will have some idea of the depths that I see in the mystery of Christ. This mystery that has now been revealed through the Spirit to his holy apostles and prophets was unknown to any men in past generations; it means that pagans now share the same inheritance, that they are parts of the same body, and that the same promise has been made to them in Christ Jesus, through the gospel. I have been made the servant of that gospel by a gift of grace from God who gave it to me by his own power. I, who am less than the least of all the saints, have been entrusted with this special grace, not only of proclaiming to the pagans the infinite treasure of Christ but also of explaining how the mystery is to be dispensed. Through all the ages, this has been kept hidden in God, the creator of everything. Why? So that the Sovereignties and Powers should learn only now, through the Church, how comprehensive God's wisdom really is, exactly according to the plan which he had had from all eternity in Christ Jesus our Lord. This is why we are bold enough to approach God in complete confidence, through our faith in him.

The word of the Lord.

Gospel Acclamation Mk 16:5
Alleluia, alleluia!
Go out to the whole world,
says the Lord,
proclaim the Good News
to all creation.
Alleluia!

GOSPEL

A reading from the holy Gospel according to Mark 16:15-20

Jesus said to the Eleven, 'Go out to the whole world, proclaim the Good News to all creation. He who believes and is baptised will be saved; he who does not believe will be condemned. These are the signs that will be associated with believers; in my name they will cast out devils; they will have the gift of tongues; they will pick up snakes in their hands, and be unharmed should they drink deadly poison; they will lay their hands on the sick, who will recover.' And so the Lord Jesus, after he had spoken to them, was taken up into heaven; there at the right hand of God he took his place, while they, going out, preached everywhere, the Lord working with them and confirming the word by the signs that accompanied it.

The Gospel of the Lord.

Prayer over the Offerings
Look, O Lord, upon the face of your Christ,
who handed himself over as a ransom for all,
so that through him,
from the rising of the sun to its setting,
your name may be exalted among the nations
and in every place a single offering
may be presented to your majesty.
Through Christ our Lord.
Amen.

Communion Antiphon Cf. Mt 28:20
Teach all nations to keep whatever I have commanded you, says the Lord.
And behold, I am with you always, even to the end of the age.

Prayer after Communion
Nourished by these redeeming gifts,
we pray, O Lord,
that through this help to eternal salvation
true faith may ever increase.
Through Christ our Lord.
Amen.

B

Entrance Antiphon   Ps 95:3-4
Tell among the nations his glory,
and his wonders among all the peoples,
for the Lord is great and highly to be praised.

Collect
O God, you have willed that your Church
be the sacrament of salvation for all nations,
so that Christ's saving work may continue to the end of the ages;
stir up, we pray, the hearts of your faithful
and grant that they may feel a more urgent call
to work for the salvation of every creature,
so that from all the peoples on earth
one family and one people of your own
may arise and increase.
Through our Lord Jesus Christ, your Son,
who lives and reigns with you in the unity of the Holy Spirit,
one God, for ever and ever.
Amen.

Prayer over the Offerings
May the offerings and prayers of your Church, O Lord,
rise up in the sight of your majesty and gain acceptance,
just as the glorious Passion of your Son was pleasing to you
for the salvation of the whole world.
Through Christ our Lord.
Amen.

Communion Antiphon   Ps 116:1-2
O praise the Lord, all you nations;
acclaim him, all you peoples!
For his merciful love has prevailed over us,
and the Lord's faithfulness endures for ever.

or   Mk 16:15

Go into all the world, and proclaim the Gospel, says the Lord.
I am with you always.

Prayer after Communion
May our participation at your table sanctify us,
O Lord, we pray,
and grant that through the Sacrament of your Church
all nations may receive in rejoicing
the salvation accomplished on the Cross
by your Only Begotten Son.
Who lives and reigns for ever and ever.
Amen.

FROM THE DIVINE OFFICE

FROM THE DIVINE OFFICE

EVENING PRAYER FOR SUNDAYS
from
The Divine Office

To facilitate the saying of Evening Prayer on Sundays, either with a group or privately, a simple order of service is given here. The changing parts of the Proper of Seasons are not given.

The psalms may be sung or said in one of three ways:

- *directly*: ie, all sing the entire psalm
- *antiphonally*: ie, two sections of the congregation sing alternate verses
- *responsorially*: ie, the congregation sings verses alternately with a cantor or leader.

Week 1
SUNDAY EVENING PRAYER II

ALL STAND.

℣ O God, come to our aid.
℟ **O Lord, make haste to help us.**

**Glory be to the Father and to the Son
and to the Holy Spirit,
as it was in the beginning, is now,
and ever shall be,
world without end.
Amen. Alleluia.**

A hymn suitable to the day and the season is said or sung.

PSALMODY

ALL SIT.

Antiphon 1
Advent: Rejoice greatly, daughter of Sion, shout with gladness, daughter of Jerusalem, alleluia.
Lent, Sunday 1: You must worship the Lord, your God, and serve him alone.
Lent, Sunday 5: As Moses lifted up the serpent in the desert, so the Son of Man must be lifted up.

Eastertide: The Lord has risen and sits at the right hand of God, alleluia.
Through the Year: The Lord will send his mighty sceptre from Sion, and he will rule for ever, alleluia.

THE MESSIAH IS KING AND PRIEST　　　　　　　　Psalm 109(110):1-5. 7

> The Lórd's revelátion to my Máster:†
> 'Sít on my ríght:*
> your fóes I will pút beneath your féet.'
>
> The Lórd will wíeld from Síon†
> your scéptre of pówer:*
> rúle in the mídst of all your fóes.
>
> A prínce from the dáy of your bírth†
> on the hóly móuntains;*
> from the wómb before the dáwn I begót you.
>
> The Lórd has sworn an óath he will not chánge.†
> 'You are a príest for éver,*
> a príest like Melchízedek of óld.'
>
> The Máster stánding at your right hand*
> will shatter kíngs in the dáy of his wráth.
>
> He shall drínk from the stréam by the wáyside*
> and thérefore he shall líft up his héad.
>
> **Glory be . . .**

Repeat Antiphon 1.

Antiphon 2
Advent: Christ our King will come. He is the Lamb that John announced.
Lent, Sunday 1: Now is the favourable time; this is the day of salvation.
Lent, Sunday 5: The Lord of hosts protects and rescues; he spares and he saves.
Eastertide: He has freed us from the power of darkness and has given us a place in the kingdom of his Son, alleluia.
Through the Year: The earth trembled before the Lord, alleluia.

ISRAEL IS FREED FROM EGYPT　　　　　　　　Psalm 113a(114):1-8

> When Ísrael came fórth from Égypt,*
> Jacob's sóns from an álien péople,
> Júdah becáme the Lord's témple,*
> Ísrael becáme his kingdom.

The séa fléd at the síght:*
the Jórdan turned báck on its cóurse,
the móuntains léapt like ráms*
and the hílls like yéarling shéep.

Whý was it, séa, that you fléd, *
that you túrned back, Jórdan, on your cóurse?

Móuntains, that you léapt like ráms, *
hílls, like yéarling shéep?

Trémble, O éarth, before the Lórd, *
in the présence of the Gód of Jácob,
who túrns the rock into a póol*
and flínt into a spríng of wáter.
Glory be. . .

Repeat Antiphon 2.

Outside Lent

Antiphon 3
Advent: Behold I am coming soon to reward every man according to his deeds, says the Lord.
Eastertide: Alleluia, the Lord, our God, is King; let us rejoice and give glory to him, alleluia.
Through the Year: The Lord is King, our God, the Almighty! alleluia.

When chanted, this canticle is sung with Alleluia *as set out below. When recited, it suffices to say* Alleluia *at the beginning and end of each strophe.*

THE MARRIAGE FEAST OF THE LAMB   CANTICLE Rev 19:1-2. 5-7

Alleluia.
Salvation and glory and power belong to our God,*
(℟   **Alleluia.**)
His judgments are true and just.
℟   **Alleluia (alleluia).**

Alleluia.
Praise our God, all you his servants,
(℟   **Alleluia.**)
You who fear him, small and great.
℟   **Alleluia (alleluia).**

Alleluia.
The Lord our God, the Almighty, reigns,*
(℟ **Alleluia.**)
Let us rejoice and exult and give him the glory.
℟ **Alleluia (alleluia).**
Alleluia.
The marriage of the Lamb has come,*
(℟ **Alleluia**)
And his bride has made herself ready.
℟ **Alleluia (alleluia).**
Glory be. . .

Repeat Antiphon 3.

Lent

Antiphon 3
Lent, Sunday 1: Now we are going up to Jerusalem, and everything that is written about the Son of Man will come true.
Lent, Sunday 5: He was wounded for our faults, he was bruised for our sins. Through his wounds we are healed.

CHRIST, THE SERVANT OF GOD,   CANTICLE
  FREELY ACCEPTS HIS PASSION   1 Pet 2:21-24

Christ suffered for you,†
leaving you an example*
that you should follow in his steps.

He committed no sin;*
no guile was found on his lips.
When he was reviled,*
he did not revile in return.

When he suffered,*
he did not threaten;
but he trusted to him*
who judges justly.

He himself bore our sins*
in his body on the tree,
that we might die to sin*
and live to righteousness.

By his wounds you have been healed.
Glory be . . .

Repeat Antiphon 3.

Through the Year

Scripture Reading
2 Cor 1:3-4

Let us give thanks to the God and Father of our Lord Jesus Christ, the merciful Father, the God from whom all help comes! He helps us in all our troubles, so that we are able to help those who have all kinds of troubles, using the same help that we ourselves have received from God.

ALL STAND.

Short Responsory
Cantor: Blessed are you in the vault of heaven.
All: **Blessed are you in the vault of heaven.**
Cantor: You are exalted and glorified above all else for ever.
All: **Blessed are you in the vault of heaven.**
Cantor: Glory be to the Father and to the Son and to the Holy Spirit.
All: **Blessed are you in the vault of heaven.**

The Magnificat: The Canticle of Mary
Lk 1:46-55

The Magnificat antiphon is recited before and after the canticle. It varies each day.

My soul glorifies the Lord,*
my spirit rejoices in God, my Saviour.
He looks on his servant in her lowliness;*
henceforth all ages will call me blessed.

The Almighty works marvels for me.*
Holy his name!
His mercy is from age to age,*
on those who fear him.

He puts forth his arm in strength*
and scatters the proud-hearted.
He casts the mighty from their thrones*
and raises the lowly.

He fills the starving with good things,*
sends the rich away empty.

He protects Israel, his servant,*
remembering his mercy,

the mercy promised to our fathers,*
to Abraham and his sons for ever.
Glory be...

Intercessions
Christ is the Head of his body, the Church, and we are the members of that body; gathered this evening to pray in his name, we say:

℟ **Your kingdom come!**

May your Church be a light to the nations, the sign and source of your power to unite all men: – may she lead mankind to the mystery of your love. ℟

Guide the Pope and all the bishops of your church: – grant them the gifts of unity, of love, and of peace. ℟

Lord, give peace to our troubled world – and give to your children security of mind and freedom from anxiety. ℟

Help us to bring your compassion to the poor, the sick, the lonely, the unloved; – lead us to find you in the coming week. ℟

Awaken the dead to a glorious resurrection: – may we be united with them at the end of time. ℟

Our Father...

The concluding prayer of the day.

Conclusion
When a priest or deacon presides over the Office and no other Hour follows:

The Lord be with you.
And also with you.
May almighty God bless you, the Father, and the Son, and the Holy Spirit.
Amen.

Another form of blessing may be used as in the Missal. The people are then invited to leave:

Go in the peace of Christ.
Thanks be to God.

When no priest or deacon is present, or in recitation on one's own, the conclusion is as follows:

The Lord bless us, and keep us from all evil,
and bring us to everlasting life.
Amen.

Week 2

SUNDAY EVENING PRAYER II

ALL STAND.
℣ O God, come to our aid.
℟ **O Lord, make haste to help us.**

Glory be to the Father and to the Son
and to the Holy Spirit,
as it was in the beginning, is now,
and ever shall be,
world without end.
Amen. Alleluia.

A hymn suitable to the day and the season is said or sung.

PSALMODY

ALL SIT.

Antiphon 1
Advent: Behold, the Lord will come on the clouds of heaven with great strength, alleluia.
Lent, Sunday 2: The Lord will send forth your sceptre of power with the splendour of the saints.
Lent, Palm Sunday: He was wounded and humbled, but God has raised him up with his own right hand.
Eastertide: He raised Christ from the dead and placed him at his own right hand, in heaven, alleluia.
Through the Year: Christ the Lord is a priest for ever according to the order of Melchizedek, alleluia.

Psalm 109(110): 1-5. 7. See above, p.1136.

Repeat Antiphon 1.

Antiphon 2
Advent: The Lord will come and will not disappoint us. Wait for him if he seems to delay, for he will surely come, alleluia.
Lent, Sunday 2: We worship the one God, who made heaven and earth.
Palm Sunday: The blood of Christ purifies us to serve the living God.

Eastertide: You have been converted from idolatry to the living God, alleluia.
Through the Year: Our God is in heaven: he has power to do whatever he will, alleluia.

PRAISE OF THE GOD OF TRUTH Psalm 113b(115)

Not to ús, Lórd, not to ús,*
but to yóur náme give the glóry
for the sáke of your lóve and your trúth,*
lest the héathen say: 'Whére is their Gód?'

But our Gód is ín the héavens;*
he dóes whatéver he wílls.
Their ídols are silver and góld,*
the wórk of húman hánds.

They have móuths but they cánnot spéak;*
they have éyes but they cánnot sée;
they have éars but they cánnot héar;*
they have nóstrils but they cánnot sméll.

With their hánds they cánnot féel;†
with their féet they cánnot wálk.*
No sóund cómes from their thróats.
Their mákers will cóme to be líke them*
and so will áll who trúst in thém.

Sons of Ísrael, trúst in the Lórd;*
hé is their hélp and their shíeld.
Sons of Áaron, trúst in the Lórd;
hé is their hélp and their shíeld.

You who fear him, trúst in the Lórd;
hé is their hélp and their shíeld.
He remémbers us, and hé will bléss us:†
he will bléss the sóns of Ísrael.*
He will bléss the sóns of Áaron.

The Lord will bléss thóse who féar him,*
the líttle no léss than the gréat:
to yóu may the Lórd grant íncrease,*
to yóu and áll your chíldren.

May yóu be bléssed by the Lórd,*
the máker of héaven and éarth.
The héavens belóng to the Lórd*
but the éarth he has gíven to mén.

The déad shall not práise the Lórd,*
nor thóse who go dówn into the sílence.
But wé who líve bless the Lórd*
nów and for éver. Amén.
Glory be . . .

Repeat Antiphon 2.

Outside Lent

Antiphon 3
Advent: The Lord is our judge, the Lord is our King. He will come and make us whole.
Eastertide: Alleluia, victory and glory and power belong to our God, alleluia.
Through the year: Praise God, all you his servants, both great and small, alleluia.

Canticle: Cf. Rev 19:1-2, 5-7. See above, p.1137-8.

Repeat Antiphon 3.

Lent

Antiphon 3
Lent, Sunday 2: God did not spare his own Son but gave him up for us all.
Palm Sunday: He carried our sins in his own body on the cross, so that we might die to sin and live for holiness.

Canticle: 1 Pet 2:21-24. See above, p.1138.

Repeat Antiphon 3.

Through the Year

Scripture Reading   2 Thess 2:13-14
We feel that we must be continually thanking God for you, brothers whom the Lord loves, because God chose you as first fruits to be saved by the sanctifying Spirit and by faith in the truth. Through the Good News that we brought he called you to this so that you should share the glory of our Lord Jesus Christ.

ALL STAND.

Short Responsory
Cantor: Great is our Lord; great is his might.
All: **Great is our Lord; great is his might.**

Cantor: His wisdom can never be measured.
All: **Great is our Lord; great is his might.**
Cantor: Glory be to the Father, and to the Son, and to the Holy Spirit.
All: **Great is our Lord; great is his might.**

Magnificat. See above, p.1139-40.

Intercessions
Through the gospel, the Lord Jesus calls us to share in his glory. Let us make our prayer with him to our heavenly Father.
℟ **Lord, in your mercy hear our prayer.**
We pray for all nations: – that they may seek the way that leads to peace; that human rights and freedom may be everywhere respected, and that the world's resources may be generously shared. ℟
We pray for the Church: – that her leaders may be faithful ministers of your word, that all her members may be strong in faith and hope and that you may be recognized in the love she bears to all. ℟
We pray for our families, and the community in which we live: – that we may find you in them. ℟
We pray for ourselves: – that in the coming week we may serve others in our work, and find peace when we rest. ℟
We pray for the faithful departed: – that through your mercy they may rest in peace. ℟
Our Father . . .

The concluding prayer of the day and blessing.

Week 3

SUNDAY EVENING PRAYER II

ALL STAND.
℣   O God, come to our aid.
℟   **O Lord, make haste to help us.**

**Glory be to the Father and to the Son
and to the Holy Spirit,
as it was in the beginning, is now,
and ever shall be,
world without end.
Amen. Alleluia.**

A hymn suitable to the day and the season is said or sung.

PSALMODY

ALL SIT.

Antiphon 1
Advent: See, the Lord will come. He will sit with princes and he will mount the glorious throne.
Lent: Lord, almighty king, deliver us for the sake of your name. Give us the grace to return to you.
Eastertide: When he had made purification for sin, he sat at the right hand of the Majesty on high, alleluia.

Through the Year: The Lord's revelation to my Master: 'Sit on my right', alleluia.†

Psalm 109(110):1. 5-7. See above, p.1136.

Repeat Antiphon 1.

Antiphon 2
Advent: The mountains will bring forth joy and the hills justice; for the Lord, the light of the world, comes in strength.
Lent: We were ransomed with the precious blood of Christ, the Lamb who is without blemish.
Eastertide: The Lord has delivered his people, alleluia.
Through the Year: The Lord is full of merciful love, he makes us remember his wonders, alleluia.

GREAT ARE THE WORKS OF THE LORD   Psalm 110(111)

I will thánk the Lórd with all my héart*
in the méeting of the júst and their assémbly.
Gréat are the wórks of the Lórd;*
to be póndered by áll who lóve them.

Májestic and glórious his wórk,*
his jústice stands fírm for éver.
He mákes us remémber his wónders.*
The Lórd is compássion and lóve.

He gives fóod to thóse who féar him;*
keeps his cóvenant éver in mind.
He has shówn his míght to his péople*
by gíving them the lánds of the nátions.

His wórks are jústice and trúth:*
his précepts are áll of them súre,
standing fírm for éver and éver:*
they are máde in úprightness and trúth.

He has sént delíverance to his péople†
and estáblished his cóvenant for éver.*
Hóly his náme, to be féared.

To fear the Lórd is the fírst stage of wísdom;†
all who dó so próve themselves wíse.*
His práise shall lást for éver!
Glory be...

Repeat Antiphon 2.

Outside Lent

Antiphon 3
Advent: Let us live justly and honestly while we are awaiting, in hope, the coming of the Lord.
Eastertide: Alleluia, the Lord our God is king; let us rejoice and give glory to him alleluia.

Through the Year: The Lord our God almighty is king, alleluia.

Canticle: Cf. Rev 19:1-2. 5-7. See above, p.1137-8.

Repeat Antiphon 3.

Lent

Antiphon 3
Ours were the sufferings he bore, ours the sorrows he carried.

Canticle: 1 Pet 2:21-24. See above, p.1138.

Repeat Antiphon 3.

Through the Year

Scripture Reading 1 Pet 1:3-5
Blessed be God the Father of our Lord Jesus Christ, who in his great mercy has given us a new birth as his sons, by raising Jesus Christ from the dead, so that we have a sure hope and the promise of an inheritance that can never be spoilt or soiled and never fade away, because it is being kept for you in the heavens. Through your faith, God's power will guard you until the salvation which has been prepared is revealed at the end of time.

ALL STAND.

Short Responsory
Cantor: Blessed are you, O Lord, in the vault of heaven.
All: **Blessed are you, O Lord, in the vault of heaven.**
Cantor: You are exalted and glorified above all else for ever.
All: **Blessed are you, O Lord, in the vault of heaven.**
Cantor: Glory be to the Father and to the Son and to the Holy Spirit.
All: **Blessed are you, O Lord, in the vault of heaven.**

Magnificat. See above, p.1139-40.

Intercessions
God is ever creative. His love renews all things and is the source of our hope. Let us turn to him in confidence:
℟ **Lord, accept our thanks and our prayers.**
We give thanks for the order of created things: – you have blessed us with the resources of the earth and the gift of human life. ℟
We give thanks for man's share in your continuing work of creation: – we praise you for your gifts to him of inventive skill and creative vision. ℟
We pray for all the nations of the world: – may those in authority work for peace and goodwill among men. ℟
We pray for all who are homeless today: – we pray for families searching for a place to live, and for refugees driven from their homeland. ℟
Life was your first gift to us: – may those who have died come to its fulness in you. ℟
Our Father . . .

The concluding prayer of the day and blessing.

Week 4

SUNDAY EVENING PRAYER II

ALL STAND.
℣ O God, come to our aid.
℟ O Lord, make haste to help us.

**Glory be to the Father and to the Son
and to the Holy Spirit,
as it was in the beginning, is now,
and ever shall be,**

Evening Prayer for Sundays

world without end.
Amen. Alleluia.

A hymn suitable to the day and the season is said or sung.

PSALMODY

ALL SIT.

Antiphon 1
Advent: See, how splendid is he who comes to save the peoples.
Lent: God has appointed him to judge everyone, living and dead.
Eastertide: You must look for the things of heaven, where Christ is, sitting at God's right hand, alleluia.

Through the Year: In holy splendour I begot you before the dawn, alleluia.

Psalm 109:1-5. 7. See above, p.1136.

Antiphon 2
Advent: The rugged places shall be made smooth and the mountain-ranges shall become plains. Come, Lord, and do not delay, alleluia.
Lent: Happy is the man to whom the Lord shows mercy; he will never waver.
Eastertide: He has risen as a light in the darkness, for the upright of heart, alleluia.

Through the Year: Blessed are those who hunger and thirst for justice, for they shall have their fill.

THE HAPPINESS OF A JUST MAN   Psalm 111(112)

Happy the mán who féars the Lórd,*
who tákes delíght in all his commánds.
His sóns will be pówerful on éarth;*
the children of the úpright are bléssed.

Ríches and wéalth are in his hóuse;*
his jústice stands fírm for éver.
He is a líght in the dárkness for the úpright:*
he is génerous, mérciful and júst.

The góod man takes píty and lénds,*
he condúcts his affáirs with hónour.
The júst man will néver wáver:*
hé will be remémbered for éver.

Week 4

> He has no féar of évil néws;*
> with a fírm heart he trústs in the Lórd.
> With a stéadfast héart he will not féar;*
> he will sée the dównfall of his fóes.
>
> Open-hánded, he gíves to the póor;†
> his jústice stands fírm for éver.*
> His héad will be ráised in glóry.
>
> The wícked man sées and is ángry,†
> grinds his téeth and fádes awáy;*
> the désire of the wicked leads to dóom.
> **Glory be . . .**

Repeat Antiphon 2.

Outside Lent

Antiphon 3
Advent: Great will be his reign and peace will be everlasting, alleluia.
Eastertide: Alleluia, victory and glory and power to our God, alleluia.

Through the Year: Praise God, all you his servants, both great and small, alleluia.

Canticle: Cf. Rev 19:1-2. 5-7. See above, pp.1137-8.

Repeat Antiphon 3.

Lent

Antiphon 3
God fulfilled what he had foretold in the words of all the prophets: that Christ would suffer.

Canticle: 1 Pet 2:21-24. See above, p.1138.

Repeat Antiphon 3.

Through the Year

Scripture Reading Heb 12:22-24
What you have come to is Mount Zion and the city of the living God, the heavenly Jerusalem where the millions of angels have gathered for the festival, with the whole Church in which everyone is a 'first-born son' and a citizen of heaven. You have come to God himself, the supreme judge, and been placed with spirits of the

saints who have been made perfect; and to Jesus, the mediator who brings a new covenant and a blood for purification which pleads more insistently than Abel's.

ALL STAND.

Short Responsory
Cantor: Great is our Lord; great is his might.
All: **Great is our Lord; great is his might.**
Cantor: His wisdom can never be measured.
All: **Great is our Lord; great is his might.**
Cantor: Glory be to the Father, and to the Son, and to the Holy Spirit.
All: **Great is our Lord; great is his might.**

Magnificat. See above, pp.1139-40.

Intercessions
In the Church, God has made known to us his hidden purpose: to make all things one in Christ. Let us pray that his will may be done.
℞ **Father, unite all things in Christ.**
We give you thanks for the presence and power of your Spirit in the Church: – give us the will to search for unity, and inspire us to pray and work together.   ℞
We give you thanks for all whose work proclaims your love: – help us to serve the communities in whose life we share.   ℞
Father, care for all who serve in the Church as ministers of your word and sacraments: – may they bring your whole family to the unity for which Christ prayed.   ℞
Your people have known the ravages of war and hatred: – grant that they may know the peace left by your Son.   ℞
Fulfil the hopes of those who sleep in your peace: – bring them to that final resurrection when you will be all in all.   ℞
Our Father . . .

The concluding prayer of the day and blessing.

NIGHT PRAYER
(Compline)

Either of these two forms of Night Prayer may be used on any day of the week.

AFTER EVENING PRAYER I OF SUNDAYS AND SOLEMNITIES

ALL STAND.

℣ O God, come to our aid . . .

Here an examination of conscience is commended. In a common celebration this may be inserted in a penitential act using the formulas given in the Missal.

Hymn
A hymn suitable to the Hour is said or sung.

PSALMODY

All sit.

Antiphon 1
Lord, have mercy and hear me.
Eastertide: Alleluia, alleluia, alleluia.

THANKSGIVING   Psalm 4

> When I cáll, ánswer me, O Gód of jústice;*
> from ánguish you reléased me, have mércy and héar me!
>
> O mén, how lóng will your héarts be clósed,*
> will you lóve what is fútile and séek what is fálse?
>
> It is the Lórd who grants fávours to thóse whom he lóves;*
> the Lórd héars me whenéver I cáll him.
>
> Fear him; do not sín: pónder on your béd and be stíll.*
> Make jústice your sácrifice and trúst in the Lórd.
>
> 'What can bríng us háppiness?' mány sáy.*
> Let the light of your face shine on us, O Lord.
>
> You have pút into my héart a gréater jóy*
> than théy have from abúndance of córn and new wíne.
>
> I will líe down in péace and sléep comes at ónce*
> for yóu alone, Lórd, make me dwéll in sáfety.
> **Glory be . . .**

Ant. Lord, have mercy and hear me.

Antiphon 2
Bless the Lord through the night.

EVENING PRAYER IN THE TEMPLE   Psalm 133(134)

> O cóme, bléss the Lórd,*
> all yóu who sérve the Lórd,*
> who stand in the hóuse of the Lórd,
> in the cóurts of the hóuse of our Gód.
>
> Lift up your hánds to the hóly pláce*
> and bléss the Lórd through the night.
>
> May the Lórd bléss you from Síon,*
> he who máde both héaven and éarth.
> **Glory be...**

Ant. Bless the Lord through the night.
Eastertide: Alleluia, alleluia, alleluia.

Scripture Reading   Deut 6:4-7
Hear, O Israel: the Lord our God is one Lord; and you shall love the Lord your God with all your heart, and with all your soul, and with all your might. And these words which I command you this day shall be upon your heart; and you shall teach them diligently to your children, and shall talk of them when you sit in your house, and when you walk by the way, and when you lie down, and when you rise.

ALL STAND.

Short Responsory
Outside Eastertide
Cantor: Into your hands, Lord, I commend my spirit.
All: **Into your hands, Lord, I commend my spirit.**
Cantor: You have redeemed us, Lord God of truth.
All: **Into your hands, Lord, I commend my spirit.**
Cantor: Glory be to the Father, and to the Son, and to the Holy Spirit.
All: **Into your hands, Lord, I commend my spirit.**

Easter Octave
This is the day which was made by the Lord: let us rejoice and be glad, alleluia.

Eastertide
Cantor: Into your hands, Lord, I commend my spirit, alleluia, alleluia.

Night Prayer

All: **Into your hands, Lord, I commend my spirit, alleluia, alleluia.**
Cantor: You have redeemed us, Lord God of truth.
All: **Into your hands, Lord, I commend my spirit, alleluia, alleluia.**
Cantor: Glory be to the Father, and to the Son, and to the Holy Spirit.
All: **Into your hands, Lord, I commend my spirit, alleluia, alleluia.**

Ant. Save us, Lord, while we are awake; protect us while we sleep; that we may keep watch with Christ and rest with him in peace (alleluia).

NUNC DIMITTIS   CANTICLE Lk 2:29-32

At last, all-powerful Master,†
you give leave to your servant*
to go in peace, according to your promise.

For my eyes have seen your salvation*
which you have prepared for all nations,
the light to enlighten the Gentiles*
and give glory to Israel, your people.
Glory be . . .

Ant. Save us, Lord, while we are awake; protect us while we sleep; that we may keep watch with Christ and rest with him in peace (alleluia).

Concluding Prayer
Sundays and Easter Octave
Come to visit us, Lord, this night,
so that by your strength we may rise at daybreak
to rejoice in the resurrection of Christ, your Son,
who lives and reigns for ever and ever.
Amen.

Solemnities which do not occur on a Sunday
Visit this house, we pray you, Lord:
drive far away from it all the snares of the enemy.
May your holy angels stay here and guard us in peace,
and let your blessing be always upon us.
Through Christ our Lord.
Amen.

Blessing
The Lord grant us a quiet night and a perfect end. **Amen.**

Anthem to the Blessed Virgin, see p.1161ff.

AFTER EVENING PRAYER II OF SUNDAYS AND SOLEMNITIES

All as above except the following.

PSALMODY

Ant. He will conceal you with his wings; you will not fear the terror of the night.
Eastertide: Alleluia, alleluia, alleluia.

IN THE SHELTER OF THE MOST HIGH　　　　　　　　　　Psalm 90(91)

> He who dwells in the shélter of the Most High*
> and abídes in the sháde of the Almíghty
> sáys to the Lórd: 'My réfuge,*
> my strónghold, my Gód in whom I trúst!'
>
> It is hé who will frée you from the snáre*
> of the fówler who séeks to destróy you;
> hé will concéal you with his pínions*
> and únder his wíngs you will find réfuge.
>
> You will not féar the térror of the níght*
> nor the árrow that flíes by dáy,
> nor the plágue that prówls in the dárkness*
> nor the scóurge that lays wáste at nóon.
>
> A thóusand may fáll at your síde, *
> tén thousand fáll at your ríght,
> yóu, it will néver appróach;*
> his fáithfulness is búckler and shíeld.
>
> Your éyes have ónly to lóok*
> to sée how the wícked are repáid,
> yóu who have said: 'Lórd, my réfuge!'*
> and have máde the Most Hígh your dwélling.
>
> Upon yóu no évil shall fáll,*
> no plágue appróach where you dwell.
> For yóu has he commánded his ángels, *
> to kéep you in áll your wáys.
>
> They shall béar you upón their hánds *
> lest you stríke your fóot against a stóne.
> On the líon and the víper you will tréad*
> and trámple the young líon and the drágon.

Night Prayer 1155

Since he clíngs to me in lóve, I will frée him;*
protéct him for he knóws my náme.
When he cálls I shall ánswer: 'I am wíth you.'*
I will sáve him in distréss and give him glóry.

With léngth of life I will contént him;*
I shall lét him see my sáving pówer.
Glory be . . .

Ant. He will conceal you with his wings; you will not fear the terror of the night.
Eastertide: Alleluia, alleluia, alleluia.

Scripture Reading
Rev 22:4-5

They will see the Lord face to face, and his name will be written on their foreheads. It will never be night again and they will not need lamplight or sunlight, because the Lord God will be shining on them. They will reign for ever and ever.

Short Responsory
Outside Eastertide
Cantor: Into your hands, Lord, I commend my spirit.
All: **Into your hands, Lord, I commend my spirit.**
Cantor: You have redeemed us, Lord God of truth.
All: **Into your hands, Lord, I commend my spirit.**
Cantor: Glory be to the Father, and to the Son, and to the Holy Spirit.
All: **Into your hands, Lord, I commend my spirit.**

Eastertide
Cantor: Into your hands, Lord, I commend my spirit, alleluia, alleluia.
All: **Into your hands, Lord, I commend my spirit, alleluia, alleluia.**
Cantor: You have redeemed us, Lord God of truth.
All: **Into your hands, Lord, I commend my spirit, alleluia, alleluia.**
Cantor: Glory be to the Father, and to the Son, and to the Holy Spirit.
All: **Into your hands, Lord, I commend my spirit, alleluia, alleluia.**

Concluding Prayer
Sundays and Easter Octave
God our Father,
as we have celebrated today the mystery of the Lord's resurrection,
grant our humble prayer:
free us from all harm

that we may sleep in peace
and rise in joy to sing your praise.
Through Christ our Lord.
Amen.

Easter Triduum and Solemnities which do not fall on Sundays
Visit this house, we pray you, Lord:
drive far away from it all the snares of the enemy.
May your holy angels stay here and guard us in peace,
and let your blessing be always upon us.
Through Christ our Lord.
Amen.

Blessing
The Lord grant us a quiet night and a perfect end. **Amen.**

Anthem to the Blessed Virgin, see pp.1163ff.

PRAYERS
FOR VARIOUS OCCASIONS

Prayer to the Holy Spirit
Come, Holy Spirit, fill the hearts of your faithful.
Enkindle in them the fire of your love.

Father,
you taught the hearts of your faithful people
by sending them the light of your Holy Spirit.
In that Spirit give us right judgement
and the joy of his comfort and guidance.
We ask this through our Lord Jesus Christ, your Son,
who lives and reigns with you and the Holy Spirit,
one God, for ever and ever.

Prayer of Self-Dedication to Jesus Christ
Lord Jesus Christ,
take all my freedom,
my memory, my understanding, and my will.
All that I have and cherish
you have given me.
I surrender it all to be guided by your will.
Your grace and your love are wealth enough for me.
Give me these, Lord Jesus,
and I ask for nothing more.

Tr. *ICEL*

Prayer to Christ Crucified
O kind and loving Jesus,
I kneel here before you,
asking you most fervently
to put into my heart
the virtues of faith, hope and charity,
with true contrition for my sins
and a firm purpose of amendment.
Help me to contemplate with sorrow
your five precious wounds,
while I remember David's prophecy:
They have pierced my hands and my feet;
they have counted all my bones.

Tr. *Stanbrook*

For the Pope
O God, shepherd and ruler of all the faithful,
look favourably on your servant N.,
whom you have set at the head of your Church as her shepherd;

grant, we pray, that by word and example
he may be of service to those over whom he presides
so that, together with the flock entrusted to his care,
he may come to everlasting life.
Through our Lord Jesus Christ, your Son,
who lives and reigns with you in the unity of the Holy Spirit,
one God, for ever and ever. Tr. *ICEL*

For Priestly Vocations
O God, who willed to provide shepherds for your people,
pour out in your Church a spirit of piety and fortitude,
to raise up worthy ministers for your altars
and make them ardent yet gentle heralds of your Gospel.
Through our Lord Jesus Christ, your Son,
who lives and reigns with you in the unity of the Holy Spirit,
one God, for ever and ever. Tr. *ICEL*

For Peace
O God of peace, who are peace itself
and whom a spirit of discord cannot grasp,
nor a violent mind receive,
grant that those who are one in heart
may persevere in what is good
and that those in conflict
may forget evil and so be healed.
Through our Lord Jesus Christ, your Son,
who lives and reigns with you in the unity of the Holy Spirit,
one God, for ever and ever. Tr. *ICEL*

In Time of War or Civil Disturbance
O God, merciful and strong,
who crush wars and cast down the proud,
be pleased to banish violence swiftly from our midst
and to wipe away all tears,
so that we may all truly deserve to be called your children.
Through our Lord Jesus Christ, your Son,
who lives and reigns with you in the unity of the Holy Spirit,
one God, for ever and ever. Tr. *ICEL*

Prayer of Saint Francis
Lord, make me an instrument of your peace.
Where there is hatred, let me sow love;
where there is injury, pardon;
where there is discord, union;
where there is doubt, faith;

where there is despair, hope;
where there is darkness, light;
where there is sadness, joy,
for your mercy and truth's sake.
O Divine Master, grant that I may not so much seek
to be consoled as to console,
to be understood as to understand,
to be loved as to love,
for it is in giving that we receive,
it is pardoning that we are pardoned,
it is in dying that we are born to eternal life.

A Prayer of Saint Richard
Thanks be to thee, Lord Jesus Christ,
for all the benefits and blessings which thou hast given me,
for the pain and insults which thou hast borne for me.
O most merciful Friend, Brother and Redeemer,
may I know thee more clearly,
love thee more dearly,
and follow the more nearly.

Prayer of Saint Thomas More for His Opponents
Almighty God,
have mercy on N. and N.,
and on all that bear me evil will and would me harm,
and their faults and mine together,
by such easy, tender, merciful means as thine infinite wisdom
　best can devise;
vouchsafe to amend and redress and make us saved souls in
　heaven together,
where we may ever live and love
together with thee and thy blessed saints,
O glorious Trinity,
for the bitter passion of our sweet Saviour. Amen.

Prayers for our Daily Work
Whatever your work is, put your heart into it as if it were for the Lord and not for men, knowing that the Lord will repay you by making you his heirs. It is Christ the Lord that you are serving.

Colossians 3:23–24

Our gifts differ according to the grace given us. Use your gift as faith suggests.

Romans 12:6

Whatever you do, do it for the glory of God.
1 Corinthians 11:31

The 'Jesus Prayer'
Lord Jesus Christ, Son of the living God,
be merciful to me, a sinner.

An Evening Prayer
May the Lord support us all the day long,
till the shades lengthen and the evening comes,
and the busy world is hushed,
and the fever of life is over,
and our work is done.
Then in his mercy
may he give us a safe lodging,
and a holy rest,
and peace at the last. Amen. *J. H. Newman*

The world, life and death, the present and the future,
are all your servants;
but you belong to Christ
and Christ belongs to God. *1 Corinthians 3:22*

For the Sick
See above, pp.1124ff.

Father,
Almighty ever-living God, eternal health of believers,
hear our prayers for your servants who are sick:
grant them, we implore you, your merciful help,
so that, with their health restored,
they may give you thanks in the midst of your Church.
Through our Lord Jesus Christ, your Son,
who lives and reigns with you in the unity of the Holy Spirit,
one God, for ever and ever. *Tr. ICEL*

For a Happy Death
O God, who have created us in your image
and willed that your Son should undergo death for our sake,
grant that those who call upon you
may be watchful in prayer at all times,
so that we may leave this world without stain of sin
and may merit to rest with joy in your merciful embrace.
Through our Lord Jesus Christ, your Son,
who lives and reigns with you in the unity of the Holy Spirit,
one God, for ever and ever.

FOR THE DYING

When the moment of death seems near, some of the following may be said:

Go forth, Christian soul, from this world
in the name of God the almighty Father,
who created you,
in the name of Jesus Christ, Son of the living God,
who suffered for you,
in the name of the Holy Spirit,
who was poured out upon you,
go forth, faithful Christian.

May you live in peace this day,
may your home be with God in Zion,
with Mary, the virgin Mother of God,
with Joseph, and all the angels and saints.

I commend you, my dear brother/sister, to almighty God,
and entrust you to your Creator.
May you return to him
who formed you from the dust of the earth.
May holy Mary, the angels, and all the saints
come to meet you as you go forth from this life.
May Christ who was crucified for you bring you freedom and peace.
May Christ who died for you
admit you into his garden of paradise.
May Christ, the true Shepherd,
acknowledge you as one of his flock.
May he forgive all your sins,
and set you among those he has chosen.
May you see your Redeemer face to face,
and enjoy the vision of God for ever. Amen. *Tr. ICEL*

The Hail, holy Queen, pp.1165-6, may be said.

Immediately after death, the following may be said:
Saints of God, come to his (her) aid!
Come to meet him (her), angels of the Lord!
℟ **Receive his (her) soul and present him (her) to God the Most High.**

May Christ, who called you, take you to himself;
may angels lead you to Abraham's side. ℟

Give him (her) eternal rest, O Lord,
and may your light shine on him (her) for ever. ℟

Let us pray:

All-powerful and merciful God,
we commend to you N., your servant.
In your mercy and love,
blot out the sins he/she has committed
through human weakness.
In this world he/she has died:
let him/her live for ever.
We ask this through Christ our Lord.
Amen.

TO OUR LADY

The Angelus
The angel of the Lord declared unto Mary,
and she conceived by the Holy Spirit.

Hail Mary, full of grace,
the Lord is with thee.
Blessed art thou among women,
and blessed is the fruit of thy womb, Jesus.
Holy Mary, Mother of God,
pray for us sinners, now, and at the hour of our death. Amen.

Behold the handmaid of the Lord:
be it done unto me according to thy word. Hail Mary . . .

The Word was made flesh,
and dwelt among us. Hail Mary . . .

Pray for us, O holy Mother of God,
that we may be made worthy of the promises of Christ.

Let us pray: Pour forth, we beseech you, O Lord, your grace into our hearts, that we to whom the incarnation of Christ, your Son, was made known by the message of an angel, may by his passion and cross, be brought to the glory of his resurrection, through Christ our Lord. Amen.

Magnificat
My soul proclaims the greatness of the Lord,
my spirit rejoices in God my Saviour;
for he has looked with favour on his lowly servant,
and from this day all generations will call me blessed.
The Almighty has done great things for me:
holy is his Name.
He has mercy on those who fear him
in every generation.
He has shown the strength of his arm,
he has scattered the proud in their conceit.
He has cast down the mighty from their thrones,
and has lifted up the lowly.
He has filled the hungry with good things,
and has sent the rich away empty.
He has come to the help of his servant Israel
for he has remembered his promise of mercy,
the promise he made to our fathers,
to Abraham and his children for ever.

Tr. *ICET*

Latin Text

Magnificat anima mea Dominum,
et exsultavit spiritus meus in Deo salvatore meo,
quia respexit humilitatem ancillae suae.
Ecce enim ex hoc beatam me dicent omnes generationes,
quia fecit mihi magna,
qui potens est,
et sanctum nomen eius,
et misericordia eius in progenies et progenies
timentibus eum.
Fecit potentiam in brachio suo,
dispersit superbos mente cordis sui;
deposuit potentes de sede
et exaltavit humiles;
esurientes implevit bonis
et divites dimisit inanes.
Suscepit Israel puerum suum,
recordatus misericordiae,
sicut locutus est ad patres nostros,
Abraham et semini eius in saecula.

Memorare

Remember, O most blessed Virgin Mary, that never was it known that anyone who fled to your protection, implored your aid or sought your intercession, was left unaided. Filled, therefore, with confidence in your goodness, I fly to you, Virgin of virgins, my mother. To you I come, before you I stand, sinful and sorrowful. O Mother of the Word Incarnate, despise not my petition, but in your mercy hear and answer me. Amen.

Alma Redemptoris Mater

Loving Mother of the world's Redeemer,
Star of the sea, and heaven's open door;
Answer the cry of all your sinful children,
Help us who fall, yet strive to rise once more.
Truly Mother of your own Creator,
Wonder of nature, Virgin you remained.
We who are sinners plead with you for pity,
Who by the angel Full of Grace were named.

Tr. Stanbrook

Latin Text

Alma Redemptoris Mater, quae pervia caeli
Porta manes, et stella maris, succurre cadenti,
Surgere qui curat populo: tu quae genuisti,

Natura mirante, tuum sanctum Genitorem,
Virgo prius ac posterius, Gabrielis ab ore
Sumens illud Ave, peccatorum miserere.

Ave Regina Caelorum
Hail, Queen of Heav'n, beyond compare,
To whom the angels homage pay,
Hail, Root of Jesse, Gate of light
That opened for the world's new Day.
Rejoice, O Virgin unsurpassed,
In whom our ransom was begun,
For all your loving children pray
To Christ our Saviour, and your Son.   **Tr. *Stanbrook***

Latin Text
Ave, Regina caelorum,
Ave, Domina Angelorum:
Salve, radix, salve, porta
Ex qua mundo lux est orta:
Gaude, Virgo gloriosa,
Super omnes speciosa,
Vale, o valde decora,
Et pro nobis Christum exora.

Regina Caeli (Eastertide)
Joy fill your heart, O Queen most high, alleluia!
Your Son who in the tomb did lie, alleluia!
Has risen as he did prophesy, alleluia!
Pray for us, Mother, when we die, alleluia!
Alleluia, alleluia, alleluia!   *James Quinn SJ*

Latin Text
Regina caeli, laetare, alleluia.
Quia quem meruisti portare, alleluia.
Resurrexit, sicut dixit, alleluia.
℟ Ora pro nobis Deum, alleluia.

Salve Regina
Hail, holy Queen, mother of mercy,
hail our life, our sweetness, and our hope.
To you do we cry,
poor banished children of Eve.
To you do we send up our sighs,
mourning and weeping in this vale of tears.
Turn then, most gracious advocate,

your eyes of mercy towards us,
and after this our exile
show to us the blessed fruit of your womb, Jesus.
O clement, O loving,
O sweet Virgin Mary.

Latin Text
Salve, Regina, mater misericordiae;
vita, dulcedo et spes nostra, salve.
Ad te clamamus exsules filii Hevae.
Ad te suspiramus gementes et fientes
in hac lacrimarum valle.
Eia ergo, advocata nostra,
illos tuos misericordes oculos ad nos converte.
Et Iesum, benedictum fructum ventris tui,
nobis post hoc exilium ostende.
O clemens, o pia, o dulcis Virgo Maria.